Laughing Matters

Laughing Matters

Comic Tradition in India

Lee Siegel

The University of Chicago Press
Chicago and London

Lee Siegel, professor of religion at the University of Hawaii, is the author of *Sacred and Profane Love in Indian Traditions*.

The University of Chicago Press, Chicago 60637
The University of Chicago Press, Ltd., London

Printed in the United States of America

96 95 94 93 92 91 90 89 88 87   54321

Library of Congress Cataloging-in-Publication Data

Siegel, Lee, 1945–
Laughing matters.

Bibliography: p.
Includes index.
1. Indic wit and humor—History and criticism.
I.Title.
PK2945.S54   1987   891′.4   87–11268
ISBN 0–226–75691–2

For my father
who, as I was leaving for India, said,
"Try to have a few laughs."

Contents

Act One: Satire

Act Two: Humor

Scene One: The Human Comedy

Scene Two: The Divine Comedy

Epilogue

Preface

Certainly if you want to understand any age you ought to read not only its heroic and philosophical books but its comic and satirical books.

Gilbert Highet, *Anatomy of Satire*

It all started quite innocently. After noticing a statement in a standard survey of Sanskrit literature that India had produced no comedy of any merit, I began to wonder why. I thought it would be interesting to look into that, to take a little time to write a brief article suggesting some of the possible reasons for that putative absence of humor. And now, five years and hundreds of pages later, overwhelmed and dazzled by what turned out to be an abundance of Indian comedy, I know that I have only just begun to scratch the surface of a great comic tradition, the depths of which remain and deserve to be plumbed and fathomed. There is a boisterous and bawdy voice, a sparkling sensibility, preserved in the literature, and yet, while Indian religious and erotic texts, heroic and philosophical books, continue to be studied, Indian comic and satirical writings (often parodies of the grand and serious literature) have been virtually ignored. Perhaps this is because India, the land as well as its cultural heritage, is most often approached and perceived with solemnity, awe, and reverence—if not with disgust or fear—and such attitudes naturally preclude an interest in mirth and wit, in laughter and zaniness.

This book is, on one level, an attempt to contribute to a broadened perception and deepened conception of Indian culture by revealing the ways in which India has laughed at itself, at its own institutions and unique experiences, as well as at the more universal human predicament. The textual resources serving that end have largely been provided by printed Sanskrit literature. But to the degree that portions of that literature preserved and recorded motifs and sentiments of oral and vernacular, folk and popular, discourse, and to the degree that representatives of that literature contributed aesthetic norms and a source of conventions to the generation of later non-Sanskrit texts, this book is about Indian traditions in a larger, more general sense. And those traditions, in turn, have presented a cultural and historical context for the examination of what I believe to be a universal experience. Though the culturally bound particulars which prompt laughter must inevitably vary from place to place and from era to era, the various structures of the comedic experience and response, formed of certain configurations of those particulars, seem to be constant across time and space. The causes of laughter, the feelings expressed in laughter, and all that laughter does to and for us refuse to change. It amazes me to laugh, here and now, over a joke (or poem or play or story) recorded there and then, a thousand or more years ago in a land that is foreign and far away. There is an uncanny intimacy in the laughter, a sense of closeness to what is distant, and as that feeling has been the pleasure of my research, so it is the point and crux of my argument.

My study of the universal experience as it presents itself within the context of Indian culture proceeds in a variety of interwoven ways, following a medley of overlapping methods: *descriptive* (a survey of the literary genres and forms which have lent themselves to the manifestation of the comic sentiment, as well as an elucidation of the theories of Indian aestheticians and rhetoricians); *causal* (a scrutiny, in terms of both form and content, of the conventions, motifs, and figurative strategies used by the comic writers to incite laughter); *modal* (following a suggestive Indian taxonomy, the comic has been divided into two modes—the humorous and the satirical—which are examined in relation to each other); *functional* (a consideration of the potential teleological, social, and psychological functions of the comic experience); *developmental* (an inquiry into the evolution of the comic sentiment within both the individual and the society—the former being a gesture towards a psychology of laughter, the latter being a beginning of a history of Indian comedy); *comparative* (the epigraphs to most of the sections of the book provide a comparative perspective to implicitly suggest the universality of the experience).

In an effort to expand the parameters of the opportunities for expression that academic exposition might afford me, I have tried to construct a scholarly comedy, a text with a tone, with a plot (in the Aristotelian sense of a "whole, the structural union of the parts being such that, if any one of them is displaced or removed, the whole will be disjointed and disturbed"), with characters (some mythological, some literary, some historical, some living, some composite), and with a theme (comedy as a way of understanding and being in the world).

The prologue, offering a contextual definition of the comic in its relationship to other aesthetic sentiments, sets the stage for the comedy by establishing two ways of laughter—*satire* and *humor*—the modal division, based on traditional Indian categories of laughing at others and laughing at oneself. Satire and humor, as I use the terms, are the two acts of comedy. And the comedy reaches beyond the stage, beyond the text, into the world. In that Indian theoreticians held that laughter has the same set of determinants in both life and in art, their formulation of the causes of laughter represents both an aesthetic of comedy and a psychology of laughter. Sharing that premise, my analyses are simultaneously of an experience that happens in the theater (or over a text) and in (or in response to) the world. And this experience, there and then or here and now, is always ambiguous—a sense of subtle and intractable connections between tears and laughter, misery and joy, informs the Indian texts as well as my own.

In the first act, after a consideration of possible ritual origins and apotropaic functions of satire, and after a discussion of some of the conventional imagery and rhetorical strategies of the mode, the inquiry into the forms and functions, the contents and contexts of Indian satirical writing is divided into three major categories, each corresponding to one of the arenas in which the Indian social theorists felt one could fulfill one's life (love and pleasure, duty and righteousness, religious practice and renunciation): *satire of manners; social satire;* and *religious satire*. In each category or arena, the aesthetic sentiment appropriate to its depiction (the amorous, the heroic, and the beatific, respectively) gives way to the comic as the satirist indicates a degradation or perversion of a traditional ideal that remains only as a mask behind which the objects of satirical laughter try to hide: affectation and lust are passed off as love; corruption parades itself as righteousness; and, in the satirical Age of Dullness, all that is left of piety is hypocrisy and cant. The satirist strips away the guises, and in the cool laughter generated by the spectacle there is a redistribution of power.

In each category of satire there is a *dramatis personae,* a typology based on the conventional objects of satirical laughter: in the satires of manners idealized, social or domestic roles (that of mother, wife, and daughter; father, husband, and son; lover and beloved) are filled and played for laughs by perverted versions of them (the horny old bawd, the venal and frigid young harlot, the naive and affected merchant's son, the dirty old man, the ascetic miser, the henpecked cuckold); the objects of social satire are comic to the degree to which they are contradictions of what they are expected to be (the corrupt king, the dishonest judge, the cowardly warrior, the diseased doctor, the stupid expert); the butts of religious satire fall into two categories—those prudes who claim to live lives of purity, morality, and service, those whose virtue is the mask of vice (the orthodox brahmins and Vaiṣṇava ascetics, and the heterodox Buddhist and Jain monks), and those antinomian adepts who flaunt their vice as a supposed sign of holiness or transcendence (Tantric sadhus, Kāpālikas, and Vaiṣṇava ecstatics).

The presentation of satire involves a discussion of its social functions (the reformation of the satiric object) and a consideration of its psychological functions (the awakening or protection of the potential victims of those objects), culminating in the suggestion that the ultimate function of satire is aesthetic, that though satire points out vice and folly, its justification on the grounds that it changes social conditions or helps people cope with corruption is a mere rationalization of its primary aim which is—quite simply—to be funny.

In the second act, humor—the other side of satire, the inversion of its laughter—is divided between two scenes: the terrestrial and the heavenly; two comedies, one human and one divine, each providing the model for and generating and reflecting the other. At the core of Indian comedy there is an irony, a revelation of the humanness of the gods and the divinity of human beings.

The human comedy has two heroes—the fool and the trickster. They are related, inverted aspects of each other. While satire attacks the vice that claims to be virtue and the folly that is accepted as wisdom, humor celebrates the virtue (or at least the delight) of roguery and the wisdom (or at least the humanness) of folly. The fool (ignorant and wise, profane and sacred; the monkey, the child, the drunkard, the clown) and trickster (the god, the jester, the con man, the crook) move and play on a variety of stages—in the heavens, the court, the city, the home, the village, the jungle—and in each linked realm a universal comedy is acted out again and again in new terms. During that comedy, sense yields to nonsense, work to play, reality to fancy, propriety to impropriety, and order to chaos. And in yielding there is renewal, the pleasures of which are expressed in warm laughter.

The divine comedy recapitulates the human. The trickster and fool, as phases of a single entity, find their wholeness embedded in consciousness as the laughing child within each adult, and that child is deified in Kṛṣṇa. As that god has been examined for the ways in which he reveals the seriousness of humor and its capacity to affirm life, so Śiva has been invoked to indicate the humor of seriousness—the ludicrousness of all human endeavors in the face of death. The two gods—one dark on the outside and light within, the other light on the outside and dark within—are, no less than the fool and trickster, aspects of each other. Comic motifs appearing in the mythology of these gods (as well as in the mythologies of Gaṇeśa, Kumāra, Kālī, Kāma, and others) have allowed me to focus on the correspondences and relationship between comedy and religion as it has been understood both within and beyond India. The sacred profanity of comedy is a leitmotif of the book.

Various visits to South Asia over a period of years yielded anecdotal material which should not be read as a systematic anthropological study of humor in contemporary India (a worthy project beyond the reach of one, such as myself, without facility in modern, vernacular languages). These impressionistic vignettes, like the modern Indian cartoons, are woven into the text primarily in order to suggest a persistent resurfacing of comic themes, motifs, strategies, and structures. They connect subject and object, past and present, literary text and personal experience, India and the West. The strands come together in the epilogue (describing a trip taken to India in 1983 with the intent to research modern Indian comedy), a portion of the book which is more about the problems of studying comedy in modern India than it is about the state of humor there—it is more autobiography than sociology. I have been duly advised that some people will be offended by this level of the text, and that I should, like many a satirist, write an *apologia* to remind the reader that these portions of the book are meant in fun and for the sake of laughter. That they are indeed meant in fun does not, however, mean that they are not meant at all. And while I genuinely do not want to offend anyone by what I have written, neither have I allowed myself to feel inhibited by a fear of that, nor to feel constrained to the degree that I would be either unwilling to record what I have seen and heard or indisposed to argue what I believe to be true.

Over the past few years I have had enormous fun reading Sanskrit satirical and humorous literature. The pleasure of translating, recounting, and writing about that literature is but an extended, magnified equivalent of the pleasure of passing on a funny joke that one has heard. And, of course, the payoff of such a gesture comes when people respond with laughter. I hope that I have done justice to the jokes, told them right, and that there are readers who find within the great corpus of Indian comedic writing, as presented here, a few good and hearty laughs.

Acknowledgments

Those who have read all or parts of this book in the various stages of its development and generously offered me criticism and encouragement, or insights and ideas, or simply (and best of all, perhaps) jokes and laughter, must, I hope, know that they have my warmest gratitude: Patricia Crosby, Mahadev Apte, Catherine Cornille, Richard Gombrich, Jacqueline Kellet, Frederique Apffel Marglin, Wendy O'Flaherty, Marilyn Pang, Graham Parkes, Juanita Wright Potter, Alexis Sanderson, Fritz Seifert, Ramanath Sharma, David Shulman, L. E. Siegel, Noreen Siegel, Burton Stein, Dorothy Stein, Sunthar Visvalingam, and Cheryl Wicker. While doing research in India a great many people were abundantly gracious with their perceptions and reflections, their hospitality and assistance: Abu Abraham, P. K. Aiyar, K. C. Aryan, the Bandyopadhyaya family, Som Benegal, Jagat S. Bright, Sudhir Dar, Ravi and Mala Dayal, Shankar Pillai, and the late Gananath Sastri. I would not have been able to conduct that research in India if it had not been for the generous support of the American Institute of Indian Studies. Further research was assisted by grants from the Joint Committee on South Asia of the Social Science Research Council and the American Council of Learned Societies with funds provided by the National Endowment of the Humanities and the Ford Foundation.

I am grateful to the following individuals, publishers, and institutions for permission to reproduce the cartoons that illustrate this book: Abu Abraham, Sudhir Dar, Prasanta Daw, Professor Thomas Donaldson, India Book House, Jaico Publishing House, R. K. Laxman, Mahua Publishing Company, Mario Miranda, Bankim Shiv Pandya, Pearl Publications, S. Phadnis, Dr. Vishnu Sarma, Shankar Pillai, Śikṣārthī, Subodh Publishers, Sushika Publishers, Sushil Kalra, the Trustees of the British Museum, Vikas Publishing House, and the *Weekly SUN*.

I also want to thank the University of Hawaii Press for permission to include here some of my translations of the poems of Amaru which previously appeared in my *Fires of Love/Waters of Peace: Passion and Renunciation in Indian Culture* (Honolulu, 1983). Portions of chapter four dealing with satires of physicians in Sanskrit literature appeared in the *Bulletin d'Etudes Indiennes* (3 [1985]: 167–193).

Prologue

The Laughter of Gaṇeśa

1

The Comic Tradition in Ancient India: The Aesthetics of Comedy and a Psychology of Laughter

Ganesh and his brother Kumar were arguing over which one of them was the swiftest, and so they decided to have a contest, a race around the entire world. The prize for the winner would be the hand of the beautiful Buddhi. The signal was given and Kumar took off like a flash. Ganesh stayed put and dallied with Buddhi. When Kumar finally returned he was surprised to find Ganesh there, and he accused him of not having run the race. Ganesh was not even out of breath! An argument ensued and Brahm was called to arbitrate. He asked Kumar where he had been and then he asked Ganesh about each of those places. Ganesh knew all the answers—he is, after all, the scribe who first wrote out all of the ancient books—including the texts on geography—for the sages. Brahm pronounced him the winner, and Ganesh and Buddhi started to laugh. Kumar was furious. He would certainly have tried to kill his brother if he had not himself been infected with their laughter. Soon everyone in heaven was laughing!

A tour guide at Ellora

Oṃ Śrīgaṇeśāya Vighneśvarāya Namaḥ!

Homage to holy Gaṇeśa, lord over the flocks of demigods, the playful attendants of Śiva; reverence to Gaṇeśa, destroyer of barriers, snags, and impediments within and without; hail Gaṇeśa, divine scrivener, honored at the beginning of books and journeys; obeisance to Gaṇeśa, potbellied, elephant-faced god, a rodent-riding comic spectacle, revered at crossroads, a lord of transitions; praised be Gaṇeśa, exuberant and worldly god, laughing and weeping god who rewards and deprives. One tusk is sharp and one is broken. The earth trembles with fear and delight as he begins to dance a comic light fantastic. The billions of stars are the spray from his trunk and the planets are pearls of ichor exuded from his temples. The red of dawn and dusk is vermilion dripping from the heavy body lightly dancing. The Gaṇas, Śiva's troops, encircle the pirouetting clown, the chubby god; they clap their hands, giggle and screech their sidereal laughter, a luminous laughter that can be brought down to earth, the place of its origin. Under the superintendence of Gaṇeśa, these Gaṇas, "the attendants of the Lord, who have play as their primary pursuit, preside over the comic sentiment" (*Nāṭyaśāstra* 6.44). In this role they are called the Pramathas—the Harassers or Shaker-Uppers. They are the cosmic clowns and jesters, mythic pranksters and fools, the zanies of heaven. Their laughter, given or found, borrowed or stolen, resounded once through the royal meeting hall, filled the lamplit theater, echoed even through the temple, suffused structures that have turned to dust and dream. That ancient Indian laughter, that distant delight, is there to be retrieved and salvaged, is there to be brought here. Diffused through vast silences, a past laughter, full of solace, awaits rediscovery that it may be remembered and laughed again as our own. This is a search for it, a research and journey, and so Gaṇeśa is invoked: *Gaṇeśasya hāsyodgamaḥ pātu vaḥ!*

The Brink of Laughter: *Comedy Sacred and Profane*

> The Wise Man fears laughter as he fears the shows and vanities of the world, as he fears concupiscence. He pulls himself up on the brink of laughter as on the brink of temptation. . . . For him who knows all things, whose powers are infinite, the comic does not exist.
>
> Charles Baudelaire, "The Essence of Laughter"

This study is a response to a startlingly simple and yet utterly disturbing rhetorical question repeatedly posed by, or attributed to, the Buddha. The young prince Gautama, before he had become a Buddha, having had a glimpse of the ultimate and gloomy transience of life, was overwhelmed with despair. His father, fearing that he might renounce the world and thereby fail to perpetuate the royal line, dispatched the women of the harem to dance for Gautama, to remind him of the luxuriant pleasures which life has to offer. But as they danced and sang, he looked upon them with revulsion. And as they laughed, he wondered, "How can anyone laugh who knows of old age, disease, and death?" (*Buddhacarita* 4.59). And later, as a Buddha, a silent sage no longer enmeshed in the world, an awakened and peaceful one beyond all tears and laughter, he reiterated the dreadful question in the presence of disciples. "How can there be mirth or laughter when the world is on fire?" (*Dhammapada* 146). There is something all too physical and chaotic, too hungry, rebellious, and evanescent about the burst or gale of laughter. It is, like any ejaculation, an explosive loss of power, a convulsive loss of control. We surrender against our will. We crack up. We die laughing.

This book is an attempt to find indigenous Indian answers to the Buddha's stunning question. The question will not go away. It is posed, however silently, to each person who dares to laugh without shame or fear. Around a thousand years ago, in some unknown and yet surely wonderful city, a comic actor standing upon a stage, no doubt grinning irreverently and gesticulating with clownish grandeur, sang a Sanskrit verse, the beginning of an answer.

> Renunciates can't count on liberation
> Just for all their lamentation;
> The road to heaven isn't blocked by jokes;
> Thus, cheerful are the wisest folks—
> Without solemnity and all it brings,
> They laugh at the very state of things.
> (*Pādatāḍitaka* 5)

Comedy delights in itself as it delights in the shows and vanities of the world, as it delights in concupiscence. Comedy beckons us over the brink of laughter as over the brink of temptation. It laughs at the Wise Man, at the Buddha as at the Christ or the Devil. It laughs for the sake of laughter and for the sake of freedom, of liberation from the constraints of righteousness, wisdom, and holiness. It laughs at freedom too and, finally, at itself. That is its great accomplishment—it takes nothing seriously. Comedy offers laughter as its alms for oblivion, a shriek of mirth to echo through the infinite silences of the Buddha.

The comic vision, in both its satiric and humorous forms, has its source, perhaps, in the very revelation that inspires the renunciation of the Buddha: satire is laughter at the vices and follies to which humanity is driven by the agonies of old age, disease, and death; humor is laughter in spite of disease, in acceptance of old age, in surrender to death. Comedy can be refuge, if not redemption; its laughter can be solace, if not release.

I went to India in an attempt to excavate ancient laughter, to piece remains together, to understand a tradition of Indian comedy. I went like Gaṇeśa, by reading Sanskrit books; and I went like Kumāra, by racing off to a distant land.

"It is a divine comedy carved in stone," the tour guide, who—like it or not—came with the price of the bus ticket, announced with a broad, betel-stained smile. His speech was intended to prepare the sightseers from Aurangabad for the vast, monolithic cave temple within the shadowed pit of Ellora. "All of life together with its triumphs and tribulations is depicted in this great monument to the excellent achievements of Indian civilization. Here you will find the gods, the demons, the people, the animals, the plants—everything. . . . Here, you must be warned, you will find the eroticism—this is quite natural to the gods. Here you will find the violence—this is also quite natural in the inevitable battle between good and evil. This is the divine comedy. Life begins and life ends, but, in the long run, life goes on."

In the heavens, underground in the Rāvana-kā-khai cavern, Gaṇeśa, the laughing god, born from Śiva's laughter (*Varāha Purāṇa* 23.5–15), exultantly gobbles sweets. Living, giggling children, no doubt unaware of the emulation, do the same and are scolded by an impatient mother. Nearby a skeletal phantom kneels in gloom as if humiliated by decay and the coldness of the stone. The tour guide, as proud as if he himself had carved it all, walks by scorpion-ornamented Kāla, the god who, as Time, is death, and by the terrible goddess Kālī, lean and all-devouring, silent and screaming. Gaṇeśa watches as Śiva plays dice with his consort; and as the god embraces her, "life begins." And Gaṇeśa looks on as Śiva disembowels a demon and collects its blood in a drinking bowl; and as the great lord dances out the destruction of the world, "life ends." Throughout this cave and others, as tourists wander, stop, stare, move on, stop again, the scampish Gaṇas, on panels, in corners, between legs, and overhead, frolic, tease, and joke, playing out their role as the naughty purveyors of the comic sentiment. Their laughter seeps through crevices in the rock, cracks in the universe, fissures in the great dream. Fat, dwarfish Gaṇas impiously pull the ears and tail of Śiva's bull, mocking power and virility. They lewdly bare their rumps at Rāvaṇa, making the wicked seem merely ridiculous. The cave is a comic phantasmagoria, a carved caricature of "all of life together with its triumphs and tribulations," a revelation of the rollicking rhythm of creation, preservation, destruction, and recreation again and again and again. "In the long run, life goes on." All the little tragedies of life, the endless episodes of failure in the struggle through the tedium of transmigration, through countless births and deaths, are essentially comic, comic through repetition, comic when viewed, like carvings at Ellora, from a distance, from above, or from below. They are comic though not always funny. The intractable persistence of life is the very essence of the divine comedy.

"The tour leader is like the guru," Mr. V. Nayak, our guide, said, his single gold tooth sparkling, his large nose wrinkling in an expression which seemed at once smile and sneer. "He takes the sightseers on the road to the tourist spots. The tourists follow him. In quite a similar manner the guru leads his followers on the spiritual path. He shows them everything. He can explain anything. So ask me anything you like."

I asked about comedy in India. "Is there some humor which you feel is particularly Indian?"

"Humor," the guru of tourism laughed with his hands upon his paunch, "is like God. You cannot explain it. Either you get it or you don't."

The Taste of Laughter: *Defining Comedy*

Comedy has been particularly unpropitious to definers.
Samuel Johnson

There is a comic way of perceiving the world and a comic mode of expressing that perception. Such expression, most simply made in the joke, may be elevated and expanded through literary techniques and devices into art, into dramatic, narrative, or strophic comedy. In the Indian context, comedy may be simply defined as that artistic form, regardless of genre, which has as its dominant aesthetic sentiment the theoretically codified and culturally conventionalized comic flavor, the *hāsya-rasa.*

Innately abiding like instincts within the human heart, according to early Indian aestheticians, there are basic emotions such as courage, love, sadness, merriment, anger, and fear. In the theater or the literary text, characters present or represent the effects of these emotions in such a way that they are transformed or enhanced to precipitate a pleasurable experience of an aesthetic sentiment, a *rasa,* in the heart of a spectator or reader. Bharata, the legendary author of the *Nāṭyaśāstra* (c. second century C.E.), the seminal Indian text on the theatrical arts, playing upon the literal meaning of *rasa,* "flavor" or "taste," used the gastronomic metaphor to explain the dynamics of the aesthetic experiences. Just as the basic ingredient in a dish, when seasoned with secondary ingredients and spices, yields a particular flavor which the gourmet can savor with pleasure, so the basic emotion in a play, story, or poem, when seasoned with secondary emotions, rhetorical spices, verbal herbs, and tropological condiments, yields a sentiment which the connoisseur can appreciate in enjoyment. Love yields the amorous sentiment, courage the heroic mood. The human emotion of mirth is enhanced into the corresponding *rasa* of comedy.

The Western theatrical curtain is decorated with the comic and the tragic masks. Under the influence of Greek forms and Aristotelian theory, Western drama is characterized by a division into comedy and tragedy. The tension between these binary forms invigorates and perpetuates each, and comedy has been largely understood in its relationship to tragedy, its polar opposite. But the Western categories fail in the Indian context. In Western terms there is no tragedy in India. There are no plays which begin in joy and culminate in sorrowful defeat, no stories of glory in grief and disaster, no conclusions to arouse pity and fear, and no catharsis of those emotions. Rather, there are heroic or romantic melodramas in which one particular aesthetic mood dominates and in which others may play a part. In terms of Western categories there is only comedy in India—the plays inevitably end happily—"life goes on."

The comic sentiment is not understood in India as a dichotomous principle in relation to a tragic one; it is rather a mood which arises out of an opposition to, or parody of, any of the aesthetic flavors. It is realized through sentimental travesty, through the intentional failure or breakdown of one or more of the codified moods of art. The comic *rasa* is experienced when something tastes funny, when representations of the emotions of love or courage or sadness fail to produce the corresponding and expected amorous, heroic, or tragic *rasa*s. The comic Gaṇas are born out of the ashes of the sublime. They mock heroes and lovers, sages and saints.

The playwright Bhāsa (c. fourth century) elicits the comic flavor through a burlesque of the tragic sentiment as his clown Vasantaka hysterically mourns the loss of some sweets. "What a catastrophe! What a calamity," he cries out again and again. "I shall moan and bewail!" His tragedy, a mere semblance of tragedy, is comic. When it occurs to him that perhaps he has not actually lost his sweets, that he may have already eaten them, he belches in order to determine whether his breath bears any of the fragrance of the confections. "Phew! Phew! Like the asshole of an old pig,

I belch only pure air" (*Pratijñāyaugandharāyaṇa* 3, opening prose). The comic Gaṇas not only lack refinement, they assault it. Comedy is an affront to delicacy. It is a deliverance from the tyranny of beauty. The comic *rasa* demands a savoring of bad taste.

The comic parodies not only the tragic, but any or all of the *rasa*s. The heroic sentiment is comically deflated as a general in a Sanskrit farce boasts of his cowardice as if it were courage. "I saw a bee today drinking juice from a red flower. . . . I put on my armor, grabbed my sword and, with the help of only a few soldiers, I captured it, tied it up with strong ropes, and skinned it alive!" When a young harlot laughs at this unheroic heroism, he provides her with a semblance of indignation and courage. "Eh, scuzzy whore! Laugh at me, huh! Okay then, come on, let's fight!" (*Hāsyārṇava,* prose before and after 1.44).

Another Vasantaka, in another play by Bhāsa, performs a burlesque of the codified aesthetic sentiment of terror. "Stand back, Your Highness! Help! Watch out!" he cries in fear. "Look, there is a serpent slithering across the ground; the lamp has illuminated its form!" (*Svapnavāsavadatta,* prose after 5.2). The royal patron laughs for it is only a garland moving in the breeze. The comic sentiment arises out of a perception that the depictions of the emotions which correspond to the aesthetic sentiments—courage, fear, sorrow, love, and the others—are not real or appropriate.

Beyond its mimicry of the conventional mood of fear, the scene of the terrified fool is a parody of the epistemological discourses of the normative, brahminical philosophical system of Vedānta. "Just as a rope is imagined to be a snake, so one's true nature is thought by fools to be the body," Śaṅkara (c. seventh century) explains. "Just as a person, out of confusion, perceives a snake instead of a rope, so the fool sees the world without knowing reality" (*Aparokṣānubhuti* 70, 95). Although comedy may have philosophical implications and ramifications, it is essentially an antiphilosophical spirit, a sentiment of perverse reaction to the seriousness of philosophy and the tedious drone of intellection. The comic Gaṇas assert themselves in rebellion, flaunting nonsense in the face of reason. Comedy plays sly jokes on truth. Laughter is blurted out when the abstract cracks like concrete, when a consciousness of lofty ideas is suddenly invaded by mundane things. Comedy mocks metaphysics with an insistent return to the physical. As the solemn and sober philosopher demeans the fool for seeing the world without knowing reality, the comedian or joker plays the fool and laughs at the philosopher for knowing reality without seeing the world.

While later commentators stressed that the comic sentiment could arise out of a mockery of any of the sentiments, including the comic itself (as when one laughs at someone for telling a joke that isn't funny, or at a parody of a bad comedian), Bharata understood comedy primarily as a burlesque of love: "The comic sentiment arises out of the amorous . . . the comic is a mimicry of the amorous" (*Nāṭyaśāstra* 6.39–40). The failure of love is the triumph of comedy.

The Erotics of Laughter: *Degradation and Unmasking*

The spheres of sexuality and obscenity offer the amplest occasions for obtaining comic pleasure alongside pleasurable sexual excitement; for they can show human beings in their dependence on bodily needs (degradation) or they can reveal the physical demands lying beneath the claim of mental love (unmasking).

Sigmund Freud, *Jokes and Their Relation to the Unconscious*

Kāma, the god who is sexual desire, is a comic power, a perverse and laughing deity, a sly trickster who makes fools of all beings. He can make Brahmā, Viṣṇu, and Śiva—the creator, preserver, and destroyer of the universe—laughable. He reduces them, according to Bhartṛhari (c. seventh century), to no more than "servants attending to the chamber pots of doe-eyed ladies" (*Śṛṅgāraśataka* 1). Kāma fills those highest gods with lowly lust for Anasūyā and, when they attempt to rape her, she curses them and "makes ridiculous objects of laughter out of the greatest deities" (*Bhaviṣya Purāṇa* 3.4.17). Kāma laughs at Śiva, the lord of ascetics, for imagining that he can overcome the power of sexuality, the very source of all power, and he laughs at all who emulate the great god. "If a man who is wise and intent upon release tries to slay me, I dance before him as he devotes himself to attaining the bliss of liberation—and I laugh at him" (*Mahābhārata* 14.13.16–17).

The satirist laughs with Kāma's contagious laughter, with a suspicious laughter at all ascetics and puritans, a lubricious laughter insinuating the hypocrisy of any attempt at renunciation. The lusty ascetic appears throughout Sanskrit comedic literature. He is seen at dawn sneaking away from the red-light district. "Carrying the mendicant's staff and wearing the ochre robes of the renunciate, he pretends to have had a vision of god," Dāmodaragupta (eighth–ninth century) laughs, "but when he thinks nobody's watching, he cunningly and lustfully gawks at women" (*Kuṭṭanīmata* 747–750). Even uncompromised celibacy may be a mere ploy, a spiritual means to carnal ends:

> The somber sages are just canting frauds
> In the ways they try to revile young broads—
> They want Heaven from ascetic fevers
> Just for the nymphs up there!—those vain deceivers!
>
> (*Śṛṅgāraśataka* 72)

Just as the hypocrisy of those who try to hide their sexuality is, through satirical unmasking, a source of laughter, so affectation, the inept attempts of those who try to display sexual suavity, is, through the subversion of the amorous mood, a stock comic theme. Commentators have referred to the character of Śākara, the boorish courtier in the *Mṛcchakaṭikā* of Śūdraka (c. fourth century), as an embodiment of the comic semblance of love, as an exemplar of the ways in which the comic arises out of a mimicry and failure of the amorous sentiment. When Śākara tries to profess his love to the beautiful and virtuous courtesan Vasantasenā, he inspires laughter rather than an experience of the erotic mood because he does it badly. The primary emotion of love becomes the basis of the comic rather than the amorous sentiment through an inappropriate use of images and metaphors, an unpoetic display of poetic figures. Dressed in gaudy attire and affecting a lisp which he thinks is fashionable, he tries to be romantic and seductive. "Why do you go, run, run away, shtumbling? Take it eashy girl, you're not going to die, shtay a bit. Alash, my shuffering heart iz burned by love like a pieshe of meat that haz fallen into a barbecue. . . . You increash my love, my dezire, my passion and dishturb my shleep when I'm in bed at night" (1.18, 21). He tries to appear all the more sophisticated by making mythological allusions, but, by getting them all wrong, he presents a mere semblance of erudition. "A mishmash of jingle-jangling shoundz your ornamentsh make! Why do you run away from me like Draupadī afraid of Rāma? I am going to take you away like Hanumān did to Shubhadrā" (1.25). When Vasantasenā tells him to stop (*śānta*), that he is tiresome, he hears "tired" (*śrānta*) and becomes delighted, understanding it as an invitation to lie down with her (prose after 1.30). "I hear the shmell of her garland!'' Śākara proclaims, ''but shince my noze iz shtuffed with darknesh I can't shee the shound of her jewelry very dishtinctly'' (prose after 1.35). He is a mockery of the true hero of amorous romances in whom sexual desire would have been transformed through refinement and courtesy into love. Śākara, no less than Śiva, is a comic victim of Kāma.

Sex is funny. It is comic when it triumphs, by asserting itself, over hypocrisy, and when it triumphs, by withdrawing itself, over affectation. Comedy delights in sex. Bawdiness, obscenity, and scatology are comic methods. ''There is a rule,'' according to Martial, ''that merry songs can't be merry unless they're a bit indecent.'' Indecency, the assault on taste, is, as the reflexive limerick indicates, an essential comic strategy:

The limerick packs laughs anatomical
Into a space that is quite economical;
  But the good ones I've seen
  So seldom are clean
And the clean ones so seldom are comical.

The Causes of Laughter: *Improprieties and Incongruities*

What we see that is ugly, deformed, improper, indecent, unfitting, and indecorous excites laughter in us, provided we are not moved to compassion.

Laurent Joubert, *Treatise on Laughter*

In delineating the theory of *rasa,* the traditional rhetoricians and dramaturgists were careful to distinguish between life and art, between the basic emotions or psychological experiences and the poetic flavors or aesthetic sentiments. In the theater the connoisseur takes a dispassionate pleasure in the passions. He tastes the amorous *rasa* without actually feeling sexual desire for the heroine or the actress portraying her. He tastes the heroic *rasa* without actually feeling hatred for the enemy of the protagonist or the actor playing that part. The comic sentiment is anomalous, however, in that we react and laugh in the same way, according to the theorists, both in the theater and in the streets. Though we do not fall in love with the beautiful heroine of a play or recoil in fear from the cruel villain, we do laugh at the ridiculous fool, the clever trickster, or the wild joker. Laughter dissolves distinctions between art and life.

Because of this unique characteristic of the comic, the traditional descriptions, categorizations, and analyses of this particular dramatic flavor provide not only an Indian poetics of comedy but also an Indian psychology of laughter. Bharata's paradigmatic list of the determinants of the comic mood as an aesthetic sentiment is, then, simultaneously a list of the potential causes of laughter as a response to actual perceptions or direct experiences of the world. "The causes of the comic include: *wearing clothes or ornaments that belong to someone else or that are unnatural [to the character or the situation]; excessive desire; audacity; trickery [or tickling]; seeing deformities; lying prattle; declaring faults*" (*Nāṭyaśāstra*, prose after 6.48). The list provides clues to the source of the laughter that must have been laughed in the cave at Ellora at the sight of the rascally Gaṇas, laughed in the theater when the burlesque verses of the clownish actor were pronounced, and laughed in the court when the girls danced for the Buddha-to-be. But these are only clues. That is all there can be. In the end, the source of the comic is as ineffable as anything sacred. "Strictly speaking," Freud in his discourse on jokes observed, "we do not know what we are laughing at."

Trickery

> The comic always involves some trickery, some lie or deception, over which we—as the perpetrators, victims, or both—laugh. If it is so that man is the only animal that laughs, it is because man is the only animal that knows how to deceive and appreciate deception.
>
> L. A. Larus, "Tricks of the Trade"

Gaṇeśa appeared to an old bawd in her dream. She lied to him, tried to trick him, to deceive him into believing that she had taken on a vow of fasting to gain his blessing. He laughed aloud. "Even in your dreams, even in respect to a religious vow, you do not fall from untruth! I am delighted with you, blessed lady, and so, because of your unwavering dedication to falsehood, you shall obtain the enjoyment that comes with mastery of the arts of great magic and trickery" (*Samayamātṛkā* 4.77–78). The elephant-headed god is a dispenser of magic, of surprise and laughter.

We might laugh at the way a trick, a joke played on someone, works, at the cleverness of the trickster and the gullibility of the tricked one, whether that person is another or oneself. The gods laugh victoriously over tricks played on demons, over celestial deceptions through which the forces of darkness are held in check; they laugh their lightning laughter at the pranks of the Gaṇas whose naked buttocks are flashed at Rāvaṇa and, through the Gaṇas, they laugh at Rāvaṇa himself. Evil is deflated and transformed into the ludicrous through the bawdy tricks of the demigods. Gaṇeśa, lord of the Gaṇas, tricks his brother, uses deception to win the race around the world, and there is laughter in the heavens. In one version of the story the trick is linguistic. While Kumāra runs around the world, Gaṇeśa merely circumambulates his mother and father and then claims his victory by explaining that "one's parents are one's world" and by citing the Vedic assertion that "he who worships his parents by circumambulating them shall obtain the merit of circumambulating the entire world" (*Śiva Purāṇa* 2.4.19.39).

On earth the poet Amaru (c. seventh century), a refined celebrant of the comedy of love, laughs at collusive lovers and a dupable girl. Erotic legerdemain, amorous trickery, becomes a determinant of the comic mood:

> Seeing his ladies on a sofa
>   (not just one but two),
> The rogue crept up behind them
>   (he knew just what to do);
> One lady's eyes he covered up
>   (as if to play "Guess Who?");
> He turned to kiss the other one
>   (who blushed a merry hue);
> But she held back her laughter
>   (and the other never knew)!
>
> (*Amaruśataka* 19)

The kissed lady's laughter is restrained in order to maintain the deception. Laughter marks the recognition of deceit. We laugh both at the way a trick succeeds and at the way it doesn't, at the way frauds fail. Amaru presents a dialogue between a lady and the friend she has sent to carry a message to her lover; the friend, returning in disarray, is questioned:

> "Why is your face all covered with sweat?"
> *"The heat of the sun posed quite a threat."*
> "But your eyes are wet; why are they red?"

> *"The words of your lover filled me with dread."*
> "But your hair is disheveled; why such a mess?"
> *"The wind was blowing; no need for distress."*
> "Your makeup is gone, rubbed all away!"
> *"Yes, rubbed off by the shawl I was wearing today."*
> "But your breathing is heavy; why are you tired?"
> *"From working so hard, doing what you desired."*
> "Very clever my friend, you've not made a slip,
> So tell me what rhymes with the bite on your lip!"
> (113)

We laugh spontaneously when we see through deceptions, when we get jokes, figure out tricks, when the guises fall away before our eyes. It is our natural delight in moments of sudden transparency that provides satire and humor with their comic appeal and method. The satirist uncovers our eyes. We see that something funny is going on. He divulges the tricks of quack doctors, the chicanery of crooked judges, the motives of lusty priests. Satire is comic exposé. Satiric laughter, the Gaṇas lewd laughter at Rāvaṇa, is protection from delusion. Humor, on the other hand, is comic recognition of our own susceptibility to trickery. Humorous laughter, our laughter at the Gaṇas, expresses a delight in illusion.

The phenomenal world was frequently described by Indian philosophers as cosmic trickery: empirical reality is *māyā,* a hoax, a joke, a deceit wherein a rope is mistaken for a snake. Seeing through the great metaphysical flimflam and epistemological bamboozlement, getting the ultimate joke then, might be liberation. Comedy might be religious gnosis, but it refuses to be so, for with liberation the comic ceases to exist. Laughter would dissipate itself in silence, like warmth into coldness or light into the darkness. And so the clown, like a bodhisattva, resists release. He uses a tenacious laughter to keep himself rooted in the world for all its delightful folly.

Tickling

> The child will laugh only . . . when it perceives tickling as a *mock attack,* a caress in mildly aggressive disguise. For the same reason, people laugh only when tickled by others, and not when they tickle themselves.
>
> Arthur Koestler, "Humor and Wit"

Abhinavagupta (eleventh century), commenting on Bharata's list of determinants of the comic sentiment, understands *"kuhaka,"* the term used for "trickery," to refer specifically to tickling, to "touching children's necks, armpits, and the like, in order to surprise them." Tickling is a kind of trick; it is, as Aristotle noted "a sort off surprise and deception" (*Problems*). The inclusion of tickling, an obvious cause of primary laughter, as a determinant of the literary mood suggests that, in some way, Abhinava considered it to be a tactile equivalent of the intellectual or aesthetic processes which prompt the laughter of comedy. "The imagination is sometimes tickled by a ludicrous idea," Darwin reflected in his study of the *Expression of the Emotions in Man and Animals,* "and this so-called tickling of the mind is curiously analogous with that of the body." Darwin understood the squirming and squealing, the writhing and wiggling, the frantic attempts to withdraw the tickled part of the body, all the normal reactions to tickling, as indicative of a defense mechanism, a vestigial motor reflex which once served survival. Comic laughter, the outward, physical response to an internal, mental stimulus, is perhaps no less a teleological defense, no less an anxious or desperate attempt to endure.

In preconscious recognition that the ticklish parts of the body are among the most vulnerable, we speak of being tickled to death. Tickling, as all children know, is an assault, "a mock attack, a caress in mildly aggressive disguise." The irony is, however, that while it may be affection disguised as aggression, it is also aggression disguised as affection-disguised-as-aggression. It is, very often, a mock mock-attack. The laughter of tickling may well arise out of a sense of relief that the aggression of the tickler is not real, is just a joke. But jokes are often—perhaps always—expressions of very real impulses and needs, very serious fears and desires. The sense of relief that laughter expresses is precarious. All laughter is, at least slightly, nervous laughter.

The ticklish zones of the body are as erogenous as they are vulnerable. As older or stronger children tickle smaller ones in mock mock-aggressive assault, so boys may tickle girls, or vice versa, in mock mock-erotic assault. Tickling is G-rated sex and violence—play sex, play violence. Play provides the context for laughter. In the game, the serious moments when seriousness is suspended, tickling establishes a relationship in which the subject asserts power, aggressive and erotic power, over the object. The laughter of the tickler is the laughter of superiority. The laughter of the tickled is an acknowledgement of submission. The harder one tries not to laugh, the more ferociously the laughter comes. All true laughter is impervious to will. The comic responses, like the comic Gaṇas, are defiant and unruly.

"I am telling you my sorrows," a lover complains to his beloved in a modern Indian cartoon, "and you're laughing at me" (fig 1). As she is being tickled she cannot help but laugh, and her laughter within the cartoon, like one's laughter over the cartoon, signals a triumph of the physical over the sentimental. The victory of the body, with its basic urges and primary impulses, over spirit, will, idea, or feeling is celebrated in and by all comedy.

The satirist is a tickler, a trickster or deceiver, a playful bully, cute and nasty, and the laughter of his audience is analogous to the laughter of children gathered around a playground spectacle of teasing and tickling. Just as an adept tickler knows precisely how to probe the armpit of his victim, the satirist probes the places

'मैं अपना दुखड़ा सुना रहा हूँ और तुम्हें हंसी आ रही है ?'

Figure 1

hidden by the object of his satire—the word Abhinava uses for "armpit" (*kakṣa*) literally means "hidden place." Satire is mock mock-attack, often obscene, at once a serious denunciation and just a joke. Effigies of doctors and lawyers, priests and monks, kings and ministers, are teased and taunted, made to squirm and wiggle, to lose control and composure. The power-laden facades of dignity fall away and the body is exposed.

Satire can persist as an aesthetic mode, as socially acceptable entertainment despite its aggressiveness, because it is funny; but it would not persist if the funniness were not serious, if the aggressiveness were not real.

Just as the child laughs when tickled, despite the torture and in spite of himself, the object of satire or the amicably antagonistic joke, can laugh at a mockery of himself. He can laugh, that is, if he has a sense of humor, humor being the capacity to laugh at oneself, at one's own peril, folly, and weakness. Satire and humor can enhance each other.

The laughter of the tickler or the satirist expresses the aggressive pleasures of cruelty; the laughter of the tickled or the humorist expresses the regressive pleasures of vulnerability. Cruelty and vulnerability themselves are frequently rendered laughable in comedy, perhaps to make the harshness of existence more endurable or, perhaps, more simply, because laughter is an expression of human perversity.

Seeing Deformities

We laugh at deformed creatures.
Sir Philip Sydney

Annoyed by some prank, Kṛṣṇadevarāya, a sixteenth-century king of Vijayanagar, sentenced his jester, the infamous trickster Tenāli Rāma, to be executed. At dusk the executioners took the legendary clown to a clearing in the forest where they buried him up to his neck. While they were away fetching an elephant to trample the jester to death, a hunchback washerman happened to pass. The poor old hunchback inquired as to what the man was doing with only his head above ground. Tenāli Rāma explained, "I am, brother, a hunchback. My hump's even bigger than yours. All my life people have laughed at me. I was, however, fortunate enough to meet a holy man. He brought me to this sacred spot and buried me like this and explained that if I would remain here for a day with my eyes closed, keeping perfectly silent, I would be cured. Dig me up and let's see if it has worked yet." The hunchback complied and, astonished to see that the jester had no hump on his back, he begged Tenāli Rāma to bury him in that very spot. Tenāli Rāma did as the hunchback asked, reminding him to keep his eyes and mouth closed no matter what. The executioners returned after dark and the hunchback's head was crushed beneath the feet of the elephant. When the king learned that his orders had been carried out, he felt remorse over the assumed loss of his dear jester. Suddenly Tenāli Rāma appeared in the hall of the court. "The king was astounded. When he heard the whole story he laughed heartily, and pardoned Rāma" (*Tenali Rama,* p. 26). The pranks of the clown led first to his punishment and then to his redemption. He laughs at the deformed man whom he has so horribly tricked. "Think of the washerman's wife," he jokes, "how lucky she is to be rid of a hunchback husband!"

In the context of a culture which assumes that congenital deformities are the result of some sinful action in one's former life, the hunchback deserves his punishment, both his sudden execution and the long torture of a lifetime as a butt of jokes. The notion of karma is an invitation to laugh at deformed creatures, to bare one's teeth and take delight in the misery of others. Compassion, as the Buddha demonstrates, knows no laughter. Comedy demands a suspension of mercy. The laughter which is tinged with sympathy is melancholy.

The inherent comic appeal of deformity accounts for the physical appearance of the theatrical clown, the makeup of the fool of Sanskrit drama, the *vidūṣaka*. "He is," Bharata explains, "a buck-toothed, dwarfish hunchback with a cleft-palate, bald head, yellow eyes, and a distorted face" (*Nāṭyaśāstra* [Nirnaya-Sagara Press ed.] 24.106). On the stage the clown parodies the pain of flesh, imitates and exaggerates human disfigurement. It is, perhaps, the sight of rigidity and gracelessness in such mimicries of deformity that prompts laughter. Awkwardness, stiffness, and ugliness are to the comic mood what finesse, fluidity, and beauty are to the amorous and heroic sentiments. It was conventional in Sanskrit drama for a king, or some other handsome connoisseur of love, to appear with his deformed, gluttonous, bald, and yellow-eyed clown. One particular hero, characteristically longing for a beloved, poetically announces the sophisticated feelings delicately anguishing his cultivated heart:

My beloved lady, it is true, will not so easily be mine,
And yet my soul finds a consolation in awareness of her feelings;
When passion has yet to find its fulfillment in the flesh,
Our longing for each other must provide me the pleasure of our love.

(*Abhijñānaśakuntala* 2.1)

The clownish sidekick, his face distorted in a sneer, lugubriously complains of the awful food he's had to eat, of not being able to sleep, and of his aching thighs. "And as if that ain't enough misery and bad luck, a pimple's sprouting on the boil. . . . The king had to run into this Śakuntalā, some sage's daughter, and since then he won't even discuss going back to town. . . . Oh, here he comes, all dolled up with flowers, bow in hand. I'll just stand here, crippled, my legs all stiff—at least I'll get to rest" (2, opening prose). Through this juxtaposition of the sublime and the ludicrous each is intensified. In my own worn and ragged copy of the text, a used edition prepared years ago for Indian students of Sanskrit, a previous owner of the book has written in English in the margin next to the poem of the king: "This indeed is *TRUE LOVE*!!!" And later, by a speech of the clown, this unknown student, whose ashes have most likely been solemnly scattered to some sacred river, wrote, "What can a fool know of love?" Perhaps a great deal, perhaps too much, so much that he cannot keep a straight face.

In the back of this edition of the play there is a list of questions taken from the Sanskrit examination administered at the University of Madras in 1931. With an ornate asterisk the anonymous student had marked one, a quote that required discussion: "In the *Śakuntalā* there is [an] elevation of love from the sphere of physical beauty to the eternal heaven of moral perfection." The spirit soars in the sentiments of love or heroism; it clunks, plops, and thuds as flesh pulls it back to earth in the comic. There is fall rather than elevation, and nothing is eternal or perfect. Awareness returns to the blemished body as a thing, lumpish and lazy. Traditional theorists list the transient emotions or subordinate states apposite to the comic, those which draw attention to the torpor and weight of the body, as "laziness, drowsiness, weakness, swooning" (*Daśaarūpaka* 4.79). In comedy the needs and limits of the body assert themselves over all aspirations of spirit. The fool knows a reality of the body that surpasses any substantiality of spirit. That knowledge is his folly, his tragedy perhaps; but it is his wisdom too, the crazy wisdom of comedy.

Abhinavagupta explains that the term "deformities" refers specifically to "missing parts such as feet and the like." The comic persona always has something missing, just as he or she always has too much of something else. Potbellied Gaṇeśa's broken tusk adds a comic touch to the iconography. That which is fragmented, which is not whole, is funny in both senses of the word. The comic figure is odd and off balance—his fall brings laughter. The success of the comic sentiment depends on a perception of failure and a sense of superiority through which one dissociates from that failure. Laughter is the sound of gloating. "All beings," Abhinava points out, "by nature, believe that they are superior to some other people at whom they laugh" (commentary on *Nāṭyaśāstra,* prose after 6.31). And Hobbes concurs that our laughter is "nothing else but a *sudden glory* arising from some conception of some eminency in ourselves, by comparison with the infirmity of others, or our own formerly" (*Human Nature*).

When the bus had pulled in to park near the caves of Ellora, the beggars, hoping for some compassion in the tourists, emerged with outstretched arms and the remains of hands. A young girl carried a man on her back, a small distorted lump of a human being, gnarled flesh without legs, a body of bruised knobs with boney arms that clung for dear life. His head arched back, unsupportable on the twisted tube of his neck, and his mouth gaped in what seemed a silent, breathless scream. And there were the lepers extending disintegrating limbs, pitiful semaphores of the sorrow of which the Buddha spoke. A fellow tourist, an American next to me on the bus, muttered with discomfort, "Jesus Christ! India! It's not real!" The pain gave way to an embarrassed and desperate smile. "Well, one thing you can say about the lepers"—he forced the excruciating joke—"they always put their worst foot forward." Compassion had not been completely suspended. I could feel, as could he no doubt, the terror, the cruelty, the iciness of comedy. His laughter was nervous and tainted with horror. But perhaps it helped.

The leper, like the disfigured clown, allows us the glory of which Hobbes spoke. A tenuous illusion of eminence is the fragile gift of comedy.

Comic deformities need not be physical. Corporeal disfiguration provides the comic metaphor for spiritual deformity, intellectual misproportion, psychological rigidity, or emotional awkwardness. The cast of comedy includes gluttons and misers, liars and lechers, drunkards and cheats. In the excessiveness with which they display their vices and follies they become caricatures of the tendencies and compulsions which are our own.

Excessive Desire and Audacity

> My lord, my true and proper baptismal name is Panurge. . . . At the present moment I feel an urgent necessity to feed. Whetted teeth, empty belly, dry throat, clamorous appetite, all are bent on it. If you will only set me to work it'll be a treat for you to see me stuff myself. In Heaven's name, order me some food.
>
> Rabelais, *Gargantua and Pantagruel*

It is not desire, the universal, which is comic but its audacious exaggeration and grotesque magnification. This inordinate desire manifests orally, anally, and genitally in gluttony, avarice, and lechery, respectively. And all three are standard comic themes.

The gluttony of the *vidūṣaka,* like his corporeal deformity in contrast to the physical perfection of his king, is made comic by its juxtaposition with the more refined appetites of the hero. When a king, too lovelorn to eat, asks his comic sidekick where they might go for solace, where he might find some distraction from the great despair of love, the all-too-orectic jester suggests the kitchen, "where we can relieve our suffering by watching them prepare five kinds of food" (*Vikramorvaśīya,* prose after 2.2). The clown is even willing to disclaim heaven for the sake of his alimentary longings—"they don't eat or drink in heaven" (prose after 3.6). When he compares the beauty of the moon to a ball of sweets, turning the conventional amorous metaphor for a woman's face into a comic trope, his patron remarks, "Eating is always the only thing that interests a fatso" (prose after 3.6).

The Gaṇas, led by tubby Gaṇeśa, have innumerable potbellies among them. With constant thoughts of food, the gluttonous Gaṇa and exemplary fatman Pumpkin (Kuṣmāṇḍa), "nourishes the happiness of his fat gut" (*Subhāṣitaratnakoṣa* 5.27). His obesity is emblematic of the glories of gluttony, the triumph of the pleasure principle, the exultation of comedy itself. In humorous comedy, chubbiness can be a sign of Pantagruelian merriment, Falstaffian exuberance, a symbol of license and plenitude, of fullness and the joyous persistence of life. Kubera, the god of wealth, is fat and comically deformed. In satiric comedy, however, corpulence often reveals decadence and rank greed, life dulled and defeated by surfeit. In a cartoon by the twentieth-century Bengali artist Deviprasad, the great weight of a wealthy woman in a rickshaw becomes a satiric symbol of the victimization of the poor by the rich as it tilts the rickshaw back, making it impossible for the thin and unprosperous wallah to pull her. Her wealth gives her the prerogative to be the passenger; but it has also made her fat, created the weight which prevents the rickshaw from moving forward. A child laughs at the ironic spectacle of self-defeat. The laughter of satire is fueled by a sense of justice (fig. 2). And in a cartoon by Mario, grossly corpulent government officials, on a mission to raise money to cope with the problems of starvation in India, board a plane as the lean and hungry look on (fig. 3). Obesity becomes a satirically revealing symbol of social and political corruption. The incongruity between what the ministers are supposed to have as their goal and their habits and intentions as revealed by their obesity is the source of a comic response. And the incongruity between the seriousness

Law of Gravity Baffled.

Figure 2

I'm afraid they're going to have a difficult time convincing anybody that there is a FOOD CRISIS in this country!

Figure 3

and the funniness of the joke enhances both the pathos and the comedy of the perception.

Obesity can signify the failure of the pleasure principle and the truth of the fundamental Indian religious dictum that craving is the cause of all suffering. This serious psychological and philosophical perception, the realization that silenced laughter in the Buddha forever, may be expressed comically:

> If the potbellied fool tries to give his beloved a kiss
> He has to give up what he really wants from his miss;
> And if he tries to do what he wants to his miss
> He gives up the joy of her nectarous kiss.
> Though his belly's too big for both forms of bliss,
> He tries both to do that and to do this
> For he's blind with desire; the moral is this—
> In trying to have both, both he must miss.
>
> (*Subhāṣitaratnakoṣa* 35.12)

Desire for more yields less. The craving of the fat man is ludicrous, absurd, and ridiculous as it becomes the impediment to its own fulfillment. The comically self-defeating tendency of desire is further illustrated by a story of a poor brahmin who had been given some grits. One day, while staring at the jar of grain that he had placed above his bed, he drifted into revery. "Hmmmm, let's see, I sell the stuff and get some goats. Yes, and they'd have little goats and the little goats would grow up and have more little goats and soon I'd have hundreds of goats! Yes, and then I could trade the goats for some cows and they'd have calves and soon I'd have cows for milking and bullocks for farming. Of course I'd have a farm and raise grain and sell the grain for gold and use the gold to buy a house. No, a mansion! No, an estate! I'd have to have servants, of course. Then some rich man is going to ask me to marry his daughter and she'll have a son. I love this boy—he is my pride and joy, the apple of my eye, a chip off the old block! Ah, but that wife of mine! She's so busy looking after the house that she has started to neglect my little boy, the heir to my fortune! She's not taking good enough care of him! I'll have to beat her!" The brahmin became so deeply absorbed in his daydream that he began to swing his arm around as if to beat the imaginary wife. He broke the jar of grits. And then he sat on the bed, covered with wheat, looking at the loss of the very little he once had (*Pañcatantra* 5.1). The brahmin is sadly funny. There is laughter "provided we are not moved to compassion." The comic spirit is not sentimental.

Excessive desire is as well represented by the miser as by the glutton. The two figures are the ludicrous extremes of craving. Humorous depictions of robust gourmands, of Pumpkin the roly-poly goblin, or Gaṇeśa himself bulging from devouring the megatons of sweet offerings daily received, are celebrations of the endearing folly of desire. We are invited to feast beneath the banner of the pleasure principle at a carnival of regression. We laugh with the glutton, the relic of the pudgy baby within each adult. The gauntness of the miser, on the other hand, is an image of craving not as folly but as vice. The image is used comically in satire to condemn excesses of acquisitive desires. We laugh at the niggard, at the terrified and wizened skeleton within each person. There are warnings rather than invitations in satire. The satirist, like the Buddha, exposes desire as the cause of sorrow and death. The comic always verges on the pathetic.

The miser is a stock character in Sanskrit satire. He is described as being less charitable than a corpse—"at least the dead give meat to fatten up the crows'' (*Subhāṣitaratnakoṣa* 39.22). ''He abstains from knowledge and is devoid of sense with his greed for profit,'' Kṣemendra (eleventh century), one of the funniest and most vituperative of Sanskrit comic writers, observes, ''and with difficulty he suppresses sensual desire and creates obstacles to sex in order to prevent his wife from making him lose his money. . . . The miser is the greatest of masters when it comes to protecting against the loss of wealth.'' The same stanza can be read as a description of the ascetic to which the poem explicitly and ironically compares him: ''He abandons money and is without intentions with his desire for knowledge; he suppresses sensual desire by concentrating his mind and avoids sexual union with women in order not to spill his seed . . . He is the greatest of masters when it comes to preventing the loss of semen'' (*Deśopadeśa* 2.36). Puns tie together the incongruous figures, one idealized, the other scorned, and the incongruity elicits laughter at both. Laughter enables us to control our awe as well as our disgust.

Avarice is asceticism gone wrong, abstinence based on attachment to the fruits of denial. Śiva practices austerities, ''wears matted hair and is covered with ashes [or, through a pun, 'is full of wealth'] and he is lord of the world,'' whereas his attendant, the Gaṇa Bhṛṅgī, ''by a quirk of fate, just withers away'' (*Saduktikarṇāmṛta* 4.3.2). Pumpkin, the bulimic fatman, and Bhṛṅgī, the anorectic skeleton, are comically incongruous sidekicks. At the marriage feast of Śiva and the goddess, Pumpkin laughs to himself, ''Bhṛṅgī's too thin to walk in the wedding procession,'' while Bhṛṅgī simultaneously thinks, ''Pumpkin's too fat,'' and both hopefully assume that they'll get more food and gifts than the other (*Subhāṣitaratnakoṣa* 5.29). The two figures, the glutton and the miser, are in opposition to each other and yet mutually dependent. As representatives of two sides of desire, they are inverted forms of each other. The relationship between them seems universally comic—they are Carnival and Lent. There is a tenacity to the comic motifs within human consciousness. The juxtaposition of fat and thin figures, of incongruous and yet dependent opposites serves a comic (and therefore mitigating) representation of psychological impulses for self-indulgence and self-denial. These twin impulses might, in part, be atavistic responses to seasonal changes, to time as a process of alternation between plenitude and famine. The comic serves to relieve, through laughter, the tensions caused by such fundamental and universal oppositions.

The glutton and the miser, Pumpkin and Bhṛṅgī, are to food what the libertine and the ascetic are to sex. Excessive sexual desire, audaciously flaunted by the lecherous lover or slyly concealed by the sanctimonious moralist, provides a major theme in Sanskrit comic literature. The lust of the ascetic is a reverberating insinuation of satire; the erotic audacity of rogues provides a bawdiness which humor celebrates. The "audacity" listed by Bharata in his enumeration of the causes of laughter refers particularly to sexual immodesty. It was a conventional quality of a particular kind of amorous hero as categorized by Bharata and the rhetoricians following him: "Although the 'audacious hero' is guilty of infidelity, he isn't afraid; although he's threatened by his beloved, he isn't ashamed; although his crime is visible in the marks on his body, he'll lie about it" (*Sāhityadarpaṇa* 3.36). And his lies make him, according to Bharata's list, all the more comic.

Lying Prattle and Declaring Faults

> I have no true story to tell since nothing worth mentioning has ever happened to me. . . . But I will say one thing that is true, and that is that I am a liar. . . . So my readers mustn't believe a word I say.
>
> Lucian, *A True Story*

"No man can compare with my father," a boy brags to his friends, "for he has observed a vow of chastity with absolute strictness all of his life" (*Kathāsaritsāgara* 61.248–251). The friends laugh at the way the lie backfires, at the boy's unintentional self-exposure, self-contradiction, and the resultant self-diminution. The liar slips, in comedy, on a verbal banana peel that he himself has dropped. The fools of comedy, attempting to inflate themselves with lies, always go too far. " 'I'm the king's right-hand man on the battlefield,' announced the police chief. 'The state relies on my pen,' proclaimed the scribe. 'The theatrical arts depend on me,' boasted the playwright. 'Gold is issued from my books,' claimed the merchant. 'I have figured out everything in the universe with my calculations,' said the astrologer. 'I have cured King Bhoja himself,' insisted the doctor. 'I've enchanted kings with the brilliance of my verses,' declared the poet" (*Samayamātṛkā* 7.45–47).

When, in an effort to aggrandize himself, a brahmin claims that "the four Vedas were composed by me," he merely draws attention to his real pettiness, his dishonesty, his utter lack of a sense of possibility or proportion (*Hāsyārṇava,* prose after 2.21). Lies reveal truths in comedy. The world of comedy is a world of prevarication: in the domain of satire, laughter, directed at liars, is a castigation of untruth as a form of vice; in the domain of humor, laughter, directed at the believers of those who lie, can be an acceptance of gullibility as a form of innocence. In either arena comic laughter arises out of the simultaneous perception of truth and falseness, out of a contradiction that makes the body shake.

As they declare their qualities, the liars of comedy divulge their faults. The revelation of faults, listed by Bharata as yet another cause of laughter, is explained by Abhinava particularly as the showing of "such faults as timidity in the case of a person who is not supposed to be timid." Comedic figures always fail in some way to be what they are supposed to be. Cowardly generals, deadly doctors, lusty monks, bumptious brahmins, stupid pandits, and wise fools, all incarnations of contradiction, are some of the naturalized citizens of the comic realm, itself a world of incongruity and indecorum. It is a domain overgrown with thick verbiage and overcrowded with lumpish forms, flesh that is ever sluggish and fat or all too nervous and thin, flesh that itches, yawns, twitches, belches, gobbles, grumbles, wobbles. Wormish inanities and trivialities eat away at the empire unnoticed. All movement—physical, mental, emotional, spiritual, gestural, linguistic—is distorted, crude, and awkward. Things stagger and fall, falter and blurt, creating perceptual disturbances which are then expressed and eased in laughter. Laughter physically relieves the mental discomfort that comedy creates. Nothing is graceful or beautiful on the comedic stage. The comic actor, the clown, fool, or jester, inspires laughter with his "buck-teeth, bald head, hunchback, lameness, and ugly grimace . . . [as] he walks like a crane, looking down and taking big strides . . . [and as] he babbles obscenely" (*Nāṭyaśāstra* 12.138–140). It would be all too painful not to laugh.

The Wrong Clothes and Ornaments

> On the way to the wardrobe I thought I would dress in baggy pants, big shoes, a cane, and a derby hat. I wanted everything a contradiction: the pants baggy, the coat tight, the hat small and the shoes large.
>
> Charlie Chaplin, *My Autobiography*

In comedy nothing fits. Everything is too tight or too loose, too small or too large, not only clothes but language, gestures, and emotions as well. Comic characters are misfits. Brahmins are described in one comic monologue rushing along "with their dhotis slipping down" (*Śāradātilaka* 117), and a foppish merchant, trying to make a grand impression in a brothel, has to keep adjusting "the all-too-long borders of his garment which keep coming loose" (*Samayamātṛkā* 7.17). In comedy everything must come loose and slip down, literally and metaphorically.

Bharata's list of the causes of laughter and the comic mood is headed by "wearing ornaments or clothes that belong to someone else or do not fit." Kṣemendra, a theorist as well as a practitioner of the comic art, amplified the item into a paradigmatic image for comic incongruity: "A girdle on the neck, a silver or pearl necklace on the hips, anklets on the wrists, bracelets on the feet . . . can only lead to laughter" (*Aucityavicāracarcā,* citation 1). A girdle worn appropriately on the thighs makes the whole form more beautiful; on the neck, by making the neck look ridiculous, it renders the entire form and everything around it ludicrous. Silliness generates itself. Laughter arises when conventional patterns are upset, when norms are perverted. Laughter flourishes on disorganization. The image is the basis of a traditional joke:

He: Hey, what's that you're wearing on your neck?
She: It's an anklet, darling.
He: But anklets are supposed to be worn on the feet!
She: Oh, in that case, it's a bracelet.

(*Paddhati* 3176)

Once upon a time there was a village farmer who just happened to dig in a spot where a thief had buried some jewelry that he had stolen from the treasury of the royal harem. Delighted with the beautiful ornaments, the simpleton took them home to his wife. "He put the girdle around her neck, the necklace around her waist, the anklets on her wrist, and the bracelets on her ears." When the people of the village saw this ludicrous spectacle they laughed heartily and told the story to everyone they met. Soon the king heard about it and he retrieved his wives' ornaments. Because the villager was such a fool, the king laughed and did not punish the man (*Kathāsaritsāgara* 61.24–30).

Clothes and ornaments engender laughter, according to Abhinava's commentary on Bharata, not only when they don't fit, or when they are worn on an inappropriate part of the body, but also when they are incongruous to time or place or when they are "contrary to the wearer's nature [or gender], age, or status." Laughter is aroused by a severance of normal connections between form and function. Expectations are subverted, comically twisted. A woman dressed in a sari can be beautiful and inspire love or represent it on the stage; a man dressed in a sari is ludicrous and inspires laughter:

My lover was unfaithful,
so I kicked him out the door;
But he came back to me at dusk,
back to me once more.
I did not know that it was he,
how could I?—after all—
He wore my best friend's sari,
and even wore her shawl!
So I thought that *he* was *she*
when *she* was *he* cross-dressed,
And I felt free to speak my mind—
secrets were confessed:
"I want to have a tryst with him,
can it be arranged?"
"That's difficult," *she* said to me;
but the voice was changed,
And *he* roared out with laughter,
and took me in his arms.
[I knew at once that it was *he*—
she didn't have such charms!]

(*Amaruśataka* 46)

The *vidūṣaka* in the *Nāgānanda* of Harṣa (seventh century), putting on a female garment that he is carrying to protect him from the bees that are swarming around him, is mistaken for a woman by a drunkard. "There is my beloved Navamālikā! She's covering her face and walking away because she's angry with me for being tardy to our tryst. I'll calm her down with hugs and kisses." The drunkard embraces the clown and tries to force betel into his mouth. When the clown repulses his advances, the drunkard, still deluded, falls at his feet in obeisance. The scene is a burlesque of love. Navamālikā enters and laughs at both the fool and the fooled (3, opening prose).

The sacredly profane humor of Kṛṣṇa, the playful, laughing god, repeatedly emerges as he is portrayed in female garb. In the final act of the *Vidagdhamādhava* of Rūpa Gosvāmin (sixteenth century), Kṛṣṇa disguises himself as a goddess to get past Rādhā's chaperon. The same poet describes Kṛṣṇa dressed as a female messenger who goes to Rādhā to convince her to stop being piqued at her beloved. "But he's a rogue and a philanderer," Rādhā insists. Speaking cheerfully in a high-pitched voice, Kṛṣṇa responds, "But he loves you." Rādhā yields. "Dressed as a woman, Kṛṣṇa was able to lead a delighted Rādhā into the woods and there, loudly laughing, he revealed himself—may Lord Kṛṣṇa protect you!" (*Padyāvalī* 248).

In the *Gītagovinda* of Jayadeva (twelfth century), a group of milkmaids, Rādhā's "circle of friends, freely laughed at dawn when they saw that Rādhā's breast was clad in Kṛṣṇa's yellow garment, and that the imperishable Kṛṣṇa was wearing her blue robe" (7.4). Dressing in darkness after lovemaking, each of the lovers put on the other's clothes by mistake.

In later Vaiṣṇava devotional literature, Rādhā and Kṛṣṇa intentionally dress in each other's clothes and the comic incident is transformed into a symbol of the ultimate unity of Rādhā and Kṛṣṇa, the devotee and the god. A joke became a doxology. Caitanya (sixteenth century), the ecstatic saint who is said to be the founder of the devotional Bengal Vaiṣṇava movement, in performances of vignettes from the life of Kṛṣṇa, would dress as Rādhā, as Rukmiṇī, the wife of Kṛṣṇa, and as the goddess, the primal mother. Comedy relies on the failure of facades. Laughter resolves the tension between what we see and what we know. The female impersonator ceases to be comic when he becomes, or is perceived to be, female, when the incongruity and contradiction between appearance and reality disappear. Caitanya's disciples, overwhelmed by his portrayals, would suck at his breasts. Laughter had turned to awe, ambiguity to faith. Caitanya provided a model which allowed transvestism to become a religious practice for the Rādhāvallabhīs and other sects in which the notion that one must worship Kṛṣṇa with a woman's passion for her beloved was taken literally. Male devotees attempted to become Rādhā in form as well as spirit; some, according to the tradition, even began to menstruate.

"Are they members of a sect?" I asked about the two transvestites who walked past. "No," the tour guide chuckled at my eagerness to see everything in India as some sort of religious phenomenon, "they are men dressed like women." "I know that; what

I meant was, are they dressed like women in order to practice *bhakti*?" He laughed again and louder, "No, no, they are dressed like women because it is funny. They go to festivals and bazaars and weddings and such and people laugh and then give them money. They are dressed like women in order to earn their daily bread." The transvestites seemed solemn despite their bright saris and lipstick. When I remarked, "No one's laughing," the guide became stern, as if my observation had been a challenge. "Of course they are not laughing. If you laugh, you have to pay and they don't want to pay. If you laugh and you do not pay, that is theft, isn't it?"

Incongruity

> In every case, laughter results from nothing but the suddenly perceived incongruity between a concept and the real objects that had been thought through it in some relation; and laughter itself is just the expression of this incongruity. . . . All laughter is therefore occasioned by a paradoxical, and hence unexpected subsumption, it matters not whether this is expressed in words or deeds.
>
> Arthur Schopenhauer, *The World as Will and Representation*

Incongruity is the basis of all the causes of laughter enumerated by Bharata. It is the essence of the comic sentiment. Abhinavagupta illustrates this with a verse which is, at first glance, hardly laughable. "I do not know how joy might be obtained," Rāvaṇa laments of Sītā, whose limbs "are not liberal with love." The demon king cries out that his "heart cannot endure without her; when her name falls upon the ear it is like a magic spell which infatuates and draws one on" (commentary on *Nāṭyaśāstra* 6.39–40). The poem is ludicrous, Abhinava explains, when one takes into account the incongruity between Sītā's and Rāvaṇa's age, social status, and appearance, and the contradiction between the conventional image of Rāvaṇa as a ferocious warrior and the suddenly revealed glimpse of him as a weakling whining with love for a woman who does not love him in return. Demonic forces, here represented by Rāvaṇa, are unmasked and degraded. The treacherous is deflated and presented as comically flimsy. The comic, whether it is in vulgar jokes or sophisticated literature, can serve a psychological function. Laughter can ease anxiety and reduce the tension caused by fear of demonic forces, those externally projected and internally repressed stimuli which threaten the ego. The hostile, painful, and deadly are rendered ridiculous and thus benign. There is the pleasure.

Abhinava sees a social function in comic perceptions of incongruity. Spectators of comic drama, hearing the derisive laughter aroused by actions or emotions which are inappropriate to a character's age, status, or situation, will naturally be discouraged from such improprieties. Such discouragement is a professed goal of satire. While moral polemics directly castigate such vices as lust, cowardice, or ignorance, satire, as comic denunciation, exposes not vice as such, but rather the specific vice of inappropriateness—the lust of monks, the cowardice of generals, the stupidity of pandits. The objects of satire are comic to the degree that their inner impulses are incongruous with their postures, or to the extent that their revealed words and actions contradict the behavior socially expected of them. The objects of humor, on the other hand—simpletons and parasites, bawds and barbers, fools and clowns—do not present incongruities between motive, action, and expectation, between inner impulse and outer expression. The fool is stupid and acts stupidly; the clown is a coward and behaves with timidity; the bawd is lusty and venal and acts accordingly. In humor the incongruity exists not within the comic figure, but between that figure and an ordered, logical, reasonable world. The improprieties of the object of humor, unlike those of the object of satire, are neither intentional nor correctable and do not, therefore, demand denunciation. The bumpkin who put the ornaments on the wrong parts of his wife's body was the object of laughter, but the good-humored king, retrieving the stolen jewelry, did not punish him "because he was as stupid as an animal."

The iconography of Gaṇeśa expresses comic incongruity. The elephant head on the human body, the broken tusk, and, above all, the spectacle of the chubby god riding his vehicle, the tiny mouse or rat, are laughable. But, according to a traditional legend, no being except the incautious moon dared to laugh at him. And when the moon did laugh at the ludicrous sight of Gaṇeśa on his mouse (or, in some versions, at the sight of Gaṇeśa falling off his little mount), the elephant-headed deity, offended by the lunar laughter, cursed the moon and declared that anyone who looked upon it would be jinxed. Gods and men, fond of moonlight, banded together to beseech Gaṇeśa to retract the curse, to let the moon come out of the lotus in which it hid. Gaṇeśa yielded, modified and limited the curse so that the moon could be observed without consequence at any time except on the fourth night of the month of Bhādrapada (August-September). From then on, anyone who looked at the moon on that particular day, Gaṇeśacaturthī, Gaṇeśa's birthday, would become subject to the ancient curse. The legend explains the ritualized custom that those who, even by accident, see the moon on that day must then provoke friends and neighbors to make fun of them, to laugh at them, and assail them with obscenities and mockery. Their laughter absolves the crime and frees its object from the curse. The folk custom reveals an axiom of comedy—to laugh at someone else (in the case of satire) or to laugh at oneself (in the case of humor) is to absolve the object of laughter from crime or sin. Laughter, just like weeping, is an expiation.

The Rhetoric of Laughter: *The Dynamics of Wit*

Wit is an arbitrary juxtaposition of dissonant ideas, for some lively purpose of assimilation or contrast, generally of both.

William Hazlitt, "On Wit and Humour"

Appropriateness was traditionally considered an absolutely essential quality in poetry. Only through a decorous use of the various tropes could the poet establish a particular aesthetic sentiment. Just as ornaments worn inappropriately, either by the wrong person or on the wrong part of the body, produce laughter, so poetic ornaments that are inappropriate, that do not fit, according to the rhetoricians, engender the comic sentiment.

Kṣemendra insisted that the poet must have wit, that he "should know how to make people in literary circles laugh" (*Kavikaṇṭhābharaṇa* 2.10). Poetic wit is the ability to prompt amusement through a playful manipulation of verbal figures, the ability to use them rightly wrongly. It is a knowledge of how to place ornaments in such a way as to burlesque and belittle one of the conventional aesthetic moods, to pervert that sentiment into comedy. Wit's razor is used to sever connections and create incongruities between form and function, content and context, cause and effect.

Poetic ornaments were categorized into figures based on meaning or sense and those based on form or sound. Rudraṭa (ninth century) subcategorized the former into figures in which descriptions are comparative, hyperbolic, punned, or natural. Any of these, if used appropriately could enhance any of the codified aesthetic sentiments. An inappropriate use would be a fault. But, Rudraṭa explains, the greatest poetic fault becomes an excellence in the case of the comic sentiment. The inappropriate becomes appropriate; impropriety is proper; incongruity is congruous with the mood of laughter.

To illustrate Rudraṭa's dictum, the commentator Namisādhu cites a malapropian verse that explains how the poetess Vikaṭanitambā got her husband. "He said 'beans' (*māṣa*) for the time period, and 'month' (*māsa*) for the pulses; he said, 'I am a shit eater' (*śakāśa*) for 'I am nearby' (*sakāśa*); when he left the *'r'* and the *'ṣ'* out of 'camel' *(uṣṭra)* [and thus said 'grass' (*uṭa*)], he was given Vikaṭanitambā [literally, 'Miss Bounteous Buttocks,' but also 'Miss Grassyass']" (on *Kāvyālaṃkāra* 5.47).

Vulgarities are normally inappropriate in poetry. Like overly abstruse terms and harsh sounding words they are, according to Bharata, as out of place in a drama or other literary composition as "whores are out of place in the company of brahmin ascetics bearing water pots and rosaries" (*Nāṭyaśāstra* 16.127). But just as every brothel in Sanskrit comic literature is certain to be visited by brahmins pretending to be pious and pure, comic diction and action inevitably abounds in the vulgar and the pedantic, that which is too low or too high. There is verbosity when simplicity would be appropriate and laconia when detail would be suitable. Great and important things are acted out or described in mundane ways while trivialities are celebrated with verbal grandeur and gestural bombast. The grave becomes light.

While none of the conventional ornaments of Sanskrit composition are inherently comic, any of them might, through the ingenuity or wit of the poet, serve to create comic incongruity.

Simile

> Wit is the Lustre resulting from the quick Elucidation of one Subject, by a just and unexpected Arrangement of it with another Subject.
>
> Corbyn Morris, *Essay Towards Fixing the True Standards of Wit, Humour, Raillery, Satire and Ridicule*

All thought, relying as it does on making comparisons, on seeing similarities and dissimilarities, must find expression in metaphor and simile. Basic as they are to all language and to consciousness itself, simile and metaphor generate and constitute poetic literature. They have the potential to establish and enhance any of the aesthetic sentiments. In the service of the comic mood, simile and metaphor can be quickly and unexpectedly manipulated by wit. In comedic literature, as in many verbal jokes, there are surprising and playful suggestions of ironic similitudes between incongruous things. Similes are used to link incongruous realms: "The tour leader is like the guru."

An ancient simile comparing Vedic sacrifice and the sexual act, the female genitalia and the lustral fire, was made solemnly: "Woman is a fire, Gautama—the phallus is the fuel, the hairs are the smoke, the vagina the flame, penetration the coal, orgasm the sparks. In this fire the gods offer semen and from it a person comes to be" (*Bṛhadāraṇyaka Upaniṣad* 6.2.13). The magical equation became a conceit in later amorous poetry, a metaphor playing upon the shape of the Vedic altar which was narrow in the middle.

for the consecration of our lord love
overflowing with holy waters
two golden fonts
her breasts
and with
her slender waist
the lady's body is a sacred altar
with deer-eyes and well-formed thighs
(*Amaruśataka* 137)

The superimposition of the image of the altar onto the woman's body elevates love, suggests a sacralization of eros, and intensifies the amorous sentiment. It makes human love all the more serious and holy. But the identical poetic conceit, the same Vedic simile, can be thoroughly comic. In a ribald farce a royal minister, charged with officiation over a ritual, enters the brothel where his king is holding court. He sees a young whore.

The hot passion of the lovely girl with deer-like eyes
Is the lustral flame in the Vedic altar, her thighs,
In the firehole where they are joined—her luscious cunt.
And her breasts are the fruit of offering up in front;
And I'll be the sacrificial priest with stirring stick

For churning a semen oblation—it's my ladle/prick.
Who'd neglect an eternal sacrifice to Love like this?
Its sacred reward comes at once and is, we know, such bliss!
(*Hāsyārṇava* 2.16)

The erotic simile from the mouth of a priest does not elevate love but degrades religion. It satirically suggests a profanation of ritual and generates, through its burlesque of the amorous mood, the comic sentiment. Comic similes frequently parody or debase noncomic ones.

Serious poetic similes became formalized in Sanskrit literature. The poet Bhartṛhari rips apart those conventional amorous similes for feminine beauty: "The bulbs which are her breasts are compared to golden pitchers; her face, that receptacle of spit, is compared to the hare-marked moon [a receptacle of nectar]; her thighs, putrid with dripping piss, are said to rival elephants' trunks. This very disgraceful form is given importance by various poets" (*Vairāgyaśataka* 16). In order to convey the comic effect of the poetic mockery, the Sanskrit clichés need to be translated into English ones:

"Lips like rubies, teeth like pearls"
  describes the oral orifice of girls;
"Hair like flax and alabaster skin"
  describes a scalp and scum so feminine;
"Limpid pools" describes just eyes:
  ideals made up of poets' lies,
Ugliness turned into beauty
  out of some poetic duty.

The comic mood arises out of the deflation of the amorous. The poet makes fun of the literary hypostatization of women. An ascetic vision is expressed with comic tonality in this direct satiric assault.

In satire, simile and metaphor serve diminution. This can be direct, as when the parasite/satirist of a monologue play, seeing the obese Mr. Hidden (Upagupta) walking down the street, asks aloud, "Is this a rolling waterpot? a big leather bag? a cask? . . . What is this bizarre thing?" (*Pādatāḍitaka* 77). The man, through the metaphor, is reduced to being a receptacle, at once empty and bloated. The human being becomes an object, a thing. And, according to Bergson's essay on laughter, "we laugh every time a person gives the impression of being a thing." Satirical attention is fixed on the body as a mechanical object, wholly dehumanized and devitalized, unsupple and unfeeling. Satire arouses laughter and disdain simultaneously.

Satirical diminution can be made indirectly through metaphor and simile, as when the *vidūṣaka* in the *Karpūramañjarī* of Rājaśekhara (tenth century) compares the poetry he has composed to musk and gold. The comic incongruity between the boast and the actuality becomes apparent when the hack recites a stanza in which he compares the whiteness of blossoms of jasmine and *sinduvāra* to that of "rice pudding and vanilla milkshakes [literally, 'strained buffalo milk']" (1.19). The bad simile, the inappropriately used ornament, causes laughter. The simile is comic because, instead of comparing the flowers to objects higher than themselves in an aesthetic hierarchy, they are compared to something lower. Similarly the comparison of Mr. Hidden with a rolling receptacle is a downward one. A comic fall takes place within, and because of, the simile. The comparison of bad poetry to musk and gold is also a fall, one that occurs in an attempt to rise. It happens outside the simile but still because of it.

The simile can be a comic rhetorical device when it tricks or tickles the mind, when it suggests something which it then denies. Through a particular Sanskrit trope known as "denial" (*apahnuti*), expectations are built and then subverted. A girl tells her friend of the "beautiful one" tugging at her hair, stroking her face, clinging to her neck, then embracing her breasts, caressing her hips, and then, finally, falling at her feet. The shocked confidante rebukes the girl for shamelessness, "Your modesty is lost!" But the girl points out that the friend simply has a dirty mind—"What is improper about putting on a dress?" (*Subhāṣitaratnakoṣa* 24.14). "What goes in hard and dry and comes out soft and gooey?" goes the child's dirty joke. Answer: "Chewing gum!" The unmentionable penis turns out to be innocent gum; a lover turns out to be a garment; a snake turns out to be a rope. Erotic expectations suddenly fizzle into comic revelations in epistemological tricks rhetorically performed. Immanuel Kant, in *The Critique of Judgement,* stressed this element of surprise in his explanation of laughter as "an affectation arising from the sudden transformation of a strained expectation into nothing." Kant, someone not usually known for his hilarity, coincidentally illustrated his perception with a joke about an Indian. "An Indian at an Englishman's table in Surat saw a bottle of ale opened, and all the beer turned into froth and flowing out. The repeated exclamations of the Indian showed his great astonishment. 'Well, what is so wonderful in that?' asked the Englishman. 'Oh, I'm not surprised myself,' said the Indian, 'at its getting out, but at how you ever managed to get it all in.' " Being a philosopher rather than a comedian, Kant felt constrained to explain the joke. "At this we laugh, and it gives us hearty pleasure. This is not because we think ourselves, maybe, more quick-witted than this ignorant Indian, or because our understanding here brings to our notice any other ground of delight. It is rather that the bubble of our expectation was extended to the full and suddenly went off into nothing."

Hyperbole

> Taffeta phrases, silken terms precise,
> Three-pil'd hyperboles, spruce affectation,
> Figures pedantical.
>
> William Shakespeare, *Love's Labour's Lost*

Hyperbole, a figure of speech indicating any exaggeration, can be used seriously for emphasis, to convey vehemence, with an understanding that the extravagance of statement is not to be taken literally. It is often employed comically in Sanskrit literature, perhaps in all literature, to create a texture of ludicrous excess. The comic mood can arise when the poet, pretending to aim at eliciting one of the standard aesthetic sentiments, overshoots the mark with verbal enthusiasm. Daṇḍin (eighth century) cites an example: "Not taking into account the predestined vastness of your breasts, the god of creation truly made the sky all-too small" (*Kāvyādarśa* 1.91). It is too much, "pil'd" too high. The poet appears to be playing at praise, pretending amorous utterance. The exaggeration, the attribution of cosmogonic significance to the breasts, turns erotic adulation into comic flattery. Again, "the comic is a mimicry or semblance of the amorous."

Hyperbole was a conventional strategy in Sanskrit panegyric literature. It was serious when a poet formally praised a king for being the greatest being in the universe. It would be comic, however, if either the poet or the king were to take the hyperbole literally. It would be comic, furthermore, if the king were to praise himself in the same terms. Comic literature abounds in extravagant self-approbation and braggadocio, in bombast and fustian.

Frequently, in attempts at self-magnification, the fools of comedy will misuse hyperbole in such a way that it backfires and yields self-diminution. Accused of being ignorant of the Veda, the jester in the *Avimāraka* of Bhāsa responds with indignation as he strives for serious hyperbole, "What do you mean, not learned in the Veda! Listen here! There is a textbook on drama called the *Rāmāyaṇa* and I was able to read five of the sayings in it in less than a year!" The fool claims to understand not only the sayings, "but what they mean as well!" (2, opening interlude).

The tour guide at Ellora explained that the size of the sanctuary was ten times as great as that of the Parthenon, that it was the most enormous example of rock carving in the entire world, and that "though it took only half as many workers to complete it as it took to build the Great Pyramid, they completed it in less than half the time!" Hyperbole demands either awe or laughter.

Paronomasia

> The child acquires its understanding of wit or pun only when it has mastered speech. . . . The child's joy at playing with the language it has just mastered lives on in the pleasure which adults find in words and is a pleasure which wit justifies before the superego.
>
> Ernst Kris, *Psychoanalytic Explorations in Art*

"You will have great difficulty in your study of humor," the tour leader warned me, "because so much of our Indian humor cannot be translated. It always involves some play on words. In India people love to play with words. Take my own name, for example, Mr. V. Nayak. It can also be heard as Vinayak, which is a name of Ganesh. This is a play on words, what the French call *un double entendre*. The French also love to play with words."

"My name, Siegel, is also a pun," I said. "You know, the bird, the Seagull. I don't find it a particularly funny pun, but when I was in school the other kids thought it was hilarious."

"Sehgal is an Indian name. Do you perhaps have some Indian blood in your distant heritage?"

"No, Siegel is a Jewish name. It means 'seal' in Yiddish."

Mr. V. Nayak smiled with utter delight, "I am so happy that you are a Jew!" He insisted upon buying a bottle of Campa-Cola for me. "The Jews have a fine sense of humor like the Hindus and the French," he laughed. "And practically all Jews know Sanskrit very well. Dr. Albert Einstein, himself a Jew, was an expert on Sanskrit and came up with his famous $E = mc^2$ only after his diligent study of the Veda."

Mr. Nayak, his finger exploring the recesses of his large ear in a circular motion, looked at me very seriously. "Are you by any chance related to the famous Dr. Albert Einstein?" he asked.

When I indicated that I was not, he roared, "Oh, that was just my theory of relativity!" I laughed not because the pun was good, but because it was so bad. As Abhinavagupta explains, the comic can arise out of the failure of any of the aesthetic sentiments including the comic itself. I suppose I laughed also because I had been tricked, because I had believed that his question was a serious one and the "bubble of my expectation suddenly went off into nothing." Puns are often used in comic literature to achieve precisely that end.

The pun seems to be the first display of wit to develop in the child, if not in the species. The child plays with sound and meaning in order to learn how to put them together and laughs as an expression of mastery when a pun is understood. The pleasures of the pun are childhood pleasures. The pun is, furthermore, a typical feature of archaic literature, of chant, invocation, curse, and spell. The pun establishes or reveals links in the universe not normally perceived and it is therefore full of magic. The powers of the pun are archaic powers.

Of the wide range of rhetorical devices in both the satirical arsenal and the toy chest of humor, the pun is one of the tropes most frequently used to establish the essential incongruity. Paronomasia can tie antithetical emotions, ideas, and sentiments together to create a comic tension. Bhartṛhari (*Śṛṅgāraśataka* 12) describes a woman's hair as "coiffed," using a word (*saṃyaminaḥ*) which also means "exercises yogic control"; her eyes are praised with a phrase (*śruter api paraṃ pāraṃ gate*) which can be construed either as "reaching beyond her ear" or as "attaining emancipation through the Veda"; he employs the word "twice born" (*dvija*) which can refer either to "teeth" or "holy men"; so too her breast is the abode of "pearls" (*muktā*) or "liberated beings" (*mukta*). Passion and renunciation are made to coexist incongruously, uncomfortably, comically. Notwithstanding the warnings of Vināyaka, it is, I think, possible to capture at least some of the semantic biformation in translation:

Your hair, my lovely lady, graceful with its unctions,
  Is a Mass so holy and so high;
And as a sacred auricle, your ear *in aeternum* functions;
  A visionary, yea a seer, is your eye.
In your mouth a conclave of wisdom teeth I count.
  Pray tell, let it be confessed,
Venerable beads play upon that splendid fount
  Which is your pure white breast.
I feel profane passion, a carnal love prodigious,
For your heavenly body, so sacred and religious.

Laughter relieves the semantic, aesthetic, and psychological tension produced by the puns' binding together of the sentiments of erotic love and religious peace. The comic arises out of a clash between those flavors. The punch line (literally, "though your body is beatifically peaceful, it truly generates carnal passion in me") releases the laughter. Suddenly the poet tilts the balance between the incongruities as he chooses sexuality over spirituality, the world over renunciation. Kāma laughs heartily at Śiva.

Puns are frequently used in poetry to enmesh the heroic and amorous moods, to link martial and erotic activities. The pun can be used seriously to suggest the congruity of sexuality and aggression. But this serious connection can be made playfully. A poet extolls the manly virtues of his king with a display of wit as he uses phrases that can be understood in two ways at once, both sexually ("O King, you delight in pulling women's hair; you seize her girdle and push her hands away suddenly in order to conquer her body") and, through puns, heroically ("O King, you seize the kingdom of the Kuntalas; you drive away the armies of Kāñcī and suddenly you pillage the kingdom of the Aṅgas"). The poet adds that when these paronomastic praises of the king are sung, "women bashfully glance at each other and enemies become afraid" (*Subhāṣitaratnakoṣa* 41.50). This stanza might also be Englished, the effect translated, if one is willing to make certain geographical—if not aesthetic—compromises:

Victoria will surrender
  and you'll lay Alberta low;
You'll knock up Regina—
  you are, dear King, *macho!*
As I sing these praises

with this punful cheer,
Three ladies are delighted
and Canada quakes in fear.

A reading of such thoroughly bisemous poems forces consciousness rapidly back and forth between two incongruous realms of experience or emotion, two contradictory levels of perception or cognition. Laughter signals a release or detachment from both realms, the arrival at a third level, a rhetorical one from which the other two can be viewed simultaneously. Consciousness focuses upon the poet's wit. The poem is neither sexual nor religious, neither erotic nor martial; it is simply clever and playful. Its primary meaning is only that it is funny. The amorous, heroic, or religious sentiments give way to the comic as the phonemic dimensions of language take precedence over the semantic dimensions, as content is eclipsed by form.

The same eclipse takes place in a punned stanza from Kṣemendra's *Bauddhāvadānakalpalatā,* a verse that he quotes in his own discourse on poetic decorum (*Aucityavicāracarcā,* citation 47). The verse can be read as an erotic poem, one typical of the amorous sentiment—it describes a woman, "all at once stealing the heart of the young man who was still with the drunkenness of love; displaying her craving for passion, she embraced his neck, scratched his cheeks with her nails, kissed and bit his lower lip, and showed her talent for arousing the pleasures of love." The same stanza can, through puns, be read as a poem of terror, one typical of the aesthetic sentiment of repugnance or revulsion—it describes a jackal bitch, and the figurative heart, the seat of the sentiment of love, becomes the literal bodily organ, a piece of carrion. "All at once seizing the heart of the fresh corpse, lying still as a drunkard, it displayed its thirst for blood; it attached itself to the corpse's throat, scratched its face with its claws, gnawed at its mouth and chewed its lips as it pulled apart its limbs." The puns, Kṣemendra explains, suggest a simile—the pleasures of love are like the terrors of death. The speaker of the poem is a bodhisattva and the simile is aptly a Buddhist one. As the women of the court danced and sang for the prince who was to become the Buddha, he looked upon them with revulsion and as they laughed, he wondered, "How can anyone laugh who knows of old age, disease, and death?" Just as the paronomastic linking of the sentiments of love and heroism, and of love and religious peace, in the previous poems actualized the comic sentiment, so the binding of the aesthetic moods of love and revulsion in Kṣemendra's stanza yields a third and more primary mood, in this case, that of religious peace. The comic and religious sentiments have something in common. The laughter of the comedian and the silence of the Buddha both express a distance from the content of experience, a detachment from love, fear, courage, anger, from all the worldly sentiments.

Just as the pun can become primary to the aesthetic effect of the poem, just as the figure itself can devour the content, so it can be used in a more passive and merely suggestive way wherein it enhances rather than eclipses primary levels of effect and meaning. In the *Gītagovinda,* Jayadeva puns on various meanings of the word *karuṇa:* as a Buddhist term it indicates the ideal of pity or compassion; as an aesthetic term it refers to the pitiful or tragic sentiment; it is also the name of a certain species of citrus tree which bears small, white, toothlike blossoms. Describing the amorous springtime, Jayadeva sings of young *karuṇa* trees "laughing at the sight of people who have grown immodest" (1, song 3, vs. 6). "To show whiteness," in reference to the display of teeth in laughter, is a Sanskrit idiom meaning "to laugh" and Bharata explains that the comic sentiment thus "has white as its color" (*Nāṭyaśāstra* 6.42). Hence Gaṇeśa, with his ever-visible white tusk, can be said to be an ever-laughing god, one who laughs even as he weeps. And the burgeoning of white flowers can be perceived, through the play on words, as joyous laughter. Nature laughs at people who have grown immodest in spring. Mirth is aroused by the triumph of Kāma, by the surrender of control to sexuality and fertility. And at the same time the tragic sentiment gives way to the comic mood—every weeping willow breaks out in the festive laughter of renewal. But there is another suggestive layer within the pun. The compassionate, despite their pity, laugh as an expression of derision at those who are incontinent. The pun, more than any other figure perhaps, allows for an expression of ambivalence. Ambivalence is inevitably at the very source of laughter just as it is at the source of renunciation.

Linguistic Ornaments

In real life a cigar is not necessarily tragic, nor do dairymen arrive in myriads. In Palindromia, however . . .

J. A. Lindon, *Worm Runner's Digest*

Within Sanskrit literature there developed a tradition of wordplay which extended far beyond the use of simple puns. Both the composition and reading of poetry became recreational activities, pure and gratuitous exercises of wit, ingenuity, and virtuosity. The poet became a verbal juggler, a grammatical acrobat, a linguistic magician, performing in a rhetorical circus. Anagrams, charades, amphibolies, puzzles, riddles, acrostics, conundrums, palindromes, tongue twisters, and the like were composed for the amusement of connoisseurs. Such linguistic ornaments, all glitz and glitter, were used for the fun of it.

The *Śiśupālavadha* of Māgha (seventh century) is a repository of such composition, of stanzas relying purely on form for their aesthetic impact. One of the stanzas, for example, is a perfect syllabic palindrome: *taṃ śriyā ghanayā'nastarucā sāratayā tayā/ yātayā tarasā cārustanayā'naghayā śritam* (19.88). A literal translation ("He was eagerly and tightly embraced by fair-bosomed Śrī, pure goddess, she of eternal beauty, her body possessed with every quality") is no translation at all since the significance, and hence meaning, of the poem is structural rather than semantic. Any attempt to translate the poem reveals a comedy of language. Certain words stand out as having palindromic potential—Śree, bosom, body, goddess, pure, possessed. But these words, if we obey the rules of the game, make demands and lead to the ludicrous: "Śree's bosom I held, no female body! As goddesses so pure (Peru-possessed dog!) say, 'Do be lame—fondle him—O SOB Seers!' " The palindromist battles against language in a comic agon. One might laugh at the triumph of language if the palindrome makes no sense; or one might laugh over the victory of the poet when the palindrome works both formally and semantically as in the case of Māgha's stanza, a verse in which one might say that "Devī lived."

Kālī, Devī in her hideous and menacing form, the skeletal goddess adorning the wall of the Rāvaṇa-kā-khai cave at Ellora, is said to have appeared once to Tenāli Rāma. Instead of recoiling in fear, the jester began to laugh when he beheld her thousand heads, her thousand gaping mouths rimmed with teeth and dripping with blood. "You dare to laugh?" the terrifying goddess asked. "Yes," chuckled Tenāli Rāma, "for something funny just occurred to me. I only have one nose and two hands and yet when I get a cold my one nose keeps both my hands busy with constant blowing, blowing, blowing. You have a thousand noses and only two hands—it must be very difficult when you get a cold." "You are a *vikaṭakavi,*" the goddess said—a "dreadful poet," or more exactly in another sense, a "drab bard." The jester laughed again, "I like that—*vikaṭakavi,* the syllables read the same forward and backward." The goddess laughed (*Tenali Rama,* pp. 5–6). The jester's wit tamed the ferocious deity. The comic sentiment transforms the world in that way. It has the capacity to transmute fear into amusement.

The Degrees of Laughter: *Misery and Mirth*

> Man suffers so deeply that he *had* to invent laughter. The unhappiest and most melancholy animal is, as fitting, the most cheerful.
>
> Friedrich Nietzsche, *The Will to Power*

The various Sanskrit dramaturgists and rhetoricians, following Bharata, enumerated particular kinds of laughter. They categorized it into six types based on degree: *smita*—the slight, restrained smile in which the teeth are not visible, but in which the eyes are opened wide with delight and the cheeks are slightly raised; *hasita*—the full but silent smile in which the teeth show, the eyes seem to grin, and the cheeks are full with pleasure; *vihasita*—laughter in which a sweet giggling sound is made as the face reddens slightly and the eyes and cheeks contract; *upahasita*—hearty laughter, a mocking guffaw in which the head and shoulders bend and move and the nose wrinkles up as the nostrils widen; *apahasita*—roaring laughter, violent cachinnation in which the eyes become wet with tears and the head and shoulders shake forcibly; *atihasita*—convulsive, hysterical, screaming laughter accompanied by copious tears and a total loss of physical control. These six kinds of laughter are subdivided into three stages which are, in turn, correlated with three classes of people: smiles (*smita* and *hasita*) are appropriate to refined people in life and noble characters in literature and drama; middling laughter (*vihasita* and *upahasita*) suits middling people and common characters; wild laughter (*apahasita* and *atihasita*) is typical of vulgar, ill-bred people and low, disreputable characters. The hierarchical classification seems to suggest a denigration of laughter and the comic spirit. Bharata is explicit. "The comic sentiment is primarily the prerogative of women and low-class people" (*Nāṭyaśāstra* 6.51). The only noble laughter in the Indian normative context is silent, the smile wherein the expansive energy of delight is contained. People or characters who are refined (socially, religiously, or aesthetically) are able to control their emotions as well as the flesh which gives expression to those feelings. They enjoy the events which occur on the stage, in the text, or in the world itself with dispassion and detachment. Their lips curl up gently into smiles as slight and faint as they are tasteful and discriminative.

Comedy doesn't care. It merely laughs at such denigrations of itself with playful assaults on refinement, control, detachment, and taste. It pushes gently curving smiles toward feral laughter. It attains its heights through being base. It shows its teeth. The exquisitely vulgar Gaṇas affirm the world with the pleasurable exuberance of laughter, with a mirth that extends defiantly beyond the restrictive bounds of propriety, nobility, and wisdom. Comedy delights in its own excesses. We laugh not only at impropriety, but with impropriety: "We laugh at a thing," Hazlitt mused, "because we ought not."

Traditional Indian attitudes toward laughter are necessarily ambivalent. Laughter is enjoyed for the ways in which it accepts the world; it is dreaded for the empty silence inevitably trailing behind it. Laughter—infectious, loud, luminous laughter—is an invitation out of the chambers of an essential human solitude; but the laughter is transparent and the solitude is not fraudulent. The great affirmation of comic laughter can never quite succeed, for although it offers a refuge from despair, it is often also an expression of great sadness. "Even in laughter the heart is sorrowful," Solomon reflected, "and the end of that mirth is heaviness." Sorrow can be the source and destiny of even the most joyous laughter. The comedic voice, speaking lightly of heavy things, punctuating melancholy with its laughter, cannot hold out against the silence.

In India, as elsewhere, laughter was recognized as a symptom of divisions within the self, of madness and epilepsy. The laughter of the epileptic expresses terror rather than delight, anguish rather than joy, a painful eruption of pent-up energy that hideously distorts the body, a screech wrenched from the heart:

> Children throw their sticks and stones:
> He sings, he shrieks, and then he groans,
> Running this way, that way stopping
> Pushed by fate, rising, dropping,
> Uncontrolled, still, then quaking,
> Teeth grinding, flesh shaking,
> Mouth foaming, amidst the crowd
> The epileptic laughs aloud.
>
> (*Śāradātilaka* 112)

The mortal King Purūravas, tormented by the loss of his immortal consort, becomes literally insane with love. He laughs as he cries out, "Like a fool I neglect the rising of anguish in my heart" (*Vikramorvaśīya,* prose after 4.3). And again he laughs the gloomy laughter of madness as a swan flees from him in fear. The king has been destined to suffer because of a curse set upon him by a celestial dance master when he, Purūravas, laughed at the dance of a heavenly nymph (*Kathāsaritsāgara* 17.20–23). Laughter is as perilous as it is protective, as dark as it is luminous. The joy of comedy is tinged with gloom, spiked with a sadness which, according to Abhinava, strikes "like a flash of lightning" (commentary on *Nāṭyaśāstra* 1.119).

Laughter very often expresses ambiguous and contrary feelings. The shaking of the body in sweltering laughter is the physical enactment of an emotional tremor. Laughter is frequently linked with weeping in Sanskrit literature. Once upon a time a psychological puzzle was put to a king: an aged brahmin, through magic powers accrued in yogic practices, left his own body to enter that of a young man who had just died; as the youthful form came to life, the young/old man began to laugh and weep at the same time. What, the king was asked, was the cause of the weeping/laughter? He wept, the king explained, when he thought of the flesh he had inhabited for such a long time for "a love for one's own body is hard to give up," and he laughed and danced with joy, "for to whom is youth not desirable?" (*Kathāsaritsāgara* 97.47). Laughter and weeping, as physical expressions of emotion, bind spirit to flesh. In the context of a religious tradition in which isolation and liberation from matter is idealized, both laughter and weeping must be demeaned. They are not so very different from each other.

In preparation for a ritual feast for the dead, a brahmin had a goat brought for sacrifice. In a previous life the animal itself had been a brahmin who had sacrificed a goat in exactly this manner and had, as a result of the action, been destined to be born as a goat and to die at the hands of a brahmin 500 times. Having been sacrificially decapitated 499 times already, the goat, realizing that it would be free from its horrible transmigratory course the moment it was slain, began to laugh. But then, thinking of the brahmin, of the destiny he was about to inherit, the laughing goat began to weep (*Matakabhatta Jātaka* [18]). Joyous laughter arose out of relief from suffering only to return to its source. Weeping and laughter move toward each other, become and generate each other.

Learning that his parents had gone blind, a boy began to weep/laugh, to weep over his beloved parents' misfortune and to laugh both over the joyous prospect of caring for them and over the irony that he, the child, would be the support of his parents (*Sāma Jātaka* [540]).

"How can anyone laugh," the Buddha asked, "who knows of old age, disease, and death?" The laughter in each vignette, the laughter of the brahmin, the goat, and the child, is qualified by tears through a realization of the all-pervasiveness of transience and the inevitability of death. But as sorrow qualifies the joy, so the laughter of the brahmin, the goat, and the child qualifies their tears and all tears. The Buddha was a *muni,* a "silent one." Laughter is an impediment to the isolation which is liberation. It must give way to silence for the sake of transcendence. But at the same time, the silence must be rummaged for the laughter for the sake of immanence, a full participation in a sad and joyous world in preparation for release from it.

A king, the Buddha himself in a former life, arranged a celebration to mark his son's marriage and consecration as successor to the throne. The ceremonial feast went on and on, lasting seven years. It continued until the delight of it became unbearably tedious and the people of the kingdom asked when it would come to an end. They ached for everything to stop. The celebration might be understood as a Buddhist metaphor for empirical existence. Even happiness, through the endless repetitions of rebirth and redeath, becomes insignificant and unendurable. Ultimately one must yearn for cessation. The king spoke to the crowd, "My son the prince has never, not in his entire life, laughed. The celebration will end only when he has done so." The world, it seems, cannot be renounced until it has been enjoyed. There can be no deliverance until there has been laughter. Troops of tumblers, throngs of jugglers and magicians, hordes of clowns and acrobats, came from all over the land to try to make the young man laugh. All of them failed. When it seemed hopeless, a divine dancer descended from the heavens and began to perform the "half-body dance." He kept perfectly still except that one hand, one foot, one eye, one ear, and even one tooth, wiggled, flickered, twitched, and wobbled. The crowd roared, hooted, and howled with laughter, rolled over and over on the ground in wild, uncontrollable delight. As the prince—in reality the god Bhadra in an earthly incarnation—watched the dancer, his eyes opened wider, his cheeks rose, and ever so slightly, he laughed at the spectacle of divine stillness made ludicrous. The festival could come to an end and the prince could accept his bride and his new role as the future king (*Saruci Jātaka* [489]). For the heavenly Bhadra to acquire power on earth and an understanding of its people, he had to laugh with the people of the kingdom. From the material of mutual enjoyment laughter constructs a scaffolding for the building of social sympathy and reciprocity. Laughter creates a complicity of shared pleasure. It beckons one to join in.

The Acts of Laughter: *Satire and Humor*

> Traditional satire excoriates folly, finding it ridiculous but also corrigible. Humor seeks, not to expunge folly, but to condone or even to bless it, for humor views folly as endearing, humanizing, indispensable.
>
> Morton Gurewitch, *Comedy: The Irrational Vision*

In the theater, confronted by the comic spectacle, the individual who laughs surrenders emotional individuality to the collective sentiment of the audience. The personal body shakes with communal amusement. We may laugh with others even without getting the joke because laughter is contagious.

Indian literary theorists divided laughter into two types. There is a laughter that arises from perceptions of ludicrous incongruities and improprieties, from laughter's own determinants (*ātmastha*); and there is a laughter that has as its only determinant the laughter of others (*parastha*). "In everyday life," Abhinavagupta explains, "one can observe people who laugh not because they have actually seen something funny, but because they see someone else laughing. . . . It is just as when one's mouth begins to water when one sees someone eating a pomegranate. . . . Laughter is infectious" (commentary on *Nāṭyaśāstra,* prose after 6.48). Each individual member of an audience generates a spark of laughter. The theatrical space blazes with a fire that intensifies as it spreads, burning up distinctions between individuals. When laughter consumes the one who laughs, the comic *rasa* is fully tasted, and the sentiment is all that is experienced. Such a pure aesthetic moment, such a comedic instant, was equated by Abhinava and others with beatification, transcendence, pure gnosis, the tasting of the absolute, *brahman.* The comic mood then, despite its own perverse resistance to the sublime, despite its intractable profanity, could be considered incongruously and ironically sacred through the dynamics of *rasa*. This irony is itself a comic one.

Unlike Abhinava, some commentators seem to have construed Bharata's laconic twofold classification of laughter to indicate "laughter at oneself" (*ātmastha*) and "laughter at another" (*parastha*). The Jain scholiast Hemacandra (twelfth century) illustrated "self-laughter" with a stanza in which Śiva considers his own form. "My garment is the hide of the elephant king; my neck is scarred with the burns of *kālakūṭa* poison; the bracelet on my wrist is the king of serpents, the jewel in it being the blazing eye of his expanded hood." Then all at once Śiva begins to laugh because "the *beautiful* appearance of my body entices the eyes of Gaurī!" The great god laughs because his ascetic, if not hideous, appearance has, ironically, become beautiful to his consort through the power of desire. Śiva is at once the laugher and the butt of the joke, the subject and the object of the comic vision. The poet invokes a sacred humor: "May the laughter of the lord of beasts, which makes his cheeks so bright and merry, protect you!" (*Kāvyānuśāsana* 2.11 [citation 109]).

The aesthetician illustrated "laughter at another" with a poem about Rādhā and Kṛṣṇa. Looking at his beloved, the god "saw a reflection of his own form, dark as a fresh rain cloud, on those splendid pitchers, Rādhā's radiant breasts; mistaking the reflection for a dark robe, he tried again and again to remove it." And Rādhā laughed at her lord. The woman laughed at the man, the human being at the god.

The two somewhat unclearly defined Indian categories, laughter at oneself and laughter at another, can be understood as roughly comparable to two Western, and no less vague, categories of the comic: *humor* and *satire*. The comic vision is formed through their convergence, through the insight of satire and the outlook of humor.

As a vision the comic is a mode of discovery. It sees the incongruities and imperfections of the world. The comic eye opens and sparkles. The pupil contracts for in comedy the world is brightly and glaringly illuminated. The myopic eye of humor sees all things as if from a distance. It is a perspective from which the sorrows of the world may appear fuzzy, insubstantial, even ludicrous. The focused eye of satire scrutinizes, peeks, peers, inspects the human fabric for microscopic blemishes. Humor gazes in unfocused wonder at the nonsense inherent in even the most somber realities. Satire, meanwhile, is ever vigilant, always on the lookout for debased realities concealed by solemn nonsense. Through a repicturing of reality from both viewpoints, comedy laughs at the world.

The comic vision is of the fundamental folly, the cosmic goofiness, pervading every living thing. Humor, as I use the term, marks an acceptance, even a celebration, of that great folly through a socially and psychologically acceptable form of regression. Satire claims to condemn and indict folly through a socially and psychologically acceptable form of aggression. If either exceeds these parameters of acceptibility, they cease to be funny. Both test the limits, go up to the edge. Comedy can, even must, be at least slightly tasteless; but the tastelessness must be relishable.

Humor gently asserts the wisdom of folly; satire petulantly exposes the folly that masquerades as wisdom, the vice that passes itself off as virtue. Satire attacks. It isn't kidding. It tells the truth as the palindrome reveals—"Satire: *Veritas!*" Meanwhile humor jokes around. It plays. It is, as the corresponding palindrome suggests, nonsense—"Humor: *OṂ*! Uh?"

While the laughter of humor is sweet and indulgent, warm and childish, gratuitous and sympathetic, the laughter of satire is caustic and cool, intelligent and mature, purposeful and bitter. Satire is sadistically and voyeuristically pleasurable; the pleasure of humor is masochistic and exhibitionistic. Satire—I put a whoopie cushion on your seat to make a fool of you; humor—I put on a pair of glasses with a big nose and mustache attached to make a fool of myself. Anything for a laugh. Humor draws near; satire pushes back. Satire is logical and controlled; humor is daft and impulsive. While humor surrenders, satire assaults. In the comic agon satire is the offense, humor the defense. Satire sees distinctions and deals with oppositions between ideals and their degraded realities; humor sees paradoxes and is assured of the unity of opposites.

The distinctions at some point begin to blur. The categories interpenetrate each other. Śiva's laughter at himself is laughter at an irony that pervades the entire universe. It is an expression of acceptance. In his cheerful laughter, as in his ascetic meditation, he is the world. When Rādhā laughed at Kṛṣṇa, the god himself, the poet claims, "laughed out of embarrassment. Kṛṣṇa, whose beloved laughed at him, triumphs!" The laughter of the gods, of Śiva and Kṛṣṇa, the laughter that blesses, would be utterly contagious if we could or would but hear it.

In the cavern at Ellora I listened for it as I watched the Gaṇas teasing the great bull Nandī. My eyes moved up to Śiva and the goddess. His mouth and her face are gone, vandalized by time. Were these laughing faces once, with cheeks bright and merry to protect the world? Did the Lord of the Universe laugh or did he weep for us?

I walked to the Viśvakarman cave and stood before the colossal Buddha. His question came back, "How can there be mirth or laughter when the world is on fire?" Still he sits, eyes closed, mouth silent, body cool. Absolutely still. But here too Gaṇas play. They cavort above, beneath, all around the Buddha, in panels and arches, on columns and ceilings, impiously flaunting and flourishing their outrageous delight. Their presence here insinuates an answer to the Buddha's eternal question. If there is neither impulse nor inclination, neither sufficient wisdom nor strength, to pursue salvation or liberation, or if there is neither conviction nor faith that redemption or release is even possible or necessarily desirable, then what are we to do? Laughter, no matter how profane or evanescent, might at least be a means to endure those terrible flames of which the Buddha, even in his silence, speaks.

"Come along," Mr. V. Nayak, Śrī Vināyaka, Remover of Obstacles, broke in impatiently, "we are ready to leave. If I had not found you the bus would have left without you. You would have been stranded. That's no joke! Not comical at all!"

Act One: Satire

The Laughter of the Sons of Bharata 2

The Forms and Functions of Satire: Idealization and Degradation

Once they had mastered the *Scripture of Dramatic Arts,* my sons began to ridicule everyone in the entire universe with farces . . . and soon they performed a satire of the Divine Sages, a play full of vulgarities.

Bharata, *Nāṭyaśāstra*

Every satirist is a bastard son of Bharata, a fallen angel of ridicule, and all satiric laughter rings with a primordial abusiveness. The myth provides a contextual Indian definition of satire: it is an aesthetic mode of attack, directed against culturally esteemed objects and characterized by degrading vulgarities in which comic laughter arises out of a sudden perception of the ridiculousness of what has been traditionally idealized.

Satire was possible only after Bharata's sons had studied the treatise on the dramatic arts. The text provided a canon for satiric aggression. Through an adherence to the norms and conventions for literary form which that scripture supplied, anarchic assault was transformed into comedy. Ridicule became an art. Satire, without its comic tone and literary context, would be merely nasty denunciation. The comedic element marks its emergence from spell, primitive invective, and ritual malediction. Satire is magical curse infused with clownish mockery—it transcends and retains features of both. The satirist is at once an apotropaic priest, whose function is to ward off evil and protect, and a jester, whose purpose is to entertain and amuse. In the world of satire autochthonous evils, mythic energies of cosmic darkness and death, have become civilized vices, mundane torpidities of dullness and folly.

The dramatic farces of Bharata's sons became satirical when their ridicule focused upon the Divine Sages, the recipients and revealers of the Veda, men transformed into gods through human veneration. Such elevated *personae,* esteemed for divinity or sagacity, are the objects of all satire. Idealization empowers them and the prestige that they are granted protects that power. Satire aims at a redistribution of power, at the equality which comes with cultivated disrespect. The laughter of the sons of Bharata made heaven seem mundane.

The Divine Sages, justly angered by the satire, condemned the sons of Bharata to be born on earth as members of the lowest caste. So too Western satire, expelled from Parnassus, had to persist without the protection or grace of a muse.

Satire is threatening; its derogatory and contumacious laughter is retaliatory. On earth the satirist, as a sacerdotal clown, reenacts the primal assault of the sons of Bharata in a myriad of forms with a multitude of voices. Satire is comic revenge for the human condition.

The Overflowing Plate: *The Forms of Satire*

Or else [the word] *satura* is derived from the plate that was filled with many first offerings from the field and garden and offered to the gods in shrines by people of an earlier time. From its full and overflowing contents the plate was called a *satura.*

Diomedes, *Grammatici Latini*

The satire performed by Bharata's sons was a *prahasana,* a "farce," and that particular dramatic form continued in its development to be a primary medium of satiric assault. Bharata's typological treatise on dramaturgy distinguishes two types of farce on the basis of the kinds of characters appearing in them. "The 'pure' farce involves comic disputes between various characters—there are brahmins, priests, monks, religious devotees; and there are a lot of wisecracks made by vulgar characters" (*Nāṭyaśāstra* 18.103–104). The ludicrousness of the venerated is divulged through a juxtaposition of high and low, of religious idealities and vulgar actualities. Ancient ideals and aspirations have become degraded in the satiric present, and these degradations and perversions hide and are protected. They are crustaceans, soft, slimy, gelatinous creatures squeezed into hard shells slowly built up over time.

The other sort of farce described by Bharata is the "mixed" farce in which "sycophants, rogues, whores, eunuchs, servants, and sluts appear in immodest costumes, making lewd gestures" (*Nāṭyaśāstra* 18.105). Such unesteemed characters are not so much the objects of satire as they are servants to the satiric intent of ruffling, challenging, and ultimately exposing stodgy pretenders to propriety with their lewdness, immodesty, and profanity, with all their comic improprieties.

Most extant farces are a combination of the "mixed" and "pure," a "modified" type described in other dramaturgical texts as including in its cast of characters heretical religious figures—monks, ascetics, and brahmins—as well as, and in comic juxtaposition to, eunuchs, harem guards, whores, and other low and vulgar types. "They dress and speak as if they were lovers" (*Daśarūpaka* 3.55), as if they were the heroes and heroines of dramas informed with the amorous sentiment, stories about the sublime transports of love.

Satire strips away poetic fancies and exposes hieratic hypocrisies and social dissemblances in wild farces, chaotic spectacles full of pratfalls and slapstick, disputes and deceptions, stuttering and raving. Movement, physical and rhetorical, is exaggerated into ungraceful and disgraceful parody, into the grotesquely comic.

The Sanskrit farce corresponds to what critics of Western classical literature classify as "indirect" satire, Menippean or Varronian satire, discourse in which the objects of satire are the characters themselves—their own words and actions serve to expose their own vice and folly. Another Indian dramatic form that lent itself to the satiric voice and vision was the *bhāṇa,* the monologue play, a form corresponding to the Western critical category of "direct" or "formal" satire, Horatian or Juvenalian satire. Speaking in the first person, the satirist exposes the vices and follies of his age. This was stand-up comedy. The form was an actor's medium in which laughter was evoked as much by the mimic and acrobatic dimensions of the play as by the script. Comedy is a physical sensibility. In the *bhāṇas* a single actor played the part of a parasite, the *persona* of the satirist, a cultured and often jaded expert in sexual etiquette and amorous arts, who earned his livelihood as a counselor or go-between for a more wealthy patron, an aristocrat or a merchant aspiring to aristocratic manners. The parasite walks through the streets of a city, frequently for the sake of conducting an erotic business transaction for his patron; he describes the people he meets, indulges in imaginary conversations with brahmins and merchants, government officials and ministers, ascetics and monks, bawds and whores, rakes and crooks, every sort of character. High and low are comically juxtaposed. People from particular states or provinces, representatives of various castes or classes, are made fun of, are tickled and teased. He mimics their gestures and speaks their lines for them. With urbanity and wit, the parasite does the satirist's dirty work as he exposes the degradations around him. He is at once a spokesman for the satirist and yet, as a part of the motley world he describes, he is also an object of satire, a satirist self-satirized, a curved mirror reflecting a distorted world. The deformities of society are, as he reveals them, at once ugly and comic.

Indian literary theory divided poetry, that literature infused with one or more of the classified literary sentiments, into that which is seen and that which can only be read or heard. The former, drama, lent itself particularly to comedy since the comic sentiment is enhanced in the theater through the infectious nature of laughter. But the latter, narrative and stanzaic literature, was no less a vehicle for satiric perception. In this seemingly later form, the satiric complicity between author and reader is more intimate; yet its laughter is muted by solitude. Satire is a term which in the Indian context must refer to an aesthetic attitude rather than to a fixed literary form, a diffused genre that pervades other specific, defined genres. It is a tone. The term describes any comic literature which attacks affectation, vanity, or hypocrisy, which strives to lay bare the lasciviousness of what seems chaste, the dirtiness of what is esteemed for its purity, the crudity of what is adored for its beauty, and the ludicrous banality of what is venerated for its sublime loftiness. Satire is a mode of exploration which leads to the discovery of profane realities hidden within sacred ideals. Cynicism is the wisdom of the satirist. The wisdom is disgruntled, even seamy. Satire is tragic, pathetic comedy. "Satire at its most concentrated," according to Northrop Frye, "is tragedy robbed of all dignity and nobility, a universal negation that cheapens and belittles everything" ("Satire"). But out of the negation comes a laughter that is its own affirmation.

The Ass in Tiger's Skin: *The Objects of Satire*

Now affectation proceeds from one of two causes, vanity or hypocrisy: for as vanity puts us on affecting false characters, in order to purchase applause; so hypocrisy sets us on an endeavor to avoid censure, by concealing our vices under an appearance of their opposite virtues. . . . From the discovery of this affectation arises the ridiculous, which always strikes the reader with surprize and pleasure.

Henry Fielding, *Joseph Andrews*

Comic laughter arises with the perception of people trying to be what they are not. Satire focuses on such affectation: on hypocrisy—a wolf puts on sheep's clothing, a dangerous person tries to appear meek or benign; and on vanity—a sheep dresses up as a wolf, an ineffectual person tries to appear powerful, even dangerous. The fur and the wool always get confused in comedy.

In India the wolf and the sheep are the tiger or panther and the ass, respectively. A washerman, in order that his ass might graze in the fields and gardens of farmers without being chased off, covered the beast of burden with the skin of a tiger so that the farmers, mistaking it for a tiger, would run from it rather than after it. The bluff of the ass is discovered in one version of the story when it brays in response to the call of a female ass (*Pañcatantra* 3.1), and in another when it chases after a farmer who, having covered himself with a rug, tries to crawl away in fear. The ass thinks the farmer is a female donkey (*Kathāsaritsāgara* 62.19–23). In both cases it is the sexual desire of the animal that gives away truth, that betrays the masquerade. And so with all objects of satire, inner impulses, desires for sex, wealth, or any other manifestations of power, break through the guises that hide them. Had the ass not been disguised it would have been merely chased away from the fields; but, in the guise of the tiger, the ass is slain. Satire demands punishment and dispenses it in the form of shaming laughter.

The mortal sin in satire is pretense, the hiding of any venal sin or the flaunting of empty emblems of sinlessness. The great crime for satire is not any particular felony except the refusal to accept responsibility for one's misdemeanors by attempting to conceal them or to attribute them to someone else. "Crooked kings blame their ministers," the satirist notes, "for their own wicked actions" (*Ubhayābhisārikā* 26). "He who falls," in satire, "blames the ground" (*Śāradātilaka,* prose after 34). The satirist himself may be guilty of the vices and prone to the follies that he castigates in the butts of his satires. "An Execut'oner am I/ Of Lust and Wanton Venery," George Wither, the early seventeenth-century satirical poet and pamphleteer, at once boasted and confessed, "Thus are Vices scourg'd by mee,/ Yet my selfe from Vice not free."

Satiric laughter is laughter at others. The satirist is like the wife of a wealthy merchant who left her husband to run away with an incorrigible thief. When the two fugitives came to a river, the woman removed her heavy jewels and expensive garments so that her roguish paramour could carry them across the water for her. The thief, of course, ran away, leaving the adulteress naked and without resources. As she was sitting on the bank weeping over the injustice that had been done to her, she saw a jackal on the shore with a piece of meat in its mouth. When a fish suddenly jumped up above the surface of the water, the jackal dropped the meat in hopes of catching the fish. At once a bird swooped down and grabbed the meat away from the jackal. The woman began to laugh, to laugh as she wept for herself as the victim of a dissembler, to laugh at the jackal for being so foolish as to give up the good meat in hopes of catching a better fish, and in so doing ending up with nothing (*Culladhanujjaha Jātaka* [374]). Though the satirist laughs at the follies and vices of others, he may weep for himself "from Vice not free" as a victim of lies and frauds. Satire is sad and bitter comedy. But surely the spectacle of the stupid jackal consoled the woman. There is a dark pleasure, expressed in satire's perverse laughter, in knowing that others are as bad, foolish, weak, or pathetic as oneself.

Something Fishy: *The Laughter of Satire*

South El Monte, Calif.—A man enraged at a group of people laughing over his inept attempts to park his car yesterday opened fire with a handgun, killing one man and wounding another.

Honolulu Star-Bulletin & Advertiser, February 17, 1985

"People willingly tolerate reproof," Molière observed in his preface to *Tartuffe,* "[but] they won't tolerate teasing. People like being bad; they never like being ridiculous." Sharp laughter is satire's weapon, wielded to cut the wicked down to size, to make vice ludicrous, to peel away surfaces, to hack through falseness, to eviscerate and expose to others all affectation, corruption, and hypocrisy.

Seeing one of his queens leaning out of the window to speak with a passing brahmin, a certain king became so enraged with jealousy that he ordered the execution of the brahmin. As the innocent was being led through the marketplace to his slaughter, a dead fish laughed at the spectacle. Hearing the laughter, the king ordered a stay of execution until the cause of the laughter could be determined. He was informed that the fish had laughed when it had an ironic thought—"all of the queens are dissolute. They have men in the harem disguised as women; and while those men indulge themselves, the king is having this brahmin murdered!" The satirical laughter of the fish led to the exposure of the faithlessness of the lusty queen, the ignorance of the cuckolded king, and the ridiculousness of the transvestite lovers. The story suggests an emendatory potential for satirical laughter—realizing his folly through the laughter of the fish, the king freed the brahmin (*Kathāsaritsāgara* 5.14–27). But reform is merely an occasional by-product of satirical laughter, the excuse for it, not its goal. The fish did not laugh in order to change the king, the queens, or the illicit lovers. With nothing to gain and nothing to give, the dead fish simply laughed at a spectacle of unrecognized folly and unnoticed vice.

In another version of the tale it is a fried fish being served as dinner to a queen who laughs, laughs like the satirist in the face of being devoured, laughs so hard that everyone in the town hears it, when the woman says, "Swāmī! I can hardly bear to look at these males [these male fish], let alone touch them" (*Śukasaptati* 6 [prose after 30]). The king demanded that his royal priest discover the reason and meaning of the laughter. Knowing that the truth, the fact that the king was a cuckold, would challenge the limits of the ruler's loyalty, the priest was afraid to disclose the cause of the laughter. The priest enumerated the things of the world of which one may have heard, but which no one has ever seen: "cleanliness in a crow, honesty in a gambler, patience in a snake, sexual satiation in women, potency in a eunuch, wisdom in a drunkard, friendship in a king" (6 [33]).

The daughter of the royal priest, appearing before the king, told him that he could discover why the fish laughed from his former minister, Mr. Flowerchuckle (Puṣpahāsa), whom he had previously imprisoned. Flowerchuckle had a remarkable gift—whenever he laughed fresh blossoms fell from his mouth. The king had once invited dignitaries from neighboring kingdoms to come and see this extraordinary feat. He boasted proudly of Flowerchuckle's talents, but in the presence of the visitors the man neither laughed nor produced any flowers. And so he had been jailed. Released by the king in order to provide an answer to the mystery of the laughter of the fish, he was questioned as to why he had not laughed for those important ambassadors. Solemnly the reinstated minister explained that he could not laugh for he had become aware of the queen's involvement in an adulterous affair. In disbelief the king, to test his wife's affections, tossed a garland of flowers playfully at her face. The queen, feigning the weakness of love, fell into a sham faint as if from the blow of the flowers. Suddenly blossoms began to gush as florid laughter from Flowerchuckle's mouth. The infuriated king demanded to know the cause of the disrespectful laughter. The frightened minister explained. "Last night she was beaten with canes by the servants [for admitting lovers into the harem room] and she didn't faint—*now* she faints!" (*Śukasaptati* 9 [prose after 79]). The minister did not laugh at her adultery but at her falseness. He advised the king to strip his wife and see the scars of the beating for himself. Stripping is a constant event in satire, suggesting the satiric method and goal. The king now understood why the fish had laughed. And in this telling of the story there is no suggestion of laughter's reformative potential. Nothing changes. Some time later the king discovered yet another man with his wife. Vice and folly, to the simultaneous despair and amusement of the satirist, are eternal.

Satire is a search for truth, the social truth which is justice and the personal truth which is honesty. The satirist, as Horace says, "speaks the truth laughing," and it is this laughing, the comic resonance of satire, that allows the truth to be uttered. When a whore in the *Śāradātilaka* of Śaṅkara (seventeenth–eighteenth century) is angered by the satirical insinuations of a parasite, the man laughs, "You aren't the only one who gets mad when the truth is boldly uttered. But, don't be angry, I was only joking" (prose after 61). Of course, the satirist is only joking when he says that he is "only joking." "Only joking" is a euphemism in satire for telling the awful truth, for being deadly serious, for venting pent-up hostility. Kṣemendra claims that he is respectful and in "no way acerbic, but that he has composed [his satirical text] just as an excuse to make people laugh" (*Deśopadeśa* 8.52). The satirist is a liar who insists on the truth.

Satire, born according to Samuel Johnson "of an unholy cohabitation of wit and malice," is the most serious of all comic forms and modes, and the most unscrupulously nasty. Satire is hostile—the Divine Sages were justified in expelling the sons of Bharata from heaven and in trying to repress them. Moral or legal prohibitions force the sublimation of direct physical assault into verbal aggression; aesthetic prohibitions or norms transform these verbal hostilities into satire. The satirist begs our pardon by insisting that he is only joking, and the laughter of the audience grants it. Satire is the literary equivalent of the tendentious joke, the funny story which, according to Freud, allows us "to exploit something ridiculous in our enemy which we could not, on account of obstacles in the way, bring forward openly or consciously; once again, then, the joke will evade restrictions and open sources of pleasure that have become inaccessible. . . . The yield of pleasure [in the tendentious joke or in satire] corresponds to the psychical expenditure that is saved" in expressing, rather than repressing, hostilities (*Jokes and Their Relation to the Unconscious*). The appeal of satire then, the pleasure derived from it, is an aesthetic experience of a release of the tension caused by the repression of aggressive feelings toward certain figures, figures endowed with enough power to demand that repression, to command veneration and esteem. The release of tension is physically expressed in laughter.

Just as the satirist excuses his hostility aesthetically by making it funny, he may excuse it morally by insisting that it serves an ethical end, that it somehow changes society for the better, that it has a corrective function.

Friends in a Corner: *The Functions of Satire*

If I ridicule the Follies and Corruptions of a Court, a Ministry, or a Senate, are they not amply paid by Pensions, Titles, and Power, while I expect and desire no other Reward than that of laughing with a few friends in a Corner?

Jonathan Swift, *Intelligencer* III

The satirist strikes a pose of good will, a posture of moral concern, to inflict his vindictive attack. The ironic *apologia* was a convention in Sanskrit satirical texts just as it was in classical and European comic literature. In the epilogue to his *Samayamātṛkā,* Kṣemendra insists that his composition is "for the benefit of good people" and that a study of it "would serve to safeguard the money of wealthy young men." Similarly, Dāmodaragupta ends the *Kuṭṭanīmata* with the assertion that he wrote it to expose the wiles of whores as a lesson to gentlemen.

Satirists, as well as countless critics and theoreticians, have argued that satire goads man with ridicule into higher moral sensibilities. Kṣemendra claims that "by laughter people are completely shamed and then they don't indulge in vice any more; my [satiric] undertaking has been for the benefit of such people" (*Deśopadeśa* 1.4). It is debatable, if not irrelevant, however, whether or not satire has ever effected any social change or institutional reform. The modern Indian satirist R.K. Laxman admits the ineffectuality of his satirical cartoons. "I have been working away at these cartoons for over a quarter of a century now, and I do not think that I can show a single instance of changing the mind of a politician from taking a mad course. . . . My efforts have not so far converted any minister to the humble ways of an honest, simple servant of the people. If I had lashed at granite with a feather with the single-minded zeal as I have bestowed on my work, by now I would, perhaps, have been able to show some faint feather marks on the rock. . . . [but] not a trace of a dent have my cartoons caused in any sphere of human activity, whether social, economic or political" (*You Said It,* vol. 5, intro.). The world does not change for the better. At best, it is stagnant (fig. 4). More often, it declines, degenerates, fizzles. The satiric tribunal cannot change that. But it can laugh at it.

The satirist and his audience revel in the sheer joy of truculence. In the corner, or in the theater, the bond of laughter made between the satirist and his audience renders them all the less vulnerable to the objects of satire, the men in the court, ministry, or senate. This is the conspiracy of comedy.

Laughter helps or changes only those who laugh. A princess suffering from an abscess in her throat is treated without success by all the physicians in the court. Her cure comes when the abscess is broken open by her gleeful laughter over a story about a monkey thief (*Śukasaptati* 41). Madam Toothey (Danturā), the old bawd in the *Laṭakamelaka* of Śaṅkhadhara Kavirāja (twelfth century), calls a doctor because her best girl, Miss Lovebouquet (Madanamañjarī) has a fishbone caught in her throat. The physician, the consummate quack, Dr. Wormbanner (Jantuketu), explains that his father was once confronted with a similar case. "A camel in the desert got a

. . . and the ruler goes on to assure his subjects that he will eradicate poverty, unemployment . . . .

Figure 4

crab caught in its throat somehow. Thick ropes were tied around the camel's muzzle and tugged on hard—suddenly the crab was dislodged from the beast's throat!" (prose after 1.22). When Dr. Wormbanner suggests the same treatment for Miss Lovebouquet, the young harlot begins to laugh at the doctor, to laugh so convulsively that the fishbone is dislodged from her throat. She is spared the dangerous cure prescribed by the authority on health. The scene may be understood as illustrative of the function of all satire. Satiric laughter is a medicine—but it treats the one who laughs, not the one who is the butt of the laughter. With pleasure it spares us of some of our need of the dangerous figures who are its object. Ultimately the satirist strives not for the unlikely reformation of the satiric object, but for the awakening of that object's victims. Satire is for satire's sake. Its power is indicative, not corrective; its appeal is aesthetic, not moral. Though satire points out vice and folly, its justification on the grounds that it changes social conditions, that it eradicates transgressions, is a rationalization of its most primary aim which is, quite simply, to be funny.

F——ing Funny: *The Vulgarity of Satire*

> The motive for telling a joke always consists of an attempt to get the approval of the audience for the underlying guilt in the offensive impulses concealed in the joke. . . . Such behavior implies that the person fears being punished for his instinctual impulses. By pretending that he is merely jesting, he hopes to avoid punishment. Usually, however, the jesting is more than an avoidance of punishment; it has an exhibitionistic quality, and is an attempt to get confirmation from the spectators, and to seduce them to participate in the jesting sexual or aggressive acts. The idea of making others laugh is a substitute for the idea of exciting them. Without the jest, this excitement would be frightening.
>
> Otto Fenichel, *The Psychoanalytic Theory of Neurosis*

The satirical drama played in heaven by Bharata's sons was "full of vulgarities. Their satire was really not fit to be performed in public—its poetry was unspeakably depraved, salacious, and abusive" (*Nāṭyaśāstra* 36.34). Vulgarity, depravity, salaciousness, and abusiveness persisted as characteristics of the satirical literature which was to evolve. "Obscenity," according to Northrop Frye, "is an essential characteristic of the satirist. . . . all great satirists have been obscene" ("The Nature of Satire"). Obscenity, scatology, bawdry, dysphemism, all contribute to the comic indecorum and brazen impropriety which serve satire's diminutional objectives. Smut is funny. Wit, poetic intelligence, and often ironic apology make it acceptably unacceptable.

Characters in Sanskrit satire have names like Mr. Prodigiousprick (Pracaṇḍaśepha, the harem guard in the *Kautukaratnākara* [sixteenth century]), Mr. Cuntface and Ms. Pussyflower (Vyañjanamukha and Yonimañjarī in the *Prāsaṅgika* of Harijīvanamiśra [seventeenth century]), and Ms. Fondafucking (Suratapriyā in the *Dhūrtasamāgama* of Kaviśekhara Jyotīśvara [fourteenth century]). And the behavior of the characters is as outrageously risqué and tastelessly lewd as their names. In the *Hāsyārṇava* of Jagadīśvara Bhaṭṭācārya (fourteenth century) Master Troublesprout (Kalahāṅkura) falls to the ground, looks under Madam Bawdbent's (Bandhurā) sari, and announces, "Hey, Bawdbent's got a beard between her legs" (prose after 1.23). He exposes himself as much as he exposes the old whore. The fact that she is a procuress already draws attention to her sexuality—his antics make his own prurience known and the bawd laughs at him: "This brahmin's a loser" (prose after 1.24). To crawl under someone's legs would be considered an ultimate expression of self-debasement; an old bawd in the *Śāradātilaka* calls out to a young man, "Hey, motherfucker, crawl under my legs" (prose after 71). The satirist himself must be vulgar, must crawl under people's legs to expose them, must reveal his own baseness, in order not to commit the very crimes he condemns—hypocrisy and affectation.

Obscenity is a quality, not a fault, in satire, an achievement, and a strategy for the transformation of the amorous sentiment into the comic. It is a method of shocking, baiting, and ridiculing Divine Sages. And yet it is because of their obscenities that the Sanskrit satirical farces have been largely ignored. They have been censured and dismissed as meritless. While the genre was always traditionally popular, and while a vast number were written and performed throughout the history of Indian theater, very few have been printed, edited, or even catalogued. The reasons are clear: the nineteenth-century Indologist and collector of Sanskrit manuscripts, Georg Bühler, wrote to Maurice Winternitz, who was composing a history of Sanskrit literature, that he had discovered a great number of satirical farces but that he had "no intention of publishing them on account of their being too obscene" (Winternitz, *History of Indian Literature*). Just as the Divine Sages cast the sons of Bharata out of heaven, more modern sages, revealers not of the Veda but of Sanskrit literature, banished bawdy satirists into academic oblivion with puritanical judgements. A basic historical survey of Sanskrit literature describes the *Hāsyārṇava* as "disfigured by unredeemed vulgarity of words and acts" and denigrates the satirical farces in general as "suffering from lack of taste. . . . There is no merit in attempting to raise laughter by deliberately vulgar exhibitions and expressions, which mar the effect of the plays even as burlesques and caricatures. The parodies of high-placed people lose their point, not only from tastelessness and exaggeration, but also from their extremely sordid and prosaic treatment. . . . Detailed and puerile coarseness is redundant and ineffective" (S. N. Das Gupta and S. K. De, *History of Sanskrit Literature, Classical Period*). The scholar is right about the plays, perhaps, but quite wrong about the nature of satire, and I would rephrase his assessment accordingly. With various modes of language and various types of characters, the satirist establishes a tension between the high and the low, the lofty and the prosaic, the refined and the coarse, the tasteful and the tasteless. The latter categories challenge the former to expose affectation and pretense. Through the use of vulgar exhibitions and expressions, through redundancy and exaggeration, satire becomes effective; the lowness of people placed all too high is revealed. There is a sudden recognition of the actual or potential sordidness, puerility, and inanity behind endless social guises of respectability and ideality.

"The spheres of sexuality and obscenity offer the amplest occasions for obtaining comic pleasure," according to Freud, as we have seen, "for they can show human beings in their dependence on bodily needs (degradation) or they can reveal the physical demands lying beneath the claim of mental love (unmasking)" (*Jokes and Their Relation to the Unconscious*). Satire is a literary method of such degradation or diminution, of such unmasking or revealing the truth of the body. That it is a comic method, that people are seduced to join in with carnal laughter, a pleasurable laughter which is itself an admission of baseness, assuages the primary aggressiveness of the activity, makes the vicious assault socially permissible. The gods mediated on behalf of the sons of Bharata so that drama could persist and continue to amuse, delight, and entertain with both its most sublime reveries and its most raucous vulgarities. Art justifies sexual and aggressive impulse and fantasy.

In satires of manners the amorous sentiment is satirically degraded into comic pornography. Pure love becomes a dirty joke. When the beautiful mask of love falls away, a lewd grimace appears on a face that is familiar. In social satire, revelations of the lust of kings, ministers, judges, and physicians act as reminders that the people in such idealized positions in the social hierarchy are basically, biologically, the same as the people who venerate them for their status. The reminder is pleasurable—the burden of the knowledge of one's own baseness is lightened in sharing it with others, particularly when those others have been previously esteemed for being beyond such baseness. One function of satire is to give that pleasure. That delight is particularly great in religious satire where we encounter endless goatish gurus, profligate yogis, wanton monks, horny ascetics—figures whose inner licentiousness is the very opposite of all outward shows and claims. Laughter arises through surprising perceptions of incongruity. And the satirist presents just those perceptions, pointing out the ways in which prurience parades as love, reprobation mimics religion, and roguery pretends to be righteousness. With vulgarities and obscenities the satirist religiously asseverates the truth of flesh and blood, the realness of earth and mud, in the face of all that claims to be spirit or heaven, truth or beauty. He points to the prick in the loincloth of the most holy ascetic, the cunt hidden by the garb of the most refined lady, and the shit that drops from the rear end of the purest brahmin. And he laughs. He laughs the truth.

In modern India, plagued as it has been by censorship, the censor is a frequent object of satirical derision (fig. 5). He personifies the puritanical propensities of the nation as well as the repressive tendencies within each individual. Satire is a reminder of the potential social and psychological dangers of morality or propriety.

Verbal propriety marks one's place in the social hierarchy. The satirist uses obscenities to remove himself from that hierarchy, to establish a vantage point from which he can laugh at the hierarchy and all respectability. The holy man does the same. A Bengali intellectual, an ardent devotee of Ramakrishna, surprised to hear

. . . and now our honored guest will speak on "The Evil of SEX in the Indian Cinema."

Figure 5

his blessed guru, the divine being himself, utter an obscenity, exclaimed, "I didn't know you knew such words!" The spiritual master explained with a laugh that he knew many of these words, more than the intellectual. Rising to the challenge, the cosmopolitan writer began to utter obscenities, and for each one he could think of, Ramakrishna would come back with one, even dirtier, of his own, until at last the disciple bowed to the saint: "In this too, you are my guru!" (personal communication from Christopher Isherwood).

The Age of Dullness: *The Cosmology of Satire*

Religion blushing veils her sacred fires,
And unawares Morality expires.
For public Flame, nor private, dares to shine;
Nor human Spark is left, nor Glimpse divine!
Lo! thy dread Empire, CHAOS! is restor'd;
Light dies before thy uncreating word;
Thy hand, great Anarch! lets the curtain fall
And universal Darkness buries All.

Alexander Pope, *The Dunciad*

Hindu cosmology, dividing time into four cosmic ages, each marked by increasing, entropic, physical, social, moral, and spiritual degeneration, provides the reference points for the Sanskrit satirist's comparison of his existing world with the world as it might be or as it once was. Implicitly or explicitly the satirist contrasts the codified ideals of the past with their perversions and degradations in the current Kali Yuga, the Age of Degeneration, Darkness, or "Dullness," the word Pope used in *The Dunciad* to describe that primordial force that weighs the world down, wears it out, and infuses it with stupidity, nastiness, pomposity, vanity, affectation, hypocrisy, and chaos. This empire of dullness is described by Kṛśānu, a malevolent *gandharva* in the *Viśvaguṇādarśa,* a satirical dialogue by Veṅkaṭādhvarin (seventeenth century). "There were, in previous ages, certain people on the surface of the earth who were pleasing enough with their fine qualities. But now, in this Age of Dullness, all people are devoid of even the slightest virtues—abundant vice runs rampant. The spirit is polluted by raging passions, envy, wrath, pride. . . . The leaders of the age have wicked attitudes" (30–31). The satirist is a jester for the apocalypse, a herald of Kalkin. The end is at hand. The satirist laughs at the thought. The word "repent" might be heard beneath the sound of that anomic laughter.

The hallowed ideals of the past, degraded in the Age of Dullness, were classified by the cultural philosophers and social theorists of ancient India. Initially they categorized three basic phases of experience (later four) in which existence on earth could be fulfilled, three desired ends of human life: *kāma*—pleasure, particularly in connection with the erotic arts and aesthetic accomplishments; *artha*—material prosperity, especially those involved with fine management in statecraft and business; *dharma*—religion, specifically in reference to virtue and morality defined in terms of duty. These three ideals provide three arenas of Sanskrit satire: satire of manners, revealing the degradation of love and the arts into vanity and affectation; social satire, divulging the degradation of statecraft and righteousness into corruption; religious satire, disclosing the degradation of piety into hypocrisy and impurity. Each of the cultural ideals has an implicitly correspondent aesthetic flavor or sentimental ideal: the amorous sentiment, the heroic sentiment, and the sentiment of peace. Within each arena of satire the comic sentiment or mood is established through the deflation of those serious sentiments by the use of ludicrously incongruous and inappropriate images, language, or characters.

The *dramatis personae* of Sanskrit satire are comic to the degree to which they betray or pervert the ideal that they ought, or pretend, to uphold. The satires of manners are populated by insincere and venal whores, by ugly women who try to appear beautiful, by inept, frigid, or impotent lovers, by effete dandies, sycophants and parasites, by poetasters and bad musicians, transvestites and dirty old men, by pretentious sons of the *nouveau riche,* and by a motley crew of supporting players—bawds, barbers, students, and rogues. Social satires reveal the true nature of kings, judges, ministers, government comptrollers, generals, policemen, astrologers, physicians. Religious satire focuses on hypocritical and sanctimonious brahmin priests, Buddhist and Jain monks, ascetics, renouncers, yogis, and devotees of every sort.

In the context of a culture in which morality was defined relatively to birth, to social or domestic role, the crime as well as the ludicrousness of the satirical objects are not in the nature of their words, thoughts, or actions as such, but in the inappropriateness of those words, thoughts, or actions. Impropriety is comic vice and comic folly. Sexual indulgence, the fulfillment of pleasure as one of the ends of human life, is charming in a courtesan and admirable in a man of the world, but comically a sin in a monk or ascetic. Conversely, while an absence of sexual desire could be the realization of a religious ideal in a holy man, it is comic in a lover or a courtesan. In satire whores pretend to be passionate, but think only of money, thoughts that would not be ludicrous in a merchant. Ascetics, priests, and monks ape dispassion, while obsessed with sexual pleasures. A judge in the *Pādatāḍitaka,* a monologue play by Śyāmilaka (c. fifth century), drifts into meditation, a perfectly good activity in a religious aspirant, while he should be hearing a court case and thus perverts justice. *Kāma, artha,* and *dharma,* are mixed up and thoroughly confused with one another in the Age of Dullness. This mingle-mangling of ideals, like the mixing of castes, is considered a symptom of the total degradation, the spiritual, social, and cultural pandemonium, that characterizes the satiric moment. Nīlakaṇṭha Dīkṣita (sixteenth–seventeenth century) complains that in this epoch of vice and folly "the gossip of women is the Veda, earning money is religion, and one's own notions are reason" (*Kaliviḍambana* 100). This chaos, the object of satiric complaint, is also the source of satiric laughter. The anarchic shuffling and jumbling of the amorous, heroic, religious, and other sentiments is the source of the comic mood, of comedy's wild laughter. As he indicates, the prevalence of vice and folly in his age, as he exposes affectation, corruption, and hypocrisy, the satirist laughs and the sound of the laughter is meant to awaken and seduce others and to relieve and soothe himself.

For their laughter, contumelious, vulgar, mocking, outrageous laughter, the sons of Bharata were expelled from heaven by the Divine Sages, but on earth their laughter provides a means to endure the fall. There is something redemptive about the comic sensibility—the way of laughter may not guide one back to heaven or back to a purer more splendid age, but it can lead to a refuge, a corner full of friends, a sanctuary of gaity.

The City of Dreadful Night: *The Setting of Satire*

Luxury hatches terrors worse than wars, avenging a world beaten down. Every crime is here, every lust, as they have been since the day, long since, when Roman poverty perished.

Juvenal, *Satires*

Satire is an urban form. The monologue plays, farces, as well as the narrative satires conventionally open with stock descriptions of the season, usually spring, followed by hyperbolic eulogies of the particular city in which the satire is set. The parasite/satirist in the *Ubhayābhisārikā* of Vararuci (c. fifth century C.E.) typically praises the splendors of the King's Road in Flowerville (Kusumapura). "It is washed and cleaned and ornamented with flowers. . . . People are shopping in the market and the palaces that line the street seem to be talking to each other as they ring out with the sound of music, the chanting of the Veda, and the twanging of bowstrings. . . . Upon glorious steeds and elephants, and in their chariots, government officials look magnificent; and promenading ladies, dressed in the finest fashions, rival the damsels in the city of the gods for beauty. . . . Life here is an everlasting festival of joy. . . . The city is an ornament upon the forehead of the goddess Earth, making her look like Heaven" (6, and prose after 5). But the descriptive paeans merely establish the ideal, the dream or fantasy of what civilization might be. They depict only the contours of the deceitful surface. Once the satirist, in this and in other plays, begins his peregrinations through the city, once the characters begin to appear, the reality behind the fancy begins to emerge, the putrid degradations begin to overwhelm the promise of an urban ideal. Satire sees the existing social order as organized chaos, a hierarchical systemization of destruction in the name or guise of civilization. Like Juvenal's depictions of Rome, like Hogarth's portraits of London, the satirical descriptions of Indian cities are invariably pictures of decay, greed, lust, depravity, and corruption. Splendid palaces are merely artful facades. Beautiful faces are but tentative masks. Fashions and uniforms are only costumes. All is pretense. Pandemonium mimics order; jungle affects city; a hungry horde poses as a society. Crowd scenes intensify the feeling of the aimlessness, squalor, and confusion that the satirist sees being passed off as civilization. The city, like each of its inhabitants, is one thing on the outside and another within. This contradiction, at once amusing and disturbing, is the central obsession of satire.

The parasite in the *Śāradātilaka* sings a proemial paean on the glories of Clangorville (Kolāhalapura) using an intricate series of sustained puns to show how the city compares with, and even surpasses, the city of the gods. "The gods are only interested in stuffing their guts, whereas here good and virtuous people care for the poor as if they were family'' (30–31). Clangorville is a beautiful pleasure resort full of lovely lotus ponds, frequented by the most handsome and sophisticated of gallants, inhabited by the most graceful of courtesans, all learned in the erotic arts and sciences. The city is rich and prosperous. The streets abound with men of learning, wisdom, and piety. In constant devotion, sacrifices are performed. But then the idealized description of Clangorville is interrupted by the ``clangor'' in the streets—the poet uses the common noun that is the name of the city, a word implying loud and indistinct noise, a chaotic din, and the satiric effect of this is a simultaneous awareness of both the common reality and the proper ideal. The clangor rises as the people, in a parody of conventional scenes of royal procession, rush to the parapets and stand on tiptoes to witness the return of their king with his mighty array of troops. Descriptions build expectations of glory and magnificence, expectations that are comically subverted with the sudden realization that this is a return not from battle, but from a hunt where the ``powerful army has killed wild animals as if they were enemies—bears were slaughtered with spears, tigers were driven out of hiding with drums, rhinos were slain with swords, and buffaloes with arrows'' (*Śāradātilaka* 35 and prose after 36). The parasite ironically praises the king for his valor, for the power of his great army, and there are gifts given in return for the praises. The slaughter of animals replaces noble battle. The image of the massacre of beasts hangs ominously over the play to suggest the deadly force of bathos, the threat posed to the innocent by the socially empowered.

Images of violence, death, and destruction abound in satire, counterbalancing its glee, infusing its laughter, and imparting a bitter aftertaste to the comic flavor. It was a convention of the satirical monologues to describe animal fights—cock fights, ram fights, battles between elephants, between trained monkeys and snakes. The descriptions serve to indicate the violence that has been covered over by civilization, that has become a divertissement, a socially acceptable bloodthirstiness. Human accomplishments and refinements are simply the guises that bestial viciousness and lust take on in the city:

beaks sharp
necks stretched
from a distance QUICK
the cocks

each aiming
to slash the face
razors on
the claws
screams in the gullet
leaping-screeching-scratching-fighting in
great swells of violence
(*Śāradātilaka* 104)

The owner of the victorious cock receives a courtesan as his prize. The cockfight replaces more heroic battles between men. Codes of honor no longer exist except as empty forms or worn-out dreams.

There is terror in satire, for satire confronts the dreadful. "To become fully conscious of the atrocious," according to Ionesco, "and to laugh at it, is to master the atrocious" (*Notes and Counternotes*). Satirical laughter is a mark of such mastery, of such sad, though jovial, triumph.

The Triumph of Laughter: *The Origins of Satire*

Comedy originated with the leaders of the Phallic Songs, which survive to this day in many of our states.
Aristotle, *Poetics*

The ancient satirical farce as described by Bharata may well have developed, in part at least, out of still older Vedic rituals, just as Attic Greek comedy seems to have evolved, through folk drama, out of more archaic Indo-European rituals, particularly seasonal rites of renewal. The vernal rite involved the dispelling of darkness (old age, disease, death, sterility, hunger, poverty, impurity, sin) and a bringing in of light (youth, health, life, fertility, nourishment, wealth, purity, blessedness), a ritual battle between the forces of life and death. The conquest of the old by the new, the beginning of spring, the lengthening of days, was celebrated with marriages and orgiastic processions. Attic comedy, and the Sanskrit satirical farce and monologue play, retained the verbal abuse and mock battles, the obscenities and lewd gestures, of ancient ritual. "The element of invective," in satire, according to F. M. Cornford, "is directly descended from the magical abuse of the phallic procession, just as its obscenity is due to sexual magic" (*the Origin of Attic Comedy*). The evolution of theurgical ritual into art, of apotropaic incantation into satire, is a process of sublimation. The evolution is from rite to drama, from magical motives to aesthetic ones. In the fertility rite evil, personified by the hosts of demons, is expelled so that the earth can be renewed; in the satirical drama vice, personified by the hosts of satirical objects, is expelled, made a laughing stock, for the renewal of the social order. The actual efficacy of the rite or the satire, the literal impact of the priest or the satirist on the cosmos or the polis is largely irrelevant—the ritual is successful, the drama has value, when the participants, dancing in the procession or laughing in the theater, experience a strengthening of the bonds between them. There can be an internal renewal despite the entropic forces of the external world.

The Vedic Mahāvrata ceremony presents one example of the kind of ritual that provided the paradigmatic forms, motives, and strategies which were transformed, redirected, and sublimated in the development of satire. The liturgy involved a mock battle for a circular white skin that seems to have been a symbol for the sun, the power of light and heat, the renewal of life and energy itself. The rite included a ceremonial episode in which a brahmin student and a harlot engaged in mutual abuse which, in the most archaic stage, culminated in sexual union, an act magically aimed at insuring fertility. The agon, the mimic contest for the symbol of power, reappears in the "pratfalls, slapstick, and disputes" of the Sanskrit satirical literature. The battles reoccur in comically degraded manifestations. The struggle for the possession of the symbolic sun, for example, resurfaces in a satirical farce, the *Mattavilāsa* of Mahendravarman (seventh century), as a comical scuffle between a debauched Śaiva yogi and a hypocritical Buddhist monk over a begging bowl. And once the bowl is won there is a prayer for prosperity, fertility, and social order.

The aesthetic amusement and comic laughter inspired by satire, preserve traces of a more primary, world-affirming joy of seasonal celebrations of the triumph of life over death.

The Triumph of Spring

Awake, the land is scattered with light . . .
And blossoming boughs of April in laughter shake.

Robert Bridges, "Awake, My Heart, To Be Loved"

A number of the surviving satirical dramas are set in the springtime and seem to have been written to be performed as a part of the celebration of the vernal festival. The bawdiness and license, the mirth and mischief, the jumbling of social and domestic roles, which typify the satires are all characteristic of the traditional Holī celebration, the orgiastic festival of regeneration. A pattern emerges in the satirical spring dramas: there is a clash between a young man (a disciple or brahmin student) and an old man (a teacher, guru, or priest) over the possession of a woman (invariably a harlot). The female is always represented in two aspects or personifications: in her fertile phase (the young and beautiful courtesan) and in her barren phase (the old and haggish bawd). The two aspects, literally or figuratively mother and daughter, are not at odds—they are one and the same, like the earth at different seasons. The battle between the men, a struggle for power, might be understood as a battle for mastery on various levels of experience: psychological or domestic (son against father, for the woman), political or social (new king against old king, for the state), and natural or cosmic (life against death, spring against winter, for the earth). The three levels correspond to my typology of satire: satire of manners, social satire, and religious satire.

The relationship between satire and the spring festival, the possible development of satire out of farce and farce out of more ancient spring rite, and the sublimation of primitive impulses into aesthetic ones, is evident in such plays as the *Hāsyārṇava*. The farce begins with conventional invocations to Śiva and Pārvatī, benedictory descriptions of the lovemaking of the ithyphallic god and the receptive goddess. The poet announces that Śiva himself commanded the composition of the satire, "a farce appropriate to the spring season, to bring joy to the hearts of clever folks" (prose after 1.3). The focus shifts from the supernal eroticism of the divinities to the earthly manifestations of the energy of fertility with conventional descriptions of the springtime: gentle sandal-scented breezes blow, creepers languorously entwine themselves around the trunks of trees, cuckoos cry out for their mates, flowers open hungrily to receive pollen-coated, nectar-drunken bees. These standard determinants of the aesthetic sentiment of love, descriptions appropriate to the amorous mood, build expectations which are suddenly subverted with the entrance of characters who are inappropriate to that mood. The royal family priest, Reverend Panzany (Viśvabhaṇḍa) and his nasty brahmin student, Master Troublesprout (Kalahāṅkura), make their way to the celebration of the spring festival which is taking place in a brothel, the house of Madam Bawdbent (Bandhurā). The movement downward from the celestial lovemaking of god and goddess to the inept sexual bungling of corrupt brahmins and lackadaisical whores, the movement from mythos to bathos, ideal to actuality, is a sentimental pratfall, a comic degradation.

The archetypal pattern is established as Reverend Panzany and Master Troublesprout are dazzled by the beauty of the young whore, Miss Moon (Mṛgāṅkalekhā): younger and older males compete for possession of the young female. Miss Moon's eyes shine brightly and dart about in playful glances like mating birds; her mouth is a lotus; her thighs are full; her firm breasts are compared to mountains; her arms are waving creepers; her pubic hair is dark like a swarm of bees seeking honey—the imagery establishes her as a representative of the fecund, anxious earth in spring in contrast to the depleted earth of winter which is incapable of bestowing birth or nourishment. That winter earth is personified by the old whore. "The old hag, Madam Bawdbent, has drooping jugs, she's sickly, menopausal, and the twinkle in her eye has been eclipsed by cataracts. . . . Her hair, her brow and lashes too, are as white as *kāśa* flowers and her teeth have fallen out from old age. Her love-box is all dried up" (*Hāsyārṇava* 1.24, 27). "The wrinkles on her body are like notches indicating the number of lovers she has had" (2.19). Master Troublesprout abuses her with obscenities:

> Crushed in the battle of love,
> her tits now sag down to here;
> Seeing what happened above,
> her twat dried up out of fear (1.24).

Assuming the obedience of student to teacher, the authority of father over son and elder over youth, Reverend Panzany instructs Master Troublesprout to act as his go-between and arrange a tryst with Miss Moon. Desiring the girl for himself, however, the boy speaks to the harlot of the evanescence of youth, the transience of the waxing moon. "Once the firmness of your breasts is gone, it won't return again" (1.48). The coy mistress is seduced—the boy kisses her and laughs at "the foolish gods who happily sipped the nectar of immortality from the celestial moon—Rāhu's leftovers" (1.49), while he quaffs the more delicious wine from his terrestrial Miss Moon. Just as Rāhu, the demon of eclipses, incited the wrath of Viṣṇu by stealing the nectar of regeneration from the moon, the young initiate provokes the anger of the old guru. The juxtaposition of the profound mythological agon with the tawdry tussle, suggesting a degradation of grandeur into triviality, accentuates the comic tone and creates the satiric tension. A verbal battle, a flyting contest typical of spring rites, ensues. The old teacher demands that the student's hand be amputated for touching the preceptor's beloved, that his teeth be knocked out for biting the girl's lip. "That organ of yours, known to the ladies as the 'pudenda-pleaser,' " the student retorts, "is to be chopped off because you claim the girl I've kissed. . . . Your hard-on is to be uprooted" (prose after 1.49). The curses are suggestive of Vedic spells: "Your member, peg-like and in-thrusting, is to fall off, is to be impotent toward women" (*Atharva Veda* 7.90.3). Magical curse is parodied in bathetic billingsgate. In a comedic dance/battle youth and age attempt to debilitate each other, to block the other's possession of the female (woman/society/earth). The struggle of the seasons is acted out by two extravagantly ineffectual characters. Again the comic arises out of the incongruity between the grandeur of the seasonal ritual and the pettiness of the buffoonish display. Comedy deals with profound things in trivial ways, with serious issues and tragic events laughingly. A character in a novel by Aldous Huxley writes in a suicide note that "every man is ludicrous if you look at him from the outside, without taking into account what's going on in his heart and mind. . . . It is a question of point of view. Everyone's a walking farce and a walking tragedy at the same time" (*Antic Hay*). The tragedy of King Oedipus is a comedy of mistaken identity. Nothing is sillier than the suffering hero. It is all a question of point of view.

The Triumph of Youth

> If tragedy . . . shows the son paying for his rebellion against the father, comedy shows the son victorious, the father discomfited. Father and son compete for the possession of the mother, and the son wins.
>
> Eric Bentley, *The Life of the Drama*

In the *Dhūrtasamāgama* the teacher, Reverend Alltown (Viśvanagara) warns his pupil, Master Malfeasance (Durācāra), that since the guru is always considered the father of the student, the boy cannot approach the guru's beloved—she is the boy's mother. The Oedipal nature of the conflict is made clear. "Damn!" the student shouts, "Dirty old man! I'll crack open that bald head of yours with a club just like it was a cooked potato" (prose after 1.35). The son challenges the virility of the father. The laughter of the sons of Bharata affronts the paternal authority of the Divine Sages.

The central plot of the *Dhūrtasamāgama* is essentially the same as that of the *Hāsyārṇava*. The setting is also the spring, "the season that captivates even the minds of sages" (1.8). As the satire commences Master Malfeasance, smitten with love, mawkishly moans, "I saw a lovely girl by a lotus pond, a playgirl, a laughing goddess, Miss Lovedart (Anaṅgasenā), and ever since I see here everywhere." His guru consoles him. "Son, I too have seen a whore, a procuress named Madam Fondafucking (Suratapriyā)—I too have been pierced by the arrow of love, right where it hurts the most" (prose after 1.16). As the farce develops Madam Fondafucking takes the role of mother—she feeds the mendicants; and Miss Lovedart, like Miss Moon in the *Hāsyārṇava,* becomes the mutually desired sexual object, the source of conflict between guru and disciple, father and son. In both plays the harlots are uninterested in their suitors. This represents a comic reversal of the paradigmatic myth of the seduction of the ascetic by the hetaera. In myth prostitutes try to seduce ascetics; in satire ascetics try to seduce prostitutes. The ascetic Ṛṣyaśṛṅga, for example, raised in the forest by an elder sage adept in austerities, kept unaware of the existence of women, performed his penances with such energy that the seasonal rains did not come. The king Lomapāda, heeding the counsel of brahmins, sent a courtesan to seduce Ṛṣyaśṛṅga that there might be an end to the drought. And after he made love to her the rains came with full force. The boy's teacher/father, realizing what had transpired, warned his pupil to return to his meditation and never again be distracted by a woman. The satires parody this model, turn it upside down in a degradation of the mythic ideal. The folk version of the story, recorded in the Buddhist *Jātakas* (but translated into English only with the funny/dirty parts deleted), anticipates the farces in stressing the humor of the story, in making it a bawdy comedy of mistaken identity. The naive ascetic, having never seen a woman, wonders what has happened to the courtesan's penis. Explaining that a bear has knocked it off, leaving a painful wound, she asks him to "kiss it and make it better" (*Naḷinika Jātaka* [526]).

In both the *Hāsyārṇava* and the *Dhūrtasamāgama* the dispute between guru and disciple is referred to a learned brahmin, an earthly sage, for arbitration, and the respective arbitrators each have their own young disciples. The conflict between youth and age is recapitulated—the judges and their young students immediately desire the harlots brought before them. In the *Hāsyārṇava,* Minister Loveblind (Madanāndhamiśra), accompanied by his student Master Wildcock (Kulāla), his sacred thread red with the rouge of whores and his eyes red from hashish, enters singing the praises of spring. "How can I survive such a springtime without a wench?" (prose after 2.6). Woman is the receptacle of immortality, both figuratively through the nectar of her kisses and literally in her capacity to bear children—he who takes possession of the female survives. The battle between the males is for immortality.

The aged band together against the young. Considering the case, arbitrating the dispute, Minister Loveblind decides that he and his peer, Reverend Panzany, should both marry the young harlot. "Draupadī, after all, was married to all the sons of Pāṇḍu" (*Hāsyārṇava* 2.19). The powerful heroine of the epic age is degraded to appear in the present epoch, the Age of Dullness, as a whore and the great warriors of the past live on in the satiric moment as piddling, dirty old men. Satire judges the present in terms of the past, assesses the banalities of reality in terms of the profundities of myth.

The old attack the young, the father laughs at the son, depreciates his masculinity and potency, his ability or readiness to possess the female:

> Since a baby could pass through that lady's hole,
> How could this stripling play the sexual role?
> His pecker's a splinter—it should be a pole.
>
> (*Hāsyārṇava* 2.20)

The young in turn band against the aged. The two students decide that they'll marry the old bawd, that they'll be able to get the girl by becoming husbands to her mother. They'll be able to make love to the younger woman while the old men are on their begging rounds. "And how much longer can these old fogies live? When they kick the bucket we'll marry the girl" (prose after 2.19).

A priest, Monsignor Maximaledictor (Mahānindakācārya), summoned to perform the marriage rite, becomes, like all the other males, immediately impassioned by the charms of Miss Moon. After the ceremony he demands his fee for the sacrifice and, accepting a bowl of hashish from the brahmin students, he sings:

Hail the beatitudes of hash!
Curious eyes begin to flash,
Fluid words start to flow like wine
And sex becomes an act divine!
(*Hāsyārṇava* 2.33)

When the two old gurus fail to come up with a payment, the priest, explaining that he has the right to keep their young wife as collateral, dances out with Miss Moon "to wield sexual weapons in the battle of love" (2.34). The burlesque dénouement makes sense in terms of archaic ritual practices: through performing the sacrifice and eating soma, the Vedic priest gained long life on earth and immortality in the Land of the Fathers. The powerful priest of the Vedic age becomes a lecherous drunkard of the Age of Dullness in satirical farce; sacred soma becomes profane hemp; hallowed sacrifice becomes a mere ploy to steal a whore. The priest/buffoon recites his own version of a Vedic hymn during the marriage ceremony:

It is a dream,
  this life on earth—
Death is sure
  to follow birth.
Knowing this,
  let there be mirth!
May those upon the fun'ral
heap,
  all drifters
  in an endless sleep,
In ancestral groves forever keep.
(2.31–32)

The Vedic priest had potent magic to protect him from death. The satirist has laughter, expressions of mirth despite the funeral heap, uproarious laughter in the face of the transience of life with all its little joys and sorrows.

The Triumph of Frogs

Brkekekex ko-ax ko-ax
Brkekekex ko-ax ko-ax
From marsh and mere

Sound again
Your fair refrain
Deep and clear,
O humid race,
Booming the bass
Cadenza
Ko-ax ko-ax.
Aristophanes, *Frogs*

There is a hymn in the Veda, a solemn chant for the regeneration of life, in which the croaking of frogs at the coming of the rains is compared to the singing of the sacrificial priests:

Like brahmins practising vows of silence
The frogs have been hibernating all year;
Now the rainy season has aroused them
And they sing aloud.
. . . .
Like brahmins singing at the soma sacrifice,
All night long, around a sea of soma,
You, the frogs, celebrate the day,
The coming of the rains.
(*Ṛg Veda* 7.103.1, 7)

While the Vedic seer's song is not comical, it expresses the same impulses to ward off evil and insure the persistence of life that are comically expressed in satire. By comparing the frogs to brahmins, the Vedic poet presumably meant to empower the priests, to insure with potently magical words their ability to bring rain and fertility, to overcome drought and death. But the simile was destined to become satirical. A grammatical commentary of the tenth century records a proverbial expression: "This frog of a brahmin just chatters!" And in a twentieth-century Indian cartoon, Nehru's opponents are compared to a chorus of croaking frogs joining him in a serenade to India (fig. 6). The comparison is not meant to empower, but to demean, to make those politicians ludicrous and thereby diminish their power and, in doing so, to insure, with satirically magical laughter, the triumph of the leader most capable of overcoming life-threatening forces within and toward India.

A courtesan in the *Pādatāḍitaka* is described appearing in her house like a nymph in the heavenly mansions playing a flute. A domestic peacock, conventionally held to become sexually

THE CHOIR—"Other organizations have emerged lately as rainy season frogs."—Jawaharlal Nehru (Dec. 9, 1951)

Figure 6

aroused during the rainy season, upon hearing her, turns its head around, "mistaking her song for the croaking of the frogs" (52) which heralds the rains. There is a shift of consciousness from the celestial realm, filled with the divine music of nymphs, to the muddy realm, noisy with the cacophonous mating grunts of frogs. The shift engenders laughter, a sense of the ludicrous, and makes the satiric point.

The magic of metaphor is satirical rather than liturgical when the chanting of brahmins and the croaking of frogs are compared in such later texts as the *Harivaṃśa* and the *Rāmacaritamānasa* of Tulsīdās. The frog, in Sanskrit satirical verse and fable, was a symbol of limited vision and self-satisfaction. Like so many of the objects of satire, the frog thinks its little puddle is the infinite universe. The satirist Nīlakaṇṭha Dīkṣita laughs:

> What is heaven? What is sky? What is earth?
> If all these really existed,
> Would they not occasionally be visible to you?
> You who are all-seeing?
> Let the perplexed jabber!
> You, O liberated frog, so truly know:

Your little well is all there is!
What could be beyond it?
(*Anyāpadeśaśataka* 99)

The Frog Upaniṣad: *The Persistence of Satire*

Thank you for sending along your ''translation'' of Pandit Gananath Sastri's *Maṇḍūka Upaniṣad*. . . . Is this a hoax? a joke? a satire? Is there such a text? Is there really a Pandit Gananath Sastri for that matter? These things should be made clear. . . . In scholarly publishing we are concerned with such quotidian things as the truth. . . . In any case, I really don't think this manuscript is suitable for consideration by an academic press.

Rejection letter from an editor not wanting to be named

Mr. Nayak, the tour guide at Ellora, had told me that I must go to see his good friend and language teacher, Pandit Gananath Sastri in Madras, that he was the author of a book on humor in the Vedic age. ''He knows everything there is to know about Indian humor, the humor of our gods, the humor of our people, the humor even of our flora and fauna! When you tell him you are the friend of V. Nayak, he will welcome you with open arms. He will care for you and all of your needs.''

Though Mr. Sastri had never heard of Mr. Nayak, he did, nevertheless, out of courtesy, sympathy, boredom, loneliness, curiosity, indifference, or some combination of these, receive me warmly. He explained, however, that he had never written a book on humor in the Vedic age. He laughed. As if assuming some disappointment on my part, he cheerfully promised that he would think about undertaking that project if I really needed to read the book. He laughed again.

He stared at me as if he recognized me, as if trying to remember when and where we had known each other before, and he smiled quite gently and always, a serious, disarming smile. And he smoked continually. ''I am happy that you smoke,'' he laughed, ''these days more and more people have lost the courage to smoke.'' While the whiteness of hair, combed straight back, made him seem old—not in a feeble way, but in the strongest sense—the thickness of it made him seem youthful, also in the strongest sense. So much about him was paradoxical.

''I am very sorry to bother you,'' I explained with some embarrassment, ''but I was told that you were an expert on ancient

Indian humor and I am planning to do a book on that subject someday. I am particularly interested in the origins of satire in Vedic myth and ritual and . . ."

As if knowing that I was just jabbering to fill the silence, he interrupted, "I can help you. Don't worry. Never worry. Have a cigarette." I soon discovered that I never needed to say anything, that he would talk on any subject, and that he could do so in English, French, German, Spanish, Italian. He knew Greek, Latin, Sanskrit, Tamil, Arabic, and many Indian vernacular languages as well. "When I was a young man, learning languages became my obsession, an obsession which I inherited from my father, a most learned pandit and a most distinguished advisor to, as well as a most devoted disciple of, the famous L. L. Zamenhof, 'Dr. Esperanto—Dr. Hopeful.' He gave me the idea that if I were to translate all the religious scriptures of the world into Esperanto, that they would all say the same thing." He laughed at himself, his father, and Zamenhof. "I quickly realized that this was not the case. I began to devote myself to translating the great works of world literature into Sanskrit. I started with the Greek tragedies and Shakespeare. But I soon discovered that these made no sense in Sanskrit. They were too discouraging; the sorrow was too vulgar and unresolved. And so I found that I had to change much more than the language of the plays. I had to transform the stories and the sensibilities which marked them. My *Hamlet,* the story of Prince Hamīlata of Śākambharī, ends with the marriage of the prince to his beloved. Tragedy became comedy. This made me see that I was translating the wrong literature, that I should devote myself to comedies alone, that they alone were translatable into Sanskrit. I began with *Twelfth Night, Dvādaśarātri*—that play, *vidūṣaka* and all, is perfect in Sanskrit. Then came the *Frogs*. That was a simple task, for Aristophanes was heavily influenced by the Veda, as the hymn to the frogs in the *Ṛg Veda,* one of the most comical of all the humorous hymns of the Veda, makes abundantly clear."

I had to stop him. "Wait, you believe that Aristophanes was influenced by the Veda? You're joking, aren't you?"

"As I started to translate the play, I was continually startled at how easily the Greek words turned into Sanskrit and how perfectly the sentiments transferred. It soon became obvious that I was not translating the play into a new language, but that I was translating it back into the language in which it had originally been written. This gave me the suspicion—the intuition, if you will—

that Aristophanes was himself an Indian who, because he was unappreciated in his own court, left India and traveled to Greece where he introduced a new form of drama, namely satire. The word 'satire' has always confounded Western scholars. Why do they not realize it comes from the Sanskrit *satūrya* which means 'accompanied by music?' Is it that they do not want to admit that comedy originated in India, that there was comedy in India thousands of years before the first Western man laughed?" He grinned at the thought and opened another packet of Charminars.

I explained to him that the frog hymn was not, according to scholarly consensus, to be understood as satirical. He laughed billows of cigarette smoke. "What do scholars ever know? Seriousness has made them blind. If a man with a sense of humor reads the Veda he laughs heartily over the drunken braggadocio of Indra [*Ṛg Veda* 10.119], over the monkeyshines of Vṛṣākapi [10.86], and over the very clever metaphysical puns in the hymn to Who [10.121; cf. the Abbott an Costello routine, 'Who's On First']. There is great humor in the Veda. Scholars simply do not get the jokes. The Vedic *ṛṣi*s knew all too well the power of laughter. They knew that it could keep evil at bay. Look here, I want to give you something. It is called *dṛṣṭi.*" He handed me a painted metal disc with a face on it, a laughing, demonic face, sticking out its tongue. "He is laughing, he is sticking out his tongue like a child. This keeps evil away, for evil does not want to be made a laughing stock. If we are afraid of demons they come; if we laugh at them they stay away. He will protect your house. He will notify the demons that you are laughing within your house. Put it on your door in Hawaii."

I asked him if he was still translating. "Yes, of course, I want to translate all the great comic writers, all the satirists, all the clowns of the pen, into Sanskrit. The comic poets alone imitate in their literary activities the activities of the gods. '*Sie haben's alle dem groszen Urpoeten abgesehen,*' Heinrich Heine said, '*der seiner tausendaktigen Welttragödie den Humor aufs höchste zu treiben weisz, wie wire täglich sehen . . .*' Or something like that. I am currently translating Heine's verse into Sanskrit. It is a very difficult task, much more difficult than Molière or Goldoni, but not as difficult as Boccaccio or Rabelais. Rabelais was the most arduous, but well worth the toil. Every page told me that I was engaged in the most appropriate of all activities. '*Mieux est de ris que de larmes éscrire,*' the old rascal wrote, '*par ce que rire est le propre de l'homme.*' "

"Am I to understand that you have translated the works of Molière, Rabelais, and Boccaccio into Sanskrit?" I asked, laughing at the outrageousness of the very idea.

"And Goldoni. Don't forget Goldoni! His *Caturavidhavāprahasanam* [*La Vedova Scaltra*] is my masterpiece. Here, I shall give you the manuscript."

I looked at the text, carefully handwritten in impeccable Devanāgarī script, in disbelief. "Who publishes these translations?"

"No one," he smiled with pleasure and lit another cigarette. "Please, enjoy a cigarette; you're falling hopelessly behind me."

"Doesn't it bother you that nobody publishes your work, that nobody reads it?"

He laughed again, flowers of laughter. "What if you write this book on Indian comedy and nobody publishes it? What if somebody publishes it, but nobody reads it? What if somebody reads it, but nobody likes it? What if you knew your book would not be published? Would you write the book anyway? If your answer is 'no,' then you should not write this book. If the answer is 'yes,' then nothing can stop you from writing it. The only things that are important are necessities—eating, sleeping, breathing, defecating, urinating—things our bodies compel us to do. Writing has to be like that. I have no choice in doing these translations. I have no choice," he laughed, "and if you have a choice about your book on humor, then don't write the book."

He laughed that kind of brawny, seasoned laughter that makes one feel, at least momentarily, entirely happy, that reassures one that there is something essentially and utterly delightful and wonderful about the world and about being alive and a part of it.

"Do you only do translations into Sanskrit?" I asked seriously. "Have you ever written anything yourself?"

He explained that he was the author of an original Sanskrit text, the *Maṇḍūka Upaniṣad* (*The Frog Upaniṣad,* a play on the names of the ancient *Muṇḍaka* and *Māṇḍūkya Upaniṣads,* I presumed). At once he presented me with that manuscript too. "Feel free to translate it into English if you like. You can publish it separately and keep all the royalties for yourself or—if you like—use portions of it in your book on Indian humor."

The afternoon before I left for Calcutta, the last time I saw Mr. Sastri, this sweetly crazed and comically brilliant smoker and philologian, we sat on a bench in his garden in the shade of a fine old tree.

Mr. Sastri wanted to know if I had ever eaten frog legs. He was amazed that I had. "What a pleasure it is," he chuckled, "to meet a man who has done such an extraordinary thing! Fantastic!"

The breeze, blowing cool and fragrant like the sandal-scented southern gusts of Sanskrit poetry, loosened little white blossoms from the branches of the tree. "You see, flowers are falling upon you from heaven, just as they rain upon the gods and heroes in our stories! What an auspicous omen!" It could not have been more than a few minutes later, just as we were beginning to discuss Abhinavagupta's theory of laughter, that a crow crapped on me from its perch in that tree. Mr. Sastri apologized for laughing. "This too, paradoxical as it may seem, is a good omen. Never wash that khurta! Keep it as it is, as a reminder of just how ridiculous we are. The crow interrupted our philosophical discussion on purpose, to show us exactly that. We should thank the crow, the black satirist who reminded us not to take ourselves too seriously."

Suddenly there were slight, delicate tears forming in Gananath Sastri's eyes. He smiled gently and took a slow, deep breath. "Please, smoke one more cigarette before you leave."

The Maṇḍūka Upaniṣad
of
Pandit Gananath Sastri
(excerpts)

OṂ! OṂ! OṂ! Praise be to Yama! Salutations to you, O Death! Without you, there would be no laughter. And praise be to Manohar Lal! Yes, salutations to you, O Cigarette-Seller (*tamākhunālī-vikrayaka*). Without you there would be no laughter for me in this world (*saṃsāra*)!

1.1. In the beginning, before there were people, when there were only gods and demons, the demon Makha, having heard that the gods were about to sacrifice Puruṣa [the primal person whose sacrificial dismemberment results in the creation of the world], laughed. It was the first laugh [i.e., the primal laugh (*ādi-hasa*)], and thus, unaccustomed to such a sound, the gods were frightened by it. The thunderous laughter filled the sky in the form of lightning, lightning which the gods, after creating the world, threw down to earth. Astonishing indeed is the behavior of gods! Where lightning-laughter stuck in the ground wheat grew. Thus, and to this day, when you eat chapati or anything made of wheat, you eat laughter.

When you eat meat, or anything made of blood, you eat tears. Thus, Yājñavalkya held that if you must eat meat, it is best to wrap it in chapati.

1.2. Makha revealed the secrets of laughter [or the comic sentiment (*hāsya*)] to Śunaḥśepha [the ancient sage, whose name literally means "dog-penis," upon whom Indra bestowed long life] who, in turn, revealed the science (*tantra*) of laughter, the blessed *Śrī-Maṇḍūka-Upaniṣad,* to his laundryman in partial payment for the loincloths which the man had washed for him. The laundryman, as is the characteristic of folks of that caste, promptly lost the esoteric text. It was not really a laundryman, but Viṣṇu who, though the power of *māyā,* had taken on the form of a laundryman. Astonishing indeed is the behavior of gods! By keeping from men the esoteric practice of laughter, Viṣṇu hoped to prevent men from becoming gods. Overpopulation in heaven was a concern.

1.3. Truth is greater even than Brahmā, Śiva, Viṣṇu and the other [gods]. The text, having been churned from the ocean of lost laundry, was discovered by a serpent (*nāga*) who, in turn, appeared to Gaṇanāthaśāstrī in a dream. At first it was difficult for Gaṇanāthaśāstrī to discern that it was indeed a serpent, for this astonishing snake had the tail of a bull, the legs of a lion, the head of a monkey, the genitals of an elephant, the body of a horse, the wings of a crow, the skin of a crocodile, and—most astonishing of all—the toupee of Gaṇanāthaśāstrī's neighbor, Mr. Śivaśaṅkar.

> *The commentary of Śaṅkarācārya on the verse:* "He would indeed be a fool who mistook this fabulous serpent for a rope. So too, he is a fool who does not know that Mr. Śivaśaṅkar's hair is not-real [*māyā*]."

[From the third *adhyāya,* "On the Kinds of Laughter"]:

3.18. There are four kinds of laughter based on animals: mynah laughter, monkey laughter, lion laughter, mouse laughter.

3.19. The mynah laughs because it hears the laughter of others; the monkey laughs because it wants to make others laugh; the lion laughs to frighten others; the mouse laughs because others frighten him.

3.20. There is, according to the *śāstra*s, a fifth kind of animal laughter: rhinocerous laughter. But the rhinocerous never laughs when any other being is present; thus it is that rhinocerous laughter has never been heard, not even by the Sages. Astonishing indeed is the laughter of the rhinocerous! It is the purest.

> *Śaṅkarācārya asserts:* "the laughter of the rhinocerous is silence." But on this, Rāmānuja is in complete disagreement. Gadācārya holds that rhinocerous laughter bears witness to the truth that all is not one, qualified or unqualified, but that all is seventeen at least.

[From the fourth *adhyāya,* "On What Is Laughable"]:

4.37. All sages agree that every word [or every object referred to by a word] beginning with the letter "*ph*" is funny: *phakka* (cripple), *phaṭa* (serpent's neck), *phaṇa* (nostril or scum), *phaṇḍa* (belly) . . . *pharuṇḍa* (green onion), *pharuvaka* (spittoon) . . . *phalāyoṣit* (cricket), *phalgu* (the red powder thrown at people during the saturnalian revels of the Holī festival), *phiraṅga* (Westerner), *phuliṅga* (syphilis), *phena* (saliva) . . . *phela* (food scraps), *pheluka* (scrotum). Astonishing indeed is the letter "*ph*"!

[From the sixth *adhyāya,* "On Satire" (*vidaṃbana*)]:

6.4. If the Self [*ātman*] is the Absolute [*brahman*], whence the sting of satire? Knowing this, the man of true holiness mocks all beings and remains unattached to the fruits of his derision.

6.9. Satire consists in declaring "That thou art" [i.e., "You are it" (*tat tvam asi*) or "You are truth" (*tattvam asi*)].

6.10. The man of true holiness laughs for he has the knowledge that the paramount truth is near-at-hand [there seems to be a pun here on the word *upastha,* which as an adjective means "standing by the side of," but which also, as a noun, refers to the *pudendum muliebre*].

[From the seventh, and final, *adhyāya,* "On the Practice (*sādhana*) of Laughter"]:

7.1. The initiate must ceaselessly mutter repetition after repetition of the supreme mantra: *Oṃ haha huṃ hahaha phaṭ haha heehee hoho huṃ.*

7.7. In the Kali Yuga laughter, the sound of the wind [fart?] of the Absolute (*brahmāntravātaśabda*), alone is liberation from liberation (*mokṣa-mokṣa*). Astonishing indeed is the way of laughter (*hāsyamarga*)!

On this verse Śaṅkarācārya remains mute.

7.8. All is sorrow, decay, and death. Thus the brahmin must chant, the tantric must whisper, the bhakta must weep, the yogi must keep silent; meanwhile the man of true holiness laughs.

7.13. But the last laugh is the laugh of oblivion.

The Laughter of Kālī

3

Satire of Manners: Affectation and the Degradation of Love

Mother! Kālī! Your body is drenched with blood,
Your mouth gleams with the peals of your laughter!
Rāmprasād

Calcutta, Kālīghaṭṭa, Kālī's Landing: the place on the river consecrated to that dark and hungry goddess, dark as the torpid clouds from the Bay of Bengal that crawled over the city and clung, and hungry as the restless fires that choked on the dead and groaned—dark and hungry as the vigilant crows, her screeching minions. Black smoke, her murky breath, seemed sentient, seemed, as it suffused the air, to hold within it an ancient and persistent desolation. It stung the eyes, stained the walls, and muddied the soul.

When the first monsoon rains came, stunned I stood for shelter in the dusky doorway of the grey temple of aching stone, her mauled and cluttered shrine. The thunder was her frightful laughter and lightning glinted from her teeth. Kālī began to dance and her sweat was in the rain. She danced her heated dance of terror; she danced the storm. It would bring the season's floods, and with them death, and with it, of course, more life. And she laughed at the endless spectacle. Dark figures—beggars, pilgrims, passersby, hawkers, loiterers, tourists, children—extras and bit players in her phantasmagoric comedy—scattered in the rain for refuge from her wrath. The voices, their myriad languages—dirges and prayers, bickerings and banterings, transactions and little conversations—were drowned out and lost in the growling of rain and in the fervid laughter. Kālī, spiritual terrorist and holy mother, danced beyond sight, offstage, in the distance, in the place where the storm came from, and in the closeness, in an unexhumed place within the heart. And as she danced the earth shuddered beneath her blood-stained feet, and she laughed again and again her wild laughter. "Kālī, with her face of terror, laughed savagely with wrath, laughed a horrible caterwaul, and the light from her teeth blinded the eyes" (*Devīmāhātmya* 7.19). It detonated a fuller and more husky storm. It pierced the ears, ripped the clouds, and shattered stubborn illusions. Phosphorescent, eerie, and incandescent, it lit up the darkness and the dread in fitful flashes. She roared, blasted, barked, and cackled. I closed my eyes to watch the dance.

"As you whirl about in dance, the nails on the skin, that elephant hide which is your skirt, scratch the moon and nectar flows from it, drips into the mouths of the skulls around your neck, reviving them, and they laugh, laugh fierce, proud laughter, wild laughter that terrifies us into praising you" (*Mālatīmādhava* 5.23). Circled by wolves, jackals, hyenas, and the dogs that prowl for bones with shreds of human meat still stuck to them, Kālī dances in the cremation grounds, laughing as she dances, spins drunken, leaps wild, waves the stained sword of time, and displays the severed head of a god. "She laughed a terrible laugh and the burst of it shattered the darkness of the night" (*Harivaṃśa* 48.33). More loudly still she laughs the mad, minatory laughter, the necrophilic laughter, the desperate, anxious howling of the storm. Grisly ornaments that mock the vanity of lovers adorn the soot-dark, dancing form: earrings made of fetuses or dead infants, the heads of elephants, and the hearts of men, a girdle of human hands, a garland strung with laughing skulls, necklaces of entrails, cobra-anklets, and bracelets formed of veins. She chews upon the flesh, sticks out the blood-stained tongue at humanity mockingly, and vomits up more acid laughter. "Kālī roared like a lioness and demons swooned around her. Again and again she burst out in feral laughter as she drank her mead and danced wildly" (*Brahmavaivarta Purāṇa* 2.19.44–45). Deformities and beauties, dreads and longings, intermingled in a holy madness.

Her body is drenched with blood—
  crimson flowers floating

on the dark waters of the Kalindi;
Her lips flow with torrents of laughter—
immortality,
nectar from the splendid moon.

(Rāmprasād 119)

Kālī is the archcomedienne of the universe, ever-laughing, the atrocious incarnation of black comedy, the source of the macabre tricks and sinister pranks that are *māyā*. Her laughter at old age, disease, and death, fills the Buddha's silence. She laughs no less at birth and youth and health. She laughs at joy and sorrow, despair and hope, at striving and surrender. She laughs at one and all, makes fun of life and death, of men and gods. The laughter gushes from her throat like blood from the lungs. Clots of it hang on her lips. Kālī's dance is an aggressive mimicry of Śiva's, a satiric parody which, like her sword, may wound, maim, or kill. And when the god is dead, she dances upon his breast, still loudly laughing. This grating laughter inspires and informs the strident, mocking jeer of satire.

In the worship of Kālī the dark forces are dealt with either aggressively, by incorporation (the mode of the Tantric hero), or regressively, by submission (the mode of the devotee). While the humorist laughs like the devotee, the satirist laughs like the Tantric adept, using laughter as both a defense against destructive powers and as a weapon, a destructive force in itself. There is hope in humor, wrath in satire, a trace of fear in both.

"This is just some joke that Kālī is playing on us. The mother teases her children occasionally." I opened my eyes. Premendra Bandyopadhyaya, the young man with whose family I was staying, smiled quite happily. His father had given him both the solemn assignment of showing me Calcutta and the heavy responsibility of protecting me from it. "I am at your disposal twenty-four hours a day, every day except Thursday at three o'clock for one hour when I must go for tea at the home of my fiancée, the beautiful Sakuntala Deb Sen." There was another burst of thunder, a flash of lightning, and a surge of thicker, darker rain. Premendra laughed. "Monsoon season is the best time to see Calcutta, the most dramatic time. Some people find this heat unbearable, but I believe it just adds to the drama of Calcutta. We must wait till the storm stops to go home. If you were to get soaked and catch a cold my father would be furious with me." I asked him about the terrifying goddess, the tutelary deity of his city. "She is not terrifying. If she were, why would people worship her? She is the opposite of terrifying—she takes away the terror. People that are worshiping Kālī are laughing and enjoying themselves just like anyone else. Why do you say, 'tutelary deity?' She is not the only god here. Every Hindu god, not to mention Allah and Jesus Christ himself, is at home in Calcutta."

"But Calcutta is named after her—Kālī-ghaṭṭa. Right?"

"No, no. Calcutta was named by some English gentlemen who arrived here when this place was just a village. They saw some peasants cutting grass and they asked them, 'What is the name of this place?' The illiterate peasants, not knowing English, thought they had asked, 'What are you doing?' The word in Bengali for 'grass' is *kal,* and so they answered, '*kal* cutting.' And that is how Calcutta was named." He laughed delightedly.

"Is that a joke or is it true?"

"A joke and a truth are not mutually exclusive. The best jokes are true and the best truths are jokes." He smiled proudly over his spontaneously generated aphorism. "Though I received my B.A. degree from *Kal*-cutting University in economics, I am a rather philosophical fellow. My head is always in the clouds. I am a basically ivory-tower bloke. This is a Bengali trait. We are the poets and philosophers of India. I am also writing poetry. 'Every lover is a poet; so too every poet must be a lover.' William Shakespeare once said those words. I am compiling a notebook of my poems, beautiful poems abounding with the sentiment of love, inspired by Sakuntala Deb Sen herself and written somewhat in the style of Shakespeare's sonnets and somewhat in the style of Rabindranath Tagore's *Gītāñjali.*" After he had recited a Bengali verse, I asked for a translation. "The poem cannot be translated. Only in Bengali can one capture the beauty of my Sakuntala. Bengali is the most mellifluous of languages, comparable only to Sanskrit and French for sublime poetic perfection."

Premendra was a sincere, honest, and absolutely kind person. And yet there was something annoying about him (maybe it was his sincerity, his honesty, or his kindness), something that made me perverse. I could not restrain myself from asking him when he had sex with Sakuntala. His ever-throbbing smile vanished for the first time since I had met him. "How could you, let alone I, even imagine such a thing? Her divine form would be soiled and sullied by the thought alone!" "Well," I persisted with admittedly bad taste, "Who do you sleep with?" He actually began to tremble. "No one! I am saving my body and soul for Sakuntala Deb Sen. If I were to even have Freudian thoughts, let alone intercourse of the sexual kind, before our marriage I would be utterly spoiled and ruined. My beloved Sakuntala would have nothing to do with me. I would not even be worthy of her surliest glances. My object in life is Love, not sexual stimulation. Love is the highest thing of all. The *Gītā* says that Love alone is worthy to be practiced. Love is the greatest religion of all. This is why Jesus Christ said, 'God is Love.' It is the source of all beauty and all truth. Love is so powerful that it can make even sex pure. Without Love, sex is profane; only with Love is sex holy. This holiness I will experience only when Sakuntala and I are united in blissful matrimony. If I were to perform carnal intercourse with anyone before that time, it would make a travesty of Love. You may think me a fool. But if I am, I cherish my foolishness. The folly of Love is blessed indeed." His smile returned and there was an easing of the rains.

The Travesty of Love: *The Sublime and the Ridiculous*

The sublime and the ridiculous are often so nearly related, that it is difficult to class them separately.

Thomas Paine, *Age of Reason*

The Sanskrit poet wrote mainly for a social group that, while acknowledging the ultimate importance of liberation from the world through an ascetic mode of being, was devoted to finding pleasure in the world through love, courtship, and all sensual delights. Human love, erotic feeling and its carnal fulfillment, was idealized. Love is described by a courtesan in Daṇḍin's *Daśakumāracarita* as "the most joyful experience possible for a man and a woman. It comes when their minds are completely absorbed in sensual things and its attendants are all of the beautiful and delightful things of this world. Out of their mutual embraces springs the fruit of love—the great delight. It is sweet just to remember it. . . . Men of high rank have undergone terrible wars and risked dreadful ocean voyages for the sake of love" (pp. 86–87). Love was valued, despite its transience, as a blessed state in which the perfection of pleasure, one of the aims of existence, could be realized and savored. In a drama by Bhavabhūti (eighth century), Rāma contemplates his wife as she lies sleeping on his lap. The cool epic hero, transformed by the playwright into a tender lover, caresses Sītā gently to comfort her, for her dreams have been uneasy. He speaks a verse often cited by traditional commentators as exemplary of love's perfection:

> Blessed is this state
> of perfect humanness
> in which we are not two
> in our joy and sorrow
> no matter what happens
> the heart rests
> age does not take away
> the taste of love
> defenses vanish
> with time
> love's essence is realized
> somehow
> we might attain
> this state
> but only once.
> (*Uttararāmacarita* 1.39)

Nothing is sacred in comedy. There are no blessed states. Satire laughs at Rāma and Sītā, at Premendra and Sakuntala, at all the enamored fools who "have undergone terrible wars and risked dreadful ocean voyages for the sake of love." As the ideal is stated, satire yawns or giggles or sneers, "yeah, yeah, yeah." But satire depends on the establishment of the ideal for its comical and critical effect. It sets up, or refers to, directly or indirectly, the ideal and then proceeds to show the ways in which that ideal has failed, gone unrealized, or been subverted. Satires of manners expose the degradations of *kāma* as pleasure, the idealized and institutionalized end in life, and the perversions of *kāma* as love, the idealized and ritualized means to that end. *Kāma*, the social and psychological ideal, is experienced or savored in Sanskrit literature as the amorous sentiment, the established aesthetic mood which, as we have seen, was held by the traditional literary theorists to be the very source of the comic sentiment.

The amorous sentiment, the flavor permeating more of the corpus of Sanskrit poetic literature than any other, was highly conventionalized, and the conceits—the kinds of lovers and beloveds, the types of appropriate emotions, gestures, words, and actions, and the stages of love in separation and union—were elaborated and meticulously categorized and classified, subcategorized and subclassified, by the rhetoricians and dramaturgists. The comic poet plays with the conventions and typologies: inappropriate sorts of characters (old or ugly people, country bumpkins, monks, priests, and the like) try, or imagine themselves, to be lovers; characters display the gestures of love and utter its poetry while seeking, in satirically exposed reality, not erotic fulfillment, but money, power, or prestige. The comic perversions of the conventions became themselves conventionalized into stock routines and old jokes. Lots of chestnuts are cracked in Sanskrit comic love literature.

The comic poet parodies the love poet—bad love poetry can be good comedy. A poet in a monologue satire has written a stanza on a wall, using all the conventional conceits for describing the spring season and evoking the amorous mood. Love poetry is degraded into graffiti. Through the poet's verbal and sentimental ineptitude, the erotic becomes comic. He produces a poem in perfectly bad taste, a travesty of love, a mere semblance of the amorous sensibility.

> Lofty laughter blossoms like flowers
> And bees are intoxicated in yon bowers!
> Oh garrulous are the girl cuckoos
> As an epiphany of holy sweat accrues!
> Love is so unrestrained and thorny
> That e'en little girls are horny!
> Yes, spring does that, it's true,
> That what e'en a million go-betweens can't do!
>
> (*Padmaprābhṛtaka* 10)

In the Age of Dullness, taste, wit, and wonder have disappeared. Poets are mere leather workers, "cobblers who stitch old lines of poetry together" as if making shoes; they round up old lines, like "cowboys looking for lost cattle" (*Padmaprābhṛtaka,* prose after 9). Kṣemendra takes the image of the ridiculous hack and transforms it into the grotesque. "The poet vomits out his verse, breathing heavily as if from labor pains." The poem is an abortion, a fetus, "unripe, immature, and covered with a membrane. . . . Night and day the poet has meditated, tearing his heart out, to come up with this shriveled-up little poem" (*Deśopadeśa* 8.18–19). The degradation of poetry is the degradation of the eros that inspires it and is represented by it. As Premendra Bandyopadhyaya said, with a modest attribution to Shakespeare, "Every lover is a poet; so too every poet must be a lover."

Making a distinction on the basis of tone, there are two kinds of erotic satire in Sanskrit literature: one is good humored and gentle as it laughs without condemnation at lovers, at their affectations as folly; the other is bad tempered and acerbic as it laughs scornfully and cynically at lovers, at their affectations as vice. Aesthetically, in terms of the literary categories, the two forms of satire are homogenous in that they both arise out of a mimicry, and a resultant deflation, of the amorous sentiment. But psychologically, in terms of judgment, they are radically different. The distinction between them reflects a larger, more general, and fundamental tension within Indian cultural traditions, the opposition of two seemingly contrary, but equally idealized, modes of being: one, the erotic, expressed in literature in terms of the amorous sentiment, affirms the world and finds fulfillment in love and imagination; the other, the ascetic, voiced in literature in terms of the mood of peace, negates the world and finds fulfillment in renunciation and knowledge. The poet Bhartṛhari formulates the conflict.

> In this world, passing, insubstantial, ever-changed,
> There are two wise ways in which one's life may be arranged:
> Sometimes there should be the piety of devotion,
> Overflowing with the nect'rous knowledge of all truth;
> No? Well, then pursue another sort of emotion—
> And touch with lust that part well hidden (and thus uncouth)
> Within the firm laps of women given to pleasure,
> Loving ladies with warm thighs and breasts beyond measure.
>
> (*Śṛṅgāraśataka* 37)

Acerbic, bad-tempered satire, pure satire, provides an alternative to both the erotic and ascetic attitudes; it is at once scornful of the pretensions of love and the hypocrisies of religion. With sensuous delight the poet of this vein of satire laughs at all piety and nect'rous knowledge; with ascetic detachment he laughs at the idiocy of lovers and the vanity of all passion. Gentle, good-humored satire, tempered satire, on the other hand, provides a reconciliation of the erotic and ascetic modes; it accepts the follies of love and religion and discovers something cheerful in the silly earnestness and sincerity with which both lovers and renouncers attempt to endure the painful ephemerality of our existence.

Good-Humored Satires of Love

I am intrigued by the pageant of human existence! We pluck a coquette; the coquette devours a man of means; the man of means has others whom he plunders. And the sum of it all is as entertaining a light-footed progression of knaveries as a man could wish for.

Alain-René Lesage, *Turcaret*

Eros invests life with irony. Love is funny because it is so serious. Or because it always seems so urgent and profound at the time. "I would give up life and limb for her," Premendra declared of the girl whom, by his own admission, he had only seen about a dozen times, always for tea on Thursdays at three o'clock, and always in the presence of the parents who had contracted the proposed marriage.

Premendra had appeared on television in a university student debate: "Arranged Marriage vs. Marriage of Choice." It was a glorious moment for the Bandyopadhyaya family, who had purchased a television in order to watch their son, when Premendra went to the heart of the matter: "The mass debate that we are having is missing the point. Neither form of marriage is better or worse than the other. In the arranged marriage there is only duty; in the marriage of choice there is only lust. Where, I ask, is Love? If Love is there, either form of marriage is heaven. If Love is absent, either form of marriage is hell. The question we must ask ourselves is simply, 'How can we learn to Love?' " Tears had come to Mrs. Bandyopadhyaya's eyes. Mr. Bandyopadhyaya had laughed, though tenderly, and said, "Love is a humorous topic *par* excellent. Quite a riot really."

In the sentimental riot of love, laughter arises over a reversal of norms, a surprising turning of things upside-down and inside-out. The comic vision is of a topsy-turvy world and love can make it so. In love a man becomes a child, a weakling, or a fool. Though gentle satire laughs at him, at the comic predicaments of love, it does not necessarily do so without approval or even envy.

She's the one who's young, so why am *I* so shy?
She's the one who ought to be afraid, not *I*.
She's the one who bears the burden of her breast,
So why do I feel *I* have to take a rest?
Her bottom should be a burden for *her* to bear,

And yet *I* can hardly move from here to there.
It's really quite amazing, the way that love assaults,
Making *me* suffer *her* charms as if they were *my* faults.
(*Amaruśataka* 34)

The failure of the amorous sentiment, its sudden crumbling, results in the realization of the comic, and it is particularly funny when the lovers themselves are the cause of the switch in mood, when desire defeats itself, when grace gives way to bungling, when banalities qualify the ideal and trivialities impede "the most joyful experience possible for a man and a woman."

The waste of time began to vex
the lover anxious for some sex—
The slip-cord in the lady's hand
was tangled in her girdle-band.
(*Śiśupālavadha* 10.61)

Acts of love, not comic in and of themselves, not humorous in experience, can be made funny through rhetoric, through witty manipulations of the language that describes love and imbues it with its essential ironies. A lady is said to survive the assault of sex only by drinking the nectar of immortality from her beloved's lips in a kiss—a metaphor is taken literally for the sake of comic effect.

The lady was embraced—she was scratched, she was bitten
in the battle of love—she was beaten, she was smitten.
This certainly should have meant her final expiration
were he not performing mouth-to-mouth resuscitation.
(*Subhāṣitaratnakoṣa* 19.28)

The perversities of love, its sweet deceits and clever deceptions, its lies, jealousies, and audacities, provide the comic poet with his material. The outrageous rogue who utters the wrong woman's name, or appears before his beloved with marks upon his body, evidence of his infidelity, is a stock figure in the comedy of love.

Once upon a time a rogue,
a very clever rake,
Appearing to his lady,
made such a big mistake:

He had not wiped off the marks
from his naked chest,
Unguent stains imprinted there
from another lady's breast!
Hoping to conceal them,
he fell at his lady's feet.
Too late! Too bad! She saw it
and started to retreat;
He stood then with open arms,
"Come, show me what you mean."
When she came close he grabbed her—
and then his chest was clean,
For as she rubbed against him
the marks were all erased;
And as he hugged and squeezed her,
then clinging to her waist,
His sins were all forgotten
in that great joyous kiss.
[The moral of the story:
ama et fac quod vis!]

(*Amaruśataka* 26)

The aggression in the battle of the sexes, its intense fear and anger, is often dissolved by laughter in the poems themselves, a conceit that suggests a functional dimension of laughter. Pride and anger can be melted away in laughter. The moment of laughter can provide a sudden transformation of, and even liberation from, the constraining self.

lying upon the bed
each looked away from the other
silent suffering
each in the heart wanted to make up
and yet they stayed
sullen proud protecting honor
and then . . .
glances mingled as each looked
at the other
from the corners of their eyes
the lovers' quarrel
crumbled with a sudden laughter. . . .

(*Amaruśataka* 23)

This laughter yields forgiveness, sympathy, and a suspension of judgment. The lovers are bound together by humor, by laughing at themselves in unison.

But there is a more acerbic laughter, laughed at others, a laughter reverberating with anger, antipathy, and judgment. It is more purely satiric. And it sounds like the laughter of Kālī.

Bad-Tempered Satires of Love

> Love is a ridiculous passion which hath no being but in play-books and romances.
>
> Jonathan Swift, "A Letter to a Young Lady on Her Marriage"

Fierce indignation, to borrow a phrase from Swift's own epitaph, tears at the heart of the satirist. His laughter is cynical, caustic, cantankerous, and bitterly realistic. Love is, in the purely satiric vision, all deceit, a self-deception as well as a deception of others. The disillusionment inherent in satiric laughter is the price paid for that freedom from illusions and delusions which is the psychological goal of satire. This kind of satire is informed with an ascetic, and yet in no way puritanical or religious, sensibility. For the satirist, as for the holy man, love is a vanity, a snare, a trap, a house on fire. He laughs at it with the indifference, if not the disgust, of a renouncer. His wit provides the perspective. "People who have savored the joy of peace," according to Apyaya Dīkṣita (sixteenth–seventeenth century), "feel disgust for the joy of love, the highest enjoyment of lovers, just as those who have tasted pure food, are revulsed by the garbage consumed by pigs" (*Vairāgyaśataka* 16).

Sanskrit satire is particularly misogynistic. Bhartṛhari irascibly describes woman as "a tornado of problems, an abode of misbehaving, a city of impetuosities, a vessel of sins, a field of doubts sown with hundreds of deceits, an obstacle to the gates of heaven, a mouth to the realms of hell, the basket of all trickery, a nectar-coated poison, a snare to all who live" (*Śṛṅgāraśataka* 45). But satiric misogyny is only a manifestation of a larger, more magnificent, misanthropy.

Behind the refined, elegant, and sophisticated manners of love, beneath amorous ideals of grace and courtliness, the satirist ferrets out brutish, petty realities. The moment of exposure is the moment of laughter. Satire sets up aristocratic illusions with lip service and convention only to suddenly undermine them. A satiric description of lovers begins sweetly:

> Wealthy lovers share an ornamental seat
>   with lovely girls as they repeat
> Clever little jokes and stories O-so-sweet
>   to all the courtesans they meet . . .

And then the dream of love is shattered, the lofty ideal is brought down to earth, with a simile: "just like bulls penned up with cows in heat" (*Pādatāḍitaka* 119). Refinement is a mere cover for coarseness and grossness. Love poetry is all cant. The *ars erotica* is affirmed to justify the crudest and most selfish hungers.

Where a beautiful courtesan, graceful with the accomplishments of love, is promised, a low-caste whore, drooling betel juice and scratching her infected loins, appears—she is like "worm-infested food upon which even dogs have shit" (*Śāradātilaka* 177). She greets a lover, not the promised gallant, but an old man who wears his turban as a loincloth. The conventional joke—garments worn on an inappropriate part of the body—suggests the comic, though not unserious, transposition of reason and lust which is a recurrent theme in erotic satire.

An "urbane gentleman," encountering the satirist/parasite of one monologue play, tries to cover his face. The literal gesture represents the sin of more figurative attempts at concealment, the crime of which all objects of satire are quilty. The laughing, mocking parasite is quick to expose him—he has been caught frequenting the lowest, and least expensive, prostitutes, those who sell themselves near the cremation grounds. The image, connecting sexuality and death, conjuring up visions of Kālī, suggests the perversion of love from the potentially life-promoting energy into a demeaning, ugly, and self-consuming obsession. The depraved rogue has, the satirist announces sarcastically, renounced those whores for a more suitable paramour—a stock comic character—the hunchback. "How can you stand to make love to her?" the parasite laughs. "Lying upon the bed, all crooked and overgrown with that hump she looks like some bird. Her breasts writhe violently after embraces, and passionately she tries to put her hips over your loins. . . . She's a creeper all right—one infested with worms. . . . She's only fit for blow-jobs" (*Pādatāḍitaka* 90–93).

The most socially esteemed women are no less vile than the sluts at the cremation grounds or the hunchback. All women, in satire, are unfaithful, inconstant, and utterly untrustworthy. They are driven to adultery by the harshness of domestic life, and they are unrestrained because no husband is "willing to be exposed with embarrassment" (*Śāradātilaka,* prose after 41). There is no valor in the Age of Dullness. When men do fight over a woman, it is awkward, pathetic, wholly unheroic, not in the least bit chivalrous. The satirist laughs at the tawdry spectacle: "They can't be merchants—if a merchant's wife gets fucked by someone else, he doesn't mention it, for fear of the shame it will bring him" (*Śāradātilaka,* prose after 166). The poet uses the crass, obscene word "fuck" (*yabh-*) in purposeful avoidance of any euphemism, any vocabulary which might lend even a trace of dignity to the scene. Satiric vulgarity is for the sake of diminution; it underscores the degradation of the erotic ideal of amorous dalliance into the reality of rampant, greedy fucking.

In the *Pādatāḍitaka* there is a Mr. Hidden (Upagupta)—his name could be applied to any object of satiric laughter. This very small-minded and enormously large-bodied man is in love with an old woman. She has gone through menopause and he is impotent, capable of "only the word 'love' " (*Pādatāḍitaka,* prose after 78). Images of sterility and sexual impotence recur throughout satires of manners as ciphers of ineffectuality and unresponsiveness on all levels of experience. The penis is a consummately comic organ: in satires of manners, lovers fail to make it rise; in religious satires, holy men fail to keep it down. It is comically unruly, always refusing—to the delight of the satirist—to obey command, demand, or reason. The satirist universally refers to it often for it—unlike the man between whose legs it resides—never pretends. The penis is always honest.

The commander of the king's army, also in the *Pādatāḍitaka,* gives all his money to the royal physician in hopes of a cure for his stubbornly flaccid phallus. A court painter takes bdellium, a drug prescribed to remove fat, in order to make himself more handsome and attractive to women. It works perfectly well. There is only one hitch—it also causes impotence. His new attractiveness has no purpose, can serve no end. Cause and effect, purpose and action, lose all connection in the absurd world of satire. The painter becomes, like something he might paint, an illusion, "pleasant only to see, like a Yakṣa in a drawing" (*Pādatāḍitaka* 13). In the bleak and horribly funny satirical vision, human beings are two dimensional. They are depersonalized. The characters of satire are phantoms, self-created illusions. They are all and only show. Obsessed with his own prestige and with the way others see him, the king's commander, "his forehead and knees calloused from multitudes of prostrations," constantly parades himself by "going from the temple to the royal palace and from the royal palace back to the temple" (*Pādatāḍitaka* 18–19).

Outer and inner always contradict each other. Incarnations of this self-contradiction and incongruity comprise the *dramatis personae* of satire. In erotic satire we encounter the impotent lover, the old person trying to be young, the hunchback trying to be sexy, the man trying to be a woman. One homosexual transvestite complains of the lover that has jilted "her." The parasite/satirist offers consolation with sarcasm, one of the most prevalent of satirical strategies.

> He who jilts you loses a festival of pleasure,
> For you have qualities that are far beyond measure:
> You don't have big breasts, but that is really okay—
> During the making of love, they just get in the way;
> You are not bothered by having to go on the rag,
> That unclean sexual hiatus, that monthly lag;
> Since you're completely immune to any impregnation,
> You do not have to fear premature maturation.
>
> (*Ubhayābhisārikā* 23)

Everyone attempts to be who and what they are not. An old man, known to the courtesans as "Old Lover-Bull" (Bharajaradgava), dyes his hair, paints his face, sucks in his cheeks, and consumes aphrodisiacs, in a desperate and futile attempt to give a "youthful appearance to his body—it was like restoring a run-down old house by plastering it" (*Padmaprābhṛtaka* 21). By trying to make himself look younger, the old man only becomes more pathetically old and comically foolish. But the objects of satire take pride in their vain pretenses; again and again they boast, "O great indeed is my prestige!" (*Śāradātilaka,* prose after 163). The hag brags of her beauty, the old man of his vigor, the dunce of his wisdom, the coward of his courage, the hypocrite of his piety. Such pleonastic ravings and self-indulgent verbal excrescences backfire and betray the speaker.

Like the old man, countless women try to defy time. And satire makes the futility of the defiance comical. One aged whore, trying to make herself look young, ties up her fallen breasts and propositions men in the street "with cunning come-ons to steal their dough" (*Śāradātilaka* 163). Kālī takes on the guise of Sātī. All is pretense and seeming. The satiric spectacle is grotesque, often as repulsive as it is comical. Another white-haired harlot, "with saggy, nail-scarred breasts, and drooping lips," ravaged by age, is encountered upon her return from the Temple of Love. "Old age had stolen her beauty, but not her wantonness" (*Pādatāḍitaka* 32). The satirist announces that when a man, a few days earlier, kissed her, one of her decayed teeth had come out and fallen into his mouth—"he had to clear his throat and spit it out" (33). The comic, in bad-tempered satire particularly, often verges on the grossly distasteful. Kṣemendra, commenting on the image of the man spitting out the old woman's tooth, explains that the poet has gone too far, that the mood of disgust has eclipsed the aesthetic sentiment of comedy. Impropriety causes the comic flavor to arise, but here, according to the theorist, the impropriety, like that of "a bouquet of flowers that has been seasoned with garlic," is too extreme (*Aucityavicāracarcā,* commentary on citation 28).

The crone, the time-withered whore in particular, always described in terms that evoke the laughter of disgust, is a conventional figure in Sanskrit satire. Madam Horrible (Vikarālā—an epithet of Kālī), the old procuress in a narrative satire by Dāmodaragupta, "has buck teeth with great gaps between them, a sunken jaw, a huge, flat nose, and the skin on her body droops around the shriveled tits that are marked with big nipples; her bloodshot eyes are sunken, and her unornamented earlobes dangle; she has a bit of whitish hair and her outstretched neck is all covered with veins" (*Kuṭṭanīmata* 27–28). The aged prostitute is an image of the inevitable decay and degeneration of all beauty as she runs along the street, "shooing away flies with her hand. . . . She has a hump like a camel, one eye, and its bad. . . . Her filthy body stinks. . . . Her voice is like an ass's. . . . She falls down again and again" (*Śāradātilaka* 69–71). All is fall, humiliation, and decay. "The hoary, wrinkled, white-haired, flabby-bodied, saggy-breasted, old bawd" (*Śṛṅgārasundara* 81) embodies the destiny of all charming, laughing, lovely ladies with full, round breasts, firm thighs, and creeper-like arms. She hovers, seen or not, over impassioned lovers, just as Kālī dances upon the copulating bodies of Kāma and Rātī, flesh burning with sex and death, as a reminder of the ultimate vanity of love, the true end of all desire and delight. And she laughs a macabre and sinister laugh.

The torrential rains that had washed the blood of the goat from the block in the courtyard of laughing Kālī's temple stopped and the crowd, begging, praying, arguing, joking, cursing, singing, laughing, moaning, reformed, reswarmed. The air was still hot as if suffused with the steaming breath of Kālī. An old woman, wrapped in dark cloth, without ornaments or vermilion in her hair, whining Bengali, reached out for alms. Premendra shooed her away. "This old woman says she's Kālī in hopes of getting our money. Probably she was a prostitute. Pay no attention to her. We must get home. Mother has prepared the meal."

The Mother of Harlots: *Comic Kālī*

A little while ago I met on the edge of the town an old bearded body called Celestina. She's a crafty witch up to every kind of wickedness. They tell me that here, in this city, more than five thousand maidenheads have been broken and repaired under her auspices. She can move the hardest rocks, and tempt them to lechery if she has a mind to.

Fernando de Rojas, *La Celestina*

Youth and age, beauty and ugliness, are juxtaposed in what became the conventional comic scene of a young harlot taking instruction in the amatory arts from an old, retired whore, a bawd or "mother." Such scenes parody the initiation of young men into Vedic study with venerable pandits or gurus. Miss Beauxarts (Kalāvatī), the young whore in Kṣemendra's *Samayamātṛkā,* a text wherein the stock comic figure of the bawd realizes its fullest satiric potential, falls at the feet of Madam Bagabones (Kaṅkālī), praises the old whore, and beseeches her for teaching. "You are creation, preservation, and destruction: Brahmā, the creator, in terms of the instruction you give to harlots; Viṣṇu, in the ways in which you manifest illusion; and Śiva, in respect to your battles with poverty stricken suitors. . . . I am devoted to you, Mother, and I seek refuge in you!" (4.11,13). The paean could be to Kālī: "O Mother, you give birth to the world, protect the world, and withdraw the world into yourself at the great dissolution! You are Brahmā, Viṣṇu, and Śiva, the Creator, Preserver, and Destroyer!" (*Karpūrādistotra* 12).

The bawd's name, Kaṅkālī (literally, "skeleton"), is an epithet of Kālī; her form too is suggestive of the hideous goddess. "She was like a hungry ghost, her emaciated body but a skull-topped skeleton, a mere contraption of bones tied together by veins and arteries; there were white spots on her bloated belly. The body was a cage, its many holes covered over with hide, a cage with a bird in it, a bird with the skill of deceiving the whole world. Her mouth was ever gaping to seize everything. . . . Her very long, sharp teeth gave her the terrible appearance of a bitch aggravated with ferocious anger at the time of giving birth. . . . She had the face of an owl, the neck of a crow, the eyes of a cat—parts borrowed from incompatible animals'' (*Samayamātṛkā* 4.2–7). Kṣemendra stresses the connection between Kālī and Kaṅkālī by invoking the goddess at the opening of his satire:

> Praise be to Kālī!
> In the dreadful hollow of her throat
> The cosmos is but a guppy squirming
> Somewhere in a stormy sea;
> Though the ancients did not know it
> Kālī is the mighty source of time,
> Proud bewilderer of all living beings.
> Praise be to her mouth—
> Horrible and gaping!

Kālī is the personification of the aesthetic sentiments of horror and revulsion. Kṣemendra evokes the essential mood: ''The cemetary seemed to be Death's pleasure garden. Drinks of blood were served in goblets made of skulls. . . . garlands formed of vulture-gnawed entrails swung to and fro as witches danced at this festival of Kālī'' (*Bṛhatkathāmañjarī* 9.2.41–43).

The hideous can inspire terror or laughter, or both at once. The link between the horrific and the comic is made apparent in Kṣemendra's portrayal of Madam Bagabones. She is the human, literary manifestation of the same uncanny power that incarnates divinely, mythologically, as Kālī. But as Kālī's terrible form inspires horrific awe, Bagabones's ugliness elicits comic laughter. In the fall from the supernal to the mundane, the dreadful becomes the ludicrous, and the sinister is silly. The monstrous and the absurd, the ominous and the fantastic, converge. Madam Bagabones is a caricature of Kālī.

Madam Bagabones is the subject, not the object, of Kṣemendra's satire. That everyone is aware that an old bawd is by nature corrupt and necessarily scheming, places such a figure outside the firing range of satire. The sight of satire is focused upon those people who imagine that their corruption is legitimate, those socially integrated deceivers whose status provides a cover for their crimes: merchants and clerks, doctors and lawyers, priests and penitents, ministers and bureaucrats, scholars and teachers, princes and kings. The old bawd's hypocrisy is not hypocritical for she is wholly dedicated to dishonesty and absolutely sincere in her duplicity. Fraud is her zealously, piously fulfilled role in life, her personal religion.

Describing the ways in which Madam Bagabones uses pretense and chicanery to obtain money from presumably respectable men, Kṣemendra exposes the unrespectable falseheartedness of those men. They are vulnerable and susceptible to Madam Bagabones's ensnarements because of their own greed for power as manifested by money or sex, because of their drunkenness, lust, pretentiousness, affectation, or dullness. Like the satirist himself, Madam Bagabones is "fair toward those whose income was fair, wicked toward the wicked, and nasty toward the nasty" (*Samayamātṛkā* 4.5).

Madam Bagabones is profoundly dishonest and, like the satirist, she is exquisitely unsentimental and cynical. The illegitimate daughter of a woman who kept an inn for travelers, she commits crime after crime, each crime leading to a predicament from which she must escape, each escape leading to another crime, another predicament, another escape. She moves from one town to another, one lover to another, one customer to another, compressing countless lives into one: she marries a farmer, a porter, a stable master, and a merchant or two or three; she sells cakes, ghee, trinkets, crooked dice, amulets, flowers, and—whenever she can—herself; she becomes a whore, a goatherd, a tavern owner, a barmaid, a wet nurse, a mendicant, a nun, an alchemist, a fortune teller, a philosopher, a magician, and an adept at yoga. As little girl and old hag, wife and widow, whore and nun, she has assimilated all phases of womanhood and experienced all the responses of men. Through her vast experience she has come to realize and incorporate into her being one basic truth: the world is a hoax. It is this knowledge, the ultimate revelation of both the yogi and the satirist, that she teaches to her discipline, Miss Beauxarts.

Her manic biography is a picaresque comedy, made comic both by the wildness of her exploits and by the outrageous way in which those exploits are recounted. It is funny in the way that a film run at high speed is crazily comic.

A lovely little girl, she became a thief quite soon:
Honored by the townsfolk during the changes of the moon,
She was invited to their homes where the little dear
Made all their sacred vessels completely disappear.
When she was only seven, her voice already bold,
Her mother started teaching her how she could be sold;
Out of greed mom tutored her to play the harlot's game,
And at the market gate, Deathtrap soon became her name.
She wore a pair of falsies and shells upon a string;
Hugs and kisses pleased her lovers—she'd do most anything.
One day a merchant's son, Master Fullofit Esquire,
Shopping for some saffron, just happened to pass by her;
He was young and handsome—he wore fourteen carat gold.
Later in a gambling joint, where drinks were also sold,
She winked her eye, raised her brow, did all that she could do
To rouse his eagerness for a nighttime rendezvous.
While clinging to his neck that night as he lay fast asleep,
(since he had had a lot to drink his snooze was very deep),
She stole his golden earrings—he still did not awaken—
And the rings from off his fingers quietly were taken.
"Help! Help!" the girl then shouted, "Oh! Oh! I have been robbed!"
As if to stop a thief, "Help! Help!" she so loudly sobbed.
Robbed and awakened, to avoid a family disgrace,
The salesman ran away, using his clothes to hide his face.
All decked out in dazzling duds, looking young and pretty,
She changed her name and moved along to another city.
Intent on picking flowers, by using all her talents,
She made love all day and night—the flowers were town gallants.
There were more lovers in her house than there were stray curs,
Coming, going, hanging out—and all of them were hers.
By day she served her lovers (the service was non-stop):
She'd pick them up in grocery stores or the florist shop,
In the park or by a well, at some refreshment stand,
Even at a friend's house—she'd pick up anyone at hand.
At dusk she'd take a lover, then she'd get him very drunk,
And tuck him into bed like a baby in his bunk,
Then she'd find another man and he'd be wildly sexed,
And when he was fast asleep, she'd go on to the next;
She'd leave at dawn to see a friend who was sick with colic—
That was just a pretext for a whore's excessive frolic.
When she missed appointments, her rich customers got mad;
She then fled to secret rooms that other lovers had.
At night she'd go to temple—but it was not to pray—
Blind with lust, the temple guard would let her in to stay.
When the man was snoring loud and sleeping like the dead,

She stole the jewels of goddess and away she fled.
Again she moved and changed her name and situation—
Baron Battlelion's mistress, Miss Sophistication.
In his home she was served heaping plates and mounds of meat;
There she fattened up on him, on all he had to eat.
As dear to him as was the witch to the epic warrior,
She so impassioned him (he should have seen a lawyer)
That she obtained the ownership of all he had accrued,
And wishing then for him to die, she caused a fam'ly feud.
By and by her wish came true: he was slain, his body found,
And once he'd been carted off to the cremation ground,
Her hold upon his house was firm, gained one way or other—
She soon became the love of Leon, her dead baron's brother.
Despite her waning youth and the rivals to be beaten
She got the lad to marry her—magic roots were eaten.
To preserve precious youth, she did all one can do—
She ate onions, garlic, ghee, milk, and fish ragout.
Death came to Leon and, fearing probate by the king,
She moved on yet once again, making off with everything.
A widow in light, white robes, she seemed most dejected;
Downward her head was bent that alms might be collected.
She spent time by a mountain stream, dwelling on the banks,
Making off'rings to ancestors, hoping for their thanks—
Sesame, sand, and sacred grass. She was quite disarming.
One day there came a cavalier—his name was Prince Charming;
At the sacred bathing place our widow got her wish,
Got that wealthy horseman as the heron gets the fish.
She knew how to win his heart, skilled from her romances;
His house was in her hands; she took over his finances.
When in a month the rich man died, standing on her feet
She claimed she wished to follow him—yet one more deceit.
The fam'ly impeded her persistence in that notion,
But she spoke like a lady, steadfast with grave emotion:
"In noble homes widowhood's honor's decimation;
With the end of honor comes love's sad separation;
By the means of funeral fire, this grief shall be no more;
'Tis a far better thing I do than I have done before."
She said it with conviction, as unmovable as stone:
Thinking of her husband's wealth, of all that she'd soon own,
She was filled with joy and that expression on her face
Was mistaken by everyone for a state of grace.
She got all her husband's fortune through the king's decree;
Then more courtiers came to court her. She knew coquetry.

(*Samayamātṛkā* 2.5–36)

Madam Bagabones is utterly irrepressible. It does not cramp her style in the slightest when the law catches up with her, and she is imprisoned.

> She made a deal with the jailer, his name was Mr. Snake;
> He made her feel right at home with wine and fish and cake.
> She held him tightly in her arms, kissed him ardently;
> By biting off his tongue, she was able to get free.
> The drunken jailer lay there, unconscious on the floor;
> She threw off her fetters and went right out the jail door.
> (2.49–51)

On and on and on it goes, *ad absurdum*. Madam Bagabones is never herself. As a little girl she disguises herself as a mature young woman; as an old woman she disguises herself as a youthful lady, using straps and corsets to support sagging flesh. As she travels throughout India, fleecing and defrauding men, she continuously changes her name and form just as the protean Kālī does: "At Kālīghaṭ you are Kālī, dear mother, and on Kailāsa you are Bhavānī; at Vṛndāvana you are Rādhā. . . . Who can understand *māyā?* . . . Who can guess what you're up to?" (Rāmprasād 30, 33).

Kālī is a caricature of *māyā*, the illusion which is this world, a deformed likeness of the world in whom all the salient features—disease and death, pain and violence—are exaggerated into blatancy. Gaṇeśa, the tutelary deity of the comic sentiment, gave Madam Bagabones the power of "great magic" (*mahāmāyā*) (4.78). This *māyā*—*māyā* as magic—provided a traditional metaphor for *māyā* as the epistemological concept: we are deceived in magic by both the power of the magician and by our own ignorance; when we are no longer ignorant, when we know the trick, the magician, despite his power, has no hold over us. Knowledge is liberation. Satire, because it unmasks and reveals realities behind pretenses, is a kind of redemptive gnosis. The satirist, like the philosopher and like Madam Bagabones, asserts that the world is a deception. Bagabones teaches the art of fraud, the science of lies, and the philosophy of illusion. She explains that only through the mastery of *māyā* can a courtesan succeed. Falsehood is propounded as a way of life. "As drunkenness destroys a woman of highbirth, so truthfulness destroys a courtesan" (4.68). "Trickery and cunning are the source of our power" (4.37). Kṣemendra uses a laconic proverbial form as a medium for cynical, satiric wit: "As a merchant is ruined by generosity, a guru by humility, and a government comptroller by compassion, so a harlot is ruined by truthfulness" (4.70). The Hindu ethical principle that defines righteousness as the fulfillment of a particular social role is turned in on itself—truthfulness is suddenly a vice and, ironically, it is good to be bad.

Kālī, as the dark embodiment of the destructive energy, is depicted conquering Śiva, a triumph that is martial and sexual: she stands upon his breast, holding his severed head in one hand and a blood-stained sword in the other; or she rides astride the god in a gruesome mockery of copulation, sapping him of his seminal power. In Kashmir, she is pictured slaying Brahmā, the personification of Vedic knowledge and justice. The Veda is obsolete in the Age of Dullness, an age of satire. The relationship between Kālī and the god, is paralleled by the relationship between Bagabones and every man she knows. Bagabones emasculates, humiliates, and impoverishes men, hundreds of them. It is revenge for the plight of women: "The charming youthfulness of girls seems to vanish all of a sudden, to be destroyed unnoticed," Madam Bagabones reflects. "A man, it seems, is like a palm tree—his youth endures. But with a woman it is different—yesterday a little girl, today a young lady, tomorrow an old woman. In old age men can have quite a happy livelihood due to all the knowledge they've acquired, but when a woman's youth is gone, she can expect nothing but alms" (8.98–99, 103). The aged harlot is a tragically comic character. "No one has any more use for an old whore than they do for an icebox in winter, a row of burning lamps at noon, or a corsage that's worn and wasted" (2.56). And so the aged prostitute becomes a "mother." The title is applied as ironically to the old bawd as it is to the raging, blood-drenched goddess. They are grotesque mothers. As a wife Bagabones is barren despite efforts to produce heirs for various wealthy husbands, but when she becomes a Buddhist nun, making her living by collecting alms, when it is most inappropriate, she is impregnated by a servant in the monastery. "When her belly got too big, it put an end to collecting alms—the new mother dumped the fetus and left for the city once more" (2.66). The horrible infanticidal image, suggestive of the dead infants that adorn Kālī's ears, is presented with amused, satiric nonchalance. Madam Bagabones is absolutely amoral and is, like a Buddha or a yogi, like the satirist himself, absolutely detached. According to the *Upaniṣads,* the man who is liberated, who has realized an identity with the absolute, is beyond good and evil. "Such a person is not worried by the thought, 'Why did I not do good? Why did I do evil?' " (*Taittirīya Upaniṣad* 2.9.1). The description of the awakened, enlightened, holy one applies ironically to Bagabones.

Maternity, normally rendering the woman all the more dependent upon men, merely gives Madam Bagabones another device and opportunity to swindle, cheat, and dominate them. Under the name Ms. Half-n-Half (Sārdhakṣīra), she hires herself out as a wet nurse—the maternal equivalent of the prostitute—for the infant son of an important minister. And thus she is well fed so that she may nourish the child. There is a comic reversal. Instead of the child growing strong from the wet nurse's services, the child becomes weaker as the nurse flourishes—Bagabones draws sustenance from him, rather than he from her. This same transposition is expressed in respect to Kālī: "I do not know," the devotee cries out to Mother Kālī, "whether I am eating you or you are eating me!" (Rāmprasād 85). A doctor, diagnosing the cause of the child's illness as a diet that is too rich and spicy, prescribes a regimen of only fish broth for the wet nurse. Surreptitiously Madam Bagabones continues to glut herself and the infant's health continues to fail. Fearing that she'll be discovered, Madam Bagabones steals some of the minister's gold and flees once more.

Madam Bagabones is the negative, degraded underside of the idealized mother, one of the most venerated of all Indian ideals. "The spiritual master," Manu declares, "stands above ten teachers, the father above a hundred spiritual masters, and the mother above a thousand fathers" (2.145). The laughter which Mother Bagabones elicits is, in part, due to the unmasking of the ideal, the disclosure of the depriving, greedy, disappointing, and frustrating mother, inevitably contained within the nourishing, protecting, and loving ideal. Hostile energies, accumulated through a domestically and socially required repression, are released in pleasurable laughter. The dreadful aspects of the mother become comic and thus, at least momentarily, benign. The dynamics of laughter are the same with respect to all idealized figures. As Madam Bagabones is the satirical representative of the mother, so her daughter, the typical courtesan of Sanskrit satire, displays the negative, fearful, suspect side of the idealized beloved.

The Daughter of Joy: *Women in Love*

These courtesans are like the sea,
All that is brought to them they take;
But though the current flows in free
No difference does it make.
Whatever enters, that they hold,
Whether it water be or gold.

Plautus, *Truculentis*

The ideal courtesan is described in the *Kāmasūtra* as possessing "beauty, youth, good markings, sweetness, a passion for good qualities, a fondness for love and lovemaking, honesty, generosity, and an appreciation for the arts" (6.1.13). The prostitute who knows the arts of love, Vātsyāyana explains, earns the title "courtesan" if she is virtuous and beautiful—"she is worshiped by royalty and men of virtue" (1.3.20–21). The text adds that, although a concern with material gain is not incompatible with love in her, since love is her profession, the courtesan should not be obsessed with money. But in satire everyone is obsessed. Obsession moves the world and sucks it into absurdity.

In stories infused with the amorous sentiment, the courtesan is depicted as loving, sincere, sophisticated, and generous. The usual example of this idealized heroine as given by the dramaturgists and commentators is Vasantasenā, the courtesan heroine of the romantic drama by Śūdraka.

Though there is no lotus in her hand
she is a goddess, Beauty;
A splendid blossom on the tree of Desire,
she is a beautiful weapon of Love.
Though she is shy in the intimacy of embrace,
she walks coquetishly on the field of Love . . .
Followed by a throng of suitors,
the envy of highborn ladies.

(*Mṛcchakaṭikā* 5.12)

Śūdraka's poetic strategy, in service of the amorous sentiment, is the contraposition of Vasantasenā with the commonplace conception of the whore. "These women," a character in the play proposes, "laugh and weep for money. They don't trust a soul and yet they make men confide in them . . . their passion lasts about as long as an ocean wave or a ridge of cloud . . . they'll have one man whom they love, while they seduce another with winks and glances, and they embrace another passionately, while they desire to make love with yet another . . . just as asses can't give birth to horses, women raised in the demimonde can't be pure'' (4.14–17). Śūdraka leads the audience from the assumption that a courtesan must be duplicitous to the revelation that she can be good and honest. Vasantasenā is wholly self-sacrificing and devoted, as genuine and gentle as she is beautiful. Satire moves in the opposite direction, from the expectation that a woman may be innocent and honest to the revelation that she is completely disingenuous and selfish. The amorous sentiment manifests itself when the ideal is actualized; the comic sentiment manifests itself when the ideal is demolished. In the face of love's insistence on the reality of ideals, satire knows only the reality of human frailty, imperfection, baseness, meanness, raunchiness, smallness, and grossness. ''How can any family man kiss the mouth of a whore?'' Bhartṛhari asks. ''Though it may seem charming, it is actually a spittoon that has been used by parasites, actors, servants, thieves, soldiers, and spies'' (*Śṛṅgāraśataka* 59). Satire is comic realism.

Kṣemendra describes Miss Beauxarts in terms which could refer to Vasantasenā or any other loving woman of Sanskrit love poetry: ''Her limbs were adorned with pearls and she was surrounded by bees hungering for the flower in her braided hair—she resembled the starry night, illuminated by the moon'' (*Samayamātṛkā* 6.4). But when the encomium culminates in the simple statement that she is gazing intently at herself in a mirror (6.4 and 7.18), vanity defoliates the beauty she admires all too much, and the burgeoning amorous sentiment bursts into the comic. The courtesan fawning over herself, looking into the mirror, becomes a vendor proudly taking inventory. The beautiful Miss Beauxarts sits upon her veranda on display, having dressed and adorned herself so as to have transformed ''her body into a piece of merchandise'' (6.5). The amorous is simultaneously transformed into the comic. The harlot is, in satire, a caricature of the sexual aspects of all women. Her greed is the greed that the male fears is hidden beneath all prettily smiling faces.

Kṣemendra uses puns to sabotage the amorous sentiment, to effect the transformation, in his description of Miss Beauxarts. ''Her breasts were ravishing (*hāriṇī*), her eyes were ravishing (*hāriṇī*), her slender body was ravishing (*hāriṇī*), and she delighted (*vihāriṇī*) in love" (*Samayamātṛkā* 7.12). "*Hāriṇī*" can mean either "lovely/beautiful" or "robbing/stealing"—Miss Beauxarts seems to be the former but she conceals, like the language that describes her, the latter. To describe a woman as beautiful would inspire admiration; to describe her as a duplicitous and avaricious thief would provoke disdain. The comedy arises out of the interplay and tension between the contradictory qualities simultaneously suggested. While neither praise nor abuse is particularly comic, both abusive praise (a device of satire) and affectionate insult (a device of humor) are. A perception of incongruity (between expression and intent, reality and ideal, object and concept, form and content) gives rise to laughter in both satiric and humorous comedy. In satire a lovely girl turns out to be a heartless thief; in humor a coarse thief turns out to have a heart that is pure and good.

An ironic vision of the world underlies the comic sensibility. Jalhaṇa (twelfth century), in his collection of often satirically didactic stanzas on prostitutes, indicates the irony of the demimonde.

> It's no sin when they act in an immoral fashion,
> And they earn their livelihood just by faking passion;
> What is considered bad in others in them is good;
> And they don't have to worry about their widowhood;
> They can rob people without fear of prosecution;
> There is happiness in a life of prostitution!
>
> (*Mugdhopadeśa* 53)

Using technical rhetorical terms from the theoretics of comedy, Jalhaṇa stresses the comic potential of harlotry as he asserts that descriptions of sexual union with whores are "above all else a burlesque of the amorous sentiment" for such union always occurs "at an inappropriate time or place for love and it is devoid of sexual propriety," and as a burlesque it is "disrespectful of domestic felicity and devoid of those qualities of beauty which are the essence of the sublime" (24).

The comic sentiment arises through descriptions of the trickery and deceits of whores, through revelations of their audacities, and through perceptions of the incongruity between the outer show of desire as love and the inner reality of desire as venality.

Love and Money

I believe that love is one of the most beautiful, warm, wonderful, and meaningful experiences that money can buy.

Steve Martin

The satirist reveals the real demands behind all claims of love: women demand money; men demand sex. Love is simply the respective need of women and men to get or use what the other has. Love is mutual exploitation.

The desire that animates the harlots in the erotic satires is never sexual, but always fiscal. Harlots merely use the arts of love to attain their real end—material gain. "Courtesans make a false show of passion out of greed for wealth" (*Kalāvilāsa* 4.20). There is no love, neither intimacy nor passion, neither playfulness nor fertility, in these texts, except in stories that set up the ideal against which the actualities are judged. There is only greed. The tension between love and material gain, *kāma* and *artha,* neither of which is comic in itself, becomes comic through unmasking, when one is discovered to be posing as the other.

This jumbling of love and money as depicted in satire, this confusion of the venal and the venereal, is perhaps symptomatic or reflective of a cultural conflict created by the establishment of commercial urban centers within a fundamentally agrarian society. The agricultural concern with sexuality as fertility becomes overwhelmed by a commercial concern with sexuality as a commodity. Villages inspire humor; cities, satire.

The satires depict the perversion of primary natural values by an overgrown, parasitic, commercial class. The lover has become a customer, and the beloved is merchandise.

The harlot is conventionally portrayed in Indian literature as venal, obsessed by wealth, gratifying her suitors "as if impassioned; but when those customers have no more money, she has her mother throw them out" (*Daśarūpaka* 2.22). Madam Deathtongue (Yamajihvā), an old bawd with "a huge protruding jaw, long, sharp teeth, and a snub nose," explains to her beautiful daughter that a harlot should never be sincere, that she, "like an actress, should feign love in order to win a man's heart; then she should take all his money from him; then, when he's broke, she should dump him and not take him back, unless, of course, he should come into cash again" (*Kathāsaritsāgara* 57). Such satire may well reflect a male fear that all women are actresses by their very nature, that all of them have the power of *māyā,* that their affections and charms, their tears and smiles, are mere show. Comic laughter, in mollifying that fear, allows us to pursue or do what we know is dangerous and absurd.

Like Madam Horrible, Madam Bagabones sermonizes, "Money transcends life itself. And it is obtained by intelligence. . . . Money is the most important thing in the world, constituting the very life of the living. . . . By money we attain wisdom, and by wisdom money. . . . Even brahminicide is absolved by money! Ah Money! Ah Money!" (*Samayamātṛkā* 4.19, 4.80–81, 4.111). The frankness of the bawd, the impropriety of the hyperbole, enforces the comic tone.

A quack doctor gave a medicinal root as a treatment to a bawd named Madam Camelneck (Karabhagrīvā). Never satisfied with a little, the old procuress, contrary to the prescripion, voraciously devoured the entire root and fell into a delirium. In her last moments, hallucinating that the sun and everything illuminated by it was made of gold, Madam Camelneck ecstatically cried out in an epiphany of greed to her daughter, "Take some! Take some!" (*Samayamātṛkā* 1.31). The image, at once ghastly and ridiculous, of the decrepit old whore overdosing herself out of greed and finding the whole world transformed into an ungraspable object of that greed, at once conveys the satirist's vision of corruption and implies his warning of its consequences.

Madam Deathtongue was hired by a rich merchant to instruct his son, Īśvaravarman, as to the wiles of courtesans. But despite his training, the young man, blinded by the dazzling light of love, lost a fortune to the duplicitous and deceitful courtesan, Miss Beauty (Sundarī). Madam Deathtongue devised a plan for revenge. Īśvaravarman returned to the house of Miss Beauty, taking with him Āla, an ape that had been fed with gold coins. The young man assured the harlot that he had forgiven her for fleecing him, assured her that because of the ape he had no more concern for money—the animal could produce money at command. "Āla," Īśvaravarman ordered, "we need money for eating and drinking and for betel; give me money for Miss Beauty and her mother, and more money to give to brahmins." The ape began to shit gold coins, much to the wonder of the harlot and her mother who, of course, immediately began to devise strategies to get the creature. But all their offers were met with a firm, decisive response: "No, I could never part with Āla." Miss Beauty groveled at the young man's feet, caressed and kissed him, begged, and finally vowed, "I'll give you everything, all I possess, everything." Īśvaravarman finally conceded and then he left town with the harlot's life-savings. For several days gold coins were produced from the rear end of the ape. But then gold turned to shit. Ape turds were all that Miss Beauty received. The harlot and her mother began to beat the ape, so enraging the animal that it turned on them, attacked them, and bit, scratched, and disfigured their faces. They fought back until finally the gold-producing monkey was dead. "When the people of the town saw the whore, her face disfigured and her wealth gone, they laughed." And when the story was told, the listeners in the larger frame story also "laughed heartily" (*Kathāsaritsāgara* 57.54–177). This laughter, the epitome of satiric laughter, is aroused as ugliness, the inner reality, hidden by beauty, the outer lie, is made visible, as the real filthiness of lucre becomes apparent, and as the deceiver becomes the deceived. That is satiric justice. Through illusion reality triumphs over illusion.

Illusion and Reality

> There's some whores lies still as stones, they think it's more lady-like or something; but I say they don't know which side their bread's buttered. Listen: if you lie still the bloke may spend half the night sweating away. But if you bash it about a bit and make like he's made you ever so happy, with a bit of luck, he'll pay up good, get out and away, and leave you in peace.
>
> A London prostitute cited by Wayland Young, "Sitting on a Fortune" (*Encounter*)

It is a satiric conceit, comic through paradox, that women of love are incapable of love. To say that a courtesan or prostitute feels love, either affection or passion, is, according to Jalhaṇa, like saying "that Death is compassionate, that there is virtue in the Age of Degeneration, that a sword is tender, that a venomous serpent brings comfort, that fire is cooling, that villainy benefits all, or that poison sustains life" (*Mugdhopadeśa* 7). There cannot be even a bit of love in a courtesan, Jalhaṇa continues, any more than there can be "sexual desire in a eunuch, bashfulness in an adulteress, water in mirages, constancy in a woman, dignity in a drunk, or religion in someone who does not exist" (9).

The whore's lack of passion or loving attachment to anyone makes her ironically comparable to the practitioner of religious renunciation. The irony became a conceit in satirical texts. Madam Deathtongue explains that they both attain the highest goal in life (liberation in the case of the holy man, money in the case of the whore) "through being the same in response to all men, the same whether the man is young or old, handsome or deformed" (*Kathāsaritsāgara* 57.64). "The whore is like a practitioner of yoga—she is devoid of both passion and desire, she is detached and does what she likes," Kṣemendra observes and, to stress the humor of the comparison, he uses puns which refer simultaneously to the religious practitioner ("She constantly indulges in meditation and is free from the constituents of nature which bind us to this world") and to the whore ("She thinks only of herself and she is devoid of merit") (*Deśopadeśa* 3.2). The satiric simile is double-edged—as whores are like yogis, yogis are like whores.

If it is funny when harlots don't feel love, it is also funny, through a surprising contradiction of the conceit, when they do. A whore, according to Kṣemendra, becomes "a butt of laughter if she actually feels passion" (*Bṛhatkathāmañjarī* 2.89). If you think she isn't in love, she is; if you think she is, she isn't. Whores are full of comic surprises. Outer and inner, show and impulse, always contradict each other in her and the contradiction is a comic one. "The harlot conceals her loins, not out of modesty, but to arouse the curiosity of others; she wears splendid clothes, not out of propriety, but in order to attract lovers. She drinks meat soup, not because she likes it, but to give her the strength to beat up men; she takes pains to paint pictures, not out of pleasure, but so that her cleverness will become famous. There is passion on her lips, but not in her heart; there is straightness in her arms and legs, but not in her nature; uprightness in her breasts, but not in her conduct. There is greatness in her buttocks, but not in her family; indolence in her gait, but not in her efforts to defraud men. She can distinguish between colors (*varṇa*) when it comes to cosmetics, but when it comes to sex, she makes no distinctions between castes (*varṇa*). She'll make love with a man whether he's young or old, whether he's impotent or long diseased" (*Kuṭṭanīmata* 305–311).

The harlot of satire is, like other objects of satiric laughter, more matter than spirit. And that quality renders her comic. Kṣemendra compares her to a marionette, an image also used by Dāmodaragupta, "a mechanical child, dancing and shaking on a string;

artificially she does everything, devoid of any real emotion within her heart" (*Deśopadeśa* 3.11). She is more a thing than a being.

The superficial moral of these satires of manners is that the courtesan is not to be trusted. "While the whore is delighting her customer, her mind is always somewhere else—cheating her father, defrauding her brothers, abandoning her son" (*Śāradātilaka* 61). But the satiric laughter here is not at the prostitute herself, the deceiver who gives delight, but at her customer, the deceived who takes delight. Satire exists not to reform the harlot, but to awaken the dupe. In his epilogue to the *Samayamātṛkā,* as already noted, Kṣemendra claims that he has composed his satire, "a work full of merriment and smiles, for the protection of the wealth of noblemen."

The deeper moral of satire is that the world itself is not to be trusted. "You're a whore!" Kabīr laughs in the face of *māyā*. The refrain occurs throughout his songs. As *māyā* is a whore, so whores are *māyā*. They are the perpetrators and personifications of illusion, and the lovers' relationship with them parallels the relationship between the individual and the world, *saṃsāra*. As the loveliness and charms of the courtesan attract the lover and then bind him to her, forcing him to pay for his pleasure with a loss of wealth and an experience of unreciprocated affection, so the beauty and delights of the empirical world attract one and bind one to it, condemning one, through that bondage, to perpetual redeath, forcing one to pay for pleasure with a reciprocal pain.

The power that the female has over the male, the power of *māyā,* is erotic, and laughter deflates eros. The capacity of satire, to provide relief, if not release, from the snare of love, to qualify desire and awaken one to the dangers of delusion inherent in passion, is a basis for its appeal, and one reason for the perpetuation of misogynistic jokes. Inherent in such jokes is the implicit suggestion that comedy may provide liberation from the snare of the less-qualified desire that binds one to the world, *māyā,* the great ontological whore. This is not to say that satire is puritanical or anchoritic—the message of satire is that, while it is perfectly reasonable to make love to the whore, it is a folly to take her, one's own feelings, or the world itself, too seriously.

As courtesans are less concerned with pleasing their lovers than they are with cheating their customers, so wives, in the satires of manners, are less concerned with their devotion to their husbands than they are with finding fresh lovers. More dangerous than the woman of love who wants money is the wife—particularly the wife who has money, the money of a rich husband—who wants love. Satire provides laughter to reduce the fear of that danger.

The Wife of Bhaṭṭ: *Adultery*

The Dean of Paul's did search for his wife
And where d'ee think he found her?
Even upon Sir John Selby's bed,
As flat as any flounder.

Anonymous seventeenth-century song

"She is a wife," Śakuntalā, in the great epic, explains, "who is skillful in the home; she is a wife who bears children; she is a wife whose very life is her husband; she is a wife who is ever faithful to her husband. . . . He who has a wife has religious rites; he who has a wife has a home; he who has a wife has happiness; he who has a wife has good fortune. . . . The faithful wife follows her husband even when he has died and gone on to another birth, for he is her lord forever" (*Mahābhārata* 1.68.39–46). The ideal wife was a paragon of unadulterated devotion, worshiping and obeying her husband as her lord.

"In previous times our cities as well as our villages, our palaces as well as our humblest hovels, indeed all places in our blessed Bharata land, were ornamented by jewels of wives. My own blessed mother was one such glowing gem." Mr. Bandyopadhyaya expounded on womanhood, marriage, and love while Premendra served us the dinner that the invisible Mrs. Bandyopadhyaya had prepared. "In former days, the days of my own youth, we had a different idea of womanhood than the one raging rampant now. Now everything is egotism and marriage has gone down a dark alley. But in former, fairer days, the marriage bondage was something sacred. Bharata land had the highest order of matrimonial relations and felicities in the world including both the eastern and western hemispheres. Why was this? In virginhood the girl performed *pūjā* in connection with all *vratas* and festivals for one purpose only—the securing of the best husband in the world. Once that husband *par* excellent was procured, the blessed wife, in strict accordance with the *Śāstras* would perform the sacred *patipūjā* [husband-worship] everyday of her blissful life to the very letter of the blessed *prayoga*. I have a book that I shall give you since you are a student of Sanskrit. It was a gift from my own blessed mother to her daughter-in-law, my own blessed wife. It has gleaned from all the *Śāstras, Purāṇas,* Epics, and *Itihāsas* the details of the *patipūjāvidhān.* When you present this book to your wife, meticulously translating all the Sanskrit for her, she will indeed be awed by it. If, with your instructions, she will but perform the worship of your feet, she will attain a bliss which I cannot even describe, which even poet laureates could not describe."

Though I feared it would shock my kind and generous host, I confessed the truth. "I'm divorced." But nothing shocked Mr. Bandyopadhyaya. "You see! Had she been performing *patipūjā* you would not be divorced! On what condition and under what circumstances could she abandon the man that she had worshiped as god?" I couldn't resist: "Under the circumstances of finding out that I had been unfaithful to her?" Nothing, really nothing, shocked Mr. Bandyopadhyaya. "What unfaithful? How can the Lord be unfaithful? Though Kṛṣṇa, the Lord *par* excellent, had sixteen thousand wives, we cannot say that he was unfaithful to any. The devotee can be unfaithful to God, but God can never be said to be unfaithful to the devotee; so it is that the wife can be unfaithful to her lord, but her lord cannot ever be said to be unfaithful to his wife. Because your wife's love was not pure, she mistook your mere dalliance with some other woman as a breach of faith. She would not have been subject to such illusions if only she had dutifully performed *patisevā* in strict accordance with the *Śāstras*! I shall give you the book in the sincere hope that your next wife will not be subject to delusion or egotism."

"God forbid," I laughed.

"Precisely!" Mr. Bandyopadhyaya shook his head.

In that aristocratic literature, with its roots in the epic, heroic tradition, when the amorous sentiment is dominant, it is always the man who is unfaithful. The vice is a manly virtue. The hero's infidelity, a robust display of virile detachment, makes him all the more attractive and it adds a poignancy to the flavor of the lady's love. When the woman is unfaithful, however, as is frequently the case in folk literature, the sentiment turns comic. The man becomes a fool. The exalted erotic hero would discard a faithless beloved. The low comic buffoon clings to her, allows himself to be duped, or refuses to recognize it. Illicit love is erotic; cuckoldry is funny. Jealous women are sympathetic and lovely; jealous men are bathetic and comically idiotic.

Hearing the gossip that his wife was a whore, a carpenter decided to test the faithless woman; he told her that he had to go away on a trip for a few days. Believing that he was truly gone, she contacted one of her lovers and bid him to come to her house late that night. The carpenter, who had hidden under the bed, though filled with the despair and anger of jealousy when the man arrived for the assignation, waited quietly to see what would happen. As the wife led her lover to the bed, her foot grazed her husband's body. Realizing at once what was going on, she quickly spoke to her paramour. "In grief over the departure of my husband I went today for refuge at the shrine of Kālī. I cannot bear to be without my lord even for a short while. The goddess appeared to me in a vision, as she frequently does to faithful wives and women of virtue. She revealed to me that my husband would die in a few months unless I intervened. I told the goddess I would do anything, that I would give my own life to save my lord, the sole object of my love and devotion. The goddess informed me that there was only one way to save him; she said that I must perform the act of sexual union with another man. Then, and only then, my husband would be able to live another hundred years. Thus I have invited you here." And then, as the man made love to the carpenter's wife, the cuckold remained under the bed. When the sexual bout was finished, he crawled out to thank his saviors. With gratitude he embraced the man, and with joy he danced about with his wife and her paramour on his shoulders and "all the people of the town laughed at him" (*Pañcatantra* 3.8).

The woman's deceitful speech is redolent of the proclamation uttered by Sāvitrī, the epic heroine often cited by traditional commentators as the perfect exemplar of wifely devotion, a woman whose love was powerful enough to redeem her husband from death. "Without my lord, I am as one who is dead. Deprived of my husband, I do not desire happiness; deprived of my husband, I do not desire heaven; deprived of my husband, I do not desire prosperity. I have no desire to live without my husband" (*Mahābhārata* 3.281.51). The contrast between the carpenter's wife and Sāvitrī is a comic contrast between ideal and actuality, exterior and interior. The adulterous woman always behaves like Śakuntalā or Sāvitrī, always wears the mask of their devotion.

An adulteress, accused by her husband of infidelity, devised a plan whereby her lover would disguise himself as a madman loitering at a temple. To publicly prove her fidelity, the woman escorted her husband to the shrine for a divine affirmation of her chaste devotion. As planned, her disguised lover, as if exter.ding his hand for alms or mistaking her for someone else, reached out and touched her. Feigning disgust, she bathed in order to purify herself, and then, performing the rites in the temple, she piously cried out: "If any man, except this madman or my husband, has ever touched me, may I be crushed by the arch of the temple! The deity of the shrine, delighted by her wit, let her pass. Like Iseult in the cognate, but hardly comic, story, the woman was declared pious, faithful, and chaste (*Śukasaptati* 15). Adultery may be morally reprehensible, but it is aesthetically pleasing, and its pleasures provide the appeal of both erotic farce and tales of illicit love. The gods, so it seems, like a good laugh even more than they like piety. On the aesthetic level, cunning can be a greater virtue than chastity, and stupidity a greater sin than adultery. The scene is a travesty of Sītā's trial by fire wherein she publicly proved her faithfulness to Rāma. It is the seriousness of that ideal that makes the parodies of it funny.

Sitting by her husband as he ate the meal that she had so devotedly prepared for him, a supposedly loving wife happened to notice a handsome man pass by the house. She told her husband that there was not enough ghee in his food, that she must rush out for some to avoid the shame of feeding him improperly. After taking some money from him, she ran off to fetch the butter. When, after some time, she arrived back home covered with dirt from making love to the passerby on the ground, she duplicitously explained that she had accidentally dropped the money in the dirt, and that she had spent hours groveling in the dirt in an attempt to retrieve it. She opened her hand and showed him a fistful of earth as if that were proof of the truthfulness of her story. Moved by the devotion of his wife, by the idea that she would dirty herself for his sake, the husband tried to console her and to assure her that he could get along without the ghee for his dinner (*Śukasaptati* 13).

The adulteress, as a stock comic figure, is always beautiful, her beauty being the disguise she wears to commit her crimes, and she always seems to love her husband. The shrew, a related comic character, is the very opposite of the seemingly sweet adulteress. She is mean, ugly, bad-tempered, and—as if her husband would care—faithful:

> Although you could encircle her hips with just one hand,
> It would take two men to reach around her vast waistland;
> Her dugs dangle down to her loins just like ringing bells;

Her face is so fright'ning, with loud laughter it swells,
A laughter that sounds like a kettledrum's rat-tat-too;
And the tormented husband is bossed about by this shrew.

(*Subhāṣitāvali* 2360).

In a modern Bengali cartoon, a devout brahmin studying the *Upaniṣads* and contemplating the philosophical commentaries of Śaṅkara, is henpecked by an ugly wife (fig. 7). It is neither the man nor the woman that is funny, but the relationship between them, their reversal of the normal or idealized domestic roles. The cartoon, in juxtaposing the abstract reality of Vedic truth with the concrete reality of domestic life, makes fun of philosophy—*brahman* is just all too useless in the face of an ugly wife. The cosmic battle between matter and spirit, *māyā* and *brahman, prakṛti* and

Figure 7

SWEET HOME.
Termagant Wife: You are a perfect fool, do you realise?
Philosophic Husband (*absentmindedly*): Yes, since I married you!

Figure 8

puruṣa, the mythological struggle for power between Kālī and Śiva, is reduced to a domestic squabble in comedy. Matter, *māyā, prakṛti,* Kālī, or the wife always seem to win in comedy. The female thrives on the battle of the sexes and she relishes it; she is more powerful than the male. The shrew with her henpecking and the adulteress with her infidelity make the man an object of laughter by effeminizing him. She's the boss (fig. 8). It is a comic castration.

Discovering the faithlessness of his wife, a royal servant stripped, bound, and began to beat her. But as he did, he felt desire replace anger and, thus aroused with sadomasochistic tantalization, he begged her not to be faithless again, to repent, and to make love to him then and there. She agreed on the condition that he would let her strip him, tie him up, and beat him. Once the foolish husband had consented to the titillating offer, the woman cut off his nose (the conventional punishment for adulterous women), stole his clothes, and left him. When the poor cuckold appealed to the king in hopes of retribution, the members of the court mocked him and laughed at him "for he had become a woman" (*Kathāsaritsāgara* 58.89–106). The man was punished for the woman's crime. The comic episode reflects normative social values. In cases of adultery, according to ancient Indian law, the husband was guilty of letting the adultery take place (*Manu* 8.317). The implicit assumption was that women can't really help being lascivious, and that it is therefore the husband's responsibility to prevent his wife from being faithless.

Didactic tales from the *Jātaka*s, the *Kathāsaritsāgara, Pañcatantra,* and *Hitopadeśa* condemn the faithless woman on moral grounds. The *Śukasaptati* purports to be a book of instructions for wives warning them against the evils of adultery. And yet, while the collectors of the stories in those texts may have soberly sermonized against the wiles of women, the individual stories framed by the larger texts, tales reflecting and preserving folk values, attack not the wantonness of women, but the stupidity of men. The husband in satire is guilty of boorishness, insensitivity, gullibility, and distraction. And he is punished with mockery and with jeering, satirical laughter. There is an implicit awareness in satire that we are responsible for our own victimization. As Vidura in the *Mahābhārata* points out, "Thieves flourish on the heedless, physicians on the infirmed, women on the lustful, priests on the religious, kings on the litigant, and wise men on the foolish" (5.33.7)—we are victims because we endow people with the power to prey on us. Satire warns us against our own natural dependencies and weaknesses, the frailties which make us absurd.

A cuckold, returning home early from a journey, discovered that his wife was not in the house. Covering for her lady, a female servant told the husband that his wife had died and been burned. The bereaved man went to the cremation grounds, took the bones he supposed to be his wife's, and performed the last rites for her under the officiation of a brahmin who just happened to be his wife's lover. The brahmin came to the man's home together with the man's wife to receive offerings of food from him. "See," the maidservant said, laughing to herself, "because your wife was so chaste and pure in life, she is able to return from the dead and eat together with you and this pious brahmin priest" (*Kathāsaritsāgara* 61.189–204). Laughter over this story creates a complicity with the wife, the lover, and the servant. It is laughter at the husband.

A woman tells her friend to watch her house, explaining that as a good wife she must go to the riverbank in the forest for water since her husband doesn't think that the water from the well is tasty. She hastens to add that the branches and brambles in the forest "might scratch my breasts" (*Subhāṣitaratnakoṣa* 24.1). The comic sentiment arises from both the reader's perception that she is going to meet her lover (that the scratches on her breasts will be from his nails) and the reader's awareness that neither the friend nor the husband knows or suspects a thing. There is comic pleasure in complicity, in seeing through and being in on the deceit. Similarly, a woman stops a traveler passing her house, "Excuse me, this morning my mother-in-law, all upset about something, went off in a huff and my husband, when he heard about it this noon, took off to try to bring her back. Tell me, you didn't happen to see him did you?" And just to make sure that he (and we) get her intentions, she adds, "You couldn't miss him—he's got a worn-out body and he limps" (*Subhāṣitaratnakoṣa* 24.22).

The comic tone is established rhetorically, not so much in what is said as in how it is said. A verse from the *Pañcatantra,* often quoted in scholastic discussions of metrics, describes an adulterous woman, using a term, "a hip-gyrating woman" (*jaghanacapalā*), that also refers to the meter in which the verse is composed. While saying that a loose woman "finds the highest joy when, at night, it is rainy and windy, the streets are empty, and her husband is out of town," the verse simultaneously suggests that the Jaghanacapalā meter will give aesthetic pleasure if used to describe rain, wind, empty streets, and travelers. Consciousness of the formal level of the poem, the reference to metrics, detaches the mind from the content, strips the perception of moral significance, and in so doing creates, through wit, a distance and lightness that are characteristic of the comic sentiment. Each stanza in the *Rasikarañjana* of Rāmacandra can, through puns, be translated in two ways—one erotic, one ascetic. The amorous mocks the religious, the religious mocks the amorous. One verse simultaneously describes an adulteress and a religious devotee: "If she desires to pursue a man other than her husband, she'll use her monthly period as an excuse to get out of union with her husband so that she can be a treasure in your heart" *and* "He, whose joy is caused by beholding icons, should desire to pursue the Absolute; if efforts for its attainment are not realized through yoga, still that joy will abide in his heart" (127). Through the deflation of each mood (the amorous and the religious, each by means of the other), the comic mood, served by the wit of the poet, prevails.

Using puns to create a comic connection between the sacred and profane dimensions of love, Kṣemendra describes the adulteress as being "like a female practitioner of yoga"; his compound "her vision was fixed in thought on the other man who abided in her heart" can also be translated "her gaze was fixed in meditation on the highest being which was established within the heart" (*Kalāvilāsa* 3.47). The comedic conceit became, through the mythology of Kṛṣṇa the cowherd lover, a theological one. The comic irony became a metaphysical one. When a married milkmaid, restrained from meeting Kṛṣṇa in the forest, makes love with her husband, she imagines that it is Kṛṣṇa—the suburban sex fantasy, even though the woman does not know it, is a meditation on union with god, and therefore, in and through her sin, she is saved from all sin (*Bhāgavata Purāṇa* 10.29).

Pater Familias: *Cuckoldry*

> A certain preacher, one day preaching to a cheerful company, inveighed against the manners of certain women and their husbands who suffered that these should indeed make them cuckold and cried out: "Yes, indeed, I know them, I see them, and I am about to throw these two stones at the head of the greatest cuckolds here," and as he made believe to throw, not a man of that congregation but ducked his head, or put his cloak, or his cape, or his arm before him, to ward off the blow.
>
> Brantôme, *Lives of the Gallant Ladies*

The English introduction to the manual which Mr. Bandyopadhyaya had given me, described the details of husband worship. "A special Mandap or Bower is erected for the sitting of her much respected husband. . . . In the midst of the Bower, a raised silver dais covered over by costly velvet is provided. . . . In proceeding with the Pooja [devotional worship] she sits like a proud queen speaking to none lest her mind may be disturbed and then gradually revives her grace and gets into usual joyous smiles and subsequently merges herself into sublime thought of love and devotion to her God-like husband. After washing his feet she reserves a small quantity of the so washed water to be taken as Teertha after completion of Pooja as consistent with the authority, *nārī patipādodakaṃ pibet* [the woman should drink the water from her husband's feet]" (*Patipūjāvidhāna,* p. 30). The woman then decorates her husband with ornaments and offers him incense, flowers, fruits, sweets, and cakes. She recites his praises and identifies him as the very highest divinity in the universe. Her lord is the Lord. As I read it, I kept trying to picture my ex-wife doing it. "The bathing in all Teerthas [sacred bathing places], the performing of all Yajnas or Sacrifices, the circumambulation of the whole of the world, the Tapas [austerities] of all kinds, the observing of all Vratas [religious vows], the giving of all important charities, the devotions of all kinds and all the virtues that exist in the world; all these as also, Guru-seva, Vipra-seva, Deva-seva [devotional service to, or worship of, gurus, brahmins, and gods], etc., will not be equal even to one-sixteenth part of the Virtue due to the Pada-seva [foot worship] of the husband" (p. 33).

"This is the *pūjā* that my blessed mother was performing every day, but especially on Friday. Now what are Hindu wives doing on Friday? They are watching television." Mr. Bandyopadhyaya grimaced. "They are watching *I Love Lucy!* Everyone in our Bharata land is watching *I Love Lucy*. Now with the satellite, even the villagers, the salts of the earth, are watching *I Love Lucy*." A sneer turned into a self-ironic smile. "What is more, even *I* am watching *I Love Lucy!* How can I do otherwise? One cannot go back to more blessed times. One has no choice in this life but to watch *I Love Lucy*."

Can a person understand the comedy of another culture? The family gathered around the television set. The Ricardoes and the Mertzes were vacationing in Miami, and Ricky and Fred had been asked to judge a bathing beauty contest. Ricky was complaining to Fred, "I've got to get Luthy out of the way—you know Luthy—she'll mess everything up!" Fred nodded, "Yeah, well you could lock her in the bathroom—if she stays in there as long as Ethel, she'll never even know the door is locked!" Though none of the Bandyopadhyaya family actually laughed during the show, Mrs. Bandyopadhyaya did occasionally cover a smile with her hand and, afterwards, Mr. Bandyopadhyaya shook his head, "There were some excellent jokes in this evening's performance. *I Love Lucy* is Indian humor *par* excellent. This evening's performance is proof of what I was saying earlier about the nature of faithfulness. Mr. Ricky and Mr. Fred may dally with the bathing beauties and it is acceptable. It is humorous. But imagine if Lucy or Ethel were ogling after some muscle-men. Would this be humorous? Would this be acceptable? My god, no! People would turn off the television in disgust."

"Ah, but it was a far cry from *patisevā* when Ethel pointed to her husband and said, 'Look the old goat is already pawing the ground.' How can that make sense in India?'' I asked, almost taunting my host. ''This is very Indian,'' Mr. Bandyopadhyaya responded. ''In every Indian film there is an old man who lusts after all the young ladies. He is a comic character *par* excellent. Perhaps the Hollywood producers took the idea of the dirty old man from our Indian films. They have, I know, been influenced by our excellent cinema and our great culture. They even call themselves 'Movie Moghuls.' ''

The Dirty Old Man

> Amorousness in the old is unseemly, one of the three things God hateth. Plutarch rails downright at such kinds of marriages, which are attempted by old men, who, already impotent in body, and laid waste by their pleasures, can sin only in fancy. . . . an old lecher is abominable.
>
> Robert Burton, *The Anatomy of Melancholy*

When an old merchant, married to a young woman, came home early one night, his wife, much to his delight and surprise, embraced him passionately—it was a ruse, a device wherein, by covering her husband's face with kisses, she enabled her lover to escape unnoticed. The text reflects on the plight of the old fool: ''An old man can neither enjoy the pleasures of love nor give them up—he is like a toothless dog that can only lick the bone'' (*Hitopadeśa* 1.5.113).

In satire the young woman, the representative of fertility, the chaotic spirit and pulse of life and sex, the wild procreant urge, constantly fools, dupes, and triumphs over the old man who seems to represent sterility, the ordered spirit of reason, institution, and law. He is an incarnation of all the worn-out authority that satire attacks. He is the moldy past—old ideas and values that will not make way for new visions. He is what is dead or refuses to die. He manifests the stodginess, hypocrisy, and straightness that satire is out to disrupt with its laughter. Satiric sympathy is with the wife of the old man, the ugly man, the dense, harsh, or stupid man.

The Buddha wondered how one, knowing of old age, disease, or death, could laugh, and yet satire laughs at these very devourers of human life. Old age is funny particularly when the old act inappropriately, when the aged try to be young. Kṣemendra tells of the ''old man who, deluded by ignorance, senility and lust, like a miser going after a bargain, wooed a lovely young girl who yearned for the touch of a man like a creeper that grows in an abyss.'' When people heard of the ridiculous old codger in love with the young girl, ''with smiles on their faces,'' they sarcastically sneered, ''This wise-guy makes a marriage for the sake of the other world.'' Though the sight of the stupefied old man, breathing heavily as if from a fever, was revolting to her, the girl's father insisted on the marriage since the old suitor was rich. The thought of the wizened old man touching her breasts, made the pubertal girl cry a storm of tears. And during the wedding ceremony, while ''the old man, his mouth watering for the fruits that were her breasts, clutched the blossom hand of that garland of a girl, the bride's eye was fixed on a young swain who was attending the marriage ceremony. She avoided the bed of the old man as if it were the executioner's block.'' When, on the wedding night, he fell at her feet, she kicked him in the mouth and knocked him out. ''When he tried to kiss her with his spit-filled mouth, she cried out, 'Shame on you! Oh, dear me! Religious devotion will be corrupted! Aren't you ashamed of yourself, old man? You're old enough to be my grandpa!' '' To the marriage bed he coaxed his ''jabbering bride with words that were suffused with the drops of spit that dripped through gaps where teeth had fallen out. When the old lecher touched her, she muttered, 'Oh god, oh god!' As if bitten by that snake in the grass, she jumped out of bed and ran from his house back to her own home. But then her relatives brought her back by force to the bedroom of the old man whose touch she considered to be the touch of a pariah. She slept under separate covers and feigned sleep at the thought of being embraced by him.''

The girl, who had already enjoyed plenty of lovers, didn't have to worry after all about the sexual advances of the old man who, though rich, was ''like a pauper when it came to potency—neither sex nor abstention from it did anything to bring his privies to life.'' Sex-play, booze, aphrodisiacs, magic herbs, all failed to revive his shriveled phallus. His health declined because of the endless enemas and emetics to which he subjected his pathetic, torpid flesh. Comedy frequently focuses on the refusal of the body to behave, to mind, to do what it's supposed to do. The girl, finally producing ''a son to carry on his name by means of the semen of another man,'' explained the pregnancy to her husband as resulting from a ''mantra for sex.'' Proudly the new old father invited all the neighbors to the birth ceremony and the guests laughed at the domestic scene, ''A shoot has sprouted from this worm-eaten, burnt-out, old tree'' (*Deśopadeśa* 7.1–25).

Kṣemendra was bad tempered—the comic tone always verges on the pathetic or the disgusting, never on the amorous. But there are also good-humored satires of old men in love with young wives. A girl who was married to a doddering old merchant could not bear the man's wrinkled flesh, his drooling mouth, missing teeth, and white hair. She was revulsed by him and she kept aloof from him. One night, however, while the old man was sleeping, the young bride, hearing a thief enter the house, grabbed onto her husband in fear. He was awakened, astonished, and delighted by what he initially assumed was a sudden sexual passion. Finally realizing that she was embracing him for fear of the thief, the old man cried out to the intruder, "Thank you! Thank you! Take whatever you like from my house in return for the great favor you've done for me in making this woman, who previously shrank from me, suddenly embrace me!" (*Pañcatantra* 3.6). His innocence, his willingness to settle for the signs of intimacy without demanding genuine feelings, reflects a kind of generosity and cheerfulness which humor appreciates and validates. He does not care about the thief. This detachment from his own wealth makes him innocent of greed, the crime perpetually perpetrated by the direct objects of satire. More despicable in satire than the old man who lusts after women is the old man who lusts after wealth. The miser, as we have seen, was a stock object of satirical laughter.

Sex and Money

> Financially speaking, there was something of both the tiger and the boa-constrictor in Monsieur Grandet. He knew how to crouch and lie low, watch his prey a long while, and spring upon it; then, opening the jaws of his purse, he would gulp down a heap of gold coins and lie torpid like a snake in the process of digestion, cold, impassive, methodical.
>
> Honoré de Balzac, *Eugenie Grandet*

Like the young wife of the dirty old man, the miser's wife is always unfaithful. "Since the wife of the miser, who is afraid of making payments, is prevented from paying brahmins to perform the ritual for obtaining a son, she spends it for the merriment of her lover [so that he will impregnate her]" (*Deśopadeśa* 2.23). Kṣemendra describes the miser, in contrast to the dirty old man, as an ascetic of sorts. Puns comically bind incongruous realms of experience together. Like the yogi, the miser "controls the senses, sleeps on the ground, is devoid of attachment, and eats not more than a handful of barley" (*Deśopadeśa* 2.2). As the yogi stores semen, the biological manifestation of power, the miser stores money, the social manifestation of power. Frugality is an austerity, a kind of asceticism. Kṣemendra emphasizes the irony.

As Kālī appropriates the power of Śiva, so Madam Bagabones extorts the power of a miserly merchant in the *Samayamātṛkā*. Mr. Shell (Śaṅka) is like a yogi—he sits still with his senses withdrawn. Like a sage he is silent (but, Kṣemendra explains, his silence comes from the fear that in conversation he will be asked how much he has given for some little bit of merchandise); like a renouncer he is deaf to the world around him (except that Mr. Shell does not listen for fear that he will be asked to share some of his profits, money he has made in breaches of contract); like a yogi his eyes are averted (except that he does so as a way of ignoring people who ask him for things). That identical outward signs can stand for divergent inward states is the continual warning of satire.

Madam Bagabones describes Mr. Shell as "very rich, an abode of avarice, the incarnation of evil" (*Samayamātṛkā* 6.31), a man so mean and nasty that he beats his own servant when she begs for money to buy spices to cook *his* dinner. While the religious ascetic deprives himself of sensual things, the fiscal ascetic deprives both himself and everybody else. Both the yogi and the miser have overcome care and emotion—Mr. Shell is completely detached and unmoved while a cat, starving to death because he has tied it up to prevent it from eating anything in his house, cries pitifully. Like a penitent, the miser has overcome vanity and exhibits no care about his personal appearance—Mr. Shell's clothes are stained, tattered, and shrunken.

Just as Kālī was able to conquer Śiva, to reabsorb the power which was primordially hers, by tempting him into dance, battle, or sexual union, so Madam Bagabones conquers Mr. Shell, takes his money, by tempting him with money, by making him believe that she would entrust her wealth to him if he would but finance her pilgrimage to all the holy rivers of India. His mistake, like Śiva's, the flaw that makes him laughable, is the conviction that the male is more powerful than the female. With a deft sleight of hand Madam Bagabones switches the box containing her fortune in jewels with a chest full of rocks. Desire, whether sexual, fiscal, or even spiritual, is vulnerability. Kālī laughs at desire, at the ways in which it backfires, at the ways in which we die from our craving to live.

Once upon a time there was a miserly merchant who never allowed himself or his wife more than a bit of barley to eat. While the glutton wants immediate satisfaction, the miser postpones it indefinitely. He saves and hoards in order to increase. Pleasure is in the ever-distant future. After years of austere living, the merchant suggested to his wife that they enjoy a milk pudding. As she prepared it, he nervously sealed the doors and windows of his house to prevent anyone from knowing about the pudding and dropping in to share it. But soon a family friend came to the house asking to see the merchant. The miser instructed his wife to tell the man that he had died. When his wife carried out the instructions, the friend, suspecting deception, began to wail as loudly as he could over the sham death, to cry so loudly that soon the neighbors and relatives came to join in the mourning. The relatives prepared to take the merchant's body to the cremation ground. If the merchant were to sit up, to expose his deceit, he would not only have to endure the laughter of his family and neighbors, he would also have to share the pudding. In utter silence the merchant, rather than facing satirical laughter, allowed himself to be burned to death (*Kathāsaritsāgara* 65.140–158).

The rich and miserly merchant is, in satires of manners, inevitably the father of a young wastrel, a parvenu dandy. The relationship between the father and the son is often juxtaposed to, and intertwined with, the relationship between the bawd and the young prostitute, and the four of them, as a group, provide a seedy caricature of the Indian family.

Sons and Lovers: *Men About Town*

AAAAAAAAAA Hey girls! Looking for fun? I could be the one!! Very handsome and highly intelligent young man with fabulous sense of humor (great dancer and radical dresser too!) seeks sophisticated lady with interests in art, philosophy, shiatsu, gourmet cooking, sex, travel, yoga, computers and/or sports. Send photo, measurements, and list of interests and goals in life. Don't be shy! I could be your guy!!!

Personal Column, *Honolulu Penny-Saver*

In satiric literature, the genteel court becomes a bawdy brothel, the courtesan, a whore, and the courtier, an inept merchant's son.

"A vulgar man with money," according to a Sanskrit proverb, is one of the "Creator's mistakes" (*Mahāsubhāṣitasaṃgraha* 675).

In the satiric literature, foolish fops ape the ideal. The refined gentleman becomes a dull dandy, rich daddy's silly boy. Elegance has been eclipsed by glitz and gaudiness. Merchants' sons, in satires of manners, aspiring for a swanky grandeur, attempt to purchase cultivation, to substitute money for breeding. They are benign specimens of the more expansive falsehood that is the object of satirical critique, the virulent falsehood that becomes truly dangerous in the more powerful figures that are attacked in social and religious satire.

The *Kuṭṭanīmata* gives a portrait of the pretentious, affected, mannered, young show-off. He has a hairdo that he thinks is fashionable, a sort of pompadour in which "his hair stands up about five inches in a thick crest," and his ear lobes are adorned with leaves cut into patterns. "His fingers are fitted with signet rings, and [like his contemporary American counterpart] he wears a lot of gold chains around his neck. His limbs are colored sort of reddish-yellow from the saffron that he had rubbed on his body." He adorns himself with garlands of flowers, amulets, and jewelry; he wears garish garments, and colors and polishes his nails. He enters the brothel surrounded by parasites and pimps, sycophants and servants, who stand around him as he reclines on cushions and stuffs his mouth with betel. Indifferent to the taste of others, he knits his brow and recites, again and again, poetry and plenty of verses, which he has memorized, in whatever manner he wishes. "He shakes his head with arrogance, from an outburst of aesthetic sentiment, as he critiques others, dismissing their verses with words like 'bravo' 'excellent' and 'that stinks.' " As he is the beneficiary of nepotism, of a father who puts in a good word for him with the king, people toady to him. He speaks of the king as if he were a friend. Though he knows nothing of the art of making decorations, he carries the tools for that craft with him to make an impression. He pretends to be adept at music, archery, and of course, the arts of love. The parasites around him praise him grandly, too grandly, calling him a great hero and a magnificent lover, a master of all the arts and sciences, in hopes that through their flattery they will obtain money or favors from the king. Outwardly he makes a feeble attempt at modesty, but he really believes all of their obsequious, canting praise (*Kuṭṭanīmata* 62–80). Madam Horrible spots him as an easy victim and teaches her daughter how to snare him.

Similarly, and no doubt inspired by the *Kuṭṭanīmata,* Kṣemendra has his Madam Bagabones pick the perfect prey for Miss Beauxarts—Master Mud, Esq., son of Mr. Shell (Paṅka, son of Śaṅka), a rich, stupid, and inept little bungler. "It looks like his face and neck are spotted with spatterings of dripping betel juice and spit, and he makes such a clatter as he moves here and there with awkward footsteps in that pair of red shoes. Such a naive boy, just the sort to scatter his wealth among whores, just rich enough not to have to worry about money, will surely ply you with the sacred offerings of commerce" (*Samayamātṛkā* 6.34).

And in the morning, after the night of lovemaking, Miss Beauxarts tells her mother about the performance of her "fiery little peppercorn," a burlesque of erotic descriptions of the union of lovers. "The maid gently tucked the boy into the high bed and at once his body became motionless—the little rascal pretended to be asleep. Trembling with a curiosity common to all women of pleasure, I embraced him. Our lovemaking was over the moment it began and he lay still once more! 'Uh-oh!' I thought to myself, fearing that he might choke to death, 'he's fallen asleep with betel still stuck in his mouth!' I moistened my hand with cold water and touched his chest to bring him back to his senses. Suddenly he got up an appetite for sex and became wakefulness incarnate—he had the sexual passion of a sparrow and he exhausted me with innumerable mountings! Too bad for me! Little did I know that, by awakening the little guy with the childish face with a taste for passion, I was forming a burning coal with my own hand. Out of mercy I did not dare inflict his body with tooth marks—I thought he'd probably cry if I did. But look here, see how he wounded my lower lip—it looks like a cherry that has been munched on again and again by a parrot! And look at my breasts—they've shrunk in embarrassment under the little fellow's all-too robust and perpetual assaults! And look at the wounds on my body—the nail scratches are all in the wrong places because of him—how am I going to keep my limbs hidden during lovemaking with more sophisticated men?" (8.4–11). And Madam Bagabones applauds the description with perfect irony. "Such is the greatness of merchants' sons!" (8.14).

The erotic bungling and amatory oafishness of young men trying to be lovers is a standard comic motif. Another whore recounts her night of love.

Listen my friend and you shall hear
Of a foolish lover who cried in fear:

> "She's dead!"
> He said,
> As he let me go, this country boy,
> When I shut my eyes in orgasmic joy!
> (*Kuṭṭanīmata* 398)

In a parody of the standard speech of the go-between to the beloved hero, Madam Bagabones tells Master Mud that he and Miss Beauxarts must have been lovers in a previous life—she is so forlorn in his absence, so fearful of losing his love, that she can think of no one but him even though the glorious "King Bhoja himself has sent emissaries in hopes of winning her favor. . . . You should be arrested for having stolen her heart" (8.20, 22). Complaining to Master Mud, expressing fears that he will abandon Miss Beauxarts, hinting that the girl might be pregnant, asserting that she has given him the best years of her life, Madam Bagabones flatly states that if he is righteous and honorable he will sign over all his money—including his inheritance—to poor, sweet, Miss Beauxarts. Master Mud consents. Once he has surrendered his wealth to Miss Beauxarts, she refuses to see him, though he grovels obsequiously. Pathetically he waits in hope of some favor from her until finally Madam Bagabones informs him that a rival lover has been murdered and that he, Master Mud Esq., "known for his bravery," is naturally suspect (8.123). It is a sign of his stupidity, typical of the vanity of the objects of satires of manners, that he would believe that others could see him as heroic. Disguised in a cotton robe, he runs away, penniless, shamed, frightened.

In satires of manners the female is inevitably triumphant. And the laughter of Kālī resounds as the cry of victory. The female principle demands submission, a surrender expressed in comic laughter. Ramakrishna would, in ecstatic trance, become Kālī's boyish lover. "He would touch Her chin by way of showing affection for Her, and sing, talk, joke, and laugh. . . . He learnt to surrender himself completely to Her will and let Her direct him" (*Gospel of Ramakrishna,* pp. 14–15).

I wanted to return to her temple. But first I had to have coffee with Premendra. It was Thursday, the afternoon that he was to visit the home of his beloved Sakuntala. He was dressed to kill in starched bell-bottom pants and an embroidered shirt. His hair was shiny bright and scented. He proudly wore the watch that his father had given him upon his graduation from Calcutta University, a deep-sea diver's watch that would "keep on ticking even at a depth of one hundred fathoms.'' He carried a box of Bengali sweets as an offering to the venerable parents of Sakuntala Deb Sen, and for the object of his love herself he was taking a cassette tape of the London Symphony Orchestra playing the Beatles' greatest hits. ''My favorite song,'' Premendra smiled, ''is that one that goes, 'All you need is Love, Love, Love. . . .' ''

Politely, and yet not insincerely, he asked me about the research I had done on the *Gītagovinda*. I explained that I had attempted a study of the sacred and profane dimensions of love as exemplified in that text. ''How can there be profane Love? That is a contradiction in terms. Love is sacred through and through. Joideb, the great Bengali poet and philosopher, illustrated this with his splendid *Gīt Gobind*. He showed the world that Love is truly divine. All you need is Love, Love, Love. That was his timeless message. That must be your message as well. Then you will enlighten your readers. Then you will be carrying on the mission of the great poets. You must help to show the world that Love is the greatest religion of all.''

Promising to do my best, I shook Premendra's hand. He laughed warmly and we parted. He went to the home of the family of Sakuntala to drink tea and eat tiffin, and I went to the Kālīghat temple to witness the sacrificial decapitation of a black goat. I saw a child laugh at the gush of blood, the rolling head, and the sudden, sacred death. Storm clouds gathered again and once more the goddess began to dance. Once more Kālī laughed her uncanny cry.

The Laughter of the Child

4

Social Satire: Corruption and the Degradation of Righteousness

The boy was brought before the demon of the brahmin caste. His mother took hold of his hands while his father held his feet. The king drew his sword to slaughter the boy. And the child began to laugh. . . .

Kathāsaritsāgara

Once upon a time a king, escorting his new bride through a forest toward home, encountered a demon of the brahmin caste, a monstrous specter with skin as black as storm clouds and hair as bright as lightning. Adorned with a garland of entrails and a sacred thread of human hair, the demon gnawed smoldering flesh from a corpse and guzzled blood from a broken skull. Vomiting hideous fire and screeching smoky laughter, he threatened to devour the king and queen. The monarch pleaded for mercy, begged the brahmin demon to let him and his queen pass.

"I shall spare you," the demon hissed, "on the condition that within seven days you bring me a seven-year-old boy, and that his parents hold him down while you, with your own sword, cut out his heart for me to eat. If this is done you shall live. If not, you shall die."

Anxiously and fearfully agreeing, the king returned home in despair, not knowing how he would be able to find such a child. The royal ministers encouraged the king and consoled him with a plan. "We shall parade a statue of a boy, a statue made of gold and studded with jewels, through the streets, and we shall proclaim throughout the kingdom that the parents of any seven-year-old boy who are willing to sacrifice their child will be given the statue as well as one hundred villages, provided that they hold the child during the sacrifice."

A seven-year-old boy of extraordinary beauty heard the proclamation. At once he decided to offer his own life that his king might live and that his parents might be saved from the miserable poverty into which they had fallen. The boy was able to assuage the initial reluctance of both king and parents. "In this act my body, something imperfect and perishable, will become a means of serving others and expressing devotion." He spoke with perfect serenity.

The boy was anointed and taken into the forest, brought before the demon of the brahmin caste. His mother took hold of his hands while his father secured his feet. The king drew his sword to slaughter the boy. The demon drooled anxiously for the young flesh. And then, all of a sudden, the child began to smile. The uncanny smile broadened and the boy laughed a loud and piercing laugh.

Struck and stunned by the laughter of the child, the brahmin demon, the king, and the boy's mother and father put their hands together reverentially and bowed to the boy in obeisance (*Kathāsaritsāgara* 94.1–137).

The boy laughed, according to the explanation given by the frame story within which the tale occurs, out of "both joy and surprise." He laughed with the joy of selfless devotion to others, the delight of transcendence. And he laughed with the astonishment of innocence, with utter surprise at discovering the greed and delusion of those others. The child had suddenly realized that the very people upon whom he had been dependent, those whose responsibility was to protect him, were in fact dangerous enemies. Dependence is fraught with peril. The mother who had once warmly held the child to her breast to nurture him was willing to coldly hold his hands during his execution. The father who had taught his son the differences between right and wrong was willing to clasp the small feet. The king, whose duty was to ensure the welfare of the people of his kingdom, was willing to slay his subject. And the child could not turn to the brahmin, for the brahmin was a demon, all hunger and thirst. The king was motivated by a fear of death, the parents by venality. All became, through impulses to preserve themselves, unreliable and jeopardous. The child had no such motivations. He subdued his elders by manifesting the very virtue—selflessness—which each of them, the brahmin, the king, the father, and the mother, was ideally supposed to display.

The satirist, like the child, sees the folly and vice that others cannot see, the degradations of understanding and virtue to which both the holders of power and the masses, who have allowed them that power, have become inured or blind. The masses always admire the king's new clothes; it takes a child to laugh at his nakedness. Satiric laughter is at once innocent and worldly wise, sanguine and cynical, constructive and destructive. Hearing it, the figures at which the laughter is directed might be awakened—their eyes might be opened to their failings, and they might repent. The brahmin demon, the king, and the parents bowed to the child. His laughter was transformative.

"When a person who is weak becomes afraid, he cries out piteously for dear life to his own mother and father. If they have passed away, it is then the king who becomes the refuge for the suffering one. If there is no king, then it is the god. The boy had all of these: his mother and father, thirsting for wealth, were holding his hands and feet; his king, desiring to save his own life, was ready to kill him; the god, a brahmin demon, was intent on eating him. Such a scene is a satire of people who are deluded about the body, who do not realize that it is impermanent, afflicted with great torments, and ultimately without a real essence. When even Brahmā, Viṣṇu, Śiva, and the other gods must inevitably perish, how can one imagine that one's own flesh can be perpetuated? Seeing just how deluded they were, that twice-born child, his perfection assured, laughed with joy and surprise" (94.130–136).

The laughter of the child suggests deliverance from the chaotic world of birth and death. Like a Buddha he knows that all must perish. Like a Buddha he is not attached to the body. Like a Buddha, devoid of thirst, craving, and desire, he is willing to die. In his acceptance of death there is a freedom from it and a sudden transmutation of terror into joy. But unlike a Buddha, the child laughed. He laughed at death, corruption, poverty, power, at the world itself. While religion might transform piteous cries into beatific silences, comedy strives to change them into mirthful laughter.

Satire tries to get us to laugh like the child with surprise, with the sudden insight into the delusion and corruption of figures of power—kings, judges, generals, physicians, and the like—people upon whom we are dependent. The child saw what the satirist always looks for—the concealment of degradations of ideals within ideals. Satire laughs when concealments fall away. And satire aspires to inspire us to laugh like the child with joy, with the delight of a freedom from dependency on those figures of religious, social, and domestic authority. Satire can be a mode of liberation.

There is, in social satire, always a tension between the amusing literary creation and a grim literal reality, a tension that is the basis of satire's aesthetic impact. The laughable fictional characters represent sinister actualities, objects of disgust and serious moral judgment.

Satire draws a magic circle, an area set apart from the degenerate society that it depicts, a place in which one has both protection from, and a clearer panoramic view of, the world of folly and vice. To laugh is to enter the circle, to join the satirist against the world. "However spontaneous it seems," Henri Bergson observes, "laughter always implies a kind of secret freemasonry, or even complicity with other laughers, real or imaginary" (*Laughter*). One function of social satire is the establishment of such secret groups, such refuges in which both hostility and despair are aligned with pleasure. But the pleasure cannot hold. The refusal to suffer cannot last. Satire is painful comedy. There is a sadness intrinsic to it, the sorrow of all transience. When the laughter ceases, as it inevitably must, the circle disappears and those who have laughed realize that they are inextricably a part of the decaying world at which they have looked in amused indignation, a world that will devour them and absorb their laughter.

The Satiric Scepter: *The Corruption of Kings*

Loud thunder to its bottom shook the bog,
And the hoarse nation croak'd, "God save King Log!"

Alexander Pope, *The Dunciad*

In India ideals of kingship were clearly and specifically established in the hallowed compendiums on the science of polity. The ideal king was "a great divinity in human form" (*Manu* 7.5). Self-controlled, modest, firm, and generous, he protects his subjects. Unlike the king who raised his sword over the child, the ideal monarch puts the welfare of his people before his own. He preserves the order of the state, the health of the social body. "The kingdom is the king," according to Kauṭilya (*Arthaśāstra* 8.2), and as its prosperity is his prosperity, so the sins of its people are his sins. Satires of corrupt kings are satires of degenerate kingdoms and satires of kingdoms in disarray are satires of inept kings.

The ideal was preserved and perpetuated by the royal panegyric, a verse form which, through lavish endowment, became conventional to Sanskrit literature. By the light of this silvery ideal, the satirist scrutinizes its leaden inversion. In the *Kautukasarvasva,* a dramatic farce by Gopīnātha Cakravartin (c. sixteenth century), King Kalivatsala (Friend of the Age of Dullness) proclaims with a thunderous beating of royal drums that vice has been made virtue throughout his kingdom, Dharmanāśa (the land where "righteousness has disappeared"). The satirist condemns not vice as such, but specifically the vice that has been made legitimate and official through an abuse of power. In social satire vice parades as righteousness and crime is made lawful. The king is described by the brahmins whom he has outrageously imprisoned after turning their homes into whorehouses. "He's a liar, an adulterer, a drug addict, a criminal collaborator—he loves vice and hates virtue. . . . What can we say of the reign of King Kalivatsala? The only truth that is spoken in his kingdom is uttered by the dumb; the only people who daily preserve virtue are the children of the barren" (*Kautukasarvasva,* pp. 60–61). Authority is tyranny.

It was conventional in Sanskrit satirical farces to show a degradation of kingship by inverting all values: bad is good, ugly is beautiful, dirty is clean, low is high, and, in effect, the dreadful is funny. Everything is reversed in the satirical mirror, turned upside-down by the satirical lens. The world makes no sense and it is precisely this nonsense, this focus upon absurdity, that makes the satiric complaint comedic. There is a total transposition of social values. One is always simultaneously conscious of the highest ideal and its most extreme degradations. The gap between the two is comically exaggerated. And in that abyss between the ideal world rendered by the panegyrist and the degenerate world cartooned by the satirical poet, the real world sits waiting to be compared, judged, and remade.

The satirical farces that present these topsy-turvy visions of society seem to be literary equivalents of the rituals of reversal during which people are permitted to mock, parody, insult, and criticize figures who normally demand respect and subservience. In the prologue to the *Hāsyārṇava,* the stage manager indicates that the play was composed for a celebration of the spring festival, a celebration, as exemplified by Holī, which would be typified by a ritualized inversion of the social hierarchy. And just as those rituals seem to strengthen and renew the social hierarchy, it may well be that satire, despite, if not through, its attack, serves to preserve social order. Satire, like the ancient vernal ritual, provides a mirthful respite from the constraints imposed by any or all social institutions, whether those institutions are good or bad, honest or corrupt, necessary or not. This freedom, no matter how transient, is full of pleasure and the pleasure is expressed in laughter.

In the *Hāsyārṇava,* King Anayasindhu (Ocean-of-Misrule) enters complaining that people have actually started being faithful to their spouses and that the venerable are being respected—virtue has begun to creep in where vice should be. It is as if he were King Carnival or the Monarch of Holī. As the rites of reversal are characterized by license, by lewd and rowdy behavior, so the satirical farces are typically obscene. King Misrule's minister, after greeting his royal lowness with his left hand (the hand associated with excrement), suggests that they hold a cabinet meeting to deal with this grave social problem of a tendency toward virtue. The governmental convocation is to be held in a whorehouse, a suggestion celebrated by the king who is anxious to make love to a young harlot since he has become uninspired by his queen's withered breasts.

> The god of love, to break young lovers' hearts,
> Shoots at them with incendiary darts
> From his mountain fortress, well protected—
> The mountains are breasts, upward-projected.
> Faced with the fall of this mammary fort
> Battered so hard in Love's battle and sport,
> Love becomes afraid and then he retreats,
> From those drooping, dropping, sagging, old teats.
>
> (*Hāsyārṇava 1.13*)

The ideal king may be carnal, may be erotically dynamic, for he is a man of the world, entrusted with the ordered perpetuation of the social body and of his own kingship in the form of sons. But he, like and on the model of Rāma, who banished his beloved Śita for the sake of the confidence of his people, must make his own desires secondary to the good of the kingdom. In contrast to any semblance of the ideal, King Misrule boasts that he has completely neglected his kingdom because his "mind has been fixed day and night on making love to other men's wives" (prose after 1.10).

The king is a fool. And it is a fundamental axiom of satire that the greater the social prestige and power of a particular figure, the more his folly is a vice. The corollary of humor is that the less social prestige and power that a particular figure has, the more his vice is mere folly.

To laugh at a fictional and absurdly corrupt king in satire is to become aware of the potential foolishness and vice of actual kings. Something known is brought to mind by satire. The satirist contributes a warning to the collective notion of kingship. "Kings who are virtuous, who are diligent in performing their duties, attain the state of Indra," according to the social theorist, "but those whose actions depart from the way of righteousness will go to the hell called Avīci" (*Kātyāyana* 9). The panegyrist, inspiring awe and confidence in the king's subjects, makes an Indra of the king; the satirist raises suspicions, tempers awe and confidence. He transposes Indra's heaven and Avīci hell. And the sight of the universe on its head is comical.

The conventional panegyrics to kings became, ironically, a vehicle for satirical defamation. Through a conceit known as "deceptive praise" (*vyājastuti*), eulogy could, by means of puns and other forms of word play, conceal blame. Stanzas utilizing this ornament are essentially comic in the way they bind incongruous attitudes together. The *Rājataraṅgiṇī* of Kalhaṇa (twelfth century) preserves examples of such deceptive paeans. "What is the difference between Pāṇini [the codifier of Sanskrit grammar] and great King Jayāpīḍa?" the poet asks. And he answers paronomastically that "the former completely explained the class of affixes forming the future passive participle (*kṛtakṛtya*) and outlined the rules for the first and second modification of vowels (*guṇavṛddhi*); the latter got things done (*kṛtakṛtya*) and increased virtue (*guṇavṛddhi*)" (*Rājataraṅgiṇī* 4.635). But the praise of King Jayāpīḍa is ambiguous. There are puns within puns. The supposed paean conceals another message: "he destroyed things and cut off virtue." Another poet answers the riddle with the same satirical figure: "Pāṇini explained the prepositions *vi* and *pra* (*vipropasarga*) and delineated the affixes of past particles (*bhūtaniṣṭha*); King Jayāpīḍa brought about a subordination to brahmins (*vipropasarga*) and the perfection of people (*bhūtaniṣṭha*)" (4.637). And again there is a lampoon lurking beneath the surface of the flattery. The attack is made comically satiric by its concealment: "King Jayāpīḍa brought about troubles for brahmins and the destruction of people."

King Jayāpīḍa was, according to Kalhaṇa, a dissolute, greedy, and cruel king. Satire is much more than protest against such oppressive and corrupt kings. Anyone can see that the king holding his sword above the child fails to live up to the ideal of kingship and anyone can denounce his behavior. The genius of satire is that it laughs at the sight. It is the laughter of the child that delivers him from the king's sword. Protest or mere condemnation would have led to his execution. And laughter, much more than denunciation, is contagious.

Kalhaṇa's chronicle of the rule of King Ananta depicts a reign rivaling Jayāpīḍa's for injustice, a reign characterized by continual uprisings, revolts, and invasions, by disorder and discontent. Ananta seems to have been extraordinarily weak and indecisive. His friends—horse dealers and betel vendors, sycophants and parasites—took constant advantage of him and repeatedly depleted the royal treasury. The king squandered his subjects' revenue in his personal pursuit of vices, addictions, and petty extravagances. His wife frequently covered his debts, not out of duty or love, but as a means, it would appear, of increasing her own power. In childhood Ananta was the pawn of his mother and in maturity he was the puppet of his manipulative wife about whom there were rampant rumors of illicit sexual relations with Ananta's prime minister. The queen convinced her husband to abdicate his throne in favor of his son, Kalaśa, who proved to be even more adept at licentiousness and misrule than his father. In the end, cheated by his friends, disgraced by his wife, publicly humiliated by his son, King Ananta committed suicide by thrusting a dagger into his rectum (*Rājataraṅgiṇī* 7.133–447).

It is, at first glance, surprising that Kṣemendra, the vituperative satirist, eulogizes this pathetic king in his epilogue to the *Samayamātṛkā,* a work focusing upon debauchery, lust, dishonesty, and the subjugation of men by women, all the degradations of society that marked the rule of Ananta: "The great king, glorious Ananta, is a hero who takes pity upon the oppressed, a ruler who is decorated with his vows of morality; his sword, a friend, has as its sole purpose the defense of those ordinances established for the sake of ending adultery. It is during his splendid reign that I, Kṣemendra, have produced this eloquent opus which is ineffectual for the preservation of proper views." On the surface of it, Kṣemendra seems to be saying that it is not necessary for him to compose a satire, that his work is "ineffectual," that since Ananta is such a righteous, compassionate, and moral king, there is no vice to expose, no corruption to attack. But satirists cannot be trusted any more than the objects of their critiques. Understanding the hyperbolic panegyric as ironic, if not sarcastic, Kṣemendra seems to be implying that the state has become so corrupt that it is hopeless to imagine that a satire would be effectual in instituting any change. By itself the eulogy might be taken as straightforward, but placed at the end of the *Samayamātṛkā,* and given the traditional Indian notion that the king was held responsible for the state of his kingdom, it insinuates the king's liability for the putrefaction of the state as depicted in the bitterly comic narrative.

The poet flatters his royal patron just as the whore flatters her customer. Flattery is lucrative. But the flattery of the satirist, like that of the prostitute, is most often an ironic expression of disdain that plays upon its object's blind self-satisfaction. The satirist's irony saves him from being guilty of the obsequiousness that he condemns in others. With satiric recalcitrance, Nīlakaṇṭha Dīkṣita mocks poets who compose odes of praise to their Lord Superbus Fadus. "Riches result from a conjunction of lies and flattery, while poverty results from truth and honesty. Poets are willing to ignore cowardice, misconduct, greed, and dullness for a fistful of rice. They are prepared to praise for no reason—poets' tongues rattle when there's nothing to praise. They'll praise anybody who gets praised by others without ever seeing the praiseworthy qualities themselves" (*Kaliviḍambana* 32–34).

A stanza preserved in a traditional anthology directly assaults a king for his arrogance. The attack is made comic through the use of puns, of a play on the words *guṇa* ("quality" or "string"), *namratā* ("humility" or "bentness"), and *stabdhatā* ("arrogance" or "straightness"). "It is really astonishing," the poet laughs, "that while the bow, with only one string (*guṇa*), becomes bent (*numratā*), you, O King, with all your qualities (*guṇa*) become arrogant (*stabdhatā*)" (*Subhāṣitaratnabhāṇḍāgāra* 102.31). A little more freely:

> While a bow is bent with but a single string,
> There are lots of strings attached to you, O King,
> And yet you don't bow or bend for anything!

Stabdhatā can also refer to the erect penis—the king was apparently hard on his subjects. The suggested obscenity adds comic thrust to the satire.

The king is not named. Samples of direct satirical attack on identifiable kings are difficult to find. Defamation does not pay as well as laudation. It is, furthermore, impossible to know whether or not any of the Sanskrit farcical satires on degenerate kings were lampoons, inferential attacks on particular living leaders. However, this is, in a sense, completely irrelevant since the comic appeal of topical references in any satire is transient. Great satire transcends the particulars which it attacks and survives as each new generation of readers brings its own particulars to the paradigms of vice and folly. We need not know about specific rivalries between various Tory leaders in the eighteenth century to delight in Swift, to understand his satires as meditations on the nature of power and authority. Corruption is eternal. Only the shapes of its avatars change. And its nameless victims remain the same over time and across nations. In the eyes of the satirist, the social system itself prevents change and hope. It encourages greed and corruption. There is a scathing cartoon by Abu Abraham, a very seriously funny statement about modern Indian society, in which a direct accusation of corruption is leveled at all members of the society whose status or power qualifies them for the fruits of corruption (fig. 9). The corrupt rulers of the land feed on the poor, are parasites

Figure 9

What do you mean "Let's go home?"
—This is our home.

Figure 10

on the very creatures they deem parasitical, and impede progress in the name of progress. The victims of that corruption grovel in the streets. Like the boy who was held down by his poverty-stricken parents so that his king could cut the heart from his body to feed it to the brahmin demon, the innocent child in a modern cartoon by Laxman is surprised by the terrible predicament in which he finds himself (fig. 10). But he does not laugh; he frowns painfully and helplessly. The laughter that might deliver him as it delivered his predecessor is offered to us in satire. That laughter is at once amused and anguished.

The Satiric Gavel: ***The Jobbery of Judges***

We say, without anyone disputing,
That he who gives the most money
Is the right, free and clear. . .
Say: He who offers ready cash
Should definitely be supported.

A judge in *Le Monde, Abuz,* an anonymous medieval *sottie*

Traditional Indian social and political theory postulates two phases of power: sacred, religious power (*brahman*) and royal, secular power (*kṣatra*). The ideal was a harmonious interaction of the two, an interdigitation of *brāhmaṇa* priests and *kṣatriya* kings that would fuse the spiritual and regal domains. Social order could be preserved in righteousness only through a collaboration of the king and his brahmin ministers, particularly his chaplain or minister of state. Originally a sacrificial priest, the chaplain became an advisor to the king on secular as well as religious issues. It was the ministers to the king, headed by the chaplain, who devised the plot of parading the golden statue of the boy through the streets to secure a sacrificial victim for the demon of the brahmin caste.

The ministers to Indian rulers interpreted their king's actions, legitimating them on the authority of the sacred texts. Ultimately they accrued even greater power—judicial power. In exercising his right to punish, the king called upon brahmins to help him pass judgement. "The king, free from anger and greed, should give justice assisted by learned brahmins, in conformity with the precepts of *dharma*" (*Yājñavalkya* 2.1). Since it was the responsibility of the brahmins to interpret those precepts, judgment in civil as well as religious issues was essentially their prerogative. And it is as judges that the chaplains and ministers in the farces are judged. They are accused of accepting bribes, altering testimony, and avoiding truth at any cost. The brahmin judge is partial, unjust, and greedy.

The king in the *Kautukaratnākara* is advised by brahmins whose names reveal their characters: Mass-of-Idiocy (Kumatipuñja), Poison-Conduct (Ācārakālakūṭa), and the guru Uncontrolled-Senses (Ajitendriya). In the *Kautukasarvasva* the chaplain Burner-of-Righteousness (Dharmānala) asks the king's spiritual preceptor Five-Faces-of-Villainy (Kukarmapañcānana) whether or not fornication is righteous. The guru explains that it is absolutely so, that the virtues of sexual incontinence are affirmed and sacralized in the holy scriptures: "Indra raped the lovely wife of the sage Gotama, just as Candra fucked the wife of his guru; Dharma himself enjoyed Pṛthā, Pāṇḍu's wife, assuming Pāṇḍu's form for the occasion; Mādhava, god himself, made love to all the wives of the cowboys. Those stupid pandits, imagining themselves to be wise, have simply said that it is a sin to commit adultery because they were jealous. . . . The sages only condemn such acts because they have grown too old to relish the pleasure themselves—it was out of envy that they forbade others what they themselves could no longer enjoy" (*Kautukasarvasva,* p. 61).

When the king in the *Hāsyārṇava* consults his minister as to what should be done about the thugs roaming the streets, the official counsels: "Arm the troops! First see that I am well protected, then arrange for the protection of the queen, and then protect the palace!" (prose after 1.40). The advice reveals not only the brahmin's selfishness and disregard for social order, it also insinuates an adulterous liaison with the queen. It is comic through a egregious reversal of normal priorities.

Satire, for the sake of laughter, shows a judge, someone who is supposed to be sober, restrained, and impartial, to be dissolute, lusty, and motivated by self-interest. In the second act of the *Dhūrtasamāgama* of Kaviśekhara Jyotīśvara there is an argument between a guru, Reverend Alltown (Viśvanagara), and his disciple, Master Malfeasance (Durācāra), over who has the right to possess the whore, Miss Lovedart (Anaṅgasenā). They turn to a brahmin, the Honorable Judge Miscarriage (Asajjātimiśra), to arbitrate the dispute. The judge insists that there are certain preliminary proceedings which must be taken care of: "First let's settle the court fees, then we can hear the legal case." Reverend Alltown offers his staff, the symbol of his sanctity. Master Malfeasance pays with hashish, the sacramental substance of his own Tantric holiness. And the judge reveals his delight:

> This removes sin, this tranquilizer;
> It's an aperitif that makes one wiser;
> It's an aphrodisiac, if I'm not wrong;
> I think right now I'll take some *bhang*.
>
> (*Dhūrtasamāgama,* p. 90)

The inebriated judge then listens as Alltown explains that Miss Lovedart herself has chosen him as her lover; Master Malfeasance replies that he saw her first and that he has already paid for her.

The Judge decrees: "The object of the litigation, one Miss Lovedart, is to be placed in the custody of the court until federal judges, appointed by the king, can make their decision as to who is the rightful party." The judge, the custodian of the court, then turns to Miss Lovedart and professes his love.

The brahmin minister in the *Hāsyārṇava,* Judge Follyprotector (Kumativarman), hears a court case in which the litigants are a barber and his customer. The barber, while paring the customer's nails, had cut him and the man jerked his hand back suddenly, whereby the barber's instrument went into the customer's eye. The judge decrees: the customer must reimburse the barber the price of the cutter. Injustice has the dangerous ring of justice. The accuser becomes the accused and vice versa. The judgment is in conformity with the values of the world as satire sees it—the nail cutter has financial value, whereas human pain, like all other feelings, does not.

A similarly unjust act of justice is satirically judged in the story of the learned brahmin whose virtuous wife chased a donkey from their vegetable garden. The fleeing donkey stumbled and broke its hoof. When its owner, a washerman, discovered the injury, he thrashed the brahmin woman. She was pregnant and the beating caused a miscarriage. The brahmin took the case to court where the magistrate made his decree: "The brahmin must carry the bundles of laundry which the donkey normally bears until the donkey's hoof has healed." But the judge also realized that the washerman needed punishment for causing the brahmin's wife to miscarry: "He must make the brahmin woman pregnant again" (*Kathāsaritsāgara* 12.205–219).

In satire innocent people have no access to justice. A stanza attributed to Bhallāṭa (ninth century) describes oppressed people who, in their appeals for assistance from their king, request an interview with his minister. They are told, "Today." At the end of the day they are told, "Tomorrow." After more waiting they are promised, "tomorrow" again. And so it goes: " 'In three or four days.' 'Tonight.' 'Tomorrow morning.' 'By noon.' 'This afternoon for sure.' ". And finally the moment arrives: "Wait here a minute. Oh, sorry, he has just gone out for a bit, but do come back again" (*Sūktiratnahāra* 219.23). The needy can never quite get through, can never cut a path across the jungles of red tape (fig. 11).

Government corruption, official and lawful corruption, seeps down to the local levels. Bureaucracy insures injustice for all. With

Figure 11

You have to apply for relief on the prescribed form in triplicate and two witnesses, one a J.P., must endorse it and all applications should be sent by registered post....

satirical sarcasm, a poet denounces the *niyogī,* a local magistrate or government official. "Whose friend is the *niyogī?*" the satirist asks:

He's a vegetarian and a teetotaler,
  But he sucks blood
  from the necks of innocents;
He solemnly fasts on Viṣṇu's sacred day,
  But he steals
  the god's rightful share;
He's an expert on Sāṃkhya philosophy,
  But he deprives
  brahmins and cows of a means to subsist;
He's a devil, a fake,
  A friend of the Age
  of Dullness and Degradation.

(*Subhāṣitāvali* 2363)

The denunciation is not simple social protest. The satirist is more concerned with the fake than with the devil; he condemns the *niyogī* not so much for oppressing the poor, for stealing from brahmins, cows, and the deity himself, but for maintaining the guise of righteousness while doing so. Injustice is condemned not for being what it is, but for wearing the mask of justice. And the contradiction between the mask and the real face is comical.

The king and his chaplain in the *Hāsyārṇava* hear another case: a brahmin explains that a fellow brahmin, visiting the home of his son-in-law, died when a fly landed on him. The man was so sensitive that the kick of the fly had killed him. What penance can be performed to eradicate the stain of having a brahmin murdered in one's home? The chaplain, Minister Panzany (Viśvabhaṇḍa), picks his nose as he listens to the account of brahminicide, the most heinous of all crimes in Indian society. As Chaplain Panzany questions the brahmin about the details, it becomes apparent that his testimony has distorted the event somewhat—actually the brahmin didn't die from the kick of a fly, he was stoned to death by the people of the town when they discovered him fornicating with a washerwoman. His Honor decrees: "The people are absolved; the washerwoman is tainted with sin" (*Hāsyārṇava,* prose after 1.40). The washerwoman, like the barber's customer and the brahmin's pregnant wife, is guilty of innocence in a world that is totally corrupt and fraudulent. In a reversal of the ideal, that the king should do penance for the sins of his people, the people endure and suffer for the crimes of their kings, prosecutors, and judges. The joke is rather horrible. The laughter it arouses is a bodily reverberation of the ambivalent feelings aroused by entrusting the guardianship of justice or any other power or authority to others. It is granted that such an entrustment is necessary, but necessity does not nullify the danger. The satiric warning is against all authorities, particularly the necessary ones. The satirist protects us from our protectors, judges our judges, and punishes those who reserve the right to punish.

Satirical castigation is a literary mode of public perambulation, one form of actual punishment recommended in the treatises on legislation for various crimes. The convicted criminal could be branded and paraded through the streets, often on an ass, to be shamed by the crowd, to be laughed at by them just as the parents, king, and demon were laughed at by the child. This chastisement was meant not only to reform the criminal, but to warn the onlookers of the perils of committing such crimes. And those onlookers, like the audience of satire, could laugh with amusement during their own warning. Such laughter marks a refusal to identify with the guilty. It epitomizes the aggressive pleasure and cruel innocence of the satiric sensibility.

"The satirist is like Paraśurāma [the sixth descent of Viṣṇu who cleared the earth of the royal, martial caste when they assumed too much power]," a Varanasi brahmin and friend explained, "He brings down the *paraśu* [the axe]. Sanskrit jokes are always cruel. They can be deadly."

The Satiric Account: *Crooked Comptrollers*

We selected your Federal income tax return for the year shown below to examine the items listed at the end of this letter. . . . It is important that you contact our office within 10 days.

A letter from the Internal Revenue Service

"The *kāyastha* gets the axe," my friend continued with a hearty laugh, "and he deserves it. These fellows were corrupt. They still are, the bastards." He began reciting and translating Sanskrit aphorisms: "When the *kāyastha* is aroused, he will fuck his mother. . . . When he sees a donkey, standing on three legs and pissing, the *kāyastha* says, 'Father, where have you been?' " The *kāyastha,* or government comptroller, an ancient equivalent of the dreaded IRS agent, was employed by kings to collect taxes and keep accounts, to supervise, audit, and certify expenditures. He became a conventional object of comic wrath and satiric vituperation. His power and authority were ominous and oppressive. "Not even criminals can survive in a place where whores, elephants, asses, monks, spies, or comptrollers live" (*Mṛcchakaṭikā,* prose after 5.7).

His capacity to uncover the dishonesty of others made him a natural victim of satiric vengeance, revenge taken with counter-insinuations of his dishonesty. He was an extortionist, a swindler, a white-collar thief, a deluder of mankind. "Delusion, which first filches our intelligence, and then robs us of everything else, hides in the mouths and pens of those accountants" (*Kalāvilāsa* 5.1).

The occupational group solidified into a caste, the origin of which was attributed to the union of a *kṣatriya* father and a *śūdra* mother; the comptroller was issued from an impure union of warriors and servants. An anonymous poet gives an etymological explanation of the *kāyastha*'s origins: the syllable *kā* was taken from the crow (*kāka*), the *ya* was taken from the god of death (Yama), and the *stha* was taken from the carpenter (*sthapati*); the government accountant derived his qualities as well as his name from them—"greed from the crow, pitilessness from Death, an ability to strike hard from carpenters" (*Sūktiratnahāra* 140.1).

"The name *'kāyastha'* is the clue," the brahmin elaborated. "What does the word mean? 'Situated in the body.' The *kāyastha* is only a body. Only hunger and lust and greed. He does not have a soul. Thus there is no morality in the *kāyastha*." Kṣemendra plays with this literal meaning of the name to give, through the pun, comic tone to his denunciation: people in this world are utterly destroyed "by the corporeal senses," a phrase which in Sanskrit (*kāyasthair indriyair*) can also mean "by powerful comptrollers" (*Kalāvilāsa* 5.9).

The obsessive meticulousness, greed, and ill-humor of scribes, tendencies associated with anality, are highlighted in the satirical descriptions. Fecal imagery abounds. Kṣemendra compares the impure comptroller to "shit that causes diseases" (*Kalāvilāsa* 5.46). Scatological references and comparisons contribute to a satirical strategy. Shit becomes a satiric symbol, an emblem of the dirtiness and stink which is ever concealed and never overcome. Scatological jokes, even more than sexual ones, emphasize dependency on the body. Sexuality can be controlled and overcome, but even the purest brahmin, or the most pious holy man, must defecate. Shit is a symbol of impurity and corruption. But it is also a symbol of the equality of man, the corporeal equivalence of the powerful and the powerless. Satiric laughter is always over revelations of that essential and hidden sameness of all beings. Thus defecatory jokes are frequently made about figures of authority. That which is idealized is suddenly degraded. "When Birbal telephoned Akbar early one morning," a joke in *Diwana* ("India's One and Only [and now defunct] Satirical Magazine") relates, "the minister-in-waiting informed him, 'I'm sorry His Majesty is sitting on the throne right now' " (no. 36, May–June 1975).

Kṣemendra amplifies the denunciation of the comptroller: "The accountant, his face splattered with the ink he uses to blot out letters, is black; erasing the top of the letter *ā*, transforming the letter *r* into a *d*, and *v* into *n*, he remakes the meanings of words." The mere accusation of fixing the books contains, through puns, a darker insult; the same stanza can be translated: "The accountant is Death, his face splattered with the ink used by that eternally voracious one—he destroys things, takes heads and bodies, and creates new terror" (*Deśopadeśa* 8.45). Kṣemendra, whose entire *Narmamālā* is devoted to satirizing the comptroller, reiterates again and again this identification between the comptroller and death. He is descended from Citragupta, Death's accountant. "Scribes do a better job of destroying the world than Death. . . . In this world, under paper banners, these personifications of death, these mathematical ogres, roam . . . and the scribblings in their accounts are as crooked as entwined serpents, crooked like the ropes of Death's noose" (*Kalāvilāsa* 5.4, 5, 10). The calculating comptroller is an incarnation of death. "Death and taxes," we say, often in a joking acknowledgment of the reality principal, in defense against the ultimacy and pitilessness of each. Laughter at the tax collector or the comptroller is laughter at death, atavistic laughter, magic, protective laughter, aimed at keeping death at bay, providing the one who laughs with a feeling, transient and yet hopeful, of immunity. Death, the ultimate mocker, he who has the last laugh, the most serious comedian of all, is mocked, laughed at, made comical. Death is a mere accountant, a scrivener, a niggling clerk.

The Satiric Sword: *Jittery Generals*

General Lee, dignified against the blue of the April sky, magnificent in his dress uniform, stood for a moment framed in the doorway. He walked in, followed by his staff. They bowed, and stood silent. General Grant stared at them. He only had one boot on and his jacket was unbuttoned. "I know who you are," said Grant. "You're Robert Browning, the poet."

James Thurber, "If Grant Had Been Drinking at Appomattox"

As the ministers and chaplain were the brains, the intellectual power, of the king, so the generalissimo and police chief were his arms, providing him with literal power.

The chief of police in the *Hāsyārṇava,* Chief Holyman-Killer (Sādhuhiṃsaka), complains that people are making a fuss just because he spends his time in whorehouses while thugs commit crimes in the streets. Chief Death-of-Lawfulness (Suśilāntaka), in the *Kautukaratnākara* protects the queen by staying in bed with her. Despite his close watch she is abducted by a lusty brahmin.

The generals in both the *Kautukasarvasva* and the *Hāsyārṇava* are both named Warjackal (Samarajambūka and Raṇajambūka, respectively)—he who is ideally a lion is actually a jackal, weak and cowardly, living off carrion, unable to fight for itself. In the *Kautukasarvasva,* General Warjackal takes a vow: "I promise that if enemy troops attack the lowlands of the eastern mountains, I will march on the highlands of western mountains." He brags that he can cut a piece of butter—an entire piece—in half with his sword, and the king feels fortunate to have such a commander of his forces: "When he walks down the street, his ears adorned with garlands of hemp, his puny body trembles for fear of being injured by the feet of the pedestrians" (*Kautukasarvasva,* p. 59). We laugh, according to Abhinavagupta, "at such faults as timidity in a case of a person who is not supposed to be timid" (commentary on *Nāṭyaśāstra,* prose after 6.48).

It is not cowardice that is funny, but only inappropriate cowardice, or the cowardice that is masked with courageous pretensions. Tenāli Rāma parodies the vainglorious bravado of army officers when he boasts that he has cut off the leg of the commander-in-chief of the enemy army. When asked why he didn't cut off the man's head, Tenāli Rāma answered, "Someone else had already done that" (*Tenali Rama,* p. 54). One laughs, like the child, with surprise.

The parasite/satirist in the *Pādatāḍitaka* meets an army officer, the son of the commander-in-chief, the kind of hero who will "strike a man when he's down, and then boast of his bravery" (43). The cowardly soldier has blood on his clothes, not the glorious blood of enemies, but menstrual blood which he claims is but "spittle, red from chewing betel" (44). Under direct satirical accusation he admits that he has indeed raped a menstruating woman. He claims that the rape was an act of valor since the woman tried to resist him. Scolded for his action, he becomes self-righteous and quotes (or rather fabricates a quote from) the *Mahābhārata* as proof of his greatness. "Only the worst of men have few enemies; only bad men escape being feared or maligned by others" (49). Satire attacks only the unrepentent. The quote insinuates the disparity between the splendid hero of the epic age and the tarnished heir to the ideal who aggrandizes himself in the current Age of Dullness.

Allusions to rape not only weaken the connection between physical force and heroism, but they also sever the association of sexuality and love. Violence and cowardice, sexuality and cruelty, are linked. A supposedly learned man, an officer attached to the royal ministry, received a Buddhist nun, a tonsured old woman collecting alms for the order, into his house. He raped her, "threw her on the ground trembling and suffering" (*Pādatāḍitaka* 137). Public office allows vice to go unpunished.

The Satiric Scalpel: *The Deceptions of Doctors*

Satire is a scourge, a whip, a surgeon's scalpel, a cauterizing iron, a strong cathartic—all in one; its mission is to flay, to cut, to burn, to blister, to purge; its object is now a culprit, a victim, a criminal, and now an ailing, submissive patient, a sick person bursting with contagion; and the satirist himself is a whipper, a scourger, a barber-surgeon, an executioner, a "doctour of physik."

Mary Claire Randolph, "The Medical Concept in English Renaissance Satiric Theory"

The Indian medical ideal was established in an ancient tradition described and codified by Caraka. The medical student was initiated into practice with solemn and lofty instructions: "You should remain chaste and eat only vegetarian foods . . . you should act selflessly, modestly, with obedience and humility . . . you should never praise yourself" (*Carakasaṃhitā* 3.8.1ff.). He was to be dedicated to the health and welfare of his patients above all else, praying every day for that end and soberly devoting his whole being to it. He was a *vaidya,* a "learned one," a master of *āyurveda,* the "Knowledge of [prolonging] Life." That special knowledge confers power, the abuse of which satire is committed to preventing. The patient or potential patient (every reader or viewer of satire) must submit to the power, surrendering, trusting, and accepting the pain which the doctor inflicts.

Satire of the medical profession is the healthy person's attempt at retaliation for past diseases; and laughter, a signal and expression of safety, when directed at the medical practitioner, gives the feeling of protection against future maladies. "We have been criticizing doctors for a long time, and we go on using them," La Bruyère explains, "Comedy and satire do not affect their income. . . . Healthy men fall ill; they need people whose profession it is to assure them that they won't die. As long as men are liable to die, and love life, doctors will be satirized and well paid" (*Characters*). There are satires of doctors because there cannot be satires of disease or death.

"When the patient is sick there are kind words and then a few payments," Nīlakaṇṭha Dīkṣita observes, "but as the patient gets better he begins to feel a mild contempt for the doctor. When he's completely well, the patient doesn't even want to look at the physician" (*Kaliviḍambana* 30). Satiric laughter voices that contempt.

The physician in Indian satirical writing is a degradation of Caraka's ideal, "a tramp (*caraka*) who is ignorant of Caraka," a hypocrite ignorant of Hippocrates according to Kṣemendra, "a wicked man (*doṣin*) who knows nothing about disease (*doṣa*)" (*Deśopadeśa* 8.35). Such quacks, "physicians who act improperly," were classified by Manu together with "bribe-takers, conartists, rogues, gamblers, fortune-tellers, and pious hypocrites" (9.258–60). The satirist is concerned mainly with the conartists and pious hypocrites. While the moralist solemnly lashes out at the rogues and gamblers as part of his general harangue against vice, the satirist jeeringly attacks only those sins which are concealed within social institutions, conventions, and norms. The sober sermons of the moralist take conspicuous vices seriously and warn those who commit crimes not to do so; the wild farces of the satirist expose covert vices, make fun of them, and warn those who do not commit crimes of those who might.

In social satire not simple wrongdoing, but the corruption of the right into the wrong, is the concern. And hypocrisy, the attempt to pass that corruption off as righteousness, is the great sin. Kṣemendra personifies hypocrisy as a sneak who slips stealthily into "the heart of a guru, an ascetic, a commissioner, an initiate, into the hearts of astrologers, servants, merchants, goldsmiths, actors, mercenaries, singers, reciters, jugglers, and physicians" (*Kalāvilāsa* 1.89–90). These are the suspects, the carriers of virulent diseases, in satire. The greater the prestige of the suspect, the greater the suspicion of the prestige. "All the woes and sorrows of the world," Kṣemendra says with comic vituperation, are due to "powerful comptrollers, naughty gurus, and ignorant doctors" (*Narmamālā* 2.77). Doctors are particularly detestable. "Physicians dry us up and are unbearable, like love in separation or a hot summer day" (*Kalāvilāsa* 9.3).

The quacks of satire, like all the butts of its recalcitrant laughter, hide within the very ideal of which they are a degradation. They conceal their vice and folly with titles and special robes, with technical language and professional accoutrements. The satirist dissects the doctor, exposes the viscera, probes the diseased brain and heart, and exhumes the gangrenous entrails that reek within.

The quack is a conventional figure in Sanskrit farcical literature not only as the object of medical satire, but also as a vehicle for more general satirical revelation. Attendant on the doctor is the imagery of disease, images which inform the satiric vision of the social body, an implicit equivalent of the individual body, as a body that is ailing. The social body is engorged, contorted, dirty, and distemperate, without harmony or control. Those who are responsible for its care and health—kings, ministers, judges, accountants, generals—are, like the quack, hypocritical. They hide their corruption, greed, and foolishness beneath the skin of their prestige. The doctor of satire may be viewed as a representative of all objects of satire, figures who have the opportunity to conceal vice and folly behind facades of respectability and authority. Hypocrisy spreads among them like a plague. And the satirist views himself as the truer physician, a specialist in social diagnostics, moral epidemiology, and the nosology of corruption.

The Mindless Medic

> Hippocrates says, and Galen proves it, that a girl who isn't feeling well is sick. You are right to put your hopes in me, for I am the most skillful and most doctoral physician in the animal, mineral, and vegetable kingdoms. . . . Don't imagine that I am some ordinary, run-of-the-mill doctor.
>
> Molière, *The Flying Physician*

In the *Bhagavadajjukīya* of Mahendravikramavarman a yogi, unbeknownst to the other characters, enters and animates the body of a dead courtesan. A doctor is summoned. "Because she's acting very strangely and unnaturally," he surmises that she has been bitten by a great serpent. "Bring all my instruments and I'll commence with toxicological procedure. [He sits down and draws a maṇḍala on the ground.] Enter the maṇḍala, coiling, curlicued son of Vāsuki! Stay! Stay! Shoo! Shoo! I'll smash your head in! Where's my scalpel?" (prose after 29). The yogi in the body of the courtesan laughs at the mumbo jumbo, at the medicaster's attempt to pass nonsense off as science. "This is a case of bile!" The self-satisfied doctor boasts, "I'll cure you of the trouble you're having with bile, phlegm, and gas." After fetching a medicine which he describes as a "beautiful pill for snakebite," he brags, operating on the assumption that more is better, that the medicine has eight active ingredients. The yogi/courtesan asks him to explain the medical science of poisons and cures. "Wind, bile, phle . . . phle . . . er, ah," he begins, "give me the book, the book" (prose after 32). After checking his manual, he again attempts an authoritative recitation and again his ineptitude is exposed. Asking how many stages of poisoning there are, instead of giving the correct answer—eight—he says, "hundreds!" Quantity again replaces efficacy in satire. In satire all things are out of proportion, carried to the farthest and most ridiculous extremes.

The foolish physician attempts to conceal his ignorance and preserve the prestige of the title of *vaidya* with instruments, pills, arcane language, technical manuals, and braggadocio. In satire titles and degrees are a substitute for, rather than an indication of, actual knowledge: "Though ignorant of physiology, pharmacology, and pathology," the misanthropic Kṛśānu of Veṅkaṭādhvarin's *Viśvaguṇādarśacampū* observes, "the physician still makes people tremble—it's the title *Doctor of Medicine*" (537). In satire it would be a crime for a physician to telephone a restaurant and make a reservation for "Doctor" whomever—satiric laughter is the revenge of the people at the bad tables.

Technical language, medical jargon, can be used to make an ignorance of physiology, pharmacology, and pathology seem like erudition. There is intimidating power in noncomprehended language. The doctor's rhetoric is an armor that safeguards status and conceals a lack of the very knowledge that it is supposed to express. The satirist cuts through the panoply and exposes the rhetoric as inflated fustian. "The world is stricken by something more sickening than illness," Kṣemendra jibes, "it is the bombast of physicians" (*Deśopadeśa* 8.34).

Just as his words, seemingly so meaningful in their technicality, are exposed as meaningless, so the doctor's medical activities, seemingly purposeful expressions of elaborate training, are reduced under satiric scrutiny to uncoordinated figetings. What seems to be order is exposed as a mere guise over chaos. Kṣemendra depicts the physician "frantically rushing to hundreds of houses, panting as if overworked, constantly wiping the flood of sweat from his brow with his hands. He arrives carrying bundles of papers—appointment slips, memoes, prescriptions. It's as if there were a lot of red tape involved in dying" (*Narmamālā* 2.69–70).

Nīlakaṇṭha Dīkṣita explains that the physician need not know anything at all. He can be ignorant of diagnostics and therapeutics and still "the women in the patient's home will provide him with all the information he needs to know" (*Kaliviḍambana* 27). "The physician should prescribe a salutary regimen which is to the patient's liking; but at the same time it should be one that is complicated and somewhat difficult for the patient to follow. If there is a cure it can be credited to the greatness of the physician; if not the patient can be blamed for not keeping exactly to the regimen" (25). And even without any knowledge of medical science he can maintain the necessary power to extract money from the patient: "the cure which comes just from drinking juices and watching one's diet, the doctor attributes to his own prescription and takes his fee" (*Viśvaguṇādarśa* 538).

Having caught a cold in India, I decided to go to an Āyur Vedic medicine shop to try out a traditional remedy. I was sold some black pellets and given solemn instructions: "Take one per day for one month and your cold will definitely be cured." When I seemed unimpressed, commenting that my cold would be gone in a month without treatment, the medical pandit suggested that I take two a day—"Then your cold will be gone in a fortnight." "Colds," I tried to explain, "don't usually last for more than a week." Undaunted and cheerful, the man recommended that I "take them all at once and see what happens." *Difficile est saturam non scribere,* says Juvenal.

The Fatal Physician

How differs, I pray, the Physician's part
From his brother, the Surgeon's healing art?
I tell you, the one by his drugs and pills,
By his knife the other, the churchyard fills:
This difference only from the Hangman's seen—
Their work is clumsy and slow, his quick and clean.

Maximilianus Urentius of Ghent, "The Physician and the Hangman"

The ignorance of doctors is their folly, but in them, as in kings and judges, folly is a dark vice. Once upon a time there was a physician who bragged to a brahmin that he could straighten the back of the man's hunchback son. Carried away by a sense of his own great powers, he bet on his success, giving the brahmin odds of ten to one. "Boasting makes a man ridiculous," according to the storyteller—the foolish doctor was unable to do anything for the boy. In his attempt to win his bet the quack "tortured the boy" with painful and insalubrious treatments (*Kathāsaritsāgara* 10.231–235). The ridiculousness of the doctor is deadly.

While the general is funny when he is a coward, when he is unable to kill, the doctor is comical in his ability to inflict death. Self-contradictions within the objects of satire are ever apparent and total. "Hail the physician," Kṣemendra sarcastically shouts, "he kills so many people with his shameful work" (*Narmamālā* 2.68). Fear of death inspires a veneration of the doctor, a desperate belief, or at least a hope, that his medicine has power. And there is the hope that that power, through the magic known as science, can sustain life indefinitely. The same dread is a source of comic disdain, of satirical laughter at the doctor. And that laughter, full of revenge for the inescapability of his ultimate failure to live up to those hopes and beliefs, is laughter in the face of death. It is a defense, however frail and fleeting, against death. It is a palliative, not an antidote or a cure. The doctor, in medical satire, becomes, like the hangman or the government comptroller, a personification of death, an effigy through which death itself can be made ridiculous. The effigy burns in the flames of laughter.

The physician in the *Kautukaratnākara* is named Vyādhivardhaka (Increaser-of-Diseases) and the doctor in the *Hāsyārṇava* is Vyādhisindhu (Illness-Ocean) son of Āturāntaka (Killer-of-the-Sick): *nomen omen est*. He who is versed in the Āyur Veda, the guardian of life, is reversed into a harbinger of death, a murderer well armed with deadly weapons, his drugs and pills. Healers are killers and medicines are poisons. The reversal, the basis of a cartoon from the *Hindustan Times* (fig. 12), is a comic one. As a doctor walks through the streets people hail him with the names of death, recite a verse to appease the god of death and keep him at bay: "[Homage] to Yama, to Death, the Prince of Justice, the Ender, to the Grim Reaper, to Time, the Taker of All Life" (*Samayamātṛkā* 1.39). Satire, like magical spell, aspires to ward off evil and death with words.

Just as a doctor is paradoxically envisioned in satire as a representative of death, so too he is seen as a personification of disease. The satirized doctors, Dr. Wormbanner and Dr. Illness-Ocean, are themselves repositories of contagion, sick and sick-

Figure 12

"Thanks for going on strike, Doctor
no medicine for seven days has cured me!"

ening, literally and metaphorically. The doctor in the *Narmamālā* "is a deadly fart and he's deranged—he's a health menace" (2.73). "It's not the disease that makes people sick," Kṣemendra sardonically notes, "it's the doctor" (2.76). Laughter alleviates the perceptual tension caused by the contradictory image of the diseased healer.

Dr. Illness-Ocean moves slowly because of elephantiasis and his swollen leg is a visual metaphor for moral edema. He hacks and coughs and, with a nervous gesture of his hand, he tries to drive off the flies attracted by the pus that his body exudes. This doesn't seem to bother his patients. In the view of the satirist, people, anesthetized and inured to social corruption, seek protection and justice from degenerate kings, just as they seek spiritual counsel from hypocritical holy men, or love from venal prostitutes. So too they rush to buy a potion to cure baldness from a medicine vendor who has as much hair on his head as there is on a copper pot (*Kalāvilāsa* 9.9).

The elaborate pharmacopoeia of the *vaidya* inspired reverence and awe in traditional India. Medicines were holy, sacralized by the Veda: "Medicinal herbs! I address you! . . . The herbs have driven away all bodily defects. . . . They have descended from the heavens and spoken: 'The living man who is reached by us shall not die' " (*Ṛg Veda* 10.97.4, 10, 17). The clever quack, playing upon the trust which his patients have in the magical power of his drugs, can manipulate the sick. That they put his medicines into their bodies or on their skin intensifies his power over them: "With nonsense nostrums—you know, those ludicrous lotions, useless oils, and insufferable pills—physicians trick the sick and fill their own potbellies," Kṛśānu jeers in disgust (*Viśvaguṇādarśa* 536).

"Sick people should get rid of medicine prescribed by stupid doctors," warns a medical text, "just like smart husbands get rid of adulterous wives" (cited in the *Mahāsubhāṣitasaṃgraha* 8257), and Caraka cautions that "a patient who wants to live shouldn't take medicine prescribed by an ignorant physician." This is particularly so since there were a great many poisons in the Indian doctor's *materia medica:* "a poison correctly prescribed can be an excellent medicine and likewise a medicine incorrectly prescribed can be a harsh poison" (*Caraka* 1.1.126–127). Dr. Wormbanner (Jantuketu), the exquisitely "ignorant physician" of the *Laṭakamelaka,* explains that he does indeed use poisons as elixirs. He magnifies the pharmacological paradox into a satiric absurdity by boasting that he is so medically talented that he can actually foster diseases with his poisons and "sound the drum of death" with his treatments (1.21). Even more profoundly ignorant, and proud of it, is Dr. Illness-Ocean of the *Hāsyārṇava.* He brags that while most doctors need medicines to kill their patients, he is so adept and knowledgeable that he can do it without the help of drugs. "Let all medicines and herbs be laid aside, for by the mere sight of me patients will give up their lives" (1.32). He claims furthermore that under his care even the sage Mārkaṇḍeya, renowned for his extraordinarily great age, wouldn't be able to survive.

The cures which Dr. Illness-Ocean inflicts upon his patients are catalogued in a grotesque parody of Caraka's therapeutics.

> Haven't you heard of this doctor's manifold skills,
> Of all of the patients he so expertly kills
> With his treatment, his medicine, his panaceas?
> In case of bad bowels and for all diarrheas

He pierces the eye with a needle—it's hot! O it glows!
He'll shove a sharp hook way up your nose
If pissing is painful, if you've got a stone.
Elephantiasized feet are cut to the bone.
He pours boiling oil as a salve when it smarts;
Or if there's trouble with his patients' hearts
He uses a vise to squeeze out their balls.
Inhalation of corn smoke is his cure for râles.
A fast or an enema, something sweat-starting
Is his cure for belching as well as for farting.
"Eat lots of ground meat," is doctor's suggestion
For any problems one has with one's digestion.
For treatment of phlegm he is punctilious—
He prescribes water—and if you're bilious
He gives hot peppers and herbs that are spicy.
For fevers he orders a bath that is icy.
Alas, with only one little mouth it's so hard for me
To enumerate all the virtues of Illness-Ocean, M.D.

(*Hāsyārṇava* 1.32)

For nasal congestion Dr. Illness-Ocean recommends putting a wasp, bee, or leech up the nose, and he advises an old bawd whose secretory malfunctions are attributed to an all-too-long life of sexual debauchery, to have an enema of "hot stinging oil" (prose after 1.35). The clyster provides another image of comic reversal.

Similarly Dr. Wormbanner, who "cauterizes the throat shut for vomiting and drains the patient of his blood to cure any fear he might have of stomach swelling" (*Laṭakamelaka* 1.21), grandly and authoritatively explains that "in case of eye disease, a hot plowshare should be inserted into the anus; then those afflictions coming from the eyes will be forgotten by the brain" (1.25). Enemas, purgatives, and laxatives are repeatedly prescribed by the doctors in satire—the digestive systems of the patients as well as of the doctors themselves are never quite working. These systems are the anatomical and physiological equivalents of social modes and systems of production and consumption, and the social satirist himself is a "doctour of physik." Satire is a literary plowshare-suppository and rhetorical enema of "hot stinging oil" aimed at purging the social body of all the crap, all the sickness, all the affectation, corruption, and hypocrisy. The treatment is embarrassing, humiliating, degrading. And it's meant to be.

The crazy, dangerous, and comically inappropriate cure appears as a comic motif as early as the second century B.C.E. in India. There is a bas-relief from Bharhut in which monkeys set about extracting a tooth from the mouth of a human (or perhaps demonic) patient. A clamp is fixed to the tooth and a rope is attached to the clamp at one end and to an elephant at the other; the moneys are poised to blow horns, bang drums, bite the elephant's tail, and use goads to get the elephant to lunge forward and thereby pull out the tooth. Doctors and dentists are like the monkeys—a little too clever and all too foolish, at once dangerous and funny.

It is natural that doctors are killers for, after all, "they become progressively more well versed in the nature of diseases only as those diseases spread and people die" (*Kaliviḍambana* 27). Our death is an educational experience for the doctor; our suffering and his expertise are directly proportional. The doctor, according to the satirist, kills us in the name of medicine, executes us scientifically, murders us respectably and legally. "Out of a desire to perfect his art," Kṣemendra wryly reflects, "the physician has killed thousands of men with his herbal treatments—thus he has become famous" (*Kalāvilāsa* 9.4). The satiric treatment is prophylactic, protection against the germ of truth within this irony.

The comic outrage is that the murderous healer expects money from his victim. "A doctor and the Angel of Death both kill," according to a Jewish folksaying, "but the doctor charges a fee." Money always makes the satirist suspicious.

The Venal Vaidya

[The Doctour of Physik] was but esy of dispence;
He kepte that he wan in pestilence.
For gold in physik is a cordial,
Therefore he loved gold in special.

Chaucer, *Canterbury Tales*

The ideal voiced in Caraka is that brahmins who become physicians practice the medical arts without charge, that they do so out of compassion; warriors were to practice medicine to help each other; members of the merchant class were permitted to earn money as doctors, but their primary impulse was still to be a concern for the well-being of the patient. Satire bears witness to the degradation of the hallowed ideals—doctors have mercantile souls.

They are infected with a concern for the wealth of the unhealthy. "The physician doesn't diagnose the disease of the sick man, he diagnoses the health of the man whose life is his money," Kṣemendra proposes. "Like a poison, a snake, a vampire . . . the physician *prospers* on flesh" (*Narmamālā* 2.71–72).

The fear of the patient must inevitably be that his health, and therefore his life, is merely a commodity, that beneath the mask of care there lurks the face of the snake or vampire. The satirist arms the patient or potential patient with a fear of this possibility to keep him aware, and at the same time he prevents the fear from becoming obsessive by mitigating it with laughter.

The comicality of the venal doctor is a function of the perception of a reversal of norms. Instead of being an enemy of disease, the physician, for the sake of profit, is an ally of illness: "sickness is what provides the physician with his livelihood" (*Narmamālā* 2.74). And, similarly, the cantankerous Kṛśānu observes, "Doctors like sickness—after all, they get lots of money because of it" (*Viśvaguṇādarśa* 537).

Kṣemendra portrays physicians as carrion eaters hovering over the dying, sneaking around them in anticipation, thriving on human discomfort: "During the great festivals in the cities and when there are marriage feasts, the physician is delighted." Joviality during the festive season is appropriate until Kṣemendra reveals the comic and repugnant impropriety: the physician's joy has nothing to do with the spirit of the time; it is fiscal delight, the result of the fact that during that period "people have to go to him because of all the overeating they do" (*Narmamālā* 2.75). Ancient laughter seeks renewal—the same joke resurfaces in a contemporary Indian cartoon (fig. 13). Images of overeating, of stuffing and gorging, pervade satire as a reminder of the perversion of the survival instinct into greed. No different is Kṣemendra's ophthalmologist: "summer is his autumn"—there are so many "sore and irritated eyes" in the hot season that he is able to harvest the fruits of his profession, to make lots of dough (*Narmamālā* 3.60). This eye doctor, furthermore, blinds his patients with an ophthalmic balm made of corn silk. References to blindness and eye disease occur again and again in satire, suggesting the real object of satiric attack—the blindness of people to the rampancy of social folly and vice.

Dr. Illness-Ocean, in the *Hāsyārṇava*, prescribes putting out the eyes of anyone with eye trouble so that they can't go blind.

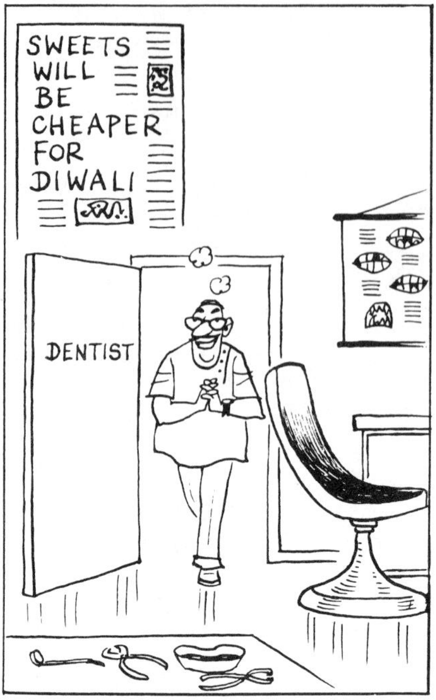

Figure 13

"Good, good ... more tooth decays!"

And the blind are enlisted to cure the blind. Madame Toothy (Danturā) consults Dr. Wormbanner about her failing eyesight. When he asks her how far she can see, the old whore answers, "as far as that fig tree." He responds, "What fig tree:" (*Laṭakamelaka,* prose after 1.24). Myopia becomes a metaphor for the spiritual and moral infirmities of the age. Satire urges its audience to see, to look carefully, and to laugh at the ridiculousness of the spectacle.

It is our blindness that allows us to be hoodwinked by the crooked quack, the venal *vaidya*—the vice is his, but the folly ours. In a burlesque of Āyur Vedic ethical discourse, a parody of Caraka perhaps, Nīlakaṇṭha Dīkṣita advises the doctor on how to extract money from a patient. "Those who are chronically ill or afraid of becoming so are a source of wealth for the physician; but there is hardly any money to be gained from people who are either too healthy or whose illness is incurable. The physician shouldn't be too reassuring—a patient won't pay unless he's afraid of dying. At the same time the physician shouldn't be too alarming—a patient won't pay unless he has hopes of surviving'' (*Kaliviḍambana* 23–24).

The foolish patient who is swindled out of his money by the clever doctor appears in Indian folk humor. One story tells of a king who had a daughter born to him and who was anxious for her to grow up, to reach a marriageable age. He called his court physicians and requested that they prepare a medicine to make her mature quickly. The doctors, ''in order to get some cash out of the foolish king,'' explained that the medicine which would make her grow quickly had to be procured from a distant land and that, as part of the treatment, the baby girl would have to be sequestered, hidden even from her family, until the medicine was brought. During the term of concealment the king frequently asked about his daughter. The doctors, in turn, continually informed him that they were in the midst of the cure, that they were procuring the magic drug. After the girl had grown up, they removed her from concealment and showed the king that they had indeed performed the task he has asked of them. The king rewarded the avaricious doctors with heaps of money (*Kathāsaritsāgara* 10.265–272).

The Physician:

He can't extend the life you've led
Though for that he'll charge his fees;
His skill's in running from the dead
And in performing moneyectomies!

(*Sāktiratnahāra* 136.6)

''At first physicians wish to take our money for what they actually do,'' Nīlakaṇṭha Dīkṣita complains, ''later they want it for the medicinal herbs they prescribe; finally they want it just out of esteem and admiration'' (*Kaliviḍambana* 28). The satirist worries about esteem and admiration. He puts a check on them by insinuating that the physician is guilty not only of murder and theft, but of other hidden crimes and vices as well.

The Dirty Doctor

''Now I just want to test these clitoral reflexes,'' said Dr. Johns, ''often enough that's where the trouble strikes first.''

Terry Southern and Mason Hoffenberg, *Candy*

In a bookstall at a railway station in India, I picked up a cheap and excruciatingly witless jokebook, K. P. Bahadur's *Humorist's Hoo's Hoo,* described on the cover as providing, among other things, "naughty keyhole glimpses of pantless . . . physicians." The same motifs which typify medical satire universally and Sanskrit writing in particular were there. Doctors are murderers (that's why "they all wear masks" [p. 3]). Of course, they are venal ("a doctor first coos and then bills" [p. 25]). But above all else they are lustful: "A girl who was asked to strip by her doctor, said to another whom she found in a similar state in the clinic, 'It's strange. I have an eye disease, and he asks me to strip.' 'My case is even more peculiar,' the other girl said. 'I'm here only to stitch the curtains' " (p. 23). The medical degree, providing the doctor with access to sex, to the nakedness of women, is a license for license. "A doctor . . . can ask you, if you happen to be a shapely woman, to strip, and proceed to give you the minutest examination, even if he doesn't eventually find anything wrong with you. . . . And after he has done so, and told you you are fit as a fiddle, you pay him twenty rupees; while if a man without a medical degree had done the same thing, you'd have slapped him hard" (pp. 1–2). Satirical laughter at the lascivious doctor belies both male envy (he is rewarded for the libidinous impulses for which the individuals who comprise the audience of satire get punished or feel guilty) and male fear (he has control over wives, daughters, and mothers). The husband of every ailing woman is implicitly, in the interest of his wife's health, a cuckold. Subliminal fear and envy arouse aggression: "Do you want to KILL somebody?" asks a large blurb on the back of *Humorist's Hoo's Hoo*—do it, it advises, "with laughter." Kill the doctor and treat yourself, the cover copy continues: "for indeed laughter is the best medicine."

A man in the berth across from mine on the train was interested to know what I was reading. "Jokes about doctors," I answered, "I'm trying to find out what people in India think is funny." "People in India do not think physicians are humorous. You should not be reading this sort of book. What is there to laugh about in it?" He told me that I must read a certain Telugu novel which depicted the plight of a middle-class doctor in rural Andhra: "He is overworked and underpaid." I explained that I knew no Telugu. "In that case you must read *The Citadel* by Mr. A. J. Cronin." If it were not for the persistence of the ideal, indications of its degradation would not be so funny.

The physician, like any representative of authority—king, priest, or father—is an ambivalent figure. Idealization augments respect and trust, which then bestow power, which, in turn, gives rise to scorn and fear. Medical satire and jokes about doctors alleviate the resultant psychological tension through laughter. "It is interesting to note, as showing the real motives or mechanism producing medical satire," according to one psychiatrist, Isador H. Coriat, "that patients under analysis, as a sign of their unconscious resistance, will often have dreams in which the physician is satirized or caricatured" ("The Psychology of Medical Satire," *Annals of Medical History.*).

As the ideal doctor is clean in every sense, so the satirized doctor is dirty—he is diseased and he is lascivious. Neither illness nor sexual desire are particularly very funny, of course—a sick patient, like an ardent lover, is a serious figure. But the incongruity between what the physician is supposed to be and what he is exposed in satire to really be, is the very basis of his comicality. And his sexuality, his concealed prurience, is particularly comical. The sexual arousal of kings, judges, professors, politicians, and physicians is universally funny.

The ideal physician, as soberly and respectfully characterized by Caraka, "should not commit adultery . . . should not treat women unless their husbands or guardians are present, and should not accept anything from a female patient without the husband's or guardian's permission" (3.8.1ff.). In the shadow of that ideal the doctors in Sanskrit satirical literature pant and leer as they ogle the bodies of female patients. Dr. Wormbanner hurries off to find some love potion and aphrodisiac to secure the amorous interests of his patient Miss Lovebouquet (Madanamañjarī):

> May the holy rites of the lovely love god come to pass!
> Whose mind is not obsessed with this gorgeous lass—
> With her beauteous jugs, with her round and hefty ass?
> (*Laṭakamelaka* 1.27)

Science provides the camouflage for prurience. Kṣemendra's version of the lusty doctor is a "glutton, a killer, a toucher of women's private parts," who is summoned by a cuckolded and henpecked comptroller to attend his wife who seems so very ill. In satire seeming always indicates its opposite—the woman is feigning illness in order to avoid all domestic service to her husband, the only man who doesn't interest her sexually. "The doctor approached her and placed his hands upon her compact breasts, breasts that were hard from being handled so often." Frottage masquerades as medical procedure, lust as diagnosis, seduction as prescription: "She cannot endure fasting and yet nutritious foods are really not suitable in such cases of colic. You'd better let her take her meals with me; I'll take care of her case. To begin with she should eat some curds mixed with brown sugar. She's frigid because her mind and body are out of harmony" (*Narmamālā* 2.76–80).

The narrator in Śyāmilaka's *Pādatāḍitaka,* encountering a physician in a red-light district, teases him with accusations of lechery. The venerable physician insists that his interests are professional, that he is merely performing his duty in administering medicine to an ailing woman. "No doubt," the narrator laughs, "the fire of love has been dampened by indigestion—you've merely prescribed a digestive tonic, a little pick-me-up—℞: *copulatus medicus*" (prose after 35). When the doctor insists that he has given her medicine to drink, the narrator laughs again insinuatingly, sure that he has indeed given her some "oral treatment" (37).

In literature infused with the erotic sentiment or mood it was a convention to compare the lover to a physician, the beloved to a patient, and passionate kisses to a medicine. In the *Gītagovinda* of Jayadeva, for example, a messenger sings to Kṛṣṇa of his beloved's amorous malady: "How can her slender body, afflicted with the fever of love, survive except by your medicine/love? You're the earthly counterpart to the Heavenly Physicians, dear to the divine healers. Stricken with the disease which is love, she will not survive without the elixir of your touch" (4.9–10). By reversing the conceit, by making the physician a lover, the satirist renders the erotic comic. While the poet of love juxtaposes sexual desire and death, makes the lover a healer in order to intensify the erotic mood, the comic poet juxtaposes sexual desire and indigestion, and makes the healer lusty in order to deflate the erotic mood—it shrivels into the comic and lies there, limp and silly.

A doctor and his female patient have a conversation which sounds legitimate: "You are afflicted," the doctor says, "by a high fever, girl; it is my opinion that fasting would restore your health"; and the patient replies, "O Lord of Physicians, prescribe mercury, since I can't undergo the fasting you have prescribed." (*Subhāṣitaratnabhāṇḍāgāra* 189.60). Presumably this could be a discussion between a doctor and a patient in the presence of a parent or husband. The seemingly professional, medical language conceals sexual innuendoes. The same dialogue can be translated erotically: "You are afflicted with the fever of love, girl," the man says, "and I believe the sacred fire [of marriage or sexual union] would make you happy"; and the girl replies, "O Lord of Physicians, give me love since I can't ignore what you've said." The puns are semantic knots that bind together comically incongruous fibers of chastity and lechery. They are also semantic windows through which to see the messy chambers of corruption behind white-washed walls of seeming.

As the doctor strips the patient, the satirist strips the doctor and proceeds to give the minutest gynecological, urological, and proctological examination. He exposes what is normally concealed in order to remind us that the figures we venerate and esteem are no different than ourselves. The pleasure of that realization is expressed in laughter. That laughter is offensive. It is supposed to be—that's the fun of satire. I didn't fully realize this when I sent this study of the satires of physicians in Sanskrit literature to my brother, a cardiologist, thinking he would laugh with enjoyment over it. He wrote back: "Next time you need a doctor, call a satirist."

The Satiric Doodlebug: *Astrologers Astray*

The State puts up with palmists, soothsayers, and those who cast horoscopes and read the configurations of the stars . . . and such people do indeed serve some purpose; they predict to men that they will make their fortune, to girls that they will marry their suitors . . . in short, for a trifling fee they will deceive anyone who wants to be deceived.

La Bruyère, *Characters*

The astrologer, a "kinsman of the doctor, is bound to pop up when the doctor collects his fee" (*Kaliviḍambana* 29). Like the physician, the astrologer knows too much, is armed with the power which comes with the recognition of his practice as a science. Like the doctor, he relies on the gullibility of people, the eagerness of people to be duped, defrauded, and embezzled. Like the physician, he is a universal object of satiric cynicism. And the satirist, like the wielder of a divining rod, looks for what is hidden beneath surfaces. The satiric doodlebug leads to the discovery of folly and corruption within the astrologer. He is a fool and a crook, a dangerous and comical combination.

There was an itinerent astrologer who, in an attempt to create a compensatory impression of prognostic proficiency, embraced his young son in public. As he held the boy close, he wept. Questioned as to the cause of his tears, he announced, "I can foretell the future. Through my great ability I have seen that my child will die in a week. Thus I weep." Seven days later, in order to prove his prophecy, he murdered his sleeping son. The people were filled with wonder, awe, and confidence in the man's astrological acumen. They paid well for his forecasts, but the wealth did not bring his child back to him (*Kathāsaritsāgara* 10.252–258). The astrologer's son, like the child offered to the demon of the brahmin caste, is the victim of authority, of its corruptions and affectations. Laughter at the astrologer is revenge for his death and for the threats made to all of us as potential victims of the same powers who so falsely weep for us.

Kṣemendra focuses upon the foolishness of the supposedly wise astrologer. He is so busy "calculating astrological forecasts by examining the position of the moon and the planets in the heavens, that he doesn't realize that his wife is balling every creep in town" (*Kalāvilāsa* 9.6). He is like one of Swift's Laputans among whom "the husband is so rapt in speculation, that the mistress and lover may proceed to greatest familiarity before his face, if he be but provided with paper and implements" (*Gulliver's Travels*). Satire is skeptical of all theoretical, abstract, or technical knowledge, of all intellectual preoccupations. The Laputan philosopher and Kṣemendra's astrologer no longer see what is before their eyes, no longer discriminate between the abstract and the concrete. The object of knowledge disappears as the knower becomes absorbed in knowing as an end rather than as a means. The satirist values simple, concrete truths, while his object always claims to know a truth that is too complicated for the rest of us. Astrology, according to Veṅkaṭādhvarin is a "great sea swollen with waves which are its many rules and the exceptions to those rules" (*Viśvaguṇādarśa* 528). The poet adds that there are but a few drops of wisdom in that vast, polluted ocean of folly.

The astrologer in Kṣemendra's *Narmamālā* is a "dimwit who has to ask fishermen whether or not it is going to rain. He carries a dirty, ragged chart about and pretends to know about the past and the future" (2.82–83). He is able to convince people that he knows something by unfolding the chart, using abstruse and technical language, "throwing in a few tidbits of common-knowledge medicine and magic'' (2.87). Like the doctor, the astrologer hides his ignorance within the venerated system, the science.

The fool can be clever; the ignorant one can be—and usually is in satire—well versed in the art of fraud. The comptroller who lost his wife to the doctor in the *Narmamālā* consults an astrologer who gives him a dismal forecast: ''Though I think you may inherit a little cash, one thing is certain—in about three years you will lose all your money. Oh yes, and also, there will be a fever and blindness and no one will help you out. After all, you have a lot of enemies. You'd better have some pea soup. You seem jaundiced—I'll cure you with a mantra'' (2.84–86). The astrologer lures the clerk into the trap, moves slowly in on his terrified prey, and then readies him for the kill. Though the astrologer knows of the lustiness of the accountant's wife through all the local gossip, he feigns divination of the knowledge through a calculation of the heavenly asterism. He pretends to ponder a chart which he draws on his slate. He raises his eyebrows again and again; he counts on his fingers. The comptroller thinks he's counting days, months, weeks. In fact he's adding up the money that the clerk has anxiously begun to hand over to him. Greed disguises itself as scientific activity. ''This wan wife of yours is afflicted by a desire for sexual pleasure. I can see by the position of Venus in the circle that she has been possessed by a ghost. When your house was empty, when she was naked, taking her bath, he took hold of her. The demon who incites sexual passion in women is hard to repress'' (2.91). The clerk pays the astrologer to discover the esoteric knowledge which everyone in town, except the clerk himself, already knows. Laughter over the episode is justice—the comptroller is as corrupt as the astrologer or more so.

As the doctor takes credit for all health while refusing blame for any sickness, the astrologer manipulates circumstances into his favor. ''No matter what befalls one through the action of destiny,'' according to Veṅkaṭādhvarin's iconoclastic Kṛśānu, ''whether good or bad fortune, the astrologer deceitfully claims to have predicted it. . . . He'll draw up a birth chart for someone, right or wrong, and if it comes true he attributes it to his own cleverness; if not, he attributes the mistake to some wrong information supplied by the client. These damn astrologers are thieves'' (*Viśvaguṇādarśa* 529–530). While we look up at the stars, astrologers pick our pockets. Astrology provides the crook with a way to steal legitimately and legally; and the victim of the crime respects and venerates the criminal. "With their predictions about sons, fortune, how long one is going to live and so forth, these damn astrologers enter house after house to continually dupe the people with money" (*Viśvaguṇādarśa* 528).

A domestic servant at a home in which I was staying received two itinerant astrologers after they had done their best to get me to pay them for telling me that I would have a long life and become very rich. The servant seemed very pleased with his session and informed me with a broad smile that he had given the astrologers several hundred rupees. They had promised him that within one week he would receive a great sum of money, enough to buy his own house, and they had assured him, furthermore, that they would return in a week and that they would give him double his money back if their prediction had not come true. In a week, the poor man's smile, like his money and the astrologers themselves, had totally vanished.

The forecasts of astrologers in satire, and frequently in the actual world, often have an ambiguity which allows them to yield a correct interpretation—"one of two things will happen on one of two days" (*Kaliviḍambana* 18). The astrologer Master Macroastrogaster (Mahāyātrika), consulted as to when a certain marriage should take place, gives his professional advice: "any time, anywhere, under any sign—*que sera sera*" (*Hāsyārṇava* 2.28). Asked when the king should proceed with a military campaign, Macroastrogaster indicates a day when the conjunction of planets suggests doom and death. He is sure to be right—either the king's army or that of his enemy will die.

In traditional India the astrologer was an advisor to the king. Nīlakaṇṭha Dīkṣita parodies serious counsel to the royal astrologer: "In order to give the king a correct reading, a proper astrological forecast, it is just as important for the astrologer to consult spies (*cāra*) as for him to divine the course of the stars (*cāra*)" (*Kaliviḍambana* 14). Two incongruous realms, the heavenly, sublime, and ordered "course of the stars" and the earthly, devious, political realm of "spies" are enmeshed in the pun, tied together by a satiric knot.

The necessity of astrological counsel to monarchs gave the ancient Indian astrologer enormous, and therefore, at least in the eyes of the satirist, dangerous, power. He could fashion the fate of the people and justify his directive by merely pointing to the stars. King Kṛṣṇadevarāya, according to a south Indian folktale, was about to set out on a campaign against a neighboring region.

There were no doubts in his or anyone else's minds that his army would easily vanquish the far weaker kingdom. Spies from the enemy's court secretly approached Kṛṣṇadevarāya's astrologer and bribed him with a substantial fortune to falsify his astrological reading, to announce to the king that it would be disasterous to proceed with an attack. The astrologer warned the king that though all earthly signs pointed to success, such a venture was clearly inauspicious—sidereal omens indicated defeat and death. Disappointed and distraught, the king called for his jester, Tenāli Rāma, to cheer him up. When Tenāli Rāma heard the story, he summoned the astrologer to court and, in the presence of the king, asked him if he was certain of his forecast.

"Absolutely certain."

"Are your forecasts always correct?" the jester asked.

"Always."

"Then tell me, will you, just for example," Rāma continued, "how long are you going to live?"

"This is easy," the astrologer smiled, "I shall live thirty more years. I am going to live to the age of seventy-four."

All at once, as instructed by the jester, the king's general drew his sword and decapitated the astrologer. The rolling head proved that his forecasts were meaningless (*Tenali Rama,* pp. 83–85). Satire decapitates—it cuts off the part of the body, individual or social, which denies the other parts, the part that schemes, that is all too clever.

"You will have a long life," the astrologer assured me, "and you will become very rich. Very, very rich!" It made abundant sense to him that, since I was going to become so rich, the least I could do was pay him generously for the prediction. He was enacting the comic prophesies of Nīlakaṇṭha Dīkṣita: "Asked how long one will live, the astrologer always predicts long life—he will be commended by those who do live long and those who don't can't complain. . . . The astrologer is appreciated, provided he tells the poor man that he will get rich and the rich man that he will get richer" (*Kaliviḍambana* 16, 18). Both the confidence man and the victim, the astrologer and the client, are motivated by greed; the avariciousness of the latter allows for the success of the former.

Dismissing the astrologer's forecast, I started to walk off. "You will write a book," he yelled. "Yes, you want to write a book. Isn't that correct? My knowledge is always correct." I turned around. He smiled proudly, sure that he had trapped his prey. The divination was discomforting—it implied that almost every Westerner walking down the street wanted to write a book. "Yes, I am writing something," I admitted, "a book about Indian comedy."

"It was not necessary to tell me that. I knew that. My knowledge is always correct. I was, you know, personal astrologer to Sri Richard Nixon." He laughed again. Then, suddenly, he assumed an air of solemnity. Closing his eyes, extending his arms, he made his pronouncement: "Everyone will buy this book. Number one best-seller! Everyone will laugh. Everyone will be happy. By means of this book you will give happiness to all literate mankind. And from this book you will make your great fortune. My knowledge is always correct." He opened his eyes and smiled again as he continued. "This comedy will become a film. Then even illiterate mankind will have happiness. What a choice comedy!"

I tried to picture the marquee over the entrance to the Grauman's Chinese Theater on Hollywood Boulevard: *LAUGHING MATTERS: COMIC TRADITION IN INDIA*. No. "No," I told the fortune-teller, "it's not that kind of book."

"Don't tell me!" he barked angrily, "My knowledge is always correct! I will tell you something else. I will appear in your book! This is certain."

"No," I laughed, "it's really not that kind of book. It's an academic book. It's about Sanskrit literature. You will certainly not be in my book."

"You are not aware of it. You do not know it. But I know it. My knowledge is always correct. I will be in your book!"

"No. I'm sorry. You won't."

"Yes. I am sorry, sir. I will."

The astrologer wanted to be paid for the divination. The inevitable Indian crowd of passersby, curious or amused or without anything else to do, was gathering as we began to haggle. I felt a tugging at my shirt and turned around. A small boy held out his dirty, cupped hand. "No food, no home," he muttered, raising the little hand toward my face. "Get away," the astrologer shouted at this competition for my money, and the child fled. I lost sight of him, but the image of the begging hand remained vivid. It was the hand of the child pariah in the cartoon who asked his mother if he could go home. It was the living hand of the boy in the legend, the hand held by the mother as the king raised his sword, the hand of the child whose redemption was to come through laughter.

The Laughter of Kāma

5

Religious Satire: Hypocrisy and the Degradation of Piety

If a man who is wise and intent upon release tries to slay me, I dance before him and, as he devotes himself to the bliss of liberation, I laugh at him.

"The Song of Kāma," *Mahābhārata*

Śiva, lord of yogis, archetypal ascetic, and perfect exemplar of the renunciatory path to liberation, performing austerities high in the Himalayas, senses controlled and desires restrained, was attacked by Kāma, the god who is sexual desire. Opening the third eye to release fiery forces, accrued, augmented, and stored through fierce asceticism, Śiva struck back. The splendid body of love was reduced to ashes. But Kāma was not destroyed. Bodiless he persists in mocking the pursuit of liberation. His laughter still resounds in the joy of lovers. Śiva must ultimately acknowledge the primacy of Kāma, the all-pervading energy of sexuality:

All hail Kāma!

"Here is mighty Lord Śiva, the world-famous ascetic:
He fears being apart from his Love (Oh, how pathetic!);
So he makes her part of himself that he can enjoy her.
And yet still people imagine that he's my destroyer!"
Kāma laughs aloud with these words (and then for good measure)
He squeezes the hand of his lover, Our Lady Pleasure.

(Nīlapaṭa, *Subhāṣitaratnakoṣa* 14.1)

While the erotic ascetic may be a potent figure, offering a mythological reconciliation of contrary impulses within the psyche and contrary values within society, the figure can also be a comical one, drawing attention to ludicrous incongruities within the self and absurd paradoxes within the cosmos. The erotic ascetic inspires awe when his austerities contain sexual energy and invest him with its power. But he elicits laughter when his asceticism is revealed to be the inevitably vain attempt either to overcome or to conceal desire. Satire reveals in order to put limits on awe. It is always skeptical of purity and chastity, of austerity and piety.

If Śiva, lord of renunciation, is in reality not the vanquisher of Kāma, but the vanquished, if he is the object of Love's laughter, there are grounds for a satiric suspicion of all those who, in emulation of the god, claim to be without passion or desire. With Kāma the satirist makes fun of them, all of them, and laughs to expose them for what they really are—no more pious or holy than anyone else, or perhaps less so for claiming to be more so.

The sobriety and rigidity, the stodginess and humorlessness, the certainty and sanctimony, which seem to be universal symptoms of religiosity, establish religion as one of the major natural arenas of satiric battle and play. Religion is comical because it is so serious and solemn.

"Of all nonsense, religious nonsense is the most nonsensical," Robert Burns wrote to Alexander Cunningham, and he asked, "Will you, or can you, tell me why a religious turn of mind always has a tendency to narrow and illiberalize the heart?" While religion may offer blessings of solace and communion, awakening and revelation, cohesion and morality, it can also be a sanctuary for the disruptive powers of ignorance and dullness, illiberality and greed. Religion provides a mask and a costume, a script of words and gestures, that can be utilized by anyone who seeks esteem, venerability, or legitimacy.

While ancient Indian society was theoretically viewed as a medium through which sacred truths could be manifested, the actual governors of real social units more often saw religion as an organizing principle by which social order could be maintained and sanctified. For that purpose religious institutions were endowed with power. The satirist was a check on that power, a guardian against its abuse.

The Sanskrit satirist wrote for a king and a court and, in this capacity, he had a social function. His ridicule had the potential to prevent religion from becoming all too absolutely hallowed, from becoming so sacred that the authority of its priests and monks was unimpeachable, so holy that the power of its representatives over those who empowered them was unassailable.

Sanskrit poets were part of a sophisticated and aristocratic social group that was devoted to finding amusement and diversion in love, courtship, and worldly delights. For the entertainment of that group, poets made an alliance with Kāma, the laughing god, to mock and parody those aspects of religion that seemed dour or stifling, those attitudes and practices that seemed to censure a life of pleasure. The poet and his audience laughed with Kāma at those who were intent upon liberation from the human condition, those who were all too sober and serious, those who attempted to deny, ignore, or repress the most natural drives. They had a creed of mirth and a faith in pleasure:

> I celebrate Kāma's sacred rite—
> It makes all the other rites seem trite.
> THE PRIEST: none is needed now by you.
> THE OFFERING: just yourself will do.
> THE ICON: it can be your misses.
> THE LITURGY: glances, hugs, and kisses.
>
> (Vallaṇa, *Subhāṣitaratnakoṣa* 14.11)

With comic irony the poet asserts the sanctity of sensual dalliance. Amaru does the same with a pun on the word *mukta,* a word that can mean either "pearls" or "liberated beings":

> Those bright pearl necklaces are playing
> On the rounded breasts of deer-eyed girls;
> And "pearls of wisdom" is a saying,
> So it must be wise to act like pearls.
>
> (*Amaruśataka* 138)

The paronomastic manipulation of the language creates a comic interplay between the amorous and religious aesthetic sentiments—the comic sentiment arises through that inappropriate juxtaposition of moods. Sex makes fun of religion.

Comedy is blasphemous. Its laughter is earthy and carnal. In that laughter, flesh confirms its reality, the physical triumphs over the metaphysical, instincts subsume ethics, and that which is human eclipses the divine. The gods are execrated, menaced, laughed out of heaven. Amaru playfully asserts that if a man takes the lower position in sexual intercourse, the face of his mistress looking down at him will preclude any need for supplicating Brahmā, Viṣṇu, or Śiva:

> The face of a girl making love on-top:
> forehead wet, weary-eyed, she nods
> As her earrings quiver and curls flip-flop;
> who on earth has need of the gods?
> Her fair face will watch over you non-stop.
> (*Amaruśataka* 3)

The sexual and the religious domains are merged in both comical and mystical poetic utterance. In mystical poetry, erotic language is frequently used to express religious experience; one discovers the religious interior or meaning of an amorous scene when sexuality becomes metaphorical for a spiritual process. The profane reveals, enhances, and vindicates the sacred. The movement of aesthetic discovery is upward. The Shulamite is realized to be, or be like, the soul, or the collective body of souls making up Israel or the Church; Rādhā, the loving beloved of Kṛṣṇa, is understood to be a representative of the soul or person who is perfectly devoted to god. In comic poetry the movement of aesthetic discovery is downward; one realizes the erotic interior or reality of a religious scene or guise. The sacred conceals the profane and is consumed by it, devoured from within.

Satire is a comic strip. It is cynical. Under its gaze, myths become silly fictions, and worship becomes ludicrous idolatry. Divine praise is sycophantic flattery, and acts of offering are unctuous attempts at bribery. Religious speculation is merely a spinning of webs of meaningless noesis. In a modern Indian cartoon, a pompous minister's sermon means nothing to a group of children (fig. 14). And it means nothing to the satirist. The highfalutin moral rhetoric is merely a string of insipid shibboleths. The satirist warns his audience against those who use such language, who adopt religious postures, those who do not laugh enough.

Satire scrutinizes pious words, gestures, and signs, looks for the ways in which sanctimony passes for sanctity, hypocrisy for piety.

. . . eradication of desires, self-abnegation and relentless pursuit of spiritual values alone will lead to the salvation of the soul!

Figure 14

Within the Whited Sepulchre: *Religion and Hypocrisy*

Woe unto you, scribes, Pharisees, hypocrites! for ye are like unto whited sepulchres, which indeed appear beautiful outward, but are within full of dead men's bones, and of all uncleanness.

Matthew 23:27

The religious satirist often sees himself as a reformer purging religion of its nonsense, an inquisitor exposing hypocrisy, an Elijah mocking the false prophets of Baal. In an Indian context the satirist could establish the religious basis of his laughter at religious endeavors with scripture: "He is called a hypocrite who controls the body through which he acts, but sits recollecting sense-objects in his mind" (*Bhagavadgītā* 3.6). There is a certain piety in satire's impious laughter. The satirist seems always aware that while nothing is more difficult or good than actually being pure and devoted, nothing is more easy, wicked, or expedient than seeming to be so.

Within Sanskrit literature the religious hypocrite, feigning austerities and devotion, using religion to acquire power, became a conventional comic character. This figure, surfacing also in both traditional and modern Indian satire, plies for that power in the form of either women or wealth. He eternally seeks what he pretends to have renounced. A typically unholy holy man of this literature is described by a harlot as she watches him in the streets of Varanasi: "Carrying a meditation mat and a mendicant's staff, wearing the ochre robe of an ascetic, he looks all about him for fear of being polluted by people touching him. The Vaiṣṇavas all love him because he acknowledges their scriptures, and he also claims to have had a vision of Śiva. He has taken a vow of silence. In my heart I suspect he's a hypocrite, a false ascetic, for when he thinks no one is watching, he cunningly and lustfully gawks at women" (*Kuṭṭanīmata* 747–750). The satirist shares the whore's suspicions.

Kṣemendra lists the kinds of men who can be recognized as hypocrites: "a man with a topknot, one with matted hair . . . one who busily recites prayers in the midst of his family and friends, one who sits in meditation on the roads that lead into town . . . a man who puts on a show at the sacred bathing places . . . one who worships the gods with many rituals and puts a very big sectarian mark on his forehead" (*Kalāvilāsa* 1.50–54). Hypocrisy incarnates as the holy man, the priest, the devotee. Hypocrisy has a multitude of avatars: "one with a shaven head, one with matted hair, one who is naked, or carries a parasol or a holy staff, one who wears ochre robes or covers his body with ashes" (1.63). The apotheosis of hypocrisy "carries sacred texts, *kuśa* grass, a water pot, a horn as crooked as his own heart, a holy man's staff, and he wears an antelope skin . . . his lips jabber prayers, his hand is braceleted with a rosary, and his eyes are closed in meditation" (1.68–70). "The cowl might make the monk," Northrop Frye observes, "if it were not for the satirist" ("The Nature of Satire"). Ashes might make the ascetic, a shaven head the mendicant, a sacred thread the brahmin.

The signs of religiosity always replace what they stand for in satire. "To make people have faith in you," according to Nīlakaṇṭha Dīkṣita, all you have to do is "have a rosary in your hand, shut your eyes every once in a while, and say 'All is *brahman*' " (*Kaliviḍambana* 90). These signs, religious symbols, enchant people, put them to sleep, and make them easy prey for the venerated thief:

"A double-quality of *tulsī* [the plant sacred to Viṣṇu, worshiped as a natural incarnation of his consort] was forgotten by Vāhata [Vāgbhaṭa, the compiler of an ancient medical text in which the medicinal properties of herbs are enumerated] when he listed its qualities: it deludes the world and it brings in cash" (85).

The objects of satire attempt to make the profane seem holy, and the satirist attempts to make the holy seem profane. Everything is the opposite of what it seems in satire. The world stands on its head. This topsy-turvydom, the absurd inversion of all values, is graphically suggested in a recurrent motif in modern Indian cartoons of the yogi (fig. 15). As up is down and down is up, so all norms, the sacred and the profane, virtue and vice, pleasure and

Figure 15

Figure 16

WILL YOU SHARPEN THE NAILS? I DID N'T
GET GOOD SLEEP LAST NIGHT.

pain, all the dualistic principles around which life in society is organized, are reversed. A yogi, taking his bed of nails to have the spikes sharpened, complains of not being able to sleep on dull nails (fig. 16). What looks like asceticism is suddenly exposed as a pursuit of comfort. Such reversal, a satiric device aimed at diminution, is often enhanced by a juxtaposition of the lofty and the mundane.

Religion, at its best and at its worst, is a dramatic art. It is make-believe. Sectarian marks and ashes are make-up; rosaries, staffs, and parasols are props; sacred threads, ochre robes, and loincloths are costumes; temples, shrines, and forest retreats are sets; scriptures are scripts. He is deemed most pious who is the most adept at putting on the show. If the act is sincere it can be a powerful ritual for the benefit of its audience. If not, it is still powerful, but the scam benefits only the actor. "He who can make himself have goose bumps or shed tears at will . . . has all the kings of the world as his slaves" (*Kaliviḍambana* 93). The satirist merely points out that the act is a comic play, that irreverent laughter is a more appropriate response, one that promises greater freedom, than solemn obeisance.

Reverence and faith render one vulnerable to the hypocrite. In a fable preserved in various Sanskrit collections, there is a wily cat who stands on the banks of the Ganges, holding its paws in zealous gestures and claiming to have purified its mind. The fame of the cat as an ascetic spread and soon a pack of mice came to it for refuge and teaching. Accepting them as disciples, the cat asked them to lead the way to a sacred spot for the performance of the holy rituals. Following behind them, the cat got fatter and fatter while the number of mice got smaller and smaller and smaller. Religious satire is a warning:

> Beware of piety, holiness, sanctity, and decorum:
> *Tantum religio potuit suadere malorum.*

A holy man, a brahmin ascetic in the *Śāradātilaka,* sneaked into the courtyard of the brothel, washed off his Vaiṣṇava sectarian markings with his own spit, took off his antelope skin, and put on the more worldly clothes that he had received as offerings. He hid his staff and water pot and concealed his sacred thread. Inner and outer never correspond in satire, one disguise replaces another. Dressed as an ascetic, the man had hidden his worldliness; clothed as a man of the world, the ascetic concealed his adopted religious station. The show is always the antithesis of the substance for which it is a substitute. The object of satire is always sneaking, always obscuring himself or some aspect of himself. Satire is a kind of literary game of hide-and-seek.

Having stashed away the emblems of asceticism, the holy man went into the brothel to make love to a harlot. The escapade was suddenly interrupted, however, by the arrival of the prostitute's patron, an officer in the king's army. Directing the holy ascetic to a niche in the wall, and placing an oil lamp on his head, the whore instructed him to stand very still. When the officer entered the room and inquired about the strange lamp, he was told that "it is just a statue, a lamp stand imported from a distant land" (*Śāradātilaka,* prose after 169). The inveterate poseur, in yet another attempt to hide, becomes an object, pure body devoid of spirit, a ridiculous thing, a piece of kitsch.

As he stood immobile in the niche, hot oil from the lamp began to drip down his face. As long as he attempted to conceal himself, he had to endure the pain, and to do so while watching the officer experience the pleasure that he had meant to have with the whore. It is an ironic image of satiric justice—the duplicitous bring their own punishment upon themselves. They deserve to be laughted at. Finally "that brahmin, that supreme ascetic, fearing that his real nature would be known, ran away, ran with the lamp still burning on his head" (prose after 169). The faster he ran, the brighter the lamp burned. In trying to escape, to conceal his actions, he appeared to be a goblin in the night. Outer appearance revealed inner nature at last. The goblin was caught and escaped execution only by confessing the truth. "Please don't tell this story anywhere," he begged, and he ran away "out of shame" (prose after 169). Satire is a comic mode for disclosures of truth. The satirist will lie to tell that truth. The satirist breaks his promise. He tells the whole story, and he makes it a funny story. Satire specializes in adding insult to injury.

The hypocrites of Indian satire fall into two categories: there are the brahmins, Buddhist and Jain monks, and Vaiṣṇava ascetics, those precisians who claim to live lives of purity, morality, and service; and there are the Tantrics, Kāpālikas, Bhairavas, and Pāśupatas, those who claim to have transcended morality and social values. They are satirical representatives of the puritanical and orgiastic excesses within Indian religious traditions, respectively. By making the excesses comical, satire limits their danger.

Brahmins are the most suspect of all, for satiric distrust is always directly proportional to the amount of power a particular person, group, or institution has, and in India the brahmin was (and is) revered by others, as well as by himself, as a human god, the very incarnation of the sacred. He was to be devoted to learning and the performance of rites. And he was, according to Manu, entitled to all and everything in the world by virtue of his high birth. The satirist inspects these custodians of the religious life. He breaks into their whited sepulchre to give us a whiff of the uncleanliness within.

Behind the Holy Thread: *Bathetic Brahmins*

All instances of the bathetic involve the reduction of some high ideal, some spiritual quality, some ineffable, to the level of the grossly substantial, the material solid thing. This materialistic drive toward the diminution of idea to thing is most obvious in the stock satiric character who substitutes some objective thing for a subjective reality: a pious expression, a cowl, folded hands, and frequent references to the Deity for true religion.

Alvin Kernan, *The Plot of Satire*

Manu, who did so much to institutionalize the ideal, also denounces its corruptions and perversions in brahmins who "neglect the study of the Veda, swerve from the rules of right conduct, and eat forbidden foods" (5.4). He warns against "the brahmin who acts like a heron—pretending to be kind when he is really dishonest and cruel, when he only wants to attain his own ends" (4.196).

In this age, the Age of Dullness, according to Kṛśānu, the cantankerous spirit of the *Viśvaguṇādarśa,* brahmins have ceased to perform the rites, ablutions, and sacrifices properly; they neglect the rules of caste purity; they are niggardly, dirty, venal, and ignorant. In Varanasi, the holiest of holy cities, the brahmin "washes, rinses his mouth, cooks his food, and anoints his icons with polluted water carried by pariahs; he eats leftovers without any revulsion, mixes with foreigners, and roams about the streets unconcerned about being touched by outcastes." The presentation of a total transposition of norms is the satiric strategy. Laughter is aroused by a revelation that the brahmin's behavior is exactly opposite of what it should be, of what it is expected to be. And the comic tone of the denunciation is reinforced with a pun. "The brahmin abandons the scriptures (*śāstra*) and lives by the sword (*śastra*)"—he abandons the Canon and shoots a cannon (*Viśvaguṇādarśa* 89).

Brahmins, the traditional purveyors of the sacred rites, invested with insuring the order and purity of the world through those rites, are satirically portrayed as corrupt. "If there are a lot of people around, the daily ritual lasts a long time," Nīlakaṇṭha Dīkṣita smirks, "but if no one is there, it is quite brief" (*Kaliviḍambana* 92). They perform their function for the impression it makes, for the gifts it brings in, and for the prestige which it affords them. As a result, the rituals have degenerated and the idealized learning of brahmins has become a mere cover for folly and ignorance.

Satirical reversal strips and exposes the most esteemed and honored figure in Indian society as pathetic and bathetic. A sadly ridiculous brahmin is encountered in the street. His wife has cuckolded him and thrown him out of his own house:

Oh, here comes a brahmin, a priestly reciter:
His hair looks like dry weeds, only much whiter;

His crooked teeth are all jagged, like broken glass;
Both his armpits are stuffed with liturgical grass;
The skin on his forehead is acned and warted,
Thus his sectarian mark looks very distorted;
With his one spotted eye he can't see very much;
One leg is missing and so he walks with a crutch;
His clothes are all baggy, all crumpled and crimpled;
His body is pustuled, is pocked and is pimpled;
And swollen big as two pumpkins his balls appear;
But he's got a chart for the holy days of the year.

(*Śāradātilaka* 82)

The brahmin ritual priest in the *Padmaprābhṛtaka* of Śūdraka (c. sixth century), "an impure man who has created a reputation of purity" (prose after 18), has a name, Mr. Strainer (Pavitraka), that reveals his nature—he is like a strainer, a sieve that, in being used for purifying, holds within itself all the impurities of that which passes through it.

The brahminness of these idiots is something else again!
They break vows of silence to mutter mantras and say "amen."
During the sacred rites they jabber with words that are profane,
And all their time is spent calculating fiscal loss and gain.

(*Subhāṣitaratnabhāṇḍāgāra* 99.22)

Brahmins, whose duty it was to be versed in the sacred literature, to attend to the sacred fire, and to preserve all sacred institutions, were, in return for those hallowed services, to be supported and maintained. They were fed. The traditional, institutionalized supposition was that there were two sorts of deities: divine deities, the gods; and human deities, the brahmins. Religious practice consisted of giving oblations to the gods and food to the brahmins. Feeding brahmins became a social obligation and religious ritual which accorded merit to the donor. A suspicious vision of brahmins, a satirical portrait of them as gut-gorging, edacious freeloaders, was perhaps inevitable in a culture that idealized them and sanctified the act of giving them gifts, particularly offerings of food. Satire warns that the hallowed guest may well be a crapulous sponger, that high birth may be flaunted as a means of legitimating and justifying the lowest, most piggish impulses and crudest hungers. The brahmins of satire are foolish, corrupt, venal, and lusty. But above all else they are hungry.

Ineffable Gluttony

Belly is God. They wear their brains in their bellies, and their guts in their heads . . . they eat till they burst: all day, all night. . . . Sea, Land, Rivers, Lakes, &c., may not give content to their raging guts.

Robert Burton, *The Anatomy of Melancholy*

The insatiability of brahmins, the most holy of men in the Indian social and spiritual hierarchy, is an ancient motif. According to the *Jātaka*s, there are four things which can never be sated: "the ocean, kings, women, and brahmins" (*Kuṇāla Jātaka* [536]). This Buddhist literature describes them feeding off kings and householders, "benefactors whom these faithless, ungrateful brahmins readily betray" (*Khaṇḍahāla Jātaka* [542]). It is most often the oral manifestation of brahminical insatiability, their intractable gluttony, that is the focus of satiric critique. A famous and surprising passage in the *Aitareya Brāhmaṇa* describes them as "gift getters, soma drinkers, food gobblers, to be tossed out at will" (7.29). And brahmin ritual priests are compared, seemingly satirically, to hungry dogs in the *Upaniṣads*. "Just as the Vedic priests walk joined together as they chant hymns of praise . . . so the dogs trot along together, sit down, and bark '*hiṃ,*' [and they howl:] '*Auṃ!* Let's eat! *Auṃ!* Lets drink! *Auṃ!* Let the gods Varuṇa, Prajāpati, and Savitṛ feed us! Lord of food, bring our food! Bring it here! *Auṃ!*" (*Chāndogya Upaniṣad* 1.13.4–5).

The immodest gourmandism of battened brahmins became a stock joke in Sanskrit drama. Brahmin *vidūṣakas* are lured, bribed, and manipulated with gifts of food. Their speech is heavily seasoned with references to, comparisons with, and suggestions of, food, particularly sweet foods. Reciting a paean to a beautiful woman, a jester delineates her charms, her courtesy and comeliness, her utter lack of vanity and anger. The rhetoric begins to soar; the erotic mood, the amorous sentiment, begins to be manifest. Then suddenly there is bathos, a satiric tactic to undermine and pervert the mood, turn it comic, bring it back to earth with laughter. "Above all else, she always greets me with scrumptious goodies" (*Svapnavāsavadatta,* prose after 2.2).

In another play by the same author, Bhāsa, a maid tells a jester that she must find a brahmin. "Why?" he asks, "what business do *you* have with a brahmin?" "Oh, nothing," she reacts coyly, "it's just that, well, I want to invite one to a feast." The brahmin jumps for the food. "Well, Madam, what do you think *I* am, some sort of mendicant?" (*Avimāraka,* act 2, opening interlude).

Two things, according to a stanza attributed to the poet Vāgura, really worry a brahmin: "how to get the funeral offerings of rich people and how slippery the road to their homes will be" (*Subhāṣitaratnakoṣa* 11.27). He is in such a hurry to consume the offerings that he fears the muddy road will slow him down. The satirist insinuates that if the brahmin were to follow his true impulses he would slip, take a comic pratfall into the muck. The poem reveals the potential muddiness of what is esteemed for its purity. It suggests, furthermore, a dark side of the comic gluttony of brahmins. Fear is embedded in craving. The appetites of brahmins are grotesque. They grow fat on the food of the dead. They devour the rice balls at funerals with the voraciousness of vultures and jackals.

Fatness can be humorous as well as satirical, a manifestation of jollity and sweetness, of an infantile cheeriness, zestiness, or simplicity. The roly-poly, pursy fool is endearingly humorous as long as he admits, as the jester in Sanskrit classical drama usually does, to his appetites. Folly confessed or displayed is folly absolved. In humor, laughter is acceptance and acquittal. But folly denied or hidden is a crime committed. Vāgura's brahmin tries to conceal his base appetites under an illusion that he is concerned with funerary rites. His socially established religious function gives him a cover for his crime. Satire is detective work and its laughter is punishment.

Depictions of the excessive corpulence of brahmins is a satiric maneuver to emphasize a comic contradiction between what such signs as the sacred thread declare them to be by birth, and what they have become since birth. But the obesity of the brahmin is not necessarily a sign of insatiability or greed. It can be a symptom of his grandeur. An Indian art historian, himself a somewhat portly brahmin, explained that a Pahari rendering of a fat brahmin which I had perceived to be a satirical caricature was in fact a very respectful portrait. "The man is fat because he has received offerings, and he has received offerings because he is a holy one, a brahmin, a god in a human body." "But," I asked, "couldn't the obesity announce that the brahmin's motives are not spiritual, that he is more animal than god, and that his fat human body bears witness to that?" "No," the brahmin answered, "he's a brahmin."

His insistence had a point. He smiled. "This is why you should not write your book on Indian humor. It is impossible for a man to understand the humor of another country. What you think is funny is not necessarily considered humorous in other cultures. And vice versa. To you this man looks funny. To me this man looks holy. What looks holy to you may look very funny to me. I think nuns look quite comical and so do those rabbis with the long curls. When I first came to America I saw a movie of Laurel and Hardy. Which is the fat one? Hardy? Yes? Well, you think this fat fellow with a Hitler moustache is funny. I watched the two of them trying to carry a piano up some stairs and each time they would almost get to the top of the stairs something would happen and the piano would slip and roll back down the stairs. Again and again they tried. And again and again the piano rolled back down the stairs. The fat man blamed the thin man. He was angry and the more angry he got, the more he seemed to get hurt. Things fell on him, and he even stepped on a nail, and all sorts of things like that. It was really quite horrible. And the worse things got for those two fools, the more people in the audience were laughing. They laughed when the fat one was angry. They laughed when he was hurt. They laughed to see him fail. 'Why?' I wondered, and I still do not know. It was the saddest movie I had ever seen, and there was nothing to redeem the sorrow. And the saddest thing of all was that this movie seemed to be suggesting that the harder a person tries to do something, the more he is destined to fail. It is not funny to suggest such a thing. It is even immoral. There was no hope for these fellows. You laugh at this spectacle of human failure. In India this would not be a comedy. I cannot understand your humor and I admit it. So why do you want to pretend to understand ours? Let's face it, all jokes are 'in-jokes.' Your study is an invasion of privacy. It could be offensive."

He laughed and, despite all cultural differences, I knew why—he thought he had me. He thought he had placed a banana peel on the steps beneath me, and he laughed to see me watch my assumptions about Indian humor and satire roll down the stairs. And I was as flustered with angry impatience as Hardy ever was. "This is rubbish. Why are you saying this to me? First of all you can understand Laurel and Hardy—they are just like Bhṛṅgī and Kuṣmāṇḍa, the thin and fat Gaṇas. The incongruous juxtaposition of the two establishes a comic matrix in which laughter is generated by the occurrence of ludicrous things. Second, Laurel and Hardy are funny because they are sad—comedy and tragedy are inextricably linked and you know it.''

''I know it is so in the West,'' he smiled with the proud grin of conviction, the smirk of an infuriating self-assuredness.

But I persisted. ''While I would admit that some of the specifics which trigger laughter are culturally relative, I simply can't accept the notion that the dynamics of comedy, what goes on behind the specifics, differ from time to time and place to place. And many of the specifics are the same. The fat man is one. Do you know the cartoons of Deviprasad, the Bengali artist? He did a cartoon of a fat brahmin who has become addicted to cod-liver oil, an image quite similar to the Pahari one. His sacred thread, rosary, sectarian marks, and pious expression, the outward signs of religiosity, have taken the place of what they are to stand for, internal convictions and sentiments. This supplantation of signs for what once was, or is now supposed to be, signifies what the satirist attacks as hypocrisy. There is nothing ambiguous about the cartoon—we are supposed to laugh at the man. He is fat and that fatness makes him look ridiculous and that helps to elicit our critical laughter. This is a cartoon by an Indian for Indians and yet I can understand it. Any Westerner can understand it. Have you read Nirad Chaudhuri's book on Hinduism? Do you remember how he describes the feasting of brahmins in Bengal and how he recounts from his childhood that some of the brahmins at those ceremonial rites of gluttony ate so much that they could not stand up after the meals? He tells a joke about it. A *joke:* There was a brahmin who had attended a feast where he ate so much that he could not walk back to his village. But since the feast had been given on the banks of the same river by which the brahmin lived, it seemed a clever idea to just put the brahmin in the river and let him float home. Drifting along with the current of the river, he happened to bump into the body of a dead cow. Reaching over and patting the carcass, he asked, 'Were you at the feast too?' ''

The brahmin did not laugh. I tried to fill the abysmal silence, the empty space after the joke that had been reserved for laughter, with an elaboration of my defense. ''All the references within this joke are to things peculiarly Indian, and yet any Westerner can get the joke and even laugh at it. There is something astonishingly universal about humor. I've been reading Indian comic literature for a while now, and I've laughed plenty of times. When I was studying Sanskrit love poetry, I don't think it ever aroused me, but

I've laughed lots at things in the farces, and I think Kṣemendra is very, very funny. I rank him with Jonathan Swift."

Now the brahmin laughed. "Lee, why are you so angry? Where's your sense of humor? I was just teasing you. But, now that you have said what you said, it is interesting to wonder if you have been laughing at the right places, and it is intriguing to note that you need to invoke Jonathan Swift in order to appreciate Kṣemendra. This is the problem that you are having: you look at this portrait of a stocky *sādhu* and you assume that his stockiness is funny. But do you know what the word for 'heavy' is in Sanskrit? It is *guru*. What you call 'fat,' I call 'venerable.' What you must realize is that it is not weight that is funny. And surely hunger is not funny. It is serious. It can be tragic for us in India, although I suspect that it might be difficult for most Americans to understand. Someone who has enough food and still craves for more is a bad person, a decadent person. In India when we meet such a person we say, '*Pahle pet puja phir kam duja*!' This is a very funny thing to say. What is funny is not the fat or hungry person per se. What is funny is what we say about this or that person, what we say and how and when we say it, how it sounds. Humor cannot be translated, so when I tell you what it means in English, you will not laugh. 'First worship your belly, then do anything else you like.' See, you did not laugh. Humor cannot be translated. This will be the major problem with your work. I liked your book on love. Love is universal as Freud has shown. Our thoughts about love can be translated. But not humor. All people of taste, Westerners as well as Indians, can appreciate *Śakuntala*. Goethe made that clear. And the *Kāmasūtra* is a universal book which every Westerner can appreciate and perhaps even learn from. I think you should give up this humor project and keep writing about sacred and profane love."

Sacred and Profane Love

A brahmin is a kind of bucking bull that is very mean and dangerous. Now cowboys ride them in rodeos. But brahmins used to be worshipped in India. People like to worship lingas (i.e., penises) in India. They probably worshipped brahmins because they have big lingas.

Student answer to an examination question on Indian Religions, University of Hawaii

In the *Āpastambadharmasūtra* the brahmin specialist in the Veda is compared to a goat, "the most horny of all creatures" (11.14.13). A brahminical reputation for lust provided grounds for comic derision in the Sanskrit farces. A brahmin named Reverend Loveblind (Madanāndhamiśra), whose "sacred thread is red with cosmetics from the bodies of whores" (*Hāsyāraṇava* 2.5), takes a harlot offstage, makes love to her, and returns to find other brahmins anxious to perform the sacred ritual. In a parody of piety, one of them explains that he is obliged to conduct the holy rites for himself. "How can I be made pure by the sacred activities of another?" (2.16). A significant theological question becomes a joke. Such blasphemy often leads to hell; in satire it is the hell of being laughed at.

Satiric laughter at prurient brahmins is not at their lust as such, but at their vain efforts to present their lechery as legitimate, religious, and proper, their empty attempts to pass the profane off as the sacred. The malevolent Kṛśānu assaults temple priests for debaucheries practiced under the protection of holy office. "They make offerings with hands that have pressed the breasts of whores, and they make recitations with mouths stained with betel juice" (*Viśvaguṇādarśa* 466).

The parasite in the *Śāradātilaka* encounters a brahmin holy man, Vedadhvaja ("he who pretends to know the Veda"), who has been seduced by a prostitute on his way to perform the sacrifices. The parasite/satirist ironically compliments him for his lack of hypocrisy—unlike most brahmin ascetics, who refrain from intercourse with earthly women so that they can make love to the more spendid courtesans of heaven, Vedadhvaja is openly depraved (prose after 93).

When brahmins try to seem sacredly chaste, they are exposed as being profanely salacious. But when they try to be husbands or lovers, they are exposed as sexually inept or ineffectual, chaste against their own will, profanely chaste. "Like death dressed up as a lover," a whore tells her friends, "some stupid brahmin tried to make it with me last night—he was totally inexperienced with women, he was inept, childish, and stiff only with fatigue" (*Kuṭṭanīmata* 392).

Brahmins make lousy lovers. They are cuckolds in comedy. It is their wives who are sexually ravenous, and their preoccupation with their own sanctity, if not with getting food, makes them unaware that their wives have other lovers. A parasite/satirist encounters a married brahmin woman by a well and tells her that he is thirsty, that he would like to drink from her "two jugs" (*Śāradātilaka,* prose after 172). Through punning the two carry on a private conversation in public—the parasite can indicate that he wants to kiss the woman's breasts by saying that he thirsts to drink from her pitchers. The puns draw comic attention to the divisions between inner and outer, private and public, truth and pretense. Language, our means of revealing ourselves, becomes another concealment, the essential crime of satire committed again.

Another brahmin wife tries to seduce the parasite/satirist even though she is menstruating, something which would normally forbid sexual intercourse. "He who rejects a woman just because she's on the rag," the highborn slut whispers with a lewd leer, "may look like a man but he's really an ape" (*Śāradātilaka* 98). The menstrual image suggests the secret and yet universal and natural pollution which satire seeks to expose.

Satire is perverse. Its depictions of brahmin women in eternally raging heat, of brahmin men, lusting or cuckolded, of rampant affectation, corruption, and hypocrisy, do not necessarily reflect external social realities. The opposite may be so—the more straight-laced, pious, and sober a group is, the more likely that its members will be caricatured as debauched, hypocritical, and silly. Satire does not care about being fair, just, or honest. It exaggerates, distorts, and overstates, all and just for the sake of laughter. The appeal of the satirical image of the depraved brahmin is the appeal of the dirty joke about the prude or spinster, the vicar, minister, or puritan. The joke is funny because it is surprising, because it bursts bubbles of expectation. Our laughter expresses the pleasure of a reassuring perception that the pure are as impure as ourselves. It is the pleasure of Kāma, the divinity or urge that makes fools of men and gods.

Revered Folly

> The author, indeed, by no means considers ridicule as a proper test of religious opinions. . . . the work is so far from ridiculing religion . . . it has [rather] a direct tendency to prevent religion from becoming ridiculous by [showing] the absurd conduct of such irregular teachers [of religion].
>
> Richard Graves, "Apology" to *The Spiritual Don Quixote*

Because the brahmin was venerated for his knowledge, his wisdom as well as his learning, satire, for the sake of laughter, displays his ignorance, his folly as well as his stupidity. The foolish brahmin is a stock character in Sanskrit narrative and dramatic comedy. The doltishness of brahmins provides the comic flavor in classical Sanskrit drama when the brahmin *vidūṣaka* attempts to display the intelligence and learning attributed to his caste. The more sagacious he tries to appear, the more his stupidity becomes apparent. The brahmin jester in the *Priyadarśikā* of King Harṣa tells his king of the many venerable brahmins in the palace, "brahmins who know four Vedas, five Vedas, even six Vedas!" The brahmin exposes his own ignorance of the fact that there are only four Vedas, and the king laughs at him. "So the quality of a brahmin is to be reckoned by the number of Vedas which he knows? Well then, come along, O great brahmin!" (opening of act 2).

The foolish brahmin is a conventional figure in folk literature. Once upon a time some thieves, spotting a brahmin carrying a goat on his shoulders, decided to get that brahmin's goat. One rushed up to him and asked him why he was carrying that "dog" on his shoulders. Imagining that the man was a fool for mistaking the goat for a dog, the brahmin shunned him. The fools of satire always attribute folly to others. Another rogue approached the brahmin and asked why he was wearing a sacred thread like a brahmin and yet carrying a dog like an outcaste hunter. Again the brahmin was astounded by such apparent idiocy and delusion, but when another, and another, and another, asked the brahmin why he was carrying the "dog," the brahmin suddenly cast the "vile dog" down and ran to take a bath. The thieves then ate the goat (*Kathāsaritsāgara* 62.62–69).

Similar stories making fun of the intellectual ineptitude of brahmins abound, as one might expect, in Buddhist texts. A brahmin complained to the Buddha: "A number of Śākyas were making merry and joking together, nudging one another with their fingers; I believe that I was the subject of their jokes" (*Dīgha Nikāya* 1.3 [*Ambaṭṭhasutta*].13). He was, no doubt, quite right. Buddhist jokes about stupid brahmins are preserved in their folk literature. A brahmin, given a horse caparisoned with a fine saddle and harness, rode the animal home and bragged to his wife of the praise that his horse had received from the people in the street. "You fool," the wife scoffed, "it is not the horse that is beautiful, but the tack. If you would put the saddle and bridle on yourself and go trotting along like a horse through the streets, the king and all the people would praise your beauty and greatness." The brahmin did as his wife suggested. The people in the streets laughed at him and his king thought he had gone mad (*Ruhaka Jātaka* [191]). Again the butt of satirical attack attempts to make his attire actually be, rather than merely represent, some quality or virtue. The attack is comic—Bharata indicated that inappropriate dress or ornaments engenders laughter.

Buddhist satires of brahmins illuminate the falseness of the front established by the brahminical reputation for erudition. The learned man who boasts of his knowledge is simply conceited; but the ignoramus who boasts of his wisdom is ridiculous. While the pomposity of the former is reprehensible, that of the latter is laughable. The brahmin, through Buddhist eyes, eyes squinting with derisive laughter, is a fool who, despite his folly, vainly persists in haughtiness, pride, and self-satisfaction. Satiric laughter equalizes. Buddhist texts utilize it to show that brahmins are no more wise, virtuous, or pure than anyone else.

Two brahmins, Vasiṭṭha and Bhāradvāja, seeking refuge in the Buddha, complained to him that they were reviled by other brahmins. "The brahmins say that only brahmins are pure. . . . Only brahmins are truly the children of Brahmā, born from his mouth, created by Brahmā as his only progeny and heirs."

"Surely the brahmins have forgotten their own past when they make such claims," the Buddha responded. "Brahmin women ovulate, get pregnant, bear and nurse children. . . . Brahmins are born from the womb like everyone else though they claim that they are the children of Brahmā, born from his mouth, created by Brahmā as his only progeny and heirs. They make a joke of Brahmā with such claims" (*Dīgha Nikāya* 3.27 [*Ajjaññasutta*].4). The commentary of Buddhaghoṣa (c. fifth century C.E.) explains that they make a "joke of Brahmā" in that their claim that they are born from "Brahmā's mouth" is an assertion that "the mouth of Brahmā is a brahmin woman's cunt" (*Sumaṅgalavilāsini* 3.862).

The Buddha compares brahmins to dogs. Once upon a time brahmins were as virtuous and pure as dogs, but now they are inferior to them. "It used to be that brahmins only copulated with brahmin women, now they copulate with both brahmin and non-brahmin women. Dogs still copulate with dogs, and never with other species" (*Majjhima Nikāya* 2.93 [*Assalāyasutta*]).

The presumptuous priggishness and vainglory of brahmins are characterized in another Buddhist text by their tedious loquacity. King Brahmadatta of Varanasi, plagued by the incessant gassy prating of his family priest, summoned a cripple from the town, one who had a reputation for being an ace marksman with his peashooter. As the brahmin began to speak, to babble and gabble on and on and on, the cripple, hiding behind a curtain in the court, began "to fire little goat turds, one by one, into the mouth of the brahmin priest who, without noticing, swallowed every one of them." The brahmin's stomach became swollen. The king, informing him that he had swallowed a blowgun magazine full of goat pellets (a euphemistic way of saying, "you're full of goat shit!"), suggested that the garrulous brahmin take an emetic (*Sālittaka Jātaka* [107]). Scatology, degradation, and reversal (the image of feces eaten and then vomited) elicit both judgmental laughter, laughter at the story, and punitive laughter, the laughter in the story. The laughter in the fictional court, like the king's laughter at his brahmin jester in the play, prompts and encourages the laughter of the reader of the story or the audience of the drama. The laughter in the court is at a particular, imaginary brahmin. The laughter in the theater or over the story is at a potential trait in all actual brahmins.

The foolishness of brahmins and the foolishness of their religion is indicated in Jain as well as Buddhist texts. A mendicant in the *Dharmaparīkṣā* of Amitagati (eleventh century) meets some brahmins who ask him how he became a monk. He explains that once, in his childhood, he had been sent to fetch some water. On his way to the well he was attacked by an elephant and had to jump for refuge into the little water pot that he was carrying. The elephant followed him into the jug and tore off his clothes with its trunk. Fortunately he was able to escape through the spout of the vessel and find protection in a Jain monastery. He was already wearing the traditional garb of a Jain mendicant—nothing. Thus he became a monk. When the brahmins laugh at him, calling him a fool and a liar, he counters that it should be obvious to them, based on the authority of their own scriptures, that he is truthful and faithful. Since, according to their own sacred literature, it was possible for the sage Agastya to drink the ocean and hang his water pot, with the entire universe within it, on a branch, surely it must be possible for an elephant to follow a boy into a jug. The brahmins must either accept the Jain's story as plausible or openly admit the absurdity and non-sensicality of their revered Epics and *Purāṇa*s (*Dharmaparīkṣā* 3).

Similarly in the *Dhūrtākhyāna* of Haribhadrasūri (tenth century), a female crook claims: "while I was dozing on my veranda one day after my bath, the passionate wind came and made love to me. Right then and there I gave birth to a son. As soon as he was born, the boy wandered off somewhere'' (5.8–10). The credibility of this is demonstrated with citations from the *Mahābhārata* and the *Rāmāyaṇa:* the wind is said to have fathered both Hanumān and Bhīma; and Vyāsa, it is claimed, walked away from his mother immediately after birth. Haribhadrasūri, bringing logic to bear on what is maintained through faith alone, satirically denounces Hindu mythology as irrational nonsense, as worthless as ''fool's gold'' (5.119).

But brahmins had their revenge on the Buddhists and Jains. It was in satire. He who laughs last, laughs best.

Under the Ochre Robe: *Buddhist Bunko*

If a satirist presents a clergyman . . . as a fool or a hypocrite, he is primarily attacking neither the man nor his church. The former is too petty and the latter carries him outside the range of satire. He is attacking an evil man protected by the prestige of an institution. As such, he represents one of the stumbling-blocks in society which it is the satirist's business to clear out.

Northrop Frye, ''The Nature of Satire''

The Buddhist monk, the Buddha solemnly instructed, ''must refrain from dancing and from singing, from attending concerts or theatrical shows'' (*Dīgha Nikāya* 1.1 [*Brahmajālasutta*].10). This injunction, this condemnation of the frivolities of the stage, would seem to have prompted retaliation from playwrights and audiences in ancient India no less than the Puritan's censure of the theater seems to have made the Puritan a conventional butt of English theatrical satire in the sixteenth and seventeenth centuries. There was always the insinuation that under the starched cover of piety and denial, Puritans indulged in excesses of the very acts which they denounced for others. Buddhists and Jains in India, like Puritans and Methodists in England, were necessarily guilty—either they were prudes or, if not, they were hypocrites. The satirist himself may be a drunk or lecher or thief; his attack is not on lust or any other vice unless it is hidden by sanctimony or self-righteousness. Satire questions all claims to moral excellence, all straight faces. The more rigidly moral or serious a person or institution is, the greater the potential for teasing, and the greater the pleasure for the teaser, the satirist and his audience. The more ticklish someone is, the greater the fun it is to tickle them. And if that person is normally serious, sober, and controlled, the fun can be exquisite. Religious satire abounds precisely because religious people do not like it. In his preface to *Tartuffe,* Molière pointed out that when he satirized "noblemen, ladies of fashion, cuckolds and doctors . . . they, along with everyone else, seemed to enjoy the portraits of themselves. But [religious] hypocrites never tolerate teasing; they become immediately incensed." The Buddhist was very puritanical, serious, and ticklish, very ripe for satire, a pleasure to incense.

The minimal moral obligation for all Buddhists, monk and layman alike, was a complete abstinence from killing, lying, stealing, indulging in intoxicants or in any form of sexual incontinence (which for the monk meant any sexual thought, action, or feeling). The monk, as one who had supposedly renounced the pleasures and comforts of a worldly life, bore the responsibility of exemplifying the ideal mode of enacting the teaching of the Buddha—he was, in addition to the five universal abstentions, to abstain from accepting money, sleeping on a high or wide bed, wearing flowers or ornaments, enjoying music or theatrical shows, and he was restricted to one meal a day, to be taken before noon. Inverting the ideal, the Sanskrit satirist portrays the Buddhist monk as a carnivorous drunkard, a lecherous thief, a brawling gambler, whose degeneracies are either hypocritically hidden or openly flaunted. The Buddhist monk became a standard and highly conventionalized character in Indian satire. He was the perfect personification of Pecksniffian prudery and religious silliness.

The traditional Indian classification of laughter into two modes, laughter at oneself (the laughter of humor) and laughter at another (the laughter of satire), was illustrated by the scholiast Dhanika (c. tenth century) with literary extracts and, as an example of "laughter at another," he cites an anonymous poem in which a degenerate Buddhist monk is typically the object of the aggressive, satiric laughter.

> O most venerable monk with a fondness for meat,
> Don't you like wine with the delicious food that you eat?
> And what goes better with wine than a loving coquette?
> But whores like money and what can a Buddhist monk net?
> Where do you get your riches, where do you come by wealth?
> By gambling or by thieving or by what acts of stealth?

Sir, you are depraved, and that is really appalling—
Tell me, what other practices make up your calling?
(commentary on *Daśarūpaka* 4.76)

In a similar stanza a Buddhist monk, asked a rather innocent question, reveals his true nature. The rhetorical structure of the poem seems to parody Buddhist dialectics and the philosophy of causation. "Why," he is asked, are his "robes so long and so loose?"

"Because I use them as a net for the catching of fish."
"You eat fish?"
"Yes, for fish with my liquor is a most savory dish."
"You drink booze?"
"Yes, but just when I'm out with whores pursuing my pleasure."
"You go to whores?"
"Yes, after thrashing my enemies, just for good measure."
"You have enemies?"
"Yes, but only those whose homes I have robbed of their treasure."
"You steal?"
"Yes, to pay off the debts I've incurred with my gambling itch."
"You gamble?"
"Yes, yes, yes! I am, as you see, a real son of a bitch."
(*Subhāṣitāvali* 2402)

The poem is comic, is ludicrous to the degree that actuality contradicts expectation, that each successive line surprises.

The narrator of Śūdraka's *Padmaprābhṛtaka,* the *persona* of the satirist, observes that the Buddha's teaching must be great since it remains untainted in spite of so many depraved and debauched monks, "just as water in a holy river remains pure despite the crows" (prose after 23). It is not religion as such that is being mocked and derided by satire, but all the crow shit that has been consecrated in the whited sanctuaries of creed and faith.

The Precept about Sexual Incontinence

If it were proper for me to unmask them as completely as they deserve, I'd show many a credulous fool what it is these fine friars really hide under their tremendously wide gowns.

Boccaccio, *Decameron*

The Buddha enjoined monks to observe strict chastity. "Putting away inchastity, the man of good conduct lives a life of celibacy and purity, averse to the base practices of sexual intercourse" (*Dīgha Nikāya* 1.1 [*Brahmajālasutta*].8). Kāma was known in Buddhist mythology as Māra—the god who is sexual desire was called Death. Love is death. "Dig up the root of thirst," the unlaughing Buddha warned, "that Māra may not destroy you again and again" (*Dhammapada* 338). Kāma/Māra triumphs over heaven and earth. That, according to the Buddha, is our plight, the essence of the human tragedy. But, according to the satirist, Kāma's dominion can also be a source for our delight, our encounter with the essence of a human comedy. And Māra, no less than Kāma, death no less than love, laughs brazenly at us, and at the defenses of religion.

"How," Ānanda asked the Buddha, "are we to conduct ourselves with regard to women?" "Don't look at them Ānanda." "But what if we have to look at them [while collecting alms]?" "Don't speak to them." "But what if they speak to us?" "Then keep your thoughts controlled!" (*Dīgha Nikāya* 2.16 [*Mahāparinibbāṇasutta*].5.9). So much for the precept. Satire watches the practice. Enter the Buddhist monk, the Venerable Mine-o'-Vices (Vyasanākara). He looks around and, seeing no one, he soliloquizes: "O crap! Damn! Without my washerwoman, the one with the beautiful big ass, this place looks tonight like a place where some buried treasure's been dug up and swiped." He sings:

> Like sacred vessels for Love's initiation rite
>   are the breasts, so lovely as they swell,
> Held together by her hand, O creeper of delight!
>   Ah, whose suff'ring would they not dispel?
> Fair-browed women, experts in the amatory arts,
> Inspire joy and quell fevers in all loving hearts
> As they elicit love, and cause sweet ambrosial rains;
> But they are, at dawn, mere memories in our brains.
> We're overwhelmed by the stench of holy books so long,
> Stories telling us just what is right and what is wrong.
>
> (*Laṭakamelaka* 2.23–24)

A Buddhist monk, encountered as he emerges from a brothel, insists that he has been there in order to "comfort Miss Server-of-Monks (Saṅghadāsā) with the words of the Buddha—she is suffering from the death of her mother." It is insinuatingly ambiguous as to just what "to comfort" means, just as it is ambiguous as to just how the girl "serves" the brotherhood. The equivocality between the incongruous spheres of experience, the religious and the erotic, creates the comic tension. "You're quite a Buddha!" the narrator/satirist of the play laughs sarcastically as a way of saying, "You're in no way a Buddha." The rhetorical tension of sarcasm, the trope in which language means the opposite of what it says, parallels and enhances the larger dramatic tension of satire in which characters are the opposite of what they appear to be. The satirist exposes that contradiction. "A monk entering a whorehouse, on purpose or by mistake," the narrator/satirist jeers, "has no more glory than the *OṂ* on Dattaka's *Treatise on Erotics*" (*Padmaprābhṛtaka* 24). A little less literally:

> A monk who goes into a house of ill repute,
> by mistake, or on purpose, or just for the sport,
> Is no more holy or sacred or absolute
> than an Imprimatur on Kinsey's sex report.

The monk slinks off in embarrassment—the satirist has given us a peek under his robe.

"Monks," the Buddha announced with detachment, "a woman who is just walking by will stop to trap the heart of a man. And she'll also try to ensnare the heart of a man as she sits near, as she laughs, talks, or sings, as she weeps, even as she is sick or dying. One must rightly say, 'Woman is wholly a trap of Māra' " (*Aṅguttara Nikāya* 3.5[55]). The satirist's audience laughs at the sight of the monks in the booby trap, laughs like the woman of whom the Buddha speaks as they rush into it, laughs at the triumph of Kāma/Māra. Once trapped the monks extol the snare, admit to the pleasures that the audience of satire has not renounced.

Embracing the consort of a yogi, a Buddhist monk becomes convinced that sexual pleasure is the basis of, rather than an impediment to, *nirvāṇa*.

> So many times I've embraced buxom sluts with passion,
> Wrapping strong arms around 'em in an ardent fashion;
> But by all Buddhas I'll swear a hundred times, I will,
> That never have I experienced so great a thrill
> As when I held this yogi's girl in close, fervent hugs,
> My delighting hands upon her firm and swelling jugs.
>
> (*Prabodhacandrodaya* 3.18)

Monks swear by the Buddha and invoke his precepts to vindicate their depravity. One recites the "nectarous words of the Buddha" in a parody of Buddhist homilies. "With the divine eye I see the joy and sorrow of the world—all conditioned things are momentary; there is no permanent self; jealousy is an impurity of the mind. *Therefore:* one should not get jealous when a monk makes love to one's wife" (*Prabodhacandrodaya,* prose after 3.9).

When the Buddhist monk in a farce tries to help to her feet a yogi's consort who has fallen down, the yogi laughs. "He claims to be a monk, but he's 'taking the hand' of my beloved!" (*Mattavilāsa,* prose after 13). As in English the phrase "take the hand of" means to "marry" in Sanskrit. The monk counters with a pun of his own, a play on the literal and figurative sense of the word "fallen"—"It is our religion to be compassionate to those who have fallen." But the yogi insinuatingly points out that he, the yogi, fell first and the monk did not offer his hand to him. The monk's hidden attraction to the woman becomes comically clear to the audience when, at first sight of her, he says to himself "Wow! what a great body this lay sister has!" (prose after 11).

Beaten back by the Buddha, Kāma/Māra returns to retake possession of the world, and the community of monks is divided. As hypocrites they join his ranks or as prigs they flee in fear. In either case the god who is love and death laughs aloud.

Once upon a time a wandering Buddhist monk arrived at a merchant's house to receive alms. Seeing the merchant's beautiful daughter, he could not help, despite his vow of silence, but sigh with lust, "Aaaah! Oooooooh! Ummmmmm!" The gullible merchant asked the monk his reason for breaking his vow. Feigning concern for his benefactor, the monk explained that he had suddenly noticed an inauspicious mark on the girl's neck, a spot which enabled him to divine that the merchant's daughter was sure to bring ruin into any home in which she resided. The distressed merchant, putting his trust in the monk and giving him power over his household, asked the representative of the Buddha what could be done to avoid calamity. Trust, in satire, is always a folly. The monk advised the merchant to place his daughter in a basket and the basket in the Ganges so that he might be rid of her. The merchant complied. Before the monk could retrieve the basket, it was discovered by a handsome prince who released the girl and put the basket back in the river with a vicious monkey inside of it. The lusty mendicant, finally finding the basket, took it to the monastery.

He closed all the doors and windows so that the girl would not be able to escape, and so that no one would be able to hear her if she tried to scream or resist his advances. When he opened the basket the monkey jumped out, bit and scratched the monk, and tore off his nose and ears. The maimed and mutilated monk, once the object of veneration and possessor of power, became an object of ridicule and derision. A wicked monk was made to look ridiculous (*Bṛhatkathāmañjarī* 3.36ff.). Satire is hostile monkeyshine. The satirist, like the feral monkey, is at once funny and destructive, marking and mutilating the object of satire in such a way as to expose him and make him a butt of laughter.

A story from the Buddhist *Jātaka*s anticipated such satirical accusations. A corrupt ascetic, ever flaunting his piety and austerities by day, would enter the chambers of women at night. When he attempted to seduce the chief queen of the king of Varanasi in this way, the clever woman marked his body with lac so that he was recognized the next day. The king, concluding that all holy men were corrupt, had them banished from his kingdom. The Buddha-to-be then descended from the heavens to teach the king that there are good as well as bad ascetics and that veneration of the good and true would increase merit and lead to heaven (*Dhajaviheṭha Jātaka* [391]). The satirist frequently says the same thing. "Religion they tell us ought not to be ridiculed," Swift asserted with an apparently straight face, "and they tell us Truth, yet surely the Corruptions in it may; for we are taught by the tritest Maxim in the World, that Religion being the best of Things, its Corruptions are likely to be the worst" (*Tale of the Tub*). But the satiric apology is always tinged with irony. The satirist does ridicule religion for, as an institution, it offers perfect concealment to its own corruptions. Though the Buddha's counsel to the king of Varanasi may be true, the king still needs to distinguish between the pious and the corrupt. The satirist provides him with the skepticism that prompts him to look for such distinctions.

A Buddha is detached and passionless. These qualities, understood and idealized in a religious context as virtues, can be seen as vices in a more social or aesthetic context. Ideals are ever degraded by practitioners. The satirist exposes non-attachment as a consecrated mask used to hide emotional dullness and an insensitivity to human feeling and need. A Buddhist layman's name, Mr. Careless (Nirapekṣa), is said to "reveal his character." As a Buddhist term the word indicates a virtue, a lack of concern with mundane things. Through the satirical character to whom it is applied, however, the virtue becomes a vice, an expression of expedient heartlessness rather than spiritual accomplishment. Mr. Careless is one of the only Buddhists in the satirical literature who seems to have control over his sexual urges, who seems to have overcome lust—he has abandoned a girl he had seduced. Asked how he can so coldly neglect her, he recites the Buddha's precept against sexual incontinence (*Pādatāḍitaka,* prose after 63). The religious injunction is used merely for self-justification. Morality, a self-serving system, is the best guise for immorality.

Ironically the satirical portrayal of the excesses of Buddhist monks is an accurate representation of the practices of certain Buddhists. In the Tantric tradition, Buddhist initiates were led through antinomian rituals, the goal of which was the conquest not of desire, but of aversion. Ritual sexual union was accompanied by the ingestion of intoxicants, meat, and other normally polluting substances. The liturgical script, though deadly serious, reads like an obscene satire. A naked woman spreads her legs, points to her genitals, and asks the initiate, "Can you stand to consume my filth, my love, to eat my shit, to drink my piss, to suck the blood from my cunt?" And she is answered, "Of course. . . . I must practice devotion to women until I realize the very essence of enlightenment" (*Caṇḍamahāroṣaṇa Tantra* 3.81–82). In what sounds like a satirical parody, the text asserts that women are the Buddha, women are the Teaching, women are the Order. Reality never ceases to be more outrageous than art, nor funnier than comedy. It could well be a monk in a satirical farce speaking when the text explains that "there is no greater sin than renunciation and no greater merit than pleasure; thus one should concentrate on pleasure, the pleasure that arises out of desire" (6.183–184). The perverse statement can be either the revelation of one who has gone beyond good and evil, or the self-justification of one who is going nowhere. It is very serious or very funny. Comedy depends on context. The comic event cannot be comic unless it is, in some sense, real, unless it refers to reality. And yet if it becomes too real, if the limits of reference are obliterated, it can cease to be comic. It can become too terrifying, painful, and tragic then. On guard against that sorrow and that fear, comedy, like a stiff drink, provides protection from that reality.

The Precept about Intoxicants

After Ch'an there is drunkenness . . . with one cup all scheming is forgotten, with three cups we feel that the world is as we like it. . . . When you come across wine, do not avoid it, otherwise practice Ch'an; the two paths lead to the same goal.

Po Chui, "Poem to Yuan Chen"

For the sake of awakening, a complete sobriety in which there is no arousal or attachment, the Buddha forbade intoxicants for the monk and layman alike, warning all who sought liberation or merit that fermented drinks lead "to a loss of wealth and to an increase in bickering, vulnerability to disease, a bad reputation, immodest acts, and intellectual degeneration" (*Dīgha Nikāya* 3.31 [*Sigālovādasuttanta*].8). Against this moral principle, a satirical monk wonders how the Buddha, in his infinite compassion and wisdom, could have not recommended—let alone, forbidden—the enjoyment of both women and wine. "It must have been that those elders, the Sthavira monks, those lazy old fogies, just to spite us younger monks, out of envy, purged the precepts in favor of women and wine from the Buddhist scriptures." The satirist burlesques the disputes between the Mahāsaṅghikas and the Staviravādins over the authority of the *Pāli Canon,* a conflict which, in the beginning at least, centered around disagreements as to the true nature of the Buddha's disciplinary precepts. The farcical monk takes a vow, a parody of the Bodhisattva vow, to devote himself to compassionate service. "I shall perform a service to the brotherhood of monks by making known to the world the complete teaching of the Buddha!" (*Mattavilāsa,* prose after 11). He resolves to search for an uncorrupted text, an uncensored scripture which records the Buddha's injunctions in favor of the enjoyment of women and wine.

Offered liquor by a yogi, this monk wants to take it but hesitates and, reminding himself to himself that "others will see," he ostentatiously declines. "It is not proper for a Buddhist monk." The satiric inference is that public censure is the real and sole basis for Buddhist morality, that the monks one might observe to be pure are so only because they are being observed.

The yogi in the farce sees through the puritanical monk's show of abstention from intoxicants. "His speech, contradicting his desire, falters—he stutters and drools!" (*Mattavilāsa,* prose after 12).

Satire always stresses contradictions between word and will, behavior and desire, outer and inner. It is this contradiction that makes the monk stutter and drool, that makes him silly.

Repeatedly this Buddhist monk recites the five Buddhist precepts of conduct. In satire, precept does not direct or define practice—it takes the place of it. "Our moral precept is to abstain from stealing. Our moral precept is to abstain from lying. Our moral precept is to abstain from sexual incontinence. Our moral precept is to abstain from taking life. . . ." At this point the audience, expecting to hear an announcement of the moral precept to abstain from intoxicants, would be comically surprised to hear that missing injunction replaced with "Our moral precept is to abstain from eating at the wrong hour" (*Mattavilāsa,* prose after 14). The comic impact of this, stressing the monk's propensity for alcohol, and exposing his willingness to adapt the teaching to his own interests, would be the Indian equivalent of the effect of hearing a rabbi reciting the Ten Commandments and replacing "Thou shall not commit adultery" with "Thou shalt not eat ham, bacon, or pork."

I invited the brahmin art historian to meet me for a drink in the bar at my hotel in Delhi. "No, no," he laughed, "Indians aren't permitted to drink in bars." I didn't understand. "But there's no prohibition in Delhi. There are wine shops all over the place, with countless Indians lined up to make purchases." "Yes, yes," he laughed again, "we can buy and consume alcohol in Delhi, but we are not permitted to do it in public. It is the same with sex. It's not what you do that counts. It's not even what people think or know you do. It's what people see that matters."

"This idealization of teetotalism in India," I suggested to my friend over a glass of duty-free Johnnie Walker in my hotel room, "is really the Buddha's fault."

"No, no," he insisted, "it is not the fault of Buddha, but of the Muslims. Buddha was a happy fellow. He did not forbid drinking, but only getting drunk."

"Well, the two go together, don't they?" I asked. "I mean, how do you know, while you're drinking, when you're beginning to get drunk?"

"When you can no longer get up off the floor," my friend smiled and poured himself another tumbler full of scotch.

The Precept about Harm

The Puritan hated bear-baiting, not because it gave pain to the bear, but because it gave pleasure to the spectators.
Thomas Macaulay, *History of England*

Despite the moral obligation to refrain from harming any living being, an injunction which implied the virtues of vegetarianism, Buddhist monks were permitted to eat meat given to them in charity provided that the animal was not slaughtered particularly for them. That provision became a comical loophole—Indian satires invariably depict monks relishing meat and fish. A monk enters the stage, bowl in hand, praising the beneficence of the lay Buddhist merchant Mr. Moneygrubber (Dhanadāsa) who has given him a luscious offering of flesh. The monk extols His Lordship the Buddha who, he explains, out of highest compassion, instructed the community of monks to enjoy themselves. The monk expounds the puritanical Buddhist precepts for religious conduct in such a way that they become prescriptions for license and pleasure. He notes, for example, that the Buddha instructed monks to dwell in *prāsādas;* as a Buddhist term this refers to the living space in the monastery, but as a non-technical word it suggests a palatial mansion—the monk clearly prefers the latter connotation. The monastic injunction to discard worldly garments and ornaments and don the ochre robe of the order becomes, in the monk's words, an instruction to "wear soft garments" (*Mattavilāsa,* prose after 11). The prohibition against eating in the afternoon becomes an invitation to enjoy a hearty breakfast. A degenerate monk, in a great hurry to return to the monastery, hungrily explains that he must "avoid eating at the wrong time" (*Padmaprābhṛtaka* 24).

The precept against harming sentient beings is applied, first and foremost, to oneself. The Buddhist monks in Sanskrit satire are religiously concerned with their own non-harm, their own cherished comforts. A yogi's young sidekick, claiming to have been born into a family of brahmins ("illiterate but proud of being high-born"), explains the advantages and disadvantages of dedicating one's life to Buddhism. "I was hungry because we couldn't afford much food, so I converted to Buddhism since those sons of bitches get to eat every morning. But eating only once a day I still kept getting hungry. So I renounced Buddhism, tore up my robe and broke my alms bowl" (*Bhagavadajjukīya,* prose after 3). Another monk boasts of his good fortune in being a Buddhist—the brethren get to live "in beautiful chambers and they have soft beds and all the food they like, not to mention the merchants' wives" (*Prabodhacandrodaya* 3.9). Monks are thoroughly greedy. One (actually someone pretending to be a monk), asked to arbitrate between a madman and fool as to who is the rightful recipient of some sweets, spits on the delicacies so that he can have them for himself. "If you don't give them to me, I'll curse you" (*Pratijñayaugandharāyaṇa,* prose after 3.1). The monk or priest can invoke powers in either curses or blessings, and he uses people's belief in those powers to reinforce his authority and to cover his deceptions.

The Buddha had explained that "to make offerings to those who are free from desire will bring great rewards" (*Dhammapada* 359). The constant insinuation in anti-Buddhist satire, implicitly or explicitly, is that the Buddhist lack of desire is the mask for a greater desire. Any apparent chastity, continence, or morality is merely a ploy to gain those offerings, preferably consisting of wine and meat, "not to mention merchants' wives."

The Precept about Lying and Stealing

> The satirical writer believes that most people are purblind, insensitive, perhaps anesthetized by custom and dullness and resignation. He wishes to make them see the truth—at least that part of the truth which they habitually ignore.
>
> Gilbert Highet, *The Anatomy of Satire*

The yogi in the *Mattavilāsa,* having lost his begging bowl and suspecting that the Buddhist monk has stolen it, demands to look under the monk's robe, a suggestively obscene request. "Let's see what you're hiding with your hands beneath your robes." The yogi insists that the Buddha ordained the wearing of ample robes so that monks could conceal things. Thinking that he means the concealing of the nakedness of the body, the monk concurs, "That's true." The mad yogi then parodies the rhetoric of Buddhism. "That's the truth of concealment [i.e., common sense], I want the real truth" (*Mattavilāsa,* prose after 11). When the monk walks with his eyes averted, as monks were enjoined to do, the gesture of humility is perceived as an expression of sneakiness. When the monk invokes praises to the Buddha, the yogi corrects him: "You mean praise to Kharapata [the patron saint and tutelary deity of thieves]—the Buddha, as if he could fool the brahmins, compiled his sacred canon by stealing his ideas from our *Upaniṣads* and the *Mahābhārata*'' (12). The accusation of the Buddha is an accusation of the monk and of all monks. The Buddha was, after all, according to the yogi, the son of Māyā, the queen whose name means ''deceit.''

> You're the son of one, or so it seems to me,
> who hid mountains and earth and the oceans whole,
> Who, deluded, denied things that all can see,
> and yet you can't even hide a little bowl (13).

As proof that he has not stolen the yogi's bowl, the monk once again recites the moral precepts of Buddhism, as if the rule prevented the crime, as if there were no hypocrisy—the most hypocritical of all assertions. The repetition of the list parodies the rhetoric of Buddhist scholasticism, the tedious manner in which moral precepts and rules of conduct were listed and relisted, cited and recited. The satire is of religious lip service.

Finally, when the monk, to prove that he does not have or need the yogi's bowl, displays his own bowl, pointing out that it is a different color than the yogi's, the yogi argues that the proof is inconclusive since Buddhists are ''adept at changing *varṇas*''—the word means either ''color'' or ''caste'' (prose after 13).

The Buddhist rejection of caste distinctions, its insistence that people of any caste might achieve awakening or release, is exposed as an expression not of the Buddha's compassion, but of his duplicity. The assertion that the hierarchical social organization of Indian society did not reflect a spiritual hierarchy was clearly, in the face of Vedic norms, a dangerously socially disruptive tenet. Buddhism threatened to transfer power from the priestly caste supported by a ruling, aristocratic warrior caste, to the community of monks, supported by a merchant class, a bourgeoisie, bourgeois in the sense that the word suggests mediocrity, false respectability, and a concern with material interests.

A professor makes fun of a Buddhist monk. ''He listens and yet has no ears; he has been born and yet he has no birth.'' By way of puns on the words *śruti* and *jāti,* the statement also means, ''He listens and yet does not uphold the Veda; he has no caste and yet he claims to be highborn'' (*Laṭakamelaka* 2.26). The satirical insinuation is that Buddhists deny caste because they are low caste.

And the notion of the Buddha as a philosophical thief is concomitant with the satirical stereotype of Buddhist monks as actual thieves, a stereotype based on the fact that Buddhism allowed thieves, gamblers, and thugs (albeit reformed ones) into the order.

The argument over the begging bowl culminates in a brawl, a fight between the monk, the yogi, and the yogi's consort. It became a Buddhist tradition for monks to shave their heads, a ritualized gesture of egolessness, purification, and, presumably, desexualization. During the fracas, the yogi's wench tries to grab the monk by the hair and pull him to the ground. But since his head is shaved, she misses, and falls herself. "O venerable indeed is the wisdom of the Buddha," the monk cries out, "for the injunction of tonsure" (*Mattavilāsa,* prose after 13). A sacrament, an outward sign of a supposed inward grace, is reduced to a convenience. Religion makes physical objects or actions (such as tonsure) symbols of ineffable realities. Comedy makes the lofty things mere ciphers of the mundane. The spirit does not exist in comic satire. There is only gross and sluggish matter. The satirist relies on the fact that his audience will laugh when a solemn and consecrated idea becomes associated with a concrete and vulgar reality. The iconoclastic poet Saraha (c. eleventh century) notes with a satirical voice that "if having an absence of hair indicates spiritual perfection, then a girl's ass must have it" (*Dohākoṣa* 7). The holy order is made up of just so many girls' asses.

With the whore's failure to pulverize the Buddhist monk, the yogi himself begins to beat up the mendicant. *"Dukkham! Dukkham!"* the Buddhist cleric screeches as a common exclamation of pain. But this expression of discomfort is, as a technical term, the First Noble Truth of Buddhism. The supposedly profound ontological insight, the Buddha's essential understanding of existence, is depreciated with slapstick into a simple "Ouch! Ouch!" (*Mattavilāsa,* prose after 13).

This play on the double associations of various terms and phrases, emphasizing the gap and tension between the holy paradigm and the perversion of it in reality, is a recurrent diminutional device of satire. In various satires Buddhist monks, assaulted or detained by adversaries, call out "Release me! [i.e., let go of me]," and in each case the rejoinder is, "Your release [i.e., your spiritual liberation] will be difficult to attain" (*Padmaprābhṛtaka,* prose after 24; *Pādatāḍitaka,* prose after 61).

The conflict between the yogi and the monk in the *Mattavilāsa,* a comic enactment of a conflict between the orgiastic and the puritanical extremes within Indian religions, is ironically compared to the battle between Śiva and Arjuna, a struggle in which both combatants are virtuous and justified, in which both the god and hero honor each other. The conflict between the yogi and the Buddhist monk is a parody of heroic battle, a burlesque agon: Arjuna fights with Śiva to acquire the god's divine weapons; the monk and the yogi fight over a begging bowl. Satire always points to the decline of heroic ideals, the triumph of vulgar banalities, the permutation of mythos into bathos.

The Precept about the Precepts

> The duty of [satiric] comedy being the correction of men by entertaining them, I believe that, in the occupation in which I find myself, I could do no better than to attack the vices of my century by portraying them as ridiculous; and as hypocrisy is, without a doubt, the most flagrant, the most improper and dangerous of those vices, I felt, Sire, that I would be rendering a service to all honest people of your kingdom if I prepared a comedy which decried hypocrites, which placed in clear view all the studied poses of these people, the hidden rogueries of these counterfeiters in devotion.
>
> Molière, preface to *Tartuffe*

In various medieval hagiographies, legendary accounts of Hindu devotional saints, Buddhist monks figure as personifications of sacrilege, blasphemy, profanation, and atheism. Caitanya, the ecstatic proponent and exemplar of a religion of passionate love for Kṛṣṇa, entered into debate with Buddhist monks and outwitted them: "Everyone began to laugh at the Buddhists" (*Caitanyacaritāmṛta* 2.9.51). In anger, wanting revenge for being made to appear ridiculous and laughable, the monks plotted to humiliate Caitanya. They offered him polluted food, telling him that it was food that had been offered to Kṛṣṇa. But before Caitanya could eat the food, a great bird swooped down, picked up the plate in its talons, dumped the food, and dropped the plate on the head of the ringleader of the Buddhists. Again the Buddhists were the object of ridicule. In repentance, the Buddhists took refuge in the teachings of Caitanya. A bit of slapstick, a play on motifs established in Sanskrit satire, became a metaphor for the Hindu absorption of Buddhism.

This assimilation included a syncretization of the legend of the Buddha into the mythology of the incarnations, or descents, of Viṣṇu. Hindu texts describe a battle between the gods and demons in which the gods, suffering defeat, sought the aid of Viṣṇu. The great god incarnated as the Buddha. Buddhism is a trick played on the demons. They shaved their heads, donned ochre robes, abandoned the Veda, and ceased performing sacrifices. Without the protection of the Veda and the power of its rituals, the demons were so weakened that the gods (or Kalkin in some versions) could destroy them. Viṣṇu, like a heavenly satirist, made fools of them.

In one rendering of the myth, Viṣṇu prophesies his incarnation as the Buddha. "At the beginning of the dark age of Iron, sitting beneath a royal tree, garbed in ochre robes, head shaven, with white teeth, as the Buddha, son of Śuddhodana, I shall delude men. I shall become the Buddha and then low-caste people will deal with the sacred. . . . Priests will neglect study and the sacrifices; there will be no offerings; respect for gurus will disappear and children will no longer obey their parents; the sacred texts will be forgotten as men indulge in deceitful practices" (*Mahābhārata* [Southern Recension] 12.348.2.41ff.). The mythological insinuation that all those who follow the teaching of the Buddha are demonic and deluded is satirical. The myth is a satire stripped of laughter.

The Veda and Vedic sacrifices, the caste system and the authority of brahmins, the guru-student system of religious instruction, the formalized patterns of both temple and domestic worship—things which, in the mainstream of Indian traditions, represented and insured order—were threatened by Buddhism. Buddhism denied the existence of a universal or personal absolute, the infinite and eternal sacredness which for Hindus was the underlying principle of all things. Buddhism, then, represented chaos—cosmic, social, domestic and personal chaos—that disintegrative state or force that is personified by the demons in the Hindu myth of the Buddha avatar.

The degeneration of traditional values is a constant concern of satire, and while the form and style of satire are often anarchic, obscene, and even manic, the message and intent are often conservative, moralistic, and even reactionary. Satire reaffirms the necessity of norms. As the heroic gods fought the demons of chaos to restore the order of the universe, the satirist attacks the earthly perpetuators of chaos to restore traditional systems of order within society. The complaint of the Indian satirist against the Buddhists and the often indistinguishable Jains was not that they were not Hindus, but that they somehow threatened the religious continuity which made Indian society seem to be a dynamically interrelated whole.

The buffoonish, hypocritical Buddhist monk persisted as a stock character in Sanskrit satirical literature even after Buddhism had been virtually reabsorbed into Hindu culture, partially through the sheer momentum of the conventions, but also, perhaps, because as a literary type he represented not simply a socially disruptive force of the past, but a psychologically disruptive force of the eternal present. Social satire is merely topical, its meaning and appeal limited by time and space, unless it also serves a psychological function and appeals to universal conflicts. One can laugh at a Buddhist monk or an English Puritan, even though one does not live in a time or place when and where Buddhism or Puritanism are particularly socially menacing, because these characters are dramatic representations of universal psychological mechanisms, tendencies, and patterns. They are caricatures of and for all institutions, persons, or psychological faculties which oppose instinctual drives or impulses for pleasure. They represent the prudes we know and hate as well as the prudes who, though we may not want to admit it, we are. It is their blatant lack of success, their ludicrously hypocritical denial of their failure, which makes them comic. Comedy celebrates the triumph of the pleasure principle, the glory of laughing Kāma.

An irony underlying anti-Buddhist satire is that, in a sense, the insights of Buddhism and satire are the same: all is unease, anxiousness, and sorrow; the cause is desire, the craving which expresses itself as lust, greed, selfishness, ignorance, and pretense. The vision that evokes compassion or pity in the Buddha inspires derision in the satirist. And through compassion and derision, respectively, the Buddha and satirist attempt to awaken people to realities behind illusions, the truth behind lies and facades. The Buddha negated the value of empirical existence, of family, society, and self, for the sake of liberation from the world of life and death. His negation was an affirmation of the possibility of liberation, of the great joy of extinction. The satirist, on the other hand, affirms the value and necessity of social, domestic, and personal interaction. His liberation is in, not from, the world.

Beneath the Saintly Nakedness: *Jaded Jains*

Tweedledum and Tweedledee
  Agreed to have a battle;
For Tweedledum said Tweedledee
  Had spoiled his nice new rattle.
    Lewis Carroll, *Through the Looking-Glass*

A servant in the *Āgamaḍambara* of Jayanta Bhaṭṭa (ninth century), searching for a representative of Jainism to enter into debate with his crusty brahmin master, realizes that he has reached the Jain gathering place when he sees plucked hairs strewn on the ground, evidence that bald monks are nearby. Through the bushes he spies a Jain monk arguing with a Jain nun. In jealous anger the female ascetic throws down her whisk of peacock feathers, the instrument used by mendicants to sweep the path before them as they walk to insure that they do not bring harm even to the smallest insect. Intent on stealing the feathers, the servant disguises himself in the robe of a nun and enters the forest clearing to claim the whisk. The Jain monk, believing that the manservant is truly a nun, tries to embrace him. Disguise is the recurrent satiric motif, and mistaken identity establishes the comic mood of the disclosure of the lust of the supposedly celibate Jains. When the real nun, returning to retrieve her peacock feathers, sees her monk/lover with what she assumes is another woman, her pique is revived and she beats up her lover with the feather broom that was meant to save insects from being hurt (act 2). The satiric justice is in seeing those who try to fool others being fooled by their own ruses.

The same text satirizes Buddhism by juxtaposing heard precept with seen practice, by counterposing the discourse of a Buddhist monk, a sermon on essential misery which permeates the world, with a picture of the Buddhist monastery as a luxurious, palatial retreat enclosing a gold statue of the Buddha. A Buddhist homily on the transience of life and the insubstantiality of all things is interrupted by the call to the morning meal. The monks rush to be served wine and meat by beautiful nuns (act 1).

The Buddhist monk and the Jain monk are, in Sanskrit satire, comic enantiomorphs. Like Tweedledum and Tweedledee, the Buddhist and the Jain are frequently depicted fighting with each other. In the *Śukasaptati* a Buddhist monk, jealous of the veneration people are feeling for a certain Jain mendicant, sends a prostitute to the hut of the Jain and then proceeds to spread rumors of his sexual debauchery; the Jain has his revenge when, after setting fire to the Buddhist's cottage, the monk emerges from the flames exposed with a whore of his own (25). The battles, physical or philosophical, between Buddhists and Jains, like the contest between the monk and the yogi in the *Mattavilāsa,* is a satiric device. In showing their attempts to defeat each other, the satirist defeats both. Similarly a Śaiva ("his body covered with ashes, muttering praises of Śiva, carrying a begging bowl") and a Vaiṣṇava ("his head adorned with peacock feathers, his body covered with sectarian markings, carrying an icon box"), arguing over which sect is better, prove the inferiority of both. Their debate focuses upon which is the cheapest, and therefore the least sacred, object—the icon box or the begging bowl (*Śāradātilaka* 63–64).

A Buddhist and Jain monk enter into casuistic debate, using absurd polemics to prove which religion is superior. Order (discrimination and common sense) disintegrates into chaos (confusion and uncommon nonsense). The Jain argues that Buddhism is self-contradictory: if, as the Buddha claims, there is no persisting self, then there is no reason to pursue liberation since the person liberated isn't the one pursuing liberation in the first place. The Buddhist monk defends Buddhist doctrine by asserting that it must be right and true since it is the teaching of the Buddha and the Buddha was omniscient. Asked how he knows the Buddha was omniscient, the monk explains that the Buddha revealed himself to be so in the scriptures. The Jain laughs, "If you think he was all-knowing just because he said he was, then I also claim to be all-knowing, and in my omniscience I say that you are my slave—not only you, but your father as well, and your father's fathers for seven generations back" (*Prabodhacandrodaya,* prose after 3.9). The satirist uses the Jain to expose Buddhism and the Buddhist to expose Jainism.

A whore's embraces have inspired the monk to renounce Buddhism and become a yogi. The Jain, beginning by admonishing the Buddhist, ends up expressing his own desire for conversion. When the woman caresses him, he too is overwhelmed by a sensual delight which mocks mystical euphoria. "Your philosophy is the only path to exultation and liberation," the Jain cries out, "I'm your slave. Initiate me into the teachings" (prose following 3.19).

Debauchery resolves doctrinal differences. The Buddhist and the Jain begin to dance, an activity forbidden to both of them by their respective religions. The buffoonish display gives physical expression to the degradation of order (composure and propriety) into chaos (uncoordinated dance) which the satire, on its most primary level, is suggesting is symptomized by Buddhism and Jainism.

A yogi offers the lecherous Tweedle-Buddha and Tweedle-Jain some booze. They invoke the precepts against intoxicants and add that they cannot drink from a vessel that has been polluted by the lips of such a socially degraded person as the yogi. But the yogi assures them that all religious authorities agree that "the mouth of a woman is always pure" (*Prabodhacandrodaya,* prose after 3.20). The aphorism, which could also be translated "a woman's face is always bright," presumably a mere secular observation on the charm of women, is passed off, through the absurd and illogical logic of comedy, as an evangelical apologia, a revelation that food or drink consumed from a woman's mouth is somehow ritually pure or sacramental. The ambiguity of the language provides the monk with a way to sanction boozing. The yogi's wench drinks from the vessel and then passes it to the Buddhist monk who jubilantly extols the drink as a glorious portion of *prasāda,* the remains of food or drink that have been offered to a god or spiritual preceptor and which are, through having been offered, pure and sacred. The profane use of sacred language is a conventional satiric conceit.

The Buddhist monk sings a paean to the wine he has quaffed from the whore's mouth:

The *bakula* blossom burgeons when sprinkled with such wine,
Sweetly scented mead from a lovely lady's luscious lips—
Not often enough, with whores, has the pleasure been all mine.
The gods thirst, I know, for heavenly nectar so divine
Only since they cannot get even tiny little sips
Of liquor from this lady's lips, a wine so very fine.
(3.21)

As the Buddhist drinks the wine, the Jain screams, "Don't take it all!" And, after sharing the liquor, he confesses his regrets that he ever "fell into the teachings of Jainism," a practice that kept him ignorant of the epiphanies of blessed booze.

Having wenched and drunk and danced, the Jain monk loses his hold on consciousness. In order to revive him, the yogi transfers chewed betel from his own mouth into the mouth of the Jain. The satiric image of contamination is comically disgusting. The monks have been stripped of their guise of purity. As satire turns veneration into revulsion, solemnity gives way to laughter.

Beyond the Hallowed Ashes: *Yogic Yahoos*

> See the sage hermit, by mankind admir'd,
> With all that bigotry adopts inspir'd,
> Wearing out life in his religious whim,
> Till his religious whimsy wears out him.
> His works, his abstinence, his zeal, allow'd,
> You think him humble—God accounts him proud.
>
> William Cowper, *Truth*

Yogis, sadhus, sannyasis, ascetics, mendicants, and renouncers, those who are utterly free from the distinctions of class or caste, from the demands of work, from responsibilities to family, friends, or community, are traditionally honored in India. And yet the veneration is always ambivalent. In exemplifying liberation from the world, they threaten norms and the values of the world. The *Śukasaptati* tells of a young brahmin who left his family to devote himself to religious austerities. Religious practice becomes irreligious when it disrupts domestic life. "One day, while the ascetic was muttering prayers on the banks of the Ganges, a bird flying over him shit on his head" (prose after 1.2).

Yogis are simultaneously respected and suspected, respected for taking the most arduous path, suspected of taking the easiest one. The distinctions between the holy man and the bum are subtle. The fraudulent ascetic, the freeloader who passes for the holy man, a stock satirical figure in ancient and modern Indian literature, expresses the cultural ambivalence toward the renouncer. While the religious tradition encourages respect, the comic tradition encourages a sensibility of incredulity. Satire is wary of all that seems holy, and it casts aspersions on all displays of renunciation. It gives us a bird's eye view of religion—it looks down on priests, monks, and yogis, and it takes pleasure in shitting on them. It apologizes for itself with claims that it only castigates hypocrisy, but as Northrop Frye has observed, "once a hypocrite who sounds exactly like a good man is sufficiently blackened, the good man himself seems a little dingier than he was" ("The Nature of Satire").

Yogis, in the satiric vision, are a thoroughly dingy lot. They are, according to the *Śāradātilaka,* "incarnations of deceit, bent on deluding the minds of people" (153). The yogi fools people with "a loincloth, ashes on the body, *darbha* grass, a garland of *rudrākṣa* beads, silence, and yogic posture," according to Nīlakaṇṭha Dīkṣita (*Kaliviḍambana* 86), and he gains a fine livelihood simply when "he performs the austerity of standing in a river until noon, worships a god in public, or wears holy vestments" (91). The ascetic practice of standing in rivers, often on one leg, created a standard association in Sanskrit literature of the yogi with the heron. He is still. He seems benign. But he's just waiting to strike, to devour some credulous fish or trusting frog.

A good many yogis were, indeed, crooks in disguise. The *Steyaśāstra,* a manual for robbers, recommends the guise of the renunciate, a guise that would enable the industrious thief to enter a strange town unsuspected, to gain access to the homes of the pious rich, and to get out of town without being noticed. And it would be hard to be apprehended since descriptions of the criminal ("he had matted hair and his body was covered with ashes") would match that of innumerable yogis. Satire bears witness to crimes of hypocrisy, committed or intended. It judges even if the evidence is circumstantial. The descriptions of its suspects fit countless holy men. Everyone in the lineup looks guilty, especially if they look innocent.

The incongruity between inner realities and outer appearances is both the source of satire's comic tone and the object of its criticism. In order to demonstrate the power of yoga to a disciple and to prove the nonidentity of the body and soul, a yogi in the *Bhagavadajjukīya* of Mahendravikramavarman leaves his own body to enter the form of a courtesan who has just died from snakebite while waiting for her lover in a garden. The comic tension is provided by the forcing together of incongruous elements, male and female, religion and sexual love. As a practical joke, the Agent of Death, the archcomedian of the universe, takes the soul of the girl and places it in the unanimated body of the yogi. A yogi with the soul of a courtesan and a courtesan with the soul of a yogi appear upon the comic stage. New guises reveal the truth, the falseness of the old guises. The yogi is really a whore and the whore is like a yogi. "Harlots are like holy mendicants," the disciple observes, "they hardly feel any love" (prose after 25). Devoid of attachment, passion, or affection, whores are what holy men are supposed to be. Full of lust, passion, and craving, holy men are what whores are supposed to be. Both feign being what they are not for the sake of alms.

When the girl's lover arrives for his tryst, the yogi (the harlot's soul in the yogi's body) tries to embrace him and begs for wine and his kisses, while the harlot (the yogi's soul in the harlot's body) rejects the lover, shuns her mother, and corrects the Sanskrit grammar of an attending doctor. All is confusion and illusion. Nothing makes sense. The audience laughs because it sees through the mistakes in identity. Satire takes pleasure in knowing what others do not know.

In dramatic satire the comic revelations of what is really going on occur through the convention of asides. A character says one thing to other characters, but reveals other things to the audience by speaking to himself. Thought is vocalized. "How can these two scoundrels be hoodwinked?" the scurrilous old brahmin Reverend Loveblind says to himself, "taking on the outward appearance of a Vaiṣṇava devotee, I'll deceive them as to who I am." Then he recites loudly and grandly for all the world to hear:

O tongue!
Forever remember to say "Hari!"
O eye!
See the entire universe pervaded by the Support of the World!
O ear!
Listen to the glorifying stories of the Enemy of Mura!
O mind!
Go to Nārāyana for refuge at once!

(*Hāsyārṇava* 2.10)

Within the play the recitation is a pretense. But from outside the play it is parody, as much a mockery as an imitation of Vaiṣṇava devotionalism. "Oh, a great sin has been made by this bit of remembering Hari," the old brahmin says to himself again, "how can I atone?" The scoundrels whom he is trying to fool, the goatish brahmin priest Panzany and his ornery student, are as adept at shamming religion as he is. "This venerable scoundrel makes his roguery apparent," Reverend Panzany thinks to himself, "I'll display some myself." And he too recites a mock devotional verse. Reverend Loveblind demands that his student enter the game of religious deceit: "Recite some Vaiṣṇava religious text." The boy obeys:

Through divine fate and the world's wicked ways as well,
Life in this blighted age has become a living hell;
Irksome abstinence destroys the body to no end;
The wisest sages knew this—what did they recommend?
They relinquished fruitless vows and troublesome rites
For the religion of wild women and sweet delights.

(*Hāsyārṇava* 2.12)

Reverend Panzany's student concurs with his own recitation, also attributed to Vaiṣṇava scripture:

Those who smear their faces with ash (and even wear it)
Say that painful austerities are full of merit;
But the Lord of Life is pleased and gives liberation
To those who enjoy flesh, fish, booze, and copulation (2.14).

Such comic attempts to establish religious legitimation for secular debauchery are most frequently put in the mouths of Śaiva yogis, wild, drunken, and lusty yogis who, rather than concealing their vice under veneers of virtue, flaunt it and call it virtue.

Skullduggery

They [the Simonist gnostics] say: "All earth is earth, and there is no difference where anyone sows, provided he does sow." And they congratulate themselves on their intercourse with strange women, asserting that this is perfect Agape.

Hippolytus, *Elenchus*

A proudly debauched yogi boasts of the pleasure and efficacy of his religious practices, the path he treads in emulation of Śiva:

What do I know about texts, spells, and meditation?
My guru's got a better way to liberation
And I stick to the path, my Tantric occupation
Of wine, girls, and women known through fornication.
To whom, I ask, is the Tantric way not appealing?
My bed is a skin and my alms are most revealing:
Alms of wine and fish and meat and sexual dealing.
And I've married a slut and she is wild with feeling.
Viṣṇu and Brahmā teach liberation with platitude,
By the Vedic path of knowledge, rites, and gratitude.

Only Śiva taught the way that suits my attitude—
Women, wine, and sex are my hallowed beatitude.

(*Karpūramañjarī* 1.22–24)

Often the wild, drunken yogis of Sanskrit satire are identified as Kāpālikas, naked, ash-covered mendicants who enacted and embodied the mythology of Śiva in his most grotesque and terrible form. Carrying begging bowls made from human skulls, wearing garlands of bones, frequenting cremation grounds, and indulging in violently orgiastic rites, they embody and convey the aesthetic sentiments of terror and disgust. "He who eats human flesh from the skull of a fine gentleman will attain the stature of Śiva and enter his domain" a Kāpālika announces, "thus spake the Lord who bears a human skull" (*Moharājaparājaya* (4.23).

The Kāpālikas as well as other Śaiva ascetics and Tantrics, taking the vow of the hero, he who is immune to terror, cultivated and displayed fearlessness by living in cremation grounds. Two such holy men, Skeletonbanner (Kaṅkālaketu) and Cremationashes (Śmaśānabhūti) in the *Āgamaḍambara* (act 3), hear footsteps and are striken with panic. That they are terrified, rather than terrifying, inverts the aesthetic mood of terror as established by the setting and turns it into the comic sentiment. Terror, like love, not comic in itself, becomes funny when someone who claims to be beyond it is suddenly, under the gaze of those who do not make such claims, its victim.

The satirized Kāpālikas use traditional religion to justify fierce and lewd practices, open expressions of anger and desire. One of them explains that one may feel free to commit any atrocity in that purification, the remission of sin, is an easy process: "The great Lord Śiva was cleansed of the sin of cutting off the head of Brahmā by taking a vow of penance, and he regained his merit after killing Triśiras by performing a lot of sacrifices" (*Mattavilāsa* 17). Religion, in satire, allows, rather than prevents, vice.

Another Kāpālika claims to have great supernatural powers: "I can change the course of the stars. . . . I can cause a flood to cover the earth and the—imagine this—I can drink up the waters of that deluge in one gulp" (*Prabodhacandrodaya* 3.14). The quest for such magical powers represents a significant trend in Indian religious traditions, and those who are able to convince others that they have attained such powers have often been venerated. Satire looks for hidden wires on the magician's stage, scrutinizes the miraculous, and focuses upon superstitions as cheap permutations of religious truth.

Holy Spirits

> Whereas Dr. Lee Siegel (herein called the permit-holder) has applied for a permit authorising him/her to consume and possess for personal consumption liquor, subject to the provisions of the Tamil Nadu Prohibition Act, and whereas the Board of Revenue is satisfied that there is good reason for so granting him/her a permit and that he/she will not misuse such permit.
>
> Liquor Permit, Government of Tamil Nadu

The Tantric yogi, according to the *Kulārṇava Tantra,* "should drink, drink, and drink again, drink until he falls down drunk on the ground; and then, when he can get up again, he should drink some more; then there will be liberation from rebirth" (7.100). The Kāpālika in the *Mattavilāsa* boasts of being faithful to this religion. In imitation of Śiva, he lives in pursuit of liberation through, not from, the senses. He compares the liquor saloon to the Vedic sacrificial ground: "The sign hanging out in front is the sacrificial post and booze is the soma; the drunkards are priests; their drunken chatter is the recitation of the sacred mantras and the barroom songs are the holy hymns; the snacks are the oblations and the mugs are the sacred vessels . . . the bartender is the patron of the sacrifice" (prose after 9). Vedic blasphemy becomes at once Tantric dogma and comic parody. The incongruous comparison stresses bathos, a satiric degradation of religious values and traditions, an absurd profanation of the sacred.

The Kāpālika, accompanied by his consort, the wench Devasomā, incites her jealous anger when he accidentally calls her Somadevā. The verbal transposition parallels the many nonverbal transpositions and reversals which occur repeatedly in satire. Transposition, whether verbal (as in the spoonerism) or physical (as in the mistaken identity motif) or philosophical (as in the assertion that profane things are sacred), incites comic laughter. In order to appease the piqued woman, the wild yogi apologizes, blames the liquor, and even promises to give up drinking. "No! Lord, no!" she cries out, falling at his feet in a parody of the devoted woman, "Do not break thy vow to do penance for my

Figure 17

sake!'' (*Mattavilāsa,* prose after 6). Spirits mock spirituality. Drinking becomes a depreciated form of religious observance, drink a silly sacrament, drunkenness a comic form of rapture, and the drunkard an ironic mystic. Inebriation is mock beatitude.

In an early nineteenth-century cartoon, the religious ecstasy of Vaiṣṇava holy men is attained by guzzling booze and smoking hashish (fig. 17), and in an almost identical modern cartoon, one renouncer shows the LSD with which he has attained his wisdom and awakening (fig. 18). The dipsomaniac or drug addict is a mock holy man. There is laughter where the incongruities converge as when Kṣemendra describes the drunkard:

> He who is drunk on wine sees one and the same thing
> In the brahmin and the cow,
> And in the elephant, the king, and the outcaste.
> He makes no distinction
> Between what's his and what belongs to others.
>
> (*Kalāvilāsa* 6.16)

The convergence occurs through parody. Kṣemendra's readers would have recognized the holy scripture:

> The wise man sees one and the same thing
> In the learned brahmin and the cow,

And in the elephant and the dog,
And even in the outcaste.

(*Bhagavadgītā* 5.18)

As that sacred text speaks of the wise man, the yogi, "who considers gold, stones, and clods of dirt to be the same" (6.8 and 14.24) so Kṣemendra speaks of the drunkard who "has attained the state of the yogi—he considers gold, stones, and clods of dirt to be the same" (*Kalāvilāsa* 6.17).

The yogi, the athlete of the spirit, because he is beyond attachment to the world and worldly things, makes no distinction between what belongs to him and what belongs to others. His detachment results from, and finds expression in, his control of the senses, his austerities, and his chastity. The drunkard, the buffoon of the body, is too drunk to make distinctions between what belongs to him and what belongs to others, and this is proven by the thieves who steal from him. He's too soused to tell a cow

Figure 18

It's called LSD. A hippy gave it to me — no more struggle to meditate, concentrate, etc.

from an elephant, a brahmin from an outcaste. And like the controlled yogi, the drunkard is truly chaste—after getting drunk "his passion is gone" (6.19 using the phrase from *Bhagavadgītā* 2.56).

"Do you like brandy?" Tukuri, the Tantric tailor of Puri, asked with a proud and broad and brilliantly white smile, "I can get you the very best. This brandy is divine. V.V.V.V.S.O.P.—one thousand V's!" The village arrack came in old Campa-Cola bottles and packed a whallop. It made Tukuri philosophical. "Brandy is god," he laughed exuberantly. But the next day the laughter was gone and he repented: "Brandy is not god. Brandy is not divine. Brandy is bad."

He smiled: "Brandy is not god. Hashish is god."

Tantric Tantalization

> In appealing his conviction on two charges of knowingly possessing marijuana in violation of Hawaii Revised Statutes (HRS) 712-1249 (1976), defendant Chuck Andrew Blake (Defendant) raises a constitutional issue. He contends that the application of HRS 712-1249 results in an unconstitutional deprivation of his right to the free exercise of a religion known as Hindu Tantrism. We disagree. . . .
>
> State of Hawaii v. Chuck Andrew Blake (1985)

"Ganja is divine. Ganja is Śiva," Tukuri told me, taking an exuberant puff on the chillum, "when you smoke ganja, you smoke Śiva. Then you are Śiva. The guru says that when you smoke ganja, Kālī smokes you."

I asked about the guru.

"Divine guru! He is god! He is Śiva! He is the husband of Kālī." As he spoke, his little daughter, Chinna, hugged his legs, crawled between them, climbed upon his lap to nestle in. "The guru is Śiva, the greatest yogi. He can do anything in the world." His smile gave way to a respectfully sober grimace and I encouraged him to go on. "Anything? Like what?"

"He can take a stone, a large stone, weighing maybe twenty k.g.'s, and he can tie a cord around this stone and the other end of the cord he ties around the penis. Then, at will, through the power of yoga, he can lift that stone right off the ground with the penis. This is divine."

"Yes," I could not help laughing, "this is divine. In fact, if we can get this guy to America and he can teach that particular yogic *siddhi* there, I'll guarantee you that he'll have more followers than the Maharishi Maheshyogi himself.'' I pictured airports full of American disciples handing out stones and chanting ''Hare Liṅga.''

My enthusiasm encouraged his. ''That is nothing! He can do greater things than that. At will, through the power of yoga, he can change himself into a bird or a snake.''

''I'd rather be able to lift the stone,'' I said, ''but still, that is rather amazing.''

Exhaling, he let his exuberance take over. ''That is nothing. He can change himself into anything. I once saw him turn himself into a sewing machine!''

''A sewing machine?''

''Singer Electric!—the kind that makes the buttonholes automatically. I swear this is true. I swear it before every god in the universe!''

When I asked if I could meet this extraordinary yogi, Tukuri assured me that I could be initiated into the Tantric mysteries, ''You are my brother, so my guru is your guru already.'' I wanted to know my guru's name.

''The guru is god. God has every name. You may call him Jesus Christ. Why not? He can walk on the water.''

After the bus ride to the village, there was a four-hour walk through the forest, four nervous hours for me since heavy rains had forced snakes out of their burrows. I looked carefully at every crooked stick on the ground. But Tuku assured me that there was nothing to worry about. ''The guru, I have told you one thousand times, is Śiva and Śiva is the god of snakes. He will not let the snakes bite you while you are coming to see him.''

When we walked into the clearing, the guru, the priest at the small shrine to Kālī became furious with Tukuri. Though he was small, he was quite muscular, and his face, despite the scars of smallpox, was curiously handsome. His hair was matted, as I had hoped it would be, and in place of the brahmin's sacred thread he wore a black rope across his chest. I assumed that his Tantric tantrum was caused by my presence, by the disciple's introduction of a foreigner, a barbarian, a *mleccha,* into the secret sanctum of esoteric mysteries.

''No, no,'' dear Tuku explained, his ever-manic mood barely daunted, ''not at all. He loves you because I have explained to him that you are from Kālīfornia, the place most sacred to Kālī where everyone is practicing the Tantra. But he is angry because you do not have a camera with you. He needs to have his photograph taken. I have told him that you do, in fact, have an excellent camera and that you will bring it tomorrow and take an excellent photograph of him with that camera.''

I didn't like it at all. In the midst of the incomprehensible Oriya conversation, I could distinctly and repeatedly hear the words ''National Geographic Magazine.''

Since Tukuri's honor was at stake, I had no choice but to make the long and, I still thought, dangerous trek once again. When we returned we were greeted by ''Mr. K. N. Mohapatra, B.A. (Honours, Bhubaneshwar),'' a village English teacher. He explained, much to Tuku's disappointment, that Guruji wanted only him to act as interpreter in our auspicious meeting. He alone had the facility to capture the ''nectar of Guruji's words.'' He wore an enthusiastically starched white dress shirt that seemed rather comically incongruous with his bare feet and loose pajama pants. He frankly stated his disappointment that I was American, not British. ''I speak only Oxford English parlance,'' he announced proudly. He was, therefore, very pleased to learn that I had been a student at Oxford. ''You must, I presume to suspect, hanker, my good sir, for fair Albion, in particular for Oxford University. The poet Mr. John Dryden could have been speaking of me when he penned the immortal lines, 'Oxford to him a dearer name shall be, / Than his own mother University.' '' I expressed my astonishment at his familiarity with Dryden, whom I kept remembering for having penned some immortal lines about religious satire being ''the check of laymen on bad priests.''

''Mr. John Dryden's poesy is only a fleeting fancy with me. My expertise, the topic of my own B.A. dissertation (Honours, Bhubaneshwar), was the poetical writings of Mr. Alexander Pope. It is an honor for myself to present you with a copy of this exhaustive fruit of my earnest erudition.'' I accepted the package with an apology that I had brought nothing to give him in return. ''Hold your regrets at bay,'' Mr. Mohapatra comforted, ''after all, Alexander Pope himself has opined, and the *Gītā* concurs, that 'to err is human and to forgive is divine.' ''

God was getting impatient. He wanted the photo session to begin. He was, my new interpreter explained, concerned at how small my camera was. He needed large photographs in ''exquisite color, so that when he is sojourning in some distant place, the people can worship his photograph in the temple.'' I promised that the pictures would be very large and very colorful. He bound up his hair to be photographed in the performance of various yogic postures and exercises; he loosened it again to pose, complete with *mudrās,* in the shrine next to ''his wife,'' the beloved Kālī. But most of all he wanted to pose with me, ''his American disciple,'' and his five dogs, ''Yudhiṣṭhir, Bhīm, Arjun, and the twins, Nakul and Sahadev.'' The dogs, I was informed through the interpreter, ''represent the five senses.'' The guru displayed his control of the senses—he could make them sit, fetch, or roll over.

The temple ritual was quite simple. Hashish was offered to Kālī. Then the *prasāda,* the divine leftovers, was smoked by one and all as we sat huddled in the shrine at the feet of the hideous mother. An old woman, with no jewelry, wrapped in brown cloth, her leg swollen with elephantiasis, grinned toothlessly like an incarnation of Kṣemendra's Madam Bagabones, as she held the smoke deep inside of herself. I asked Śiva/Christ about Tantra. Were the left-hand practices still performed? Was there ritual copulation? Did he initiate students into those practices?

He spoke for a long time. He would talk very rapidly and then he would stop and close his eyes and then he would wait and then he would suddenly laugh and open his eyes and begin speaking quickly again. The discourse was embellished with ritual hand gestures. I waited anxiously for the translation. Mr. Mohapatra turned to me and smiled, ''In the words of the immortal Mr. Alexander Pope, 'Fools rush in where angels fear to tread.' That is not all that the great poet noted. In his fulsome wit and wisdom he also surmised—and on this the *Gītā* is also in 101 percent agreement—that 'a little learning is a dangerous thing.' Such words merit our devoted contemplation lest they become but pearls before swine.''

That was all I could get out of my interpreter. That, and the copy of his dissertation.

Tukuri smiled his eternally enduring smile all the way back to Puri. ''Well, now you have met god. So now you must be a happy man. Happiness is my gift to you. Happiness and laughter! Rām! Rām!''

Late that night, in my room, removing the newspaper wrapping from the other gift I had been given, Mr. Mohapatra's dissertation, I read the title: ''The Wit of Alexander Pope and the Wisdom of the *Bhagavad Gītā:* a Comparative Exegesis with a Profound Preface by His Holiness Śrīmad Bhakti Sādhaka Syām

Sundar Mohanty and an Insightful Introduction by Dr. Bauribandhu Dās, M.A., B.L., Ph.D., Retired Law Secretary to the Government of Orissa.'' I thumbed the yellowed pages. I noticed a quote from Pope and, before going to sleep, I copied it out.

> Laugh then at any, but at Fools or Foes;
> These you but anger, and you mend not those.
> Laugh at your friends, and, if your Friends are sore,
> So much the better, you may laugh the more.
> To Vice and Folly to confine the jest,
> Sets half the world, God knows, against the rest;
> Did not the Sneer of more impartial men
> At Sense and Virtue, balance all again.
> Judicious Wits spread wide the Ridicule,
> And charitably comfort Knave and Fool.

Act Two: Humor

Scene One: The Human Comedy

The Laughter of the Weaver

6

The Fool: The Wisdom of Folly

One night a stray camel wandered through a field in a village and in the morning the young people asked an old weaver in that village what the strange footprints were. The old man began to weep and as he wept he began to laugh. "Why do you weep? Why do you laugh?" they asked. "Why do you laugh and weep at the same time?" The weaver explained it. "I cry because I wonder what these poor children will do for someone to explain things to them when I am dead. And I laugh because, as for these footprints, I don't know—I really don't know—what they are!"

Panjabi folktale

"In order to truly understand humor, you must look back to your childhood," Gananath Sastri had explained. There was a warm and honied breeze in the overgrown garden in Madras, and Mr. Sastri offered me one of his Charminars. "I'm not finished with this one yet," I held up the half-smoked cigarette. He insisted that I smoke a fresh one.

"Every time we laugh, what is it other than the little child in our heart breaking loose and jumping for joy?" With gentle delight he recollected that child within himself and I could see the boy with bright black eyes and an even more glistening, though thoroughly naughty, smile. The child was puffing on a cigarette. "I started smoking when I was six years old. I was a terrible child," he laughed. "I stole cigarettes like Kṛṣṇa stole curds."

He lit a cigarette. "To hear genuine Indian laughter you must visit the villages. You won't hear real laughter in our cities. Before my father was appointed at Presidency College we lived in a village of weavers. I remember a fellow in our village called Gada. Every village has such a fellow—a 'village idiot.' You must have one, just as you must have a well. You cannot be a self-respecting village without one. Everyone always laughed at Gada. One day a man, holding out ten paise in one hand and one rupee in the other, asked him whether he wanted the ten or the one. And Gada took the ten paise. The man told the story at a meeting of the village council and everybody had quite a laugh over it. After that people would test it for themselves. Just to tease the fool, they would hold up a one-rupee note and a ten-paise coin and ask, "Do you want the ten or the one?" And Gada always took the ten paise and people always laughed at him for that. And when they would laugh, he too would laugh. He always laughed when others laughed. Some folks postulated that he took the coin rather than the note because he was so stupid that he thought the metal was more valuable than the paper. Others assumed that he was simply fooled by the numbers, that he reasoned that ten must always be greater than one. Whenever any visitors came to our village they would inevitably be introduced to Gada and shown the prank. They would laugh at Gada. And Gada would join in and laugh with them. He was a veritable tourist attraction. Perhaps it seems cruel to you, all this laughing at Gada. But people actually liked Gada. He was quite harmless. Even after we moved from the village I would frequently return to see my grandparents. On one of these visits I was informed that Gada was dying. Everyone was very sad. The old fool had given them such great amusement. And I think that they felt bad because they had laughed at him all the time. I went along to his place, a mere hut, and, yes, he was very sick. He was weeping. 'Don't cry, please don't cry,' I begged him. And he explained the reason for his tears. 'I feel very sorry for what I have done. I have cheated these happy people who have been so kind to me. I have deceived them! Of course I know that one rupee is worth more than ten paise. Any fool knows that! The first time I chose the ten paise over the rupee note, it was because I didn't want to take advantage of the man's generosity. But then, when everybody started offering me that same choice, I always chose the ten paise because I knew that if I were to choose the rupee, people would stop offering me the choice at all. And so, by always choosing the ten paise, I earned a great many rupees!' Realizing at that moment that Gada was the wisest man in my entire village, I could not help but laugh aloud. And when I laughed, Gada laughed. Even as he wept, he laughed. He always laughed when others laughed. The fool couldn't help himself. There is something very powerful for me about the laughter of Gada. I can hear it even now."

Laughter provides and expresses a feeling, however momentary, of power. In exposing real or potental hypocrisy, in stripping away revered political, social, and religious guises, satire reveals socially and psychologically empowered figures as powerless. Authority squirms in its nakedness. By implication and insinuation, satire retrieves a power that has been given away or accrued through pretense and affectation. Satiric laughter expresses the exquisite pleasure of that sudden, though often transitory, reclamation. I laugh when the one who seemed greater—stronger, wiser, or holier—than I, turns out to be no different, no better, than I am. My laughter voices an amusement arising from the sense, real or not, that I have retaliated against the external or internal forces, symbols, or personifications of repression.

Satire, by definition, focuses upon figures with a high social status; humor deals with the lowly—fools and clowns, tricksters and knaves. And power is still the issue. While the hypocrite has too much power, the fool has not enough. If the hypocrite represents that which represses, the fool embodies that which is repressed. And the trickster is the fool fighting back, the dimwit who is clever, the weakling who is strong, the rogue who is righteous.

There is a theory, following Hobbes, that explains laughter in terms of the pleasure inherent in a feeling of superiority over some object of our laughter. And this theory is commonly invoked to explain the comedic nature of the fool. The fool gives me a sense of power. I feel greater—stronger, wiser, or holier—than he. But this is not to say that the object of our laughter cannot be ourselves, a former us, or some contained aspect of ourselves. Though we may laugh at the fool with relief that we are not fools, that laughter is always, I would suggest, informed with at least a partial sense of identification, with a realization that we have been him and that we still are him in those moments when the defenses are down. The pleasure of humor is enhanced by the relaxation of those defenses. The pleasure is diminished when there is no identification with the object of laughter, when humor provides no relief from the stresses and strains of ego. In humorous laughter we have the luxury of being superior to ourselves. Such laughter simultaneously expresses feelings of safety and peril, of knowledge and ignorance, power and powerlessness.

The comic appeal of the fool is contingent upon the lure of regression, the temptation to be a child, a little fool again, free from the restrictions of reason or rule, sense or civilization. The moment of identification with the fool is a moment of freedom and of innocence regained in impulsive laughter. The fool laughs when happy, cries when sad. Like the weaver he is prone to weep for others and to laugh at himself just as we laugh at him. If he has vices, it is not by design. He does not have the skill or intelligence it takes to be vicious or hypocritical. He is what he seems. "The fool couldn't help himself." He is without malice. "People actually liked Gada. He was quite a harmless fellow." The fool is appreciated, though not emulated, and valued, though not esteemed, because he acts out our folly for us. "If others had not been foolish," William Blake mused, "we should be so" (*Marriage of Heaven and Hell*).

While satire attacks the folly that is concealed, humor merely points to a folly that is already apparent. There is no accusation of hypocrisy in humor—the fools of humor are too stupid to connive or to realize their potential as hypocrites. They themselves, not other members of society, are their victims. It is hard for them to harm others unless they are trying to help them; and it is hard for them to harm themselves even if they try. A fool in a modern Gujarati cartoon, trying to commit suicide, beats the tree to which the noose is tied rather than the donkey on which he stands (fig. 19).

Once upon a time in a Buddhist monastery there was a dull-witted Buddhist monk who, as he was collecting his alms, was bitten on the knee by a dog. He rushed back to the monastery, climbed to the top of the building, and rang the great bell. The monks gathered beneath him to find out the cause of the commotion. "Why do you sound the gong at this hour?" they asked. The monk answered, "I have been bitten by a dog. I realized that each of you would ask me what happened to my knee and I would have to tell each of you the story of the dog. That would take a great deal of time. So I decided to call you together so that I could save time by telling you all at once" (*Kathāsaritsāgara* 65.132–140). There is a certain sense to his senselessness, and a certain childlike sweetness to his naiveté.

A satirical pamphlet, the *Bharaṭakadvātriṃśikā* (c. fifteenth century), makes fun of Bharaṭakas, Śaiva mendicants with hair matted and worn in long twists. In one of the stories a Bharaṭaka named Somaka, thatching the roof of his hut in the rainy season, fell and was injured. When people asked him how he had become so badly banged up and bruised, "the fool would climb up on the

Figure 19

roof and show them. 'This is how I fell and this is how I was injured.' " He did this again and again until his injuries were so compounded that he was not even able to stand up any more. From then on "people laughed as they passed his place" (6).

The stories are jokes, ancient equivalents of the American "Polack" joke, the English Irishman joke, the modern Indian Sikh joke, jokes that are in no way satirical, in no way demanding a change in behavior. "How many Bharaṭakas," the Jain compiler of the jokes seems to ask, "does it take to change a lightbulb?"

There is a didactic posture taken in much of the literature of folly, a moral overlay that constitutes the repressive perspective on the fool. It encourages dissociation: "Thus you see that in this world fools never succeed at becoming anything but objects of the laughter of ridicule, while the wise are ever honored" (*Kathāsaritsāgara* 61.55). The voice is always distant, detached, and rational. It strives to transform our laughter at the fool into a warning to ourselves against folly. Satiric warnings against vice are legitimate, but warnings against that which cannot be helped are superfluous. There is another voice in the stories, the warmer, more human, voice of the fool himself. It cries out for sympathy. It beckons us to weep for the fool. The censure of the didactic layer of the fool stories and the pain of the psychological level are resolved on the aesthetic level in comedy. Like the weaver, like Gada, we laugh as we weep and weep as we laugh, laughing and weeping for the fool we are, the fool who ultimately is everyone.

The recognition of our own essential folly is the goal and object of humor. The function is a teleological one—a sense of humor, an appreciation and affirmation of folly, has the power to preserve and enhance life. So Erasmus's Stultia, Lady Folly, explains that she, Folly and folly alone, keeps men from committing suicide.

What's So Funny: *The Foolish Fool*

In sum, no society, no union in life, could be either pleasant or lasting without me [Folly]. A people does not for long tolerate its prince, or a master tolerate his servant, a handmaiden her mistress, a teacher his student, a friend his friend, a wife her husband . . . a partner his partner . . . except as they mutually or by turns are mistaken . . . and soothe themselves with the sweetness of folly.

Erasmus, *In Praise of Folly*

The first joke I can remember hearing as a child was about a moron who had thrown a clock out of the window in order to see time fly. Later he tiptoed past the medicine cabinet so as not to awaken the sleeping pills. Folly was consummated in death—he jumped off the Empire State Building to make a smash on Broadway. The jokes were troubling and full of anguish. I pictured a thin, boney-cheeked boy, bald except for a wisp of hair on the very top of his head, wearing pants too short for his lanky legs. I could see him lying on the pavement, broken and drenched with blood. And I shuddered as I forced a laugh, a signal that I understood. The moron's mistakes were always mistakes in language. He lacked the ability to move from the syntactic or phonemic level of language to the appropriate semantic level, the very ability which the child, at the age when these jokes are told and heard, is under pressure to master. Laughter relieves the cognitive pressure momentarily, but the jokes that inspire it contain a terrible message: know or die.

The moron of my childhood has had a multitude of incarnations. The same simpleton lived in ancient India. The lore is universal: Why did the moron, a village servant, take the door off its hinges and carry it into town with him? Because his master told him to "keep an eye on the door of his shop" (*Kathāsaritsāgara* 62.209–211). Why did the stupid servant wrap the clothes around the trunk when it rained? Because his master told him not to let the trunk in which his clothes were kept get wet if it started to rain (62.193–196). A cart driver requested the assistance of a fool in fixing his cart. The fool asked what he would be given for his services. "Nothing at all," the man answered. The fool then helped him and, when the job was done, he turned to the man and said, "Okay, now please give me 'nothing-at-all' " (61.326–328). The fool reveals a comedy of language, a farce of mistaken identities. He shows the limits of words and grammar, their inevitable failure as precision instruments for the categorization, conceptualization, and communication of reality. The folly is shared by all who speak.

The farce is due not only to breakdowns in language, but to failures in logic as well. The comic literature of fools, pointing to the absurdities to which reason may lead us, implicitly suggests the ultimate impossibility of certain knowledge or unassailable wisdom. Logic leads the fool astray. There was once a Bharaṭaka guru who had two problems—he had a back that was hunched and a student who was stupid. The student, going to town one day to collect alms, saw a carpenter in his workshop rubbing bamboo with sesame oil and then heating the bamboo in the fire. The stupid Bharaṭaka asked the carpenter what he was doing. "Straightening out this bamboo." "What makes one thing straight ought to make something else straight," the ignoramus thought to himself, "I'll use this very remedy to help my guru who is all bent out of shape with arthritis and rheumatism." The idiot went to his teacher's hut and set the venerable man, who was already anointed with oil, on fire. When people heard the loud screams of the poor old holy man, they rushed to help him. "Idiot!" they cried, "You are killing the old man! Don't do this to your guru!" But the fool responded proudly to their scolding. "Sirs! You are the fools! You are, haha, the sons of fools! I am making my crooked guru straight!" The story is cautionary—it illustrates the way in which those who call others fools are inevitably fools themselves. Folly is relative. We are all Bharaṭakas, Polacks, Irishmen, and Sardārs. The storyteller explains that those people were fools indeed: "If they were wise they wouldn't have let the Bharaṭaka go" (*Bharaṭakadvātriṃśikā* 4).

Another well-meaning Bharaṭaka, wanting to bless someone, tried to say "May love (*bhakti*) befall you." But since his version of Sanskrit was simply Gujarati with Sanskritic endings, his blessing came out as a curse: "May an oven (*bhaṭṭhi*) fall on you" (21). And yet another foolish disciple, in the same text, procures a homeopathic herb, a deadly poison unless taken in small amounts, for his guru. He so loves his guru that he tells him to take it all, hoping he will get better immediately. The old ascetic dies (12). The fool knows no proportion. Everything is done, said, felt, and shown in excess in comedy. A fool reasoned that since salt makes food taste better, it would be a good idea to swallow a whole handful—he gagged and choked (*Kathāsaritsāgara* 61.39–44). The backfiring of intention is a comic spectacle.

A foolish cotton merchant, seeing a goldsmith in the market purifying his gold in fire, decided to purify his cotton in the same manner (*Kathāsaritsāgara* 61.28–31). A foolish seller of expensive aloe wood, finding no customers for his valuable commodity, decided to burn his wood and sell it as charcoal (61.2–6). A foolish sesame farmer, discovering that roasted sesame seeds tasted better than uncooked ones, reasoned that if he were to roast all of his seeds before planting them he could harvest a crop of preroasted seeds—nothing grew (61.7–9). A group of foolish date farmers, noting how easy it was to get the dates from the palms if they cut the trees down, reasoned that it would be wise to cut down all the trees to harvest the dates. The next year they had nothing (61.32–35). A fool reasons: everyday he gets a pail of milk from his cow; if he does not milk her for a month, it stands to reason that he'll be able to get thirty pails of fresh milk at festival time. It makes sense, but he gets no milk and everyone laughs at him (61.44–49). Reason defeats the fool. By trying to do, the fool undoes; by trying to fix, he ruins. "He cuts the udder to get the milk" (*Mahābhārata* 12.72.16). The fool always has something right, but it always goes all wrong. As reason consumes the fool, so it threatens us all, and humor thus insists that it is not to be trusted. The dreams of fools, their hopes and aspirations, always come to nothing. The bubble always bursts and we laugh. "In this world fools never succeed at becoming anything," the *Kathāsaritsāgara* laughingly insists again and again, "but objects of the laughter of ridicule."

The imagery of these stories—the burnt cotton and aloe wood, the sesame seeds rotting in the ground, the field of date palm stumps, the dry cow—is the imagery of death. The Bharaṭaka gurus are killed by the reasoned and devoted efforts of their students. The moron of my childhood fulfilled the dreadful Oedipal fantasy when he put his father in the refrigerator in order to have "iced pop." Through the fool we are seduced to laugh at disaster, chaos, and death. Laughter momentarily works things out.

In a brief essay on humor, Freud tells a joke about a criminal who, being led to the gallows on a Monday morning, says, "What a way to start the week!" The man is a fool. He sticks by the pleasure principle, unable—or if able, refusing—to capitulate to reality, even in the face of death. It is a part of the fool's function to reveal what is funny about the deadly serious. He discovers for us a source of pleasure within our pain. Freud distinguished between the kind of jokes that provide an outlet for aggression (what I have classified as satire) and those that are purely humorous, as exemplified by the man on his way to the noose. He considered humor the finer mode of the comic. "What is fine about it is the triumph of narcissism, the ego's victorious assertion of its own invulnerability" ("Humour"). The cry of victory is a loud laugh, a laugh at death, the death of the fool with whom we have identified.

A fool grabbed onto the tail of Nandi, Śiva's bull, and rode it up to heaven where he then feasted on the ambrosial delicacies of Kailāsa. Though enthralled with the delights of heaven, the simple man missed his friends on earth. And so he rode the bull back down to the terrestrial realm and insisted that those friends come to heaven with him. They all held on to Nandi. On the return journey one friend asked, "How large did you say the sweets in heaven are?" Enthusiastically the fool stretched out his arms to demonstrate the size, let go of Nandi, and fell to his death (*Kathāsaritsāgara* 65.177–199). The story is told for laughs. Another simpleton was stuck high in the branches of a tree. Trying to rescue him, another man also became stuck in the tree. The second man began to sing both to bring people to them for help and to wile away the time until such help came. When the song was over, the first man applauded and, in so doing, fell to his death (65.200–212).

Falls are universally funny. But there must be sympathy, even admiration, for those who fall—if not, the laughter is just too nasty. The two simpletons are motivated by generosity, enthusiasm, and friendliness without a trace of self-interest or greed. They are the martyrs of folly, acting out not only our potential ignorance and stupidity, but also our potential innocence and goodness as well.

Just as the fool turns reason into nonsense, just as he makes disaster a source of amusement, so he inverts everything. "Fools, with unknowing hearts, turn everything upside down" (*Kathāsaritsāgara* 62.203). A foolish servant, fetching oil as directed by his master, was stopped on the road by a well-meaning man who pointed out to him that there was oil leaking from the pot. In order to inspect the pot, to find the small leak in it, the moron turned the pot over and all the oil poured out (*Kathāsaritsāgara* 61.188–192). Everything is topsy-turvy in humor as in satire. Comedy stands on its head to look at the world.

From that vantage point the social hierarchy is inverted. Once upon a time there was a foolish girl of the *caṇḍāla* caste, the very lowest group in the Indian social hierarchy, a girl who thought herself too good for marriage to another *caṇḍāla*. With the resolve that she deserved the greatest of all men, she decided to marry the king. But when she went to inspect her future husband, as he came out of the palace in a royal procession, she saw that he bowed to a wandering ascetic. If the king would prostrate himself before the holy man, it stood to reason that the mendicant was a greater man than the king. And so, now intent on marrying the ascetic, she followed him, pleased that she had not mistakenly married someone as lowly as the ruler. Trailing her chosen fiancé to a temple, she saw him bow down before the idol of Śiva. Reasoning that Śiva must be greater than the holy man, she vowed to marry the god. But then, when a dog came along and raised its leg to piss on the idol, she reckoned that the dog must indeed be greater than the Lord of the World. She was intent on marrying the dog. Following the cur to the house of a *caṇḍāla,* she watched it settle at the feet of the pariah. She reasoned that the *caṇḍāla* was surely the greatest man in the world, greater than the king, the holy man, the god, and the dog. She married him and lived happily ever after (*Kathāsaritsāgara* 61.208–214). The triumph would not be possible without the grace of folly.

Fools are endearing because they, unlike the objects of satire, mean well. Premendra Bandyopadhyaya told me a joke: "Did you hear the one about the brahmin whose wife sent him to the bazaar to buy an umbrella?" The woman carefully instructed her husband. "Whatever the price he asks, only pay half of that." The man asked the price of the umbrella. "Eight rupees," the merchant answered. "I'll give you four," the man said, following his wife's instructions. "What do you think I am?" the merchant snapped. "I sell things at fair prices. But since you are a friend, I'll give it to you for four." "Okay," the customer smiled, "I'll take it for two rupees." The umbrella salesman became furious. "It is worth eight rupees. I was willing to give it to you at half price. Now you want to give me only two rupees! You are a cheat and an ingrate! Take the umbrella for two rupees! But don't come shopping here again." "I'll give you one rupee," the brahmin said, remembering his wife's words. Now the merchant became so enraged that he threw the umbrella at the brahmin. "You insult me! Get out! I never want to see your face again! Take the damn umbrella for nothing! Take it and get out!" The brahmin smiled, "May I have two of them, please?"

Jokes, passed on for pleasure in social intercourse, travel around the world like venereal disease. I had heard the same joke as a child, but then it was about a Jew whose wife had sent him to buy a stewing chicken. I told Premendra that. "How can this joke be funny," Premendra asked with a genuinely quizzical expression, "if it is not about a brahmin?" Premendra is, of course, a brahmin. The fool, to be truly humorous, must, in some way, be ourselves.

"Seeing the reflection of the sun mirrored in the water in a pot," Śaṅkara, the wise philosopher, solemnly sermonized, "the fool thinks it is the sun" (*Vivekacūḍāmaṇi* 218). The philosopher insinuates that all who fail to realize that the objects of our perception are but dim reflections of the eternal *brahman* are fools. The phenomenal world, the empirical self, and the relationship between them all are all illusory. The interaction tricks us, plays epistemological pranks and jokes on us. It makes fools of us. This monistic Vedāntic position, always fashionable in Indian intellectual life, links us with the fool. Intellectual apprehension of worldly things, any knowledge save that of the one *brahman,* is folly. We are all fools then, and the comic stories of imbeciles and noodleheads are Vedāntic parables, allegories pointing to the silliness of ordinary perception and knowledge. The fool acts out our metaphysical ignorance and our painful entanglement in the endless round of birth and death.

Beholding drops of water on a lotus leaf, the fool thinks they are pearls. One fool "tried to take the drop of water from the leaf, but it disappeared from his fingertip. So distressed was he that he couldn't sleep,'' Bhallaṭa laughs, ''for he kept trying to figure out where that pearl had gone'' (*Bhallaṭaśataka* 96). ''Life is as fleeting as water on a lotus leaf,'' a laughless hymn attributed to Śaṅkara asserts. ''Abandoning love, anger, greed, and delusion, realize 'I am the Self'—fools lack that knowledge'' (*Dvādaśapañjarikāstotra*). Wealth and affection, power and ritual, friends and lovers, family and community, are but false pearls, drops of water on a lotus leaf, transient and insubstantial. It is folly to imagine otherwise.

Traveling by boat, a certain fool dropped a silver vessel overboard. ''I'll remember this spot,'' the fool thought to himself, ''and I'll retrieve my treasure on the way back.'' During the return journey he looked closely at the currents and eddies. Suddenly he dove into the water. When he surfaced empty-handed, his fellow travelers asked him why he had jumped out of the boat. He explained. ''I remembered that wave from before.'' They all laughed at him (*Kathāsaritsāgara* 61.278–281). In Vedāntic terms all our worldly actions are just such leaps into the sea, in that the very fabric of empirical existence is as changeful as the waves watched by the fool. Change is the essential quality of the world and the source of all illusion. Only *brahman,* the Self, is permanent and therefore real.

A fool went to a tank to quench his thirst. Seeing the reflection of a gold-crested bird in the water, the moron mistook it for real gold and entered the tank to get the riches. Desire is the fetter and the enhancer of delusion. When the fool grabbed at the gold, stirring up the surface of the water, it suddenly disappeared. As soon as he stood on the bank again, he saw the gold again. Once more he entered the tank and once more the gold disappeared. Again and again he tried. Repetition, engendering a sense of absurdity, is both a characteristic of comedies and of the great comedy of birth and death, the ontological farce of creation and destruction. We are born only to die only to be born yet again and yet again; the universe is created only to be destroyed only to be created yet again and yet again. The story is a parable about the desire for wealth—all gold is fool's gold. The storyteller notes that foolish people, deceived by false impressions, are both a laughingstock to their enemies and a source of sorrow to their loved ones (*Kathāsaritsāgara* 62.187–192). We laugh at the boy and yet the laughter is tinged with sorrow. He is at once an enemy, a part of ourselves that threatens to hold us back, and a loved one, a part of ourselves that is innocent. Humor is the resolution.

The Indian moron joke stories seem to illustrate the Vedāntic vision, and yet comedy always turns back on itself, laughs at what it has established as true. There are jokes about Śaṅkara. "During his great tour of victory, Śaṅkara became the teacher of the King of Kāñcī. Everyday he would explain to that monarch that the world is but an illusion, that it is woven from the threads of *māyā,* that nothing—not the reverent subjects in his kingdom, not the beloved wives in his harem, not the valued gold in his treasury—is real but *brahman.* The king instructed his minister, 'Tomorrow when Śaṅkarācārya arrives, place a cobra in a food basket and have that basket delivered to him with his meal. We shall see if this philosopher himself really believes that everything is an illusion.' The plan was set in motion. Śaṅkara opened the basket and the snake crawled out. The philosopher screamed, leapt to his feet, and jumped out of the window. The king, waiting for him there in the courtyard, was laughing. "So all is illusion, eh, Guruji?" "Yes, indeed," Śaṅkara calmly answered, "all save *brahman,* the real Self." The king laughed. "If that is so, what about the snake? Why did you scream and jump out of the window?" Śaṅkara smiled, "What snake? What window?" (told by Gananath Sastri). We are prompted first to laugh at Śaṅkara and then at the king. Both are right, both are wrong, both have a certain wisdom, both a certain folly. Assumptions, all assumptions, are the common object of such laughter.

Kālidāsa

> He who lives without folly is not as wise as he thinks.
>
> La Rochefoucauld, *Maxims*

Mr. Sastri continued his recollections of his childhood with all the enthusiasm, irony, humor, and embellishment of a true raconteur. His eyes were the eyes of a child, extraordinarily beautiful in their setting beneath white brows. Forgetting about the cigarette burning in the ashtray, he lit another. He refused to smoke mine because "of the damned lie on the package—nothing is 'duty-free.' "

I looked at the crow in the tree, turning its head from side to side as if listening to the stories, opening and closing its beak as if mocking us.

"When I began studying Sanskrit my father told me a little story about the great Kālidāsa. Imagine it—Kālidāsa was a dullard as a child, a noddy, a boob, a driveling ignoramus! He could not learn one iota of Sanskrit. He was an orphan raised by cowherds. But he was a happy boob! Why? Because he was an ardent devotee of Kālī. And the ardor of his religious conviction filled him with joy. He would go to her temple and there he would dance for her. It looked just like jumping around, but it was the best dance he could do. When he saw her hideous form, he would whistle and laugh and shout, 'How beautiful you are, Mamma!' Then he would cry. Then he would sing and everyone laughed at him. 'Mamma, mamma, your baby needs you! Mamma, mamma, don't spank your little baby. Mamma, mamma, give me sweets!' Over and over again he would cry out, '*Muñca maṃ! jāva ajjūe saāsaṃ gamiśśaṃ* [(Prakrit) Release me! I shall go to my mamma].' The priests and pandits shook their heads. 'What a silly bumpkin this Kālidāsa is,' they said. He slept by the door of the temple in order to be near his mother. And one night Kālī appeared to him in his dream. 'Of all my devotees, you are the most sincere. So great and uncompromised is your devotion that you let them laugh at you for my sake. In your folly you are the wisest of all. For this devotion, I will give you the gift of eloquence and intelligence. You will be the greatest of all poets, the supreme jewel in the garland of jewels adorning the court of King Vikramāditya.' And when he awakened from that dream, he was wise and Sanskrit flowed mellifluously from his lips. He had the knowledge of all joy and of all sorrow. He had the gift of praise, and Vikramāditya gave him one lakh for each syllable that he wrote. He attained what all men aspire to—wit and wisdom, fame and fortune, the love of women and the respect of men. But with these boons came attachment to the world and the sorrow that must accompany such attachment. Kālidāsa, the wise poet, met a fate from which the foolish devotee would have been spared. In Śrī Laṅkā, a courtesan, jealous and designing, poisoned the bard. The poet's friend Kumāradāsa found him on his deathbed. He asked him, 'Of all of your works, which is the greatest, which is the most perfect?' And Kālidāsa answered, 'Only one line in all of my dramas and *mahākāvya*s is of real merit—*Muñca maṃ! jāva ajjūe saāsaṃ gamiśśaṃ* (Release me! I shall go to my mamma).' These were Kālidāsa's last words. This line is uttered by the child of Śakuntalā at the end of the *Abhijñānaśakuntalam*. Taken at face value, in the context of the play, this line is not great, certainly not the greatest line in the play, let alone in Kālidāsa's works as a whole. What then did the poet mean? This line was the only remnant of his former, foolish but holy, self. It was the simple line that he had always sung to Kālī. And because he uttered those words on his deathbed he went immediately to heaven, transported by his blessed mother, Kālī!" Gananath Sastri lit another cigarette.

I asked him if he believed that the story had any historical validity. He laughed a laugh that seemed to have been curled up in his gut, a laugh that woke up startled, leapt from the throat, through the mouth, stretching in midair to pounce with a growl and a bark, a laugh that chewed up what I had said. "What story does not have validity? History is only that which happens to have happened. These things are not any more true or untrue than those events which just happen not to have happened."

"Then anything goes?" I challenged.

"What a wonderful idea!" He laughed and continued. "After my father told me this story, he posed a question to me: 'Would it be better to be Kālidāsa, the foolish devotee and ever-happy simpleton, or Kālidāsa, the enlightened poet, prone to all of the sorrows that accompany the joys of this world?' Which would I choose? Now you must remember that he asked me this question just as I was beginning to study Sanskrit. I did not know what to say. I tried to reason it out. Since my father was a learned pandit and a poet himself, I suspected that Kālidāsa-the-poet must be the correct answer. But since the end of the story suggested that the learned bard himself would have chosen to be the happy dullard, I guessed that Kālidāsa-the-fool was the correct answer."

"Was that the right answer?"

"No. My father told me that I must aspire to be truly learned so that someday I would realize that I was truly a fool. With that realization happiness would come. Then he made me learn all the case endings for the Sanskrit nominal forms."

Mr. Sastri looked chagrined. "I'm still not happy with the question. I am still not sure about the answer. The question raises a multitude of paradoxes and problems, a myriad of confusions and conundrums. I still haven't figured it out. Who is wise? Who is a fool? Touchstone in one of the plays which I have translated into Sanskrit, that humorous drama by the Kālidāsa of Britain, voiced the essential paradox: 'The fool doth think he is wise, but the wise man knows that he is, himself, a fool.' Here's the gist of it: if I think I am a fool, I am wise; if I think I am wise, I am a fool. But what if I know the paradox? Then when I think I am a fool, I am actually thinking that I am wise, so I am a fool once again. On the other hand, if, still knowing the paradox, I think I am wise, I am actually thinking I am a fool, which by the previous proposition, means that I am wise. Or does it? I cannot figure my way out of it. I am a fool! I mean truly a fool. I really do think I am a fool, but I do also think it is wise to think of oneself as a fool. That is why I am such a fool—because I think I am wise. No. I am a fool. No! Yes! I don't know!" He laughed again, "I really can't figure it out."

"You must be too wise to figure it out!" I joked.

"You fool!" he snapped, aping anger.

"Thanks," I laughed.

"No, I meant it," he said with a gravity, real or pretended, which was almost instantly obliterated by his laughter.

The Joke's on You: *The Wise and Holy Fool*

If any man among you seemeth to be wise in this world, let him become a fool, that he may be wise. For the wisdom of this world is foolishness with God.

I Corinthians 3:18

Yājñavalkya, the paradigmatic sage of the *Upaniṣads,* mentions a group of men whom he considers to be *paramahaṃsa*s, the highest of holy adepts. "The marks of holiness are not seen on them and the behavior of holy men is not displayed by them. Though they are not mad, they behave like madmen." Among these men Yājñavalkya lists one, Jaḍabharata, whose name means Bharata the Fool (*Jābāla Upaniṣad* 6). The holy man, the wisest of men, often appears to be a fool. His wisdom is not flaunted as such. His insights are extraordinary and strange. The wisest of men, like the most foolish, live outside the social hierarchy, beyond normative values and conventional behavior. People, less wise and less foolish, laugh at them.

A begging bowl on the road—
  broken, the scrap-filled skull,
  left by the dense and dull,
Yet used by sages—
  they know truth in the heart,
  the real Self—That Thou Art;

It was his—
  by simpletons repulsed and scorned,
  naked, matted-hair unadorned,
And he danced—
  at the crossroads children, sweet but cruel,
  clapped their hands and laughed at him—
THE FOOL.

(Bhartṛhari [Kosambi ed.] 418)

While the notion of the wise fool or holy madman is an ancient one in India, that figure only became a model of religiosity and a conventional literary character with the flowering of devotionalism in the medieval period. The natural purity of the simple heart, rather than the purity of brahmins attained through birth, the purity of yogis attained through discipline, or the purity of sannyasis attained though renunciation, became the ideal. The gods rewarded loving faith. Vernacular stories of the medieval devotees stress their natural folly. Sur Dās, Kabīr, Tulsī Dās, Caitanya, Tukuram, and others often refer to themselves as fools, as *mahā*fools in relation to god. As Kālidāsa was said to be a dolt who, as a reward for his devotion to Kālī, was given the gift of eloquence, so Pāṇini, the systematizer of Sanskrit grammar, was said to have been a dullard as a child. Because of the sincerity of his devotion to Śiva, he was granted intelligence. Mahīpati, the compiler of the *Bhaktavijaya,* legends of the great devotees, assures his audience that he is a fool: "I am mentally dull and stupid. I ain't never read the *Purāṇa*s and I don't know no Sanskrit. But that don't matter to Kṛṣṇa—he just loves stories about his devotees" (1.8–9). And he consoles his fellow fools with the revelation that Kṛṣṇa came to earth "in this Age of Dullness to redeem fools, numbskulls, and ignoramuses" (1.5).

Caitanya once happened upon a man reading the *Bhagavadgītā* aloud in a temple. As he read everyone around the man laughed at him for he mispronounced all of the words. The man himself was weeping and trembling, and Caitanya asked him which words had made him cry so. "I don't know the meaning of any of the words," the rube confessed, "but as I sound them out I see Kṛṣṇa in Arjuna's chariot. He is holding the reins in his hands and he is speaking to Arjuna and he looks very beautiful. The vision makes me weep with joy. Caitanya smiled at the holy fool: "You are an authority on the *Bhagavadgītā*. You know the real meaning of the text" (*Caitanyacaritāmṛta* 2.9.93–103). That fool was wiser than any pandit.

Such irony is an essential dimension of the comic revelation. Satiric irony, as we have seen, always involves the conflict between a reality of some wise, holy, or in some other way venerable, appearance with another, more real, wholly contradictory, and concealed reality of squalor, depravity, or degradation. The irony of humor, an inversion of the irony of satire, points to the potential wisdom, purity, and holiness of the masses of people, of the poor, the humble, and the unnoticed. It asserts that the meek shall inherit the earth. The cynicism of satire might add that they'll only inherit it because they won't have enough courage to turn it down. But while satire denounces and rebels, humor accepts and surrenders. Satire negates, laughs a nasty "no" in the face of all promises and ideals. Humor affirms, laughs its exuberant "yes" in the face of all that is dark and miserable. Most often comedy is some mixture of the two. It laughs, "yes! no! yes! no! I don't know!" And it laughs again.

A religious irony central to devotionalism questions the relative significance of human learning and knowledge. "For the wisdom of this world is foolishness with God." Love, a natural impulse within every human being, no matter how foolish, could be transformed into the highest wisdom by the grace of its object. Knowledge, discipline, and rites were detrimental if they threatened that natural emotion. Love, the source of all folly, was suddenly the matrix of wisdom. "If any man among you seemeth to be wise in this world, let him become a fool, that he may be wise."

A bald fool was sitting beneath a tree one day when, for no reason, a bully threw an apple at him. It hit him on the head. The man did nothing. Angered by the man's lack of reaction, the thug threw another, another, and another. Still the man, whose head was now dripping with blood that "looked like a crown for the king of fools," did nothing. Asked why he didn't fight back, let alone duck, the man answered, "They were such delicious apples." And everybody laughed at him (*Kathāsaritsāgara* 61.48–55). The fool is humble and grateful. Folly is virtue comically exaggerated.

Another fool found a lost purse full of gold. A wiser, smarter, more clever person would have run off with it, but the fool stood inspecting it, happily counting the money. He stood there grinning for so long that the owner returned and took the purse from him (*Kathāsaritsāgara* 64.28–31). The fool is good, even if it is only because he does not possess the cunning to be bad.

Once upon a time there was an old guru who had five devoted students, noodleheads one and all. While their spiritual preceptor was sleeping, they discussed what gift they might give him as a token of their respect. One suggested that since he was so old and weak, and yet still went from village to village teaching, that they should get him a horse. Unanimously agreeing that it would be a fine and fitting gift, they pooled their money and went to town to buy the best horse they could afford. They sat down by a tree to rest in the shade when a man carrying a bag of watermelons came by and began to talk to them. Typically, the fools were honest and utterly guileless. They told that roguish melon vendor what they were doing. "What a fine coincidence," the watermelon man said, "I am, in fact, a horse seller. I have many excellent horses, strong ones for work, fast ones for racing, all sorts of well-bred horses. So how much money do you have?" They told him the truth. "Well, you can't really afford a very good specimen with only that much. But I'll tell you what you can afford—you can afford a horse egg! Then you can hatch your own horse and raise the animal for your teacher, a steed that will serve him for many years." Enthusiastic over the idea, the fools asked if he happened to have any horse eggs. "Yes, I just happen to have one right here," he smiled, holding out a watermelon. "It's the very best horse-egg I have." The foolish religious students, handing over all their money, took the "egg" to their guru. The old man was pleased with the gift and touched by his students' generosity. "I have never seen a horse egg before. But live and learn, I say. I shall sit on it myself tonight. Let us bring it with us to the village where I am to speak this afternoon." Two of the students carried the horse egg. As they came over a hill, one of them tripped, and the watermelon was dropped. It rolled down the hill and split open against a tree trunk. A rabbit, resting by the tree, jumped with fright and ran off. "Look, there goes the tiny horse that was in the egg!" one of them cried. "Our master's horse, so fast, so lightning fast, is gone!" They wept with sorrow over the accident. But the guru assured them. "Do not weep. That horse was too fast for me—that was a horse for a warrior, a prince, or a god, not for an old guru. Such a spirited animal might have run away with me or thrown me off. By dropping the horse egg you probably saved my life. I thank you. I rejoice in your kindness and in my good fate" (retold by M. A. Jagendorf, *Noodlehead Stories from Around the World*).

There is a poignancy in humor wholly absent from satire. It arouses sympathy. The currents of humorous laughter within the ocean of comedy have an undertow of melancholy. Needing water for his ablutions and fire for his sacrifice each morning, a fool decided to mix the fire and the water together. Both were ruined and everyone laughed at him in his sadness and disappointment (*Kathāsaritsāgara* 61.9–13). But those who laughed did so with the banal wisdom that fire and water do not mix. The greater wisdom, the wisdom that the fool has but does not know he possesses, is that they do. The fool is less successful but no more foolish than Brahmā who placed the raging fire of Śiva's asceticism into the depths of the ocean where, according to the myth, it continues to burn:

> The fire is immersed in water,
>   the sea in which it's drenched,
> And yet it does not perish,
>   for its thirst is never quenched;
> The ocean is consumed by fire,
>   the flames that it contains,
> And yet it is so very vast
>   that every drop remains.
> Wondrous is the fire and wondrous the sea,
> Thoughts of their greatness completely dazzle me.
>
> (*Subhāṣitaratnakoṣa* 1198)

Only fools can comprehend the great and subtle mysteries. Only fools are capable of the great faith, the act of make-believe, that all religions demand. The notion of a Christ, crucified and then resurrected, was, according to Paul, utter "foolishness to the Greeks." And the Greeks were, above all else, wise.

Cūlapanthaka

> There were two boys there who had placed one long piece of wood at right angles to another, and they were seesawing up and down. Brother Juniper went there, took one of the boys from his place, and sat down and started to go up and down. . . . A number of those [watching him] said: "What kind of stupid sheep is he?" After they had all left, Brother Juniper was quite consoled because many had mocked him.
>
> Fioretti

Buddhist hagiography contains tales of a Thera named Cūlapanthaka, brother Little Walker, who, after his initiation into the order, proved to be such a bonehead that he was unable to learn even a single stanza of the Buddha's teaching after months of study. Many of the monks laughed at the intellectual ineptitude of his efforts. The fool's brother, Big Walker, was so embarrassed by his sibling's stupidity that he urged him to leave the order. But Cūlapanthaka explained that, even though he could not memorize the Buddha's words, and even though he did not understand them, he so loved to listen to those words that he had no intention of returning to the life of a layman.

Out of shame over his younger brother's foolishness, Big Walker, whose responsibility it was to call the monks to hear the Buddha speak, refused to inform Little Walker whenever the Buddha addressed the monks. Cūlapanthaka's feelings were so deeply hurt, his sense of worthlessness became so great, that he resigned himself to leaving the order. As he was walking sadly along the road, the Buddha met him and asked where he was going. Cūlapanthaka explained to the Buddha that he was too great a fool to be a worthy disciple. The Buddha smiled and gave Cūlapanthaka a piece of cloth, instructing him to use it to wipe the sweat from his brow. Doing as he was told, Cūlapanthaka soon noticed that the cloth became dirtier and dirtier. "I have made this cloth that was clean dirty. All compounded things are impermanent!" At once he grasped the essence of the Buddha's teaching. At once the fool became wise (*Cullakaseṭṭhi Jātaka* [4]; *Dhammapadatthakathā* 4.180ff.).

Those who laughed at Cūlapanthaka did so on the assumption that they were superior to him, wiser than he. That was their folly. The muted, humorous laughter that the story intends to evoke is laughter at oneself over the realization that oneself is no wiser than the fool. Tradition notes that, in a previous birth, during the life of Kassapa Buddha, Cūlapanthaka had been a very learned monk, and that he had been reborn as a dolt because he had once laughed at a monk who was having trouble memorizing scripture. He needed several lifetimes of stupidity to purge himself of the arrogance that comes with knowledge.

In another previous incarnation he was also a nitwit. He went to study with a religious preceptor, but despite the sincerity of his heart, he could learn nothing. The teacher, not unsympathetic with the simpleton, taught him a special charm: "You try, you try! What are you trying to do? Even I know that." Awakened one night by some thieves creeping into his house, the stupid student muttered the magic words and at once the thieves fled. The story came to the attention of the king of Varanasi. As the monarch was waiting for his barber to sharpen the razor for his shave, he recited the words aloud. At once the barber fell at the king's feet and, begging for mercy, confessed that he had been bribed by the king's generalissimo to cut his throat. The king banished the general and made Cūlapanthaka his commander-in-chief (*Dhammapadatthakathā* 1.250ff.). Being a fool can have its rewards. A more explicitly humorous variant of the same story is told in the Bengali folk tradition. A certain noodlehead, hearing of the great rewards the king gave for poetic composition, tried to write a verse. But he could not think of anything, not a single line of poetry, until one day, while watching a pig wallowing in the mud and then rubbing itself against a tree, he spontaneously happened to utter aloud:

> *Rubbing, rubbing, dipping, then rubbing with might and main,*
> *What your rubbing's all for, is easy enough to explain!*

The fool was delighted and scratched the words onto a palm leaf. "I've written a poem! I'll take it to the king and maybe he'll reward me!" When he arrived at the palace, he became suddenly embarrassed by his efforts. "I'm a fool. The king will probably have me banished for insulting him with such a poem." He threw the poem down and ran away. Later that day, the king went into the garden to have his shave. While the barber was sharpening his razor, the king happened to notice the palm leaf with the poem on it on the ground. He picked it up and read it aloud. The barber, thinking the poem referred to his rubbing the razor against the sharpening stone, thought that the king knew what he was about to do, confessed that the queen and chief-of-police had bribed him to assassinate the king. After having his wife and her lover beheaded, the king sought out the fool who had written the poem and made him his court poet. The poem wasn't so stupid after all (after the retelling by W. McCulloch, *Bengali Household Tales*).

The irony of triumph through folly is stressed in the story of the humble, and therefore blessed, simpleton Cūlapanthaka as retold for children in a Japanese educational comic book. "What a fool you are!" one monk exclaims, "you'll never attain awakening. Go home!" Poor little Panthaka feels disgusted with himself. "Why am I so foolish?" he asks, with a self-effacement that is natural to the holy fool, an attitude encouraged within Japanese Buddhism. Children tease Cūlapanthaka, taunt him by asking him to add one and one. When he cannot, the children laugh, "he's a fool!" The fool fulfills his social function only when we, like others, laugh at him; he fulfills his religious function only when we, unlike others, cease laughing. The story of Cūlapanthaka, like the stories of all holy fools, reconciles the social and religious responses: we laugh and yet we don't; we know why the others find him funny, and yet we take him seriously. Compassion can arise out of the same perceptions that yield the comic sentiment. Buddhism teaches the transformation of all sentiments, love and fear as well as mirth, into compassion. And so the Buddha, the most serious of beings, he who asked the crucial question—"how can there be laughter?"—appeared to Cūlapanthaka and explained to him that "no one is a fool who is aware of his own foolishness." The piece of cloth given to the fool by the Buddha in the Indian legend becomes a broom, a conventional Japanese Buddhist symbol of the perfections of patience and effort, in the comic book. As he sweeps, and sweeps, and sweeps, little Panthaka tries to repeat the words of the Buddha. Other monks laugh at him, but he does not care. Suddenly the perfections of patience and effort give way to the perfection of understanding. And Cūlapanthaka laughs aloud. He gets the meaning of the Buddha's words, as one gets a joke—with a sense of surprise, a relief of tension, and a resultant delight.

Laughter can signify either folly, as does the laughter of the monks at Cūlapanthaka, or wisdom, as does the laughter of Cūlapanthaka over the sudden revelation of the truth. But that wisdom, in a Buddhist context, demands silence. As Cūlapanthaka stands in reverence before the Buddha, the laughter of his delight turns to the tears of a greater joy (S. Chida, *O Shakasama*).

The comic book explains that the fool, Cūlapanthaka, became one of the most distinguished of the Buddha's disciples. The Buddha looked upon him as Saint Francis looked upon the seemingly foolish Brother Juniper. The Saint could not help but joke: "I wish I had a whole forest of such Junipers."

Ramakrishna

Let the little children come to me; do not stop them; for it is to such as these that the kingdom of God belongs. I tell you solemnly, anyone who does not welcome the kingdom of God like a little child will never enter it.

Mark 10:14–15

It was Mr. Bandyopadhyaya who first interested me in Ramakrishna, "a holy man *par* excellent." He gave me a portrait of the saint with instructions to contemplate the "bliss of his smile." I confessed that the smile looked rather like a frown to me. "So it must seem to one who does not know the blessed teachings of the blessed saint," he laughed wryly, almost grimly. "The comedy of life appears to some as a tragedy."

The lore of the saint, at least in Mr. Bandyopadhyaya's telling of it, was familiar. "When he was a lad in school, both his teachers and his schoolmates thought he was a dullard. This was because book knowledge meant nothing to him. Life was the only book he wished to study. While his brother, Ramkumar, was mastering Sanskrit and all of the Vedas, Ramakrishna was making images of the gods. They were the toys with which he played. Unlike other children, his play was divine. His toys really were gods. Just as people thought he was a fool when he was a child, so they thought he was a drunkard or a madman when, later in life, he would worship—he would shake all over, he would fall down, jump up, fall down again. He would go silent. Then he would laugh, then cry, then laugh again. Ramakrishna was a saint *par* excellent."

Mr. Bandyopadhyaya kindly gave me a copy of *The Gospel of Ramākrishna*. "This will help you in all of your confusion." I was startled. "Do I seem confused?" Without any reluctance, my host, though we hardly knew each other, said that, yes, I was confused about several things: "religion, politics, women, and money. You are also very confused about India." I blushed as I laughed, "Is that all?" Premendra looked down at the floor as if out of embarrassment either for his father or for me. "No. You are also very confused about humor. I have met many people who are confused about religion and politics, about women and gold. And I have met many foreigners who are confused about India. But you are the only person whom I have ever met who is confused about humor. You are always asking questions about that topic!"

"That's because I hope to write a book about it."

"In India we write books about topics that we understand. You want to write a book about something you don't understand. Is that not a foolish endeavor?"

I admitted my folly and promised to read the *Gospel of Ramakrishna*.

Ramakrishna, I learned, was fond of recounting a story of a boy who posted a letter to god addressed to heaven. He explained that the boy's folly was holy. "A perfect knower of God and a perfect idiot," the saint would say, "have the same outer signs" (p. 792). Folly was for him not something to overcome, but something to rediscover, or to attain through the grace of god. Ramakrishna stressed that he who has seen god becomes a fool. "He laughs, weeps, dances, and sings. Sometimes he behaves like a child, a child five years old—guileless, generous, without vanity, unattached to anything, not under control of any of the gunas, always blissful. Sometimes he behaves like a ghoul: he doesn't differentiate between things pure and things impure; he sees no difference between things clean and things unclean. And sometimes like an inert thing, staring vacantly: he cannot do any work; he cannot strive for anything" (p. 269). Like the fool or the child, the truly holy person, for Ramakrishna, has no sense of order, caste, hierarchy, or distinction. "He doesn't discriminate about caste. If his mother tells him that a particular man should be regarded as his elder brother, the child will eat from the same plate with him, though the man may belong to the low caste of a blacksmith. The child [like the fool, the drunkard, the madman, or the holy man] doesn't know hate, or what is holy or unholy" (p. 171). The *paramahaṃsa,* the greatest of all sages, according to Ramakrishna, is no different than the most foolish of all fools—"he doesn't keep track of his whereabouts. . . . He cannot distinguish between a stranger and a relative" (p. 491).

The fool has a potential for an experience of god that is denied to the more sensible, judicious, or certain. "God cannot be realized by a mind that is hypocritical, calculating, or argumentative" (p. 672). The fool is gullible. Like the swindled fools who bought the horse egg for their guru, the truly holy person trusts the world. He is like a little child. "He becomes as quickly detached from a thing as he becomes attached to it. You can cajole him out of cloth worth five rupees with a doll worth an anna" (p. 171). Total trust, foolish trust, is both a symptom of, and the means to, sanctity.

Once upon a time a certain foolish herdsman was befriended by some con men. They told him that they had arranged for him to marry the daughter of a very rich merchant in a nearby village. The fool was so happy that he gave them money to repay them for making such a fine match for him. When the sharpers told him that the marriage ceremony had been performed, the guileless herdsman became so elated that he gave them more gifts. Soon they informed him that his wife had given birth to a son for him. In complete joy he gave them all of his wealth. The crooks left town. One day people in the village, seeing the herdsman weeping, asked the reason for his tears. He was not crying, as they had expected, over the loss of his wealth. "I am sad because I miss my son," he said, and all the villagers laughed at him (*Kathāsaritsāgara* 61.17–24). There is something holy about the man. He is wiser, in a sense, than the fools who duped him. He is profoundly gullible, but gullibility is, after all, only a vulgar term for faith. Ramakrishna would certainly have done the same. He played the part of the fool. "I don't want *brahmajñāna* [knowledge of the absolute]," he would cry out, "I want to be merry. I want to play. . . . I don't know the Vedānta; and Mother, I don't even care to know" (p. 373).

The great Bengali holy man would worship his own penis as the personal, corporeal manifestation of the universal, cosmic *liṅga*, the image of Śiva. While we, in the West, imagine that the *liṅga* is a phallic symbol, Ramakrishna understood the phallus as a liṅgic symbol. Everything is a symbol of god for the holy fool.

"I am the greatest of all fools," Ramakrishna was fond of announcing with laughter sometimes, but often with tears (p. 407). The question is whether the announcement is a confession or a boast, or both, or neither. The statement is humorous if it is serious, serious if it is humorous.

"It is appropriate that you study this gospel of Ramakrishna," Mr. Bandyopadhyaya smiled ironically, "for it was Ramakrishna who brought you into our home." It was true. I had made reservations to stay at the Ramakrishna Mission upon arrival in Calcutta, but when the superintendent saw my bottle of Johnnie Walker, he informed me that neither alcohol nor tobacco were permitted in the Mission. I immediately contacted the Bandyopadhyayas, relatives of a friend in England, for suggestions as to where to stay. "You must stay with us!" Mr. Bandyopadhyaya insisted. "These bloody fools! Ramakrishna would not approve of what they have said to you! He himself noted that the holy man is no different in his mode or manner than the drunkard."

One of the glories of strong drink is that it gives all humanity access to the wisdom and holiness of folly.

Feeling No Pain: *The Drunken Fool*

Shalom, my friend, has an exceedingly kind nature and he oftentimes helps people when he is able to do so. His only fault is a love of strong drink, but this craving saves him from every other sin.

Niflaoth ha-Yeheidi

The Buddhist monk who heeds the Buddha's injunction against intoxicants by hiding his fondness for wine is an object of satirical unmasking. The Kāpālika who flaunts his drinking with the claim that it is sacramental, that what is merely enjoyable for the rest of us is a liturgical act for him, is equally, but differently, a target of satire's merry scorn. Exposures of hypocrisy and a self-righteous dissembling give rise to satiric laughter. The gentler and more sympathetic laughter of humor is prompted by the drunkard, he who without pretense, excuse, or shame, drinks and gets happily drunk. The drunkard is a fool, subject to illusions, but capable, as the cartoon by Śikṣārthī suggests, of delighting in those illusions and in his sweet folly (fig. 20).

The drunkard hides nothing. Wine dissolves all concealments. In drunkenness his weakness, folly, and vulnerability are plainly seen. The drunkard, without claim to superiority, even flaunting his foolishness, is never prudish, sanctimonious, or judgmental.

Figure 20

There is a poignancy to the humor of the universally comic character. The poet Rāmakṛṣṇa laughs at him.

> Cast a glance for a moment, look to your right,
> Here comes a booze-bibber, a disgusting sight:
> Helter-skelter he weaves; he stumbles and trips,
> Shooing away the flies that swarm round his lips,
> Gibbering gibberish, barfing up liquor,
> Surrounded by kids—oh look how they snicker!
>
> (cited *Mahāsubhāṣitasaṃgraha* 3833)

The unabashed drunkenness of the wino is a humorous folly rather than a satiric vice. The drunkard hurts no one but himself. Most often he is a good man, if only because he is too drunk to commit any real sins or crimes. "He pursues vice with great difficulty," Kṣemendra muses (*Kalāvilāsa* 6.22). He has trouble misbehaving even when he wants to. A whore tells her colleagues of a lover "who, under the influence of wine, seemed dead as he lay there on a part of the bed, his sleep wholly unobstructed. Thus my night went by with pleasure" (*Kuṭṭanīmata* 394).

"Folks ridicule the drunkard," the Jain poet and monk Amitagati (tenth century) warns—they laugh because or in spite of the inevitability that "he is bound to have hassles and he is sure to lose his job; wealth vanishes from him; he gathers up stain and he tosses out sexual potence" (*Subhāṣitasaṃdoha* 579). The poet indicates the folly of the lush, the source of his comedic appeal, the way in which his drunkenness turns the world upside down: "Ah! The dipsomaniac regards the king as a servant, and a servant as the king; he thinks a well is the ocean, and that the ocean is dry" (505).

It became a convention for the drunkard, often the *vidūṣaka* after a bout of boozing, to provide the comic relief in typically melodramatic Sanskrit plays. Bharata provided a description of the ways in which drunkenness was to be enacted to bring out its full comic effect, and he classified the kinds of drunkenness appropriate to various types of characters. "People who are drunk will sing or laugh, some will sleep, others will use harsh words. Light intoxication is characterized by a smiling face, a pleasant feeling, a joyful body, slightly faltering words, and a delicately unsteady gait. Medium intoxication is characterized by rolling eyes, drooping arms or arms restlessly thrashing about, and an irregularly unsteady gait.

Excessive intoxication is characterized by loss of memory, an incapacity to walk, vomiting, hiccoughing, burping, spitting, and a thick protruding tongue'' (*Nāṭyaśāstra* 7.39, 41–43). Certainly a great deal of the comic impact of the drunkard was dependent on the actor's ability to imitate the gait and speech, to master the apparently uncoordinated movement. Spectacles of loss of control inspire laughter.

The physical and verbal improprieties of the drunkard, represented by the acrobatic abilities of the actor and the rhetorical skills of the poet, the incongruities between what the lush attempts to do and what he can do, epitomize the more general improprieties and incongruities which the literary theorists posited as the causes of the comic sentiment. Describing a ''lady who left her house blind drunk'' with vocabulary from the canons of literary criticism, technical terms used by the rhetoricians to explain the comic sentiment, the poet Bhikṣāṭana says that ''people laughed at her as they laugh at the works of a hack poet'' (cited in the *Mahāsubhāṣitasaṃgraha* 3876). Both the soused lady and the bad poem have ''their ornaments in all the wrong places.'' The same phrase (*padaskhalana*) explains that ''her feet stumbled'' and that the bad poem was full of ''misplaced words''; one word (*aprasanna*) indicates that she's ''not gracious'' and that the poetaster's words are ''not clear.'' The bad poem and the drunk lady are both comic. They've got things all wrong.

Kṣemendra describes one tippler who, in his drunkenness, strips off his clothes and pisses. ''With cupped hands he drank the moon as it appeared in his urine'' (*Kalāvilāsa* 6.20). The comic image plays upon both the occasionally Tantric practice of drinking urine and the poetic conceit of drinking the moon from a wine cup.

cool Reflections
  in the Wine
sulking Women
  drink the Moon
penetrating
  Anger's Mine
their Hearts
  the Mead
    until soon
Women's Souls begin to shine.

(*Amaruśataka* 120)

Drunkenness is frequently considered a grace in women, an enhancement of the amorous mood and erotic sentiment. Irāvatī, a loving lady of the harem in the *Mālavikāgnimitra* of Kālidāsa, entering the stage drunk, utters a proverb, "Drunkenness is particularly an ornament for women." Her lady-in-waiting agrees—"What was a proverb, you've made a truth" (prose after 3.12).

While wine is ever censured in the normative brahminical, dharmic texts as abhorrent, something anathema to an idealized control, wine was a popular delight in everyday life. Secular literature abounds with descriptions of sumptuous drinking parties at which people were enthralled with the sweet wonders of wine. "They drink wine there: it snaps the chains of modesty round the women of the harem; it is the whole sum of the life of Love; it is the attendant of loveplay. With wine their faces are flushed red, like lotuses opened and blushing from the rays of the sun" (*Kathāsaritsāgara* 110.127–128).

Communal drinking is play. Glasses and goblets clink; bottles and pitchers are passed; deep laughter, lush eloquence, and resonant songs flow from wet mouths. The energy of camaraderie overflows at drunken festivals as flushed and exultant drinkers form a holy community, a revelrous, though ephemeral, communion. Drinking, like humor, establishes friendship, fun, the erosion of barriers, and the filling of abysses. Drunkenness coalesces and harmonizes. It lends an innocent decadence to love. At certain ancient weddings, according to *Gṛhyasūtras* of Gobhila, the Indian bride's body was rubbed with rum and the priest sang out: "O Love, I know your name—drunkenness is your name."

Wine:

in the midst of love's ladies
  oh to drink that wine,
shaken as one befuddled passes it,
  remaining in the cup she drinks,
dripping from her mouth,
  clinging to her lips,
is to know the taste,
  is to savor love.

(*Dhūrtaviṭasaṃvāda* 61)

Wine is infused with the spirit of celebration, the spirit which humor constantly affirms. The drunkard, the fool, and the humorist rediscover irresponsibility and regression. The drunkard is a child, whole and undivided, a child tasting paradise, a child sweet and selfish, immaculate and crude, joyous and desperate. The ancient bar was a setting for fun, a place for jokes, comic banter, and warm laughter. "Liquor shops should consist of many confortable rooms furnished with cots and seats," Kauṭilya soberly explains. "The drinking house should possess comforts appropriate to the changing seasons and there should always be garlands of flowers and scents and perfumes" (*Arthaśāstra* 2.25).

The drinking saloon was a temple consecrated to Balarāma, Viṣṇu's descent as the drunkard, the avatar of inebriation and tutelary deity of tipplers and swillers. "May the divine wine guzzler, he who bears the plow, purify you within the drinking taverns!" (*Saduktikarṇāmṛta* 1.48.4).

Balarāma

> We run with the god of laughter; labor is joy and weariness is sweet, and our song resounds to Bacchus.
>
> Euripides, *The Bacchae*

Varuṇa, for the sake of some recreation for Balarāma, sent his consort, Varuṇī, the goddess of wine, down to earth where she concealed herself within the hollow of a *kadamba* tree. When Balarāma smelled the liquors flowing from the tree, with exuberant thirst he quaffed the wine. Then, in drunken stupor, he called the Yamunā river to come to him that he might bathe. And when his command was ignored, he used his plowshare to drag the river to him. The tortuous course of the river is explained by the staggering of the drunkard (*Viṣṇu Purāṇa* 5.36; *Bhāgavata Purāṇa* 10.65; *Harivaṃśa* 83).

Balarāma is invoked in the *Nāgānanda* of Harṣa as a comic parasite staggers soused onto the stage, followed by a servant bearing a wine pot. The carouser stammers and slurs. "As far as I am concerned there are only two gods—Baladeva, who eternally drinks booze, and Kāmadeva who brings about sexual union for folks. My life is fulfilled since my beloved lies on my chest, and because my mouth is filled with lotus-scented wine!" (*Nāgānanda* 3, opening scene).

In Balarāma, Kṛṣṇa's irascible brother, the quarrelsome Plowman, god becomes a rummy. Drink is to Balarāma what sex is to Kṛṣṇa. The bibulous incarnation is a comic one, full of surprises and incongruities. God is so soused he can hardly speak. He is a fool, humorously human and comically confused.

"Why's the earth sp-sp-spinning around?
  Why's the moon fa-fa-fa-falling down?
Kṛ-kṛṣṇa, te-tell me quickly
  Why are our tribesmen la-la-laughing?
Boo-booze!
  Le-le-let go of my mou-mou-mou-mouth!"
May the Ploughholder,
Sputtering this drunken stutter,
    Bestow prosperity upon you!

(*Subhāṣitaratnakoṣa* 6.24)

And the poet Lakṣmīdhara laughs, "Balabhadra is victorious!" It is humorous, ironic laughter over the theophany of a stinko god:

Rum-drunk and more irascible than ever
from tripping over all the cattle,
        Balarāma,
persistently kissing her, hugging her,
and yanking the garment from her breasts,
just couldn't get it up for Revatī—
It seems that he was too crocked on wine!

(*Saduktikarṇāmṛta* 1.48.1)

His drunkenness is beatific. There is a comic intersection of mundane folly and transcendental grace. Implicit in his mythology is a divine dispensation and a shower of blessings for drunkards and fools.

Speech sputtering, word mumbling,
Body boozily bumbling,
Clothes ramble-scramble crumbling,
Revatī held hands fumbling,
Eyes blinking bloodshot, tumbling,
Leis laden with bees rumbling
Blotto from breath so humbling:
        Balarāma!
May his drunken stagger save you!

(*Saduktikarṇāmṛta* 1.48.2)

Balarāma was the slayer of Dvivida, a monkey as scampish and rascally as the god. The ape, who amused himself by "defiling the sacred Vedic fires by pissing and shitting on them," happened to come upon Balarāma, surrounded by playful women and drunk as usual, in the forest. The monkey chattered and jabbered in a mockery of the deity, and the women, "enjoying the joke, burst out in wild laughter." Aping the gestures of lovers, the animal winked his eyes, puckered his lips, and then, finally, exposed his genitals to the ladies. He snatched up the wine jug, laughed at Balarāma, and made great fun of him. The god lost his sense of humor. Humorous laughter was subverted into something terrible. "Balarāma broke Dvivida's neck with his hands, and the ape fell down and vomited up torrents of blood" (*Bhāgavata Purāṇa* 10.67.6–25).

The humor of both the monkey and the drunkard is the humor of nonsense. There is an innocence in nonsense and a relief from the pressures of sense and sensibility. The appeal of both is the appeal of pure instinct, of deliverance from repression, guilt, morality, rationality, and, above all, seriousness. The moment of laughter expresses the momentary pleasure of such a redemption.

The monkey, a universal comic archetype in the great allegory of human folly, fulfills the fool's role throughout Indian literature. He is clever and yet stupid, human and yet bestial, devious and yet innocent. It is the contradictions within him that make him humorous.

Monkeyshines: *The Allegorical Fool*

At a great gathering of all the beasts the monkey got up to entertain his friends by doing a dance. So nimble were his feet and so amusing his gestures and grimaces that all the animals roared with laughter. Even the lion, the king of beasts, forgot his royal dignity and rolled on the ground with glee.

Aesop, *Fables*

There is a bas-relief at Bharhut of two monkeys. One of them has a pitcher of water, the other holds a plant that he has pulled from the ground. This stone cartoon from the second century B.C.E. illustrates a kind of moron joke. "Why did the monkey pull up the tree? To get to the root of the matter." The royal gardener had left some monkeys in charge of watering the plants in the king's garden.

The leader of the monkeys addressed the herd. "We don't want to waste any water, so let's pull up all the plants by the roots and give the most water to those having the roots which reach deepest into the ground. . . . With a desire to do good, the fool only does harm," the moral goes (*Ārāmadūsaka Jātaka* [46]). The comedy of folly is the farce that results from the sense of incongruity provided by the severance of aim and result. The monkeys are allegorical personifications of human folly.

When some monkeys entered a temple that was under construction, one of them noticed a wedge driven into a wooden beam for the sake of splitting it. "One of the silly monkeys, playing around, hopped onto the beam. His balls just happened to hang down into the crack in the beam. Thinking to himself that someone had driven the wedge in where it didn't belong, the monkey pulled it out with his hands" (*Pañcatantra* 1.27–32). The superficial moral of the story—"mind your own business"—is conveyed in an image that is at once comic and horrific, an image that taps into deeper and darker layers of consciousness where the story perpetuates a fantasy that castration will result from breaking the incest taboo. The comic story, like its many variants in jokes from many cultures, serves the teleological function of validating the fear that preserves the socially and domestically valuable taboo, while simultaneously serving the psychological function of relieving the tension caused by that fear through laughter. Castration jokes arouse anxiety and relieve it. The arousal is in content, the relief in form.

An ancient, perhaps comic, variant of the joke occurs in the *Ṛg Veda*. The simian Vṛṣākapi, "Mr. Macho-monkey,"the son of Indra according to the commentator Sāyaṇa, tries to seduce his father's wife who, insulted by the sexual advances, angrily threatens to cut off his head. She teases him: "He's not so macho—his prick dangles between his thighs." The refrain of the hymn asserts the power of the father—"Indra is the greatest of all!" (*Ṛg Veda* 10.86).

From the Vedic period on, the monkey is often the allegorical personification of lustiness, of sexual desire unhampered by conscience, reason, or propriety. Comedy, thriving as it does on erotic impropriety, makes much of the monkey. He is the fool and champion of sex.

"Ever hear the one about the monkey that fucked the Buddha in the ear?" In a life previous to the one in which he was to become fully awakened, the Buddha was born as a brahmin who, after devoting himself to Vedic study, retired to a Himalayan hermitage where, on the banks of the Ganges, he practiced fierce austerities, immersed himself in deep contemplation, and mastered the perfection of patience. Each day when he would sit down in meditation, "a rambunctious monkey came along, stuck his prick in the ear of the Buddha-to-be and fucked away as the consummately detached Buddha-to-be remained calm and tranquil. One day a tortoise, crawling out of the river to have a nap in the sun, fell asleep with its mouth open. The randy chimp, seeing the open mouth of the tortoise, promptly jumped off the head of the Buddha-to-be and quickly treated himself to some fellatio. Thus rudely awakened, the tortoise bit down on the monkey's prick." Screaming with pain, holding the tortoise that refused to loosen its grip on his penis, the monkey hopped about, howling for help. The Buddha-to-be emerged from his deep meditation and laughed at the monkey. "Who is this wandering around holding a begging bowl? Is it a brahmin seeking offerings of food or a monk collecting alms?" The monkey cried out, "Help! I'm a fool! Please! Release me!" The dirty joke becomes a Buddhist parable. Desire, particularly sexual desire, is the cause of pain. Through suffering one seeks refuge and release. The holy one joked, "The tortoise is a member of the Kassapa clan, and the monkey is a member of the Koṇḍañña clan. Between these two clans intermarriage is permissible. Now that the marriage has been consummated, you, Mr. Tortoise, can let him go." The monkey freed his prick as soon as the tortoise laughed (*Kacchapa Jātaka* [273]). The moment of laughter is, in comedy, a moment of release. Comedy, like Buddhism, has freedom as its goal.

Such "prettie Allegories stealing under the formall Tales of beastes," according to Sir Philip Sidney, "makes many more beastly than beastes." The allegorical monkey is comic only to the degree that he is human or that he provides a perspective on human folly which he either personifies or indicates through contrast. The nonhuman figure, the monkey, like Swift's Houyhnhnms, can voice an entirely etic and objective perception of human behavior. "Begin to heare the sound of vertue," Sir Philip advised, "from these dumb speakers."

The Buddha-to-be in a former life was born as a monkey who, as a baby, was captured by some woodsmen and given as a gift to the king. For several years the monkey lived in the palace doing tricks and amusing the king. Monkeys are, by nature, funny. They are incongruously human. The king was so pleased with the monkey's antics, with all the merriment and laughter he had inspired, that he decided to release the monkey. Again, laughter yields freedom. The king instructed the woodsmen to let the monkey loose just where they had found him. Asked by the other monkeys to speak of where he had been, the royal monkey insisted that he did not dare tell them about the ways of men. But, under the pressure of their pleading, he finally gave in. "Human beings, royalty and brahmins as well, are fools. Blindly they say of everything, 'This is mine, mine!' They are fools, blind to the transience of things" (*Garahita Jātaka* [219]). Human beings are, by nature, funny. They are incongruously bestial. Monkeys may be foolish, but their folly is wisdom compared to the folly of humanity, our folly. Comedy makes monkeys of us all.

The monkey in Indian fables personifies either folly or cleverness, taking the part of either the fool or the fool's inverted double, the trickster. A monkey, the figure assumed to be foolish, outwits the human being, the figure assumed to be wise, in another story in which the monkey is used to indicate the greed of human beings. A certain greedy king had a son who had some pet monkeys. One of the monkeys, clever as he was, realized the palace was too dangerous a place, made so by the basic inhumanity of the people there. He sought refuge in the forest. The tale could be a religious parable indicating the necessity of renunciation for the sake of liberation from the world; or it could be a psychological parable indicating the necessity of leaving the house of the father for the sake of liberation from one's own childhood. Eventually the king, at the advice of his court physicians, had his son's monkeys killed to use their fat as a medicinal balm for his horses. Learning of the fate of his brethren, the monkey in the forest decided to take revenge. He went to a marvelous lake in the forest that was inhabited by a man-eating monster that wore a garland of pearls around its neck. The monster grabbed the monkey. "Wait," the monkey cried, "I can get some really delicious human meat for you if you will but give me your pearl necklace to use as bait." The monster agreed, and the monkey took the necklace to the king who was dazzled by the beauty of the pearls. "Oh king," the monkey says, in a modern Indian version of the *Pañcatantra* (*Human Folly and Other Stories*) prepared for children, "I will lead you deep into the woods where there is a wonderful lake. Whoever bathes in it will come out with his neck adorned with a pearl necklace like the one

I am wearing." The king and all of his men were devoured by the monster. While the stories of the monkey as fool warn the son against transgressions against the father, stories of the monkey as trickster indicate a potential for the triumph of the son over the father, the triumph which is maturity.

The Buddha-to-be in a former life, according to the *Jātaka* variant of a story found in the *Pañcatantra* and other collections, was a monkey. He used to frequent an island in the river where mangoes and other fruits grew wild. He would jump from the shore, to a rock, and then onto the island to eat his fill. A crocodile, urged on by his wife to catch that monkey so that they could eat its heart, climbed onto the rock and lay perfectly still so that the monkey, unable to see him, would jump onto his back. But the clever monkey, noticing the unusual height of the rock, became suspicious and decided to investigate. "Hey rock! Hello there! Hello! Hello rock!" The crocodile/rock remained silent. "Hey rock," the monkey shouted, "every day you say hello to me—what's wrong today, why won't you answer?"

"Hmmm," the crocodile thought to himself, "I'd better talk or he'll suspect I'm not the rock." "Hello Monkey, what's up?"

"Oh, I was just wondering who or what you are and what you're up to."

"I'm a crocodile sitting here waiting to catch you and eat your heart."

"Oh, I see. Well then, I guess I had best surrender to my fate—open your mouth and I'll jump in." When the crocodile opened his mouth, the monkey jumped onto his head and then sprang to the bank and ran off laughing (*Vānarinda Jātaka* [57]).

The clever and triumphant monkey is divinized in the mythology of Hanumān. If the monkey is comic to the degree that he is human, he is both more so and less so to the degree that he is divine.

Hanumān

> "What sort of wisdom are you hoping to learn from me?" the Patriarch asked. "I leave that to you," Monkey laughed. "Any sort of wisdom—they're all the same to me."
>
> Wu Ch'eng-en, *Monkey*

"Hanumān is in no way comic," the Delhi art collector and historian insisted. "Why are Westerners always considering him ludicrous. He does not inspire laughter. He inspires awe and reverence. For the Mahāvīra Melā at Aliganj, the devotees crawl to his temple on their stomachs. Their knees and palms bleed with devotion. They are not laughing! They are weeping, weeping with joy! What is Hanumānji, the greatest of warriors, the greatest of yogis, the greatest of *bhaktas*? He is obedience, service, simplicity, devotion, self-control, strength, and humility." The man showed me a selection from his great collection of drawings and paintings of Hanumān. "The only thing humorous about Hanumānji is that Westerners think he is humorous. The *Rāmāyaṇa* itself proclaims, 'Hanumān is perfect; no one equals him in learning, in mastery of the scriptures, in austerity, or in strength.' What is funny?"

I tried to answer: "What about when Indra attacked Hanumān with his thunderbolt and wounded him, and Hanumān's father, the wind god, took revenge by flying into the mouths of the gods, staying in their bellies and afflicting them with flatulence. The idea of constipated gods suffering from gas is surely comic." The collector grimaced, not finding the idea of divine farting at all funny. "Flatulence is not humorous. Have you never been afflicted with this terrible condition?"

"What about the story of Hanumān's birth [*Rāmāyaṇa* 7.35]? Isn't it funny when the famished baby monkey jumps out of his mother's arms up into the sky to devour the sun, mistaking it for a piece of fruit?"

"No!"

"What about all the other stories in which Hanumān doesn't know his own strength, like the story of how he knocked over all the sacrificial implements and dishes in the hermitages of the great sages [7.36]. Surely that was meant to be funny."

"No!"

"Isn't it funny when he sets Laṅkā on fire with his tail?"

"No!"

"What about when the monkeys destroy Madhuvana [5.61]? Isn't it funny when they get drunk in the orchard?"

"First of all, they are monkeys. Perhaps monkeys are humorous to some. Gods should not be humorous. Hanumān is a god who seems to be a monkey to the ignorant. He is in no way humorous. But, second of all, the monkeys that desecrated the grove are not humorous in any case. They show us, by their example, the foolishness of a propensity toward liquor. Such a propensity allows greed, lust, and other vices to get the better of us. The result is always destruction. We should not behave like those monkeys who, in their drunken state, were laughing and laughing. Rather let us model our behavior on that Hanumān who was ever devoted to Lord Rām. Hanumān is in no way humorous."

Despite my informant's insistence to the contrary, it is hard not to see many of the episodes in the mythology of Hanumān as serious epic versions of once comic folktales. The *Rāmāyaṇa* is heroic rather than comic. It is moral and didactic, sober and brahmanic. Aubrey Menon suggests that brahmins kept rewriting Vālmīki's tale to get it to say the very opposite of what the original poet originally meant. Menon wrote his own ironic version of the epic in which he attempted to retrieve what he believed to be the original mood, to rediscover and reestablish its lusty humor. Menon's modern, witty version ends with Rāma questioning Vālmīki as to what he believes is real. The sagacious poet smiles. "There are three things which are real: God, human folly, and laughter. Since the first two pass our comprehension, we must do what we can with the third."

Hanumān, the tutelary deity of wrestlers, is the Baby Huey of Indian mythology. His inability to assess his own strength leads to countless comic incidents. In the epic his battles are heroic, but they retain a trace of a possibly originally comically slapstick character, and this is played upon in popular reenactions of stories from the epic. I sat in the theater in Delhi. The exuberant laughter of the audience was as loud as the fierce pounding of the drums. The shadow puppets from Andhra danced with wild energy on the other side of the bright white screen. As the jaws of the demonic crone Surasā opened and closed mechanically, a dexterous switching of puppets made it seem that Hanumān was growing larger and larger, that he would at once fill the screen, overwhelm the theater, the city even. The monkey whirled around like a rimless wheel, his arms, legs, and tail the spokes. He pummeled the *rākṣasī* with those spinning limbs. Suddenly tiny, he flew in and out of her mouth. Then he was large again. With each change in size there was more laughter, louder drums. The folk spirit of Andhra infused the deadly serious and gravely moral epic with manic magic, transformed it into a Punch and Judy show. The slapstick violence and comic hysteria provided that kind of atavistic spectacle in which one can still sense the rites out of which comedy must have emerged. It seemed to be a frenzied celebration of fertility, a raucous ritual for the subduing of demonic forces and the joyous renewing of the world. The animal slew the hag. The laughter in the theater turned to applause, the darkness to light.

The burning of Laṅkā also brought gales of laughter. When I told the art collector about the evening, he shrugged his shoulders. "Such performances help children appreciate the *Rāmāyaṇa*." He hesitated and smiled ever so slightly, "children and Westerners perhaps."

Mendicant actors dressed up as Hanumān frequent religious fairs in India. They play the god for laughs and, in return for entertaining the crowds with divine monkeyshines, they receive offerings to that god. Improvised performances of the antics of the god are but individual spin-offs of more formalized plays based on the *Rāmāyaṇa*. Caitanya is said to have taken the part of the simian god in dramatizations of the story of Rāma.

Such dramatizations transform the epic in many ways. There is the transformation of an aristocratic sensibility into a folk one and the transformation of the ideal of duty into the ideal of devotion. There are also instances of a transformation of tone or sentiment from the heroic into the comic. In one performance (based on *Rāmāyaṇa* 6.128), Sītā gives Hanumān a necklace of jewels for him to take to Rāma. The prop is a garland of grapes. The monkey bites into them and then throws them away. Asked what he is doing, he explains that the splendor of the jewels makes him think they contain the holy name of Rām and so he opens them. But they are discarded when he finds nothing within. "Things that do not contain the name Rām," the monkey announces, "are of no use" (*Rām Līlā* as recorded by Norvin Hein, *The Miracle Plays of Mathura*). The episode reverses a conventional comic motif from the literature of folly in which some animal, often a monkey, mistakes a ruby, or some other jewel, for a pomegranate seed, a grape, or some other piece of fruit.

The Monkey:

He held you up and pawed you,
He sniffed you and he licked you,
He nibbled and he gnawed you,
Finding no juice, he flicked you;
O Ruby!
I know that it surprised you,
But be grateful for your fate;

He could have pulverized you—
You could be what he just ate.
(*Saduktikarṇāmṛta* 4.18.3)

The folly of the monkey in the poem is that he throws away something of value because it is not what he expects it to be. He is fooled by appearances. So is Hanumān. But while the monkey throws away the jewel because it is not a piece of fruit, Hanumān throws away the jewel (which is a piece of fruit) because it does not contain the holy name. Hanumān's folly, a variation on the profane folly of the monkey, is a holy folly, a folly greater than wisdom, the folly of loving devotion. The spectators laugh and their laughter affirms the irony of the wise fool, an irony that stresses the irrelevance of discrimination and knowledge in comparison to a simple and yet total devotion to god. Hanumān is the key character in a divine allegory, one who, by example, promises salvation not from folly, but through it.

Hanumān is to Rāma in the folk dramas what the *vidūṣaka* is to the king in classical Sanskrit drama, a devoted sidekick whose antics serve to intensify the power of the hero.

A Scholars' Conference: *The Theatrical Fool*

I'm a fool, that's no mistake;
Yet I too have some remarks to make.
Anonymous German Carnival Play

Director (*Sūtradhāra*): Enough, enough. The audience requests me to present the play called *A Scholars' Conference* (*Paṇḍitasamāgama*), a rather undramatic work made tolerable only by the presence of the *vidūṣaka*—the fool, clown, or jester of Sanskrit drama, the mocker, messer-upper, disgracer, or spoiler. The work is full of shameless plagiarism—all the words of the characters themselves are taken straight from their own books! And here they come now—a procession of pandits! What could be the meaning of this? What do professors have to do with fools? What is a fool? Perhaps my wife, author of *The Fool,* knows. [*Looking-off-stage*] My wife, you whose breasts resemble the sinus lobes on an elephant's forehead, you whose thighs resemble the plantain, you of exquisite buttocks and *bimba*-lips, if you are truly back there, join me on stage.

Actress (Enid Welsford): A Fool is a man who falls below the average human standard, but whose defects have been transformed into a source of delight, a mainspring of comedy. . . . As a dramatic character he usually stands apart from the main action of the play, having a tendency not to focus but to dissolve events, and also to act as intermediary between the stage and the auditorium.

Director: Well said, my dear. But with the *vidūṣaka* specifically we are concerned. Surely in a book about comedy in India there must be some statement about the *vidūṣaka*. This dramatic figure has attracted a good deal of scholarly attention. Practically the only things written about Indian comedy have been written about him.

A Voice Off-Stage: Come on, come on, this is getting dull.

Director: Ah, the voice of the *Vidūṣaka* himself. So, my dear, let us be off!

[*Exeunt both. The Vidūṣaka enters—he has protruding teeth, a bald head, and a hunched back. His face is distorted and he walks with a limp.*]

Vidūṣaka: When I heard there was going to be a conference of scholars, I rushed right over. What is a conference after all but an excuse to eat and drink and gossip; and those are the three things I like to do the most. Oh, here come the boys now! But keep in mind that "I'm the only real scholar here—after all my father-in-law's father-in-law used to haul the books around in some fellow's house" (*Karpūramañjarī,* prose after 1.18).

[*Enter Professors Bhatt, De, Huizinga, Jefferds, Keith, Kuiper, Schuyler, Siegel, and Suntharalingam wearing academic gowns.*]

Professor Siegel (author of *Laughing Matters*): Let's start with the obvious. The *vidūṣaka*, a brahmin who acts contrary to brahminical norms, is the sidekick of the dramatic hero—a lover or warrior—and the comedy of the *vidūṣaka* balances the play.

Professor Huizinga (author of *De vidūṣaka in het indisch tooneel*) [*playing around as he speaks*]: The *vidūṣaka* is a counter-stroke of the spirit of the play itself; the loftiness of the sentiments comes out the more strikingly by the contrast of his vulgarity. . . . His clumsiness manifests itself in his committing silly blunders in the very circumstances in which all depends on him—blunders with which he gets his friend into trouble, especially because he always lets his tongue run away with him.

Vidūṣaka [*laughing*]: Professors are experts on runaway tongues!

Siegel [*to Vidūṣaka*]: It's remarkable that you can get away with impertinences like that whether to kings or professors. It is, I suppose, only because you're willing to play the fool.

Vidūṣaka: "I'm not such a big fool that I don't know the right time and place for a joke!" (*Mṛcchakaṭikā,* prose after 3.23). That's more than I can say for you guys!

Siegel: Careful—you need us to be funny! And if you're not funny you get cut from the book or play!

Vidūṣaka [*snickering*]: And you need me not to be dull. Without me the hero is lost. Thus one has described me:

> He is comic at parties,
>   and yet ferocious in war;
> He is a guru when there is sorrow,
>   and yet rowdy at other times;
> He makes for a festival within my heart . . .
>   Ah, but why all this babbling?
> He is my flesh indeed
>   split, it seems, in two!
>
> (Bhāsa, *Avimāraka* 4.27)

I am at once the hero and an alternative to him. We are one and yet, and yet . . .

Professor Jefferds (author of "Vidūṣaka versus Fool: A Functional Analysis"): The *vidūṣaka* does offer an "alternative" to the hero, one that is strongly felt in the totality of the *rasa.* He speaks for and embodies certain fundamental human urgencies. His pusillanimity, his suspicion of the ideal in any form, and particularly his notorious and perpetual hunger are expressive of self-preservation, security in retrogression, the stability of consolidation—in contrast to his master's idealism and predisposition to incautious expansion, externally referent progression.

Siegel: Yes, the *vidūṣaka* stands in relationship to the king like Pancho to the Cisco Kid, like Gabby Hays to Hopalong Cassidy, like Andy Devine to Wild Bill Hickock. Without the comic sidekick, the goodness, nobility, and grandeur of the hero would be unbearable. The *vidūṣaka*, in his buffoonish imperfection, makes the perfection of the other characters tolerable and real. The disgracer highlights the grace of the hero.

Jefferds: But unlike so many of the "boon companions" of world literature—Sancho Panza and the rest—the *vidūṣaka* is almost purely a figure of "fun," important not in that he qualifies the "meaning" of the main action, but for his modal impact on the whole. . . . The hero is desire in self-transcendence, the *vidūṣaka*—especially in his food orientation—is desire as subsistence, every cycling back to safety and satiety. . . . He is, in his burlesque embodiment of appetite, an antic distortion of life, a fun-house mirror that mocks but does not actually modify the original.

Vidūṣaka [*holding his sides with laughter*]: A mirror! Yes a mirror! "In my case, brahmin that I am, everything's backward like a reflection in a mirror—the left's over on the right and the right's over on the left" (*Mṛcchakaṭikā,* prose after 1.16).

Siegel: As the hero of the drama is the champion of love, of the spirit, so the *vidūṣaka* is the champion of hunger, of the body. As the king represents an abstraction and affirms an ideal, the *vidūṣaka* represents and affirms concrete realities—he kvetches, he moans, he whines, he laughs. He's hungry, he's tired, he's uncomfortable. And the comic sentiment, mood, or flavor arises out of his deflation of the principle, usually amorous, sentiment of the play. There is a comic dialectic in Sanskrit drama, a contest between ideals and realities, spirit and flesh, heaven and earth. And at the same time there is a cooperation in the contest, there is a bond made between these oppositions. The *vidūṣaka* serves a function—he provides for an aesthetic resolution of the tension between spirit and flesh.

Vidūṣaka [*breaking wind*]: Yeah, yeah, yeah. Why does Siegel do so much talking? He should give the others a chance, especially since he's stolen most of the his ideas from them anyway.

Professor Kuiper (author of *Varuṇa and the Vidūṣaka*): It may be suggested that the original full function of the *vidūṣaka* in the dramatic performance not only consisted in cooperating-in-contest with the hero, but also in purifying the king, as the sponsor of the performance, by taking upon himself the latter's impurity. . . . Only a brahmin was able to redeem the king from evil by accepting the role of scapegoat.

Vidūṣaka [*rubbing his belly*]: God, I'm hungry. With all these Dutch professors around you'd think there'd be some chocolate. No! Not a bit! Not even any Edam cheese!

Professor De (author of "Wit, Humor and Satire in Ancient Indian Literature") [*disgruntled, scowling at the Vidūṣaka*): The *vidūṣaka*'s attempts at amusing [us] by his witticisms about his gastronomical sensibilities were originally unavoidable concessions to the groundlings; but much of his wit [has] lost its flavour which we must believe it once possessed, while most of his oddities [have become] fatuously conventionalised into mere buffoonery.

Vidūṣaka [*picking his nose*]: *Mere* buffoonery?

De: The outworn jests of yesterday's literature, like the exposed relics of yesterday's feast, leave us cold today, even repel.

Vidūṣaka [*gesticulating wildly*]: Did you say feast?

Professor Bhatt (author of *The Vidūṣaka*): The dramatists have shown the *vidūṣaka*, as a brahmin, to be very fond of food. . . . The *vidūṣaka* symbolizes the uneducated, stupid, pretentious Brāhmaṇa who was a social parasite. There certainly was much to ridicule about such a class of brahmins. Their pride and privileges coupled with enormous ignorance, their clinging to ritual formality which often concealed hypocrisy and selfishness, their apparent piety which became only an excuse for irrepressible greed—all these were fine subjects for ridicule, satire and comic treatment.

[*While this is being said, Professor De is looking quite uncomfortable.*]

Siegel: While the *vidūṣaka* is a brahmin, a low brahmin not qualified to perform the rituals, the satirical element is only indirect or vaguely implicit. Unlike the usual objects of satire, the *vidūṣaka* has no real power, and he laughs at himself and invites others to do the same—that is how he survives. We laugh at him, and through him at the king and at ourselves as well. I am sure that many a brahmin has laughed over the *vidūṣaka*, laughed at themselves with fine humor and . . .

Professor Schuyler (author of "The Origin of the Vidūṣaka and the Employment of This Character in the Plays of Harṣadeva") [*grabbing Professor Siegel by the neck and placing a hand over his mouth to prevent him from continuing*]: The *vidūṣaka* originated not in the court drama under the influence of the Brāhmaṇa caste, but in the earlier plays of the different tribes of India. These primitive efforts are presumed to have been for the most part farces, their characters were doubtless taken from the actual life of that time. It was in this way that the priest-ridden people had an opportunity to express their hatred of Brāhmaṇas which, no doubt, they early embraced. By making the *vidūṣaka* a degraded and contemptible wretch, who nevertheless was a Brāhmaṇa, they could give a farcical element to their rude and formless plays and at the same time take revenge on the privileged class.

Vidūṣaka [*scratching his armpit*]: Yeah, yeah, yeah.

Siegel: That seems rather overstated. Although I think you are right in suggesting a popular origin for the *vidūṣaka*.

Professor Keith (author of *The Sanskrit Drama*): The popular origin of the *vidūṣaka* is obvious but the question is whether this origin is religious or secular.

Kuiper: The relationship between the hero and the *vidūṣaka* has its origins in the ambiguous relationship between Indra and Varuṇa. The *vidūṣaka* impersonated Varuṇa.

Doctor V. Suntharalingam (author of "Abhinavagupta's Conception of Humour"): The *vidūṣaka* is not merely Varuṇa but Brahmā with an exaggerated Varuṇic aspect; which accounts for the confusion of the Brahmā and the Varuṇa symbolism in the *vidūṣaka*. . . . In delving into the complex symbolism of the *vidūṣaka*, more and more of his features show themselves to refer back, directly or indirectly, to a central function of being the institutionalized transgressor of brahminical norms and taboos, especially founded on the pure/impure opposition which sustains the Hindu socioreligious hierarchy. The *vidūṣaka* is a comic figure precisely because he reenacts this transgressive function, in a purely symbolic mode, before an exoteric audience in the public social setting of the Sanskrit drama, where these taboos still have all their binding force. Since a unilateral valorization of breach of taboo is ruled out under these circumstances, there is instead an ambiguous expression that permits the spectators to participate, indirectly and partially—almost unconsciously—through sympathetic identification with the *vidūṣaka*, in these violations; yet, at the same time, the spectators dissociate themselves from his actions under the contrary impulse of fear, shame, disgust and other negative emotional attitudes. . . . It is this "bisociative" structure of the exoteric perception of the *vidūṣaka* that is responsible for humor and laughter; and because laughter is so pleasurable and relaxing, we are prepared to tolerate the absurd, nonintegrated, asocial behavior of this *avaidika* buffoon.

Vidūṣaka [*yawning*]: You boys better hurry up with this. We're already on page . . . [*pauses and looks at upper corner of this page*] . . . Egads! Already on page 290 and we still have to get through a chapter on the trickster, another on Kṛṣṇa, and one on Śiva, not to mention a completely self-indulgent epilogue! Siegel doesn't seem to know one of the cardinal rules of comedy: keep your routine short. Let's go.

[*Exeunt Omnes*]

The Laughter of the Jackal

7

The Trickster: The Righteousness of Roguery

A tiger attacked and severely wounded a jackal. Then, grasping the neck of its prey in its jaws, the tiger ran off toward its lair, dragging the poor jackal along. The jackal, its flesh dripping with blood, suddenly laughed aloud through tears of anguish. "Why are you laughing?" the tiger asked. "I am laughing," the jackal answered, "because Vyāghramāri, the demoness who feeds upon tiger flesh, was just about to eat me. Since she could not find a tiger in the forest, she was going to settle for jackal meat. Just then you saved me from her! And now she is, no doubt, following the trail made by my blood. And when she catches us she will eat you and I shall be spared!" Suddenly releasing the jackal, the tiger dashed off and the jackal's laughter, previously feigned, became quite genuine.

Śukasaptati

For a wicket the boys had painted three streaks on a wall incrusted with a patchwork of peeled posters urging the election of the Congress Party for the good of the nation; a discarded board, pared down at the end, was their bat. I picked up the bald and dirty tennis ball that had rolled to my feet and tossed it to the small boy, the ubiquitous Indian urchin who was approaching me with wide eyes and a timid smile. "Cricket?" he asked. Whispering to each other, radiating an infinite potential for mischief, the other boys came cautiously. I tried to explain that I didn't know how to play cricket, that Americans just didn't do that. When the child unexpectedly threw the ball back to me and I dropped it, the team burst out laughing. One of the boys, lunging forward to pick up the ball, blurted out something in Hindi which I did not understand, and the others laughed louder still as they ran off, and the game went on. The game persists forever. The players change, time-outs are taken, the field moves, the rules fluctuate, but the game goes on.

Gaṇésa, patron god of the comic mythos, once joined a group of boys just like these to play with them just like this. They divided into teams to take the parts of gods and demons and turn cosmic battle into earthy fun. One boy threw a ball up into the air, another caught it, then climbing up and on to the shoulders of the other, he threw it again. Another caught it and, in wild, sweet, playful laughter the game went on (*Gaṇésa Purāṇa, Uttarakhaṇḍa* 93). Comedy is inevitably a quest for the rediscovery of childhood's laughter and the sense of play that threatens to forsake us if it is not guarded well.

Implicit in the comic sense of life is the notion of a metagame—unseen, unplayed, unfelt—an eternal game upon which personal, domestic, and social structures are built in a work that is but distraction from the play. Comedy is access to the primal game, is seduction and invitation to play. The comic sensibility continuously informs existence with the festive spirit of play as it simultaneously recovers that exuberant spirit. Comedy is at once revel and revelation, and the logos that is revealed in laughter is a controlling principle that exists to make sure that things go out of control, a pervasive power insuring that the destiny of all beings is realized in a discovery of their own absurdity—not the solemn absurdity of the philosophers, but the mirthful absurdity of children and clowns.

There is always a trickster in the game, a joker in the deck, to prevent the rules from becoming oppression, the contest from becoming tedious or dull in losing its surprises or enchantments. This universal character of comedy, a prophet of the comic logos, is the laughing herald of renewal. He keeps us on our toes. The trickster is a criminal for the fun of it. He's a rogue whose cleverness absolves him of his crimes, a crook whose crookedness makes others straight.

Through his lies, pranks, games, and jokes, turning the world upside down, the trickster—divine, human, or bestial—in the heavens, court, market, village, or jungle—is the guardian of humor, prompting us to laugh at ourselves, to take nothing seriously, to realize that profundities are but vain inventions of desperate intelligence. He exists in order to remind us of the game, that the game is all.

A Game of Tug-of-War: *The Divine Trickster*

Every generation occupies itself with interpreting the Trickster anew. No generation understands him fully, but no generation can do without him. Each had to include him in all its theologies, in all its cosmogonies, despite the fact that it realized that he did not fit properly into any of them, for he represents not only the undifferentiated and distant past, but likewise the undifferentiated present within every individual. This constitutes his universal and persistent attraction. And so he became and remained everything to every man—god, animal, human being, hero, buffoon, he who was before good and evil, denier, affirmer, destroyer and creator. If we laugh at him, he grins at us. What happens to him, happens to us.

Paul Radin, *The Trickster*

The agon: gods and demons, *deva*s and *asura*s, powers of light and darkness, energies of order and chaos, take their sides over the abyss to play the game of tug-of-war. That abyss essential within each heart, through the psyche is directed out, projected onto cosmos so that it may be infinite, eternal, and more real than any human thought or fragile feeling.

"The gods and demons, issued from the creator, are engaged in contest against each other. [Round one:] the demons win and begin to divide the stakes, our world; [round two:] the gods trick the demons out of their winnings, this world, the sacrifice" (*Śatapatha Brāhmaṇa* 1.2.5.1–10). The rounds are endless, the game persists day and night, through heat and cold, in joy and sorrow, across fields of life and death. "The gods found refuge in the day, the demons in the night, and they were of equal strength, indistinguishable" (*Aitareya Brāhmaṇa* 4.5). The tug and pull on the rope of time, the push and take of fear and desire, back and forth, provides the tension that infuses and perpetuates creation, preservation, and destruction. "The manifold creations of the worlds and their infinite destructions are but games, played again and again" (*Manu* 1.80). Existence is sport, a game of chance, a play, a magic show, "a divine comedy" as the tour guide at Ellora had said.

In play, in fun and jest, Viṣṇu uses the power of magic, *māyā,* to enter the game, to dance on the rope, and tip the balance in favor of the gods. He descends in illusive forms to trick the demons and amuse himself. The comedic spirit animates the avatars of Viṣṇu. "God played the part of the boar just so that he could have fun goofing around in the primal waters" (*Matsya Purāṇa* 248.64). Kaṃsa, ultimately the butt of Viṣṇu's trickery, teases the god, laughs that "the only way he can kill his enemy is by tricks" (*Viṣṇu Purāṇa* 5.4.4).

Viṣṇu is a trickster, a magician, a practical joker. And trickery, as we have seen, was understood in Indian literature to be one of the paradigmatic causes of laughter (*Nāṭyaśāstra,* prose after 6.48).

The Riddle of the Man-Lion

Question: Which would you rather—a lion eat you or a tiger?
Answer: I'd rather the lion eat the tiger.

Anonymous riddle

The demon Hiraṇyakaśipu had won a round in the great cosmic game, had amassed so many points, so much power, that he was assured by Brahmā, the divine referee, that he could be killed neither during the day nor during the night, neither by man nor by beast, neither indoors nor outdoors. Failing to realize that only rounds can be won, that the game itself, being endless, can never be wholly claimed, and with humorless confidence in his own invincibility, Hiraṇyakaśipu, champion of the demons, claimed dominion over the universe and demanded the devotion of gods, demons, and men, of players and spectators alike. But his own son, Prahlāda, an ardent devotee (or sportsfan) of Viṣṇu, resisted. His unswerving loyalty and constant immersion in contemplation of the god so angered his father that Hiraṇyakaśipu tortured him, that good and pious demon, and threatened him with death. "Where is Viṣṇu?" the jealous captain of the teams of demons yelled. And his son answered with holy calm, "Everywhere." "In this pillar?" Hiraṇyakaśipu asked with sarcastic laughter. "Yes," answered Prahlāda with religious conviction and uncanny calm. "Then I shall slay him," the father announced mockingly as he struck the pillar with his royal bat. Viṣṇu, the protean trickster, taking on the bodily form of a man with the head of a lion, burst from the pillar. And there, in the pillared doorway to the palace (neither indoors nor outdoors), and then, at dusk (neither during the day nor during the night), the demon was slain by the man-lion (the god who was neither man nor beast). *Score:* gods 1; demons 0.

By being everywhere, Viṣṇu is neither inside nor outside; by being eternal he exists during neither day nor night; by being god, he is neither man nor beast. Through a prank, the form of the man-lion becomes an expression of the omnipotence, omnipresence, and eternity of ultimately formless divinity. The trick makes a fool of the demon who imagined that he understood the game, that he could not be beaten. The trickster discovers and reminds us of the loopholes in reality and the semantic pleats in the language that creates and represents the illusion which constitutes that reality. The trickster has access to hidden pockets in space and secret compartments in time.

The myth contains incongruities, surprises, tricks, lies, deformities, the characteristics of comedy enumerated in Bharata's seminal list of the causes of laughter. It is a practical joke. And, indeed, as he rushed toward the demon, "the man-lion screeched and roared with piercing laughter" (*Bhāgavata Purāṇa* 7.8.28). The shrill sound of it pierced Hiraṇyakaśipu's ears as the flashing gleams of it dazzled his eyes. Laughing, the god disemboweled the demon screaming. But what causes laughter in gods can cause fear in other beings. "Every being in the entire universe, hearing the horrible roar of the man-lion, became terrified" (*Liṅga Purāṇa* 1.95.18). There is a close connection between the fearful sentiment and the comic. Laughter often voices the relief that occurs when something fearful suddenly ceases to threaten. Implicitly the god promises the devoted that their fear may become mirth and their cries laughter. The horrific visage of the avatar is the comic mask of a trickster, a face worn to play the great game.

The myth of the man-lion is a joke, and the outwitted Hiraṇyakaśipu is the butt of it. The joke has the form of an enacted set of riddles: Who is neither man nor beast? When is it neither day nor night? And where is it neither inside nor outside? The demon is riddled to death. Though many riddles are not comic, they often share in the structure of jokes and rely on the same verbal mechanics as they bring incongruities together, as they surprise and tease. "What is it that has a neck but no head, that has two arms but no hands, and can take away Sītā (and it isn't Rāma or Rāvaṇa)?" one Sanskrit riddle asks; and since *sītā* as a common noun means "cold," the answer is "a shirt" (*Subhāṣitaratnabhāṇḍāgāra* 185.22). Laughter is generated upon hearing the answer, upon realizing that one has been linguistically tricked. We laugh at a riddle when we suddenly get it, seeing sense in some nonsense or nonsense in some sense, when we break through a previously experienced misunderstanding or ignorance. We laugh at ourselves. The god bestows such laughter, so holy and profane.

The Festival of the Dwarf

Child: Mummy, what's the magician doing?
Mother: He's putting on a blindfold.
Child: What's a blindfold, Mummy?
Mother: Something you wear so you cannot see.
Child: Why's he wearing one, Mummy?
Mother: So he can tell us what he's looking at.

Corinda, *Thirteen Steps to Mentalism*

Through the performance of sacrifices, Bali, the grandson of Prahlāda, increased his kingdom to such a degree that it encroached upon the celestial abode of the gods (*score*: gods 1; demons 1). Viṣṇu, enlisted to join the game and tilt the balance once again, playfully manifested as a dwarf, a universally conventional comic persona, often the form of the *vidūṣaka,* to trick the demon and arouse the laughter of the gods. As the magician puts on the blindfold to show how much he can see, so Viṣṇu became small in order to reveal his immensity.

The dwarf stood before Bali, the new captain of the demons, known for his sense of fair play, and asked him for a piece of land, as much as he could cover in three strides. The trickster played the fool and Bali laughed at him—"you have the intelligence of a child" (*Bhāgavata Purāṇa* 8.19.18). Bali said he might ask for much more than land, but the dwarf stuck to his terms. "And Bali laughed heartily as he said, 'Take as much as you wish' " (8.19.28). But Bali's laughter turned to awe as the dwarf revealed his true dimensions and repossessed the universe by taking three strides, one over the earth, one across the sky, and a third which spanned the heavens. Viṣṇu asserted his dominion over the universe, the whole game board, in another practical joke. *Score:* gods 2; demons 1.

In satire the supposed giant is exposed as but a dwarf; in humor the supposed dwarf is revealed to be a giant.

In some versions of the myth, Viṣṇu leaves hell for Bali and makes him ruler over it. According to a South Indian tradition, Bali, exiled to the nether region, supplicated Viṣṇu and requested that he be able to return once a year to see his beloved people. And during the Malayalam month of Chingam, the late-summer period at the end of monsoon designated as the time of that return, the people of Kerala feel constrained to laugh, to joke in displays of festive delight that their anciently righteous king might be assured of their great joy. The jungles are lush, the rivers full, the harvest in, and faces are radiant. Song and dance celebrate that abundance. The festival of Onam is played out with snakeboat races and boxing matches, holy games to enact the myth. Vāmana the dwarf is worshiped and Bali is adored in mirth. The sacred is experienced as fun, the holy is known in play, and throughout the day laughter is the prayer of the people. The comic spirit is affirmed and sanctified in such festivals throughout India.

When I inquired at a travel agency in Delhi about arrangements to go to Kerala to witness and participate in the Onam festival, the agent, seemingly personally offended that I had not yet seen the Taj Mahal, insisted that I buy a package trip to Agra and Fatehpur Sikri. "You must go nowhere else until you have seen the Taj." I explained that I particularly wanted to see the Onam festival because I was interested in the mythology of the dwarf. "It so happens that the very hotel at which I was planning to book accommodation for Madam and yourself is less than one furlong's distance from a Vāman temple. And at that temple, at this very time of year, they are having a Vāman festival. You can attend those festivities and see the Taj Mahal to boot—two proverbial birds with one proverbial stone!" He further insisted that we would not be able to find any accommodations in the villages of Kerala. "Besides, I am not so sure that this festival is still being celebrated. It is a sign of modern times that festivities are rapidly becoming obsolete. If you must go to Kerala, wait until spring and you can go for the elephant festival. I can make arrangements for your stay at Trichur at that time."

The man at the desk in the hotel in Agra explained that he knew of no Vāman temples in Agra, and certainly of no festival honoring Bali or the dwarf. He smiled rather sympathetically as he listened to the story of how I had been tricked. "Well, at least he wasn't completely dishonest. He wasn't lying altogether." The kindly man seemed to be trying to contain the unkind smirk of laughter. "There is, in truth, a Taj Mahal in Agra."

A Game of Pachisi: *The Royal Trickster*

Be the first player to move all four of your playing pieces Home and you win! It will take some skill, it will take some luck! . . . Players of all ages can have fun playing Pachisi, the Classic Game of Ancient India!

Directions to a Pachisi game

I went from shop to shop trying to find a game of pachisi so that we, sitting in the garden at our hotel and feeling the presence of the shamelessly romantic Taj Mahal, could play the game that the great Moghuls played. Akbar, they say, played it with lovely women as the pieces, carnal tokens on great marble courtyard-boards at Agra and Fatehpur Sikri.

"Not only do I not have such a game for sale," the proprietor of a little book and magazine shop informed me, "but you will not find bloody pachisi anywhere in Agra.'' He argued that I should settle for cards. When I explained why we were particularly interested in playing pachisi, he assured me that Akbar was ''a card bloody sharper himself, a master of all card games and the inventor of new ones. He invented bridge. He enjoyed challenging foreign ministers and ambassadors to play cards with him. Whoever lost the game had to crawl around on all bloody fours and bray like an ass. Akbar never lost! He made those ambassadors laughing bloody stocks.''

When I finally agreed to purchase cards from the man, he produced a used deck held together by a rubberband. I expressed a certain disappointment that they were Western-style cards. ''What do you mean? They are Indian bloody cards! See!'' He pointed to the back of the top card which was decorated with a mildly comical, mustachioed maharaja, the logo of Air India. While warning me that one of the cards, the king of hearts, was missing from the deck, he assured me that ''that is no problem—I have taken the pains to mark one of the jokers as such. The joker is wild, you know. The joker can be any card. In this deck he is the king of bloody hearts.'' A metaphor suddenly ignited his imagination and the fires of it shone in his eyes and gleamed in his smile. ''The joker is what we are calling Brahman.'' Metaphysics suddenly overwhelmed him. ''The joker is all cards which is why he can be any card. So it is with Brahman. Brahman is a joker—he can be Śiva or Kṛṣṇa or Allah or Jesus Christ or Confucius or whatever bloody god.'' The fire would not go out. He explained caste in terms of the four suits, karma in terms of the hand of cards we are dealt, heaven as winning, renunciation as folding, different religions as different kinds of games, and so on and on and on until I finally agreed to buy the deck. I even consented to agree that this deck, used and missing a card as it was, was indeed superior, philosophically at least, to any other deck which I might have purchased from some other merchant in that its joker/king would be a constant reminder to me of the essence of Hinduism. With the assertion that we would ''be able to learn everything one could wish to know about the great Moghuls for ten rupees—less than one bloody dollar,'' he also insisted that we buy the Amar Chitra Katha comic books on Akbar, Humayun, Babur, and Jahangir.

Amidst the comics for sale I noticed several on Birbal (1528–1583), a poor brahmin writer of Hindi verse who, through the exuberance of his wit and the tirelessness of his charm, became one of Akbar's favorite courtiers. In folk legends, told aloud throughout north India, the courtier had become a royal jester, a trickster in the court, a joker in the deck.

The bookseller ordered tea. "You are interested in Birbal?" You have come to the right place. I know so many stories of Raja Birbal." In addition to telling us each and every one of those stories and to selling me three comic books—*Birbal the Wise, Birbal the Clever,* and *Birbal the Witty*—he convinced me that I needed to buy a reader for children entitled *More About Birbal.* After I agreed to pay him for the text, he explained that I would not really be able to understand "the bloody wit of it" unless I also purchased its companion volume, *All About Birbal,* a booklet reassuringly described in the puff on its dust jacket as a collection of "fun-filled stories."

The arrival of the tea prevented escape. "So many of these stories are mere fairy bloody tales. You have bought only children's books. You are adults, are you not? You must purchase adult books. Besides, you will not have a clear understanding of the importance or purportance of the legends without some historical background. You are fortunate indeed to have come to my shop. In some other shop you might have ended up empty bloody handed, or at the very best, with only a deck of cards!" I had no choice but to purchase P. N. Chopra's *Life and Letters under the Moghuls,* which I was told was "a very rare first edition," a reprint of Vincent Smith's *Akbar the Great Moghul* (which ironically—and I swear this is true—turned out to be missing pages 170–174, the pages describing Birbal), a guide book to Fatehpur Sikri, an American edition of a collection of short stories by Rabindranath Tagore, "winner of the Nobel bloody Prize," a book, *Indian Ribaldry* by Randor Guy, which I was told "every American will appreciate," and a paperback, published in England, entitled *Jesus Died in Kashmir*—I cannot remember how he convinced us we needed that one.

The collection of Tagore's stories included one, "Bidushak," about a court jester, the *vidūṣaka* to the King of Kāñcī. Returning from conquest in Karnat, the king was accompanied by his counselor and jester. If the brahmin counselor, the *purohita,* in ancient Indian society invested the king's rule with divinity, the brahmin jester, a *vidūṣaka* of sorts, invested it with humanity. Passing through a village near the palace, the king, counselor, and jester noticed some young boys playing with little toy soldiers, and in that war which was their game Karnat was the vanquisher, the boys explained, and Kāñcī was the loser. "The counselor's face became grave; the king's eyes became bloodshot; the jester broke into laughter." To teach the boys a lesson in authority and to remind the people of his kingdom of his power, the king had the boys tied to a tree and caned. When the jester asked for his ruler's permission to leave the court, the king inquired as to the reason for the request. "I am able neither to kill," said the jester, "nor to destroy. By the grace of God, all I can do is laugh. If I stay at the Emperor's court, I shall forget how to laugh." The court jester has the function in the story of reminding his king of the importance of humor, and the function beyond the story of reminding the reader of the same thing.

The humor of the jester in the comic literature of India always tempers the power of the king who, as the representative of *dharma,* law and order, rule and righteousness, is potentially dangerous. The trickster personifies that chaos which, in the long run, preserves order, and that freedom from rules which, in the long run, sees that rules serve rather than oppress. As the cool wit of the satirist scrutinizes the righteousness of kings to make sure that it is genuine, the warmer humor of the jester serves to prevent real righteousness from becoming cold, institutional, or inhuman. The jester reminds the king that he but enforces the rules of a game, a reminder that inspires detachment, a freedom from the anger and oppressiveness which come with an unqualified identification of the kingdom with the ego of the king. The jester strives to make the king laugh at himself. The comic spirit, of which the jester is a courtly representative, subliminally but constantly asserts the value of such self-irony in all people.

Whether or not there were ever in India true court fools, clowns of the European type with actual court office, is largely irrelevant. The roguish jester of the court, scheming behind merry pranks, became a conventional literary figure. Daṇḍin describes one such parasitical joker, a childhood playmate of the king. "He was adept at singing, dancing, and playing various instruments; he was always after strange women; he was very clever at telling dirty jokes, and skillful at making puns, riddles, and such; he knew how to lampoon people and to make folks roar with laughter" (*Daśakumāracarita,* p. 255).

The legends of Birbal emerge through a recasting of history in terms of the literary conventions, the transformation of a biography into a comedy, the hero of which is part *vidūṣaka* and part rogue. With an interest in the actual spark of the court, the life of Akbar's parties, I went to Fatehpur Sikri. I was anxious to enter the house of Birbal the joker, to run my fingers along its walls and look out through its windows. I harbored hopes of hearing resonances of a distant, drunken, and luxurious laughter, of being able to imagine spicy jokes of enamored courtiers and enraptured courtesans.

Hawkers and peddlers, tour guides and beggars, greeted us as we descended from the cramped chaos of the overheated bus. "Come, please, come, please, come at once. It will be the sight of your life," a young man yelled at us with enormous urgency. He wanted us to pay him to dive off the high wall of the mosque into the shallow reservoir below it. "Just like Acapulco," he kept repeating. "I will dive headfirst and headlong just like Acapulco. I'll do it just for you. Fatehpur Sikri is the Acapulco of India!" Beyond the display of high diving and perhaps the heat, the comparison of the Mexican city where bikini-clad, Margarita-drinking Americans drive around in pink jeeps to this dry, desolate, now austere, but strangely beautiful place seemed ludicrous. At night jackals—and ghosts we were told—roamed through the empty courtyards, prowled the forsaken harem and durbar rooms, crouched in shadowy portals, sniffed the dusty treasuries. They howled in the night. Or was the eerie screeching really the laughter of the ghosts? Did Birbal still have jokes to make?

Crossing the great courtyard where Akbar had played pachisi with women as the tokens, making our way to Birbal's house, we talked as we walked, trying together to construct a vision of the court, a sumptuous place of exotic joys, a life of "romantic bemusement and enraptured disorientation" as my companion called it, "a world consecrated by art and dedicated to exquisite purities of form." Our conversation covered the red sandstone with carpets and pillows, and our reveries filled the porticos and windows with fine muslins and variegated silks.

"I don't see Akbar as a person who would enjoy humor or care about jokes," she said as we sat for rest on the floor, beneath a disintegrating bower of tendrils, leaves, and flowers subtly carved into the red stone, in the upper story of Birbal's house. She had read the chronicles of the Court, the accounts of travelers, and the books the bookseller had convinced us we absolutely had to buy. "He seems to have been a somewhat cold, dispassionate, and detached man, perhaps because he lived in a court full of intrigue, in a world of extreme mistrust.'' We looked out over the dry fields of stubble where a lake once was.

''Birbal's house,'' she explained to me, ''was not really Birbal's house. It was probably the residence of one or two of Akbar's favorite queens.'' I was disappointed with the news, but it seemed somehow appropriate that Birbal's house was not really Birbal's house, just as the stories about Birbal are not really stories about Birbal. Travel in India, for me at any rate, teaches a lesson—one that is constantly affirmed in Indian philosophy—that very little, perhaps nothing, is what it is. It's the lesson of the trickster.

Birbal and the Comedy of Intolerance

Leane he was, hollow eyde, as all report,
And stoop he did too; yet in all the court
Few men were more belov'd than was this foole,
Whose merry prate kept with the King much rule.
. . . .
The King would ever grant what he would crave,
For well he knew Will no exacting knave:
But whisht the King to doe good deeds, great store,
Which caus'd the court to love him more and more.

Robert Armin, *Nest of Ninnies*

''As emperor I meet only wise and learned men,'' Akbar, realizing that there might be some wisdom in folly, complained to Birbal one day. ''Show me the ten greatest fools in the kingdom.'' Birbal brought him an assortment of morons, figures typical of the traditional fools of Indian literature: one man, riding a horse, carried a bundle of wood on his head as he traveled along because he reasoned that the bundle would be too heavy for the horse if he carried it behind him on his saddle; another, a muezzin, after making the call to prayer, ran after his voice to see how far it would carry; another looked at night for a ring he has lost, not where he had dropped it under a tree, but in a clearing where the brighter light would make it easier to find. Birbal brought eight such fools to the king who then reminded the jester that he had been ordered to bring ten. ''There are ten,'' the trickster laughed, ''including you and I—the two biggest fools of all—you for giving me such a foolish order and I for obeying it'' (*Birbal the Witty,* pp. 1–16). Laughter filled the court (fig. 21). His willingness to make a fool of himself gives Birbal license to make a fool of the king.

Figure 21

The relationship between the king and his jester, the authority figure and the trickster, is that of players in a game. The king can, and always does, lose to his opponent, but because the defeat is qualified by the ludic spirit, he has no choice but to laugh. To do otherwise would be to be a bad sport. As long as he observes the rules of the game, the jester can make a fool of the king—it's just in fun, just a game, just play. Comedy is always just comedy, and by being so it can get away with being outrageous, offensive, immoral, immature, squalid, inane, tasteless, nasty—whatever—as long as it's funny. By being just comedy, comedy becomes more than comedy.

The historical Birbal is credited with having had sufficient influence at court to act as a liaison between Akbar and his Hindu subjects, to protect them from Muslim prejudices. The legendary Birbal is a player in a different sort of game, a comic contest which persists tragically to this day, the battle between Indian Hindus and Muslims. "There was a Muslim minister in Akbar's court who hated Birbal," many of the stories begin. "He could not understand why Akbar made such a fuss over a Hindu" (*More About Birbal,* p. 45). In one such story, Muslim courtiers, jealous over the affection that Akbar extends to Birbal, enlist the aid of the Muslim royal barber in a plot to kill Birbal, an attempt to win the game that was life at court. The cosmic game of tug-of-war between demons and gods becomes a social game of tug-of-war between Muslims and Hindus. The Indian comic book casts the Hindus as the home team, and the Moghuls are the visitors—the depiction of them is clearly a Hindu caricature of Muslims. While shaving Akbar, the barber asked his emperor if he ever wondered how his father, Humayun, was faring in heaven. He assured the great Moghul that he knew of a way to find that out. "You could send a man up. I know a magician who frequently transports messengers to heaven and brings them back alive. He would be happy to be of service to you. With his assistance you could send an ambassador to heaven. It should be a wise and witty man. You could send Birbal. No one is wiser or wittier than he." Delighted with the idea, Akbar gave the barber and the Muslim magician permission to proceed. A great pyre was prepared on which Birbal was to be immolated so that he might rise to heaven with the smoke. Thanking Akbar for the honor of being chosen for such an important mission, Birbal requested some time to prepare himself for the long journey. And during that granted period he secretly dug a tunnel from his house to the place where the pyre had been assembled. On the day of his departure for heaven, as he mounted the pyre, Birbal asked that extra straw and kindling be placed over him to make the fires burn all the brighter and hotter. As the fire was set, Birbal surreptitiously crawled down into his tunnel and proceeded happily home. The rejoicing of the Muslim ministers, courtiers, and attendants was shattered when, after a month, Birbal reappeared in court. "Your father is doing very well in heaven, Sire. There is only one thing that displeases him—it is absolutely impossible to get a really good shave or haircut up there. There are no barbers in heaven—they must all be in hell. Your father has only one request. He asked me to tell you to please send the royal barber up to him as soon as possible." Akbar carried out Humayun's request (*Birbal the Wise,* p. 19; *All About Birbal,* pp. 36–42). *Score:* Hindus 1; Muslims 0.

The competition between Muslim courtiers and Raja Birbal, the playful brahmin gadfly, seems to have been quite real. The pious, even zealous Sunni Muslim, Badaoni, in his history of the court frequently refers to Birbal as "that bastard." The rather stern and apparently bigoted chronicler detested Birbal for tempting his emperor with heretical ideas.

Akbar assigned Badaoni the task of translating the *Mahābhārata* into Persian. The Muslim scorned the Hindu text as a garbage bin of "puerile absurdities." So much for history. Birbal, the bookseller informed me, took up the task "which the Muslim could not, of course, perform adequately. The Muslim, despite the injunctions of the Koran, made a bet with another Muslim, wagering one crore that Birbal would not be able to accomplish the task. But Birbal was such a clever brahmin! He spoke to Akbar about the project. 'Instead of merely translating the great *Mahābhārata,* I shall do something better. I shall write a version of the epic based on your own life, one *Akbar-Mahābhārata,* complete with an *Akbar-Gītā,* not to mention numerous *Akbar-stotras!*' The ruler, egotistical as all rulers are, could not resist. He gave Birbal crores and bloody crores to complete the project. After one year Birbal told Akbar that the epic poem was complete, but that before anyone could read it, he needed to show it to the begum, Akbar's favorite wife, to whom the new *Mahābhārata* was dedicated, for her approval. Granted admittance to the harem, Birbal took a massive book with him, an enormous manuscript which, between its beautifully decorated covers, contained only blank pages. 'In this *Mahābhārata,* Akbar is Yudhiṣṭhira, the son of Dharma, the very incarnation of truth, courage, and justice. He is the very perfection of rulership. And you are Draupadī, the beautiful one. It is to you that this *Mahābhārata* is dedicated. So you will decide who can have the honor of reading the text to the court.' The begum, flattered by the words of Birbal, smiled and asked him to read some portion of the text to her, some part in which her beauty was described. Birbal complied with a smile. 'Muhammad Hakim, prince of Kabul, the bloody Duhśāsana of the earlier and more inferior Hindu epic, grabbed Draupadī-begum by the hair and dragged her along the ground, all the while spitting on her and calling her "bloody slave" and "bloody slut." He invited the soldiers of his army to come and touch the various parts of her body. He ripped away her veil, her dress, every bit of clothing, to help them decide which part they wanted to touch. All of the soldiers were laughing and . . .' 'Stop!' the angry queen shouted. 'Burn this work at once!' After destroying the blank manuscript as the begum ordered, Birbal went to Akbar and told him of the fate of the *Akbar-Mahābhārata,* complete with *Akbar-Gītā*. The Muslim scribe lost his bet." The bookseller laughed heartily. *Score:* Hindus 2; Muslims 0.

Raja Birbal, the brahmin, the Hindu devotee of Sūrya, was so wise, witty, and clever that Akbar decided that he too wanted to become a brahmin. Birbal tried to convince him that it was enough that he was a good man, but the Moghul insisted. "I want to be a brahmin, Birbal, and not even you are going to stop me. Arrange for a ceremony." Birbal did arrange something, but not exactly what had been requested. Claiming that he was taking Akbar to the house of a holy man who would be able to turn the Moghul into a Hindu brahmin, Birbal escorted Akbar along the bank of the Yamuna where they encountered a man who was scrubbing a donkey. Akbar asked what he was doing. "I am changing my ass into a horse. Just this morning a holy man [Birbal in disguise] explained to me that if I stood by this river and scrubbed my ass very hard, it would turn into a horse." Akbar laughed at the fool. "It won't work. It can't work." And then Birbal laughed, and Akbar realized he had been tricked, that he could not become a brahmin any more than an ass could become a horse. And Akbar, his sense of humor regenerated, laughed at himself for being so foolish, for being such an ass. The message of the story as it is told in the children's book is moral: "It is enough to be a good man and a good king." The message discerned by the bookseller was less superficial: "A Hindu can become a Muslim if he so wishes; but a Muslim cannot simply decide to be a Hindu. It is a question of birth. The only way an ass can be transformed into a horse, is by performing his duties as an ass throughout his life. He must carry his heavy loads obediently. If so, he will certainly have the opportunity to be born as a horse in his next life." *Score:* Hindus 3; Muslims 0.

In the South Indian variant of the story, it is the king's barber who wants to be a brahmin. Capitulating to royal command for the sake of a tax exemption, the court priests perform an elaborate ritual for the barber. Tenāli Rāma mocks them by performing the same ritual for a black dog "to turn the dog white" (retold by David Shulman in *The King and the Clown in South Indian Myth and Poetry*). The story of Birbal makes fun of Muslims; the story of Rāma makes fun of brahminical ritual. One story, with a potential for endless variants, can serve a variety of social functions while maintaining a single psychological function, that of inciting laughter, of bestowing pleasure.

When I asked the bookseller, who had ordered another round of tea spiked with profound amounts of sugar, why he so disliked

Muslims, he became incensed. "What? I love Muslims! They are my bloody brothers! We Hindus believe that all religions are true. All gods are but manifestations of the Brahman. It is the Muslims who believe that only their religion is the correct one. They are close-minded, bigoted, and highly prejudiced." He hesitated, seemingly realizing that there was something contradictory in what he was saying. He smiled slightly. "I love Muslims despite their bigoted nature." He laughed and ordered more tea. *Score:* Hindus 4; Muslims 0.

A benevolent but brazen brahmin from Varanasi told me a slew of jokes in which Muslims were the butt of laughter. *"Ajab hāl dekhā Mussalmām ke ghar kā! Pahantī haiṇ sir pe to kahtī haiṇ burkā!"* He explained it through unrestrained laughter. "*Bur* is 'cunt' in Hindi, *burka* means 'of the cunt.' So you see, we are playing on the word *burka* which refers to the garment with which Muslim women cover their heads: 'I saw a strange thing in the house of a Muslim—they wear it on their head but they say it's for the cunt!' " He laughed again and then became gravely serious. "You must promise me not to tell this joke in your book. The Muslims will kill you and kill me too. They have no sense of humor." A good-humored Muslim from Dacca told me that before Muslims entered India, there was no humor at all. "Muslims brought humor to India. The Hindu, particularly the brahmin, because of his diet, thinks in abstractions and abstractions can never give rise to laughter."

Never in the legends, but finally in history, did a Muslim have his revenge on Birbal. Badaoni had the pleasure of recording the Hindu's death in his chronicle: "Birbal who had fled from fear of his life was slain and entered the row of dogs in hell and thus got something for the abominable deeds he had done during his lifetime" (*Muntakhab-ut-Tawarikh* [Lowe trans.] 2:361–362).

Akbar, who had rather foolishly permitted Birbal to lead an army against rebellious tribes in the northwest, was so overcome with grief over the death of his mirthful companion that he could neither eat, nor drink, nor appear in public, nor function in any other way for days. A Hindi verse, attributed to Akbar, is said to have been recited by him upon hearing of the death of Birbal:

When I was melancholy
Birbal gave me everything
except more sorrow to bear.

That he bestows now.
And so it may never be said.
that Birbal did not give me all.
(my trans. following that of P. N. Chopra,
Life and Letters under the Mughals, p. 388)

"Birbal's body was never found," the bookseller whispered as if confiding a secret. "But some say that he had just volunteered to lead the army in order to free himself from Akbar's court. He was tired of cheering up these bloody Moghuls all the time. So he led the army to the Khyber Pass, but he did not go into battle himself. As a Hindu he was prone to practice *ahiṃsa,* after all. While all the soldiers were senselessly killing each other, Birbal was happily making his way to Bengal where he became the jester for a Hindu king. He was known in Bengal as Gopal. Bengalis tell jokes about Gopal to this very day. Here, you can purchase these illustrated stories of Gopal from me."

The story, passed on or invented by the bookseller, perpetuates the motif, recurrent in so many trickster cycles, of Birbal outsmarting death. Just as he escaped from the burning pyre in the story of the barber, so he escapes, in countless variations on the conceit, from gallows, poisonings, and innumerable attacks and attempts to execute him. It is the trickster's mission to make a fool of death, and in fulfilling that mission he performs a psychological function, allowing us to laugh heartily and confidently at death, to suspend our quotidian understanding of reality. As a representative of one species of comic hero, he invites us to laugh in celebration of fertility as he escorts us to a merry carnival consecrated to the renewal of life in joyous laughter.

The bookseller's conviction that Birbal became Gopal reflects a refusal to believe that such a figure, the trickster, can ever die or succumb in any way to anything dark or dismal, a refusal inspired by the stories themselves, stories affirming a perpetual triumph of life over death. Informed that his jester, Tenāli Rāma, had been bitten by a cobra and was dying, King Kṛṣṇadevarāya "laughed loud and long. 'Rāma is dying again so soon!' " Assuming that his death was but another amusing trick, the monarch went to visit him. He stood before the still and ashen corpse. There was no laughter to be heard. "What! Is he really dead? Impossible! He is feigning! See the smile on his face!" The king shook the body of the dead clown. "Friend, get up and speak to your friend. You cannot be dead, you who had such a joy for life!" (*Tenali Rama,* p. 122).

The trickster continually strives to trick mortality, to outsmart all or any endings. Like a Christ or a Buddha, his exploits promise a way out. Once when Tenāli Rāma was sentenced to death for some felonous trick he had played on the king, he asked to be given the right to choose the form of his execution. Granted that last wish, he chose to die of "old age" (*Tenali Rama,* pp. 39–40). The king laughed, and in laughter forgave the jester. The trickster would die if he were not funny. Laughter preserves and generates life. It is absolution. On another occasion when Tenāli Rāma was sentenced to death, he asked his executioners to let him pray in the river before his death. Begging him not to pull any tricks on them, they agreed. "All right," the jester assured them, "stand near me with drawn swords, and cut off my head on my slightest attempt to escape." They stood on either side of him as he pretended to pray. After a long while he suddenly yelled "cut" and dove into the water. In confusion the executioners swung their swords and decapitated each other (*Tenali Rama,* pp. 37–39).

In the end, the trick goes stale, the laughter dies out; neither Birbal nor Tenāli Rāma nor Gopal of Bengal can save himself from death. But they can, and repeatedly do, save others. The spirit of comedy transcends individuals in its triumphant celebration of the perpetuation of the greatest eros, an exuberant life-force larger than any one who lives or dies. Comedy demands faith in that telic power or eternal energy.

The court jester continually redeems victims of the king's wrath or rashness by mitigating the king's authority with humor. In satire the potential victims of that authority are rescued as they laugh at the authority; in humor those victims are saved as the authority is made to laugh at himself. Repeatedly the stories end with Akbar doing just that and admitting, "You have saved me from punishing an innocent person Birbal. Release the poor man" (*Birbal the Clever,* p. 17). Humor, in affirming what is human, seeks to make justice humane.

Akbar was once given a handsome and eloquent parrot that he came to prize and adore above all the pets in the palace. Ordering the servants to care for it well, he warned them, "He who ever tells me that the parrot has died, will himself be put to death." The servants did their best to care for the bird, but one day they found it lying dead on the bottom of its golden cage. In fear of the Moghul's anger, they told Birbal of their predicament. "No problem," Birbal laughed. He went to Akbar and told him just how wonderful his bird really was. "The parrot is a veritable yogi! He has entered into perfect *samādhi*!" The king, anxious to behold the parrot's beatitude for himself, became furious at the sight of the bird on the floor of the cage. "The bird isn't in *samādhi,* you fool! He's dead." The royal trickster smiled, "Your Highness must die, according to your own decree, for telling you that the parrot is dead." The king had no choice but to admit his folly—"I sometimes say foolish things"—and to laugh the humorous laughter which is directed at oneself, and in that laughter to forgive his servants, his jester, and himself as well (*More About Birbal,* pp. 11–14). Similarly, in a rash fit of rage over all the demands of the many brother-in-laws that he had acquired through hundreds of political marriages, Akbar ordered all the brother-in-laws in the court to be executed. In response to the decree, Birbal had a golden gallows constructed. Akbar asked him whom it was for. "The golden gallows are for you. You too are a brother-in-law" (*All About Birbal,* p. 68). Birbal makes the king see that the plight of his servants and subjects is his own plight. Implicitly, the Hindu jester teaches the Moghul king an ancient Indian ideal of kingship: "The happiness of the king lies within the happiness of his subjects, his welfare within theirs" (*Arthaśāstra* 1.19). The king and the state, the collective body of the king's subjects, are one and the same. Humor has the capacity to establish and affirm that identity.

Akbar is said to have sentenced a poor brahmin to death for some inconsequential misdemeanor. When Birbal appeared in his chamber, the irritated king was in no mood for laughter. "I suppose you've come about the brahmin. But it's no use. You are always trying to tell me what to do. Now if you say anything to me I shall do exactly the opposite." Birbal smiled, "I think you should execute the brahmin. In fact, I think you should hang his whole family and take away all they possess." Shocked at Birbal's harshness, Akbar listened as the jester recommended a long list of severe punishments. He broke out in laughter when he suddenly realized that he had said he would do "exactly the opposite" of what Birbal told him to do. Hearing his own intentions through the mouth of the jester, he realized his folly. The topsy-turvyness of comedy provides perspective on statecraft. The humor of this story, the parrot story, and so many others in the king-and-jester cycles plays on a creation of severance between language and intention. Language is taken so literally that it no longer communicates what it was meant to express. And as they cease to mean what they say, words become comical. The jester finds the loopholes of absurdity in language.

"Let's not be too literal," is the suggestion in many of Birbal's pranks. "Let's not be afraid to change our minds." From such suppleness alone, achieved through good humor, is a real righteousness, beyond ideals and the letter of the law, possible. As satire shows the degradations of ideals that hid behind ideals, humor shows ways in which ideals can be made real, how they can be invigorated by a recognition of the folly that is, at least in the comic vision, the essence of human spirit, and how they can encompass the frailty that is the essence, in the comic as well as tragic vision, of human flesh.

"Birbal was a master of disguises. He could make himself look and sound like anyone," the bookseller explained to me. "He was like the joker in a deck of cards. The joker is wild. He can be any card." In satire the goal was repeatedly to see through masquerades, to laugh when guises (rogues disguised as kings, sluts as loving ladies, libertines as holy men) failed. In humor we laugh at the way a ruse works, at the way we, or representatives of ourselves, are fooled by a trick, verbal or gestural. Birbal as a trickster was adept at guises. And he used falseness to establish the truth. In order to expose the corruption of a palace guard, Birbal disguised himself as a poet from a distant province and, when stopped by the guard at the gate and asked for a bribe in order to be admitted to court, he explained that though he had no money he would give the guard whatever literary award the generous Akbar bestowed upon him. The greedy guard admitted the disguised Birbal to the durbar where he read his poems before the king. Akbar, completely fooled by Birbal's makeup, costume, and voice, was so impressed with the verses that he offered him any prize that he wished for. "I would like a hundred lashes of the whip." Assured by the poet that this was really what he wanted, Akbar duly agreed to comply. "Thank you, Your Majesty. There is only one thing more—I promised to give my payment to the guard at the gate to your palace" (*All About Birbal,* pp. 21–24). Through dishonesty, honesty is promoted. The irony is a comic one.

Life at court, if not in the world itself, is seen in the stories as a game wherein all of the players are out to trick the others. The winner is the trickster who outtricks the other tricksters.

In a frequently told story, another instance in which a truth is revealed through an untruth, Akbar himself takes on a disguise that he may wander through the streets and discover people's opinions of him. He was accosted and insulted by a stranger. "Do you know who I am?" Akbar, displaying the royal signet ring, asked the man. "I am Akbar!" The stranger grabbed the king's ring and ran with it. "Thief, thief!" Akbar shouted, and some passersby tackled the man in flight. "Fools!" the thief yelled, "Don't you know who I am?" And he showed them the signet ring. As they bowed before him, begging forgiveness, the real Akbar fearfully ran back to the palace. Upon return he found the ring waiting for him, with a note from Birbal warning him not to leave the palace alone ever again. Akbar laughed at the prank, grateful for the lesson he'd been taught by being tricked (*Birbal the Witty,* pp. 23–28; *All About Birbal,* pp. 28–32).

"Birbal's disguises were so good that he could fool any bloody one. He fooled the Bengalis when he was Gopal. He fooled the Tamils when he was Tenāli Rāmaliṅga. You must purchase these comical books about Rāma of Tenāli as well. You cannot understand Birbal unless you understand Rāma."

The bookseller prepared my bill. "Who knows who else Birbal has fooled! Who knows? Perhaps he is now Kushwant Singh!" he laughed. "Who knows? You could be Birbal disguised as an American tourist, tricking me right now!"

"Who knows?" That question is what the trickster teaches us to ask constantly and eternally, to ask with a laugh, a twinkling laugh over the impossibility of epistemological or ontological certainty.

As I paid the bookseller the almost three hundred rupees I now owed him, I couldn't help but marvel at the fact that though he had swindled me, I found him completely likeable. The loss was worth the entertainment, just as in a game. The trickster pleases us despite ourselves as he makes fools of us. He pleases us by making fools of us.

"Who knows?" I thought to myself, "this bookseller could be Birbal, the immortal trickster, tricking me, making up these stories himself, lying to me both to get some cash for himself and to teach me some truth."

"Who knows?" you might wonder, "maybe this bloody Lee Siegel is Birbal, maybe he has fabricated these anecdotes about the bookseller."

Who knows?

Gopal Bhar and the Comedy of Imperialism

Then Eulenspiegel turned, ran away, and left the crowd, one part cursing, the other part laughing and saying, "There goes a charlatan; but still he spoke the truth."

A Pleasant Vintage of Till Eulenspiegel

The guidebook to Fatehpur Sikri which I had purchased from the bookseller turned out not to be a guidebook at all. The book, *Fatehpur Sikri Is A Hindu City,* is rather a diatribe against Muslim political, religious, and aesthetic imperialism. The author, Hansraj Bhatia, "Member of Institute for Rewriting Indian History," argues that people all over the world have been tricked, duped, and hoodwinked "by fanatic Muslims" into believing both that the Hindu palace known as the Taj Mahal was built as a tomb by Shah Jehan, and that the Hindu township of Fatehpur Sikri was built by Akbar. The history of India, as we know it, is, Mr. Bhatia explains, "India's History as Written by its Own Enemies," an imperialistic fraud, its real history having been "warped, twisted, turned topsy-turvy or even obliterated during 1,200 years of continuous alien rule in India." The fraud, initially perpetrated by Muslims, was perpetuated by the English with such force that Indians have blindly accepted it. "Archaeology and Tourist departments functioning under the British have bluffed people." Mr. Bhatia, who refers to Birbal with unintentional humor as "Akbar's court stooge," is offended by the merriment of the figure, understanding his comedic posture as a bending over backward to the oppressor, his laughter as a betrayal of people.

I recognized the sentiments in the book. An Indian graduate student, studying engineering at the University of Hawaii, attending a lecture that I was delivering on my research on Indian comedy, surprised me with bitter reproach. "How can you write about comedy in India, about anything in India? We don't want to know what you have to say. First you come to India and destroy our culture, make fools of us, make a joke of our nation, a laughingstock of our flesh and blood. And now you want to say we are funny? Now the white man dares to laugh at us, the joke he has cracked at our expense? You have no business writing a book about Indian comedy. Do you think that because you know a little Sanskrit that you understand anything at all about India or that you have the right to laugh at our culture and traditions?"

I tried to reassure him that I meant no harm, that I realized the limits of my understanding, that I had a sympathy for all victims of imperialism, and that he was, in my opinion, taking my research all too seriously. I urged him to try to have a sense of humor about what I had said and what I was doing. Apparently my response seemed patronizing. " 'Have a sense of humor' is euphemistic for 'turn your back, bend over, let yourself get raped, abused, and humiliated,' " he answered. " 'Have a sense of humor' means 'shut your eyes, ignore injustice, and endure oppression.' " That he is right is one of the horrors of comedy. Humor, like love, drunkenness, or religious faith, is a dangerous pleasure—it makes us vulnerable just as it soothes our wounds and protects. Comedy makes a joke of intolerance and imperialism, makes light of oppression and injustice, for the funniest things are things that aren't funny.

Humor is all surrender. And even satire, which, on the surface, has the capacity to attack oppressors, can be said to be a reactionary mode of comedy, allowing the release of energies of anger which would, in the serious minds of the socially conscious, be better directed toward reformation or revolution. Comedy sponsors a reformation of oneself, rather than society; attitudes are restructured so that life in society, for all of its inevitable injustices, can be endured. The comic revolution is within; for it satire provides the weapons of offense, humor the armor of defense. Humor is a mode of sympathy with the victims of injustice, the cosmic injustices of old age, disease, and death, the social injustices of poverty and unobstructed abuses of power. In a cartoon by Mario, a middle-class Indian searching his pockets in vain for change to give to a beggar sits down next to that beggar (fig. 22). The absurdity of the fiscal hierarchy is exposed; there is a realization that, though we may try to turn our backs to it, we are all victims of any injustice that exists in the society in which we exist. In laughter one sees the relativity of wealth and poverty and the identity of oppressor and oppressed. The joke teaches precisely what countless renouncers have taught with gravity. The cartoon can illustrate the dynamics of humor. In the same way that I become disassociated from the objects of satiric laughter, I become identified with the objects of humorous laughter. Humor dissolves strife. It reconciles. And this process of reconciliation can be seen in the comic stories of Gopal Bhar, jester and sometimes barber to Rāja Kṛṣṇacandra of Kṛṣṇanagar in eighteenth-century Bengal. The rāja, in owing allegiance both to his Hindu subjects and to the Imperial Muslim

Figure 22

nabob of Murshidabad, is continually faced with conflicts of obligation. He has the responsibility of keeping the peace, of reconciling the internal needs of the people of Kṛṣṇanagar with the external demands of the nabob. It is Gopal, the clown and trickster, who through his comic wit and playfulness inevitably enables the rāja to perform this function. The clown could never himself rule as a king for the king must—above all else—be serious; and yet the king cannot rule effectively, humanly, without the perspective on the world which comedy bestows. Like the *vidūṣaka* of Sanskrit drama, the court jester or royal trickster of the legends is an externalized aspect of the ideal king himself.

The nabob, the representative of the Moghul Empire in Bengal, once ordered Kṛṣṇacandra to inform him as to exactly how many stars there were in the heavens. If the impossible command was not carried out, the mahārāja would die and his Hindu subjects would fall directly under Muslim rule. In despair, the king summoned his jester to cheer him up. Hearing the cause of his patron's sorrow, Gopal laughed. "No problem! Tell the nabob that in order to obey his command you will need one crore [ten million rupees] and one year's time. I will take care of everything." The governor gave the money to the mahārāja who, in turn, gave it to his jester who, spending every paise of it, treated himself to a year of luxurious living. When the year was over Gopal appeared on behalf of his mahārāja before the Moghul with seven sheep. "There are the exact number of hairs on these sheep as there are stars in the heavens, hair for hair, star for star." The governor sneered, "And what number is that?" Gopal smiled. "You did not explicitly ask for a number. You asked to be informed as to 'how many' stars there are. The mahārāja has kept up his part of the bargain." Despite his fury, in the presence of so many witnesses in the court, the nabob had no choice but to admit that the mahārāja had fulfilled the command. "But why did you need a whole year to complete the mission?" the mahārāja asked Gopal. "It took that long to find the sheep with the exact number of hairs," the jester answered, and the king and all of his courtiers broke out in laughter (told by K. N. Bandyopadhyaya; cf. *Gopal the Jester,* pp. 28–30; in the version told by Edward Dimock in *The Thief of Love,* the mahārāja must also measure the circumference of the earth; the same story is also told about Birbal but in addition to the number of stars he must also locate the center of the earth [*More About Birbal,* p. 49]).

In another story, Rāja Kṛṣṇacandra, put in a similar predicament, urges Gopal not to make light of the situation. "This is not a matter to joke about," the king moans. "Perhaps my very life is at stake" (*Gopal the Jester,* p. 5). But the compulsion of comedy is to laugh the loudest when life is at stake, and because it is at stake, to make jokes when things are most serious. The conviction of comedy is that life is won only through mirth and laughter.

The comic stories of Gopal arose, presumably in reaction to the imperialistic presence of Muslims and then the English in Bengal, and the appeal of the stories can be understood in terms of the ways in which laughter eases the tensions created by such social situations and political predicaments. But beyond their historical reference, the stories might be understood psychologically. The mahārāja has the function in the social arena that is served by the ego for the larger psyche. And Gopal helps the mahārāja in precisely the same way that a sense of humor aids and protects, enhances and yet contains, the ego. Humor has the capacity to define the ego in terms of pleasure and to assert the glory of pleasure before the stony face of reality.

During the season when hilsa-fish abound in the rivers of Bengal, "fisherman could think of nothing but hilsa-fish. Fishmongers sold nothing but hilsa-fish. Householders could talk of nothing but hilsa-fish. And in the palace too the courtiers could discuss nothing but hilsa-fish." The king challenged Gopal to see if he could get anyone to stop talking about hilsa-fish for even five minutes. "Let me see you buy a huge hilsa and bring it to the palace without anyone asking you a word about it." Gopal shaved half of his face, smeared his body with ashes, donned old rags, bought a hilsa-fish and proceeded through the town toward the palace. No one who saw him mentioned the hilsa-fish he was carrying: "Look at that man! Isn't he comical!" a child asked. "He must be a madman," a brahmin commented, and his companion answered in whispers, "Hush! I think he's a mystic." The courtiers conferred, "The man has lost his mind." "I think it's one of his crazy jokes." The comments are revealing—the madman, the mystic, and the clown display the same outward signs. All three are free from the institutionalized values and norms that regulate the social structure. Madness, the division of the ego suggested by Gopal's half-shaven face, is a threat to the productivity of the individual; renunciation, the rejection of society suggested by the ashes and tattered clothes on Gopal's body, is a threat to the productivity of the community. The trickster clown is a madman who is sane, a renouncer who is firmly rooted in the world, a child who is mature—"The children of the town loved Gopal for he often joined them in their pranks" (*Gopal the Jester,* p. 9). The clown turns chaos into order, and order into chaos. He turns a threat to society back on itself, as he brings the community, the collective body of hilsa-fish-possessed individuals, to its senses with a trick, a joke, with laughter (*Gopal the Jester,* 22–27; fig. 23). Comedy, as the king's reaction implies,

Figure 23

expands the parameters of possibility. The expansion can be social or psychological, or both at once.

The Moghul governor, camped with his army near Kṛṣṇanagar, happened to notice a great and wonderful bull grazing. Hungry for beef, the nabob resolved to eat the husky animal. He ordered his servants to tie it up and prepare it for slaughter. The bull, that magnificent mountain of beefsteaks, had been consecrated by the mahārāja to the memory of his father in a ritual requiring that it be left free to wander at will, to graze where it wished, for a full year. The nabob's action would destroy the efficacy of the rite and dishonor the father of the mahārāja. The very idea of consuming the bull was, furthermore, both physically repugnant and spiritually repulsive to the vegetarian Hindu ruler and the subjects of Kṛṣṇanagar, the city of the cowherd god. The mahārāja, grievously sorrowful over his inability to change the situation, confessed his sense of terrible helplessness to Gopal. "No problem!" Gopal laughed, and going to the nabob, he explained that he wanted to thank him on behalf of all of the people of Kṛṣṇanagar for capturing the bull. "We are grateful to you, for this is an evil bull with evil habits," the trickster explained. "You see, my good sir, above all else this bull enjoys eating human shit. Whenever we go to the field in the morning to have our morning defecation, this bull, impatient for the excreted goodies, charges the defecator with his horns. Out of fear the entire town is constipated! Once you kill this shit-eating bull, which we as pious Hindus cannot slay, we will be able to have our morning dumps in peace. Thank you, sir! One thousand times thank you!" The governor was revulsed with the thought that he was going to eat a bull that had grown fat on human feces. He, in turn, expressed his gratitude to Gopal for saving him from that meal, and he ordered that the bull be freed (after the retelling by Edward Dimock in *The Thief of Love*).

Excremental imagery abounds in comedy. Scatology, as we have seen, was a satiric method, and shit a satiric symbol of the hiding of fundamental corruptions and of a universal dirtiness denied. It is no less a feature of humor, particularly the humor of the trickster. Caca, as every child and Frenchman knows, is funny.

Tenāli Rāma and the Excremental Comedy

One of the young men at the table said, if the organ of epic was the phallus, of tragedy the testicles, and of romance the vagina,

> what was the organ of comedy? Oh, the anus, Angelica replied instantly, with a bright smile.
>
> David Lodge, *Small World*

I had a friend in England, a medical student from Madras, now a pathologist in Florida, who, making fun of the Bengali tendency to palatalize all sibilants in such a way that *s* sounds like *sh,* told me, laughing almost uncontrollably, about a Bengali guru. In an address to potential devotees in London, the holy man had spoken with a serene smile on his face, "The word *Upaniṣad* is meaning 'shitting near debotedly.' No matter where you are shitting, imagine that you are shitting debotedly near me." The tension between the loftiness of what is intended and the baseness of what is heard made my friend laugh. I asked him if modern Indian jokes were generally very scatological. He shrugged, thought a moment, and then smiled. "There is some such humor. Basically it is funny when a brahmin steps in shit, but it is really rather sad when a harijan does."

"But you're a brahmin," I laughed. "Is it funny when you do?"

"I suppose shit is funnier on the other guy's shoe than it is on your own unless you have a very, very good sense of humor. I do have a sense of humor—one has to in medicine. The sickest jokes are the healthiest. Life would be intolerable without them."

When a brahmin steps in feces he becomes a harijan for the moment; he knows what it's like to be a pariah—the social hierarchy is turned on its head and there is pleasure in that; when a harijan does the same he is only reminded of the devastation of his lot, the hierarchy is validated and there is the sadness of resignation in that.

Satirical scatology has brahmins stepping in shit to reveal the ways in which they are not as pure as we might imagine; humorous scatology reminds us that we are not as pure as we imagine, that we are, like everyone else, shitters from birth to death. And laughter resolves our embarrassment, the embarrassment that comes with the realization that we are human. Laughter affirms humanness for what it really means, for all its stinkiness and filthiness. Humor's interest in defecation is a regressive one, bestowing the pleasure of return to a period of nondiscriminative delight. Baby Kṛṣṇa and his brother Balarāma, the divine tricksters, much to the aggravation of their parents and to the amusement of others, "crawled about in the cowpens, right through all the cow shit, on their hands and knees" (*Viṣṇu Purāṇa* 5.6.11).

"There are a lot of shit jokes about Tenāli Rāma," my friend explained. "I heard them as a child. They are very dirty. Rāma is always shitting somewhere where he shouldn't, always defiling what should be kept pure. And as children we thought that was very funny."

I complained to him that all my sources for stories about Tenāli Rāma, the legendary jester at the court of Kṛṣṇadevarāya, were clean. "They're all published by the Indian government. The excrement has been washed away. And in becoming clean, the jokes cease to be funny." I was consoled with a recollection of one of Rāma's excremental exploits. Once after a great feast in the palace, the courtiers were discussing what was the greatest pleasure possible for mankind. "Sex," said the poet; "gold," said the treasurer; "god," said the priest. "You are all mistaken," said Tatachari, the brahmin minister to the king. "He who has found god, finds no pleasure in sex or gold. There are, furthermore, beings who have found happiness without god. One can live without sex, gold, or god. But who can live without eating? We enter this world hungry. The pleasure of food is our first and greatest pleasure. And even when we are dead, it is for food that we wait in heaven. Are our sacrifices to the gods not the serving of food? Is our worship in the temple not the serving of food?" The praise of food, a typical expression of brahminic priorities in comic literature, won the approval of everyone in court, everyone but Tenāli Rāma. "Shitting gives greater pleasure than eating," the trickster laughed. Tatachari and the others were disgusted by the vulgarity of the jester and no one would agree with him. Later, when Tatachari went into one of the palace chambers alone, Tenāli Rāma locked the door behind him. The brahmin pounded on the door, demanding to be freed. Having gorged himself at the feast, his stomach was in agony and his bowels begged to be relieved. "I shall let you out as soon as you tell me what will give you greater pleasure—shitting or eating?" The brahmin had to reverse his earlier decree about the source of human happiness. He, like the poet, the treasurer, and the priest, had to admit that their philosophical speculations were nonsense. Tenāli Rāma proved that they were all full of shit. Comedy always balances, tells the underside of the story, shifts the focus from the mouth to the anus (following the version of P. K. Aiyar; cf. *Tenali Rama,* pp. 58–59, in which it is the king who is locked in the room).

Kāma, artha, and *dharma*—love and art, wealth and politics, justice and religion—are just so much crap in the comic vision.

The Buddha instructed disciples to meditate on the body as a "bag of shit" so that they might cultivate revulsion for the flesh and move from a concern with worldly things to a desire for release. Comedy prompts the same meditation, but it is for the sake of delight, for a reminder of what is most basically human. Allusions to excrement are comic to the degree that they provide a sudden switch in consciousness from a lofty ideal to an incongruous, mundane reality. In a modern cartoon by Vishnu, a minister makes a rousing plea to India's "dumb friends," a phrase with a semantic potential for reference to more sacred cows than those literally intended by the speaker—"Make more dung" (fig. 24). The seriousness of the participants at a conference on alternate energy sources is undermined by the fact that no matter what they decide, say, or do, reality is at work—cows are, without theory or reflection, contentedly eating and defecating.

In satire we laugh at impurities that need to be cleaned up; in humor we laugh at impurities that are natural and at any absurd attempts to try to clean them up. The journalist Gokki, writing in a now-defunct Indian humor magazine, explains that while visiting England he was constantly mortified by people who had read V. S. Naipal. "Everyone asked me, 'Why do you Indians defecate so much all over the place?' I almost wished our Government would launch a massive defecation control programme along the lines of family planning. I daresay our media genuises would come out with something as imaginative as in the family planning campaign which

"...and in conclusion, I have a rousing call for our dumb friends. Make more dung..."

Figure 24

could be plastered all over the countryside. Something like, 'When you've had one shit, that's it' " (*Diwana,* October 1974, p. 18).

While the Muslim courtiers are the foils for Birbal, the nabob for Gopal, it is Tatachari, the brahmin *purohita,* who is the enemy of Tenāli Rāma. He is the straightman for the crooked clown. The chaplain is a representative of a purity which is recognized as order and sanctity; the trickster is the harbinger of an impurity which is chaos and yet freedom. He is funny the way crow shit on a white kurta is funny.

One day, while Tatachari was bathing (an act emphasizing his role as an examplar of purity in the stories), Tenāli Rāma stole his clothes. The trickster informed the brahmin that he would return the clothes only if he would consent to carry him on his shoulders past the king's palace. The priest had no alternative but to accept the humiliation. When Kṛṣṇadevarāya, who had not yet met Tenāli Rāma, saw his royal priest humiliated in that way, he was furious and he ordered his guards, "My guru is being shamed! You will find him outside the palace carrying a man on his back. Tear the man from his shoulders and beat the scoundrel soundly. Then bring my beloved guru to me." Meanwhile Rāma, suspecting the king's response, slipped down from Tatachari's shoulders and fell at his feet. "I have wronged you, sir." To make amends for my sins, I shall carry you now." The guards rushed out, pulled the priest from the trickster's back, and made obeisance to the clown. Tenāli Rāma was escorted to the king who was sufficiently amused by the account of what had happened to make Tenāli Rāma his court jester (*Raman of Tenali,* pp. 12–20).

My Madrasi friend told me that when he was a child he and his friends had taken great delight in pulling tricks on an old brahmin in Adyar. "We were really cruel," he laughed. "We were little Tenāli Rāmas. One day, with a small shovel we gathered up some shit from the field which was the most popular site for morning ablutions in the area. This we wrapped up in newspaper, the *Madras Mail,* and we soaked the package in kerosene. This little gift was then placed on the hallowed doorstep of the venerable V. V. Subrahmanyam and ignited. He was our Tatachari. 'Help! Help! Fire! Fire!' we cried out from a safe hiding place, and the holy brahmin came running out and, seeing the fire threatening his house, he stamped on the package with his feet." I heard of the same prank as a child in Los Angeles. Tricks, jokes acted out, seem to travel like jokes, or, also like jokes, they arise from a seemingly universal level of consciousness to which children and clowns have access.

The childish prank recapitulates a motif that is the basis for another story of Rāma. One day while the king and his jester were taking a stroll, Rāma accidentally stepped in some excrement. As Rāma tried to wash the filth from his toe, the king insisted that he would never be able to remove the stain and defilement with water—"the only way to get rid of it is to cut the little toe off." The king, disgusted by what he saw and smelled, warned Rāma never to enter his private chambers, never to step on his delicate and precious Persian carpets with that disgusting toe. The jester tried to indicate to the king the absurdity of his insistences. "We don't wash ourselves any better when we answer our own calls," he said, but the king was adamant. "That is our own filth. Another's filth can be cleansed away only by cutting off the defiled part."

Rāma then played a prank to enlighten the king. He covered a pit of human excrement over with a layer of turf and the turf was planted with the most beautiful rosebushes that he could secure—pink, white, and red roses, fragrant and full. When he invited the king to see the magnificent flowers, his Majesty could not help but want to smell them. Stepping near the bushes, Kṛṣṇadevarāya sunk into the pit of soft, warm excrement, sunk in up to his neck. "I'll save you," Rāma shouted out with mocking laughter, "I'll get a sword and cut off the polluted part. I'll make a clean cut right at the neck!" The king had no choice but to admit that a good washing would be sufficient to cleanse his body. The jester would have been executed for what he had done except that the king was amused by the cleverness and naughtiness of the trick (*Tenali Rama,* pp. 47–49). Rāma's improprieties are comic, comic because they are improper. Shit is, in the anecdote, a symbol of a more general impurity, figurative as well as literal, and the king, the guardian of justice, is made to realize that he too is potentially guilty of all crimes.

Kṛṣṇadevarāya had commissioned a painter to decorate the walls of his palace with a mural which he proudly showed to Tenāli Rāma. Rāma squinted and scratched his head. "I can only see half of this woman." The king explained that that was because she was rendered in profile. But the jester was still not satisfied. "I see only the head of this fellow." Pointing out that it was only because the rest of the man's body was outside the picture, that he had been drawn in close-up, the king informed Tenāli Rāma that in beholding a work of art, one must use one's imagination. Several months later Rāma announced that he had been studying fine arts and that he wished permission to paint a mural for his king. Flattered by the poet's generous offer, Kṛṣṇadevarāya consented. At the unveiling of the masterpiece, in the presence of all the courtiers and courtesans, Rāma proudly revealed an enormous greenish blob on the wall. "What is this ugly thing?" the king asked. "Ugly!" Tenāli Rāma snickered, "You must not be using your imagination. I have painted a beautiful horse, a swift and wonderful steed with a full mane and an exquisite face. Of course, you can't see the face, because I have drawn the horse from the back. One must use imagination in viewing art. It is morning and the horse is relieving itself. Because I have drawn a close-up, a detail, all one can see is the horse shit. Ah, but one must use one's imagination—just beyond that horseshit is the horse's rump, and in front of that the rest of the body, and in front of that the splendid head. "When Ramāliṅga was awarded the prize for the most original and thought-provoking painting, the entire court was dissolved in laughter" (following the version of Randor Guy, *Indian Ribaldry,* pp. 105–107; cf. the nonscatological version retold by David Shulman, *The King and Clown in South Indian Myth and Poetry,* wherein the jester simply paints various parts of the body on different parts of the wall). The satirical dimension of the story, the aspect which makes fun of the pretenses of artists, recurs frequently in modern Indian cartoons; the cartoonist makes a joke of modern art (fig. 25). On the satirical level the story simply says that aesthetics, talk of imagination and such, is just crap, that it can be used for the sake of patronage, to pass off shit as gold. But the satire, focusing our perception on the degradation of art, is tempered and balanced by humor, by the childish delight it takes in horse manure.

The excrement in the stories serves as a reminder that while we aspire to art, we are eternally trapped by biology. I am told that a certain Chirquin, a nineteenth-century Urdu poet, once stood before a meeting of poets reading his ghazals. "*Goo! Goo!*" they cried, "Shit! Shit!" "If it is shit, you want," the poet laughed, "it is shit you shall have." And Chirquin dedicated the rest of his creative life to filling Urdu literature with shit, with poems about it. Sitting to defecate, after half an hour, he cries out in one of his poems, "Where are you? Why won't you come out? Don't be afraid, I won't eat you!" (Ramanath Sharma, personal communication). The poems challenge taste as they were meant to do—they

Figure 25

are dirty in every sense of the word, disgustingly and delightfully dirty. They require, like so much comedy, a suspension of taste, sophistication, maturity, propriety, and sensitivity. Laughter expresses the pleasure experienced in such moments of relaxation and release.

While the fool of folk literature is often epicene, the trickster is most often priapic. His erotic escapades, like his fecal frolics, are celebrations of fertility, of fundamental tropisms, urges, and powers. I asked my South Indian informant if there were sexual jokes about Tenāli Rāma. "Many. Many! He usually screws Tatachari's wife or daughter. One day he went to Tatachari's house and asked if he could please stay with him, for his own house was filled with visiting members of his family. Tatachari consented but warned Rāma not to go near his daughter . . ." My friend's wife, also a physician, stopped him and scolded him with a laugh, "You're telling him the joke you heard in the pub the other day. You are just changing the farmer's daughter into Tatachari's daughter. Just admit that you don't remember any such jokes about Rāma. What if you were diagnosing Lee and he were to mix things into his urine specimen, some sugar or beer or something? It would throw your whole analysis off. Lee is doing research—cultural diagnosis so to speak. Just because it is on humor, that does not mean that it is not serious. You must not put him on the wrong track. This is not a funny joke to play." He laughed off what his wife had said. "Okay, okay, it's not about Tenāli Rāma but it is funny nevertheless." He grinned. "A medical diagnosis must be correct. There shouldn't be anything funny going on. On the other hand, it is more important that a book on humor be funny than that it be correct or true." He laughed and turned to me for an approval of what he had said. I gave it with a smile, but turned to a book for my specimen of Tenāli Rāma's sexual wit.

One day some women were watching Tenāli Ramāliṅga bathe. His head was shaved except for the brahminical topknot, and as he performed his ablutions, he shook his head to prevent any water from entering his ears or nose. One of the women started to tease him, "O learned Brahmin, be careful when you bathe. I've been watching you for some time and the way you've been shaking that head, your poor little tuft will fall off and there will be nothing left on your head." The other women giggled. "Dear woman," replied Rāmaliṅga, divesting himself of the scant loincloth he was wearing, "God, in his infinite wisdom, has taken care to see that no such thing takes place—he has created a strong root here for the tuft upstairs." Pointing to his phallus, he laughed, "The root is strong as you can see for yourself and so, set your fears at rest, woman" (*Indian Ribaldry,* pp. 36–37). While the pleasures of satire are voyeuristic, the pleasures of humor are exhibitionistic. The trickster shows off. He doesn't care what others think as long as they laugh.

I was surprised that my friend asked me to refrain from using his name if I were ever to write up the stories he had told me. "Is that because you've made them all up?" "No, no," he insisted with an ironic smile. "My father would be furious with me for telling you such stories, stories which in his mind would hardly be representative of his beloved Tamil culture. He considers himself an expert on Tamil literature. But he would refuse to admit there was any fecal matter in that body of literature. If he were to read your work," my friend laughed heartily, "the shit would hit the fan."

I wrote to the father, also a physician, explaining that I, a friend of his son, was writing a book on Indian comedy and I asked him for references to comedy in Tamil literature. "Your book on humour cannot succeed until you have studied Tamil," he wrote back to me. "Tamil is the wellspring from which all Indian humour has sprung. This humour is not translatable, for so much of it depends upon the subtle nuances of meaning of which Tamil, above all other languages, is capable. When you have learned Tamil, the oldest (if not the sweetest) language in the world, I shall cheerfully supply you with the texts that you will require. I enclose a very humourous piece by Kavimani. Keep it before you. It will be an inspiration for you to learn and an excellent place for you to start."

The small green pamphlet with a cartoon of a man's laughing face on the cover, a comic story or essay by Kavimani, sits in front of me on the desk as a symbol of the wealth of Indian vernacular literature to which I have no access. I don't know the language, not even the script. It makes a fool of me. I sense, with a certain, odd pleasure, that the face on the fading cover is laughing at me, for all that I don't know, can't know, for all of the laughter that cannot be mine. I stare at the face and cannot help but smile back at it.

A Game of Chance: *The Plebian Trickster*

In this surprising trick, I will instruct you how to do the Hindu Shuffle which is very useful in many other card tricks. A deck of cards is shuffled Hindu fashion and backs of cards freely shown to be blue in color. Deck is fanned face up and a spectator asked to select any card. Upon turning his card over it is a red card. The deck is turned over and fanned and the whole deck has red backs.

Harlan Tarbell, *The Tarbell Course in Magic*

"Poker?" W. C. Fields asks a rube in *My Little Chickadee*. "Is that a game of chance?" the innocent questions in return. Fields shuffles, "Not the way I play it." The cheat has comic charm. The rogue, as long as his crimes are for the sport of it and not solely for the monetary fruits of trickery, can be a comic hero, the champion of mirth. When Tenāli Rāma was a child, his teacher warned his guardian uncle: "He is extremely intelligent but diabolically mischievous. If he drops his pranks, he will become the greatest logician and scholar of India. If he drops his learning, he will become the greatest gangster of India" (*Tenali Rama,* p. 2). Scholarship or logic, like real gangsterism or crime, would require Tenāli Rāma to take himself and others seriously, and it is the trickster's mission to demonstrate that nothing is serious, that existence itself is a rollicking farce and crazy game. Adopting a purely comic posture in the world, Tenāli Rāma drops neither his intelligence nor his pranks—he becomes a pandit amongst pranksters, a learned mischief-maker. He commits all the crimes that are censured in the objects of satire—he's a liar, a thief, a cheat, a lecher, and anything else that ruffles the order of things—but he does it for us rather than against us, in fun rather than for self-aggrandizement or gain, for the sake of freedom rather than repression. He acts out our own suppressed impulses, premoral, childhood urges, naughty and fun. And by making us laugh with the pleasure of recovering those impulses, he is forgiven. Guilt is resolved. The delightful transport of humor is in such moments of forgiveness, innocence, and moral suppleness. He helps us savor the perfect joys of our imperfection.

In emulation of courtiers, bourgeois heroes in Sanskrit literature pursue pleasure and the arts—the brothel is their court, and their jester or *vidūṣaka* is the *viṭa,* a hired sidekick who cajoles his patron with jokes and cultural counsel. These rogues, conventional comic characters, were commissioned to instruct aspiring libertines in the ways of roguery.

A wealthy traveling salesman in the *Kalāvilāsa* of Kṣemendra, fearful that his son might fall into the hands of rogues and squander his fortune, takes the boy to one such *viṭa,* Mr. Wizard (Mūladeva), "the prince of rogues, an expert in trickery" (1.9), so that he can be educated in the crooked ways of the world. In a parody of the rite whereby a brahmin boy is initiated into Vedic study, Mr. Wizard accepts the youth as his disciple and introduces him into the sacred mysteries of roguery, chicanery, and hypocrisy. "Listen, my boy, and learn the very crooked core of all the arts of the tricksters" (1.39). That essence of trickery is hypocrisy, and Mr. Wizard extols that satiric vice as a virtue for the sake of humor. " 'Hypocrisy' is a magic word, a wishing jewel capable of securing anything that one desires. Rogues use it to get power or to take over fortunes. . . . Snakes can be caught by the power of spells, innocent deer by traps, birds by snares, and men by hypocrisy. Viva Hypocrisy, a magic wand, victory on earth, deceit within the human heart!" (1.42–45). The irony is extended to comic extremes as hypocrisy is praised as the essential power and glory of the universe. "Viṣṇu as a dwarf conquered the universe through hypocrisy" (1.95). Hypocrisy came into the world as a boon to mankind. "Having gazed at the world of mortal men, the creator, with divine insight, saw that men needed help. He noticed that, because they were so concerned with being honest, they weren't able to get any real pleasure out of such things as money. And so the creator closed his eyes at once, immersed himself in deep meditation, the magic trance, and created Hypocrisy, a vessel of honor, for the prosperity of mankind" (1.66–67). And then admiring Hypocrisy, his son, the creator laughed and took the newborn divinity on his lap, and all the other gods made obeisance. The creator dispatched him to earth where, according to Mr. Wizard, he appropriately incarnated in the "language of tribals, the vows of southerners, the politics of Kashmir, and all things Bengali" (1.86). He entered the hearts of "gurus, ascetics, commissioners, teenagers, religious initiates, astrologers, doctors, servants, merchants, jewelers, actors, soldiers, singers, reciters of religious texts, and magicians" (1.89–90), all the figures satirized by Kṣemendra. It is not hypocrisy that is bad, but greed—"be on guard against greediness" (2.1). It is greed that separates the righteous rogues from the unrighteous ones, the subjects of humor from the objects of satire. In satire the seemingly righteous turn out to be villains; in humor the seemingly unrighteous turn out to be heroes. Comedy brings those heroes and villains together, pits them against each other in a game that is won by bluffing, by cheating, by loading the dice and stacking the deck.

Kṣemendra's Mūladeva, our Mr. Wizard, often *viṭa* to a certain Mr. Moon (Śaśin), is a stock figure in the folktales preserved in the various Sanskrit collections. This popular and delightfully devious rogue was sometimes identified with Karīsuta the legendary author of the *Steyaśāstra,* a treatise on the fine art and exact science of theft. He is a thief, riddler, practical joker, gambler, and libertine. He is a master of disguises. And he is a magician. With magic he turns himself into a dwarf (suggestng his equivalence to Viṣṇu as the trickster god) and delights the people of Ujjayinī with magic tricks (the *Vṛtti* of Devendra on the *Uttarādhyāyanasūtra*).

There is a close alliance between comedy and magic ("the net of Indra" as it is known in India). While many styles of magic elicit wonder or awe, other styles have laughter as their goal. At the magic show we experience the pleasure of humor, of laughing at ourselves, laughing at the way the magician fools us, tricks us with his trick, traps us with the net. Mr. Wizard's implicit mission is to reveal the true nature of the world as a magic show.

In the show the trickster himself can be tricked, tangled in his own net. It is sometimes impossible to tell the audience from the performers, the spectators from the players. That's the fun of it. The *Kathāsaritsāgara* culminates with a story, a comic cognate of *All's Well That Ends Well,* in which the trickster tells the tale of how he himself was tricked.

The Confessions of Mr. Wizard

[Paraphrased from *Kathāsaritsāgara* 124]

> By turning the world playfully upside down, by putting down the mighty from their seats and—though only in jest—exalting them of low degree, the trickster makes apparent the frailty of human existence and the proximity of laughter and tears. Quintessence of the absolute comic, he transports us into worlds where imagination and make-believe triumph. [And] he is sacrificed for daring to be both Satan and Savior.
>
> Edith Kern, *The Absolute Comic*

Since we had heard that the people in Patna are real wits, Moonie and I decided to go there to see for ourselves just how clever they are. I'll tell you one thing—you can't get a straight answer in Patna. Just outside the city I asked an old broad who was washing clothes by the river, "Where do travelers stay here?" Taking "here" to mean literally "there" by the river, she put me on and answered with her idea of a joke. "Ducks here stay on the banks, bees here stay in the lotuses, and the fish here stay in the water—travelers don't stay here. Travelers, by definition, are people who don't stay."

No sooner had we entered town than we saw this little boy sobbing and crying over a bowl of hot porridge and Moonie turned to me and said, "How foolish this child is! Tears are vanity. He should stop crying and enjoy his porridge." And all at once, the snot-nose kid started laughing, laughing at Moonie and me. "You're the fools—I'm just crying to clear my sinuses while I wait for my porridge to cool down."

No sooner had we left him than we saw a foxy girl up in a mango tree picking the fruit and we asked her if we might have some. "Do you guys like to eat your mangoes hot or cold?" Wondering just how she was going to produce hot mangoes straight from the tree, I said that we liked eating them hot. She threw a couple of them on the ground and we picked them up, blew the dust off of them, and ate them, thinking she was crazy. But she just laughed at us. "You guys said you liked eating them hot, so I threw them on the ground and you blew on them just like they were hot—you got to eat them in the way you said you like to eat them!" I like clever girls, girls with a sense of humor, a sense of fun and games, a girl who can make a joke. But she had tricked me, made a fool of me, Mr. Wizard, a rogue who has dedicated his life to tricking others, so I hatched a little prank of my own. I decided to marry her.

Moonie and I, disguising ourselves as brahmin students, went to the house of her father, a local pandit, and explained to him that we had come all the way from Magicville to study the Veda. He agreed to teach us and, as is typical of a dedicated professor, he vowed to give us all that we wished of him. Little did he know that what we wanted was not his learning, but his daughter. He had given his word and so, even though I had tricked him, he had to give her to me—that's one of the rules of the game and brahmins play by the rules.

On our wedding night, as we crawled into bed, I laughed. "Remember me? The guy who liked eating his mangoes hot? We'll see who has the last laugh!" Then she laughed. "Yes, we'll see, my dear. Do you really think that *you,* a country bumpkin, could ever trick *me,* a city girl?" "Yes, darling," I laughed back "Yes, indeed! This marriage has been a trick—I the trickster, you the trickee—I'm going to leave you in the morning! He who laughs last, laughs best."

Years later in a casino in Ujjayinī, I was playing dice—gambling is my profession, play my work—when this little kid walked in and right up to the circle of gamblers. The boy could not be beaten. I had never seen a better player in my life. He won the shirt off every back in the house and—believe it or not—he gave every cent of his winnings to the poor. That's the mark of a real gamester, one who plays for the game and not the money. Anyway, I went home broke and tired and went to bed. In the morning, when I woke up, my mattress was on the floor. While I had been sleeping someone had stolen my bed out from under me, *me* the author of the *Steyaśāstra, The Joy of Theft!* But that afternoon in the market, at the used furniture dealer's stall, I saw my bed. That young brat was selling it! I rushed forward to stop the deal. "I'll buy the bed," I said. The boy looked me square in the face and laughed. "I wouldn't sell you this bed for anything, not for a million rupees. But I'd give it to you, if you could outsmart me, if you could fool me, trick me, or come up with a joke I don't know, or a riddle or conundrum I can't solve."

I couldn't help but accept the challenge with a laugh—after all, I'm Mr. Wizard, professional trickster, magician, and riddler *extraordinaire*. "A certain king, with a certain vessel that had a silver lining, sprinkled the body of a certain female, who had been the beloved of a certain bore, and thereby ended the great famine that had plagued his kingdom. True or false?"

"True," the boy laughed. "The word 'bore' which you meant for me to hear is really a 'boar,' the Boar-avatar of the trickster god Viṣṇu, whose beloved female is the earth which, when sprinkled with the rain that comes from a cloud, a vessel with a silver lining, gives forth the wheat that is used to produce the food that puts the end to the famine. That was an easy one. Now I'll tell you one," he laughed. "And if you can solve it, I'll give you your bed back. If not, you must obey the command I give you."

When I agreed, he laughed again. "A certain shrimp, taking certain steps to make the world shake, ended up in heaven. True or false?"

"False," I laughed with foolish confidence, and he laughed with the triumph of his trick. "True! The divine trickster, Viṣṇu, became the dwarf—or a 'shrimp' as people often call such little guys—to outwit Bali with his three steps, the first of which made the whole earth shake and the last of which placed Viṣṇu in heaven. You lose and must, therefore, obey the command I now give you. You are to come home with me to Patna and live there with my mother as my father."

His mother laughed when I walked through the door. She was the girl who had picked the mangoes, the woman I had married. "Do you remember a certain courtesan in Ujjayinī named Sumaṅgalā?" she asked. "That was about ten years ago. You loved her well. My disguise fooled you, didn't it? I seduced you and kept you lusting after me just long enough to get what I wanted—to be pregnant. And why did I want that? So we might have a son, the child of two tricksters, a child who, through such fine breeding, would be capable of helping me to trick you into coming back to me. Remember what you said on our wedding night, the night you thought *you* had tricked *me*? 'He who laughs last, laughs best!' "

The three of us—father, mother, and son—could not help but laugh. We roared with laughter, laughed and laughed together as one big happy family.

A Game of Hide-and-Seek: *The Animal Trickster*

Eve'y time I run over in my min' 'bout the pranks er Brer Rabbit . . . hit make me laugh mo' en mo'. He mos' allers come out on top, yit dey wuz times w'en he hatter be mighty spry.

Joel Chandler Harris, *Nights with Uncle Remus*

The beasts of the forest, terrorized by a vicious lion who was slaughtering them both for food and for his own amusement, appeared before that lion with a pact. "Your Majesty, what's the point of this purposeless killing? You are going to destroy us all and thus you will have no food left. Your actions are bad for you as well as for us. If you put a stop to this, we promise that one of us will come to you every day to be voluntarily eaten." The lion agreed, and each day one of the animals, for the sake of sparing the others, would go to the lion and allow itself to be devoured. One day it was the hare's turn. He was as spry as his American cousin, Brer Rabbit, and as full of pranks. When he showed up late for his appointment with death, the hungry lion was angered. But the rascally hare explained. "Sorry, I'm late—it's not my fault. I was detained on my way here by another lion. I told him he couldn't eat me, that I was reserved for your dining pleasure. But he just said you were a thief and that he would eat me and the rest of the animals in the forest as well. I defended you. But he's out to get you. He only let me go on the condition that I come and get you, that I bring you to him so the two of you could fight it out in order to decide which of you really has dominion over this forest." The infuriated lion, anxious to take his revenge on the intruder to his territory, followed the little hare to a well in which the hare claimed the other lion was residing. The lion, peering into the well, imagined that his reflection there was indeed another lion. When he growled, the echo of his voice supplied the roar of the other lion. The lion jumped into the well and drowned. The beasts of the forest had a great laugh over the trick of the hare. The storyteller concludes with the amoral moral of comedy: "He who has wit, has power" (*Pañcatantra* 1.257).

The trickster is a devilish savior. Through his cleverness and wit he redistributes power, turns society around so that the strong feel their weakness and the weak their strength. The turning is comic. The laughter it arouses expresses the relief of a primary anxiety. While satire exposes the ways in which the strong oppress the weak, humor shows the ways in which the weak can have their just revenge. Trickery and deceit, the vices of satire, are the virtues of the trickster, the source of his success on our behalf, and the wellspring of his humorous appeal.

The animal stories in the *Pañcatantra, Hitopadeśa, Kathāsaritsāgara, Jātaka*s, and other collections constitute a comic allegory in which society is depicted as a jungle. That literary transformation is for the sake of amusement. The *Pañcatantra* declares itself to be a book on polity and rulership recited by a clever brahmin for the entertaining edification of the sons of a king. Serious lessons are imparted with comic tones, tempered with humor, enlivened with satire, enriched with wit. The introduction to a children's edition of the *Pañcatantra* promises that the stories will convey important moral lessons to the children of India in a form that will be acceptable to them. "Nowadays, children do not like to read goody-goody stories which teach not to do this, that and the other." But of course, no one likes to read goody-goody stories and no one likes to be told not to do this, that and the other—moral polemics exist in literature not because anyone likes to read them, but only because some people like to write them. The real value of the stories is not in their serious (and often trite and obvious) lessons, but in their humor. The primary object of the stories is not the explicitly stated didactic or moral one, but rather the implicit, aesthetic, and amoral one. Morality is merely invoked to legitimate comic pleasure. The lion who drowned in the well was a victim of a deadly trick played upon him by an unscrupulous and wholly dishonest hare. It is a story of injustice passed off as a parable of justice, and the injustice is justified to the degree that it is amusing.

A mother goat who had escaped slaughter in the world of men sought refuge with her kids in the forest. A hungry tiger there, hearing the bleating of the little goats, slowly approached. The mother saw the tiger out of the corner of her eye and, as her only hope to save her offspring, she spoke to them in a voice loud enough for the tiger to overhear. "Why are you still crying out for food? Can you still be hungry? I've already fed you five tigers, your favorite meal, not to mention the two bears, the rhinoceros, and those buffaloes! But—okay, okay—stop crying, there's a tiger coming now. I'll kill him so you can have some dessert." Hearing the bluff of the mother goat, the tiger backed off in fear, turned, ran for dear life, and hid beneath a tree. A monkey in that tree asked the tiger why he was trembling so. When the tiger told the monkey the story of the tiger-eating goat, the monkey laughed at the foolishness of his fellow beast. "That was a trick. Come along, I'll go back there with you and show you." But the tiger was terrified. "No. When we get there you'll escape—you'll go bounding up a tree and I'll get eaten." The monkey laughed, "I won't leave you. Don't worry. We can tie our tails together so you'll be assured I'll stay by you. Come, come—you're a tiger. You don't need to be afraid of a little she-goat and her kids." And so the tiger and the monkey, their tails tied together, returned to where the mother goat was hiding. And when the goat saw them, she shouted out to the monkey, "You rascal, where have you been? Monkey, I've been waiting for you all day! My kids are hungry and you promised to bring me some tigers! What—you've only brought one little tiger with you? You promised to bring several—the kids are famished!" In terror the tiger turned and ran, dragging the monkey with him as the mother goat calmly continued to suckle her trembling little kids (after W. McCulloch, *Bengali Household Tales,* and M. Stokes, *Indian Fairy Tales*).

Again morality is hardly at work. The tiger in his need to eat has done nothing wrong and the monkey speaks the truth. And yet they are punished and the lying goat is triumphant. The irony, that through the power of wit the weak can be stronger than the strong, is a comic one, one that pleases, consoles, and soothes all that is weak within us. The laughter of humor is inevitably a confession of frailty. But it is a celebration of frailty as well.

Near the entrance to the Taj Mahal a man with a mongoose on a leash and a cobra in a bag insisted that if we were to pay him we would enjoy the pleasure of seeing the two animals fight. As a crowd gathered in hopes that we would provide funding for the public show, I insisted that I was not interested in the spectacle. A stranger from the crowd, the animal trainer's shill perhaps, urged me on. "You will be quite amused by the little mongoose. He is unafraid of the big snake. But he tricks the snake. He pretends that he is afraid so that the snake will think he can eat him up. And once the clever mongoose knows the snake is confident, he shows his true mettle. He beats the snake! It is very, very amusing. There is nothing like it in America I am sure." I tried to explain that I would not consider watching the death of a snake particularly amusing. "Don't worry! The snake will not die. The mongoose will not die! No one will die! Think about it—if one of the animals were to die, the owner of them would lose his livelihood. He won't let that happen, I can assure you. Furthermore the audience would not be pleased. He will separate them. Don't worry, it is just for fun. It is just for amusement. It is just a game. Don't be a bad sport. Give the man his twenty rupees. Treat yourself, madam, and all of these poor people gathering here to have some fun. You can afford it, they cannot. They want to laugh just like you. Everybody wants to have a laugh! Isn't it so?"

Act Two: Humor

Scene Two: The Divine Comedy

The Laughter of Kṛṣṇa

8

The Preserver: The Seriousness of Humor

Kṛṣṇa burst into loud laughter and as he laughed his body seemed to become a roaring fire with throngs of gods flaring from it like flashes of lightning.

Mahābhārata

Tukuri's small daughter Chinna shyly, at the persistent behests of her exuberantly smiling father, brought me the calendar, crudely printed with the words "TUKURI PURI TAILER DELUX. TEMPLE ROAD. PURI ORISSA. INDIA. PIN 752001" under the glaringly garish and glossy picture of the infant Kṛṣṇa being carried in a basket across a stormy sea by a noble Vasudeva. The pudgy baby, clutching his father's forefinger, smiled sweetly. The little girl jumped back from me to hide behind her seated father, as if seeking the very safety enjoyed by the god. "She loves Kṛṣṇa!" Tukuri laughed happily, pointing to the kitschy image of the deity. "I never know what date it is, Lee Baba, because she is always stealing my calendar. How can I get angry with her when Kṛṣṇa, his divine self himself, is also always stealing things from his mother and father? She is naughty, but so is Kṛṣṇa!" Little eyes peered at me over the father's shoulder. As I held out the calendar, the small girl summoned the courage to retrieve it quickly from me. She hesitated and, when our attention was on her, she kissed the picture of the infant god, giggled, and skipped away with him in her little arms.

The god is disarming. One minute he is the epitome of cuteness—a Kewpie doll; and then he is all terror and glory, an infinite power with a multitude of blazing eyes, and tusked, gaping mouths, a thousand raging arms, and a myriad of shining weapons raised, "the imperishable support of the cosmos, the unchanging guardian of eternal righteousness" (*Bhagavadgītā* 11.18). A little girl cuddles him and smiles; a warrior on the battlefield makes obeisance with terror and awe. The ardent Līlāśuka Bilvamaṅgala (c. fourteenth century) surrendered to the mystery of this god. He marveled that though Kṛṣṇa was only a child he could lift a mountain, that though he was dark he could dispel all gloom, that though he was a philanderer he could absolve our sins. And pondering the uncanny, contradictory nature of the deity, he asked, "What's with you?" (*Kṛṣṇakarṇāmṛta* 2.73). Embodied incongruities and paradoxes make Kṛṣṇa a comedic god—an ontological joker and divine trickster.

Bharata's list of the causes of laughter and comic sentiment reveals the comedy of the mythology of Kṛṣṇa: trickery or tickling (he tricks the cowherds and teases [teasing being a nontactile mode of tickling] their wives and daughters); seeing deformities (he taunts the hunchback Kubjā for her crooked form); excessive desire and audacity (he rapaciously makes love to sixteen-thousand women); wearing inappropriate clothes or ornaments (he dresses in women's clothes to gain secret access to Rādhā); lying prattle and declaring faults (he steals butter and curds, outlandishly lies about it, and blames others for the havoc his pranks create). His improprieties are essentially comic, and the comedy enhances the appeal of the deity. The god, smiling softly or laughing uproariously, sanctifies mirth. "When shall I behold your face," Bilvamaṅgala cries out for a vision of the grin of god, "your lips—red as the dawn and eternally smiling?" (1.44). The poet hears his lord's laughter, "sweet and soft as honey" (1.46), and he sings or whispers, "I am absorbed in the ruby lips, shimmering everlastingly with a gentle laughter that voices an abundance of the joyous sentiment that is so natural to him" (1.59). The smiles and laughter dazzle, stun, beguile, enliven, intoxicate, soothe, console, and promise an everlasting joy.

A Christian theologian appropriately explains that while humor may help us to cope with immediate and superficial problems, "it must move toward faith or sink into despair when the ultimate issues are raised. That is why there is laughter in the vestibule of the temple, the echo of laughter in the temple itself, but only faith and prayer, and no laughter, in the holy of holies'' (Reinhold Niebuhr, ''Humour and Faith''). But in the shrines of Lord Kṛṣṇa—those made of words as well as those made of stone—this has not always been so. The echoes of a splendid laughter in his temples have, for many, had their source in the very heart of the holy of holies.

Peek-A-Boo Baby Kṛṣṇa: *Humor and Regression*

> Perhaps we ought even to carry simplification still farther, and, going back to our earliest recollections, try to discover, in the games that amused us as children, the first faint traces of the combinations that make us laugh as grown-up persons. . . . We are too apt to ignore the childish element, so to speak, latent in most of our joyous emotions.
>
> Henri Bergson, *Laughter*

The first smile is a smile of recognition. And it is a breakthrough, a new consciousness, and an initiation into pleasures outside the self. Perceiving the mother in a hazy world, seeing a face that is known, that intimates warmth and fullness, that prepares the infant to be held, fed, and wholly pleased, the baby smiles a smile that makes the mother smile a bright, reciprocal smile that expands that of the child. The tender pleasure of each amplifies the pleasure of the other. Mother and child establish a warm circuit of joy. And sweet smiles in time give way to laughter, softly diffused joys to bursts of delight. Humor recovers that primary laughter as it awakens the baby within, reviving infantile feelings of safety. Humor is regression and defense, a search for a security that threatens to be lost in the past. Humor discovers, rediscovers, or invents a holy infancy and makes a sanctuary of it. Kṛṣṇa is the Indian embodiment of that divine baby, that idealized image of what we might have been and known, that pure pleasure. And throughout India at the end of summer, Janmāṣṭhamī, Kṛṣṇa's nativity is celebrated. The image of the crawling baby is bathed in sweet mixtures of milk and curds, fruit, spices, and tulsī leaves. The idol is a toy—the playful god is a doll played with, placed in a swing, rocked to and fro, hymned with songs, laughter, jokes, and praises full of mirth and desire. The mythology of the divine baby, enacted in rituals and such festivals as Janmāṣṭhamī and Holī, provides social license and psychological legitimacy for regression. It pronounces regression holy.

Kṛṣṇa is a god of and for children, sanctifying childhood; and within adults he preserves childhood, makes it last a lifetime. For the theologians of the medieval devotional movement, who transformed classical aesthetic theory into a system of religious psychology, the myths of the divine baby were meant to inspire the sentiment of parental affection, to awaken the instinctual smiles of mother and father, and focus that affection, expressed by those smiles, upon the infantile god. As they modified the rhetoric of literature into a rhetoric of devotion, laughter had to have a place in their codification of religious sentiments. "A fully developed joy of laughter [inspired by the playful deeds of Kṛṣṇa] is discussed by experts with the term *hāsyabhaktirasa,*" Rūpa Goswāmin explains—"the devotional sentiment of comedy" (*Bhaktirasāmṛtasindhu* 4.1.6).

The myths, rituals, and iconic dolls at once represent the god as an infant and the infant—each and every infant—as god; they establish a sacrality for infancy—his and ours alike. Natural innocence, absolute freedom, unmitigated pleasure, unbounded desire, and undetermined potentiality are hypostatized in the holy baby, the resplendent ideal worshiped in India as Kṛṣṇa. The myth activates a dream, charts the geography and topography of a land of milk and honey. The heavenly Vṛndāvan, where Kṛṣṇa plays eternally, is an inner refuge remembered with fantastic fancy and fabrication, a lost land of infancy where gratification was immense and immediate, a land of big rock-candy mountains. The myth is nostalgic, utopian, and romantic, full of astonishment and wonder, magic and mirth. It makes an apotheosis of childhood and a symbol of the child. And the symbol, by the grace of Kṛṣṇa, is a sacred one. Within the temporally and spatially bound adult, the god enacts the triumph of the invincible child, naughty and innocent, and utterly free from consciousness of time. The baby represents wholeness to consciousness divided and liberation to spirit contained. The child is the symbol of renewal, a symbol formed of fear for the sake of unqualified happinesses and illusions of deathlessness. "When I am face to face with death," Bilvamaṅgala cries out, "may he appear before me—the baby boy, making mischief at the breasts of the milkmaid" (*Kṛṣṇakarnāmṛta* 3.37). The poet, longing for dread to give way to solace, oblivion to succor, tears to laughter, invokes the image of Kṛṣṇa, the baby/god. Devotedly, he recollects the image of the divine infant lying upon a cot of leaves, "sticking his lotus-foot into his lotus-mouth with his lotus-hand'' (2.58). It is an image of freedom from empirical realities, an emblem of self-reality, self-gratification, self-dependency, and self-happiness—states attributed to gods, feelings projected onto speechless children.

The infant feels the omnipotence which the god, in the minds of his devotees, actualizes and fulfills. Baby and god are, contain, and subsume all. When Yaśodā looked into the mouth of her baby she saw there ''the entire cosmos—heaven, sky, and the whole earth with its mountains, lands and seas; she saw the winds, lightning, the sun, moon, and stars; she saw air, earth, fire, water, ether. . . . Within her boy's open mouth she saw all of life . . . the village in which they lived, and she saw herself'' (*Bhāgavata Purāṇa* 10.8.37–39). In the Purāṇic accounts, Kṛṣṇa's older brother and the other boys of the village tattle on Kṛṣṇa, tell his mother that he has been eating dirt. When Kṛṣṇa denies it, Yaśodā checks his mouth as if she will punish him if indeed she catches him in a lie. The inversion of the power structure existing between parent and child is naturally comic. And Bilvamaṅgala makes the implicit humor explicit—Yaśodā has her vision ''when Kṛṣṇa's mouth was wide open with laughter. The butter he had eaten had become Mount Kailāsa, the dirt he had consumed had become the earth, and the milk he had drunk had become the cosmic Ocean of Milk.'' Surely Bilvamaṅgala, though not an essentially jolly devotee, is joking when he adds that ''when his mom saw all this, she became really worried about his digestion'' (*Kṛṣṇakarṇāmṛta* 2.62). The incongruities between the banality of dyspepsia and the magnificence of cosmic vision, between puerility and divinity, temporality and eternity, smallness and infinitude—paradoxes resolved by the god and the baby—prompt laughter and an astonishment that is at once sacred and profane.

In the act of humor we laugh with admiration and an idealization of childhood, of its folly and mischief, its charming transgressions. We laugh at the child we still are or wish to be under the pressures of adulthood.

Humor celebrates what satire disdains. Its laughter expresses the pleasure of relief provided by regression into infantile feelings of omnipotence, illusions that, like baby Kṛṣṇa, we contained the mother, the pleasure, the world. Humor idealizes childhood just as it makes folly a mode of wisdom, vulnerability a strength, and roguery a virtue. The silliness, smallness, and scampishness of the child become graces pleasurable to remember or behold.

As transgressions are chastised in satire, they are exonerated in humor. While satire, the predatory mode of comedy, exposes degradations of ideals, humor, with its exultant tenor, establishes, promulgates, or accepts them. The roots of both phases of the comic sentiment are embedded in childhood experience. The singsong "naa-na-naa-na-naa-naa" laughed by children at other children, at their more childish childishness (when they wet their pants, suck their thumbs, or do not know what the other children know), is the prototypical laughter of satire. The "ha-ha, hee-hee" of delight in nonsense in oneself or the world echoes in the developed laughter of humor. In both cases comedy bestows a happiness and freedom associated with childhood. Freedom is the goal of comedy just as it is of religion; it is the aim of both satire (freedom from others) and humor (freedom from or in oneself).

Comedy offers a special and frivolous freedom that threatens to disappear if taken too seriously. Comic satire is all disruption; humor is indulgent and absurd; farces are all chaos. Anything goes. Comedy's robust and real laughter cannot be contained. The comic liberation is from the intellectual order of reason and logic, and from social order too—hierarchy, responsibility, and injunction. The comic hero, like or as the child or god, is beyond the law. He has the freedom to which the holy man aspires. The toddler is silly and naughty, a little fool and a little rogue. The pranksome misbehavior of Kṛṣṇa, allowed to him as a baby just as it was allowed to us, is a source of laughter, an expression of a pleasure taken in awakened memories of an immunity to censure or punishment. The mythology of the god is a mythology of childhood. And childhood provides an access to the god.

Adulthood brings the responsibilities of *dharma*—righteousness, propriety, virtue, duty, rules and the observance of them. *Dharma* is a logos, the principle of order in the home, society, and the universe. It is the force that holds the world together. In the meantime, comedy cracks the world up. Its heroes—the naughty child, the rogue, the fool, the theatrical clown, the court jester, the trickster, and Kṛṣṇa—break the codes, behave inappropriately and without propriety. The heroes of comedy challenge *dharma* with their transgressions and, in so doing, prevent it from becoming stale or static. Chaos graces, humanizes, warms, and softens order.

The small child breaks rules and things, overturns feelings and objects; he is the champion of a life-affirming disorder. He makes a mess, and it is a source of delight. The innocence of the baby, like the divinity of the god, is redemptive. Yaśodā placed her little baby Kṛṣṇa under a cart so that he might sleep while she went to the river to bathe. The infant god, crying for the teat, wiggling his hands and feet about, kicked over the milkwagon and all the butter pots and milk jugs in it were broken. Hearing the noise of that destruction and the hungry cry of the baby, Yaśodā raced back to him as quickly as she could, "her body drenched with flowing milk, like a cow whose calf is tied up. Not knowing how the cart had been overturned, she was at once afraid and pleased—'What will your father say?' " (*Harivaṃśa* 50.7–10). "The cowherds, shouting 'uh-oh, uh-oh,' came running only to find the little baby lying on his back in the crib. 'Hey, who overturned the cart?' they asked some children. 'Don't look at us—the baby did it,' the kids exclaimed. 'We saw him—he was crying and he kicked the cart over!' " (*Viṣṇu Purāṇa* 5.6.2–5).

Kṛṣṇa, as baby and as god, cannot be punished. As a toddler he cannot be restrained. "Binding Kṛṣṇa around the waist with a cord, Yaśodā tied him to a mortar and impatiently she said to him, 'Go on, get away if you can, you naughty little rascal!' And then she set about her chores and housework. But while she was occupied, the lotus-eyed one, dragging the mortar with him, went in between two twin *arjuna* trees, and the mortar was lodged there, crosswise between them. The two great trees, heavy with lofty branches, broke and fell. The people of Vraja, away at the time, when they heard the cracking sound, came and saw the two magnificent trees fallen and the little boy, bound around his belly with a cord, was in between them. His laughter was white with the rays of his newly appeared baby teeth" (*Viṣṇu Purāṇa* 6.13–19). In the *Harivaṃśa* too, attention is given to the laughter of the toddler, a laughter inviting reciprocal laughter. "Sitting in the midst of the debris, having revealed his divine power, the little child laughed." The infantile laughter is the laughter of omnipotence; the illusion of all infants is the reality of Kṛṣṇa. And again Bilvamaṅgala takes refuge from the phenomenal world in the noumenal world of the almighty god, the realm of myth (the collective past) and memory (the personal past). With joy he visualizes "the toddler with ringlets, his little body all dirty from playing in the mud, his mother worn out from chasing after him amidst the cows" (*Kṛṣṇakarṇāmṛta* 2.77). He visualizes the smile, hears the giggle, and it inspires him with joy and allows him laughter.

So that the smile is not forgotten, the laughter not stifled, the infancy of Kṛṣṇa is enacted in folk performances, *rāslīlās,* throughout India. The overturning of the cart and the pulling of the mortar are standard scenes in the repertoires of the troupes of actors who spark village laughter with their mystery plays. There is a comic theophany. There is holy laughter, no different from the most profane, when a milkmaid catches Kṛṣṇa stealing butter and drags him to his mother for a spanking. The laughter makes god real. It makes him one of us.

The waggish child is the precursor of the heroic Kṛṣṇa, the slayer of demons. The erotic Kṛṣṇa, the lover of the milkmaids, is no less present in the baby. He is fondled, cuddled, suckled, and snuggled by fleshy, breasty, carnal, fecund, laughing mothers. All is tumescence. All is delight.

When the little baby Kṛṣṇa cried,
  milkmaids would put him to their breasts;
And in the confusion lips rubbed lips,
  neck to neck,
  forehead upon forehead,
  cajoling eye to eye;
And all at once he'd giggle
  breaking out in goosebumps—
May the god whose flesh is languid
  with love
  preserve the world!

(Divākara, *Saduktikarṇāmṛta* 1.51.4)

Again infancy is idealized as a world of pure and immediate delight, a rapturous realm without denial or repression, an endless orgy of orality, a delirious paradise of polymorphous pleasures. Humor is a mode of identification with the giggling baby, and laughter is a signal that the identification has been successful.

The milkmaids thought he was just an innocent little baby,
  and so they kissed him
    (and he loved their lips),
  and so they cuddled him
    (and he hugged them,
    till their necks were red),
  and so they bounced him on their laps
    (and he touched their cunts).
May little Kṛṣṇa, swami of little rascals,
  take our sins away,
    far, far away!

(*Kṛṣṇakarṇāmṛta* 2.69)

Memory and myth contain other female figures: austere mothers, laughless women, sources of denial, punishment, disillusionment, and auguries of death. The mythology of Kṛṣṇa names one such female Putanā, the "Putrid One" or "Mrs. Stinky." She and Yaśodā, the hideous depriver and the beautiful giver, the deadly poisoner and the vital nourisher, are two phases of a more whole and real mother, dark and light aspects of the moon in the vast space of consciousness.

Mrs. Stinky

Begin, my little infant, knowing your mother with laughter.
Virgil, *Ecologues*

The hideous devourer of babies, using the power of magic to transform herself into a lovely woman, entered the village of the cowherds and asked Yaśodā if she might suckle the infant Kṛṣṇa. "Her evil nature was hidden by a sweet demeanor, like a deadly sword concealed in a scabbard. Yaśodā, dazzled by her beauty, thought she was a good woman and so she consented" (*Bhāgavata Purāṇa* 10.6.9). "All children who are suckled by Putanā in the night die. But Kṛṣṇa grabbed her breast with both hands and squeezed it, bit her nipple and sucked the milk out of her, and then he sucked the very life out of her. Screaming, her sinews torn apart, the hideous Putanā fell upon the ground dying" (*Viṣṇu Purāṇa* 5.5.8–9). Her true nature was revealed: "Her teeth were plowshares, her nostrils caves, her eyes dark pits" (*Bhāgavata Purāṇa* 10.6.16). The breaking through concealments, the exposure of degradations hidden within ideals, is a motif familiar in satiric comedy. There is laughter at Putanā because in trying to trick Kṛṣṇa she was outtricked. But when the vile ogress is burned, her flesh smells like sandalwood. Because she offered her breast to Kṛṣṇa, even though her intentions were evil, she was saved, delivered despite herself. The soteriological irony is comic. There is a tonal shift in the religious myth from the satirical to the humorous.

The *Purāṇa*s find the humor of the incident in the reactions of Yaśodā and the other milkmaids who are afraid for the baby. The innocence of milkmaids is comic. As they pick him up, perform rites for his protection, nurse him, and put him to sleep, humor arises out of the tension between the sense of danger that they feel and the understanding on our part that everything is all right, that the Almighty cannot be harmed. It is comic, according to Sanskrit literary theory, because it is a "mere semblance of the sentiment" of fear. One laughs at the realization that what seems threatening really isn't. And such laughter recapitulates one of the earliest experiences of laughter.

The mother discovers that the baby will laugh at a sudden "peek-a-boo," at being surprised, scared by a sharp "boo," and then relieved by a peek at the familiar, softly smiling face. There is an increase in arousal and tension followed by an abrupt arousal decrease and a relief of tension expressed in laughter. The laughter of the baby makes the mother laugh and her laughter makes the baby laugh all the more. It's the first game, the first joke, and it links fear and laughter inextricably in consciousness. This very laughter may later serve as a mitigation of fear and a recapture of infantile feelings of safety and trust. The myth makes fun of Putanā and illustrations of it make her a caricature of danger through which protective, apotropaic laughter is aroused. Laughter makes Putanā benign. It makes a joke of real terror.

As I rummage memory for clues to the development of this laughter, Mrs. Bartz, my fourth-grade teacher, her hair as red as Putanā's, appears, stern, severe, and smileless. The mother figure, seemingly devoid of affection, wielded power and exhibited authority. "No talking. Stop laughing! Go to the principal's office." She was the enforcer of rules, the precision priestess of knowledge charged to initiate us into solemn mysteries of greater intellectual and social maturity. And the funniest joke at the school, the endlessly repeated joke that could make any fourth-grader laugh, was a simple play on the sound of her name—"Miss Fartz." The utterance exposed the Putanā, "Mrs. Stinky," beneath the teacher's mask, revealed the bodily processes, rude sounds, and rank odors, hidden by the teacher's posture. To make a farting sound behind her back was to refer to her, and if one preceded that raspberry with the word "Mrs." it was wildly hilarious. It undermined authority as the suck of Kṛṣṇa deflated Putanā's illusion of beauty. Laughter, expressing the joy of irreverence, made Mrs. Bartz benign. Like the flatulence we imitated, such laughter relieved internal pressures.

Mrs. Bartz can be blamed for this book. She assigned each child in the class a project, gave each student a country of his or her own and a mission to find maps and pictures, paste them in a notebook, and write a report about that assigned land, its resources and industries, its culture and history, its religions and arts. Going up and down the rows, Mrs. Bartz distributed countries to us in alphabetical order from Afghanistan to Zanzibar: "Joey Zimmelman—Iceland. Mike Friedman—India. Lee Siegel—Ireland. Sheri Sheridan—Israel . . ." The quintessentially cute Sheri Sheridan (those *i*'s were dotted with little hearts) insisted that she trade with me, that she have Ireland since she was "going to Ireland this summer and the project will help to prepare me for the trip." I was willing to switch, but once the nations of the world were up for grabs, Mike Friedman demanded Israel because his parents had just returned from there and, bragging about all the trees that were planted there in his name, he explained that we would all benefit from his presentation on Israel since he had many valuable souvenirs to show us. Mrs. Bartz made me take India. This book is an appendix to that project, that unfinished, never-finishable, utterly futile attempt to figure out a culture. If not for Sheri Sheridan, this book would no doubt be about Irish humor and satire. To explain a function of laughter, I'd be quoting the poet Carpre who, in the Old Irish *Second Battle of Moytura,* when asked by King Lugh what power he might wield in battle, answered, "I will satirize them and shame them, so that through the spell of my art they will not resist warriors." And if not for Mike Friedman, this book would be full of jokes about moyels, rabbis, overbearing mothers, yentas, and such. But the book would be the same. The content of the jokes would be different, but not the delineations of the structures, patterns, or functions. The status of laughter might be different in Ireland, Israel, and India—in Christian, Jewish, and Hindu contexts—but the sound of it is the same. "Men have been wise in different modes," Dr. Johnson observed, "but they have always laughed in the same way."

Childish Things: *Humor and Play*

> The child is making an image of something different, something more beautiful, or more sublime, or more dangerous than what he usually is. One is a Prince, or one is a Daddy, or a wicked witch or a tiger. The child is quite literally "beside himself" with delight, transported beyond himself to such an extent that he almost believes he actually is such and such a thing, without, however, wholly losing consciousness of "ordinary reality."
>
> Johan Huizinga, *Homo Ludens*

"When I was a child, I spake as a child, I understood as a child, I thought as a child," Paul wrote to the Corinthians, "but when I became a man, I put away childish things." The apostles of devotion to Kṛṣṇa have often done the very opposite. "All at once, overwhelmed with the emotions of childhood, Caitanya began to play childhood games, even crawling around on his hands and knees like a baby," Vṛndāvanadāsa's hagiography happily explains. "Then he jumped up and around and laughed out loud" (*Caitanyabhāgavata* 2.8.174–175). The devotees themselves may be mature, savoring the sentiment of parental affection inspired by Kṛṣṇa or Caitanya, by the child actor in the village play or by the dollish idol in the temple, home, or heart. They laugh at the childhood pranks with "the devotional sentiment of comedy." They laugh at Kṛṣṇa's theft of butter from the homes of the milkmaids, one of the most popular and explicitly comedic of the scenes from the mythology of Kṛṣṇa as portrayed in folk drama. And they laugh at stories of Caitanya doing the same and, undoubtedly, at recollections of the transgressions of their own childhood when they were no different from the god. They laugh when the milkmaids tell Kṛṣṇa's mother just how naughty he is, for it is a description of their own, former and universal naughtiness, an account of everyone's theft from the cookie jar, everyone's incontinence. "He shits and pisses in our homes just when we've cleaned them! He does things like that and then he even steals from us, and then he comes and sits next to you like a good little boy, innocent through and through" (*Bhāgavata Purāṇa* 10.8.31). The laughter is full of a nostalgia for a time of freedom from control, continence, and order. Laughter alleviates the pressures of conscience and morality, and allows for a socially acceptable appreciation or indulgence of socially unacceptable feelings or actions. Kṛṣṇa is the liar, the thief, the cheat—which is to say, the child—in all beings. "If you try to scold him," the milkmaids complain, "he just laughs at you! He's come up with some new and clever ways of stealing, of getting to the sweet milk, yoghurt, and butter—if the jars are hung high up, out of his reach, he constructs a scaffolding, using the kitchen chairs and tables, to get at the goodies. If that doesn't work he uses a slingshot to break the pots!" (*Bhāgavata Purāṇa* 10.8.29–30). In America Dennis the Menace is merely funny; in India he is god.

The descriptions of the bucolic childhood of Kṛṣṇa in the *Harivaṃśa,* and throughout the *Purāṇas,* repeatedly stress his laughter, the sound and joy of it. Laughter becomes a sacred utterance, the expression of a divine carefreeness and godly delight. Vṛndāvana is a world of perpetual play and eternal amusement. Playfulness is the godliness of the gods in heaven, and the fun of it, by the grace of myth, pervades the world. Nature itself, the trees, clouds, mountains, rivers, birds, and animals all laugh the full and fertile laughter of renewal.

The comic sensibility is crucial to the effect of the *rāslīlās*. those motley comic operas which bring the god, in the flesh of a young boy, to village after village. For the sake of laughter the character of Mansukhā was introduced into these spiritual vaudeville shows. Formed out of the traditional *vidūṣaka* of classical Sanskrit drama, this foolish bungler and rustic brahmin draws laughs as Kṛṣṇa's comic sidekick. "Now there you go ridiculing me again," he dolefully, but comically, kvetches in a *rāslīlā* recorded by Jack Hawley, "Ridicule, ridicule, that's all I get!" *(At Play with Krishna)*. By providing the audience with a needed object for their pent-up ridicule and a gracious subject for their delight, the character performs his function. He acts out their own folly for them, their own limitations and pretensions, their humanness for all its absurdity. And despite Mansukhā's folly, Kṛṣṇa seems to love him, to love to tease and taunt him, but to love him nevertheless. It's fun to have him around.

Slapstick

> A slapstick consisted of two flat pieces of wood which, when applied, for instance, to somebody's buttocks, produced a cracking or slapping sound. . . . There may be some connection between this and the tradition of the Vice cudgelling the devil; and, further back, the demons of the medieval Mystery Plays coming on with fire-crackers exploding in their tails.
>
> J. A. Cuddon, *A Dictionary of Literary Terms*

As the perfect happiness and eternity of each childhood, real or fantasized, is inevitably jeopardized by new forces, needs, or figures, so the idyllic childhood of Kṛṣṇa is threatened by demons. The demons, most often in the form of various gigantic animals, are sent by Kaṃsa, Kṛṣṇa's evil uncle, perhaps the dark but shimmering shadow of a parent, psychologically separated from that parent for the sake of the idealization requisite for filial love and respect. The appeal of the mythology of Kṛṣṇa's childhood battles with these demons, a mythology often informed with a comic tone as established by the conventional assertion that Kṛṣṇa slays the demons in play and for fun, is the appeal of *Tom and Jerry* and countless other similar cartoons in which the child is offered the pleasure of laughing over the ways in which an ominously large and potentially dangerous figure is tricked so that his own aggression backfires. In plotting to eat Tweety the canary, poor Sylvester the cat ends up flattened behind a slammed door, or under a falling tree or moving steamroller. Again and again he is killed, and again and again he is resurrected for comic delight. So too Kaṃsa's aggression toward Kṛṣṇa is reformed again and again—now as a whirlwind, now as a giant crane, or snake, or ass—only to be destroyed again and again by the little child. Both the narrative and dramatic depictions of these battles are, like the repeated agons of Tom and Jerry or Sylvester and Tweety, comic. The signal is Kṛṣṇa's own laughter. Caught in the coils of the venomous serpent Kāliya, "Kṛṣṇa's face was bright with laughter. He laughed and at once slipped out of the clutch of the snake" (*Viṣṇu Purāṇa* 5.7.43); attacked by the terrible bull Ariṣṭa, "Kṛṣṇa laughed playfully with scorn" (5.14.10).

The demon Pralamba disguised himself as a herdsman boy and came to join in the games that Kṛṣṇa, his brother Balarāma, and the other boys were playing. When in one of the games Balarāma had to carry Pralamba on his shoulders and the horrible demon assumed his true, monstrous form, Balarāma pretended to be afraid and called out for help. The scene burlesques the conventional sentiment of fear, and, as we have seen, such parodies were held to establish the comic sentiment. There is laughter in the knowledge that Balarāma is not really afraid or in danger. "And Balarāma laughed as he squeezed Pralamba between his knees . . . and the demon vomited blood as his brain oozed from his broken skull" (*Viṣṇu Purāṇa* 5.9.34–35). And when at the final battle Kaṃsa, the commissioner of all these demons, ordered the destruction of the child god, "Kṛṣṇa laughed aloud at him, grabbed him by the hair, and smashed him on the ground" (5.20.85). The slaughter of the demons and their leader is slapstick comedy making laughingstocks of mythic demons, silly images of real fears. It is play.

As Kṛṣṇa the laughing child cudgels demons to death in play, so all children, in play, go into battle. And they laugh at the vanquishing of demons formed by imagination. Religious myths and children's games are both make-believe, making one believe, aiding in the discovery of new dimensions of reality. Fantasy, a rich source of humor, is necessary to an understanding or endurance of what really is.

Of the many connections between play and laughter, a crucial one in the development of the comic sensibility is rooted in childhood endeavors. Children play for the sake of mastery. Games (physical play), jokes (verbal play), and fantasies or make-believe (psychological play), serve to reduce the anxieties that are aroused by the pressures upon the child to master the physical, linguistic, and emotional skills expected of an adult. While the laughter of children expresses the pleasure of the reduction of anxiety as well as the delight of mastery, adult laughter revives such feelings of relief and mastery, comfort and safety. Nervous laughter is the result of the attempt to laugh without those feelings, in hopes that the effect will engender the cause. Kaṃsa laughed nervously when he faced Kṛṣṇa in battle.

The mythology of the childhood of Kṛṣṇa offers children like little Chinna access to the god, a means of affection for, or identification with, him. And as those children mature, the god resurrects the divine child within the human adult. The comedic elements in the mythology, reawakening childhood laughter and reactivating primary feelings of mastery and power, fortify consciousness against new anxieties, new pressures, and new demons. The god is he who has total power, mastery of all things in the universe. And thus he laughs. The devotee yearns for a share in that supernal power, a taste of that ambrosial laughter.

Benny Hill in Vṛndāvan: *Humor and Sex*

> Many a green gown has been given;
> Many a kiss, both odd and even:
> Many a glance too has been sent
> From out of the eye, love's firmament;
> Many a jest told of the keys betraying
> This night, and locks picked, yet we're not a-maying.
>
> Robert Herrick

As we stood in the harem room within the eighteenth-century palace of the Mahārāja of Mattancheri in Kerala, staring at the mural depicting Kṛṣṇa's loveplay with the milkmaids, I felt the presence of the guard behind us, looking at us looking at the scene of Kṛṣṇa's sexual sports. The reclining god, smothered in Gopī-groupies was not the delicately sexual Kṛṣṇa who sports with milkmaids in Kangra paintings, not the muscular, sensual Kṛṣṇa of stone or bronze sculpture playing his flute, not the boldly erotic Kṛṣṇa of the *Purāṇa*s, not the elegantly amorous and sophisticated Kṛṣṇa of poetry, but a raunchy Kṛṣṇa, a funky god, a porno star, sex-crazed, sex-amused, sex-silly.

"Do not mistake this mural for something gross and physical," the guard, posted to prevent further effacement of the mural—further additions of lewd graffiti or further scratching out of lewdness already there—said with the authority that came with the uniform. He stood between us. "Foreigners are tempted to see here only lowly things—sensuality, passion, a depiction of the world of the senses. But we Hindus are knowing that this is not the case. This is symbolical, metaphysical, and entirely religio-philosophical. This is an allegorical representation of the Lord instilling in the souls of his devotees the Peace-which-Passeth-All-Understanding. This is what we call *sat-cit-ānanda*—the Bliss-of-Union-with-the-Eternal."

It was as if he could read my dirty mind. I could not see Vṛndāvan in Mattancheri, could not see the forest of divine love for all the obscene trees of adolescent sexual fantasy. Amidst crudely drawn bulls mounting cows, rams banging ewes, stags humping deer, birds doing it, and bees doing it, bowling-ball-breasted girls of various colors pushed and shoved their way into the crowded orgy. Pointing to Kṛṣṇa's toe jammed into the crotch of one of the girls and disappearing into her vulva (while the big toe of his other foot tickled the nipple on the swollen breast of yet another milkmaid), I asked, "What does that symbolize?"

"This is a depiction of the *līlā* or Divine Play of the Eternal Lord. This is *māyā* or Divine Illusion. He is not doing what you are thinking He is doing! Such is the way of the Divine Lord."

The hands of the six-armed Divine Lord were kept busy in this Divine Illusion. I pointed to the hand that delved into the loins of one lady and another hand tweaking yet another ripe-red nipple in foreplay, and affirming his ideas about foreigners, I asked what those actions meant spiritually. He clearly sensed my skepticism and it disgusted him. "Look here, this is the Blessed Lord, the very God who appeared to Arjun in his hour of need on the Field of Righteous in the Blessed *Gītā!* This is Bhakti Yoga! This is a depiction of the Divine Bliss which is attained by the Soul in its Divine Love for the Blessed Lord. The females are representing Souls in Eternal Dalliance with the Absolute Divine Godhead!"

"Oh, now I see it," I said, in an effort to make my companion laugh. She didn't—it would have been, like most laughter, rude. I continued to scrutinize what I could only perceive as a rather cutely pornographic depiction of sex play, naughty and fun, more silly than sordid, a sort of eighteenth-century precursor to a dirty movie about a wild and crazy guy in a hot tub with a bunch of Playboy Bunnies, commissioned by some wealthy Mahārāja for the amusement or titillation of himself, his women, or his friends. I imagined the laughter that must have been aroused in this room—I could hear dirty giggles, and not a single prayer.

We were essentially stranded at our hotel, the Bolghatty Palace Tourist Bungalow, because a Japanese tourist, who had come there to play golf, was willing to pay the boatman a hundred rupees for the short, one-rupee ride across the water from Bolghatty Island to Ernakulam. The boatman wouldn't work for less and so pride kept us captive, making us wait for Mr. Sato to get us to the other side. We spent our time drinking on the veranda, watching Mr. Sato trying to play golf which amounted to observing his five Indian caddies look for golf balls in grass that had not been cut in months. A crow, landing on the ornate, wooden balustrade, holding a used condom in his beak, tugged at the thing with his foot. As the mysterious, rubber treasure slipped loose from the crow's claw, it slapped the bird in the face. He dropped it and flew away, leaving the condom on the floor of the veranda. Two waiters stood over it, staring at it in amazement, wondering what to do about it. Our eyes met their eyes and we laughed. Everything to do with sex is funny.

An Indian businessman, also stranded by his refusal to pay the boatman the outrageous going-price of transport, joined us for a drink and asked us if we had made the trip to Periyar Lake Wild Life Sanctuary, "an ideal place to get back to nature—Mother Nature!" We explained that all we had seen was the Mahārāja's Palace at Mattancheri. "Excellent palace! Excellent art!" he smiled. When I told him about the guard's interpretation of the mural, he laughed. "No, no," he laughed again as he collected his thoughts. "The mural is a homage to Kām, the Cupid of India! We in India are very enlightened about sexual matters; or we were until the coming of the puritanical foreigners. Muslims and Brits! They're not like Americans—they are prudes through and through. The Gāndharva marriage—basically free love—was practiced in India two thousand years before there even existed a California! Two thousand years before your Dr. Sigmund Freud, our Vātsyāyana, brilliant author of the *Kāmasūtra,* the *Holy Scripture of Sexual Love,* discovered the libido; two thousand years before your Dr. Havelock Ellis, our Vātsyāyana discovered the sixty-four positions for copulation; two thousand years before your Drs. Masters and Johnson, our Vātsyāyana discovered the clitoris!'' He smiled proudly. ''The mural of Kṛṣṇa and the Gopīs has a deep message to it. The message is that sexuality is divine. The ancient Indian knew that sexuality is the very woof and warp of life, the source and meaning of existence, not to mention the method of supreme bliss. The guard was mistaken. This mural does not portray the Bhakti Yoga, but rather the Tantra Yoga! I am myself a practitioner of this highest, most difficult, most esoteric, and most sublime of all disciplines.''

A cat, cautiously creeping up on the condom that still lay on the floor, suddenly pounced and ran off with it. Mr. Sato, appearing on the veranda with a broad smile, bowed and asked if we wished to join him in making a journey to town. We accompanied him on his tour of Cochin and, at the synagogue on Jew Street in Jew Town, he politely asked if I would take a photograph of him and my companion together. I focused carefully on the Buddhist, wearing the yarmulke provided by the temple, standing next to the gentile woman, in front of the Jewish Temple in India. ''Say cheese,'' I said, and they laughed.

I mulled over the two interpretations I had of the mural at Mattancheri, one that the sex wasn't really ordinary sex, but that it was Divine Love, and one that the sex wasn't really ordinary sex, but that it was Divine Sex. In either case, in light of *bhakti* or *tantra,* the mural was sacred and was meant to inspire some sort of beatitude. But the more I thought about it, the more I felt the humor of the mural, the humor of the revelation that its sex was profane sex, an ordinary fantasy about an ordinary, but perhaps lucky, guy at an ordinary orgy with ordinary girls. It is, I think, a cartoon of Kṛṣṇa, not making fun of him, but rather tapping the sexual fun that he often personifies. Whether or not the ''ancient Indian,'' to which the businessman had referred, knew that ''sexuality was divine,'' he did certainly know that it is funny. It is especially funny when it's taken seriously whether by the *bhakta,* the tantric adept, or the sexologist. And so the farces make fun of ethereal devotees and lusty yogis. And Kṣemendra, in his parody of the *Kāmasūtra*'s categorizations of sexual love in the *Samayamātṛkā,* laughed at Vātsyāyana. So have audiences of the Hindi film *Utsava* in which Vātsyāyana appears as a Peeping Tom. Throughout the film he is seen peering into bedroom windows, making notes towards his classic classification of sexual postures. At one point, the funniest moment in the film, he turns away from a window in amazement—"I can't include *that* position in my *Kāmasūtra*—no one would believe it is possible!" And the modern audience roared with an ancient laughter.

Panty Raid

Appearing on charges of first-degree burglary, James "Bucky" Buchanan, offensive tackle for the Saracens, pleaded innocent in court today, explaining that "the whole thing was just a joke. Sure, I took the bras and panties from the Pi Phi house. But I didn't really steal them, I was going to give them back. It was just a Panty Raid. My Dad did the same thing when he was in college and no one thought he was a criminal." The defendant was found guilty as charged. Judge Morton Lee suspended Buchanan's sentence but added a warning: "This does not mean that the court finds felonies funny."

The Daily Scimitar 11/23/76

The girls of the village went to the Yamunā to bathe and, while they played in its dark and cool waters, laughing and joking, each within her heart longing for Kṛṣṇa, the adolescent god, followed by other cowherd boys, happened to come along. The clothes of the girls were strewn about on the banks of the river. "Kṛṣṇa quickly gathered up the garments and climbed a *kadamba* tree that grew by the river. 'Hey girls!' Kṛṣṇa laughed out loud, laughed as he joked with them and teased them, 'Come on—out of the water—come here and get your clothes!' And Kṛṣṇa's teenage buddies laughed over the joke he was playing on them. 'Hey, I know you're tired from practicing religious vows. So come on, come and get your saris. I'm not kidding you. I'm not teasing—I wouldn't do a thing like that. My pals can vouch for me—I'd never tell a lie! Come on, you sexy babes—come and get your clothes, all at once or one at a time.' The girls, madly in love with Kṛṣṇa and well aware of the trick he was playing on them, looked at each other blushing and giggling. Coyly, shyly, embarrassed by Kṛṣṇa's joke, they sunk down in the river, shivering in its icy waters. 'Please Kṛṣṇa,' they cried out, 'Please return our clothes, we're freezing to death. Stop playing this naughty trick on us. You're a good-looking guy, and we'll do whatever you want, but please give us our clothes. If you don't, we'll report you to your dad, Nanda, the chief!' The blessed lord spoke, 'If you mean what you say—that you'll do what I want—then come here and get your clothes.' And the girls, shaking with cold, teeth chattering, came out of the water and up onto the bank. When they tried to cover their private parts with their hands, Kṛṣṇa laughed at their modesty, threw their saris over his shoulder, and continued the tease. 'This is serious. Since you went skinny-dipping while you were supposed to be observing a religious vow, you must perform a rite of expiation—you must place your hands on top of your heads and then bow. And then you'll get your clothes back!' " (*Bhāgavata Purāṇa* 10.22.9–19). "Bow" is a euphemism for "bend over," a religious command for a prurient request. The blatantly bawdy, sexily funny, scene has, in Indian art and literature, been repeatedly told, drawn, and enacted for laughs. A modern cartoonist, in a parody of traditional illustrations, has one of the milkmaids surprise Kṛṣṇa by getting out of the Yamunā in an anachronistic (and therefore comic) bikini. She consoles the god: "Listen Kṛṣṇa—don't worry—there will be a time when topless bikinis come into fashion" (fig. 26).

Medieval commentators provided devotional glosses of the text, interpretations like that of the guard of Mattancheri, to sanitize the material and make it serious. The comic scene of teenage voyeurism became a solemn allegory of the blessed lord's pure impulse to see the true self beneath the garment of the ego of his devotee. The comic vitality and carnival spirit of the story was subsumed in the sober hermeneutic process wherein the playful folk deity was assimilated into the Absolute. Theology is universally laughless.

In literature and art, in the court as well as the village, beyond the puritanical purview of the pious, however, Kṛṣṇa remained randy and rakish, a prankster and joker, a comic and utterly human god, a champion of fun and the funny, making the world a stage for a great, joyous comedy. Māgha describes that deity, spreading mirth and bestowing the blessing of laughter, as he entered Mathurā. The echo of the welcoming drums seemed to be "the laughter of the buildings there," raucous, amused laughter at the comic sight

Figure 26

of the women who rushed to greet him "with only half their make-up on, trying to hold up their slipping dresses" (*Śiśupālavadha* 13.31). "Ho-ho-hosannah!" the multitudes cry out at the coming of this sweet and comic lord. Hosannah in the highest. Hosannah in the lowest.

The incongruity of the aspects of Kṛṣṇa—the blessed lord (the object of serious devotion) and the raunchy cowboy (the object of humorous laughter)—itself had comic potential for poets. The juxtaposition of the religious and the amorous, of piety and sexuality, was a comedic device. The essentially clever, witty poet Rāmacandra writes a superficially devotional verse in which Kṛṣṇa is invoked:

> He displays violence in battle
> for the sake of the highest beatitude—
> Why does he not simply desire
> to firmly fix Mukunda, Lord Kṛṣṇa, in his soul?

Is there any greater means to happiness,
  any better way to cross over the ocean of existence?
(*Rasikarañjana* 13)

The very same stanza, if the words are divided differently, can be read erotically. While the man fights battles or worships god, a loving lady laughs:

Feeling the same love for all men,
  She laughs aloud over the pleasures she's had—
Why does she not desire to decorate herself
  with jasmine flowers?
Is there a greater means for courtesans
  to increase their treasure
  than in giving others pleasure?

The tight semantic interweaving of the dichotomous sentiments produces the fabric of the comic sentiment. Laughter alleviates an aesthetic tension. A parallel tension, resulting from a syncretization of traditions and an assimilation of various regional deities into a national one, informs the larger mythology of the god. It is essentially funny that "the eternal Lord of gods, the undying abode of the living, He who is both all that is and is not, and beyond both, He, the primal god whose manifestations are infinite" (*Bhagavadgītā* 11.37–38) is born as a plump little baby in a cowherd village. And it is funny that as a child he is liar and thief, and that as a young man he spends his time seducing the girls of that village and making cuckolds of the men. Such a god was well-suited to humorous depiction. The adulterous nature of his trysting with the milkmaids of Vraja provided ample opportunity for dirty jokes and an abundant source for a religious humor that was thoroughly naughty, but in no way blasphemous.

Kṛṣṇa's aggressive and sexual impulses are always playful: battle is contest; sex is foreplay. Both bubble with mirth and sparkle with festive laughter. Sex in the mythic forest of Kṛṣṇa's youth is all fun and games. Games of erotic hide-and-seek, of sexual peek-a-boo, and amorous catch-me-if-you-can are exuberant rituals for a celebration of life as it might be, full of happiness—not the transcendental bliss of the theologians and saints, but the earthy, fleshy joy of village cowherds and milkmaids.

Satire produces its snickering laughter with revelations of sex hidden; humor generates its more hearty laughter with sex laid bare. Satire peeks through keyholes; humor throws the doors open wide. Humorous laughter is a great hooray. And it reverberates throughout the mythology of Kṛṣṇa.

"Although their parents tried to stop them from going out, the milkmaids were so anxious for the delights of love that they snuck out into the night in search of Kṛṣṇa. They had great fun together in such amusing ways. In pairs these sexy girls sang songs about Kṛṣṇa and, with eyes fixed upon him, they mimicked his walk and burlesqued the way he played. . . . The girls of Vraja had fun making parodies of his lusty laughter and his gawking glances. They imitated his song and dance routines. . . . 'Ha-ha, ha-ha,' Kṛṣṇa laughed so soothingly, and when they heard the sound of that laughter they were overwhelmed with mirth. Their braided hair fell loose and disheveled, spreading in delight over their breasts. They were eager to make love. And that is how Kṛṣṇa spent his moonlit nights in autumn—playing the merry games of love" (*Harivaṃśa* 63.24–35).

Kṛṣṇa teases and tickles the girls, makes them laugh their delicious laughter, and they jive him in return. "One bonnie-assed lass came up to him to whisper something in his ear—a mere ploy to kiss the cheek that bristled with delight" (*Gītagovinda* 1, song 4, vs. 5); another did an imitation of Kaṃsa in hopes that he would join into the game and wrestle her to the ground; another pretended that she had to fix the braids of her hair—"a mere pretense to raise her arms up high and show off her breasts" (*Gītagovinda* 2.12).

The comedy of love is a comedy of pranks, put-ons, and pretenses, a comedy of errors and of honied deceits. Infidelity, for all its chaos, is a perpetual theme of comedy, not only in its satiric mode, but in the humorous as well. In satire adultery is inevitably symptomatic of a larger falseness pervading and degrading all of society; it is the force of cosmic dissolution that characterizes the age. In humor it is an expression of the uncontrollable truth of eros that pervades and animates all of nature; it is the energy of preservation, the creative tropism.

Lady waiting for her lover:

"Here comes Kṛṣṇa, wearing his garland of forest flowers!
Oh, god! Here comes my husband too!"

Her friend and confidante:

"Remember, my friend, Pāṇini's grammar:
'In case of conflict
[between two grammatical rules of equal strength]
choose the latter.' "

(*Sūktimañjarī* 61.12–13)

The comic sentiment, aroused by the milkmaid's conventionally comedic dilemma, is enhanced by the learned reference to Pāṇini (*Aṣṭādhyāyī* 1.42), by the incongruity between cool grammatical dictum and the inappropriately erotic end to which it is being applied. If the lady is well-versed in grammatical literature, she will be aware that commentators have glossed "the latter" (*param*) with *iṣṭaṃ*, suggesting that she can choose whichever lover—her husband or Kṛṣṇa—she wants the most, "the one that will bring the desired result."

A friend of the suffering Rādhā tries to cheer her lady up with a little joke, to soften the torment of erotic passion with laughter over the silliness of sexual pursuits. The verse begins seriously enough; the pitch is amorous:

First a hug and then a kiss,
  and then they scratch each other's bodies,
And then, aroused with love, they bounce about in union,
  and they come. And they are pleased.

But then the punch line:

But when they spoke, they recognized each other!
  A husband and a wife—each sneaking off
    to a tryst with another—
Had come together in the darkness, by mistake.
  Embarrassment modified their pleasure!
    Wouldn't you say?

(*Gītagovinda* 5.5)

The commentator Kumbha explains that "pleasure" (*rasa*) also refers reflexively in the verse to the amorous sentiment, and that through impropriety and surprise the amorous sentiment has been modified into the comic sentiment. If planned and plotted adultery is funny; accidental fidelity is even funnier.

Mistaken identity is a recurrent motif in both satiric and humorous comedy, both Western and Indian, ancient and modern. Comedy relishes mistakes, confusions, and all pandemonia, the stuff and fun of love.

"When foreigners and even certain lowly Indians perceive this depiction of the Divine Lord as some picture of a lustful lecher," the guard at the Mattancheri Palace had said with a wry laugh, "it is a case of mistaken identity." This mistake in identity is even funnier when it goes the other way around.

Blueboy and Pinkey: *Humor and Love*

What is love? 'Tis not hereafter;
Present mirth hath present laughter . . .
William Shakespeare, *Twelfth Night*

In that Indian love stories conventionally end with hero and heroine united to live happily ever after, they fall into the traditional Western category of comedy. And in the Indian system, as we have seen, the comic sentiment arises out of the amorous. Love is full of present mirth and laughter. In satires of manners love's sweetness always conceals other motives. Satire laughs at women pretending to love men in order to take their money; and it laughs at those young men, inevitably the sons of merchants, trying to play the lover's part, shamming sophistication, using manners to conceal their innate doltishness and insurmountable asininity. Though the laughter, prompted still by incongruities between feeling and behavior, still occurs when concealments fall away, the humor in the comedy of eros is different. Love is humorous, by courtly convention, when lovers hide their real infatuation and sincerest adoration in pretenses of jealousy and anger.

In bed together
He mentions the name of another lady
by mistake—her rival!—and at once
She rolls over, turns away, feelings hurt
and angry despite his desperate flattery;
He becomes silent, slighted by his lady,
such an innocent girl;
She then turns back to check on him—
"He can't be tired . . . *can he?*"
(*Amaruśataka* 22)

And the lover thoroughly enjoys his beloved's anger. He makes fun of the gods, laughs at them for going to all the trouble of churning the cosmic ocean to secure the nectar of immortality when it is available from any angry woman's lips. His irony and irreverence are humorous.

> Brow-bending, finger-shaking, lip-biting,
> Eyes lowered, the piqued lady's fighting
> "Don't! Stop! Cheat!" the angry lady hisses;
> But there's divine nectar in fierce kisses—
> How stupid of the gods to have churned the ocean
> For immortality's ambrosial potion!
>
> (*Amaruśataka* 36)

Love is all folly and roguery, paradox and perversity, and the self-contradictory nature of its impulses and expressions provides much of the humor of Sanskrit court poetry. "He won't let me sleep!" a lady angrily declares, and then, "rolling over as if trying to doze, she made room for her lover to join her in the bed" (*Amaruśataka* 21). Love is a pretty game—an aristocratic amusement—played for the fun it. Lovers tease each other and play erotic pranks; they laugh with love and inspire laughter.

> When she saw the room was empty
> she rose softly from the bed;
> Long she watched her lover's face,
> not knowing his sleep was feigned;
> Fearlessly she kissed him and then
> his cheeks bristled with delight—
> Modestly she bowed her head and
> her laughing lover kissed her.
>
> (*Amaruśataka* 82)

Jayadeva, court bard to King Lakṣmanasena of Bengal, a witty poet, unfairly accused by myself and others of extremes of devotionalism, transformed Kṛṣṇa, the transcendent lord, killer of demons, charioteer on the Field of Righteousness, and rustic playboy, into a courtier, a man about town, a city slicker adept in the game of love. When Rādhā, following the conventions of courtly tradition, puts on a display of pique, Kṛṣṇa teases and flatters her, tries to seduce her with wit. "All right, if you are *really* angry with me," he says with humorous irony, and really want to punish me for my infidelities, "shoot me with arrows—your fingernails; bind me with chains—your arms; or bite me!" He adds that by such punishments "all the conditions of pleasure will come to be" (*Gītagovinda* 10, song 19, vs. 2). The joke is that while he explicitly means her pleasure (the moral pleasure of punishing someone who has wronged her), he implicitly refers to his own pleasure (the masochistic, sexual pleasure he will derive from being scratched, hugged, and bitten in love).

In a comic stanza attributed to Jayadeva, Kṛṣṇa the heroic god, lifting up Mount Govardhana to protect the cowherds from the storms sent by a jealous Indra, calls Rādhā to him. "My arm is breaking from the weight of this mountain!" He feigns weakness and she asks, "How can I help you, darling?" He asks her to raise her own arm, to help him hold up the mountain. It's a comic ploy—"At once his glances fell upon Rādhā's boobs, exposed to him when her shawl fell from her shoulders as she lifted up her arm" (*Saduktikarṇāmṛta* 1.60.5). The humor is enhanced by the incongruous juxtaposition of Kṛṣṇa's divine, heroic, and miraculous power with his human, erotic, and prurient interests. Unlike the conventional object of satire—the puritan whose pure acts or words are juxtaposed with clues to his lubricious intentions—Kṛṣṇa laughs at himself: his lust, because he is god, is divine. So too is his laughter. It seems uniquely Indian that part of the deity's function should be to amuse. His appeal is that he laughs at himself. E. M. Forster was startled by this, by India's divine comedy. "There is fun in heaven. God can play practical jokes on Himself, draw chairs away from beneath His posteriors, set His own turban on fire, and steal His own petticoats when He bathes. By sacrificing good taste, this worship achieved what Christianity has shirked: the inclusion of merriment. All spirit as well as matter must participate in salvation, and if practical jokes are banned, the circle is incomplete" *(A Passage to India)*.

Knock-Knock

"Knock! Knock!" "Who's there?" "Amos." "Amos who?"
"A mosquito!"
"Knock! Knock!" "Who's there?" "Anna." "Anna who?"
"Another mosquito!"
"Knock! Knock!" "Who's there?" "Stella." "Stella who?"
"Still another mosquito!"
Dmitri and Sebastian Siegel

As Kṛṣṇa teases Rādhā, Rādhā teases Kṛṣṇa in the humorous game of love. When Kṛṣṇa asks Rādhā to get into his "boat" (*tari*), Rādhā pretends to hear "tree" (*taru*—in the locative case the phonetic distinction vanishes). Kṛṣṇa, falling for the trick, changes case and repeats the word—"No my 'boat' (*taraṇi*)"—but again she plays the fool, pretending to have heard "sun" (*taraṇi*). Yet again, Kṛṣṇa invites her into his "boat" with a different word (*nau*) which, in turn, she pretends to understand as the genitive dual form of the first person pronoun, a reference to "the union of the two of us." The joke goes something like this:

Kṛṣṇa: Want to go for a ride in a boat?
Rādhā: In a-bout how long?
Kṛṣṇa: Not "about!" *"A boat"*—you know, a scull.
Rādhā: A skull! How horrible!
Kṛṣṇa: Not "skull!" *"Scull"*—you know, a launch.
Rādhā: You want to have lunch?
Kṛṣṇa: Not "lunch!" *"Launch"*—a boat with a sail.
Rādhā: Lunch is for sale?

"I worship Lord Kṛṣṇa, the unconquerable," the poem ends, "Kṛṣṇa who laughed when he was conquered by the words of Rādhā" (*Padyāvalī* 269). Rādhā's teasing is a semantic tickling; the wordplay is foreplay. It is funny that the unconquerable is conquered, that the female outwits the male, that the milkmaid outtricks the Lord.

Similarly, in a poem attributed to Cakrapāṇi, Rādhā again teases Kṛṣṇa by pretending to misunderstand his words. Hearing a knock on the door at night, she asks, "Who's there?" And when Kṛṣṇa says his name, "Keśava," she, pretending to take it as the common noun ("someone with long hair"), asks, "Why are you so proud of your hair?" He tries to explain, uttering another one of his names, "Śauri." Again, feigning to have understood the word as the common noun meaning "son of a warrior," Rādhā teases with a question—"What does a father's virtue have to do with the character of his son?" Kṛṣṇa keeps playing the game. He identifies himself as "Cakrī," (literally "the bearer of the discus," but also a word for a "potter"). "Then why haven't you delivered the milk pots I asked for? May Hari, teased and left speechless by a cowherd's wife, protect you!" (*Padyāvalī* 282). It is the Sanskrit equivalent of the children's "knock-knock" joke. That these jokes were compiled by Rūpa Goswāmin, a devout worshiper of the blessed lord, suggests that, at least in some areas of the medieval Indian religious milieu, humor was thought to enhance devotion. The jokes were not blasphemous in that context, not sacrilegious as they would be in a Christian context. It is difficult to imagine the Book of Common Prayer containing a poem in which the Nazarene knocks upon Mary Magdalene's door and, asked "who's there?" responding, "Emmanuel," only to be teased, "A manual laborer?" "No," a jokey Jesus would answer, the "Savior," to which a mirthful Mary would counter, "Save-your jokes for someone else!" But in Indian religious traditions, knock-knock jokes seem to have been conventional. There is one inscribed upon a temple at Khajuraho:

Knock! Knock!

Pārvatī: Who's there?
Śiva: Digambara [literally, the "Sky-Clad" one].
Pārvatī: Why are you naked?
Śiva: No, no, baby, it's me—Śūladhara [the "Trident-Bearer"].
Pārvatī: Yuck! Why bear weapons when you should be carrying peacock feathers?
Śiva: Come on, you know me—Maheśvara [the "Great Lord"—the Omnipotent].
Pārvatī [looking at his crotch]: Even if you were wearing clothes it would be obvious [that you are omni-potent]!

(*Epigraphica Indica* 1:140.3)

Such jokes and word games revive a childhood pleasure, the pleasure of reducing the anxiety created by the pressure to master language in play. The Sanskrit poetic tradition is heavily laden with lightness, ornately laced with such semantic games, linguistic jokes, and verbal play. Elaborate alliteration, onomatopoeia, and other such verbal plays and ploys, invest a tone of humor into the poetic diction:

lalitalavaṅgalatāpariśīlanakomalamalayasamīre
madhukarakaranikarakarambitakokilakūjitakuñjakuṭīre
When sandal-scented-southern currents clutch climbing-cloves
When bee-bands buzz as cozy-cuckoos coo-coo in coppice-coves

(*Gītagovinda* 1, song 3, vs. 1)

Sound overwhelms sense, rhyme absorbs reason, as the *"la-li-la-la-la-ko-la-la . . . samīre"* rubs up against the *"ka-ka-ka-ka-ko-ki-la-kū-ku . . . kuṭīre,"* as soft, dental *l*'s yield to hard, guttural *k*'s.

Syllables are intertwined like the creepers to which they refer; phonemes are intermingled like the sounds of the bees and cuckoos. There is a subtle and pleasing comedy of language played out for the amusement of connoisseurs.

The poetry about Kṛṣṇa, written for such aesthetes, preserved the essential and primary humor of the god, transformed the folksy humor of the villages in which the mythology of the cowherd arose into the sophisticated humor of the court. The devotion of cowherds and aristocrats could accommodate laughter; the sacred could accommodate the profane.

Hare Kṛṣṇa: *Humor and Devotion*

To recall this, to recall this incredible relation between mud and God, is, in its own, distant, adumbrating way, the function of comedy.

William F. Lynch, *Christ and Apollo*

The judge, smiling himself, raised his gavel to silence the laughter in the courtroom that had been prompted when I, the "expert witness" in a case against a member of the Hare Kṛṣṇa organization who was accused of attempting to smuggle $30,000 worth of jewels through the United States Customs, tried to explain that the fourteen-carat gold Dunhill cigarette lighter was in fact a "religious object," as sacred as any gold crucifix, and therefore exempt from duty.

"A cross is a religious object for Christians on the basis of what it symbolizes," I explained in what seemed an appropriately professorial tone. "The lighter would be a sacred object, in the context of the tradition of the devotional Hinduism practiced by the members of ISKON, on the basis of function. They use the lighter to light the lamps and incense in the shrine."

"Wouldn't the flick of a 89¢ Bic do the job just as well?" the prosecutor pointedly joked. "Or does it have to be a *gold* lighter, a $200 lighter?"

I tried to explain that as members of the Hare Kṛṣṇa movement, they were—in their hearts—milkmaids in love with their god, and that like any smitten lover they would want to buy the very best for the beloved. The more serious I tried to be, the more amusing it seemed to the court. And it became difficult to keep the straight face necessary for the credibility of my testimony. Bharata's dictum (as amplified by the commentary of Abhinavagupta), that "wearing clothes or ornaments that are inappropriate to the wearer's nature, age, or status, or inappropriate to the time when or place where they are worn," gives rise to laughter and the comic sentiment, was being tested by the defendant, a Caucasian American, his head shaven except for the curly topknot, the devotional markings of the sect bridging his nose behind his glasses and climbing up his forehead, his neck garlanded with tulsī beads, his pale body swathed in light orange robes. He looked completely ridiculous. Comedy is a matter of jumbling contexts, taking the serious content out of its own serious context and putting it in another equally serious, but less appropriate, context to create a comic relationship. The displacement can make either the content or the context funny. A perfectly serious and holy act of chanting in Vṛndāvan becomes a consummately silly spectacle in a waiting room outside a Honolulu courtroom. The Hare Kṛṣṇas are ludicrous, as is attested by the many Hollywood films in which they appear for the sake of a laugh. It is funny when a Jewish kid from California tries to become a *bhakta* and express his love for Kṛṣṇa. It is, no doubt, just as funny when another one tries to become a pandit and write about Kṛṣṇa. People at cocktail parties, who ask me what I do, often laugh when I answer honestly.

"Last year we made a pilgrimage to Vṛṅdāvan. We chartered a plane. A whole plane full of devotees," the accused told me. He smiled, "We did *kīrtan* and, way up in the sky, we could feel the divine ecstasy. Wow! Someone shouted out that we were flying to Vaikuṇṭha to see the Lord. And everybody began to laugh and chant 'Hare Kṛṣṇa' and then everybody got up and began to dance. The jet was bobbing around in the sky, shaking with our bliss. The pilot had to ask us to sit down. He was worried that we would bring the plane down. But Gopīnāthadās told him that Kṛṣṇa was watching over us and delighting in our divine mellow. He told him that the plane would not go down, that we were so high that our highness would keep the plane up. And all the devotees laughed and chanted 'Hare Kṛṣṇa.' " He laughed, perhaps trying to mitigate or conceal the fear of imprisonment, with a laugh of faith in the Lord. It was sad laughter, forced and fragile, not a roaring from the guts, but a more mirthless laughter that seemed to have been learned like the Hare Kṛṣṇa *mantra*. It seemed more an expression of bewilderment than of amusement. The joy was solemn.

I asked Narahariswāmī, a spokesman for the Honolulu Hare Kṛṣṇa Temple, about laughter and humor. "All of our earthly moods are perverted versions of the spiritual mood of eternal ecstasy." The devotional insight is an inversion of the comic perspective which sees all things spiritual as perversions of the earthly, of what is delightfully muddy. The divine is a perversion of what is human. The transcendental is a vain abstraction of the immanent. Narahariswāmī explained that *rāslīlā*s depicting Kṛṣṇa's comic pranks were performed at the temple and laughter was encouraged. "The people enjoy the shows. When they laugh it fixes their minds on Kṛṣṇa. It draws them in. It attracts them so that they can move on to meditation on Kṛṣṇa. It's a mundane device for a spiritual goal." Devotion enables one to move from the mundane to the heavenly, from the flesh to the spirit; comedy enables one to return to earth. It saves us from salvation and delivers us from the temptations of the spirit.

Devotion, not the spontaneous religious exuberance exhibited by Bilvamaṅgala or Caitanya, or expressed by the audiences of village *rāslīlā*s or court recitations, but the institutionalized devotion of the *sampradāya*s and *maṭha*s, orthodox religious communities and schools, the pious religiosity of the theologians and renouncers, of the medieval commentators on the *Bhāgavata Purāṇa* and the guard at the Palace of Mattancheri, demands silence within the holy of holies. Their devotion transforms the butter, the curds, the clothes of the milkmaids, the flute—all the props of the rowdy comedy—into symbols. The mythology of Kṛṣṇa takes on a higher, more serious meaning; and faith, rather than amusement, is the goal. Comedy is iconoclastic—it smashes the symbols as Kṛṣṇa broke the milking pots; it shatters all higher meanings. We laugh at the ultimate insignificance of apparently significant things.

Within the history of the religion of Kṛṣṇa there has been a dialectic at work between the theologian and the comedian, one that balances the god and creates an invigorating tension. The theologian, stressing the absolute divinity of Kṛṣṇa, makes the god serious; the comedian, emphasizing the absolute humanness of Kṛṣṇa, makes the cowherd funny. The more divinely serious he becomes, however, the greater his potential for comedy, for comic revelations of his humanness; conversely, the more comic he is, the greater his appeal, the greater his potential for being taken seriously. Comedy vitalizes, then, the very devotion of which it makes fun. It preserves what it seems to destroy.

"If the plane would have crashed, that wouldn't have mattered. We would have been happy," the accused devotee continued with a delicate and tentative smile. "Even if we would have all died, it would have been for Kṛṣṇa. We would have been chanting 'Hare Kṛṣṇa.' We would have died laughing."

Dying of Laughter: *Humor and Liberation*

Verrius witnessed that Zeuxis, the very excellent portraitist, died from laughing ceaselessly over the grimace of an old lady that he himself had painted.

Laurent Joubert, *Treatise on Laughter*

After a dissolution of the universe, Indra, a frequent butt of laughter in the *Purāṇa*s, began to rebuild the heavens and to construct a sidereal mansion for himself there, a palace grander than all others as a monument to his own greatness. To humble the Vedic god, Kṛṣṇa took on the form of a young boy and, surrounded by other children, all laughing and smiling, he surveyed the heavenly construction site. The divine child shook his head. " 'No previous Indras have been able to complete such a construction.' Indra [the anachronistic god, buffoon, and heavenly laughingstock], drunk with an illusion of grandeur and prosperity, bellowed with laughter over the words of the boy" (*Brahmavaivarta Purāṇa* 4.47.96–97). Indra's laughter was the laughter of self-complacency, of self-confidence which is one of the many illusions a sense of the comic may offer the ego. Such laughter expresses feelings of triumph and invulnerability. But his laughter was interrupted by the louder laughter of the child who had noticed a line of ants passing by them. "Why are you laughing?" Indra demanded. "What is the meaning of this laughter?" And the boy explained: "I laughed at the sight of those ants there. But don't ask me why—the explanation of my laughter, though it is a source of wisdom, also contains the seeds of sorrow." But Indra beseeched the boy for an answer. "Why did you laugh?" And smiling Kṛṣṇa consented to reveal a cosmological comedy: "I laughed at the sight of the ants, moving single file in a line, for each one of the myriad ants, in a previous birth, has, through good deeds, been an Indra. And in the great course of time, after a long series of births, each has, through bad deeds, become an ant again. Through their deeds and actions beings may go to one of the heavens or one of the hells, places of delight or realms of desolation. Through their actions beings are born as pigs or rodents, born from the wombs of beasts or eggs of birds.

Through their deeds beings may become trees or insects, brahmins or gods. One can, through one's action become Indra or Brahmā, a master or a servant, happy or sad, beautiful or deformed. . . . All these states, all things animate and inanimate, are but ephemera, transient as things in a dream. Joy and sorrow are as momentary and fragile as bubbles" (4.50.122–130). The laughter of the child was the inversion of Indra's proud laughter, the laughter that arises with the loss of self-complacency, with the revelation of the essential vulnerability of all beings, the fundamental evanescence of all things, the ultimate absurdity of all endeavors. We are, in the eyes of a laughing god, no more than ants, parading our way through a great cosmological round. As individuals, conscious only of ourselves and what is around us, we cannot see the line, the grave teleological pattern in which we are trapped with our illusions of meaning.

The source of the child's laughter was his transcendence. The very sound of it burst all bubbles of illusion and humbled Indra. His haughty yearning for wealth and glory yielded to a longing for liberation from the magnificent and ludicrous wheel of time. Rather than seeking mastery over the insubstantial and ever-changing universe—the endless tedium of birth and death, creation and destruction, triumph and failure, joy and sadness—Indra sought release from it. Laughter awakened Indra to his own folly and the folly and futility inherent in all activity. As defined by Indian cosmology, seen from the distant viewpoint of the god, watched with detachment and considered without sentimentality, all human actions and aspirations are in essence comical. Wisdom is getting the joke. But, as Kṛṣṇa warns, the very source of that wisdom, and the laughter which expresses it, is sown with seeds of sorrow. The vision of ants could have brought tears rather than laughter. We are as funny as we are sad, and as sad as we are funny. Until liberation is attained, until there is nothing at all, humor, the sensibility displayed by the child god, is, in the face of ultimate things, one—if not the only—alternative to despair.

The Laughter of Śiva

The Destroyer: The Ambiguity of Truth

9

Empyreal darkness consumed by light—
  the gleaming of the splendid teeth,
    the halfmoon shining—
Radiant laughter in the night,
  echoes of the frenzied dancer,
    Śiva, across rainclouds:
May it protect you!

Saṅghamitra, *Saduktikarṇāmṛta*

Night, dark and silent: and suddenly the poet hears Śiva's wild laughter in thunder, sees the incandescent flash of his teeth in bright lightning, and feels the effulgent joy of his divinity in a coming of the fecundating rains. Myth invests nature with sentiments that the poet recuperates and keeps alive. The myth or poem, like the dream or joke, is an invisible truth that comes to be seen only in its guises: Śiva's dance in the movement of the planets; Śiva's three eyes in the sun at dawn, at noon, and at dusk; and Śiva's laughter in a rolling of monsoon thunder, a howling of winter wind, then in a gurgling of the waters of springtime, and always in the crackling of fire. The flames are teeth barred in laughter, laughing as they consume the corpse upon the pyre, the oblation on the altar, the food in the hearth, and the world at the end of time. Śiva holds the fire within himself in fierce austerities that store and regenerate the energy of life, and then, supplicated by gods or human beings, he releases it in mythic battle, ritual dance, sexual union, and in wild laughter.

"When the twentieth cycle of the ages occurs," Śiva, enumerating his incarnations, proclaims, "then I shall be known by the name Aṭṭahāsa, the 'Loudly Laughing One'—a form that people will adore'' (*Liṅga Purāṇa* 1.24.94–95). He is Rudra, the ''Howler,'' and the howl, the ambiguous, strident screaming of an ambiguous, frenetic god, is at once screech and laughter, the cry/laugh of creation/destruction. Śiva is an uncanny embodiment of infinite paradox, and his devotees praise him as such: ''far, far away and yet so very near . . . infinite and infinitesimal . . . the oldest and the youngest . . . all there is and transcending all'' (*Śivamahimnaḥstotra* 29). Paradox is the power of Śiva, the god who both sits still in enstatic trance and writhes in ecstatic dance. Covered with ashes, Śiva is said to be light on the outside, but dark within—he is, in that respect, like comedy itself.

The god inspires awe to the degree that his being represents a resolution and assimilation of paradoxes; he inspires laughter to the degree that the paradoxes are self-contradictions. His father-in-law and enemy, Dakṣa, points out those contradictions within the god to mock and belittle him, to make a joke of Śiva's divinity: ''If he really is an ascetic like he's supposed to be, why does he carry weapons? And he's supposedly married, but he's not really a householder since he lives in the burning grounds. He has no caste. He's neither male nor female, and yet he can't be said to be a eunuch either, since everybody worships his penis'' (*Skanda Purāṇa* 4.2.87.29–35). Dakṣa's enumeration of the paradoxes inherent in the god is meant to elicit laughter at Śiva, to denigrate him as only laughter can. When Bhṛṅgī, Śiva's skeletal attendant, worried silly over ''the contradictions in his lord,'' lists the same contrarieties, it is Bhṛṅgī who is the object of laughter: ''If he's a naked ascetic why the bow? And if he's got weapons, why the ashes of renunciation on his body? And if he's got those ashes on, why the shapely woman? And if he's got her, why does he hate Love?'' (*Subhāṣitaratnakoṣa* 5.33). Bhṛṅgī is comical because he doesn't ''get it,'' doesn't understand the mystery of his master, the ironies quintessential to the mythology of Śiva. The understanding of myths is like an understanding of jokes, a comprehension rooted in physiological, psychological, and social ambiguities and ambivalences. Their meaning is beyond their explication.

The mythic Śiva makes the heart ache and tremble with a devotion that is at once fear, love, wonder, dread, anxiousness, resignation, and hope.

> You dance for the redemption of the universe:
> yet the earth fears that it will crack
> at once beneath the pounding of your feet;
> yet the star-studded sky fears the peril
> of the flailing of your arms,
> as fierce as iron bars;
> yet the heavens,
> whipped by waving locks of your matted hair,
> trembles too.
> Your great power is perverse indeed!
> (*Śivamahimnaḥstotra* 16)

As Kṛṣṇa is a playful lover, an obviously funny child and joker whose hilarity and frivolity has had serious implications and ramifications, Śiva the more obviously austere and solemn figure, is more esoterically funny, a renouncer and an ascetic, all terror and grandeur, whose very seriousness has had comedic potential for poets and mythmakers. Both gods laugh and have been laughed at, and yet the tones of all this laughter are diverse. Kṛṣṇa, the drinker of milk, giggles; Śiva, the drinker of poison, roars. The devotee laughs warmly, the yogi wildly, the villager heartily, the poet wittily. Laughter, no less than tears, links heaven and earth.

Human laughter is broadcast into the realms of myth and the echoes of it are heard again on earth as resonances of a divine laughter—or is it the other way around? Did the laughter of Makha become the golden wheat upon the earth (*Taittirīya Āraṇyaka* 5.1.3), or did the wheat, celebrated in harvest ritual, inspire a joyous laughter, deeply felt and utterly human, that could only be understood and explained as something miraculous and utterly divine?

Risus Populi Risus Dei: *The Ambiguities of Holiness*

Something wonderful has happened to me. I was caught up into the seventh heaven. There sat all the gods in assembly. By special grace I was granted the privilege of making a wish. "Wilt thou," said Mercury, "have youth or beauty or power or a long life or the most beautiful maiden or any of the other glories we have in the chest? Choose, but only one thing." For a moment I was at a loss. Then I addressed myself to the gods as follows: "Most honorable contemporaries, I choose this one thing, that I may always have the laugh on my side." Not one of the gods said a word; on the contrary, they all began to laugh. From that I concluded that my wish was granted, and found that the gods knew how to express themselves with taste; for it would have been hardly suitable for them to have answered gravely: "Thy wish is granted."

Søren Kierkegaard, *Parables*

Comedy is an uncertainty principle. It proves relativity with each laugh. It tosses a pie into the face of truth, any truth, all truth. It finds truth dull, profundity tedious, and soaring spirit a mere party-pooper. Comedy challenges notions of meaning, strives to undermine all hermeneutics and epistemologies, and exposes the ambiguities inherent in any knowing or feeling. In the world of comedy, absurdity itself is the logos. The senselessness of the universe makes comic sense. Laughter expresses the comic understanding that nothing is ever really understood. "We should call every truth false which was not accompanied by at least one laugh," declares Nietzsche's Zarathustra. Laughter qualifies truth by highlighting its essential ambiguities.

In its challenges, strivings, exposures, and disruptions, comedy is, by nature and conscious intent, profane, a mockery of the sacred and a rebuttal to holiness. But against its own aims, ironically and in self-contradiction, by its own law of eternal topsy-turvyness, it participates in the sacred. "Perverse indeed is the power" of comedy.

A person's life recapitulates the holy ritual of Vedic sacrifice according to esoteric utterance—"When one laughs and eats and makes love, he joins in the sacrificial chant and recitation" (*Chāndogya Upaniṣad* 3.17.3). Laughter then, no matter how profane the cause, no matter whether one wills it or not, or knows it or not, can be sacred utterance, a phatic chant, a magic and wordless hymn of renewal.

Low comedy—human laughter from the streets at the gods, laughing up in order to bring down—converges with high comedy—divine laughter from the heavens, at all human endeavors, laughing down in order to elevate—to create a comic middle ground: an exuberantly quaking place where nothing grows stale. As the laughter of the gods is a sign of humanness, the laughter of men can be an expression of godliness. In laughter the human and the divine are merged. All is ambiguity. Just as laughter represents enmeshment in the world and all that is low about us, it can also represent transcendence, a detachment, all that is high. In comedy high and low are continually transposed so that we cannot tell one from the other. That's part of the fun of it.

Low Comedy

People who tell anti-clerical or even anti-god jokes or who express themselves sacrilegiously concerning God and the clergy are not necessarily irreligious people, nor do their jests and mockeries, however broad, necessarily express any serious anti-religious feelings. More often, and profoundly, it is the reverse.

Gershon Legman, *Rationale of the Dirty Joke*

Jokes or comic vignettes in which gods are belittled often suggest a proud assertion of the ultimacy of the human ego and imagination. Laughter can be an arrogant proclamation of omnipotence; it expresses a fragile illusion of power.

Most often jokes against gods are not so much against those deities as against those who worship them. Comedy, as in the satires of Hindu mythology in such Jain comic texts as the *Dharmaparīkṣā* and the *Dhūrtākhyāna* (in which, as we have seen, the flagrant logical absurdities of the *Purāṇa*s are put on display), has the potential to make light of the gravity of others, to expose belief as a folly second only to the wider folly of seriousness itself.

"What's the use of worshiping the gods?" asks the *vidūṣaka* in the *Mṛcchakaṭikā,* making fun of religious ritual. "They don't bother to show any favor no matter how much you worship them anyway" (prose after 1.15). Rather than denying the existence of the gods, the comically rhetorical question merely challenges the seriousness, the literalness, of the pious in relationship to their deities. The laughter inspired by the *vidūṣaka* questions conventional understandings of what godliness really is. Such irreverent laughter can justify itself religiously with a claim that its function is a stripping away of superstitions for the sake of a truer and more vital religiosity.

Religious jokes often mark a personal or social transformation in religious consciousness. Old religious sentiments or practices, no longer effectively functional, are buried in laughter. What was a powerful myth becomes a funny joke. Thus Indra, after the Vedic period, is depicted in ludicrous terms, as a fallen, anachronistic, outmoded, and useless god, fearful and greedy, addicted to soma, lustful to the core, and cursed, as the result of his attempt to rape the wife of the sage Gautama, to bear upon his body a thousand vulva-shaped marks, signs that make him a laughingstock. *"Il a l'air con,"* as the French say with a laugh or sneer. The Purāṇic depictions of Indra as a buffoon are in no way blasphemous, but are, rather, entirely normative, affirming a new religious consciousness and focus, a revitalized sacred hierarchy. Indra's fall into absurdity elicits a laughter that expresses a freedom from old beliefs and practices without challenging the system as a whole, enabling the system to continue to provide cultural continuity. When Indra falls, it is to make way for the Buddha, Kṛṣṇa, or Śiva. Laughter signals, allows for, and generates changes in individual and collective attitudes. Without the comic perspective, the *risus populi* infused from below, myth and ritual would stagnate. Indra is, in the *Purāṇa*s, a rather silly god. His status in those texts is akin, in some ways, to that of Saint Peter in the endless jokes that are set at the Pearly Gates—the disciple who was given the keys to the kingdom of heaven has become an overworked doorman. The jokes shake off religious obsolescences.

A comic poet, contemplating the mythological tradition, comes to a mock-theological conclusion:

> Lakṣmī sleeps on a lotus;
> Śiva sleeps on the Himalayas;
> Viṣṇu sleeps on the Milky Ocean—
> The gods must be afraid of bedbugs!
> (*Subhāṣitaratnabhāṇḍāgāra* 364.13)

The goddess, Śiva, and Viṣṇu—the three great deities around whom the three major sects of Hinduism are formed—are objects of laughter as the banality of their motives is exposed with comedic logic. Cosmic logoi are reduced to homely practicalities, and the divine is made grossly human. But the belittling process of the comic poem can be a religious affirmation, a proposition of a way in which to understand divinity. That the gods are human, makes them all the more accessible. The mythology of Śiva often establishes just such a humanness and the revelation is inevitably comic. "The Bengalis subject Śiva to a slapstick mythology: when all the gods are on parade, going to a wedding, Viṣṇu on his Garuḍa bird buzzes Śiva, whose clothes are held up by snakes; the snakes, shying from the bird, slither away into the bushes, and Śiva's pants fall down" (Wendy O'Flaherty, *Women, Androgynes, and Other Mythical Beasts*). The motif was conventional in the comedy of Śiva—Pārvatī smiles, restraining a laugh, when, again in fear of Garuḍa, Śiva's snake-belt sneaks off and the great god's loincloth slips down (*Subhāṣitaratnakoṣa* 4.40).

The accidental falling down of pants is universally comic. We laugh at exposures, at the sudden, surprising encounters with improprieties, things normally concealed—the sound of flatus, the smell of the bowels, or the sight of the genitals—at a time or in a place that is inappropriate. The spectacle of Śiva's phallus, the *liṅga,* is appropriate and serious in the temple where it is worshiped as the god, but inappropriate and comic when it is seen, still on the god, in the wedding march or when he is (as when Pārvatī laughs at him) in a contemplative pose.

The *liṅga* is an object of reverence and mockery, a subject of myth and joke, the symbol of the god's mysterious divinity and of his blatant humanness. One myth, already considered, explains the origin of *liṅga*-worship in terms that make the connection with the comic explicit: Śiva appeared before Anasūyā, the wife of the sage Atri, with his penis in his hand, ready to rape her. She cursed him, proclaimed that in the future he would be worshiped as the *liṅga,* and would thus be a "great laughingstock" (*Bhaviṣya Purāṇa* 3.4.67–78). The curse made "a real prick" out of Śiva. Obscene invectives, with their origins in magical curse, are meant, with their essential impropriety, to illicit laughter.

The mythology of the *liṅga,* always verging on phallic humor, reveals a formal and functional relationship between myth and joke, both of which are authorless, growing, changing, and being edited with each retelling, until they give voice to a collective understanding. In the mythic tone, the voice explains the origin of *liṅga* worship and the devotional function of the castration of Śiva. In a predominant cycle, Śiva, the mendicant god, enters the Pine Forest and seduces the wives and daughters of the sages there. In retaliation they castrate him, directly, through curse, or by making him castrate himself. The myths of the Pine Forest are, in content and structure, strikingly similar to the common joke of the traveling salesman who seduces the farmer's wife or daughter. The salesman and the god embody sexual desire unrestrained by vows of marriage or ascetic practices. The sages and farmer are representatives of social norms and repressive forces. The myth and joke serve to resolve the fundamentally opposed modes of being. A farmer, in an old and tasteless joke, catching a traveling salesman making love to his wife, knocked the man out. The salesman woke up in the barn with his prick in a vise, the handle of which had been broken off. Seeing the farmer sharpening a knife, the salesman cried out, "You're not going to cut it off are you?" "No," the farmer laughed, "you're going to do that—I'm going to set the barn on fire." The farmer acts out the very injunction quoted by the sages when they cause the castration of Śiva: "A man who is so wicked and without shame as to seduce another man's wife must be castrated. . . . If it is the wife of his spiritual preceptor [or host] that he has seduced, he must cut off his own penis and testicles and carry them around with him in his hands until he dies" (*Skanda Purāṇa* 6.245.32–42).

The surprise which makes the story of castration so funny in the joke and the implicit conclusion of the myth ("and that is how the *liṅga* came to be worshiped on earth") which makes the same story of castration religiously meaningful are the pretexts allowing for the telling of the stories themselves. The myth and joke have their power and humor respectively in the ways in which they tap human consciousness for the anxieties over castration that seem to be imbedded there. Such anxieties can then be alleviated in worship or laughter. Jokes are funny myths, and myths are serious jokes.

Laughter directed at Śiva, or any other god or traveling salesman, any figure whose pants slip down, whose penis is cut off, who falls in any way, is inevitably laughter at ourselves, at our own fears or ideals. "His ornament is a human skull that scares people; his attendant is Bhṛṅgī, a skeleton; and all he owns is a very old ox. If this is the shape that Śiva—the most venerable of all the gods with the crescent moon upon his forehead—is in, what can we expect for ourselves?" (*Subhāṣitaratnakoṣa* 40.12). The poet's sardonic laughter is simultaneously directed at Śiva and at humanity, at the god as an image of human potential and limitation. The words for "the crescent moon upon his forehead" are paronomastic, meaning also, in reference to the human condition, that "cruel fate will prevail" against us. And for this, the gods laugh at us.

High Comedy

> He that sitteth in the heavens shall laugh: the Lord shall have them in derision.
>
> Psalms 2:4

"God laughs on two occasions," according to Ramakrishna. "He laughs when the physician says to the patient's mother, 'Don't be afraid, mother; I shall certainly cure your boy.' God laughs, saying to Himself, 'I am going to take his life, and this man says he will save it!' . . . God laughs when two brothers divide their land with string, saying to each other, 'This side is mine and that side is yours.' He laughs and says to Himself, 'The whole universe belongs to Me, but they say they own this portion or that portion' " (*The Gospel of Ramakrishna,* pp. 105–106). The Lord has us in derision whenever we assume or presume to ultimately do or have anything. The seriousness with which we take ourselves makes us ridiculous. The revelation of the final futility of human action or possession, according to Ramakrishna, inspires laughter in the heavens. All human endeavors, when seen from the heights of Mount Kailāsa, become comical. And so Ramakrishna taught a way of laughter—to see the world as the gods see it without forsaking one's own humanness. Laughter was for him a mirthful expression of freedom-in-bondage, detachment without disinterest, and transcendence-in-being.

In projecting laughter on to the heavens, in creating a pantheon of gods who laugh, Indian mythology sanctifies laughter. And its divine laughter, the roaring of paradise, is merciless. It is a response to all tragedies as comedies. In a preface to *Saint Joan,* George Bernard Shaw noted that while angels weep over the cruel and unjust murder of the martyr, "the gods laugh at the murderers." The laughter of the gods is at the ignorance and folly of men, the laughter which comes with the suspension of compassion that is concomitant with a conviction that there is no difference between the murdered and murderer (*Kaṭha Upaniṣad* 2.19; *Bhagavadgītā* 2.19). There are no crimes or tragedies in the parade of ants.

The poet Sāgaradhara invokes the protection of Śiva's face—"the poison [in his throat], the fire [in his eye], and the laughter [in his mouth]" (*Saduktikarṇāmṛta* 1.20.3). Laughter, like poison and fire, devours. It kills. And yet each of the poems included in the section of the *Saduktikarṇāmṛta* devoted solely to the laughter of Śiva ends with the phrase, "May the laughter of Śiva protect you!" (1.8.1–5). These invocations of laughter, the call for its protection, guidance, and blessings, suggest not only a belief in the power of the god, but a faith in the power of laughter itself to transform and strengthen.

Charades: *The Ambiguities of Language*

Cool, I sport. O amateur banjo, you sly comedian.
Coo, lisp, or to a mate urban joyously come, Dian.
No, uncle-and-auntless be, as ties deny our end.
No unclean, dauntless beasties' den you rend.

Edwin Fitzpatrick, *The Rubaiyat of Charades and Palindromes*

The ambiguities in the mythology of Śiva—the apparently simultaneous idealizations of passion and renunciation, eroticism and asceticism, the preservation of the world and a liberation from it—are reiterated by the poet Rāmacandra in the *Rasikarañjana* in a series of duplex stanzas, anagramic charades, in which, as we have seen, the same letters, in the same order, have two different and incongruous meanings. The ambiguities of the language recapitulate the ambiguities of the god which, in turn, recapitulate unnameable paradoxes inherent in being itself. The two serious meanings of the poems, because of their surprising incongruity-in-simultaneity, yield a single, comic meaning. Laughter expresses a resolution and delivers the mind, at least momentarily, from the conflict in values.

As Śiva can be both ascetic and lover, depending on how we look at (or divide) him, so a single poem, depending on how we divide (or look at) it, can advise us to emulate either the yogi or the seducer of the wives of the sages of the Pine Forest. The body of the poem is like the body of the god.

One should strive at once
  to be devoted to the Absolute Self—
Damn the man who worships Śiva only occasionally,
  only in distress.

Or:

One should try to get another man's wife
  to do what he wants to do;
Damn the man who overcomes desire with pain,
  who settles for one wife,
    who conquers himself.

(*Rasikarañjana* 18)

In another stanza the poet, with one phrase, simultaneously says that he worships Lord Śiva ("I worship Bhava [Śiva], the one who angered Dakṣa, the very splendid god who wears an elephant hide") and that he worships Kāma, the enemy of Śiva ("I am so pleased by what you do, O carnal god [Eros], that I worship you alone, you who agitate the mental faculties) (*Rasikarañjana* 30). Language presents, creates, and resolves a fundamental mythological, psychological, and teleological tension. One phrase, again depending on how it is divided, means both: "A man with heretical thoughts in his heart will not experience the appearance of the Lord at Varanasi"; and "What teenage girl, placed on the heart of her lord, with a true thought, will not get to make love?" (*Rasikarañjana* 116).

These exercises in wit, puzzles to be deciphered, provided fun for the riddled imaginations of connoisseurs. The amusement, the laughter, was in figuring them out (try "amiabletogether") and in generating them. As one makes the effort, strange worlds emerge from the language. The meaning of meaning is questioned. I try to emulate the poet, to translate the spirit rather than the letter of the verbal charades:

> Thechaplainwasbeatifican-
> dearthysextonitestallsinsex-
> communicationsaintsoveryearnestimateyouratonementogodasoft
> womanslaughtersend.

In the sacred dimension the words indicate one zealous churchman ranting with another: "The chaplain was beatific and earthy: 'Sexton! I test all sins!' 'Excommunication?' 'Saints over-yearn!' 'Estimate your atonement—O God—as of two manslaughters.' End." The same letters can be divided into a profane dialogue between a man and woman after lovemaking: "The chap, lain, was beat: 'If I can dear.' 'Thy sex tonite stalls. In sex, communications ain't so very earnest.' 'I mate, you rat on men!' To god a soft woman's laughter send." And when that mocking woman laughs, "Ha! Thy eros escapes?" her lover retorts, "Hath ye roses? capes?" I switch from the sacred/profane ambiguity to the Indological realm with no better luck: "Hand? *Liṅga*-penis! Manu, alas, as Śiva granting all eons It, is a yogee" is also "Handling a pen is manual! As ass I, vagrant in galleon, sit: I say, 'O gee!' "

In the same way that the charades tease the reader or hearer, the goddess teases the god, uses language playfully, jokingly employing linguistic tricks to tickle him with language. In another variant of the knock-knock joke, when the god arrives, Pārvatī asks, "Who's there?" and Śiva answers with various of his names, to each of which she responds as if the word has been used as a common noun: "I am Śulī ('one who suffers from stomach cramps')"—"then see a doctor"; "I am Nīlakaṇṭha ('one with a blue neck [i.e., a peacock]')—"then sing a note"; "I am Paśupati ('the chief of domestic animals [i.e., a bull]')—"But you don't have horns"; "I am Sthāṇu ("immovable" [i.e., a tree])—"Then how did you come here?" The poet invokes the protection of the "Moon-crested Lord, who was defeated by the verbal wit of the Goddess" (*Subhāṣitāvali* 103). The male god outwitted, whether with words, dice, or sexual play, by the female is always comic in the literary depictions of Śiva and Pārvatī, or Kṛṣṇa and Rādhā, or any human couple.

Again the female teases the male, sets language up as a barrier: when he asks her why she is being so "hard" on him, Pārvatī (whose name means "daughter of the mountain") explains that hardness comes naturally to one born of a mountain (something like saying, "My Dad's name is Rocky"). When he asks her why she is not more loving toward him, using a word for love (*sneha*) which also means oiliness or greasiness (something like the English word "lubricious"), she says that a man who smears his body with ashes can't also anoint it with oil. When he says that her jealous anger is "fruitless," she explains that it is because Sthāṇu (this name of Śiva is also a word for "post") can't bear fruit (*Subhāṣitaratnakoṣa* 4.6).

In this kind of comedy, words are more than sounds that communicate—they are objects manipulated, things in which multiple meanings converge and from which multiple responses are generated. The comic poet plays with words and, like the magician, he uses them to create a spell.

Liṅga Franca

"When *I* use a word," Humpty Dumpty said, in rather a scornful tone, "it means just what I choose it to mean—neither more nor less."

"The question is," said Alice, "whether you *can* make words mean so many different things."

"The question is," said Humpty Dumpty, "which is to be master—that's all."

Lewis Carroll, *Through the Looking Glass*

In an Indian legend, told in a variety of versions and contexts, a thoroughly despicable and sinful criminal, fleeing from the law enforcers, was shot with an arrow. "*Marā! Marā! Marā!* (Death! Death! Death!)," he cried out, and he was immediately redeemed and delivered into the highest heaven, for, despite his unrepented crimes, in uttering the words "*marā-marā-marā*" he was also, even though he did not realize it, even though he did not untangle the charade, crying, "Rāma! Rāma! Rāma!" The invocation of the name of god was his salvation. The medieval story is usually told to illustrate the power of devotion and the religious irony that intent does not matter. But more fundamentally the story illustrates the power of language, the mystery of sound. One word can be worth a thousand pictures.

The irony central to this story, comedic though not necessarily funny to all hearers of the legend, is the basis for a similar legend about a hunter who on Mahāśivarātri was, like the criminal, saved in spite of himself. The charade in this story is iconic rather than verbal. "Once upon a time there was a cruel hunter named Gurudruh ("Foe-of-the-Venerable"), a tribal, a man of no caste, without learning or religious conviction. He was a poacher and thief, heartless and wicked to the core. One day—it just happened to be Mahāśivarātri, though the hunter did not know it—he went into the forest in search of prey, but none was to be found. In the evening, still without catch, as he bathed in a forest pond, he thought to himself, 'Surely some animal will come to this pond to drink. All I need to do is climb this tree here by the pond and wait.' Under the tree, which just happened to be a *bilva* or wood-apple tree, there was a rock which just happened to be shaped like the *liṅga*. When the hunter climbed the tree some of the *bilva* leaves fell down upon the *liṅga* and some of the water on his body also dripped onto the stone. Though the hunter did not know it, he had just performed the worship demanded on Mahāśivarātri—the offering of water and *bilva* leaves to the Śiva-*liṅga*—and for his action Śiva redeemed him" (abridged and paraphrased from *Śiva Purāṇa* 4.40.1–102). The gods, in the devotional tradition, play not only jokes on us, but jokes for us.

As the verbal charades suggest that we do not ever really know what we are saying, so this story implies that we do not ever really know what we are doing. That we move through the world so unaware, as such utter fools, makes a comedy of human existence. Laughter as an understanding of that, as a response to the great comedy, is attributed to the gods. They get the joke that people take seriously.

In Varanasi, on Mahāśivarātri, I asked a shopkeeper who sold toys, including little wooden gods, brightly painted and typical of Varanasi, directions to the Cantonment where I had an appointment to meet some friends of my parents who were traveling in India. The verbal map was labyrinthian. "Is it in walking distance?" I innocently asked. "Of course. Delhi is in walking distance provided that you have the time! Isn't it?" I was forced to agree with a laugh. "Don't go to the Cantonment today. Today is Mahāśivarātri. Just stay here. Stay all night long! Just chant the name of Śiva." He laughed as he repeated the holy name "Śiva! Śiva! Śiva!—go on, say it!" I didn't want to say it; it seemed embarrassing somehow; it felt wrong. "Say it—Śiva! Śiva! Śiva!" His insistence, despite a warm smile and easy laugh, was annoying. "No. It's not really for me to say. I'm not in any way a Hindu and. . . " His laughter interrupted me. "You do not have to be a Hindu to say 'Śiva.' It doesn't matter in the slightest. You do not have to be a Hindu to be saved!" He told me a variant of the story of the hunter. "Once on Mahāśivarātri there was a wicked man in jail, a man who did not believe in god. Imagine this—even though he did not believe in any god, he hated them all! How ridiculous! How comical! All night long the pilgrims were chanting 'Śiva! Śiva! Śiva!' and the bad criminal could not sleep. He was so angry and so cantankerous that he yelled out of the window of his cell, 'Damn you! Damn you! Stop making such a noise. I cannot sleep with all your damn Śiva! Śiva! Śiva! All I hear is Śiva! Śiva! Śiva!' " The toy merchant laughed. "Because he said that name of god, he was saved! Straight to heaven, in a flash!"

Selling me two little wooden dolls, one representing Śiva, the other representing Pārvatī, he told me the festival was in honor of their wedding. A book said that it commemorated Śiva's manifestation as the *axis mundi,* the transformation of the *liṅga* into a pillar of fire which could not be measured by either Brahmā or Viṣṇu. Someone else said it meant nothing special—"It is simply a chance to fast, to stay up all night, to buy things, to see people, and finally to have a feast that tastes all the better for the fast." Festivals are like charades in action, ambiguous movements, the meanings of which are dependent upon how they are taken apart and put back together.

His and Hers: *The Ambiguities of Sex*

Only one with a carnal nature deeply appreciates the ascetic ideal.
Edward Dahlberg, *Reasons of the Heart*

Śāradātanaya (fourteenth century) speaks of an ancient drama, composed by the god Brahmā himself, performed by the sons of Bharata, depicting the burning of Tripura, the lawless Triple City of the demons. Each of the aesthetic sentiments—the amorous, the heroic, the terrible, the tragic, the comic, and the rest—were, according to the rhetorician, present in the play, and generated by the activities of Śiva in his various forms and moods—the lover, the archer, the skull-bearer, the dancer. Śiva is the source of all the sentiments, aesthetic as well as religious. As the one ineffable and transcendent god takes on various forms, moods, and postures, so a single aesthetic sentiment, the sentiment beyond all sentiments, itself transcendent and ineffable, manifests in the play in correspondence with the emotions stirred up by the god. As the lover of the goddess, Śiva personifies the amorous sentiment. And "the comic sentiment," Śāradātanaya explains, "is said to be produced from the amorous. Thus, the ladies-in-waiting to the goddess burst out in loud laughter when Śiva, his hair matted in ascetic locks, wearing his serpentine ornaments, his eyes blazing with fire, his body covered with ashes, longed for sexual union with the goddess" (*Bhāvaprakāśana,* p. 57). The incongruity between outer, ascetic appearance and inner, erotic motive, the ambiguity essential to the god, sparks laughter. The two aspects of the god represent two antipodal forces seemingly imbedded in all things as the energy of creation and the energy of destruction, and two corresponding antithetical ideals within Indian cultural history—the passion which affirms and perpetuates the world and the renunciation which denies it and delivers one from it. Laughter resolves inevitably mixed feelings; it is comic relief. The god himself laughs at the incongruities that he embodies and at the irony that the signs of his asceticism are wholly erotic:

"A deadly cobra is the bracelet worn upon my wrist,
And from drinking primal poison my neck is in a twist;
My eye's a blazing fire and I wear but elephant hide,
And yet I look handsome to Gaurī, my enticing bride!"
May the wild burst of laughter that the Lord of Beasts then made—
A blush of joy upon the cheeks—be for your constant aid!

(Rudraṭa, *Saduktikarṇāmṛta* 1.8.1)

This verse, as already indicated, was cited by the Jain rhetorician Hemacandra, in his discussion of the distinction between "self-situated-laughter" and "other-situated-laughter" (the categories which I have construed as "humor" and "satire," respectively), to illustrate "self-situated-laughter," laughter at oneself, arising in oneself (*Kāvyānuśāsana* 2.11). Śiva, then, is the perfect exemplar of humor, and he, the Lord of the Universe, in laughing at himself, laughs at all things.

The comedy based on Śiva's laughter at himself is played out in the testing of Pārvatī, the trick that Śiva plays on her in order to discover her motives in loving him. In Kālidāsa's version the god disguises himself as a young mendicant who has taken a vow of chastity. He approaches Pārvatī in the forest where she is practicing austerities and asks the reason for her penances. A lady-in-waiting explains that Pārvatī is attempting to win Śiva through the performance of austerities. "You gotta be joking," the hermit-in-disguise laughs (*Kumārasaṃbhava* 5.62). And when Pārvatī expresses her sincerity, the mendicant makes fun of the god. Śiva makes fun of Śiva. The reader, knowing what Pārvatī does not know, is in on the joke. Śiva points out how ludicrous they will be together. "People are going to laugh at you riding on an old bull in the marriage procession when you should be on a royal elephant" (5.70). He enumerates the incongruities that will make them an absurd couple: "Your wedding dress, embroidered with geese, and his loincloth, an elephant skin dripping with blood . . . your lac-red footprints, marks that ought to be left on the flower-carpeted floors of a palace, left instead on burning grounds that are strewn with human hair; and what could be more incongruous than this—the meeting of your breasts, dusted with sandalwood bath powder, and the chest of three-eyed Śiva, encrusted with ashes from funeral pyres! . . . His body is disgusting; nobody knows who his parents are; and he's so poor he goes around stark naked! He isn't the sort of guy a good girl like you deserves—forget about him" (5.67–73).

The sages of the Pine Forest say the same sorts of things about him. They laugh at Pārvatī and call her a fool, asking what a girl like her is doing with a guy like him: "He has no family or breeding. He's ugly and goes around stark naked. He hangs out with ghouls and goblins. . . . Sure, he married Sātī, but the fool couldn't even support her—all he could do was think about (or meditate upon) himself. He only married because of what people would say if he didn't. . . . You'd be better off with Viṣṇu." And "when Pārvatī, the mother of the world, heard these words, she laughed" (*Śiva Purāṇa* 2.3.25.46–55). Her laughter was, at once, the laughter that rejects—a bitter laughter at the sages—and the laughter that accepts—a sweet laughter at Śiva. It was, furthermore, laughter at herself.

In the conflict between the ascetic and erotic ideals, the comic poet always cheers for the triumph of sex. He makes fun, as we have seen, of all spiritual pursuits in order to affirm the flesh, and that affirmation is made when his audience physically responds with laughter. Hārṣa burlesques the wise or holy man. "The sage feels that both sexes ought to occupy themselves with sexual pleasure; even Pāṇini said '*apavarge tṛtīya.*' " (*Naiṣadhacarita* 17.70). The sexual meaning of the phrase, that "liberation is for eunuchs," makes a comic mockery of the actual, technical meaning of its original usage by Pāṇini (*Aṣṭādhyāyī* 2.3.6), a reference to the use of the instrumental case termination on a word denoting time to express continuity and accomplishment.

Sex is the energy of comedy. Just as Kāma, Desire, laughed at Śiva, so *kāma,* desire, laughs at all mortal beings. A bull laments the ridiculousness of the predicament in which his sexuality has put him.

> If I, a bull for breeding, were to be castrated,
> I could not please a cow or make a calf;
> But if I keep my balls, so clearly indicated,
> people always look and they always laugh.
> (Ratnabhūti, *Subhāṣitāvali* 2355)

Another poet uses a juxtaposition of his beloved's body with the ascetic form of Śiva, and the act of lovemaking to the suggested austerities of the god, to create a comic incongruity. He asks her to make her breasts naked, using a word ("skyclad" [*digambara*]) which is one of Śiva's names; he promises to scratch those breasts, to mark them with the nailmark termed "the crescent moon" in the *Kāmaśāstra,* a simultaneous reference to the emblem worn on Śiva's forehead; her breasts are "firm" (*ugra*), a word conventionally used to refer to Śiva in his terrible aspect. As the Ganges flows from Śiva's hair, so a pearl necklace, bright and pure like the Ganges, rests on her breasts: in Śiva's case the Ganges is like a pearl necklace; in her case a pearl necklace is like the Ganges (*Subhāṣitaratnabhāṇḍāgāra* 318.2). In comedy, religion is banal and sex is almighty. Everything, like everyone, is mixed up. The profound and the trivial, the heavenly and the mundane are comically transposed.

The Androgyne

Then Eryximachus said, "My good man, look what you are doing! You are playing the fool . . . You compel me to keep a watch on your speech and look out for something laughable. . . ." And Aristophanes answered, with a laugh, "Quite right, Eryximachus, I take back what I said . . . I am not at all afraid I may say something laughable, for that would be clear gain and natural to our Muse—but lest the things I say may just be ridiculous. . . . At first there were three sexes, not two as at present, male and female, but also a third having both together. . . . There was then a male-female sex and a name to match, sharing both male and female, but now nothing is left but the title used in reproach."

Plato, *Symposium*

"The body of Śiva, splendid as fire, was half male and half female. By his own will he divided himself in two, into a woman and into a man" (*Liṅga Purāṇa* 1.70.325). The seminal image of the androgynous god is pregnant with theological and psychological meaning and power; it is a serious emblem of a proposed metaphysical unity beyond apparent dualities of existence, a spiritual or psychological hint or directive to the divided psyche, a prompt to seek a more holy or healthy wholeness. But it is also a humorous image of comic incongruities inherent in presumed and profound unities, a directive to laughter. The poet Sārvabhauma makes fun of the highfalutin hermeneutics that extract an esoteric ontological truth from the image of the divine androgyne when he asserts that Śiva only made the goddess a part of himself because "he was afraid of having two bellies to maintain," two mouths to feed (*Paddhati* 64). The lord of the universe is reduced to a bourgeois householder with money problems like everybody else. Creating, preserving, and destroying the universe is no bigger deal, in comedy, than making ends meet at home. In comedy the banal eclipses the profound, the immediate overwhelms the ultimate. The rupee or dollar, the banana peel, the big nose, the crow shit, the stinking fish, the fat belly, the smelly cheese, the belching frog, the bottle of rum, the whoopie cushion, the wart, the panties, the dirt, the bowels, the genitals—not any Absolutes—are truth; things alone—not ideas—are real in the comic vision.

As an idea the androgyne offered the philosopher a theological, cosmogonic metaphor, but as a literal and bizarre incarnation of biological incongruity, the androgyne had, for the Sanskrit poet, abundant potential for the establishment of the comic sentiment. The figure, providing an intensification of the comedy of the transvestite, is a walking mistaken-identity. Kumāra, the infant god of war, sits on his androgynous parent's/parents' lap in a state of thoroughly comic confusion.

> This is my Mommy! No, this cannot be her—
> There is a prickly, red beard on half of this face!
> This must be Daddy! No, oh, it's hard to be sure—
> A breast on the chest of a dad is quite out of place!
> I can't figure it out: Why, what, or who?
> A man? A woman? Not one of those two?
> (Rājaśekhara, *Subhāṣitaratnakoṣa* 5.20)

Laughter at Kumāra recollects the curiosity and confusion of early childhood, of the phallic stage in the development of the ego when jokes about what daddy had and mommy hadn't were funny, when laughter alleviated the anxieties that were concomitant with the struggle to understand anatomical as well as social sexual differences and distinctions. Laughter at Kumāra's confusion is laughter at the *kumāra,* "the child," within. It is humorous laughter, laughter at oneself, at what one once was.

"What has sixteen arms, fourteen balls, and a pussy?" was the childhood joke, and the answer—"Snow White and the Seven Dwarfs"—made comic sense in terms of what I knew in Mrs. Bartz's fourth-grade class. In terms of what I know now of the many-armed androgynous deity, another punch line would do just as well: "Śiva, carrying four cans of tennis balls."

In evocations of the amorous sentiment, the two—lover and beloved, man and woman—experience a sense of unity, a metaphorical oneness: in two bodies they have one will and urge, one spirit and self; and sexual union is the enaction of the metaphor, the experience of a mystery, the merging of feeling and flesh. The comic sentiment is a travesty of the amorous and a reversal of erotic conventions. The mythology of the androgyne, repeatedly asserting that Śiva made the goddess one with him in order to enjoy her eternally, provided the groundwork for a comedy, a sex farce, in which two wills, spirits, or selves, are caught in one body. The figurative language of love—the amorous metaphor of oneness, the sexual simile of unity—becomes the literal language of comedy. The comic battle of the sexes is waged within a single form. Śiva, despite the presence of the goddess in his body, is unfaithful; his performance of the daily worship of twilight, personified as Sandhyā, is but flirtation. The lips of the androgyne tremble—his part of the lips because he's muttering the praise/flattery of the prayer/solicitation, her part because she's jealous and piqued (Śaṅkaradeva, *Saduktikarṇāmṛta* 1.28.1). The goddess doesn't want to put up with all this divine nonduality or sacred wholeness stuff any more. The *coincidentia oppositorum* may symbolize the primordial totality of the cosmos or psyche to mystics or Jungian psychologists, but it's just a bother to the goddess.

> "So let another goddess try to live this way,
>   Bowing down to a rival, Ms. Twilight, each day,
> Trapped in your body and trying there to share you,
>   And supporting the Ganges up in her hairdo!"
> Umā thus complained with furied behests;
>   But Śiva held tightly onto his/her breasts,
> As she struggled then to get herself free.
>   May the great arm of Śiva protect you and me!
>
> (Mayūra, *Saduktikarṇāmṛta* 1.28.5)

To restrain her, Śiva has to grab himself; to make love to her would be either masturbation or an impossibility. The poet Chittipa chuckles over the sexual frustrations of the androgynous Śiva "whose body is coalesced with that of his beloved—it's like simultaneously being apart and making love: he can't see the loveliness of her mouth, nor can he have her kisses; he can't unbuckle her belt, nor can he fondle her crotch. May the Enemy of Love protect you!" (*Saduktikarṇāmṛta* 1.28.2). The invocatory epithet is an ironic amplification of the prevalent comic allusion to the backfiring of Śiva's destruction of Kāma. "People call Śiva my destroyer," Kāma laughs, "but he's made the goddess a part of himself so he can enjoy her!" (*Subhāṣitaratnakoṣa* 14.1). Kāma laughs at Śiva the family man, the god who is comically like us. Śiva and Pārvatī, with their boys Gaṇeśa and Kumāra, are, in the comic vision, just older and more persistent versions of the Cleavers with Wally and the Beaver.

The Sacred Sit-Com

> The frivolous have rightly cracked jokes about a God who seemed to take a more than spiritual interest in a carpenter's wife. The birth of a divine son in a stable is touching but also funny, suggesting a farce . . .
>
> Chad Walsh, "On Being With It"

The gods take part in a domestic comedy, the conventions of which were established in literary celebrations of the sweet follies of human love. The *anima mundi,* the *śakti,* the power and mother of the universe becomes, in the thoroughly human divine comedy, a shy young girl who makes Śiva gently laugh.

> May Gaurī bless you!
> The first time they made love,
> anxious, she had rushed to him;
> But when she beheld his face,
> a natural shyness made her run from him;
> Coaxed along by women's words,
> persuasions to return to him,
> She bristled with delight—more and more—
> When Hara, laughing, held her close to him.
>
> (Harṣa, *Ratnāvalī* 1.2)

Kālidāsa makes much of the young bride's coyness and the tone is lightly comic: when Śiva undresses the goddess, she shyly covers his eyes; he then simply opens his third eye to inspect her nakedness and she, with only two hands, can do nothing about it (*Kumārasaṃbhava* 8.7). The humor is in the shift from the mythological associations of the third eye with the idea of powerful, mystical insight, to the realization that he uses that eye, the eye that incinerated the god of love, to indulge in loveplay. The organ of divine vision becomes the organ of a lustily playful voyeurism.

Śiva plays little love-tricks on Pārvatī—he has Bhṛṅgī and Kālī dance to frighten her so that she'll jump up on his lap in terror and cling to him, so he can make love to her (*Kumārasaṃbhava* 9.49–50). By the conventions of Sanskrit comedy, her fear, because it is without real cause, is comic. The incongruity between the sentiments of fear, revulsion, and love yields the comic sentiment. The sentimental incongruity parallels the mythic incongruity between the erotic god and the ascetic god, and the incongruity that causes laughter in the circle of Pārvatī's ladies-in-waiting when they see ashes on her breasts the morning after her night of love-making with Śiva. Reversal is the basis of the humor—the women laugh because the ashes that usually indicate austere penances suddenly mark happy sexual indulgence (*Subhāṣitaratnakoṣa* 5.10).

The mother-in-law, a universally comedic persona, enters the cosmic comedy in an elaboration of the jokes based on Śiva's appearance. Menā, Pārvatī's mother, waits at the betrothal rite to meet her perspective son-in-law. Each of the gods, invited as guests, arrives in turn, and each one is handsome or fine in some way. With each arrival Menā smiles, "Oh, this must be Śiva!" And each time she is told, "No, this is Viṣṇu" or Indra, or Vāyu, or Kubera. Brahmā arrives. "Surely, this is my son-in-law!" Menā gloats. "Wrong again!" And when Śiva finally walks in, escorted by his ghoulish sidekicks, with his ashes, matted hair, skulls, in his elephant-skin underwear, Menā faints (Śiva Purāṇa 2.3.43.1–63). It is the comic farce that occurs when the Hell's Angel shows up at the home in Southampton to meet the mother of his debutante bride.

As in any domestic farce, squabbles between husband and wife form a motif in the comedy of Śiva and Pārvatī. The lord of the universe is at once a henpecked husband (Pārvatī gets angry at him for looking so awful, for being addicted to hashish, and for gambling) and a roguish lover (cheating on his wife in illicit trysts with Sandhyā, Gaṅgā, and others). The battle between this manifestation of Punch and Judy is a game, funny not serious, and all the funnier in proportion to the degree that it is taken seriously. Śiva keeps losing all he has to his wife in games of dice. Bhṛṅgī asks Kumāra what Dad has lost lately: "His bull, his drum, his snakes, the moon, and [since he didn't have a shirt on his back] his ashes" (*Subhāṣitaratnakoṣa* 5.28).

Comedy continually stresses the ordinariness of the extraordinary god. The god fares no better in the highest heaven than does any man in any home. Just as some middle-class businessman might come home and bore his wife to tears with tales of the office, so Śiva, in a South Indian legend (recounted in a comic book, *Tales of Shiva*), puts Pārvatī to sleep with a tedious discourse on the Veda (this is a joke anyone who has been married to a Sanskritist can understand). The husband's pride is hurt and, in a petty anger worthy of Ralph Cramden, he yells at her. "The Vedas are not for you! You are no better than a common fisherwoman. May you be

Figure 27

born as one!'' Pārvatī vanished from Śiva's sight and reappeared on earth as a baby in a fishing village. The punch line of the joke is a god saying, ''Whoops!''

Poor Mom—she can't even have any privacy in the bathroom. ''One day when Pārvatī was taking her bath, Śiva, after scolding Nandin [their pet bull] who had been posted to guard the door, barged in. When the beautiful lady, the mother of the world, was suddenly interrupted by Śiva, she jumped up, completely embarrassed'' (*Śiva Purāṇa* 2.4.13.15–16) and Śiva laughed (fig. 27). His laughter further annoys the goddess. She confides in her son, that Dad is a joker who laughs at all and sundry: ''He's going to laugh at you, just because you have the head of an elephant, just like he always laughs at me'' (*Skanda Purāṇa* 1.2.29). And, of course Pārvatī is right. Śiva does laugh at Gaṇeśa and at their other son, Kumāra—the six-headed Skanda or Kārttikeya, the god of war—as well. The boys, like Wally and the Beaver, inspire a laughter that people know within their own homes. In a reclamation of lost innocence, one laughs at them as at one's own children or at one's own childhood.

Gaṇeśa, about to suck his mother's breasts, suddenly ''became utterly confused and reached up with his trunk to touch the sinus lobes on his own forehead, making everyone laugh'' (*Saundaryalaharī* 72)—in his naiveté, the idealized blissful innocence of infancy, he thinks the great round globes on his own forehead must have been somehow transferred to his mother's chest. The comparison between a woman's breasts and the sinus bosses on the head of an elephant was a conventional one, a trope often used comically to link incongruous realms of experience. Kṛṣṇa, in battle with the war elephant of Kaṃsa, looked at the ferocious animal's forehead and ''was reminded of Rādhā's swollen breasts. He broke out in a sweat and closed his eyes.'' Kaṃsa, mistaking the symptoms of sexual arousal for symptoms of fear in battle, cried out, ''Victory! Victory! Victory!'' The joke is on Kaṃsa—his yell brought Kṛṣṇa to his senses and the god killed the elephant (*Gītagovinda* 10.8). Mistakes—Kaṃsa's of affect and Gaṇeśa's of object—are funny. Kaṃsa's mistake allows us to laugh at a personification of wickedness, Gaṇeśa's at a personification of innocence. Mistakes of the latter kind typify the humor of the divine children. When Skanda sees a peacock (the animal that is to become the vehicle and totem of the young god) with its head tucked under its wing in sleep, he asks his father, ''Who chopped off that bird's head?'' Śiva laughs and his laughter reassures his son—Kumāra laughed in turn. ''May that laughter protect you!'' (*Subhāṣitaratnakoṣa* 5.26). Divine ''kids say the darnedest things'' too.

> ''Mommy, tell me, what is that
>   in the palm of Daddy's hand?''
> ''That's jujube fruit, my little darling.''
>   ''He won't give it to me!''
> When his mother said, ''Go and get it,''
> Little Guha forced open the hands
>   clasped in twilight meditation;
> Śiva's trance was broken,
>   thoughts were interrupted,
>   and he laughed.
> May the burst of his laughter protect you!
>   (*Saduktikarṇāmṛta* 1.8.3; *Subhāṣitaratnakoṣa* 4.30)

The humor of the poem, like all humor perhaps, affirms innate and natural impulses. Laughter signals a shift in ideals, a change in consciousness over the poem that is concomitant with the alteration of Śiva's thought in the poem. We move from the religious to the secular, from the metaphysical to the physical, from an adult as piration for liberation to the infantile hunger for something sweet. Humor stresses the ultimacy of the child, of simplicity, and naturalness. In the epistemology of comedy the jujube—not *brahman* or any other absolute—is real, and we can know that by asking not the philosopher or mystic, but the child or the fool.

Little Skanda, sitting on his daddy's lap, counts the teeth in the mouth of the deadly cobra that Śiva wears around his neck: "one, nine, two, ten, five, seven . . ." (*Kumārasaṃbhava* 11.45; cf. *Subhāṣitaratnakoṣa* 5.25)—the child knows the names of the numbers but not what those names mean. In his innocent ignorance, he knows what more maturely learned people may not know—that there is nothing to fear, that Śiva, for all his fearful signs, even in his most terrible aspect, blesses and comforts. The comedic axiom that it is funny when a character is afraid of something benign or isn't afraid of something dangerous, has religious ramifications in the context of the comedy of Śiva. Skanda, again on his father's lap, "counts the ornamental skulls of Śiva's necklace with curiosity, as if they were a row of geese" (*Subhāṣitaratnakoṣa* 5.23). The provision of a refuge from terror is a function of comedy no less than it is a function of religion. The laughter of Śiva, as the poets reiterate, "protects."

Funny Bones: *The Ambiguities of Death*

> If I were to laugh, it would be as if lightning and thunder were laughing as they broke the clouds; the fire burning inside me would scorch my lips, and I would perish in the furnace of my mirth.
>
> Nizami, *Layla and Majnun*

"Let the whole world willingly be under the power of Kāla, the Grim Reaper," Nīlakaṇṭha Dīkṣita ends his comedic satire on the Age of Dullness, "but what can Kāla do to us if we have taken refuge in the Reaper's reaper?" (*Kaliviḍambana* 101). Death makes fools of us, but Śiva, death's reaper, makes a fool of death. His laughter, as the laughter of transcendence, has the power, according the poet Vaidyagadādhara, to deliver us from gloom. The apocalyptic vision is illuminated by divine laughter.

> May the terrible Lord Śiva deliver you from dread!
> When all living things were drowned in a single sea
> When the world was flooded, when every being was dead,

There and then did Śiva dance with the black Kālī;
Then and there he loudly laughed in a playful tone,
And driven by his gleaming teeth, the darkness went away.
There in the waters then the god's reflection shone;
"Who are you," asked the god, "What have you to say?"
(*Saduktikarṇāmṛta* 1.18.4)

As Śiva laughs, the nectar from the moon upon his forehead trickles down and brings the skulls around his neck to life. They join in his laughter which then makes him laugh all the more. The darkest vision is made light by the blazing circuit of laughter.

May the torrents of Śiva's laughter,
all-pervading, glorious
With great waves rivaling river currents,
rushes of the rainwater cleansing heaven,
Protect you!
He laughed without restraint at the spectacle:
the human skulls around his neck,
rattling, brought to life,
By drops of nectar trickling from the moon—
the crest upon his head—as his body quaked.
(Vācaspati, *Saduktikarṇāmṛta* 1.8.4)

White Comedy

For within the hollow crown
That rounds the mortal temples of a king
Keeps Death his court, and there the antick sits,
Scoffing his state, and grinning at his pomp.
William Shakespeare, *King Richard II*

The skull, the face of death, eternally laughs with a shrieking silence at the living. The conceit of the laughing skull in Sanskrit poetry followed naturally from the common usage of the phrase, "showing the whiteness of one's teeth," as an expression for laughter.

Here is the face—
Where are the honied lips
and where the sidelong glances?
Where is the silken banter,
and where the brow
arched like the bow of love?

This disappearing act is a magic trick,
  The joke of the skull
    atop the ascetic's staff;
  And thus the skull loudly laughs,
    teeth bared in laughter,
    the murmuring sound of laughter,
      the whispering wind,
Laughing, it seems, at those who are blind with love.
(*Subhāṣitaratnakoṣa* 48.26).

The wind that scatters the crematory ashes is the sinister laughter of the skull that mocks the stirrings of passion and the futilities of love. Bleached white by the sun, carried by an ascetic in emulation of Śiva, the skull grins like the skull of Yorick, that "fellow of infinite jest," who jibed and gamboled, and whose "flashes of merriment" made so many people laugh. But the skull, as the emblem of death, laughs at renunciation as well as passion, for death obliterates distinctions, wipes away all things, makes a comedy of all endeavors. Death is the ultimate banana peel, the final whoopie cushion. Neither the practice of yogic breath control nor the study of sacred texts gives one power over death.

Though controlling breath, that vital part,
And expounding scriptures learned by heart,
  Gurus die—their souls must part—
  Just like the passing of a fart!
(*Subhāṣitāvali* 2305)

"Death laughs at the man who watches over his body and guards his wealth," another poet reflects, "just as an adulterous woman laughs at the husband who has parental affection for 'his' son" (*Subhāṣitāvali* 2309). Death, like the illicit lover, like wealth and the earth, laughs at the very responses that death itself prompts within the human heart.

Wealth laughs
at those who make of money an obsession;
Earth laughs
at those who says "this land is my possession!"
Illicit Lovers laugh
at the guy who thinks his kids are kids he's made;
and Death laughs
at the king who on battlefields is afraid.
(*Bhartṛhari, Subhāṣitatriśatī* [Kosambi ed.] 382)

The bone-white comedy, in which death is depicted laughing at human beings, is an attempt to accept reality, to come to terms with the limits of human hope. It is balanced by a soot-black comedy in which human beings laugh, in response, at death in an attempt to evade reality and assert an omnipotence of the self and the pleasure which that self finds in the world. The ultimate goal of comedy is, perhaps, a reconciliation and alliance of reality and pleasure—to begin laughing at death as it laughs at us, and to end laughing with death, with the feeling that it laughs with us.

Black Comedy

In Sardinia, aged parents were expected to laugh when immolated by their children; in Phonecia, it was children who were immolated, but here too the parents were expected to laugh; and in India, laughter was *de rigueur* when mounting the ritual pyre.

David Victoroff, "New Approaches to the Psychology of Humour"

The Buddha's question remains: "How can anyone who knows of old age, disease, and death, laugh?" The comic answer is that there is a way of laughter that salvages amusement out of despair, that deals with sorrow by taking a perverse and even eerie pleasure in it. Nowhere is the defensiveness of all laughter more apparent than in black comedy. Laughter is a weapon against reality, against the ultimacy of time and death. As Rāvaṇa wields a scimitar called Candrahāsa, "Moon Laughter," so he who laughs, who in the darkness of despair shows his teeth, white like the moon shown in the night, lifts a sword. It cuts up. It defends in its attack. It makes a travesty of death and a raucous joke of the apocalypse.

Pārvatī, intent on playing a trick on Śiva, a little game of "Guess Who?" came sneaking up behind the god and covered his eyes with her hands. At once the cosmos was overwhelmed with darkness. "You goofy girl!" Śiva reprimanded her, "just for the sake of a joke, you, in your silliness, have destroyed the universe" (*Skanda Purāṇa* 1.3.1.3.50–52). The world ends not with a bang but a chuckle. This version of the Indian Armageddon is but a banal bedroom farce, a little comedy of errors, a childish girl's innocent game. The biggest joke of all is that life and death, or creation and destruction, are taken seriously at all. In the comic vision, absurdity is the fundamental and ultimate principle at work in the universe, and nothing, absolutely nothing, not even comedy, is ultimately or absolutely serious.

Figure 28

Laughter at death is a fearful pose of fearlessness. It is nervous laughter. The modern Indian cartoon of a beggar who has starved to death (his corpse pitifully attended by his small, hungry child) is from a book called *Laugh It Off*—the title suggests the desperately defensive function of comedy (fig. 28). But the sloughing off of agonies, the alleviation of the pain, is inevitably transitory; rather than making the cause of sorrow go away, it, just for a moment, turns from the sorrow as if in hopes that, when it turns around again, misery will have vanished. The mortality which defines life, the end inherent in all living cells, is extracted, exorcised, and objectified in jokes about death. The laughing one makes an effigy "out there" of his own death and, as if in some ancient apotropaic rite or festive carnival, death is mocked with brazen shows of excoriating laughter to keep it at bay.

Jokes about the death of another allow the laughter to gloat about what has not yet happened to him. They focus and intensify the hostility that is at least a subliminal aspect of all comedy. Asked the difference between tragedy and comedy, Mel Brooks once explained, "It is a tragedy if *I* cut my finger; it's a comedy if *you* fall in a sewer and die." Comedy is seemingly heartless. It gives respite from compassion and relief from the burden of sympathy. But in the ephemeral respite there can be a renewal, and in the defiant gloating, an acceptance of what is sure to come. Humor has the capacity to brace and prepare. The appeal of the criminal who, on the way to the gallows on a Monday morning, joked, "what a way to start the week!" is in the suggestion that it is possible to laugh at one's own death, to laugh upon the pyre, to laugh like the child held down by his parents, like the fool, the trickster, or the god—to die laughing, and in that last cry of mirth to be delivered from all fear and from all sorrow.

Black and White and Read All Over: *The Ambiguities of Comedy*

For thence,—a paradox
Which comforts while it mocks,—
Shall life succeed in that it seems to fail.

Robert Browning, *Rabbi Ben Ezra*

I found my parents' friends at the Hotel de Paris in the Cantonment. The man, a retired urologist from Los Angeles, and his wife, on a tour of South Asia, were very enthusiastic about India. "People told us we would hate India," the woman smiled, "that all the disease and poverty would get to us. But that hasn't been the case. We have had the most wonderful time. Sure, you have to keep your sense of humor or things can get pretty hectic, but that's true no matter where you travel. Everyone has been so good to us here in India. We haven't gotten sick. The only bad thing that happened didn't actually happen. Bill was taking pictures of the bodies being cremated at the burning ghats and these soldiers came over and stopped him. I was afraid they were going to put him in jail." Bill cut in with a laugh, "Imagine her coming to visit me in the Banaras jail with a file concealed in a chapati!"

The doctor was very jovial. He joked about the Śiva-*liṅga,* said he wished he had had one hanging outside of his office when he was still practicing urology, "the way the old watch repairmen used to hang big watches out in front of their shops." He laughed a friendly, American laugh that made me feel completely at ease as only laughter can. "So what are you doing here in India. Are you studying their religion?"

I explained that I was working on a book on comedy, on humor and satire in Sanskrit literature. Bill laughed again. "Comedy! That's really a hard one! I'd imagine it's pretty difficult to write about. I mean, we don't really know what makes a person laugh. If we did, anybody could be a comedian. There are so many things going on at once. It's quite an enigma, really. You tell a joke at one party and everybody laughs; you tell the same joke, in the same way, at another party and nobody laughs and you feel like a fool. Why is that? I mean, what makes people laugh?"

"A lot of people have theorized about it," I explained, slightly self-conscious about my all-too-serious, professorial tone. "I think it is safe to say that we laugh at the chaos created by incongruous or inappropriate things, words, gestures, at surprising or improper sights, sounds, or smells; we laugh, that is, provided that such ordering principles as sympathy or anger, fear or desire, don't prevent it. Oh yes—also provided that disinterest does not interfere."

"That sounds pretty good, but is it true?"

"Probably not," I laughed to ease the inappropriately intellectual turn in our talk.

"I've always wondered about why we laugh over certain jokes. When you're a urologist you hear lots of jokes about what you do." As he said it, his wife laughed out loud as if remembering a joke—a dirty one.

"I'm kind of interested in the physiology of laughter. Isn't it funny that if I tell a story in a certain way it can somehow, even if you don't want it to, affect your adrenomedullary activity!" He laughed at the thought. "I suppose a lot of people have studied that. I'll stick to travel and golf, and leave the study of comedy to you. But I'd look into the physiology of it, if I were you. That's where the answers are."

Assuming that talk of my research was boring these people, I asked about my parents. But the doctor wanted to talk more about laughter. "I remember reading once in a medical journal about the outbreak of something they were calling 'laughing syndrome' in Africa, in Uganda I think. It's very interesting—it was like a plague, a laughing plague affecting thousands and thousands of people. It only affected the women though—young women and teenage girls first, and then their mothers, and soon the grandmothers, the old women. It was an epidemic—schools had to be closed down. Girls with the laughing disease had to be quarantined so that the other women wouldn't catch it, just as if it were being spread by some laughter-bacteria. The laughter was *literally* contagious. But no one could find any physical cause. People who caught the disease would laugh so hard that they had to be strapped down. Some women even died—they'd choke while laughing, or just die from the exhaustion, or because they couldn't stop laughing long enough to eat or drink. That article really stuck in my mind. I wonder if anybody ever figured it out." Another round of drinks was just what the doctor ordered.

"Instead of writing about humor in ancient India," he continued with enthusiasm, "you ought to write about humor now. Edit a book of modern Indian jokes. Yes, I think you ought to study what people in India think is funny today. That would be really interesting."

His wife agreed with him that Indians seemed really good-humored. "Let me give you an example. When we arrived in Delhi, there was quite a scene at the baggage pickup. This Texan had lost his luggage, and he was mad as hell. The man from the airlines just smiled happily and said, as if it was going to comfort the Texan, 'No problem! No problem at all! Your bags are absolutely safe.' 'Then where the hell are they?' the Texan yelled. And the Indian kept smiling. 'They are safe somewhere: safe in Bombay perhaps; safe in Calcutta possibly.' Oh, speaking of Texans meeting Indians. Did you hear the story about the Texan who gets seated next to the Sikh on the airplane? 'What are you?' the Texan drawled. 'I am Sikh,' the Indian replied. 'I'm sorry to hear that, I hope you're feeling better soon.' 'No, no, sir, I am not *sick* as of body, I am *Sikh* of religion.' The Texan slapped his back, 'I'm kinda sick of religion myself!' " Bill laughed, "That's what you call a 'sick joke,' " and his wife rolled her eyes over the pain of the pun.

The doctor, suddenly noticing someone enter the lobby bar of the hotel, jumped up and waved his arm. "Mr. Nayak! Mr. Nayak, come over here! We want you to meet someone." The big man trundled toward us, exposing his gold tooth and wrinkling his large nose with a great, friendly smile. I recognized him immediately.

"Lee, I want you to meet Mr. Nayak, the leader of our tour. This gentleman knows everything there is to know about India! Mr. Nayak this is Professor Siegel from Hawaii—he's here to learn about Indian humor. Maybe you can tell him some jokes."

"This is an unbelievable coincidence!" I laughed in amazement. "The world really is very small. We've met before. Several years ago. You wouldn't remember, but I remember it clearly. I took a tour of the caves at Ellora and you were the guide. Maybe you do remember. We had a talk. I was just beginning my research on comedy and you suggested that I go to meet your language teacher, Pandit Gananath Sastri in Madras. I must thank you for that introduction. I took your advice—what a wonderful, fine man. What a great sense of humor!"

"You didn't hear?" Mr. Nayak asked with an expression of genuine sadness. "The good pandit has passed away. Too many cigarettes, I suspect. Also, he was a drinker on the sly. Whatever the reason, it is a great loss." I was stunned by the news. I could picture him vividly beneath the white-blossomed branches of the shade tree in his garden, laughing as he smoked a Charminar, laughing as he told some outrageous lie, laughing as he wove some philosophical irony, laughing as he came up with some preposterous proposition—that Aristophanes was an Indian who had fled to Greece; that the *Mattavilāsa* was the oldest comedy in any written language; that Rāma had, in his exile from Ayodhyā, gone to Egypt where he was known as Ramses—"why not, after all he had an airplane." I never knew when he was being serious and when he was joking. I couldn't believe that he was dead, that this was not some joke.

"Mr. Nayak has a great sense of humor," the doctor continued. He put his hand on the tour guide's shoulder. "I'm trying to convince Professor Siegel here, that he ought to write about humor in modern India. People don't care about Sanskrit. Americans would like to know what makes Indians laugh today."

Mr. Nayak agreed. "Yes, absolutely. You will find a wealth of material. There is humor all around us." He thumbed through the newspaper he had been carrying under his arm until he finally found a small news item. He read it outloud. "An old fellow brought into court on a charge of stealing chickens was told by the judge that he should have a lawyer. 'But I don't want no lawyer.' 'Why not?' asked the judge. 'Well, judge, because no matter what happens I want to enjoy them chickens myself.' " The doctor, his wife, and the tour guide laughed heartily, but I was distracted still by thoughts of Gananath Sastri. I wanted to talk about him, but death was too intimate a subject. It was more appropriate to keep joking, to laugh some more.

I declined an invitation to dinner and said goodbye, explaining that I had some other people to see. "I'm leaving for Delhi tomorrow morning, and then back to Hawaii."

As I walked away from the hotel at dusk a dog followed me, keeping a distance from me as if afraid, but barking fiercely as if unafraid. Some boys threw a stone at the animal and then ran after it, laughing as they imitated its bark. Their laughter faded and it was suddenly quiet with an eerie twilight silence, not the absence of sound, but rather a booming, deafening silence. I felt I was hearing the silence of Gananath Sastri, the quietness of death itself. I did not know him well enough to feel a right to mourn for him, and yet I felt a loss and a sense of helplessness and loneliness. I thought about how much fun it would be, if he were still alive, to do that study of modern Indian comedy, of satire, humor, and jokes. "With his extraordinary knowledge of languages, he could give me access to the vernacular humor of modern India. We could travel together and laugh, laugh a lot. I didn't know he was a drinker. So much the better—we'd laugh all the more."

Thinking about laughing made me all the sadder. Or was it that my laughter in the lobby bar of the Hotel de Paris had emptied me somehow? There is no solidity or solidarity of feeling in laughter. I thought of those girls in Uganda wretching with horrible laughter. I thought of the apocalyptic laughter of Śiva and of the hissing laughter of the skulls around his neck. There is, perhaps, an ambiguity to all laughter, traces of guilt or fear or melancholy or cruelty or nakedness or despair or something else that is utterly joyless in all expressions of joy. Laughter mocks the one who laughs. And yet we laugh, I think, for laughter "comforts while it mocks . . . and succeeds in that it seems to fail."

That night at dinner someone said, "You must come back soon." "I want to," I answered. "And I want to come back to Varanasi. I will come back. As soon as I finish my research on ancient Indian comedy, I want to come back to study the comic tradition in modern India."

Epilogue

The Laughter of Kumāra

10

The Comic Tradition in Modern India: In Search of Laughter

Ganesh and his brother Kumar were arguing over which one of them was the swiftest, and so they decided to have a contest, a race around the entire world. The prize for the winner would be the hand of the beautiful Buddhi. The signal was given and Kumar took off like a flash. Ganesh stayed put and dallied with Buddhi. When Kumar finally returned he was surprised to find Ganesh there, and he accused him of not having run the race. Ganesh was not even out of breath! An argument ensued and Brahm was called to arbitrate. He asked Kumar where he had been and then he asked Ganesh about each of those places. Ganesh knew all the answers—he is, after all, the scribe who first wrote out all of the ancient books—including the texts on geography—for the sages. Brahm pronounced him the winner, and Ganesh and Buddhi started to laugh. Kumar was furious. He would certainly have tried to kill his brother if he had not himself been infected with their laughter. Soon everyone in heaven was laughing!

The tour guide at Ellora

The immigration official at the Delhi airport carefully read my passport, pausing now and again to look up and scrutinize me with a severity verging on suspicion. Under interrogation I confessed the purpose of my visit, producing a letter from the Government of India's Ministry of Education and Culture as substantiating evidence: "I am directed to inform you that the Government of India has approved the research project entitled, 'The Comic Tradition in Modern India,' to be undertaken by Prof. Lee A. Siegel."

"Satire and humor?" the official grimaced.

"Yes, you know, comedy, jokes, and that sort of thing. I want to find out what is funny in India."

Punctilious, bureaucratic acrimony yielded to a more genuine, personal antipathy. "What is funny in India! India is not a funny place. Life is difficult here. It is difficult to get along. It is a struggle, not a laughing matter.'' Abruptly he handed my passport and papers back to me and signaled me to move along.

Perched in the night and cold, dark shawls hanging like ready wings at their sides, owl-eyed taxi drivers awaited their helpless prey—passengers in need of rides at four in the morning—a weary, confused, and disoriented quarry.

Settling into the taxi, I noticed Śiva grinning on the dashboard. And as we pulled out into the dark and silent night, seeing heavy clouds roll softly across the half-moon, I could not help but be reminded of the poem: ''Radiant laughter in the night, echoes of the frenzied dancer—may the laughter of Śiva protect you!''

The presence of Śiva was far more comforting than that of a solemn Jesus would have been. It was, after all, the mirthfulness of Indian religion, the laughter of their gods, in contrast to the gloom and sorrow of my own heritage, the wailing of wanderers, that had drawn me to India.

The taxi driver was as quiet as the empty streets, but I imagined that he too would soon be laughing, chuckling with other drivers in the morning over how much I had overpaid him, gloating over the spoils of the nocturnal hunt.

Out of deep darkness the lights of another taxi came closer, closer, closer still. They did not stop. Glass shattered, the seat buckled, the door reached in, and as we rolled sideways everything seemed to twist, crack, and groan. Time stretched, snapped, stopped, started again. Suddenly I was standing outside the wreckage. The two drivers were yelling and screeching as they beat upon each other, and the wild cries drew people out of the night—dark figures bringing their own chaos, clamor, and violence with them. There was no way of telling whether they were breaking up the fight or joining in. There was a convulsive tangle of bodies, shoving, punching, kicking, grabbing, pushing, amidst broken glass and torn metal. Searching for my suitcase in the mangled cadaver of the taxi, I discovered that it had burst open at the seams in the collision, and I had but a single, terrible thought: ''The scotch! The scotch! O God, I hope my duty-free bottle of Johnnie Walker isn't broken!'' I retrieved it—it was safe.

Compelled to get as far from the wreck as possible, completely unaware of where I was going, I walked away as quickly as I could. I realized that my hand was drenched with blood, and I speculated that at least one rib was cracked or broken. There was blood in my mouth. I forced myself to move faster. ''Quickly, quickly—run for your life.''

I wanted, more than anything, to be able to laugh. I could not. I wanted to strut like Johnnie Walker, to tip a top hat like his, and laugh as I walked, to laugh a great, drunken, uproarious laugh at myself, the pained man who had come to India to study laughter, and to laugh a wild, mad, black laugh at the bleak irony of being driven from the airport free of charge by a poor taxi driver who would not laugh in the morning after all, the man who in losing his taxi must have lost his livelihood and hope. I took a swig of the scotch and wished I could get back to the driver, to sit with him atop the destroyed car, drinking scotch and laughing until dawn. We would laugh together with the sweet and roaring laughter of Śiva, the rapturous laughter that protects and redeems. With all anger calmed, we would laugh at the whole world. We'd laugh like Kumāra and Kālī, like the weaver and the jackal. We'd laugh like children and fools. But I dared not go back and I could not laugh.

"India is not a funny place. Life is difficult here. It is difficult to get along. It is a struggle, not a laughing matter." I pictured the immigration officer's mirthless face. Perhaps he understood his India as some great, grieving mother, a land of endless, haphazard collisions and senseless crashes in which there are only victims, a realm in which one is forced by inexplicable circumstances to limp along in pain, unsure of where one is going, uncertain of how serious the wounds are. But would he, or the taxi driver, then not want, as I did at that moment, to laugh, to quake and howl as the hyena howls at the disappearing moon of dawn?

To Get to The Other Side: *Finding the Field*

A person cannot laugh heartily in a strange country.

Joyce Hertzler, *Laughter: A Socio-Scientific Analysis*

Five hours and half a bottle of Johnnie Walker later, I sat in the bank manager's cluttered office, marveling, as I waited for my fellowship check to be cashed, at the number of rubber stamps on his desk. "Tea?" the manager asked perfunctorily as he settled back into his chair with an almost formal attempt at comfort, that standard gesture that indicates that the transaction at hand will take a very long time to complete. He sat beneath a portrait of Gandhi. His face was expressionless. "What is your topic of research?"

"I'm doing a study of humor in India."

The blank look became a frown. "We are not a humorous people."

"I have trouble believing that," I said with the self-assurance that only a visitor in India can afford. "I've been to India before and have found lots of humor. I've found a vast amount of comic material in Sanskrit literature and, what's more, most of my Indian friends and colleagues seem to laugh a lot. They all seem to have a sense of humor. And the Hindu gods . . ."

The frown deepened as he interrupted me. "No, we are not a humorous people. This is not a good topic for research. I suggest that you do your research on the law of karma in Indian philosophy. Humor? Why have you picked such a topic? You don't seem such a humorous fellow yourself."

"Well, I'm normally more jovial," I said defensively, trying to smile, "but I have a splitting headache, and I think I've broken a couple of ribs, and I haven't slept for two days, and . . ."

He cut my all-too-doleful jeremiad short as his deep frown stretched into an uncomfortable sneer. Not quite aggressive enough to be a scowl, this sneer seemed not so much aimed at me personally as at the world in general. "Yes, you will do your research on the law of karma. Excellent topic. It is a serious topic. Many brilliant minds have worked on this topic. What minds have worked on the topic of humor?"

Still struggling to sustain a grin, feeble proof of good humor, I attempted to explain that it was precisely because so little attention had been given to Indian comedy that I was undertaking the project. The sneer unfolded into a forlorn stare. "Now, listen to what I am telling you! We are not a humorous people. If we were, would I need to have this sign on my desk?" His finger pointed to the printed plaque: *SMILE!* "If we were a humorous people, I would not be needing this sign because everybody would already be smiling. They would be laughing even! But, no, every day people come into my office and they sit just where you are sitting and they are always serious. Always. They are tense. But at least there is one good thing—I myself have an excellent sense of humor. I must. Otherwise I would come to blows with the customers. But I am the exception to the rule."

"Does the sign work? Do your customers smile when they see it?"

"No. Never." The forlorn look folded back into the frown.

"But your films," I said with all the cheerfulness I could muster, "there are comic films."

"Only two percent. Maybe one point five or six. And they are no good. It is always the same—an old man gets drunk and chases a young girl. Do you call that comic?"

I laughed out loud, my first laugh in India, and the motion of the laughter made the pain in my ribs expand. I winced and his frown deepened again.

"Well, why do you think this is?" I asked in order to assure him that I was taking him seriously. "Why aren't Indians more humorous?"

"They don't have the time," he answered, the frown melting into expressionlessness once more. And, offering another cup of tea, he explained the law of karma in Indian philosophy to me.

During my initial twenty-four hours in India I was told three times that what I had come to study did not exist. After the immigration official and the bank manager, there was the author and newspaper editor, renowned for his wit and humorous social commentary, Kushwant Singh. When I was introduced to him on the first night of my visit as "the American writing the book on Indian humor," he responded with a rolling, sonorous, generous laugh, "There isn't any!" But unlike the remonstrations of the official and the banker, his chortling denial of the existence of modern Indian comedy presented a comic paradox. It was itself an ironic display of Indian humor. "It promises things," I smiled to myself as I sat in bed finishing my bottle of Johnnie Walker.

Funny Business: *Finding Texts*

The humour of a people is in their institutions, laws, customs, manners, habits, characters, convictions—their scenery, whether the sea, the city, or the hills—expressed in the language of the ludicrous.

Westminster Review, London, December 1838

In the morning, with hopes of finding some satirical and humorous writing, some comic novels, joke books, or cartoons, anything that might shed light on what is considered funny in India, I set out for Connaught Circus to rummage the many book stalls and shops there. Entering a large store, a deep bibliopolic cavern with books from floor to ceiling and mysterious side and back rooms filled with more books in bundles, I asked to see the "humor section." With a smile and a swivel of the head, the young salesman led me to a shelf of picture books on India and pulled out a volume on the Taj Mahal. "Beautiful book. First rate. Everyone is buying this. Look at the photograph of the Taj by moonlight." I explained that I was not interested, that I wanted books that were comic. The smile persisted and the head rolled more loosely on the neck. Led to another part of the store, I was shown an illustrated edition of the *Kāmasūtra*—he no doubt thought I had said I wanted something "*kāmic*."

"Have you heard of the *Kāmasūtra?*" he asked, thumbing the pages of the text to show me the illustrations and lingering at the images of fellatio at Khajuraho. "Of course I've heard of the *Kāmasūtra,*" I answered with the beginnings of impatience. "Everybody in the world has heard of both the *Kāmasūtra* and the *Bhagavadgītā*. But I'm not interested in that. I'm looking for humor. Do you have anything funny."

"Of course we have the *Bhagavadgītā*. Yes, we have many translations of the blessed *Gītā*. It is our Bible you know. Beautiful book, but not so humorous." I stopped him from getting it. "Look, I don't want the *Kāmasūtra*, or the *Bhagavadgītā*, or the Bible for that matter. I want something that is funny. Do you have any books that are funny? You know, funny as in 'ha ha ha.' "

"No problem!" he smiled and, with enormous pride, he produced from out of the depths of a back room a book which he presented to me with a ceremoniousness befitting a triumph in cross-cultural understanding and international relations. He handed me a copy of *Dennis the Menace*.

"No, no, I'm not interested in Western humor. I want samples of Indian humor."

"What is the difference? Humor is something universal, isn't it? Man laughs all over the world. And this book is only three rupees. You must buy it. Beautiful book! First rate!"

I insisted on something Indian.

"I am an Indian, am I not? To me Dennis is a most funny little fellow. Every Indian loves Dennis. What a rascal! This is a most beautiful example of Indian humor."

I suppose that he was as exasperated by me as I was by him, that we were both trying to be pleasant despite respective impulses to physically assault one another in a mutual fit of frustration and rage. His stamina was greater than mine. But then, my rib was cracked. He continued to smile even as I snapped, my rising tone betraying the shallowness of my pretense to patience, "Look, I want to buy a book that is funny by an author who is an Indian writing for other Indians. Do you or do you not have such a book?"

"Of course. Many books! Beautiful books! No problem. Be seated please. Do you want tea?"

"No, I want some samples of Indian . . ." My voice, now quavering with aggravation, reached for the salesman who turned and went to fetch the manager.

"Yes? What is it that you want?" the old man asked with a glower. He had a diffident seriousness about him that contrasted with the smile of the salesman in much the same way as his dhoti contrasted with the younger man's bell-bottom pants. In the two of them traditional and modern India seemed juxtaposed. I tried to collect myself. Almost calmly I explained, "I want something by an Indian that is comic."

"Karmic?"

"No," I struggled to restrain hysteria, "comic." And the old man pointed to the copy of *Dennis the Menace* lying on the counter. "No, no," I muttered, "I want something Indian. Something Indian. INDIAN COMEDY! Do you understand? Indian!"

Now both heads were swiveling. I somehow trusted the old man—there was something distinctively venerable about his long face. I followed him to the shelves of Indological books with faith that, buried amidst all the volumes on the law of karma in Indian philosophy, all the translations of the *Bhagavadgītā*, the books on ancient Indian aeronautics, and the teachings of countless gurus and yogis, I would find some samples of Indian humor. The two men watched as I perused the shelves. I suspected that they thought me mad or drugged or both; and so, when I saw a copy of my own all-too-serious *Sacred and Profane Dimensions of Love in Indian Traditions: the Gītagovinda of Jayadeva*, I seized upon an opportunity to restore or establish my credibility. "I wrote this book," I smiled, pulling my book from the shelf, and with a forced nonchalance, I asked if they had sold many copies of it.

"Not a single one!" the manager grumbled dispassionately. "Don't buy that book. You said you wanted a book by an Indian. That book is not by an Indian." He pulled a book from the shelf. "Buy this book. *Autobiography of a Yogi.* Paramahamsa Yogananda was an Indian." He took my book away from me and put it back on the shelf. "I'm the author of that book," I said and, from the expression on the manager's face, I immediately realized that he thought I was claiming to have written *Autobiography of a Yogi.* Without a word he turned and walked back to his desk, no doubt wondering what he had done in a past life that had made him deserve such a customer, such an annoying crank from a mad foreign land.

Still smiling, the young salesman asked which book I was buying: "The *Kāmasūtra* by Vātsyāyana, The *Bhagavadgītā* by Śrī Kṛṣṇa himself, *Dennis the Menace* by Mr. Hank Ketcham, *Sacred and Profane Gītagovinda* by Mr. Lee Siegel, or *Autobiography of a Yogi* by Paramahamsa Yogananda. I know the name of the author of every book we have in the shop. Go ahead, ask me the author of any book here."

"I'm not buying any of them. And I have no interest in quizzing you!" I snapped with an admittedly obnoxious defiance worthy of Dennis, and with an anger that would have been frowned upon by Paramahamsa Yogananda. For the first time the salesman's smile faded slightly and with utter sincerity he asked, "Why not?"

Another salesman in another shop tried to lure me into purchasing *The Complete Comedies of William Shakespeare* and various plays by Kālidāsa with the earnest suggestion that these would be quite useful to me if I would but modify the topic of my research and write a comparison of the *vidūṣaka* in *Śakuntalā* and the fool in *King Lear*. When I remarked that I doubted that *King Lear* was included in *The Complete Comedies of William Shakespeare*, the salesman assured me that he could sell me *The Complete Tragedies of William Shakespeare* "in a matching binding."

In another shop, when I asked if they had any "humor or satire," I was proudly informed that "yes, we have both Hume and Sartre. In fact, we have books by all the major philosophers—Plato, Aristotle, Śaṅkarācārya, R. Descartes, Mr. Bertrand Russell, and Dr. Sarvepalli Radhakrishnan."

In the next store I was shown children's books—some comics (*Tarzan, Archie, The Phantom,* as well as the Amar Citra Katha illustrated tales of Śiva, Kṛṣṇa, Rāma, and the Goddess), a juvenile version of selected stories from the *Pañcatantra* (complete with study questions designed to reinforce timeless moral lessons), and a copy of *Dariba, the Good Little Rakshasa*. It was as if only prepubescent beings were either capable of frivolity or allowed to indulge in it. The shop had no humorous books for adults.

I asked another bookseller why there was no comedic literature by Indians in any of the shops. "There is no money in it," was the response. "A man might read a joke book standing in the shop, but if he is going to spend good money on a book, money that he has worked hard to earn, it must be a good book."

"Can't a humorous book be good?"

"No. It is just a laugh. What does it teach you? How does it help you to better yourself? Such a book isn't serious. Isn't it?"

I thought of the way in which Sanskrit books traditionally begin with the invocation of the deity, and reflected that perhaps a book in India, by its very nature, must be a solemn thing, not so much a medium for ideas, feelings, and information, as a sacred object, a symbol of learning, an icon of wisdom, consecrated to Sarasvatī. Thinking of the Sikhs' adoration of their book as Lord Scripture, the holy residence of supreme authority, I considered the idea that the very notion of a funny book might be a contradiction, a funny idea. I offered my theory to the bookseller excitedly, with the feeling that I was verging on a profound insight into Indian culture.

A laugh dismissed my hypothesis. "No, no, no. We have many funny books in India. Many, many, many humorous books. Mostly they are in Tamil and Telegu and Malayalam and Kannada, and also in Marathi. There may be some in Bengali and Oriya, though I am not one hundred percent certain. There are also many in English. But you won't find them in these shops. I already told you that—there's no money in it."

When I asked where I might find these English-language texts, he tried to make me guess, and when I confessed that I could not, he gave me a hint. "It is so obvious. Where would a man want to read a humorous story? When would a man want to have a good belly laugh over a cartoon? When and where would he have the time and penchant for such things?" I couldn't guess. "It is obvious," he laughed. "It is *so* obvious. He would not have the penchant at home. He would not have time at the office. He would have neither the penchant nor the time in the company of his acquaintances. I am certain that you can guess. It is *so* obvious."

He withheld the information until my tantalization was apparent, until the suspense hurt as much as my cracked rib. "It is *so* obvious," he laughed again. "When he is traveling by train, of course! You will find humorous books, so many in both Hindi and English, if you go to the bookstalls at the railway stations."

I didn't have time to go to the train station. I needed to return to my hotel in Sundar Nagar to get ready for a dinner party at the home of some friends, a get-together that would be attended by urbane and cosmopolitan Indians involved in publishing and journalism, the foreign service and academic life. I looked at the newspaper in the hotel lobby to see what comic films or plays might be on in Delhi that week. I could find only *Airplane*, the American parody of disaster movies, described in the advertisement as "a rolicking tamasha headed for keeping you high with laughter." Nothing listed in the television schedule was supposed to be funny. Remembering watching *I Love Lucy* at the Bandyopadhyaya home a few years before, I asked the desk clerk if it was still shown. "Yes," he smiled happily, "all the time. Best show! Best!"

"People in India watch *I Love Lucy* and think it is amusing," a frustrated writer for Indian television was to tell me later. "But if we were to produce our own version of it, as I have very much wanted to do, people would say, 'That is ridiculous. A wife would never do such a thing. This show is not funny at all. It's quite stupid.' And it's the same with films, books, magazines, with everything. Humor is a foreign concept. It is not Indian."

Life of the Party: *Finding Methods*

Part of the problem lies in the difficulties of gathering humor data in other cultures by using the traditional methodological technique of participant observation used in fieldwork. The gathering of humor data requires different skills and preparation.

Mahadev Apte, *Humor and Laughter: An Anthropological Approach*

"This is the American writing the book about Indian humor." My introduction at the party was to become a sort of eponym throughout my visit to India that provided people with a clue to my character. It prompted a smile in some, a frown in some, and a look of bewilderment in others. A pattern, that was to solidify during my stay, began to emerge at the party: if I asked about Indian humor, I was told there wasn't any; if I asked why there wasn't any, I was told there was an abundance of it, that there was a vital comic rhythm to the pulse of Indian life. Most agreed that I would not find much in Delhi. I would have to go to Bengal or Rajasthan or Andhra. Wherever I went, as soon as I said I was looking for examples of humor, I was sent somewhere else. "You must go to Banaras—the Banarsi-wallah has the perfect sense of humor, the humor that comes with a detached outlook on life." And if I was not referred to another place, it was to another time. "I had a friend who was always making jokes. What a great man, a veritable comic genius. His mere presence would make everyone laugh. He was one of the funniest men who ever lived. He was always laughing. I would like to introduce you to him. It is too bad, but he died some time ago. I would certainly have introduced you to him."

My "mere presence" at various parties and get-togethers seemed to inevitably inspire debates as to which state had the richest comic sensibility. "The humor in Kerala is the most intelligent," the doctor from Trivandrum insisted, "while that of the Panjab is far too obscene. The Tamilian's humor is too political, and the Bengali's is too cruel. Parsis have the best sense of humor, I must admit. Hindus are too philosophical. Muslims are too devout. Christians are too Samaritan. Go to Bombay and talk with some Parsis. Most other Indians take themselves too seriously."

Drinking a glass of rum and hot water, whimsically garnished with a kumquat, I sat with a sociologist from Delhi University who had traveled in the United States. She demurely challenged my assumptions, if not my presumptions, with warnings about the difficulties of trying to understand the humor of another culture. "How can you expect to judge Indian humor? What are your standards?"

Recollecting the gracious Indian informants who, while I had previously been working on ancient Indian comic forms, had suggested that I return to study humor in modern India, and explaining that I did not intend to judge, I attempted to justify my project. "I am not looking for material that I think is funny. That's irrelevant. I want to discover what Indians think is funny. I simply want to gather impressions and present them as such. I won't claim to have any objective understanding of India."

She asked me if I had seen the article in the *Los Angeles Times*, "that horrible piece that appeared quite appropriately on a Friday the thirteenth, by that horrible man, Tyler Marshall." I understood her vituperative diatribe against the author, an attack as fiery and energized as Durgā's assault on the buffalo-headed demon, as an indirect (and therefore courteous, but nonetheless severe) caveat, an admonition that I not undertake my study. The offending article, "India—The Funny Bone Stays Numb," which I later secured from the author, reported that a satirical, tongue-in-cheek column by Art Buchwald about Mao Tse-Tung had appeared as a serious and factual news story in an Indian newspaper, something that could have caused an international incident if the Chinese Embassy could have made any sense of it. "The editor's blunder was not hard to understand," the correspondent explained, "for in India humor is rare—and easily misunderstood. . . . The lack of humor is also evident among the educated elite. . . . Although Indians are generally fond of music, the dance, and other art forms . . . they seem to care little for humor. Humor exists in India, but its quality is poor and its influence in easing the routine of life is negligible" (*Los Angeles Times*, August 13, 1982). The article seemed an imperious, journalistic equivalent of the Amritsar massacre, the author an avatar of General Dyer, and the words were bullets. It aroused anger and indignation in Indian readers; it brought out an antipathy for any foreigner claiming any understanding of India. One letter to the editor described the column as "biased, racist, untrue, and most offensive." The author was admonished to "leave India now! . . . And let the people progress with dignity, lest they be choked with the thorns of your cruel criticisms." "The man," another letter announced in reference to Marshall, "is getting desperate. He had to come up with something to keep up his nit-picking about India and her people. He must have stared at the wall for a long time wondering, 'Now what shall I get them for this time?' Marshall is plainly a frustrated man. If he is capable of some dispassionate introspection, he will find that it is he who is lacking in a good sense of humor" (*Los Angeles Times*, August 28, 1982).

I was still trying to justify myself to the sociologist. "I think it is important that I try to write about humor in contemporary India. Too often, I think, foreign Indologists write only about the wonder that *was* India. We study the ancient monument without looking at what has become of it, without reflecting on the ways in which the past inspires the present, the ways in which history persists." My statement started from the best of intentions, but as I uttered it I realized that I was implying the very opposite of what I meant, that I was suggesting that I had come to India this time to look at the ruins of the ancient comedy I had previously researched. I tried to soften the impression of impudence and impertinence with stories and asides that I fancied to be at least mildly funny. I told her about the bookstores. The sociologist did not crack a smile. She wanted to know if I thought it was funny when Peter Sellars did his imitation of an Indian accent. I swallowed my kumquat. If Tyler Marshall was General Dyer, I was Cripps—I meant well, but still I was a foreigner who did not—who could not—understand the values and needs of a modern India.

I was rescued by a Sardār, a magnificently husky and warmly laughing Sikh, a turbaned Falstaff, who pulled me into a corner to tell me jokes, mostly one-liners, delivered first in a melodious Panjabi and then in a literal English translation. His mouth was so full of rum, betel, laughter, and a thick accent, that I could hardly tell where the Panjabi ended and the English began. But still, even though I didn't understand most of the jokes, I found myself holding my rib and laughing uproariously. The delivery, the comedic kinesthesia—the inflated gestures, the improper modulations of the voice, the naughty glimmering of the eyes—was worthy of the best of stand-up comedians. It was evidence that comedy is form, not content.

"Look, there is no humor in India. None. That is why I am always in trouble. I joke and no one can take it. No one knows what I am talking about when I joke. Look, if you really want to hear jokes, you'll have to come to my house. But I am warning you, you'll only find three things there—rum, books, and empty bottles. . . . Look, I read your book on sacred and profane love. Actually I only read the profane parts. I'm writing a book too. It's called *Pubic Hair*. Why not? Walt Whitman called his *Leaves of Grass*."

Our host, offering each of us another drink, looked at me quizzically and asked, "What happened to your kumquat?"

Most of the Sardār's jokes alluded to the enormity of Sikh penises, organs shaming any Śiva-*liṅga*, magnificent members wreaking havoc on brahmin women. "Look, the Sardārji had to stop fucking the brahmin woman—he had already put out one of her eyes!" I didn't get a lot of them. "The brahmin woman's cunt is so holy that you have to bow to it before you fuck it!" "The brahmin fucks so well, the bed doesn't creak." "The old Panjabi was fucking the cook from behind while she prepared the meal. He had smoked so much charras that he couldn't ejaculate. Too bad—the dinner was burnt."

After he left the party, his niece said softly and tenderly of him something that is perhaps always true: "Beneath the buffoon is a serious, sensitive soul." Though he was the only one at that party who actually told jokes, there was a discussion of jokes inspired by my presence. "Americans tell jokes, but that doesn't mean they have a sense of humor," someone said. "Jokes are most often cruel, unnecessarily cruel. Perhaps our most common joke in India is the Sardār joke. Such humor tries to justify racism and make it permissible. These anecdotes are the Indian equivalent of your Polish jokes, the Brit's Irish jokes. They are cruel and ignorant. They are indecent."

I was solemnly warned never to ask a Sikh for the time, or even to so much as glance at my watch in the presence of a Sikh, at midday. There were various explanations. "It is because at noon, when the sun beats directly down on the Sardār's turban, it makes him become crazy, stupid, and utterly foolish." "No, no—it is because of that old joke. At exactly high noon someone asked a Sardārji the time. He looked at his watch. 'I don't know. I think one of the hands of my watch is missing.' " "No, that's not the joke. Two Sardārs met on a street corner in Delhi at noon one day. 'Look at the moon,' said one of them, pointing into the sky. 'That's not the moon,' the other replied—'that is the sun!' As they argued a third Sardārji happened along. 'Settle this for us—is that the sun or the moon up in the sky?' The third man shrugged his shoulders, 'I don't know, I'm just visiting Delhi.' " Even the woman who had said that Sikh jokes were cruel and indecent laughed. Her husband asked if any of us had heard about "the Sardār who had a photograph of himself on the wall. He had written under it, 'In this picture I am laughing.' "

I wanted to collect jokes in India, to classify them according to motifs, but generally I found it difficult to get people to tell them. Certainly this reveals more about the nature of jokes and their relationship to intimacy than it does about cultural characteristics of India. Perhaps a study of a society's jokes, done by an outsider, is too meddlesome a project, too invasive, too threatening in that it may appear, because of the nature of comedy, to be but a masked attempt to study that society's pettiness and ignorance, its cruelties and indecencies. It is, furthermore, simply unfair to ask someone, anyone, to tell you a joke, to give you an example of something they think is funny. It threatens a balance of power. Wanting to be fair as well as tactful, I decided that I must, as a methodological strategy, tell some jokes, that my jokes might remind them of one they had heard and that my own self-exposure might allow them to risk making fools of themselves as well. I adapted some American jokes to the Indian setting, transforming Western figures into South Asian ones. It was a mistake. At another party, a week or so later, I told one of my jokes to a group of Indian academics. From the very outset I could feel a growing gloom, could see icicles forming on the walls, and could sense the impossibility of a laugh over the punch line, a line that was seeming so very far away. But telling a joke is like boarding an express train—you have to go on to the end of the line, no matter where it's going. "There was this man," I started out cheerfully, "who was so devoted to Indira Gandhi that he had her portrait tattooed on his thigh, right next to his groin. He came home to show it to his wife. He dropped his dhoti and, pointing to the tattoo, asked her how she liked it. 'The one of Indira is not a very good likeness,' she said, 'but the portrait of Zail Singh [the Sikh president of India] next to it is perfect.' " Since I am certain that everyone at the party knew both what the president of India and the male crotch look like, I conclude they got the joke, but, even so, there was not a laugh, not a smile, not even a friendly glance. In perfect unison they paled, gasped, winced. The express train was derailed. One of the professors was composed enough to change the subject to a discussion of the pros and cons of Westernization.

I did, despite myself, hear some jokes in India. In the satirical mode it was common to make the political regime in Pakistan the object of the laughter. "General Zia issued a stamp with his portrait on it—he wanted his face in everyone's home. When Zia asked his Postal Minister why no one seemed to be using the stamps, the official explained that they were not sticking to the letters. 'Is the glue bad?' Zia asked. 'No,' the Postal Minister explained, 'the people are spitting on the wrong side of the stamps.' " Jokes in the humorous mode, India laughing at herself, were more poignant. There was baleful laughter over the frustrations of Indian life. "A fisherman caught a fish and gave it to his wife. She would have made a curry, but she couldn't afford the masala; she would have fried it, but she couldn't afford the ghee; she would have roasted it over a fire, but she couldn't afford the fuel. So the fisherman threw his catch back in the sea. The fish jumped up above the surface of the water, laughed, and shouted out patriotically, *'Jai Hind!'* "

Driving me back to my hotel after the party, my friend related a comment made to him by the man who sold him his betel each day, a bit of sidewalk banter which my friend had transformed into a morsel of Oxonian common room wit with convincing grace. "One day he seemed to be ignoring me. He served up the *pān* to the other customers first. When I questioned him as to why he was serving them ahead of me, certainly one of his best customers, he replied, 'It is precisely because you are one of my best customers that I am serving them first—you won't mind waiting.' That is the sort of humor one finds everyday in India. You must loiter around the *pān* shops, the tea stalls, the bazaars and markets. Go to Old

Delhi. There you will find the Indian comedy. It is alive and well, I can assure you." The sociologist with whom I had been talking at the party had said the same thing to me and to my compatriot in her own letter to the editor of the *Los Angeles Times*: "Perhaps he might like to take a trip on the buses and trains, or visit lower-class shops and eating places. I have worked among poor sweeper women in Delhi, where an earthly sense of humor underlies an acceptance of their lives."

I was counseled to wander through the Kabari bazaar on any Sunday. There, outside the great walls of the Red Fort, I would be sure to see jugglers and magicians, mummers and montebanks, clowns and buffoons, performing for a few paise, and there, mixing with the people, I would hear jokes and jibes, and though they would be in Hindi, I would at least be able to bear witness to the laughter and feel the joy. And I was assured that the National Circus was nearby in the Parade Ground.

Cartoons: *Finding Sources*

Last year Indians came third (after English-Canadian and British readers) in the league table of the number of jokes and fillers published in the international edition of the Reader's Digest—320.

Dhiren Bhagat, "The Sad, Sad Story of Indian Humour," *Express Magazine* 8/7/83

As I walked to the railway station in hopes of finding the humorous literature that the bookseller had promised would be on sale there, I looked and listened for smiles and laughter in the streets, for the humor underlying an acceptance of a life that is often bleak. Block after block, stumbling in potholes, stepping in cowdung, enjoined to give a little bakshish, asked where I was from, dodging hysterical traffic, I watched as I moved.

Some young boys were laughing as they threw stones at a sow. It was that nasty laughter, at once satanic and innocent, of which only children are capable. The pig, her udders heavily swollen with milk, her bristles thickly caked with mud, her eyes hazed with dark slime, was gobbling excrement in the streets. Flinching and grunting when the rock hit her side, she gulped up the shit all the more quickly and desperately, giving the impression that though she wanted to run from the children, she simply could not give up this fine meal. Another stone struck the sow on the head. The boys laughed more and the animal snorted, took a last large mouthful, let out a delayed squeal, and bolted.

I stopped at a tea stall for something to eat. No one was laughing. I bought a *pān* and lingered at the shop while I chewed it. No one was laughing. I watched a sweeper work without a laugh or a smile, and I thought of the joke about the Sardār who had written under his photograph, "In this picture I am laughing." When I heard the joke, I had assumed that it simply referred to the beards worn by Sikhs, that one couldn't see the laugh through all the hair. But now the joke took on more ominous ramifications—perhaps all the faces in the crowd, the faces in the tea stall, the faces in the *pān* shop, were not as laughless as I perceived them. Perhaps I was all too foreign and all too distant from Indian culture to see humor where it flourished. How could I tell the difference between comedy and tragedy, the sun and the moon? Like the Sardār of the joke, I was, after all, "just visiting Delhi." Perhaps I should, indeed, have been investigating the law of karma in Indian philosophy or comparing Kālidāsa and Shakespeare.

But just when things seemed bleak, I discovered, to my utter amazement and delight, that the bookseller had been right—there were joke books for sale at the train station. I bought everything: K. P. Bahadur's *Humorist's Hoo's Hoo*, Jagat S. Bright's *Playboy Jokes* and *Gems and Jewels of Jokes*, the cartoons of Laxman reprinted from the *Times of India*, as well as a cartoon book by Mario and two by Sudhir Dar. The salesman told me about a humor magazine, *Diwana* (literally, "Mad"), that was "quite a riot of jokes and humor." Unfortunately he did not have a single copy, but he assured me that I would find it if I went to the bookshops around Connaught Circus. "Millions of people in India are reading *Diwana* each month."

While I was at the station I bought a ticket for Varanasi. I wanted to return there for Mahāśivarātri. There I could pay homage to Śiva, Aṭṭahāsa, "the Loudly Laughing One," the dashboard deity whose laughter may well have saved and protected me in the taxi accident.

Back in my hotel room, reading the books I had just purchased, I caught myself doing exactly what I had vowed to the sociologist I would not do—I was judging the quality of the humor. I hated every single joke on every single page of *Humorist's Hoo's Hoo*: "A teenager is a girl who wagers she'll stay a virgin and loses. . . . A spinster is a woman who spins invitations and no one ministers. . . . A whore is a woman who is greatly bored. . . . Intercourse is an entry between monthly courses. . . . Lovemaking is an act in which love is maid.'' The book abounded in flaccidly adolescent and torpidly naive endeavors to be wildly bawdy and cleverly risqué. Most of the jokes, like the poorly executed drawing of a naked blond on the cover, rested on the widespread Indian assumption that all Western women are ''greatly bored.'' The jokes in that jejune book were about as funny to me as my joke about Zail Singh had been to the Indian professors. I felt the sheer joy of forbidden ethnocentricisms, the crepuscular pleasures of prejudice, bias, and intolerance, as I fantasized feeding the book to the sow that had been stoned by the young boys. To stay myself from blaming all of India for *Humorist's Hoo's Hoo*, I read a story by R. K. Narayan. I would turn to Narayan, let him take me to Malgudi, whenever I found myself believing the immigration official, Kushwant Singh, the Los Angeles correspondent, and others, whenever I was tempted to suspect that there was no outlet for humor in India, that the comic vein in Sanskrit literature, the ancient tradition of mirth that I was studying, had shriveled, dried up, and disappeared. Narayan's humor is deeply humane, his satire sweetly sympathetic; his comic perspective is at once sentimental and sophisticated. The irony of Narayan became my assurance that comedy persists in contemporary India. Each night, in bed in the hotel room, protected from the unrealness of reality, the confusion of the streets, I'd read his stories, drink a rum-cum-kumquat, and even softly laugh.

And each morning I'd search the *Times of India* for the cartoons of R. K. Laxman, Narayan's brother. Laxman's drawings are full of penetrating satire and melancholy humor. I had purchased six books of Laxman's cartoons at the railway station and found the experience of reading them all at once, over six hundred cartoons, a gloomy one. And the funnier the cartoons were, the greater the gloom. His comic vision is a spectacle of corrupt and fatuous ministers, forlorn and homeless pariahs, impoverished and subjugated villagers, people trapped in a senseless world of famines and food shortages, adulterated medicines and black money, union corruptions and hopeless protest, inflation and overcrowding, and red tape, sticky and tangled, preventing any movement forward. The only unity is in the sense of disunity (fig. 29). Nothing works. Everything is chaos.

The cartoons expose realities that are themselves so overexposed that one becomes inured to them. A policeman bending

What I like is the people's unity in this matter!

Figure 29

over a large can, an oil drum or garbage bin, looks menacingly at the poor man within it, a discarded human being who must justify his squalid existence: "I am not hiding here, I am living here" (*You Said It* 2:23). There is laughter in the face of misery, satiric laughter at a society that allows injustice, and humorous laughter of sympathy for those who must endure injustice.

"India is not a funny place. Life is difficult here . . . a struggle. Not a laughing matter." Again and again people warned me not to expect to find ebullient laughter, mirthful joking, any gleeful sense of the comedy of life, in a country plagued with serious social problems. "Life indeed looks a grim affair," Laxman wrote in his preface to the first volume of *You Said It*, "in which any attempt to joke to relieve the gravity would appear as out of place as a juke-box in an operation theater." But Laxman's cartoons, like his brother's stories, seemed ample proof that suffering may engender comedy, and that comedy, in turn, may offer deliverance from the misery of social oppression as well as redemption from the essential despair that comes from being human.

One of the Indian professors with whom I had spoken seemed to imply that I was playing the jukebox. "How can you do research on humor when there are so many serious problems to be dealt with? Humor is a luxury that India cannot quite afford yet, although some of the rich are importing it for their own use, like the Mercedes cars and their Johnnie Walker. The rich people can afford to have a sense of humor. Why shouldn't they? But what about the poor man whose crops are ruined by famine, the poor man who is reduced to begging in the streets? Have you asked him if he has heard any good jokes lately?"

"What about Jewish humor?" I asked to counter his assertion that oppression and humor were somehow incompatible. "Didn't the suffering in the ghettoes of Europe produce a rich comic tradition?" It was a tactless question that, quite unintentionally, sounded once again like I was using my research to establish my own cultural and ethnic superiority. "You are a Jew?" he asked. "Well, there is a difference. The Jews had hope. You have to have hope that things will get better in order to laugh. So many people here have no hope. They don't believe the politicians." I tried to argue that laughter might bring hope, but my words were but more coins in the jukebox.

In one of the cartoons of Mario Miranda, a rich business man (who has, no doubt, just had a shot or two of Johnnie Walker) emerges from his limosine (a Mercedes most likely) and, passing by one of those poor men reduced to begging in the streets, holds up a newspaper for the frowning poor man to read: "Prohibition soon for the uplift of the poor" (fig. 30). The cartoon at once confirms and contradicts the professor's opinion, for it is at once miserable and comical—it is, as it were, terribly funny.

"If you expect to find humor, not the jokes of a few Westernized cartoonists and writers, but the real humor of India, you must go into the villages." Again and again I encountered that idealization of Indian rural life, a Gandhian legacy perhaps, a projection of all positive values and virtues on to villagers, a romantic belief in their simple grandeur. Safe from the perils and evils of Westernization, technology, urban overpopulation, and television, they are the real people, full of basic human emotions and natural wisdom. Though they lack the electricity to watch *I Love Lucy* and the literacy to read *Dennis the Menace*, they laugh exuberantly,

Figure 30

just as they work, just as they play. That's what I heard, but I never had the opportunity to meet them.

In Laxman's vision of Indian village life, the peasant rarely laughs. He stands ill-clad, starving, and in the hopeless presence of government ministers. *"Jai Hind!"* laughs the fish. Amidst the misery and corruption, the squalor and injustice, rural and urban, Laxman draws a witness to the absurdities of Indian society. He is a lone and silent figure, a small man in a checkered coat and dhoti. Through the spectacles resting on his bulbous nose, he gazes at India with a slightly amazed, slightly worried, and slightly confounded look. Laxman has named him the "Common Man," and the dust jacket of the sixth volume of *You Said It* describes him as "no mere cartoon figure of fun, but Everyman, the soul of Modern India." He sees factories that work without producing anything in order to employ labor, dams built where there are no rivers, injured people carrying stretchers on which they would be lying if there were not personnel shortages in the hospitals, and ministers announcing that their corruption is in the best interest of their country. This witness, "the soul of modern India," says nothing. He does not make a sound, not even a whimper, and certainly not a laugh. He sees much that is funny, but little that is amusing.

Circus Acts: *Finding Directions*

"They had no idea who I was other than some weird blond person," Goldie Hawn says of her first trip to India. "We just began to communicate and laugh. Despite the poverty, they're very happy people. I found myself laughing all through India."

Newsweek, February 14, 1983

Heeding my friend's suggestion, I walked to the Kabari bazaar on a Sunday in hopes of seeing professional buffoons and street comedians there. I planned to attend the National Circus. As I moved I felt as though I was wandering through a series of Laxman cartoons. I was the recurrent tourist, the awkward outsider. In one of his drawings, a tour guide speaks to a group of such naive visitors from abroad, gathered at the portal of an ancient temple: "So much for our rich past! As for the future we visualise in the Plan a two percent decrease in prices" (*You Said It* 3:86). So much for the rich tradition of comedy in ancient India.

On the way to the bazaar I stopped at each book and newspaper stall to inquire about India's only humor magazine *Diwana*. Each vendor laughed with surprise as they told me they didn't have any copies. Each suggested another stall which would surely carry it. As I searched fruitlessly in place after place, the elusive magazine became for me a kind of symbol of comedy in modern India—something that was surely there, something that everyone knew about, that everyone had seen, but something that could not be found when you wanted it. It was something eternally elsewhere.

As I walked along I noticed that there was, in fact, laughter in the streets—people were laughing at me. And it was laughter well deserved, for certainly I was as ridiculous as any Pantaloon, any fool or *vidūṣaka*, as I tried to make my way through the chaos of the streets, stepping out into the road only to jump back in fear of mad and rabid vehicles. I walked cloddishly in the hallowed dung of cows and the polluting feces of pigs, dogs, and human beings—shit sacred and profane. The sleeves of my proudly purchased Khadi Khurta were too short, and I surely appeared as foolish as any Indian clown in his outsized Western waistcoat. The foreigner is always a buffoon. I had been shown a Rajasthani painting of two Europeans, an old caricature of two men displaying tiny reptilian teeth through stupid and salacious grins. Touching pointed, drooping noses with chalky fingers, draping their arms around each other, they were a spectacle meant for derisive, satiric laughter. I realized that that was what I looked like. My notepad, pen, and camera were merely the zany props in my academic gag show, my burlesque imitation of a professor.

It did not seem to me that I walked into the bazaar—rather it seemed to come toward me, to open its mouth and swallow me up like some great serpent, Śeṣa himself, the thousand-headed serpent king of the infernal regions. But where did he come from? Where did the border between bazaar and nonbazaar lie? Śeṣa is called Ananta, "the Endless One."

Hawkers peddled their goods and people pushed, shoved, and reached to touch the merchandise. There were pickpockets and policemen, beggars and Sunday strollers, tourists and transvestites, fortune tellers and soldiers, food vendors and cows, junkmongers and at least one snake charmer, his serpent lying lethargic beside its basket, a microcosmic Śeṣa at home within its lord. There were no clowns or jesters, no mummers or buffoons, as my friend had promised, unless I just did not see them, or unless this whole bazaar was the hippodrome, the great comic act, a Sunday festival of fools. Perhaps the poor were just thousands of Emmett Kelly's Weary Willies, tramps to make us laugh; the soldiers and police were Keystone cops; the shoppers were shills; the cows, pigs, and mangy curs were the tigers, elephants, and trained poodles of this national circus with its myriad of overlapping rings.

My friend had said that the National Circus would be nearby, and the complementary guide to weekly events in Delhi, the little magazine nestled up to the Gideon Bible in my hotel room drawer, confirmed my faith that the circus would truly be there. I stopped to buy a plastic water bottle from a vendor of such goods, a bottle I planned to use for rum both in restaurants that served no liquor and on the train to Varanasi, a white bottle with pictures of Western-style clowns on each side. The man did not want to sell it to me. He sang the praises of a metal one, a vacuum-sealed thermos that would be more appropriate for a man of my obvious means and social stature. "Foreigners are always boiling their water," he smiled, proud of his knowledge of the ways of the world, "and this world-class thermos will be keeping your boiling water ever-hot." I was not sure, then or ever, whether I was hearing a joke. "No, I want the one with the clowns on it. And I want to go to the circus—is it nearby?"

"Connaught Circus?"

"No, the National Circus."

I walked in the direction in which his finger, sure and precise as a compass needle, pointed. I stopped to ask directions again, just to be safe, and another finger pointed, and then another, and another, and another. I followed finger after finger after finger—light fingers and dark fingers, big, fat fingers, and scrawny, little fingers, clean fingers and dirty fingers, fingers that seemed experienced with callouses and cuts, fingers that seemed wise with wrinkles and steadiness, fingers that seemed to know the world, to have touched, poked, and penetrated it. I suddenly found that I was back to where I had started, that I was standing in front of the vendor of bottles. And he had a worried look, a fear perhaps that I was back to complain about my bottle. I too had a worried look, an expression of fear that I was lost in a labyrinth, caught in the eternal meandering of Śeṣa's coils. Like my search for *Diwana*, it was a miniature version of the great runaround, the quest for the comic: "You must go to Andhra. . . . You must go to Kerala. . . . You must go to Bengal. . . . You must go to Banaras. . . . You must go back to Delhi." And that maze was, in turn, a miniature version of the still greater runaround, the endless cycle of birth and death itself.

Pointing to the clowns on my bottle, I asked a child, "Circus? National Circus?" With a giggle and an enormous smile, he led me through the labyrinth, through the morass of flesh and food, clothes and utensils, bottles and locks, religious objects and medicines, infinite things for sale, this way and that way to a sudden clearing. Grandly the boy pointed to the sign: NATIONAL CIRCUS. The boy's smile was infinitely and wonderfully proud, the look of one who knew what others did not know.

But the sign was all there was. It curved over a locked gate beyond which was nothing—a desolate lot, a fenced and forsaken field of dirt and rubble. "Was the circus here?" I asked the ubiquitous Indian loiterers. "Where is it now?" Shoulders shrugged and heads wobbled ambiguously. No one knew. No one cared. With an air of consummate authority, a coolness that suggested that everything was under control, a policeman informed me: "The circus should be here. The sign says, 'National Circus.' Therefore the National Circus should be here. It most definitely should be here." Suddenly a man appeared and grabbed the boy, my little guide, by the arm. He jerked the small limb violently, slapped the child fiercely, screamed at him, barked, snarled, and struck him again and once again. Like the boy who let his mother and father hold him down for the king to cut out his heart, the boy who laughed in the ancient legend, the child endured it, submitted to it in silence. And perhaps he too would someday laugh.

The National Circus, like *Diwana*, like modern Indian comedic forms—like God, or Truth, or Reality for that matter—was not where it was supposed to be. Maybe it once was; maybe it would be again; or maybe I had missed the point—maybe the immigration official at the Delhi airport had really been the circus doorman and the entry visa he had checked so carefully was my ticket to the real National Circus.

The fence around the empty lot contained the fragile dream of a circus—phantom elephants, ghost trapeze artists, invisible bareback riders, eidolons of mirth. The laughter of ethereal crowds had faded to the brink of silence. A painted poster remained to decay, the portrait of a clown much like those on my water bottle, a poor man's Bozo, with a bright red ball of a nose and a white-rimmed smile. In his floppy, formless, green hat and green bowtie, the clown was posed outside a great globe-shaped cage. The main bars of the cage were the lines of latitude and longitude, and within the sphere motorcyclists were racing around and around. It was a strikingly apt metaphor for the Indian conception of empirical existence, a metaphor to express the law of karma in Indian philosophy. The phenomenal world, *saṃsāra*, is a great cage in which we are trapped. Through birth after birth, death after death, we race around and around and around, up and down, this way and that way, without really going anywhere. And outside this prison of rebirth and redeath is the holy man, he who is liberated, a Buddha. And the Buddha of the poster, beholding the cage, was laughing. The liberated one was a clown, a holy fool.

A vision of the clown or joker as the holy man or saint, a man of the world but not in it, had been central to Raj Kapoor's tearful movie *Mera Naam Joker*. The clown in the film is asked his age. "The yogi and the joker," he smiles, "have no particular age." They transcend time and space just as they transcend loathing, greed, and terror. The clown in the film, like the clown on the poster and the clowns on my flask, like my hotel, like Campa-Cola, and the elusive *Diwana*, like so much else in modern India, was based on a Western model. But there are traditional Indian clowns. When I had been in India previously, not looking for comedy, but doing research on love poetry, I had seen some street players, dressed like fallen holy men, build a fire, perhaps in mockery of Vedic ritual. One squatted over the fire, pretending to be oblivious to it, until his seat was in flames. He ran around, chased by another clown with a bucket of water to put out the fire. And the scruffy crowd laughed a universal and hearty laughter. Where were they when I needed them? They were in Tamil Nadu—*komāḷīs*, wearing conical hats, bells on their feet, cowrie shells across their mouths, jumping about, lewdly dancing, singing obscenities. They were in Kerala—*bārāṅgadis* who showed up at festivals, weddings, or other such gatherings, in crazy costumes, sometimes with dead fish hanging around their necks or from their ears, to perform slapstick routines and earn a living from the coins tossed to them. They were in Maharashtra. They were in Bengal. They were in Karnataka. Or they were in the past. The unappreciative and humorless Abbé Dubois described them: "They perform obscene and ridiculous farces in the streets, with boards and trestles for their stage; or else they exhibit marionettes which they place in disgusting postures, making them give utterance to the most pitiable and filthy nonsense." With complete self-confidence, the revulsed Abbé proceeded to do what the *Los Angeles Times* correspondent had been accused of, and what I was struggling not to do. He judged the performances and drew conclusions about Indian culture based on those judgments. "These shows are exactly suited to the taste and comprehension of the stupid crowd which forms the audience. Hindu players have learned from experience that they can never rivet the attention of the public except at the expense of decency, modesty, or good sense" *(Hindu Manners, Customs, and Ceremonies).*

As I made my way from the empty lot to the Red Fort, I passed a small crowd of men, a crooked fidgeting circle of bodies around a magician, a circle that seemed to breathe and pulsate rhythmically as the bodies forming it pushed closer to see and then pushed back to give the magician more room. He held up a lime for all to see. He cut it in half with his knife. Blood oozed out of it as if from flesh, and the eyes of the circle widened with wonder if not with a trace of fear. This was not an amusing entertainment, a funny trick—it was a serious display of power, a solemn miracle over which only the magician would laugh. The magician is the manipulator of *māyā*, the conjured mirage which is this whole world. He holds Indra's net in his hand. He pulls pigeons from pans, flowers from handkerchiefs, jewels from ashes. He proves that what we imagine to be the void is, in fact, plenum.

Abhinava Rides Again: *Finding Theory*

Now the first of these topics, the essential nature of laughter, the way it is occasioned, where it is seated, and how it comes into being, and bursts out so unexpectedly that, strive as we may, we cannot restrain it, and how at the same instant it takes possession of the lungs, voice, pulse, countenance, and eyes—all this I leave to Democritus.

Cicero, *De Oratore*

I walked through the gardens of the Red Fort and into the pavilions where I tried to imagine Akbar lolling by the cool fountains of once pellucid waters, drinking opiate wine and laughing dreamily over some joke just wisely cracked by Birbal.

I looked down over the marble balustrade and gazed at the stretch of space that had once been the Yamunā. The river was not there where Akbar had watched it flow. Like the National Circus, like Akbar and Birbal, and the laughter of the court, it had vanished and only dust remained. And in that dust a trained monkey jumped up and down as its master menaced it with a stick. Another man had a bear muzzled on a leash. Yogis with matted hair, imitating the divine form of Śiva, squatted nearby, watching the animal imitate human form and gesture. The bear danced in a circle, waved its forelegs about in a learned mockery of supplication, a silent way of calling out, "*bakshish, sab, bakshish*." It stood on its hind-legs and the forelegs seemed like arms. The gesture seemed like a cry for help from a human being trapped by some wretched curse or trick within a bear's body. "Beneath the buffoon," the woman at the party had so gently said, "is a serious, sensitive soul."

As I watched the bear—the only stand-up comedian I could find in India, a buffoon more melancholy than any Pierrot—a small man dressed in a Sunday suit, sporting a wide tie much like that worn by the clowns on my water bottle, appeared from out of the crowd, a manifestation of Laxman's common man, an avatar of some comic Gaṇa. This man whose curse it was to seem like every other man, this incarnation of the crowd itself, sidled up to me and posed the eternal question, the basically friendly but ultimately annoying query that all foreign visitors must endure many times each day: "You are from vhich countṛy?"

"America."

"Excelleṇṭ place! Vhaṭ a happy coincidence for all concerned! You are a ṭourisṭ and every ṭourisṭ is neediṅg a hoṭel. I am verkiṅg for a five sṭarr hoṭel! You vill mosṭ cerṭainly be comiṅg ṭo my hoṭel! Iṭ is a mosṭ excelleṇṭ place!"

I curtly explained that I had accommodations, that I was not exactly a tourist, that I was in India doing research for a book on Indian comedy.

"Ph.D. thesis?"

"No," I insisted without the grace of self-irony, "a book."

"You are a sṭudeṇṭ aṭ vhich universiṭy?"

Lacking the spontaneous good humor to lie, to simply tell him what he surely wanted to hear, that I was president of Harvard University, I told him the truth which, like many truths, was neither humorous nor impressive. After insisting that the University of Hawaii was not in America, he proceeded to enthusiastically delineate the details of his own *curriculum vitae,* garnished with references to various degrees, honors, and awards earned by sundry members of his family, a clan ornamented by a host of "V.I.P.'s" and even a few "V.V.I.P.'s." He questioned me about my family, trying to determine, I suppose, if there were any V.I.P.'s, V.V.I.P.'s, or V.V.V.I.P.'s in the Siegel-*kula.* Despite the fact that we were, alas, just a bunch of P.'s, he cheerfully followed me as I turned away from the marble balcony. He ignored my farewell. "I can help you," he announced happily. "You are an imporṭaṇṭ man, a great scholarr. I am only verkiṅg aṭ a five sṭarr hoṭel. You are haviṅg the knowledge of the books. I am only haviṅg the knowledge of life. I vill ṭell you everythiṅg abouṭ the humorr based on my humble knowledge, but iṭ vill be your duṭy, usiṅg the knowledge you have gleaned from me, ṭo ṭesṭ the hypothesis. Lisṭen ṭo vhaṭ I am ṭelliṅg you. If you are doiṅg your verk mosṭ scieṇṭifically, you vill cerṭainly be geṭṭing the Ph.D. Buṭ you musṭ be knowiṅg vone thiṅg above all else: Vhaṭ is ṛdiculous ṭo vone man, is noṭ ṛdiculous ṭo anotherr. For example, you vere laughiṅg aṭ the sighṭ of the bearr."

"No, I wasn't laughing at it," I snapped crankily after a hard day of looking for laughs in Delhi, "and neither was anyone else."

"Exacṭly!" he smiled as he directed me, pointing to where he wanted me to walk. "These people ver noṭ laughiṅg because in Indiā a dancịng bearr is a mosṭ common sighṭ. Iṭ is noṭ ṛdiculous. You vere laughiṅg because in Americā iṭ is noṭ a common sighṭ and iṭ is, therefore, ṛdiculous. Leṭ us ṭake another example of the aforementioned hypothesis. In Indiā ve are noṭ laughiṅg vhen ve are seeiṅg the ladies in their saris. But in Americā you are always laughiṅg ṭo see such a sighṭ."

"We don't laugh at women in saris in America," I insisted. I was thoroughly grumpy, my rib ached, and I was confused about what I was doing, unsure at that point whether there was any humor left in either India or myself.

"Exacṭly!" he said solicitously, continuing to direct where I had to go and what I had to see within the Red Fort. "And the obverse is ṭrue. I read in the *Reader's Digesṭ* thaṭ a man in Americā boughṭ a car and iṭ ṭurned out ṭo be a lemon. In Americā this vas ṭaken seriously. Buṭ in Indiā, iṭ is laughable. Ve vould think iṭ quiṭe ṛdiculous ṭo pay ṭen thousand dollars for a piece of fruiṭ. Once again iṭ is proven: vhaṭ is ṛdiculous ṭo vone man, is noṭ ṛdiculous ṭo anotherr. Buṭ iṭ is noṭ thaṭ simple. Vhaṭ is? There are, most scienṭifically speakiṅg, three kinds of humorr. There is the humorr thaṭ is primary—the child is laughiṅg aṭ the ṭoy. There is the humorr thaṭ is secondary—the parenṭ is laughiṅg aṭ the child laughiṅg aṭ the ṭoy. Now you are knowiṅg the humorr thaṭ is primary and the humorr thaṭ is secondary. Vhaṭ is the humorr thaṭ is the third form?"

Marveling at the way in which the spirit of aesthetic classification in Sanskrit rhetoric persisted in this little man, I confessed that I did not know. "Exacṭly! No vone is knowiṅg thaṭ! Thaṭ is beyond science! Thaṭ ve cannoṭ be askiṅg. Thaṭ vould be goiṅg ṭoo deep for morṭal man!"

As we walked through the Hayat Baksh Bagh, the "garden bestowing life," walked where perhaps Tansen and Surdās may have strolled amidst crimson, saffron, and purple blossoms, discussing poetry, music, and philosophy, we surely must have been a comic spectacle: a short, plump Indian, dressed in a Western suit that was pressed to a shine, lecturing a foreigner, too lanky for his rumpled khurta, carrying a water bottle with clowns on it. We might have passed for a cross-cultural version of Abbott and Costello. And I wasn't sure which one of us was Bud and which was Lou.

On and on and on and on he rambled, pontificated, and gushed explanations. "There are, furthermore, three kinds of laughṭerrs. There is the laughṭerr in the mouth, throaṭ, and nose. There is the laughterr in the chest and lungs. There is the laughṭerr in the stomach and bovels. Some vould add a forth—laughṭerr in the enṭire body—buṭ this is nothing more than a combination of numbers vone through three." I tried my best to refrain from grabbing him by the throat and shouting, "Shut up and leave me alone!" I could not be so rude, however—by that time he had, after all, invited me to come and live in his home with his family. "Don'ṭ vorry, the cook will noṭ be puttiṅg ṭoo many spices in your meals." He looked at me almost lovingly. "Iṭ is so excellenṭ thaṭ karma has broughṭ us ṭogetherr like this! Isn'ṭ iṭ?" Since I could devise no way to escape from him gracefully, I was hoping that karma was going to take us apart. "The imporṭanṭ thiṅg ṭo rememberr is thaṭ vhaṭ is ṛdiculous ṭo vone man is noṭ ṛdiculous ṭo anotherr. For example, in Americā you are having uṭiliṭy; in India ve are haviṅg fuṭiliṭy!"

I thought it would be polite to laugh, but it made him wince uncomfortably, look at me anxiously and with a fear, I suppose, that he had made a fool of himself. I tried to reassure him that I was not laughing at him, but at his joke, his play on the sound of the words. He smiled tentatively as he reiterated the *śloka* several times more, his confidence picking up momentum with each round. Then he offered paraphrastic commentary, a *chāya* worthy of any ancient pandit. Through a deft, though somewhat abstruse, manipulation of logic, he concluded that while Americans are rich and Indians are poor, Indians are spiritually advanced while Americans are wholly materialistic. This explained national differences in humor.

As we passed through the arcade of shops, the corridors where vendors of curios have replaced armed Moghul guards, I became increasingly nervous and worried as to how I was going to get rid of this irksomely chipper philosopher. But as we emerged from the fort, his philosophical discourse suddenly ended. He extended his hand abruptly, lowered his eyes, rolled his head slightly. I could not tell whether he was smiling or frowning. "Here you vill be geṭṭiṅg a ṭaxi; here I vill be geṭṭiṅg a bus. Good luck on your Ph.D. Remember all vhaṭ I have been teachiṅg you. You are my friend always." We shook hands and he vanished into the clamorous throng, absorbed by the mass of dusty bodies squeezing into the overburdened passageways of Old Delhi. His moment as a *penseur*, a pandit, a V.I.P., was over. "Vhaṭ is ṛdiculous ṭo vone man, is noṭ ṛdiculous ṭo anotherr"—I sensed that his motto was more than a cliché meant to reveal the mysteries of comedy to me. It seemed a request that I not judge him and that I not judge India.

Perhaps the words offered him some solace, if not a justification for his life and for the absurdity of all life.

Through the dust, smoke, haze, and diffused gloom of dusk, the setting sun seemed more immense and more violently red than ever. The minaret of the Jama Masjid was a solemn silhouette.

It was a "dry day" in Delhi, but I knew of a restaurant that served beer in teapots on such days. "More tea?" the waiter winked and smiled. The persistent pain in my ribs registered on my face, and the waiter asked what was wrong. "Oh," he responded to my explanation. "You need a different kind of tea in that case. A medicinal tea!" He brought me a teapot of what passes in India under other circumstances for brandy.

Happily drunk, I made my way to the theater to see a puppet play, a comic permutation of the "Goose That Laid the Golden Egg." The goose was a cow and the eggs were gold turds, the "laying" of which incited wonderfully naughty laughter from the gathered children. Cow shit is apparently funny even in a country that uses it and worships it. Cows themselves, however, are not so funny. "Are cows sacred in India," I jokingly asked someone, "because they say *OṂ* backwards?" I suppose that if he would have understood the joke he would not have answered, "No. The cow is sacred because she is the mother. She is all the pilgrimage places in India. She is all the gods at once." It occurred to me that if this intelligent man could not tell that I was joking, it might well be that I would not be able to tell if he were joking, if his answer had been a witty rejoinder. Perhaps I had, unknowingly, been hearing jokes every day.

In order to get the invitation to the puppet show I had gone to the academy sponsoring the event. An administrator at the cultural institute, after questioning me about my work, soberly asserted that there was little comedy in India. "Of course there is the vulgar humor of the streets, the lower-class jokes of the cinema, the crass stupidity and infantile humor of comic books, cartoons, and television. But all of these things are foreign. They have come to India with industrialization, modernization, and Westernization. The young people want comedies just as they want transistor radios and calculator machines. There has never been any humor in India. India is traditionally a spiritual nation."

Assuming that he was not joking, I insisted that I had found an abundance of satire and humor in Sanskrit literature, and that my scholarly goal was to bring it to light, to make it known, to let it be appreciated. He shook his head. "Of course there is the gentle smile of Kālidās, the subtle wit of the *Pañcatantram*, the sublime playfulness of Lord Kṛṣṇa. But this is not comedy. Sanskrit is a lofty language, too lofty to accommodate such a trivial thing as a joke. Sanskrit is not a funny language."

I tried to tell him about the wild farces and hilarious monologue plays, about Kṣemendra and Dāmodaragupta, about the raunchy wit and magnificent vulgarity of which Sanskrit was capable, but he refused to hear what seemed to him like an insinuating slur against a glorious culture. "Of course it is true that there is always laughter among the lower classes. And it is true that one can joke in the lower languages. But not in Sanskrit. That is why the *vidūṣak* speaks Prakrit—how could he amuse us in Sanskrit, the perfect language, the sacred language, the language spoken by the gods, the language from which all other languages have descended? It is only the lower types who are interested in comedy, who spend their time making jokes. Did Buddha go around laughing? Did Śankarācārya make jokes on his Tour of Victory? Did Jesus laugh? No. Who was always laughing? Nero and Joseph Stalin! Aristotle says that comedy is an inferior thing for inferior minds and such other sages as Rāmānuja and Abhinavagupta concur." He gave me the tickets to the puppet play. "Of course, there will be humor in the play, but this is because it is for children, and people who are not so well educated, or for people who have been influenced by the West. This is popular theater. It is not art, not *sāhitya*."

Another administrator told me the exact opposite of what his colleague had said: "The greatest comedies of all have been written in Sanskrit. The *Mṛcchakaṭikā* is the most humorous of plays. With such profound psychological insight the ancient playwright creates humorous situation after humorous situation. I always have a good laugh at the part when the gambler runs away from his creditors and hides in the temple." He laughed quite genuinely as he recreated the scene for me. "There are more comedies in Sanskrit than in any other language, though most have not been preserved. It is not only our great literature that has this humorous element. All the arts in ancient India were used to express the comic *ras*. It can be found in the music, in the painting, everywhere."

I inquired about comedy in the visual arts, and he excitedly told me about a friend who possessed a large collection of ancient cartoons. He assured me that if I used his name I would be shown the works. I telephoned the man and he graciously invited me to his home. We sat over tea. "I am sorry, but I don't have a collection of ancient cartoons. Nor do I know of any such pictures." But to fill the awkward silence and make the best of the situation, he explained Indian comedy to me just as he would have explained the law of karma in Indian philosophy had I heeded the bank manager's advice to study that subject instead. "There is humor in India, in the people. But there is no place for it to exist in the society. We have personal humor, but no outlets for it. In ancient times it existed in the temple and the court. Then in medieval India it existed in the temple, the court, and the red-light district. But where can it exist now? Some years ago, if you went to a wedding, all the women, the relatives of the bride, would shout obscenities at the family of the groom. It was good-natured. They would make dirty jokes and everyone would laugh. There was so much joking and playing around then. But now there is nothing of the sort. India is a puritanical country. That is why people don't show their innate humor. They are ashamed of it just as they are ashamed of sex and the consumption of alcoholic beverages. The people who do it don't talk about it. Forty years ago it was a common thing to see someone carrying a box and in the box there was a piece of wood shaped like the genital of a man. There was a string and if you pulled it the genital would stand straight up in the air! Everyone would laugh if you pulled that string. This was a common object; every carpenter was selling them. But I haven't seen one for many, many years. Now everyone would pretend to blush at the sight. They would try not to laugh. They would appear scornful. India is a hypocritical country. Still, I myself am a free man—you see I can tell you about such things even in the presence of my daughter. I don't believe in hiding anything. I want her to know everything."

The daughter, sitting rather formally in silence, seemed bored by her father's speech. When he left the room, she explained that actually Indian humor had flourished and that people had been happy and mirthful until the suppression of that comic spirit by capitalist imperialism. She was working on her master's degree at Jawaharlal Nehru University, a study of "The Oppression of the American Negro."

Her father returned. "India is not a poor country as you may have imagined. It is a rich country. The problem is that because so many people are using all the riches, India seems like a poor country. All of our problems have to do with overpopulation. Because of overpopulation there is competition. Everyone is trying to beat everyone else out of something. So how can there be humor? If you make a joke, if you show humor, if you laugh, you are showing weakness, or you are showing you don't care, or you are showing that you are like everyone else. When you laugh, you let down your guard and then people can take advantage of you. So you see, you cannot have humor without birth control.'' He stared at me intently, seriously, quizzically, almost fiercely for a protracted moment of silence, and then he suddenly laughed.

I kept thinking about the man's daughter. How could she write anything about American black culture that had any bearing on reality, that was not completely superficial, trivial, naive, and meaningless? Imagining her arriving at Kennedy airport in her sari, explaining to a black immigration official that she had come on a grant from the Indian Institute of American Studies to write a book about his oppression, I felt lost and utterly confused about what I was doing in India.

Mad Laughter: *Finding Out*

One gets absolutely no sense from his text [this epilogue] that there are flourishing traditions in, for example, Marathi and Bengali, or highly humorous traditions of public poetry readings. Not to speak of ongoing traditions of humorous riddling, joke telling, narration of humorous tales, etc. The way he went about his search for humor in modern India was fundamentally flawed, as it took place through the medium of English exclusively, dealt heavily with the printed word (in English) and with chance street and cocktail-party kinds of encounters instead of the complex web of family and community relationships and institutions, within which humor both public and private certainly flourish today.

Anonymous reader's report on *Laughing Matters*

I had given up hope of finding any copies of *Diwana* when, going by taxi to Shankar's Doll Museum in search of Shankar Pillai, India's most venerable cartoonist, I happened to notice a sign on a nearby building: *DIWANA*. Like comedy itself, when I looked for it I couldn't find it, and yet when I stopped looking, when I least expected it, it was there. But since I had also seen the sign for the National Circus, I entered the office somewhat skeptically. I learned why I had not been able to find any copies of *Diwana* at the newstands: ''We had to close down just as Shankar had to stop publishing his *Weekly*. There's no money in humor. People don't take it seriously. Business won't advertise in a humor magazine because they think people will mistake the ad for a joke. Besides, the government controls the media, and the government has no sense of humor. The government is the joke. You can sneak a joke or two past the censor, but not a whole magazine full of them. There was a little humor before the Emergency and a growing interest in it. But the Emergency killed it. We all move more cautiously now.'' I was reminded of a cartoon by Abu Abraham that the censor had refused to pass (fig. 31).

The editor showed me a special satirical supplement to the *Weekly Sun* (6:22 [1983]), a spoof of the New Delhi International ''Fillum Pestival,'' carrying an apologetic explanation: ''This is a parody, satire, lampoon, pasquinade, squib, meant only as a joke, jest, revel, lark, for the fun of it, not to be taken seriously, with no malice or spite intended.'' And further down the cover, mocking the cautionary warning on cigarette packets, there was a box: ''Laughter is *not* injurious to health.''

Figure 31

"You see," the editor said with wry resignation, "we have to print this sort of explanation on anything that is supposed to be funny or people will take it seriously. That kills half the humor right there. People don't know when you are joking. Jokes are taken as insults. In America you make friends by telling jokes; in India you make enemies. There are, for example, people who want to kill me for printing this." He held up a parody of the poster for the film *Gandhi* which was playing in Delhi at the time (fig. 32).

We talked about the film. I wondered whether or not Gandhi had a sense of humor. A lot of Indians seem to believe he did. "He met Charlie Chaplin in London," I was told as if that were proof of something. I had heard that when asked what he thought of Western civilization, he had answered, "I think it would be a good

A 20-YEAR DREAM COME TRUE!
Boloneya Pictures
takes great pride in announcing
THE WORLD PREMIERE OF
MANOJ KUMAR'S FILM
CHURCHILL
with an Unknown Indian
NIRAD CHAUDHURI
as Winston Leonard Spencer Churchill
Difficult to believe Nirad Chaudhuri is not an Englishman
. . Deserves an Oscar' –Times
'A dazzling left-handed tribute in reverse
to Britain from India' –Guardian
TO REMIND A FORGETFUL WORLD A GREAT
FIGURE WHO RESOLUTELY STOOD FOR EMPIRE
"I have not become the King's First Minister to preside
over the liquidation of the British Empire."

Figure 32

idea.'' A tribute printed in *Shankar's Weekly* in October of 1949 stressed that ''Gandhiji knew how to laugh. He laughed at everyone. He laughed in Noahkali, he laughed in Calcutta. . . . He could laugh when he began one of his fasts and again when, breaking it, he observed the officious and solemn ceremonialists who surrounded him. . . . Gandhiji would laugh because the individual was essentially ludicrous in his understanding of collective man. . . . [He was] a man of supreme humor, one who laughed and liked laughing not because man is small but because men never know how small they are.''

In the novelized version of *Mera Naam Joker*, Rajoo the clown studies a poster of Gandhi: ''A small, thin, darkish man. Very big ears. Small eyes peering through round glasses of steel-rimmed spectacles. A loincloth, and bare above the waist. . . . Looked like a joker. In the picture there was a child too, who was dragging the Mahatma by catching hold of his bamboo staff. The child and the Mahatma were both laughing, making each other laugh. So Gandhiji, too, was a 'joker!' ''

I looked at the cover of a copy of the Hindi version of *Diwana*—there was Rāvaṇa, the ten-headed demon-lord of Laṅkā, and each one of those heads was that of someone familiar—it was the face of *Mad Magazine*'s Alfred E. Newmann. Most of the comedy in *Diwana* was social satire, using parody of Indian films particularly to poke fun at politics and occasionally at religion. In a lampoon of the Indian version of the film *Zorro*, the hero holds a dagger with a Z-shaped handle to his forehead and takes an oath: ''I'm Zero! I'm Zero! I swear by the Z-sign that I will bring Zocialism to India!'' (36 [May-June 1975]). There was an impish, naughty wit at work in the parody of the film *Siddhartha*, a mockery of Western understandings of Indian spirituality: ''*Shitdhartha* . . . a tangled yarn of Hermann Messe . . . the screwed up story of a brahmin boy's search for the meaning of life'' (35 [April 1975]). At one point Shitdhartha crosses a river with a mystic ferry man, a holy sage who offers the young aspirant a revelation: ''Some day you will come back . . . everything comes back. Everything!'' Contemplating the eternal return to the source, Shitdhartha answers: ''Alas! you have not seen the toothpaste tube. The paste does not return to the tube.''

A mock movie review simultaneously laughed at Indian films and Indian mythology. The film was *Hari Darshan*. ''If you are the type who goes in for the westernized glamour and dishoom type fights then this movie is not for you. But if you are on an intellectually higher level, see it. . . . The movie begins by showing the different avatars of God Vishnu and the reason for His assuming them. The photography is wonderful. They even show underwater shots of Lord Vishnu as a turtle and of demons flying. And how they managed to photograph Prahlad in the middle of a blazing fire is a mystery but a really superb mystery. As a layman I didn't understand it but I sure appreciated it. Based entirely on Hindu mythology the movie is a tribute to the religious minded producer. . . . It's a movie that must be seen by all (especially in this Kaliyug) if not for its technical superiority then at least for the lesson it teaches one and all. After the movie one comes out with a feeling of admiration, reverence and great inner peace'' (29 [October 1974]).

Diwana folded. The comic vision and voice were there but the society seems to have lacked the particular aesthetic norms and conventions necessary for the voice to be heard or appreciated. ''The curse of India,'' Shankar Pillai said, ''is its lack of humour.''

In the first issue of *Shankar's Weekly*, the only humor magazine to ever enjoy any success in India, there was a drawing of India personified as a distraught woman surrounded by screaming, bickering children (fig. 33). At her side a puckish Shankar was trying to give laughter's sweet solace. ''*Shankar's Weekly* makes its appearance [in May of 1948] with a modest claim: it will help you laugh. Other peoples of the earth have been laughing heartily, even in the midst of their struggles, but we seem to be a nation in perpetual mourning. . . . Ours is a humourless generation, a procession of colourless puppets. Years ago it seems, we lost our gift of laughter and gained an unhealthy seriousness. At best we simper and grin, yawn or giggle; we seem to think it is vulgar to laugh and we never laugh at ourselves. . . . We must laugh or we must die. . . . We have become a nation ashamed to laugh and afraid of laughing.'' The theme of India's lack of humor provided a recurrent refrain in Shankar's publication. But, like Kushwant Singh's jolly denial of the existence of the comic in India, *Shankar's Weekly* simultaneously provided evidence for both the presence and the absence of Indian humor. In an early issue of the *Weekly* there was a letter to Shankar written by Jove from his throne on Olympus: ''India was fashioned by my powers to be a country without humour. Hence all the high philosophy and eternal Nirvana. . . . India was never assigned for laughter. It was assigned just three yajnic tasks: (a) sacrificial poverty, (b) self-mortifying squalor, and (c) Nirvanic yawns'' (February 4, 1951).

Figure 33

Shankar was a close friend of Nehru's, and the prime minister seems to have accepted, even indulged and encouraged, the cartoonist's satirical criticism. "I gladly pay tribute to Shankar," Nehru wrote, "and I hope that he will long continue to enlighten us and amuse us and pull us down a peg or two" (reprinted in *Shankar's Weekly Souvenir*). Though he satirized the head of state, just as Birbal and Tenāli Rāma had supposedly made fun of Akbar and Kṛṣṇadevarāya, respectively, his cartoons were taken not as an assault upon the leader, but rather as an attempt to amuse the leader and his followers.

"There is humor in India," Sudhir Dar, an Indian cartoonist whose work has appeared in the American *Mad Magazine*, said over lunch, "but it's hard to find because it doesn't get published, produced, or distributed. Humor just doesn't pay. The publishers won't subsidize comic writing. The television people are not willing to encourage the art, to pay talented writers to develop comedy. Comedy is a gamble. Why should film producers take that gamble when melodramas pay off so well?'' Our talk was interrupted by the sudden appearance of a friend of his to whom I was introduced, once again, as ''the man writing the book about Indian humor.'' The woman laughed—''Well, you're having lunch with one of the only people in India with a sense of humor.''

After lunch I went to a movie that I had been told had ''a great deal of humor.'' But, as in most Indian films, the humor was there only for comic relief from the ponderous melodrama, the ''dishoom type fight scenes,'' the manic songs and dances, the kittenish attempts to get sex past the censor. The comic element in Indian films is conventional—a hero, pitted against some villain, and in love with some maiden, will often have a thick and blundering friend, a cowardly and yet sweet sidekick, to draw a few laughs from the rapt audience. He is the cinematic descendent of the *vidūṣaka*.

Toward the end of the film, protected by the darkness, the boy in front of me, awkwardly lackadaisical, put his arm around the girl next to him. Slowly, ever so slowly, her head tilted toward his shoulder. It almost touched. The film ended with a song, and the girl followed the boy out of the theater. She could not be expected, by the rules of social propriety, to laugh on the street any more than she could be expected to walk arm in arm with her boyfriend in a public display of inner desire or delight. Laughter, like love, is kept in the dark. It is there, but it is hidden.

The next evening at a dinner party I saw the man who had recommended the film. ''I thought you said it was funny!''

''Didn't you think the older brother was funny?'' my Indian colleague smiled as he answered for me. ''No, I suppose you didn't. Indians and Americans expect different things from a film. I remember seeing that movie with Sophia Loren and Peter Sellars in which Sellars is supposed to be an Indian doctor. I imagine that in America everyone thought that Sellars's Indian accent was quite amusing. No one laughed at it here in Delhi. But they roared with laughter when he tried to say a few words in Hindi. Of course, everybody here liked Sophia Loren. She's built like Hema Malini. Sex is more easy to translate than humor. There is a new Hindi film coming out that I hear is very, very funny. It's about a talking car. It was inspired by your own *Herbie the Volkswagen* movies.''

''I hope I don't miss it,'' I said, trying to tease him in the way I assumed he was teasing me. ''I'm leaving for Varanasi in two days, and I would not want to forsake the opportunity of hearing a car speak Hindi just to witness the marriage rites of Lord Śiva by the banks of the Ganges."

"Don't worry," he laughed. "Don't worry about missing anything by going to Varanasi. Everything is in Varanasi. If people can find God and Truth there, surely you can find humor there. And be sure to have a bath in the Ganga. And drink some of her waters. No need to boil it! Don't worry about getting sick. In fact, if you do get sick, really sick, and happen to die, so much the better for you—he who dies in Varanasi goes straight to heaven! Did you hear the joke about the man who died in Varanasi? Before Yama led him to heaven, the man asked if he could visit hell. Yama consented to take the man on a tour of the place. Hell didn't seem so bad—people were joking and laughing and having a jolly time of it. Then Yama took the man to heaven and, in contrast to hell, it seemed a rather dull place—beautiful and peaceful but not much fun. No one in heaven joked or laughed. So the man asked Yama if he could return to hell and reside there instead of in heaven. Yama agreed to it and the man was thrown into hell. This time there was no joking. There was no laughter. Demons tortured the man with red-hot pokers. They put him on a spit over a blazing fire. The man cried out to Yama, 'What happened? Hell seemed like such a nice place before. Everyone was laughing. What happened?' Yama laughed: 'That was because you were on a tourist visa. Now you're a resident!' "

The man laughed robustly and I joined in nervously, unsure of what the joke was meant to say to me. Something about the nature of the perceptions of nonresidents in India? Something about the nature of comedy and laughter? Or nothing at all? He laughed again. "Good joke, good Indian joke, isn't it?"

Bright and Gay: *Finding the Guru*

Were I on Indian soil,
  Soon as the burning day was closed,
I could mock the sultry toil. . . .
    John Gay, *The Beggar's Opera*

When I had gone to the railway station to purchase my ticket to Varanasi, I had found several joke books by Jagat S. Bright for sale there as well as a slew of "How-to-do-it" books by the same author, guides for those wanting to learn how to play cricket, write business letters, read palms, practice yoga, give public speeches, improve memory, live long, and kiss ("controversies regarding kissing and more than 101 ways of kissing explained"). Though I only know how to do two of those things with reasonable ease, I bought only the joke books and the author's *Dictionary of Indian Quotations* in which I immediately looked up "Humour." The sought-after entry, appearing between "Humility" and "Hunger," was a quotation from Rabindranath Tagore: "Humorists have a knack of making themselves felt even in the dark."

One of the joke books ("jokes to jilt your jaws and tilt your balance with rip-roarious laughter") contained an obviously foreign limerick that seemed particularly peculiar in a book compiled by an Indian for Indian readers:

> The poor benighted Hindoo,
> He does the best he kin do;
> He sticks to his caste
> From first to last,
> And for clothes he makes his skin do.

In the telephone directory I found a "Jagat S. Bright" listed in Rajouri Gardens. I asked him about the jokes he had collected and written. "Do readers laugh at themselves, laugh at the 'poor benighted Hindoo,' when they read that limerick, or do they laugh at the English, at the way foreigners view Indians?"

"I don't know, I really don't know," Jagat S. Bright laughed. "I just don't know. I've written so many books—over seven hundred I think—and lately I haven't done any joke books. I hardly remember those books, you know. Lately I've been thinking about other things. I have been wondering: What is the meaning of this life? Why is a man born? Why does he die?"

The tiny, turbaned man with wisps of whiskers, crooked teeth, and eyes filled with delight, laughed as he spoke, laughed even as he said the things most serious to him. "Everyday I pray to *all* the gods to remove *all* the sorrows of *all* the people for *all* times."

He was more enthusiastic about my project than anyone else had been. But then, he was enthusiastic about everything. "To study comedy is to study life," he reflected. "Life is a comedy, you know. And to study humor is to study how to live life. Humor is not a thing, but a way of knowing things. It is a spirit in the heart of a man. Humor is not what a man says or does. It is a gesture of his hand, the look in his eyes, the way he walks down the street, even the way he curls up for sleep. It's very mysterious, you know. If a man has humor, then everything is funny. But for the man without humor, nothing is funny. The man whose heart is filled with humor is the perfect man. What else can the perfect man do but joke and laugh? He looks at the newspaper and laughs, looks at the people in the street running around and around, and he laughs. He looks at his family and he laughs out of love. He looks at himself in the mirror and he laughs then too. That is how a man ought to live, like Kṛṣṇa, always laughing, always joking, like all the gods. The gods are comedians, you know. Think of the tricks they play on us. Whenever I wait for the number 58 bus, the 59 always comes along. It never fails. If I decide to wait for the number 59, the 58 is sure to come. It is the same with everything in life, not just buses, but everything—I could be waiting for money, for a friend, even for death, for anything. Life is a comedy, a series of jokes, you know. And the gods are laughing at these jokes all the time. The Veda says this. William Shakespeare says this. John Gay says it. I think I put this quotation in one of my books—on John Gay's tombstone there is a joke:

> Life is a jest and all things show it;
> I thought it once, but now I know it!

The frail little man, sweetly laughing, seemed to rise in his seat, transported by the thrill of philosophy, uplifted by the delight of his revery. "I have not read any books by John Gay, you know, only what he wrote in the *Oxford Book of Quotations*. I don't need to read his books. I know what they would say. He is one of my favorite authors. I like his name; it is like my name. A man should always be like us—Bright and Gay! And I like the name of his book, *The Beggar's Opera*. It is a comedy, you know. Life is comic opera and everyone in it is a beggar: the prime minister is a beggar for votes; the business man is a beggar for money; the priest is a beggar for god; the lover is a beggar for the beloved; the film star is a beggar for fame; the scholar is a beggar for knowledge; the newborn baby is a beggar for his mother's milk; and the dying old man is a beggar for heaven. And, of course, the beggars are beggars. And you and I are beggars too. Life is a beggar's comic opera because everything within it is relative. Everyone is a beggar in respect to someone or something else. Only the Absolute is not a beggar. How can it be? Nothing is beyond it, you know. What can it beg for? It is perfect. The Absolute laughs at the relative, laughs at everything and everyone. How can it be otherwise? And that is why the perfect man laughs at everything—he is one with the Absolute. He is the man of perfect brightness and perfect gaiety. The perfection is what Buddha called nirvana. The enlightened man is always laughing because the spirit of lightness is in his heart. That spirit is humor, you know. He knows the meaning of life and he knows why a man is born and why he dies. He knows all of these things and what does he do? He laughs! That is why I am sure that your study of comedy and humor will lead you to nirvana."

I laughed with surprise at the sudden discursive turn from life and the gods to me and my little project. I protested adamantly, assuring Mr. Bright that I was not in the least interested in what Shankar had called "nirvanic yawns," that my goal was not in any way to become enlightened, but just to become aware of what was considered funny in India. "All I want is to gather some data for a scholarly book about comedy. Well, there is one other thing I want—I want to have a cigarette. Do you mind if I smoke? Do you have an ashtray?"

"The attainment of an ashtray may be much more difficult than the attainment of nirvana. An ashtray, you see, may be found nowhere in my house; nirvana, on the other hand, may be found at any time in any place." He rose to search for an ashtray for me. As none could be discovered, he suggested that I move my chair outside the door, and "the world can be your ashtray." He moved his own chair up to the door and then, with him sitting in the house and me sitting outside of it, he continued to speak as I smoked.

"There was a prince named Siddhartha and he lived in a great palace, surrounded by every luxury. One day he went out of the palace for a ride and he saw an old man on the road. He became very depressed because he had never seen old age before. The next day he went for another ride and he saw a sick person and he became more depressed. The next day he saw a dead man. He was very upset, so confused and distressed. Once he became aware of old age and disease and death, he could not find happiness in the palace. He lost his sense of humor, you know. He decided to renounce every luxury and to leave the palace, to go into the forest. He wanted to understand why a man is born and why he dies and what his life means. He wanted to know why there is so much sorrow in the world."

His monologue was punctuated by my attempts to butt in. Each time I tried to tell Mr. Bright that I was familiar with the story of the Buddha, he countered my intrusion into the legend: he ignored it with an increase in the volume and velocity of his speech; or he dismissed it with a little chuckle; or he deflected it with the words, "And now for the best part of the story." I had to yield to the Buddha, to smoke another cigarette, and another, and another, as the young mendicant talked to holy men in the forest, performed penances, and resolved to sit beneath the Bodhi tree until he understood. I ran out of cigarettes just as Māra dispatched his daughters to seduce Siddhartha and his sons to terrify him.

Mr. Bright stood up, beaming, holding his hands in the air majestically. "And then do you know what happened?"

"Yes!" I began, seizing the opportunity to join in. "He . . ."

"Wait," the little man stopped me. He sat down, looked straight into my eyes, and smiled. "This is the best part of the story. He felt neither fear nor desire. What a moment! He had become Buddha, you know!"

I rejoiced in the enlightenment of the Buddha—that is, I was relieved that the long and familiar story had come to an end. I stood up. "Is there any place nearby where I could buy some cigarettes?"

"Wait," he smiled. "Sit down. This is the best part of all. Now I shall explain how your study of humor will lead to nirvana." I knew it would be quite a while until my next smoke.

"You come from America. It is like a big palace with every luxury. But for some reasons you left that palace to go on a search. I don't know why. Maybe you heard some jokes, and you asked yourself why you laughed, why certain things are funny. You wanted to find out what laughter is, what humor is, and what comedy is. Just as Buddha talked to the holy men and philosophers, you are asking people who seem to have a sense of humor, and people like myself who have written joke books, to tell you about comedy. You listen to jokes; you try to tell jokes yourself; you laugh; but still you do not understand what humor is. And so you keep looking for the answer. Just like Buddha! Even if you don't think you are looking for nirvana, even if you don't want enlightenment, your search is leading you there. It cannot be otherwise, you know. Buddha himself said it—happiness and unhappiness, pleasure and pain, are just two sides of the same coin. Opposite paths lead to the same place. The search to find out why life is a comedy must lead to the same place as the search to find out why life is a tragedy."

I was extremely embarrassed by his words and once again I protested. "I'm not trying to find out why life is a comedy. I'm just looking for information for a scholarly book on the forms and functions of comedy in India. That's all. Really."

He laughed. "But the form and function of comedy is the nature of comedy, and the nature of comedy is the nature of life. What is a scholarly book? A book that is superficial? A book that has nothing to do with life? A book that has footnotes? Trees must not be killed to make the paper for such a book. A scholarly book, if it is a good one, can be about important things, you know. Try to write about important things. And promise me, please, that you will put no footnotes in your book. I don't like footnotes."

I promised.

"And promise me one other thing," he smiled. "When you go to Banaras tomorrow, be sure to make a sidetrip to Sarnath. It is not far away. That is the place where Buddha explained the meaning of suffering. In that place you will understand the meaning of laughter." Jagat S. Bright laughed as he said it, and the laughter lingered in his eyes. I was absolutely sure that he had said all of this just to console me, to assure me that my research was not insignificant. I am convinced that if I would have contacted him because I was working on a book about cricket, business letters, palmistry, yoga, public speaking, memory, or kissing, any of the hundreds of things he had written about, he would surely have been able to explain how my research on any of those topics would lead to Buddhahood.

He walked me to the bus stop where I waited for the number 59 to take me back to Connaught Circus. Of course the number 58 came first.

On the bus, thinking over all that Jagat S. Bright had said, I could not help but remember a joke I had heard before leaving for India. There was an American who wanted to know, "What is the meaning of this life, and why is a man born, and why does he die?" He left America and went to India in search of a teacher, a guru who could answer such ultimate questions. He heard of a man who was said to be the most wise and holy teacher in India, a guru to gurus who lived in a cave high upon a Himalayan peak. The American climbed the mountain. Nothing could keep him from his goal. After years of searching he was finally there. And just as I had sat outside the door of Jagat S. Bright's house in Rajouri Gardens, my compatriot sat outside the cave of the guru. He bowed in obeisance.

"Please, O greatest of gurus, O knower of truth, tell me, what is the meaning of existence? What is life all about?" From within the cave, the guru, breaking a vow of silent meditation, spoke for the first time in many years. "Life," he said, "is a fountain." The American wanted more. "I don't mean figuratively. I mean *really*. I do not want parables or metaphors. I want the Truth. Please tell me, what is *really* the meaning of life?" The guru poked his head out of the cave, frowning with bewilderment. "You mean to say that life *isn't* really a fountain after all?"

In his search for the meaning of life, my fellow American became the straightman in a joke; in my research on the comic, my quest for jokes and laughter, I heard about the meaning of life. I was really not concerned about whether or not life is a fountain, a jest, or a bowl of cherries or cheerios for that matter. What concerned me was whether or not the rich comic tradition of ancient India persists in modern Indian society. Clearly there was folk humor, and I had met countless individuals who were very funny, who possessed great senses of humor, but it was difficult to locate contemporary cultural manifestations of the comic sensibility. Where were the social outlets for the universal and clearly felt sentiments? Comedy seemed to have no status. A year after this trip to India, I received news of a "World Humour Conference" held in Hyderabad, a city "now recognized," according to the pamphlet for the conference, "as the humour capital of India." The sober, even stern, pamphlet further explained a goal of the conference as the establishment of an international union of humor. "It is hoped that it will be like the Olympic movement which will provide an avenue for all nations to sublimate their aggressive instincts and thus provide an invaluable instrument for promoting peace and understanding." Perhaps I should have gone to Hyderabad. I heard about it too late. Why was comedy so inaccessible to me on that trip? Why did so many good-humored Indians tell me there was no humor? Why was it so hard to find comic plays, films, books, magazines? "Why aren't any of these people laughing or joking?" I asked myself as I sat in a restaurant that evening after visiting Jagat S. Bright.

In restaurant after restaurant, I had been repeatedly struck by the dreariness of the clientele, by the way in which throngs of straight-faced middle-class men consumed their food in public with dutiful solemnity and obligatory gravity under the cool light of fluorescent bulbs, light that makes all edges and corners sharp, that casts no shadows, that has not a trace of the golden glow of sun or fire. Occasionally a band would play rock music, although no one ever paid the slightest attention to it. Occasionally there would be women, but there was distance in their presence. Eating may be a pleasurable necessity, but it seemed to me, sitting alone in restaurants in Delhi, that it was never an amusing entertainment—the pleasure seemed biological, not social. Eating was serious business. Where was the nocturnal, public fun, the laughter in the streets at night? "India" according to my 1978 *Fodor's Guide*, "is not a place for nightlife."

Seven men, apparently business associates or employees from a single office, gathered at a nearby table, demanded service in abusive tones, placed their orders gruffly, and spoke soberly about politics. The previous night I had eavesdropped on a group of German businessmen eating at the Imperial Hotel—they had joked obscenely, laughed loudly, drunk beer with a vulgar and yet friendly exuberance. Joking offered a means of finding refuge from the formalities of business transaction, a way of making bonds, opening channels, finding points of equality. The Indian businessmen did not laugh, did not joke, did not drink beer, did not slap each other on the back. Rather than trying to break barriers, to establish a sense of equality and feelings of complicity, these dour men worked to reinforce the hierarchy of the office and of birth, the subtle and complex stratification of humanity that seems fundamental to all aspects of Indian life. Each man, in turn, told the others how important he was. "I am beholden to my father for my fine sense of music. He was one of the greatest musicians of Lucknow, as was his father before him, and his before him, into days of old." Like ancient warriors arrayed for battle, they recited their lineages. "And my father, hailing from Hyderabad, was a most important physician, but my professors encouraged me, due to my natural talents, to pursue the M.Sc. degree." One showed that he was greater, more prestigious, than another; another acknowledged the superiority of yet another. As they spoke the hierarchy became clear, and each clung to his place upon it like a bird in a flock upon a telephone wire. They defined and redefined it. And as I ate my solitary meal a theory formed. While there is, undoubtedly, lots of private humor, laughter behind closed doors, social conventions for joking and public outlets for the comic are difficult in India because of the sacrality of the hierarchy, the power with which it pervades all experiences and interactions. One is always in the presence of inferiors or superiors, and often in the presence of both. One is rarely, if ever, with an equal. It is not respectable to joke or laugh in the presence of inferiors, and not respectful to do so in the presence of superiors. Respect is too strong an ideal, perhaps, in modern India for there to be an abundance of public, socially acceptable, and readily available comedy. Respect is anathema to the comic. The clown, the fool, the holy man, the foreigner, the outcaste, and the child—anyone outside of the hierarchy—can joke and laugh. But within it, the comic spirit is too dangerous, too irreverent, indecorous, and indecent. Humor, laughter at oneself, is self-exposure, a shedding of one's own guises, a thoroughly unrespectable gesture; satire, laughter at others, exposing all hierarchy, tearing guises off all that claims to be superior, is an absolutely disrespectful response to the world. And India seems to cling to the hierarchy and to worship it.

As the men talked mirthlessly about colleagues, about business, about the elections, it occurred to me that perhaps they could not afford to joke. India seems quite conscious of itself as a nation in transition, a potentially powerful nation, hungry for the fulfillment of that potential, a nation that takes itself very seriously. The responsibility for growth and progress seems to be carried on the shoulders of each individual. To laugh or joke or surrender to the innate silliness of being human might give the impression that one is not working hard enough with enough earnest concern for oneself, one's family, and one's nation. To laugh or joke might be, or appear to be, complacency or frivolity, a dangerous attitude in a hungry land.

My analytic reverie was suddenly shattered by a loud laugh. I turned to the table of men and they were smiling. Two were still chuckling over some joke that had been told, a joke that I had missed because I had been jotting down my hypothesis about hierarchy in my notebook. I tore out the pages. India is impossible for me to figure out—as soon as I have enough data to form an idea, as soon as an understanding of something begins to take shape, a new bit of data inevitably forces its way in and consumes all other axioms and postulates, destroys the surest of my assumptions. As soon as I realized from daily experience that all scooter-taxi drivers were evil, heartless mercenaries whose sole purpose in life was to cheat me, to overcharge me because I was an ignorant foreigner, one came along and offered me a free ride. Perhaps, in his generosity, he was the most evil of all—he took not my money, but my precious illusion of the possibility that sense can be made of the world, that India can be fathomed. Perhaps his kindness was a practical joke.

I thought about the contest between Gaṇeśa and Kumāra. Gaṇeśa won—he knew the world through studying the ancient texts; Kumāra lost by racing off and actually going around the world. "I should have stayed home like Gaṇeśa," I thought, "and spent my time in the Sanskrit collection of the University of Hawaii library." The past seemed more real than the present. I could comprehend an ancient India—the rich fiction of scholars, the sprawling dream of poets, a vivid reality constructed from random fragments of truth. But in the present tense the country in which I found myself refused me understandings, held them back as if to tease me. And Buddhi, she whose name means "knowledge" or "comprehension," the goddess who had laughed at Kumāra, at all his efforts, seemed to laugh at me as well.

I decided to walk back to my hotel, following the directions given by the waiter, directions proffered with authoritative sureness, directions by which I promptly became lost. I thought I recognized the dome of Humayun's tomb and I made my way toward it as I knew how to get to the hotel from there.

I was depressed, lonely for people with whom I could laugh, discouraged about my research, unsure of what I was doing or why I was doing it. I felt that I had lost all sense of humor. It was hard to imagine laughing.

It was not Humayun's tomb, nor any tomb I knew. Crumbling, overgrown with weeds and wild brush, the ruin was as dark as death. It seemed to devour, rather than reflect, the moonlight. The night was cold and deeply silent. I was tired, lost, and my rib still ached. "Who is buried here?" I wondered. Sad news that had come from home would not let go. I sensed the doom in all things, the odorless, tasteless, silent, invisible melancholy that all beings breathe, the subtlest wastes of joys consumed.

Suddenly there was a sound, a quick and startling noise. I thought it was a laugh. "Was it a laugh? Is there someone living in that tomb, some homeless castaway or holy wanderer?" I wasn't sure—perhaps it was a cough, a sneeze, a groan, or perhaps I had just imagined it. "No, there was laughter in the tomb. I heard it." I pictured a pariah there, one of Laxman's impoverished victims, dreaming in his Moghul monument of sweet pleasures, and laughing in that dream. I imagined that it was the echo of some ancient laughter, the last reverberations of the drunken laughter of some court fool. I imagined then that there was a laughing ghost in there, a comic *preta*, the spirit of Indian comedy. I had studied the classical monument and now I stood before the ruin, the tomb of the Pramathas, the guardians of the comic mood. I listened. There was not another sound. The still and silent darkness refused to issue any further signs of life.

The Last Laugh: *Finding the Way*

Now suddenly he could laugh. First Ha then Ho, then Ha Ha HAR, HAAAAA! Laughter!

James Purdy, *Cabot Wright Begins*

As the train pulled out of Old Delhi Station I took a swig of rum from my clown bottle. Outside the windows of the train the face of Indira Gandhi, the serious visage on the millions of election posters that wallpapered the vast home of the multitudes living on the streets, sped past again and again. The epigraph in one of the books that I had brought with me to read on the train, L. R. Prabhakar's *In Lighter Vein*, was attributed to her: "What would life be if one were not able to see the funny side?" The irony now seems painful.

Despite the assurance of the bookseller that people read funny books on trains, I seemed to be the only one doing so. And the sad thing was that my funny book wasn't funny at all. It began with an austere polemic on the value of humor in our lives, a sober sermon on the importance of seeing the lighter side of misery and misfortune. This was followed by an essay on midgets which thoroughly confused me: "Among the various freaks of nature," Prabhakar wrote, "perhaps the birth of midgets is the most ludicrous and fun-provoking." Was the author actually saying that midgets are funny, that we should be grateful to them for providing us with an opportunity for laughter? Or was he being ironic, trying to be funny himself by saying they were funny? Were people supposed to laugh at the actual physical deformity of midgets, or at the posed (or real) aesthetic deformity of the author? I couldn't figure it out. I took another pull at my clown bottle, put the book away and, amidst the already snoring men in my compartment, I read some jokes from *Diwana*, jokes which seemed to be telling me something. "Patanjali once asked Aryabhatta what was zero. Aryabhatta said nothing." Where I heard no punch line, where I heard no laughter, where I thought there was silence, was that actually a joke? I took another drink. "When William Saxbe, American Ambassador to India, went to present his credentials to President Fakhruddin Ali Ahmed, he rushed forward with his outstretched hand, crying, 'I'm Saxbe, I'm Saxbe!' A shocked attendant, unused to such unconventional behavior on so solemn an occasion, exclaimed, 'Be silent!' The Ambassador stopped in his tracks and advanced more slowly saying, 'Oh, sorry. I'm Sax-e, I'm Sax-e.' " Was I as naive as my ambassador in both my behavior and understanding? I took another gulp of rum and looked at the grinning face on the bottle for an answer.

I arrived in Varanasi, the holiest of Indian cities, the sacred destination of ardent pilgrims, ancient and modern, with an empty bottle, a hangover, and a bag made heavy by all the light reading I had hauled to the capital of the Hindu religion. A porter, a scrawny, cadaverous, little man, frail with age, bent over by what must have been sixty, seventy, even eighty years of carrying other people's burdens, attempted to take my bag from me. As I tried to explain that I was quite able to carry it myself, one of the men who had slept in my compartment frowned, "Why deprive the man of his livelihood?"

He placed my bag on his head and made his way on skinny, scratched legs to the stairs that rose up to the ramp that crossed over the tops of the trains. "No, no. There is really no need to go ahead with this. I'll pay you. I'll carry the bag and you carry the water bottle. Okay? I'll pay you."

Ignoring all protestations, standing at the foot of the stairs, bracing himself for the ascent that he must have made literally millions of times before, he looked up, then bowed his head and started the climb. He strained to raise a foot and place it carefully on a step; he hesitated, shifted balance, and with all his might hauled the other foot up to give it rest next to its twin. He breathed heavily through his toothless mouth, drooling slightly. With an agonizing slowness he forged on. Meager shreds of muscle were taut and trembling. His sweating body was at a right angle to his legs. He reached for the handrail to steady himself. People raced past us, darting up the stairs, dodging us like racecars swerving to miss wreckage on a speedway.

I followed the old porter with simultaneous feelings of compassion ("How can I let this poor and aged man carry my bag?"), impatience ("Come on, you old goat—get a move on it!"), and embarrassment ("I must look like the worst and most inhumane sahib of the British Raj, or the most crass of ugly Americans."). I was surrounded by a hungry pack of rickshaw wallahs and self-appointed hotel-agents. "No, I don't want a rickshaw. No, I don't want a hotel room. No, no, no. I don't want anything. I just want to get to the top of the goddamn stairs." I kept asking the porter if I could help him with my bag. But he was impervious and totally absorbed in his struggle. One foot rose, sought firm ground, and waited for the other foot to follow. His breath was but wheezing groans. Fearful that he might have a heart attack, I persistently tried to take charge of my luggage, but it was like trying to convince Sir Edmund Hilary to turn back three quarters of the way up the icy slopes of Mount Everest. "Maybe he wants to die," I thought. "He wants to die in Varanasi so he'll go straight to heaven, so he can get Yama to carry his luggage." Still, I didn't like the idea of my bag being used as the suicide weapon.

He stopped and held the rail. Sweat rolled down the martyr's bowed and quivering legs. The summit was only two stairs away. He took a deep, rasping breath and then, with a sudden surge of energy, he seemed to leap up the last two steps. He spun around smiling over his victory, grinning a toothless grin over this giant step for all mankind. He wiped his brow, the smile gave way to a little chuckle, and he almost jauntily made his way along the over-ramp, as if anxious to face the easy stairs descending onto the platform by the station hall.

All night I could hear the *bhājans* to Śiva, laughing lord of the universe, passionate supplications rising up to the moon, the crescent adorning the hair of god. I pictured him as he had appeared on the dashboard of the taxi—his white skin, his red hair, his serpent necklace, and his cartoon smile—and I wondered where that icon was: in some junkyard, watching over endless wreckage, or redeemed, once more moving through the streets, god resurrected in Devdas' Auto Repair Shop?

Multitudes surged toward the Viśvanāth Temple, pushed through the chaos or surrendered to it, as they sang the midnight litanies, marriage chants for the happiness of god and goddess, droning cries for benediction. "May the laughter of Śiva protect and bless you!"

And at dawn lepers lined the pathway down to the ghats, "poor benighted Hindoos," extras in the beggar's opera, heaped upon the ground, displaying their wretchedness, the dark whiteness of their disease, holding out their bowls and crying for alms if not mercy, as if each passing person might manifest the Lord of Infinite Compassion. The lepers gave each one the opportunity to give, to be a god, or—better still—to be a human being.

A naked child, squatting in the dirt, scratched the ground, picked up a pebble to show it to the old woman in her wooden cart. Her face was half-devoured by the goddess of disease. Through the hideous, white-spotted beggar's mask, reddened eyes spotted me coming and the bruised, numb stump of a foot was raised, and pale pink knots of flesh that were once dark brown fingers reached for what could no longer be grasped. The other hand held a chillum of hashish slowly smoldering with dreams. The child pushed his way into the yawning lap of a man who then picked lice from the child's hair.

Her eyes followed me, she waited for her cue, waited until I was near, to cry out, "Hallooo . . . Bonjorrr . . ." The man and the child laughed at her. She repeated the parody with embellishments, "Hallooooo Mastarrr . . . Bonjorrrrr Mosurrr . . ." She laughed a crackling, throaty laugh, a laugh erupting with an uncanny glee, an outrageous and painful delight, part mockery and part resignation. It seemed an assault on misery and hopelessness, a rebellion against karma, a desperate outcry against desperation. Might the laughter of Śiva, like the touch of Jesus, like the sacrifice of birds over running water, cleanse the leper, purify the pain, turning all sorrow into joy, all lamentations to jubilations?

People made their way down to the Ganges to bathe at dawn after an all-night vigil, a night of songs that had beckoned Śiva to carry them in his arms into his heaven. In a boat upon those holy waters, the boatman wanted to know what I wanted to buy: "Banaras saris? Gold? Silver? Jewels? Lacquer toys? Opium? Heroin? Shawls? No? Film? Chocolates? Anything? Valium?" If I didn't want to buy anything, surely I wanted to sell something: "Camera? Calculator? Duty-free liquor? Film? No? Anything? Valium?"

It was impossible to convince him that I wanted neither to buy or sell anything. In his vision of the world to buy and to sell is to live, is to inhale and exhale. Refusal is merely a bluff, an attempt to hold out for a better price. My only device to get him to stop talking and to start rowing was to agree to go with him to his cousin's handicraft shop. "But I can't go today. I'm going to Sarnath today. I'll come back tomorrow and go with you then."

Like the ferryman in *Diwana*'s parody of *Siddhartha*, he seemed willing to believe that "everything returns. Everything!" I thought of the boatman the next day as I squeezed the toothpaste out of the tube onto my toothbrush and, despite the small tugs of conscience, I sustained my resolve not to return.

As he rowed toward Maṇikarṇikā Ghāṭ he kept saying with a big smile, "Dead bodies, no photographs. . . . Dead bodies, no photographs!" Perfumed corpses, washed and wrapped in white winding sheets, waited patiently for the consuming embrace of fire. One was carried upon a bamboo stretcher to his pyre. A log was placed upon the body so that it could not writhe in the heat. The fire was set at the head. The skull must burst in the flames to free the soul. "Who was this person? What dies with him?"

I thought of Gananath Sastri. I missed him. I could see him on the pyre. Did laughter explode from his skull with his soul to curl into the sky with the thick smoke, with the smell of sandalwood and human flesh, to diffuse itself throughout the heavens? "Run!" the dead are implored in the ancient hymn. "Run by the right path, past the four-eyed, brindled dogs, guardians of the gateway to the other world, run and join the blessed fathers who rejoice at the feast with Yama" (*Ṛg Veda* 10.14.10). Did he drink at the feast of Yama, and joke and laugh, and smoke Charminars, and joke and laugh some more, and did his presence there make Death and all who have died come to life with laughter? Surely he would have. Surely he would laugh if he could, would laugh with Kṣemendra, Dāmodaragupta, Nīlakaṇṭha, Birbal, Tenāli Rāma, Kālidāsa, Amaru, with a thousand ancient poets and dramatists, with a million dead clowns and comics, with ten million fools and tricksters gone. He'd laugh with John Gay—"Life is a jest and all things show it; I thought it once, but now I know it." As the boat neared the shore, I imagined that I heard his fine, strong laughter. It came from the pyre, rose into the sky, melodic, sweet, and beautiful. I could hear it clearly, perfectly, and it made me very happy at that moment.

I sat in the ruins of the monastery at Sarnath, the excavated rubble of ancient Buddhism, thinking of Jagat S. Bright, of what he had said and the way he had laughed. I tried to picture the Buddha filling empty, human-shaped spaces there, delivering his first sermon to the world, explaining to the gathered that all is suffering, that the reason for this great, all-permeating sorrow is thirst, the impulse to survive. Laughter is transient. Joy and mirth are as full of dread as they are unreal and insubstantial. The Buddha did not laugh in Sarnath nor did those who listened. "How can there be mirth or laughter when the world is on fire?" the Buddha asked. "How can anyone laugh who knows of old age, disease, and death?"

I tried to answer the Buddha. "Jagat S. Bright can laugh! So can Kushwant Singh and Shankar Pillai! So could Mahatma Gandhi and Ramakrishna! So do Gaṇeśa and Kālī, Kṛṣṇa and Śiva, and countless other gods and goddesses. There can be a way of laughter, a comic faith, a creed of mirth. There must be. The old porter at the top of the stairs and the poor leper in the dust of the streets had laughed. And I heard the laughter of Gananath Sastri, the laughter of a dead man. If the aged and diseased can laugh, if the dead, even though it be in dream or memory, can laugh, who cannot?"

I wanted to laugh in the face of the Buddha, to tickle the upturned, sacred soles of the contemplative Buddha's feet, to make the peaceful, pious smile on the cool sculpture in the museum at Sarnath turn to wild, hilarious laughter, the warm and jubilant laughter which suggests that despite the transience of things, despite all suffering and sorrow, all is delight, and the cause for the great, all-pervasive joy of which we are sometimes forgetful, like the cause of sorrow, is the ache and thirst to live. "We must laugh," Shankar said, "or we must die."

As I sat in the back of the taxi on the way to the Delhi airport I realized that for the first time my rib no longer hurt, that I had been in India just long enough to heal.

I stood in line, documents in hand, waiting to be questioned by the government official behind the desk, ready to show that everything was in order, that I had registered and deregistered with the police, that tax forms were properly completed. He looked at my passport and read over my papers and then, without expression in his voice or on his face, he asked me what the topic of my research had been.

Taking a deep breath, unfolding the letter of explanation, I said it for the last time: "The comic tradition in India—you know—humor, satire, jokes, and that sort of thing."

"Comedy?" he smiled with surprise. "Humor?" he laughed. "Excellent topic! We have so much humor in India! Such a funny place!"

He handed my passport and papers back to me and signaled me to move along and to return home.

Bibliographic Essay

The puritanical scholarship of the pioneers of Indian studies created an impression that, while there was ample truth and beauty, elegance and wisdom, in Sanskrit literature, there was little humor or satire. The standard surveys of Sanskrit literature by S. N. Dasgupta and S. K. De (*A History of Sanskrit Literature* [Calcutta, 1962]), Arthur Berriedale Keith (*A History of Sanskrit Literature* [London, 1920]), Maurice Winternitz (*Geschichte der indischen Literatur* [Leipzig, 1904–1920]), and others, lacking of any appreciation of vulgarity, perpetuated the assumption that the vast literature was devoid of a comic sensibility. Perfunctory discussions of such established comedic genres as the *prahasana* and the *bhāṇa* inevitably contained stern and sober judgments of those ribald texts. S. K. De's essay "Wit, Humour and Satire in Ancient Indian Literature" (in *Aspects of Sanskrit Literature* [Calcutta, 1959])—to the best of my knowledge the only survey of traditional Indian comedy to date—despite an explicitly intended gesture of approbation and recognition, implicitly reaffirmed the relative absence of hilarity in that literature. And that notion continues to be recapitulated. Gayatri Verma, for example, concludes a recent study of the comic element in the plays of Kālidāsa with the assertion that "coming to Indian literature and especially Sanskrit literature, we find that humour of the finest flavour is not found" (*Humour In Kalidasa*) [Delhi, 1981]). This misconception remains to be obliterated.

Against the predominant tendency to ignore or censure the comic tradition in Sanskrit literature, Sunthar Visvalingam has written a doctoral thesis on "Abhinavagupta's Conception of Humour: Its Resonances in Sanskrit Drama, Poetry, Hindu Mythlogy and Spiritual Practice" (Banaras Hindu University, 1983). This work (soon to be published by SUNY Press) provides the only systematic account of traditional Indian theories of comedy and laughter beyond the brief and technical essay by Har Dutt Sharma, "Hāsya as a Rasa in Sanskrit Rhetoric and Literature" (*Annals of the Bhandarkar Oriental Research Institute* 22:103–115). Another doctoral dissertation dealing with comedy is S. S. Janaki's *A Critical Study of the Caturbhāṇi and an Account of Bhāṇas in Sanskrit Literature* (Oxford University, 1971). Based on that dissertation she has published "Le piu recenti composizioni teatrali di tipo *bhāṇa*" (*Atti della Accademia delle Scienze di Torino. II Classe di Scienze morali, storiche e filologiche* 107 [1973]: 459–490).

Other studies giving attention to the comic include the charming, although not entirely convincing, essay by Walpola Rahula, "Humour in Pali Literature" (*Journal of the Pali Text Society* 9 [1981]: 156–173), as well as such disappointingly inconsequential articles as G. H. Godbole's "Role of Humour in Classical Sanskrit Plays" (*Indian Literature* 21 [1978]: 101–113) and G. S. Amur's "Laughter in Sanskrit Poetics" (*Journal of the Karnatak University* 7 [June 1963]: 229–242).

Richard Salomon's article, "Kṣemendra as Satirist: A New Look at the *Deśopadeśa*" (*Acta Orientalia* 44 [1983]), is an insightful piece of scholarship augmented by fine samples of translation. While most of the studies of Kṣemendra, Dāmodaragupta, and other writers of comic narratives have, for the most part, totally ignored the essential comic core of the texts (e.g., Ajay Mitra Shastri's *India as Seen in the Kuṭṭanīmata of Dāmodaragupta* [Delhi, 1975]), several articles other than Salomon's have considered the satirical dimension of Kṣemendra's writings: J. R. A. Loman, in "Types of Kashmirian Society in Kṣemendra's *Deśopadeśa* (*Adyar Library Bulletin* 31–32 [1967–1968]: 171–184); Om Bajaj, "Kṣemendra as a Social Reformer in the *Deśopadeśa*'' (*Journal of the Oriental Institute of Baroda* 13 [1963]: 221–231).

The lack of material on comedy in Sanskrit literature has reflected a corresponding paucity of interest in humor in Indian culture more generally. David Shulman, however, in *The King and the Clown in South Indian Myth and Poetry* (Princeton, 1985)—a brilliant analysis of kingship in terms of comic themes appearing in South Indian stories of political order and its transformations—provides us with a wealth of perception into both Indian culture and the meanings of the comic processes. Mahadev Apte, in his cogent anthropological study of *Humor and Laughter* (Ithaca, 1985), uses occasional Indian material in support of his arguments. Other anthropologists working in India have given some attention to humor and laughter: J. Brukman, '' 'Tongue Play': Constitutive and Interpretive Properties of Sexual Joking Encounters among the Koya of South India'' (in Mary Sanches and B. Blount, eds., *Sociocultural Dimensions of Language Use* [New York, 1975]); A. Sharman, '' 'Joking' in Padhola: Categorical Relationships, Choice, and Social Control'' (*Man* 4 [1969]:103–117); and V. P. Vatuk, ''Let's Dig Up Some Dirt: The Idea of Humor in Children's Folklore in India'' (in *Proceedings of the Eighth International Congress of Anthropological and Ethnological Sciences,* vol. 2 [Tokyo, 1968]).

Of the various issues related to comedy, humor, and satire, the figure of the *vidūṣaka,* the clown or fool of Sanskrit drama, has been the object of the most extensive Indological attention. There are, of course, discussions of that figure in the standard surveys of Sanskrit drama: Arthur Berriedale Keith's *The Sanskrit Drama in Its Origin, Development, Theory and Practice* (Oxford, 1924); Sten Konow's *Das indische Drama* (Berlin-Leipzig, 1920); and Sylvain Lévi's *Le théâtre indien* (Paris, 1890). And the previously cited studies by David Shulman and Sunthar Visvalingam contain interesting and original analyses of the *vidūṣaka*. Visvalingam's arguments are in reaction to the rigorous study by F. B. J. Kuiper, *Varuṇa and the Vidūṣaka: On the Origin of Sanskrit Drama* (Amsterdam, 1979). Other books devoted to this *dramatis persona* include G. K. Bhat's *The Vidūṣaka* (Ahmedabad, 1959), and two studies by J. T. Parikh—*The Vidūṣaka: Theory and Practice* (Surat, 1953) and *Sanskrit Comic Characters* (Surat, 1952). Important articles include the recent and judicious ''Vidūṣaka versus Fool: A Functional Analysis'' by Keith N. Jefferds (*Journal of South Asian Literature* 16 [1981]: 61–73) and the rather antiquated ''The Origin of the Vidūṣaka and the Employment of This Character in the Plays of Harṣadeva'' by Montgomery Schuyler (*Journal of the American Oriental Society* 20 [1899]: 333ff.). Johan Huizinga, whose classic "study of the play element in culture," *Homo Ludens* (London, 1949), has influenced so much of what has been written in the last several decades about comedy (including my own study), wrote his doctoral thesis on the theatrical jester: *De vidūṣaka in het indisch tooneel* (1897).

For stories about the legendary court jesters, the tricksters Tenāli Rāma, Gopal Bhar, and Birbal, I have, beyond oral resources, used comic books from the Amar Citra Katha Series: *Birbal the Wise, Birbal the Witty, Birbal the Clever; Raman of Tenali, Raman the Matchless Wit; Gopal the Jester, Gopal and the Cowherd.* The renditions of the mythologies of Kṛṣṇa and Śiva as presented in this same series are occasionally informed with a lightness that reflects a traditional Indian sense of humor in respect to the Hindu pantheon. Further accounts of the adventures of Tenāli Rāma are given in David Shulman's study of South Indian clowns (as already cited), in A. S. Panchapakesa Ayyar's *Tenali Rama.* (Madras, 1947), and in Randor Guy's *Indian Ribaldry* (Delhi, 1967). Eunice de Souza has recounted many of the comedic legends of Birbal in her two volumes for children—*All About Birbal* (Bombay, 1969) and *More About Birbal* (Bombay, 1973). Several stories about Gopal of Bengal are retold with wit and sparkle by Edward C. Dimock, Jr., in *The Thief of Love: Bengali Tales from Court and Village* (Chicago, 1963).

Maurice Bloomfield, in his devotion to examining motifs in Sanskrit literature, dealt with the trickster in his "The Character and Adventures of Mūladeva" (*Proceedings of the American Philosophical Society* 52 [1913]: 616–650); and his "On False Ascetics and Nuns in Hindu Fiction" (*Journal of the American Oriental Society* 44 [1924]: 202–242) is of particular interest to the study of religious satire in Indian folk literature.

Studies of the mythology of Kṛṣṇa, because of the essentially ludic nature of that god, often deal with comedic themes, with the issues of play, the trickster, and the role of mirth in religious belief and practice. This is the case particularly in David Kinsley's *The Divine Player: A Study of Kṛṣṇa Līlā* (Delhi, 1979), and in two books by David Hawley—*At Play with Krishna: Pilgrimage Dramas from Brindavan* (Princeton, 1981) and *Krishna the Butter Thief* (Princeton, 1983). Dealing more generally with Hindu mythology,

Wendy O'Flaherty's analyses are always graced by her inimitable and exuberant wit—her *Women, Androgynes, and Other Mythical Beasts* (Chicago, 1980) is, in particular, a mine of Indological fun.

A significant amount of Sanskrit humorous and satiric literature remains uncatalogued, unprinted, and unstudied. And of the published works, much remains to be translated. While the majority of the translations of the comic texts that do exist are characteristically humorless, there are some notable exceptions. Some very funny Sanskrit poetry has been cleverly translated by John Brough in *Poems from the Sanskrit* (London, 1968); and Daniel H. H. Ingalls's monumental translation of the *Subhāṣitaratnakoṣa* (*An Anthology of Sanskrit Court Poetry* [Cambridge, Mass., 1965]) contains many stanzas informed with the comic sentiment. While translations of such important comedic texts as the *Dhūrtaviṭasaṃvāda, Kaliviḍambana, Karpūramañjarī, Padmaprābhṛtaka, Śāradātilaka,* and *Ubhayābhisārikā* are acknowledged below in the bibliography of Indian texts cited, other translations deserve to be mentioned. The comic pitch is preserved in Arthur Ryder's translations of the *Pañcatantra* (Chicago, 1956) and the *Daśakumāracarita* (*The Ten Princes* [Chicago, 1927]); the *Kathāsaritsāgara,* upon which I have relied for so many jokes and folk tales, was delightfully and carefully translated by C. H. Tawney and edited in ten volumes by N. M. Penzer as *The Ocean of Story* (London, 1924–1928). The *Jātaka*s were brilliantly translated by E. B. Cowell (Cambridge, 1895–1913) although the dirty (i.e., funny) parts are either omitted or rendered into Latin. Michael Lockwood and A. Vishnu Bhatt have translated the *Bhagavadajjuka* of Mahendravarman (Madras, 1978), and the edition of that king's *Mattavilāsaprahasana* by N. P. Unni includes a drab literal translation. The *Viśvaguṇādarśacampū,* the satiric poem of Veṅkaṭādhvarin has been well translated into French by Marie-Claude Porcher (Pondicherry, 1972). There is also a French translation of the *Samayamātṛkā* by Louis Langle (*Le Breviare de la Courtisane* [Paris, 1920]), following the German of J. J. Meyer (*Das Zauberbuch der Hetären* [Leipzig, n.d.]), which, in turn, became the basis of E. Powys Mathers rendition, *The Harlot's Breviary* (in *Eastern Love,* vol. 2, [London, 1927]). Langle's translation of the *Kuṭṭanīmata,* published with his translation of the *Samayamātṛkā* is far more witty than the almost incomprehensible English translation by B. P. L. Bedi (*The Art of the Temptress* [Bombay, 1968]). Richard Schmidt attempted a translation of the *Rasikarañjana* in German (Stuttgart, 1896). In general translators have shied away from Sanskrit comic literature because, it seems, they have felt it was trivial, distasteful, pornographic, or untranslatable. I share in that feeling, but, in my case, those qualities have drawn me to that literature and inspired my attempts to translate it. The translations of the texts cited in this book are my own.

Bibliography of Indian Texts Cited (by title)

Abhijñānaśākuntala of Kālidāsa. Edited with an English translation by C. Sankara Rama Sastri. Sri Balamanorama Series, nos. 32, 42. Madras: Sri Balamanorama Press, 1947.

Āgamaḍambara of Jayanta Bhaṭṭa. Edited by V. Raghavan and Anantalal Thakur. Mithila Institute Ancient Texts Series, no. 7. Darbhanga: Mithila Institute, 1964.

Aitareya Brāhmaṇa. Edited with the commentary of Sāyaṇa by P. S. Sāmāśramī. 4 vols. Calcutta: Bibliotheca Indica, 1895–1906.

Amaruśataka of Amaruka. Edited with the commentary of Arjunavarmadeva by Mahāmahopādhyāya Pandit Durgāprasād and Kāśīnāth Pāṇḍurang Parab. Kavyamala Sanskrit Series, no. 18. Bombay: Nirnaya-Sagara Press, 1900.

Aṅguttara Nikāya. Edited by R. Morris and E. Hardy. 5 vols. London: Pali Text Society, 1885–1900.

Anyāpadeśaśataka of Nīlakaṇṭha Dīkṣita. Edited with an English translation by Nagaraja Rao. Mysore: Sudharma Publications, 1973.

Aparokṣānubhuti of Śaṅkara. In *Śrīśaṅkaragranthāvali* (q.v.) 10:383–402.

Āpastambadharmasūtra. Edited with the commentary of Haradatta by Mahadeva Sastri and K. Rangacharya. Government Oriental Library Series, no. 15. Mysore: Bibliotheca Sanskrita, 1898.

Arthaśāstra of Kauṭilya. Edited by R. S. Shastry. Government Oriental Library Series, no. 54. Mysore: Bibliotheca Sanskrita, 1919.

Aṣṭādhyāyī of Pāṇini. Edited by Brahmadatta Jijñāsu. 3 vols. Amritsar: Ramalal Kapur Press, 1964.

Atharva Veda. Edited with the *Gopatha Brāhmaṇa* by Sūryakānta. Kāśī Saṃskṛta Granthamālā, no. 166. Varanasi: Chowkhamba Sanskrit Office, 1964.

Aucityavicāracarcā of Kṣemendra. In *Kṣemendralaghukāvyasaṃgraha* (q.v.), pp. 11–62.

Avimāraka of Bhāsa. In *Bhāsanāṭakacakra* (q.v.), pp. 109–190.

Bhagavadajjukīya of Mahendravikramavarman. Edited by P. Anujan Achan. Trichur, Kerala: Mangalodayam Press, 1925.

Bhagavadgītā. See *Mahābhārata*.

Bhāgavata Purāṇa. Edited with the commentary of Gaṅgāsahāya by Pāṇḍeya Rāmateja Śāstrī. Varanasi: Pandita-Pustakalaya, 1965.

Bhaktavijaya of Mahīpati. Translated by J. E. Abbott. Poona: Scottish Mission Industries, 1926.

Bhaktirasāmṛtasindhu of Rūpa Goswāmin. Edited by Shyam Narayana Pandey. Kanpur: Sahitya Niketana, 1965.

Bhallaṭaśataka of Bhallaṭa. Edited by S. Vasudeva Chariyar. Madras Sanskrit Series, no. 2. Madras: Ramacandra Iyer, 1898.

Bharaṭakadvātriṃśikā. Edited by Johannes Hertel. Forschungsinstitut für Indogermanistik Indische Abteilung, nr. 2. Leipzig: Sächsische Forschungsinstitut, 1921.

Bhāsanāṭakacakra. Edited by C. R. Devadhar. Poona Oriental Series, no. 54. Poona: Oriental Book Agency, 1962.

Bhāvaprakāśana of Śāradātanaya. Edited by Yadugiri Yatiraja and K. S. R. Sastri. Gaekwad's Oriental Series, no. 45. Baroda: Oriental Institute, 1968.

Bhaviṣya Purāṇa. Edited by Śrīrāma Śarmā. 2 vols. Bareli: Saṃskṛti Saṃsthāna, 1968–1969.

"Bidushak" of Rabindranath Tagore. In *The Housewarming and Other Selected Writings*, pp. 299–300. Edited by Amiya Chakravarty. New York: New American Library, 1965.

Brahmavaivarta Purāṇa. Edited by Śrīrāma Śarmā. 2 vols. Bareli: Saṃskṛti Saṃsthāna, 1970.

Bṛhadāraṇyaka Upaniṣad. See *Upaniṣads*.

Bṛhatkathāmañjarī of Kṣemendra. Edited by Sivadatta and K. P. Parab. Kavyamala Sanskrit Series, no. 83. Bombay: Nirnaya-Sagara Press, 1931.

Buddhacarita of Aśvaghoṣa. Edited with an English translation by E. H. Johnston. Reprint (2 vols. in 1). Delhi: Motilal Banarsidass, 1972.

Caitanyabhāgavata of Vṛndāvanadāsa. Edited by Kaliprasanna Vidyāratna. Calcutta: Vasumati Karyalaya, 1908.

Caitanyacaritāmṛta of Kṛṣṇadāsa Kavirāja. Bengali text with an English translation by A. C. Bhaktivedanta Swami Prabhupada. New York, Los Angeles, London, Bombay: Bhaktivedanta Book Trust, 1975.

Caṇḍamahāroṣaṇa Tantra. Edited with an English translation of chapters 1–8 by Christopher S. George. American Oriental Series, vol. 56. New Haven, Conn.: American Oriental Society, 1974.

Carakasaṃhitā of Agniveśa. Edited with an English translation by Ram Karan Sharma and Vaidya Bhagawan Dash. 2 vols. Chowkhamba Sanskrit Series, no. 94. Varanasi: Chowkhamba Vidyabhavan, 1976–1977.

Chāndogya Upaniṣad. See *Upaniṣads*.

Daśakumāracarita of Daṇḍin. Edited with four commentaries by Nārāyaṇa Balakṛṣṇa Godabole. 7th ed. Bombay: Nirnaya-Sagara Press, 1913.

Daśarūpaka of Dhanaṃjaya. Edited with the commentary of Dhanika and the subcommentary of Bhaṭṭanṛsiṃha by T. Venkatacharya. Adyar Library Series, no. 97. Madras: Adyar Library, 1969.

Deśopadeśa and Narmamālā of Kṣemendra. Edited by Pandit Madhusudan Kaul Shastri. Kashmir Series of Texts and Studies, no. 40. Srinagar: Research Department of Jammu and Kashmir State, 1923.

Devīmāhātmya [from the *Mārkaṇḍeya Purāṇa*]. Edited with an English translation by S. Shankaranarayanan. Pondicherry: Dipti Publications, 1968.

Dhammapada. Pali text with an English translation by S. Radhakrishnan. Madras: Oxford University Press, 1950.

Dhammapadatthakathā. Edited by H. C. Norman. 4 vols. London: Pali Text Society, 1970.

Dharmaparīkṣā of Amitagati. Edited by N. Miranow. *Abhandlungen für die Kunde des Morgenlandes*. Leipzig, 1903.

Dhūrtākhyāna of Śvetāmbara Haribhadrasūri. Prakrit text edited by A. N. Upadhye with the Sanskrit version of Saṅghatilaka and an Old Gujarati version by Jina Vijaya Muni. Singhi Jain Series, no. 19. Bombay: Bharatiya Vidyabhavan, 1944.

Dhūrtasamāgama of Kaviśekhara Jyotīśvara. Edited by Christian Lassen in *Anthologia Sanscrita*, pp. 66–96. Bonn: H. B. Koenig, 1838.

Dhūrtaviṭasaṃvāda of Īśvaradatta. Edited with an English translation by Manomohan Ghosh in *Glimpses of Sexual Life in Manda-Maurya India*, part 2, pp. 17–44. Calcutta: Manisha Granthalaya, 1975.

Dīgha Nikāya. Edited by T. W. Rhys Davids and J. E. Carpenter. 3 vols. London: Pali Text Society, 1890–1911.

Dohākoṣa of Saraha. Edited with a French translation by M. Shahidullah in *Les Chants Mystiques de Kāṇha et de Saraha*. Paris: Adrien-Maisonneuve, 1928.

Dvādaśapañjarikāstotra of Śaṅkara. In *Śrīśaṅkaragranthāvali* (q.v.) 11:282–287.

Gaṇeśa Purāṇa. Poona, 1876.

Gītagovinda of Jayadeva. Edited with the commentaries of Kumbha and Śaṅkara Miśra by Telang and Panshikar. Bombay: Nirnaya-Sagara Press, 1949.

Gospel of Ramakrishna by M. [Mahendranath Gupta]. Translated from Bengali by Swami Nikhilananda. New York: Ramakrishna-Vivekananda Center, 1942.

Gṛhyasūtras of Gobhila. Edited with a commentary by Chandrakanta Tarkalankara. 2 vols. Calcutta: Bibliotheca Indica, 1880.

Harivaṃśa. Edited by V. S. Sukthankar, S. K. Velvakar, and P. L. Vaidya [as the "appendix" to the *Mahābhārata*]. Poona: Bhandarkar Oriental Research Institute, 1969–1971.

Hāsyārṇavaprahasana of Jagadīśvara Bhaṭṭācārya. Edited with a Hindi commentary by Īśvaraprasāda Caturvedī. Vidyābhavana Saṃskṛta Granthamālā, no. 103. Varanasi: Chowkhamba Vidyabhavan, 1963.

Hitopadeśa of Nārāyaṇa. Edited with an English translation by M. R. Kale. 6th ed. Delhi: Motilal Banarsidass, 1967.

Jātaka. Edited by V. Fausbøll. 6 vols. London: Pali Text Society, 1877–1896.

Kalāvilāsa of Kṣemendra. In *Kṣemendralaghukāvyasaṃgraha* (q.v.) pp. 219–271.

Kaliviḍambana of Nīlakaṇṭha Dīkṣita. Edited with a French translation by Pierre Sylvain Filliozat in *Oevres Poetique de Nīlakaṇṭha Dīkṣita*. Publications de l'Institut Français d'Indologie, no. 36. Pondichery: Institut Français d'Indologie, 1967.

Kāmasūtra of Vātsyāyana. Edited with the commentary of Yaśodhara by M. P. Durgāprasād. Bombay: Nirnaya-Sagara Press, 1900.

Karpūrādistotra. Edited with an English translation by Arthur Avalon (Sir John Woodroffe) with an introduction and commentary by Vimalānandasvāmi. 3d ed. Madras: Ganesh and Co., 1965.

Karpūramañjarī of Rājaśekhara. Edited by Sten Konow with an English translation by Charles Rockwell Lanman. Harvard Oriental Series, no. 4. Cambridge, Mass.: Harvard University Press, 1901.

Kathāsaritsāgara of Somadevabhaṭṭa. Edited by M. P. Durgāprasād and Kāsīnāth Pāṇḍurang Parab. 3d ed. Bombay: Nirnaya-Sagara Press, 1915.

Kātyāyanasmṛti on Vyavahāra. Edited with an English translation by P. V. Kane. Bombay: Reprint from *Hindu Law Quarterly,* 1933.

Kautukaratnākara of Lakṣmana Mānikyadeva of Bhuluya. Summarized by Carl Cappeller in "Zwei Prahasanas." *Gurupūjākaumudī: Festgabe zum Funfzigjahrigen Doctorjubilaum Albrecht Weber,* pp. 59–63. Leipzig: Otto Harrassowitz, 1896.

Kautukasarvasva of Gopīnātha Cakravartin. Edited by Rāmcandra Tarkālaṃkara. Calcutta, 1828. Summarized by Carl Cappeller (see *Kautukaratnākara*).

Kavikaṇṭhābharaṇa of Kṣemendra. In *Kṣemendralaghukāvyasaṃgraha* (q.v.) pp. 63–84.

Kāvyādarśa of Daṇḍin. Edited with a Sanskrit commentary of Vidyabhusana Rangacharya Raddi Shastri. Government Oriental Series, no. 4. Poona: Bhandarkar Oriental Research Institute, 1970.

Kāvyamālā: A collection of old and rare Sanskrit Kāvyas, Naṭakas, Champūs, Bhāṇas, Prahasanas, Chhandas, Alaṇkāras, etc. Edited by M. P. Durgāprasād, Kaśināth Pāṇḍurang Parab, et al. Bombay: Nirnaya-Sagara Press, 1886ff.

Kāvyālaṃkāra of Rudraṭa. Edited with the commentary of Namisādhu by M. P. Durgāprasād and Kāśīnāth Pāṇḍurang Parab. Kavyamala Sanskrit Series, no. 2. Nirnaya-Sagara Press, 1913.

Kāvyānuśāsana of Hemacandra. Edited with two anonymous commentaries by Rasiklal C. Parikh and V. M. Kulkarni. Bombay: Srimahavira Jaina Vidyalaya, 1938.

Kṛṣṇakarṇāmṛta of Līlāśuka Bilvamaṅgala. Edited with an English translation by Frances Wilson. Haney Foundation Series, no. 14. Philadelphia: University of Pennsylvania Press, 1975.

Kṣemendralaghukāvyasaṃgraha. Edited by Vidyaratna E. V. V. Raghavacharya and D. G. Padhye. Sanskrit Academy Series, no. 7. Hyderabad: The Sanskrit Academy, Osmania University, 1961.

Kulārṇava Tantra. Edited with an English reading by Taranatha Vidyaratna. Madras: Ganesh and Co., 1965.

Kumārasaṃbhava of Kālidāsa. Edited by Sūryakānta. Delhi: Sahitya Akademi, 1962.

Kuṭṭanīmata of Dāmodaragupta. Edited with a Hindi translation by Narmadeśvara Caturvedī. Mitra Prakasana Gaurava Granthamala, no. 5. Allahabad: Mitra Prakasana, 1961.

Laṭakamelaka of Śaṅkhadhara Kavirāja. Edited by Pandit Kapiladevagiri Sāhityācārya. Vidyābhavana Samskrta Granthamālā, no. 87. Varanasi: Chowkhamba Vidyabhavan, 1962.

Liṅga Purāṇa. Edited by Śrīrāma Śarmā. Bareli: Samskṛti Saṃsthāna, 1968.

Mahābhārata. Edited by Vishnu S. Sukthankar et al. 21 vols. Poona: Bhandarkar Oriental Research Institute, 1933–1960.

———. (Southern Recension) edited by P. P. S. Sastri. Madras: V. Ramaswamy Sastrula & Sons, 1931.

Mahāsubhāṣitasaṃgraha. Edited by Ludwik Sterbach. 5 vols. Hoshiapur: Visvaranand Vedic Research Institute, 1974.

Majjhima Nikāya. Edited by V. Trenckner. 3 vols. London: Pali Text Society, 1887–1902.

Mālatīmādhava of Bhavabhūti. Edited with an English translation by M. R. Kale. Delhi: Motilal Banarsidass, 1967.

Mālavikāgnimitra of Kālidāsa. Edited with an English translation by C. R. Devadhar. Delhi: Motilal Banarsidass, 1966.

Maṇḍūka Upaniṣad of Gananath Sastri. Unpublished manuscript (author's collection).

Manudharmaśāstra. Edited with the commentary of Medhātithi by Gaṅgānātha Jha. Calcutta: Bibliotheca Indica, 1932.

Matsya Purāṇa. Edited by Śrīrāma Śarmā. Bareli: Saṃskṛti Saṃsthāna, 1980.

Mattavilāsaprahasana of Mahendravarman. Edited by Ganapati Sastri. Trivandrum Sanskrit Series, no. 55. Trivandrum: Government Press, 1917.

Mera Naam Joker by K. A. Abbas (after the film of Raj Kapoor). Delhi: Hind Pocket Books, n.d.

Moharājaparājaya of Yaśaḥpāla. Edited by Muni Chaturvijaya. Gaekwad's Oriental Series, no. 9. Baroda: Central Library, 1918.

Mṛcchakaṭikā of Śūdraka. Edited with the commentary of Pṛthvīdhara and an English translation by M. R. Kale. 2d ed. Bombay: Booksellers' Publishing Co., 1962.

Mugdhopadeśa of Jalhaṇa. In *Kāvyamālā* (q.v.) 8:125–135.

Muntakhab-ut-Tawarikh of Badaoni. Translated into English by S. A. Ranking (vol. 1) and W. H. Lowe (vols. 2–3). Calcutta: Asiatic Society of Bengal, 1925.

Nāgānanda of Harṣavardhana. Edited with an English translation by Bak Kun Bae in *Śrī Harṣa's Plays* (pp. 49–223). Bombay: Asia Publishing House, 1964.

Naiṣadhacarita of *Śrīharṣa*. Edited by Nārāyaṇa Rāma Ācarya. Bombay: Nirnaya-Sagara Press, 1952.

Narmamālā of Kṣemendra. See *Deśopadeśa and Narmamālā*.

Nāṭyaśāstra of Bharata. Edited with the commentary of Abhinavagupta (*Abhinavabhāratī*) by M. Ramakrishna Kavi et al. 4 vols. Gaekwad Oriental Series, nos. 36, 68, 124, 145. Baroda: Oriental Institute, 1926–1964. [This edition cited unless otherwise indicated.]

———. Edited with the commentary of Abhinavagupta (*Abhinavabhāratī*) by Pandit Śivadatta and Kāśīnāth Pāṇḍurang Parab. Kavyamala Sanskrit Series, no. 42. Bombay: Nirnaya-Sagara Press, 1894.

Pādatāḍitaka of Śyāmilaka. Edited by G. H. Schokker. Indo-Iranian Monographs, no. 9. The Hague: Mouton, 1966.

Paddhati of Śārṅgadhara. Edited by P. Peterson. Bombay Sanskrit Series, no. 37. Bombay: Government Central Book Depot, 1888.

Padmaprābhṛtaka of Śūdraka. Edited with an English translation by Johannes Reinoud Abraham Loman. Amsterdam: Uitgerij De Driehoek, 1956.

Padyāvalī of Rūpa Goswāmin. Edited by S. K. De. Oriental Publications Series, no. 3. Dacca: University of Dacca, 1934.

Pañcatantra. Edited and reconstructed by Franklin Edgerton. American Oriental Series, vol. 2. New Haven, Conn.: American Oriental Society, 1924.

Patipūjāvidhāna. Edited by Lodd Govindas. Poona: Aryabhushan Press, 1918.

Prabodhacandrodaya of Kṛṣṇamiśra. Edited with an English translation by Sita Krishna Nambiar. Delhi: Motilal Banarsidass, 1971.

Prāsaṅgika of Harijīvanamiśra. Summarized by George Artola, "Harijīvanamiśra and His Short Sanskrit Plays." *Samskrita Ranga Annual IV,* Madras, 1965.

Pratijñāyaugandharāyaṇa of Bhāsa. In *Bhāsanaṭakacakra* (q.v.), pp. 57–108.

Priyadarśikā of Harṣavardhana. Edited with English translation by M. R. Kale. 4th ed. Delhi: Motilal Banarsidass, 1977.

Rājataraṅgiṇī of Kalhaṇa. Edited by Vishva Bandhu, part 1 (*Taraṅgas* 1–7). Woolner Indological Series, no. 5. Hoshiapur: Vishvaranand Vedic Research Institute, 1963.

Rāmāyaṇa of Vālmīki. Critically edited by J. M. Mehta. Baroda: Oriental Institute, 1960–1975.

Ramayana as told by Aubrey Menen. New York: Charles Scribner, 1954.

Rāmprasād. *Chants à Kālī de Rāmprasād.* Bengali text edited with a French translation by Michel Lupsa. Publications de l'Institut Francais d'Indologie, no. 30. Pondichery: Institute Francais d'Indologie, 1967.

Rasikarañjana of Rāmacandra. In *Kāvyamālā* (q.v.) 4:96–148.

Ratnāvalī of Harṣavardhana. Edited with an English translation by M. R. Kale. 3d ed. Bombay: Booksellers' Publishing Co., 1964.

Ṛg Veda. Edited with the commentary of Sāyaṇa by F. Max Müller. (Indian edition) Chowkhamba Sanskrit Series, no. 99. Varanasi: Chowkhamba Sanskrit Series Office, 1966.

Saduktikarṇāmṛta of Śrīdharadāsa. Edited by Sures Chandra Banerji. Calcutta: Firma K. L. Mukhopadhyay, 1965.

Sāhityadarpaṇa of Viśvanāthakavirāja. Edited with a Hindi commentary by Nirupana Vidyalamkara. 2 vols. Meerut: Sahitya Bhandara, 1974.

Samayamātṛkā of Kṣemendra. Edited by M. P. Durgāprasād and Kāśīnāth Pāṇḍurang Parab. Kavyamala Sanskrit Series, no. 10. Bombay: Nirnaya-Sagara Press, 1888. See also *Kṣemendralaghukāvyasaṃgraha,* pp. 349–416.

Śāradātilaka of Śaṅkara. Edited with an English translation by Fabrizia Baldissera. Bhandarkar Oriental Series, no. 14. Poona: Bhandarkar Oriental Research Institute, 1980.

Śatapatha Brāhmaṇa. Edited with extracts from the commentaries of Sāyaṇa et al. by Albrecht Weber. Chowkhamba Sanskrit Series, no. 96. Varanasi: Chowkhamba Sanskrit Series Office, 1964.

Saundaryalaharī attributed to Śaṅkarācārya. Edited with an English translation by W. Norman Brown (as *The Flood of Beauty*). Harvard Oriental Series, no. 43. Cambridge, Mass.: Harvard University Press, 1958.

Śiśupālavadha of Māgha. Edited with the commentary of Mallinātha by Pandits Haragovinda Śāstrī and Bhagavanadatta Miśra. Vidyābhavana Saṃskṛta Granthamālā, no. 8. Varanasi: Chowkhamba Vidyabhavan, 1961.

Śivamahimnaḥstotra of Puṣpadanta. Edited with a Hindi translation by Radhelala Trivedi. Varanasi: Chowkhamba Vidyabhavan, 1966.

Śiva Purāṇa. Edited by Śrīrāma Śarmā. Bareli: Saṃskṛti Saṃsthāna, 1966.

Skanda Purāṇa. Edited by Śrīrāma Śarmā. Bareli: Saṃskṛti Saṃsthāna, 1970.

Śrīśaṅkaragranthāvali. 11 vols. Srirangam: Vani-Vilasa Press, 1952–1960.

Śṛṅgāraśataka of Bhartṛhari. In *Subhāṣitatriśatī* (q.v.), pp. 56–110.

Śṛṅgārasundarabhāṇa of Īśvaraśarmā. Edited by K. Raghavan Pillai. University of Kerala Sanskrit Series, no. 214. Trivandrum: University of Kerala, 1965.

Subhāṣitaratnabhāṇḍāgāra. Edited by Nārāyaṇa Rāma Ācarya. 8th ed. Bombay: Nirnaya-Sagara Press, 1952.

Subhāṣitaratnakoṣa of Vidyākara. Edited by D. D. Kosambi and V. V. Gokhale. Harvard Oriental Series, no. 42. Cambridge, Mass.: Harvard University Press, 1957.

Subhāṣita[ratna]saṃdoha of Amitagati. Edited with a Hindi translation by Balchandra Sidhant Shastri. Sholapur: Jain Samskriti Samrakshaka Sangha, 1977.

Subhāṣitatriśatī of Bhartṛhari. Edited with the commentary of Rāmacandrabudhendra by U. L. S. Panshikar. Bombay: Nirnaya-Sagara Press, 1917.

———. Edited by D. D. Kosambi (as the *Śatakatrayasubhāṣitasaṃgraha*). Bombay: Singhi Jain Series, no. 23. Bombay: Bharatiya Vidyabhavan, 1948.

Subhāṣitāvali of Vallabhadeva. Edited with a Hindi paraphrase by Ramacandra Malaviya. Varanasi: Ananda Bandu, 1974.

Śukasaptati. Edited with a Hindi and Sanskrit commentary by Ramakanta Tripathi. Haridas Sanskrit Series, no. 269. Varanasi: Chowkhamba Sanskrit Series Office, 1966.

Sūktimañjarī. Edited by Baladeva Upadhyaya. Vidyābhavana Saṇskṛta Granthamālā, no. 142. Varanasi: Chowkhamba Sanskrit Series Office, 1967.

Sūktiratnahāra of Sūrya. Edited by Śambaśiva Śāstrī. Trivandrum Sanskrit Series, no. 141. Trivandrum: Government Press, 1931.

Sumaṅgalavilāsini of Buddhaghoṣa. Edited by T. W. Rhys Davids and J. E. Carpenter. London: Pali Text Society, 1886.

Svapnavāsavadatta of Bhāsa. In *Bhāsanaṭakacakra* (q.v.), pp. 1–56.

Taittirīya Upaniṣad. See *Upaniṣads*.

Tenali Rama. Stories retold by A. S. Panchapakesa Ayyar. 4th ed. Madras: Orient Publishing Company, 1957.

Ubhayābhisārikā of Vararuci. Edited with an English translation by T. Venkatacharya and A. K. Warder. Madras: V. Sambamurthy, 1967.

Upaniṣads. Eighteen Principle Upaniṣads. Vol. 1. Edited by V. P. Limaye and R. D. Vadekar. Poona: Vaidika Samsodhana Mandala, 1958.

Uttararāmacarita of Bhavabhūti. Edited with the commentary of Ghanaśyāma by P. V. Kane. Delhi: Motilal Banarsidass, 1962.

Vairāgyaśataka of Bhartṛhari. In *Subhāṣitatriśatī* (q.v.), pp. 111–175.

Vairāgyaśataka of Apyaya Dīkṣita. In *Kāvyamālā* (q.v.) 1:91–101.

Varāha Purāṇa. Edited by Gautam Chaman Lal. 2 vols. Bareli: Saṇskṛti Saṃsthāna, 1973–1974.

Vidagdhamādhava of Rūpa Gosvāmin. Edited by Bhavadatta Śāstrī and Kāśīnāth Pāṇḍurang Parab. Kavyamala Sanskrit Series, no. 81. Bombay: Nirnaya-Sagara Press, 1903.

Vikramorvaśīya of Kālidāsa. Edited with an English translation by C. Śaṅkara Rāma Śāstrī. Sri Balamanorama Series, no. 52. Madras: Sri Balamanorama Press, 1954.

Viṣṇu Purāṇa. Edited with the commentary of Śrīdhara. Calcutta: Vangavasi Steam Machine Press, 1887.

Viśvaguṇādarśacampū of Veṅkaṭādhvarin. Edited with the commentary of Balakṛṣṇa Śāstrī by Surendra Nath Shastri. Vidyābhavana Saṇskṛti Granthamālā, no. 98. Varanasi: Chowkhamba Vidyabhavan, 1963.

Vivekacūḍāmaṇi of Śaṅkara. In *Śrīśaṅkaragranthāvali* (q.v.) 10:1–100.

Vṛtti of Devendra on the *Uttarādhyāyanasūtra.* Edited by Jacobi, "Ausgewählte Erzählungen in Māhārāṣṭrī," pp. 56–65.

Yājñavalkya Dharmasūtras. Edited with the commentary of Mitra Miśra by Narayana Sastri Khiste and Jagannatha Sastri Hosinga. Chowkhamba Sanskrit Series, no. 62. Varanasi: Chowkhamba Sanskrit Series Office, 1930.

Illustration Citations

Figure 1. Śikṣārthī. *Phaiśan Pareḍ* [Fashion Parade] (Delhi: Subodh Publishers, 1968), p. 160.
Figure 2. Deviprasad. *The Cartoons of Deviprasad.* Edited by Prasanta Daw (Calcutta: Mahua Publishing, 1978), p. 39.
Figure 3. Mario. *Sketchbook* (Bombay: Pearl Publications, n.d.), p. 29.
Figure 4. Laxman. *You Said It* (Bombay: India Book House, 1967–1979), 5:2.
Figure 5. Mario. *Laugh It Off* (Bombay: India Book House, 1974), n.p.
Figure 6. Shankar Pillai. *Shankar's Weekly* (Delhi, December 9, 1951).
Figure 7. Deviprasad. *The Cartoons of Deviprasad,* p. 8.
Figure 8. Mario. *Are You Ready, Miss Fonseca?* (Bombay: Jaico Publishing House, 1979), n.p.
Figure 9. Abu Abraham. *The Games of Emergency* (New Delhi: Vikas Publishing House, 1977), n.p.
Figure 10. Laxman. *You Said It* 1:81.
Figure 11. Laxman. *You Said It* 5:6.
Figure 12. Sudhir Dar. *This Is It!* (New Delhi: Vikas Publishing House, 1976), n.p.
Figure 13. Sudhir Dar. *This Is It!,* n.p.
Figure 14. Laxman. *You Said It* 1:74.

Figure 15. S. Phadnis. *Hasari Gelari* [Laughing Gallery] (Poona: Suvichar Prakashan Mandal, 1969), p. 61.
Figure 16. Sushil Kalra. *This Dilli!* (New Delhi: Sushika Publishers, n.d.), n.p.
Figure 17. Pahari School of the early nineteenth century. London, Trustees of the British Museum (1949 10-8 021).
Figure 18. Laxman. *Science Smiles* (Bombay: India Book House, 1982), p. 80.
Figure 19. Siva. *Manataranga* (Ahmedabad: Sahityanidhi, 1969), p. 128.
Figure 20. Śikṣārthī. *Phaiśan Pareḍ,* p. 164.
Figure 21. Illustration by Ram Waeerkar. *Birbal the Witty* (Amar Chitra Katha Series, no. 152; Bombay: India Book House, 1982), p. 28.
Figure 22. Mario. *Laugh It Off,* n.p.
Figure 23. Illustration by Souren Roy. *Gopal the Jester* (Amar Chitra Katha Series, no. 237; Bombay: India Book House, n.d.), p. 27.
Figure 24. Cartoon reprinted from *Swarajya* in *Vishnu and His Cartoons*. Presented and privately printed by Vaijayanthi Mala.
Figure 25. Sudhir Dar. *Out of My Mind Again* (New Delhi: Vikas Publishing House, 1977), n.p.
Figure 26. Śikṣārthī. *Phaiśan Pareḍ,* pp. 122–123.
Figure 27. Illustration by C. M. Vitankar. *Ganesha* (Amar Chitra Katha Series, no. 89; Bombay: India Book House, n.d.), p. 2.
Figure 28. Mario. *Laugh It Off,* n.p.
Figure 29. Laxman. *You Said It* 4:22.
Figure 30. Mario. *Are You Ready, Miss Fonseca?,* n.p.
Figure 31. Abu Abraham. *The Games of Emergency,* n.p.
Figure 32. *Weekly SUN* (Special Supplement) 6, no. 2 (1983): 6.
Figure 33. Shankar Pillai. *Shankar's Weekly* (Delhi, May 23, 1948).

Index of Indian Texts and Authors Cited

Subject Index